CG International Series

Nadia Magnenat Thalmann
Daniel Thalmann (Eds.)

Communicating with Virtual Worlds

With 394 Figures, Including 150 in Color

Springer-Verlag
Tokyo Berlin Heidelberg New York London
Paris Hong Kong Barcelona Budapest

Prof. NADIA MAGNENAT THALMANN
MIRALab, Centre Universitaire d'Informatique
University of Geneva
24 rue du Général-Dufour
CH-1211 Geneva 4
Switzerland

Prof. DANIEL THALMANN
Computer Graphics Lab.
Swiss Federal Institute of Technology
CH-1015 Lausanne
Switzerland

Cover picture:
Design: Agnes Daldegan
MIRALab, University of Geneva and CGL, Swiss Federal Institute of
Technology, Lausanne

ISBN-13: 978-4-431-68458-9   e-ISBN-13: 978-4-431-68456-5
DOI: 10.1007/978-4-431-68456-5

Printed on acid-free paper

Preface

This volume presents the proceedings of COMPUTER GRAPHICS INTERNATIONAL '93 (CGI '93), the Eleventh International Conference of the Computer Graphics Society (CGS), CGI '93 has been held in Lausanne, Switzerland from June 21-25, 1993 under the theme *Communicating with Virtual Worlds*. Since its foundation in 1983, CGI conference has continued to attract high quality research articles in all aspects of computer graphics and its applications. Previous conferences in this series were held in Japan (1983-1987), in Switzerland (1988), in the United Kingdom (1989), in Singapore (1990), in the United States (1991), and in Japan (1992). Future CG International conferences are planned in Australia (1994), and in the United Kingdom (1995). CGS also organizes each year *Computer Animation* in Geneva, an international workshop and Computer-Generated Film Festival. Two new CGS events are planned in 1993: Pacific Graphics '93 in Seoul and MMM '93, an International Conference on Multi-Media MOdeling in Singapore.

The invited papers and the refereed papers included in this book represent the state of the art in Computer Graphics and its role in Virtual Worlds. The book presents original research results and applications experience to the various areas of Computer Graphics. This year most papers are related to user interfaces, Virtual Reality, parallel processing, rendering techniques, image processing and geometric modelling. The refereed papers were selected, after peer review, from a large number of papers submitted from around the world. Countries represented in this volume include Australia, Austria, Belgium, China, Denmark, France, Germany, Israel, Italy, Japan, Korea, New Zealand, Sweden, Switzerland, Taiwan, United Kingdom, and United States This wide international coverage of research confirms the truly international characteristic of CGI.

This volume concludes with a listing of the CG International '93 program committee and the technical reviewers. This annual Conference has been organized this year by the Computer Graphics Society, the Swiss Federal Institute of Technology in Lausanne, and the University of Geneva with the cooperation of the British Computer Society, IEEE Computer Society, Eurographics and IFIP WG5.10.

NADIA MAGNENAT THALMANN
DANIEL THALMANN

Table of Contents

Part I

User Interface and Virtual Reality

Future Directions in Advanced User Interface Design

Aaron Marcus

Abstract

Future industrial products incorporating micro-computers will require advanced user interface (UIs) to enable the products to be useful and the users to be productive. These UIs will incorporate innovative input and display technologies, such as multimedia and three-dimensional displays, as well as new approaches to metaphors, mental model, navigation, look and feel. These technology advances present challenges and opportunities for designers of human-computer communication and interaction. The design of metaphors is discussed in greater detail.

Key Words: cultural diversity, human factors, metaphors, semiotics, user interface design.

Introduction

In the coming decades, work and play products will need to account for large amounts of data and functions that products will make available through embedded networked computer systems communicating with human beings and with each other. These developments will affect the product development team's task of communicating increasingly complex information through new technologies. Successful user-interface (UI) design requires that the designer achieve effective communication of the following components [Marcus, 1990]:

- *Metaphors*: Fundamental terms, images, and concepts that are easily recognized, understood, and remembered
- *Mental model*: Appropriate organization and representation of data, functions, tasks, roles, and people
- *Navigation schema*: Efficient movement in the mental model via menus, dialogue boxes, etc.
- *Look*: High-quality appearance characteristics that effectively convey information and appeal to the user
- *Feel*: Interaction techniques that operate efficiently and provide an appealing perceptual experience.

As developers build future user interfaces, they need to remember lessons learned from the past about successful communication. This article discussed issues from the perspective gained by the author from more than twenty-five years of developing user interfaces.

Some aspects of effective user interface design are likely to remain viable, in particular, the importance of simple, clear, and consistent communication [Marcus, 1992]. Developers will need to search for and use effectively a collection of metaphors to convey the high-level attributes of the product, its data, or its functional capabilities. They will also need to analyze existing use scenarios or develop alternatives that convey a well-organized mental model and an efficient navigation scheme. In this development process, it is helpful to determine diagrammatic depictions of the fundamental "nouns" and "verbs" of the product (its high-level data objects, data labels, and functions) that are useful in conveying the logic of the product in a manner that makes sense to users. This approach leads to visualizations that can be naturally and relatively easily incorporated into user interface building tools. All of the essential components of metaphors, mental model, and navigation schema must help users gain rapid access to data and functions but at the same time not lose their comprehension as they "fly" through the conceptual space of the user interface. Developers also must account for the look and feel of advanced UIs. For increasingly diverse user groups, they must provide functional, aesthetically pleasing displays and efficient interaction with new input and output display devices. The technology changes have a direct impact on look and feel.

This article will summarize the impact of some new technology directions and explore the topic of metaphor design in detail.

UI Development Objectives

In the coming years, performance and productivity improvements will be important to product success. Front cover articles in major news weeklies, books, and newspaper articles report growing dissatisfaction with incomprehensible products [Norman]. By improving the user interface design, especially by providing better metaphors, mental model, and navigation schema, UI developers will make it easier to for users to understand the work flow embodied in products, especially in cooperative work environments. Clear organization of data and functions will also make it easier for colleagues in product development groups to develop documentation, training, and marketing materials.

The objectives of UI development in this decade include not only making products that are easier to learn and use, but also easier to produce and maintain through object-oriented, computer-aided software engineering techniques. Developing complex UIs for complex applications means that multi-disciplinary teams must be organized. The team must develop detailed user interface standards and specification documents, conduct usability testing, and provide templates that ensure good practice.

Without careful analysis and design, developers can overuse or misuse techniques that lead away from cognitive simplicity, clarity, and consistency in product development. For example, in the 1970s, when color first became widely available on CRT's, product developers abused or overused color, for example, using too many highly saturated colors in information displays. The same pattern often occurs with new techniques, if developers are not sensitive about how to achieve effective communication. Although a cautious approach to the use of new visualization techniques is generally recommended, one may contrast that conservative view with a very exciting and dramatic development for computers. UIs will eventually respond to stylistic and cultural influences as product developers reach out to more diverse audiences, especially as *computer* products become *consumer* products. These developments are noticeable in the new pen-based computers and the personal digital assistants (PDAs) that Apple and others have developed [Thomas *et al*].

Technology Challenges

Throughout the industry and specifically in research and development centers, many developers are searching for new technologies and techniques that affect the user interface design of products. Some of the future design issues [Marcus and van Dam, Marcus and Galle] include the following:

• Products must satisfy existing national user groups, but they must also reach out to new customers in a fractured global economy that recognizes national, regional, local, and cultural diversity. Pressures to localize products in terms of language, color, symbolism, even metaphors and mental models will increase.

• Large corporations with major investments in hardware platforms and application software are trying to cope with migration and portability, or cross-platform, cross-graphical user interface (GUI) issues for current commercial GUIs. At the same time they are trying to keep an eye on the approaching new technologies for human-computer communication and interaction. Although cross-GUI application builders have emerged, they do not automatically build good user interfaces. Developers face the need for guidelines and templates embodying good practice based on theory and design principles.

• Industry standards are beginning to emerge for some aspects of GUIs. The international Standards Organization (ISO) has formed committees developing color standards and icon standards, while the IEEE is examining cross-GUI specifications. Within the constraints of commercial GUIs and in the free-for-all of non-standard GUIs, corporations are looking for the means to establish strong corporate and product identities.

• Even within the constraints of established GUI paradigms, it is possible to design a specific identity by carefully selecting innovative metaphors, unique mental models, engaging appearance of dialogue boxes, and novel interaction devices. Future design developments also are focusing on providing increasingly sophisticated tools for building GUIs and widget sets, or libraries of typical GUI parts, including the much needed libraries of complex controls, like dials and gauges, and real-time data display devices for charts, maps, and diagrams.

• User-centered, task-oriented design has become a necessary basis for better products. The user interface design community is responding by educating developers about usability testing before, during, and after product development and by providing tools to help gather data, conduct tests, and to analyze the results.

To better appreciate the changes ahead for user interface design, it is useful to examine some user interface design issues posed by specific technology developments. Each of them presents new design challenges to product developers.

Sound

The addition of sound attributes to the UI is a significant change. Sara Bly's research [Bly] in the 1980s demonstrated that acoustic plus visual cues aid communication. Gaver's and Blattner's research [Gaver, 1986 and 1989; Blattner] examined how voice, music, realistic or concrete sounds, and abstract sounds could aid in reporting data or establishing rapport. In order to be successful with these two modes of communication, i.e., reporting vs. building rapport, together with gender-specific speech output, developers will probably require expertise in how women vs. men communicate. The work of Deborah Tannen [Tannen, 1986 and 1990], which discusses how women and men communicate differently in conversation is a useful and provocative source of information on this subject.

Every UI object can have possible sound attributes. In addition to graphic designers and animators, user interface development teams will need to hire a musician or sound effects technician. In a few years, the idea of looking at a computer screen with the sound turned down will seem as odd as looking at a movie today with no soundtrack playing. As one can assert for every technology development, using sound well will require significant skills for developers. Libraries of sounds, templates, and significant amounts of training will be needed for both developers and users to take advantage of this new technology.

Video

The addition of digital video in multimedia presentations and compound documents in general is a significant step forward in technology [Winkler], but the presence of video can be a step backward in effective communication. If a typical user of a communication/work product can monitor 9 football games or soap operas from a 500-channel satellite- or cable-fed tuner in the background of a spreadsheet display, the video can distract from and compete with other information in the display. Animated video is very compelling, especially video showing human faces or moving objects. On the other hand, video *does* catalyze the possibility of new metaphors for data display, like the news announcer or the weather reporter, i.e., human-like agents that provide summaries of data.

As with sound, every GUI object may have possible video attributes, which will necessitate significant changes in UI software, e.g., small video inserts might appear within scroll bars. Most people do not have significant experience editing and composing video; to exploit this technology, both developers and users will require significant skills. They will benefit from libraries of video content plus templates of communication content with built in video attributes, plus extensive training, including on-line help.

Three-Dimensions and Virtual Reality

Virtual reality and three-dimensional displays present a challenge to conventional two-dimensional GUIs. The developer must position any desktop or window in three-dimensional space. Developers and users might ask a question that would be nonsense for today's GUIs: what does the *back* of a dialogue box look like? (See Figure 1.) Most current GUIs have no answer.

New input and output devices like the Data Glove™, the Data Suit™, Eye Trackers™, etc., [Green *et al*] challenge the notions of conventional dialogue boxes and control panels. Researchers are exploring novel three-dimensional approaches to how they enable command/control and information visualization, for example, the three-dimensional widgets for CAD/CAM user interfaces developed by Andries van Dam and his colleagues at Brown University [Snibbe] or the Information Visualizer developed at Xerox PARC (see for example [Card], [MacKinlay], and [Robertson]).

The complexity of spatial displays and spatial tools for user interface design deserves careful study [Marcus, 1987, Ellis]. Interdisciplinary teams will be necessary to effectively exploit the new virtual reality technologies and transform them from exotic toys into practical tools. As with all of the new technologies discussed, exceptional skills, which most architects and jet pilots have, will now be required first by developers and then by users. Once again, libraries, templates, and training will catalyze truly useful systems.

Agents

The Friend21 Project in Japan [Nonogaki, Hirose] envisions a variety of highly complex, sophisticated programs called agents that are associated with metaphors. The Newton project of Apple [Thomas *et al*] is also exploring this approach. The Friend21 project envisions multiple agents grouped into agencies [Uede] that may even compete with each other to take on tasks in a society of agents.

Researchers like the Thalmanns [Thalmann] demonstrate the capability of depicting convincing images of Marilyn Monroe interacting with Humphrey Bogart; this capability suggests that highly anthropomorphic agents can be developed. Several of the so-called Cyberpunk science-fiction writers explore this approach and other user interface themes in their work (see, for example, [Gibson, 1984 and 1988], [Rucker, 1986 and 1988], [Sterling], and [Vinge] and the report on user interface design issues of these science-fiction writers in [Marcus *et al*, 1992].

If there are many agents with their associated attributes to choose from, imagine the challenge for the user interface developer or user to pick the right ones. Once again the constant challenges of these new technologies manifest themselves. Developers and users will require skills most do not now possess. Developers will need the assistance of skilled professionals from a variety of disciplines, and users will require and benefit from libraries of parts, templates, and training.

Work Flow and Cognitive Organization

The work flow of many products lies in the decision-making expressed in dialogue boxes. Most current GUIs provide too little design assistance of work flow and information organization; as a result, the layout and content of menus and dialogue boxes are often too varied, uncontrolled, and cluttered, without providing options for alternate and simultaneous views of content for different levels of expertise, different cognitive styles, or different cultures (for the possible impact of multi-cultural influences, see, for example, the work of [Hall], [Doi, 1973 and 1986], and [Neustupmy]).

Cognitive scientists like Don Norman [Norman] have challenged developers to think more carefully about fundamental cognitive processes. As reported by the *Wall Street Journal* [Wall Street Journal], one-third of American VCR owners have given up programming their VCRs, abandoning a primary functional capability of the device, because they cannot understand the instructions and controls. If users are going to cope with multimedia, hypertext, or virtual reality functions that developers are trying to add to desktop or pocket devices, significant improvement in work flow and cognitive organization must be accomplished.

Depicting structure and process effectively often requires optimizing hierarchy, rate, and comprehension. Miller's magic number from human factors 7±2 [Miller] is useful in the beginning: for short term memory and quick decision making, as in the upper levels of mental models, e.g., expressed as menu hierarchies, 7±2 often is a useful limit. However, after three levels of 7±2, the challenge is to hide complexity and reveal it at the right time, in the right place, in the right form. Then users can achieve both a high rate of speed through the mental model and retain comprehension when they arrive at their destination. Effective use of visible language (e.g., typography, layout, and color) can help achieve this level of communication, especially when developers recognize the built in needs and rhythms of real users doing tasks like searching, remembering, musing, and deciding.

Among commercial GUIs in the near future, many new approaches to dialogue box design will emerge as professional designers are able to work along side of programmers to develop products. Improved skills are already being demonstrated, and specific training materials are beginning to appear, like Shiz Kobara's book on detailed Motif design [Kobara], which can set an example for what is needed for each of the GUIs.

Metaphors and Metaphor Design

Metaphors, substitutions of one item for something else, help users understand and remember things. As two linguists explain: "the way we think, what we experience, and what we do every day is very much a matter of metaphor" [Lakoff and Johnson].

Future user interfaces will feature multimedia, hypertext, three-dimensional display, possibly with virtual reality characteristics, and agents, all added to the mixture of technologies available in the user interface. The resulting "hypermedia" user interfaces are likely to exacerbate a situation that already challenges current

UI design: users have trouble understanding how to use complex tools offering a variety of functional groupings and databases [Norman].

User interface discussions often cite the use of the desktop metaphor as a successful approach to communicating an operating system's functions to the average computer user. A single metaphor cannot solve the communication challenge of future user interfaces. Even in the traditional "desktop" there are multiple metaphors present, e.g., the so-called trash can sitting on the desktop. This device has been used widely by many personal computers. Metaphors, like all aspects of user interface design, can be assembled, designed, and evaluated. Metaphors are usually already present in the users' work environment. In interviews with users, the first words out of users' mouths or sketches out of their hands are often the verbal terminology, visual imagery, and the concepts through which they themselves understand the essential roles, tasks, functions, and data.

The Friend21 Project in Japan has made multiple metaphors and special metaphor management software, called metaware [Nonogaki], part of its research program for several years. They envision that these multiple metaphors will control associated agents [Uede] and appropriate means of data display to convey complex information to vast numbers of people who ordinarily would not be using advanced computer technology.

Some of the new metaphors revolve around displaying agents as human-like beings [Apple], e.g., the automated news announcer. As this technology progresses, developers will encounter strong productive or counter-productive reactions from users depending on how they utilize expertise from sociology, psychology, and anthropology. For some cultures, even showing anthropomorphic images breaks a cultural taboo and may result in violent protest. In situations that do not create cultural dissonance, developers will need to adapt these metaphors subtly to user's needs. For the example of data newscasters, some people may prefer a young woman; others may prefer an older man.

As with the other technologies, using metaphors successfully requires significant skills in addition to libraries, templates, and extensive training to solve the communication challenge. Metaphor, in fact, is just one of several devices in the communication techniques called rhetoric, which in turn is a topic of the discipline of semiotics, the science of signs [Eco].

Semiotic Dimensions

In order to better understand the place of metaphor in semiotics and its role in communication, consider the four dimensions of semiotics: lexical, syntactic, semantic, and pragmatic.

- Lexical: Production
- Syntactic: Combination
- Semantic: Reference (e.g., product semantics)
  Rhetoric (i.e., tropes)

      ...

      Metaphor

      ...

- Pragmatic: Consumption

These terms are used in other disciplines in other ways. In UI discussions, they may be defined in this manner:

• The *lexical* dimension refers to the production of signs. The primary question is: how can one make the visible language primitives such as elements of points, lines, and areas that contribute to shape, size, color, texture, and orientation?

• The *syntactic* dimension refers to combinations of visual attributes and determines the ease with which visual signs can be distinguished and identified. Here one asks: is one sign bigger than another? Is it red or blue? Is it regular in its location or not?

- The *semantic* dimension addresses the every day sense of the word's "meaning" (i.e., denotation and connotation) by specifying the qualities of the visual sign that allow it to represent, or refer to, an object, process, or concept. Here one asks: Is the sign intuitive? Is it accurate?

- The *pragmatic* dimension refers to the consumption of signs, to whether the sign will be perceivable and understandable to the intended audience. Here one asks: Can one read it from a typical viewing distance ? Does the sign appeal to the viewer? Does it seem alien or foreign?

Taxonomy of User Interface Metaphors

Because human-computer communication has always been an unusual, unnatural experience, people have always used some kind of already familiar devices as metaphors to help computer users understand and remember what data and functions the computer makes available. Following are some typical metaphors:

- Character-based user interfaces (CUIs):Typewriter, teletype machine
- Graphical user interfaces (GUIs): Desktop, folders, paper documents, pushpins, trash cans
- Pen-based user interfaces (PUIs): Paper, pen, drawing, handwriting
- Virtual reality user interfaces (VRUIs): Flying, pointing, touching

In the CUIs of the 1970s, when the user looked into the screen, one was supposed to imagine that one was using a typewriter. In the GUIs of the 1980s, when one looked into the screen, one was to imagine that one was looking down at a desktop. Recently PUIs have been introduced that emphasize handwritten note taking and data entry exemplified by the functions of the Sharp Wizard pocket electronic organizer or the paper-and-pen diaries that many people carry. VRUIs have emphasized many of the terms, images, and concepts of flying, e.g., roll, pitch, and yaw, to manipulate a three-dimensional cursor or to move through virtual space.

Noun-Object Metaphors of Collection

In designing metaphors, it is useful to consider some of the terms, images, and concepts used often to refer to collections of data or objects. These are the "nouns" of the visual-verbal communication in the user interface. Below are some typical examples:

- Desk: Drawers, files, folders, papers
- Publication: Books, newspapers, newsletters, articles, figures, forms
- Photography: Albums, photos, photo brackets/holders
- Television: Programs, channels, networks, commercials
- Compact disk, cassettes: Tracks
- Jukebox: Records, tracks
- Deck of cards: Cards, games, game rules
- Film: Rolls, slide trays, shows, reels, movie
- Boxes: Compartments
- Tree: Branches, trunk, leaves, roots

Over the years, applications have used many of these metaphorical concepts. For example, some hypertext systems use the concept of cards, like that embodied in the HyperCard product from Claris. In designing metaphors for new systems, one should examine the user community to determine what seem to be the natural metaphors for collections before one begins to impose yet another artificial one, or a metaphor transposed from some other very different realm.

Verb or Action Metaphors

Some of the typical verb's of human-computer interaction and how they are made real or concrete are listed below. The basic verbs of interaction were originally analyzed by Foley and Wallace [Foley and Wallace, Foley *et al*]:

- Browse: Rapid replacement, scanning lines, window shopping, thumbing through books

- Select: Touch item, grab item, lasso item, place finger on item and slide
- Delete: Throw away, destroy, lose, recycle, shred
- Valuate: Rotate knob, slide pointer, twist, spin

Each of these can be symbolized and acted out in many different ways. For example, Delete is sometimes pictured as a trash can, garbage can, black hole, paper shredder, or even a goat. This approach can generate many novel, interesting, and potentially useful ideas. One must recognize the potential value of an idea, prepare a simulation or prototype, test its usefulness, and implement a practical version. Imaginative insight and as well as market testing can narrow the range of useful directions. Eventually techniques for inventing and evaluating will become more algorithmic as the work of Iwayama and his colleagues suggests [Iwayama *et al*].

Cultural Diversity of Metaphors

As the computer industry attempts to take computers out of data processing centers and off the desktops of office workers and into the shirt pockets, wallets, or purses of consumers, computers as they have been known for forty years will change radically. In their place will arise "smart" knowledge processing and communication appliances, in which computers will be invisible, but ubiquitous components.

Among the Cyberpunk science fiction writers (see, for example, [Gibson, Rucker, Sterling, Vinge]), Sterling has predicted the appearance of computers as textiles, which he calls *furoshiki*, (after the Japanese cloth wrapper used for wrapping presents) that can be wrapped around the user, or placed onto other objects in order to "scan" them [Marcus *et al*, 1992; Rucker, 1988]. Matsushita has already announced the development of rugs in which loudspeakers are imbedded [Pollack]. Examples of metaphors used in past products include the following:

- Clerical staff: Desktop, counter
- Engineers, scientists: Laboratory workbench
- Middle class consumer: Pocketbook, library, VCR control
- Homeowner: Closet, kitchen counter, basement/garage workbench
- Stockbroker: Trading room desk, floor
- Shopper: Market, bazaar, mall

Extending the realm of human-computer communication will lead to a search for the optimum metaphors to communicate to culturally diverse users who, as consumers, will be far less patient with computers. Until recently, user interfaces were built by, and for, well-educated white males between the ages of 20 and 40. The make-up of that user community, if not the developer community, does leave out most of the human race, and the developer community unconsciously may incorporate certain biases. In the future, whatever the makeup of the developer group, user interfaces will be directed toward specific target audiences that are more complex in their diversity than the ranges developers now often use, i.e., naive, occasional, intermediate, expert, and guru, or office-worker vs. special operator, e.g., of CAD/CAM systems or process control systems. Examples of possible future target markets include the following:

- White male adult Western engineer (default standard)
- European adult male intellectual
- White American woman
- Afro-American adult
- Children
- International-style designer

Future development will need to incorporate more culturally diverse considerations into every aspect of user interface design. The idea that marketing and business communications need to be adjusted to achieve success has certainly taken hold in US-Japanese business circles (see, for example [Doi, 1986], [Hall], [Neustupny], and [Rowland]). It follows that cultural differences may be incorporated into the verbal and visual aspects of the user interface. The following is a preliminary scenario of how cultural diversity would affect, for example, the Print dialogue box design (See Figures 2-4):

The European male adult intellectual might prefer a classical approach to font selection, e.g., the user of serif type in axial symmetric layouts. Elegant bronze European vs. utilitarian American building identification signs are an example of this approach. A young male African-American adult concerned with preserving ethnic identity might prefer more vibrant colors than typical white users. For corroboration, one can examine the attire of US television talk show hosts Arsenio Hall vs. Jay Leno. The colors, for example, of the indigenous architecture and clothing of the Ndebele tribe in Africa [Courtney-Clarke] give an indication of color sets unlike those typically encountered in European Western society. Children may want dialogue boxes similar to US television programs like *Sesame Street, Mr. Rogers' Neighborhood*, or, for boys, perhaps more like Teenage Mutant Ninja Turtles™, rather than what many children-oriented educational software products provide them. International-style designers, who have inherited the Bauhaus traditions, consequently might prefer the simple clean lines of asymmetric, sans-serif typography and layout over more traditional typefaces and axially-centered layouts.

The white American woman, able to process more complex levels of detail than the average male counterpart, according to some popular notions (differences in female brains have been noted regarding non-spatial pattern matching, see e.g., [Kimura]), might prefer a more detailed presentation, and one with less "harsh" rectangle boxes favored by male architects and engineers, especially those containing terms like Kill, Trash, Abort, etc. For corroboration, consider the shapes and colors of male and female electric shavers or perfume bottles, or a female car designer's views about cars [Heiman] (Figure 2).

These sketches are intended not to provide immediately testable examples, but to illustrate the general approach. This topic has only recently entered the discussions of the user interface design community; however, other product design professionals have already debated the issues (see, for example, the discussion of gender differences in [Heiman]). The user interface design community may benefit from statistics of specific user communities in order to be able to analyze the amount of diversity in their make-up and to determine what differences might be required to account for this diversity, e.g., in the metaphors, mental model, navigation, look, or feel.

New Computer Metaphors

As computers move into the consumer realm, metaphors like the following are likely to become more prevalent (see, for example, references to Apple's Personal Digital Assistant and to others illustrated in [Thomas]):

- Personal assistant
- Wallet, pocket pal
- Cloth, clothing, necktie, glove
- Pens, wands
- Cards (credit/debit card, smart card)
- Telephone
- Eyeglasses

Among the basic questions to evaluate metaphors are these:

- How might people understand grouping and acting upon the objects of new, complex applications?

- Are the metaphors appropriate to the user's culture?

- Are the metaphors hard to conceptualize?

- Do the metaphors make it easier to understand things, i.e., to learn?

- Do the metaphors make it easier to act, i.e., to use?

Figures

Figure 1: A sketch of a complex, three-dimensional user interface, with implied multimedia attributes (Illustration from [Marcus, 1992], © copyright 1992 Addison-Wesley, used with permission).

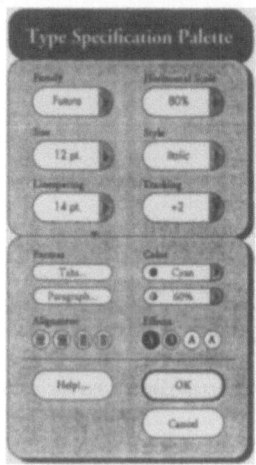

Figure 2: A sketch of a culturally diverse dialogue box described in the text intended for white American adult females (© copyright 1993, Aaron Marcus and Associates).

• Are there multiple aspects to command/control that the metaphor makes easy by combining many into one? (For example, the research of van Dam and his colleagues explores the concept of a "magnet" as a 3D CAD/CAM cursor for altering parametric surfaces, a device that simplifies changes in many different attribute settings [Snibbe *et al*].)

• Are the metaphors easily extensible?

• How many different metaphors are used? Can one limit it to 7±2 major metaphors, following Miller's "magic number" from human factors [Miller]?

• Do the metaphors add appeal? Do they add charm? Do they misdirect or deceive?

Conclusions

This article has attempted to describe technology impacts on user interface design and to explore one aspect in particular, metaphors. The era in which one programmer, or even one discipline, can provide all the necessary skills for user interface design is coming to a close. Teams of designers from many disciplines, for example, animators, video programming directors, musicians, cognitive psychologists, and content experts, will be necessary to develop applications and their embodiment within products. As implied throughout this article, professional communication analysts and designers will be called upon to invent new formulations and to refine already existing embodiments of data, functions, tasks, roles and people within user interfaces. As hardware and software continue to develop in the 1990s, new metaphors will take hold in the general public and in specialized areas of use. Especially important will be the metaphorical devices by which complex products are made more understandable, learnable, memorable, and appealing.

Acknowledgments

The author acknowledges the assistance of his staff in preparing this article. This article is based on an article in preparation for a May 1993 special issue of ACM *Communications* on user interface design; the tutorial "Graphic Design for Advanced Graphical User Interfaces" at ACM's SIGGRAPH-92 conference, Chicago, July 1992; his presentation at the International TRON Conference, December 1992; and the article "Future User Interface Design Issues" in the TRON-92 *Proceedings* [Marcus, 1992].

Bibliography

Andersen, P.B., *A Theory of Computer Semiotics*, Cambridge University Press, Cambridge, UK, 1990.
Apple Computer, Inc., "Knowledge Navigator," video created by Apple Creative Services, Cupertino, CA, 1990.
Baecker, Ronald J. and Aaron Marcus, *Human Factors and Typography for More Readable Programs*, Addison-Wesley, Reading, 1990.
Baker, Sheridan Warner, *The Complete Stylist and Handbook*, Thomas Y. Crowell Company, New York, 1976.
Blattner, Me'era, D. Sumikawa, and R. Greenberg, "Earcons and Icons: Their Structure and Common Design Principles," *Human-Computer Interaction*, Vol. 4, No. 1, 1989, pp. 11-44.
Bly, Sarah, "Presenting Information in Sound," *Proceedings*, Human Factors in Computer Systems Conference (15-17 March 1982 Gaithersburg, Maryland), 1982, pp. 371-375.
Card, Stuart K., George G. Robertson, and Jock D. Mackinlay, "The Information Visualizer An Information Worskspace," *Proceedings*, ACM/SIGCHI-91 (27 April-2 May 1991 New Orleans, Louisiana), 1991, pp. 181-188.
Courtney-Clarke, Margaret, *The Ndebele Tribe*, Rizzoli International Publications, New York, 1986.
Doi, Takeo, *The Anatomy of Dependence*, Kodansha International, New York, 1973.
Doi, Takeo, *The Anatomy of Self: The Individual versus Society*, Kodansha International, New York, 1986.
Eco, Umberto, *A Theory of Semiotics*, Indiana University Press, Bloomington, 1976, ISBN 0-253-35955-4.
Ehses, Hanno H . J., "A Semiotic Approach to Communication Design," *The Canadian Journal of Research in Semiotics*, Vol. 4, No. 3, 1977, pp. 51-77.
Ellis, Steve, ed., *Proceedings*, "Spatial Displays and Spatial Instruments," NASA Conference (21 August 1987), Publication 10032, 1989.

Feiner, Steven, Jock Mackinlay, and Joe Marks, "Automating the Design of Effective Graphics for Intelligent User Interfaces," Tutorial Notes, ACM/SIGCHI Conference (3-7 May 1992, Monterey, CA), 1992.

Foley, James D., Andries van Dam, Steven K. Feiner, and John F. Hughes, Computer Graphics: Principles and Practice (2nd Edition), Addison-Wesley, Reading, MA, 1990, 1174 pages, ISBN 0-201-12110-7.

Foley, James D. and Victor L. Wallace, "The Art of Natural Graphic Man-Machine Conversation," *Proceedings of the IEEE,* Vol. 2, No. 4, 1974, pp. 462-470.

Gaver, William W., "Auditory Icons: Using Sound in Computer Interfaces," *Human Computer Interaction,* Vol. 2, 1986, pp. 167-77.

Gaver, William W. , "The SonicFinder, an Interface that Uses Auditory Icons," *Human Machine Interaction,* Vol. 4. No. 1, 1989.

Gibson, William, *Neuromancer,* Ace Science Fiction Books, New York, 1984.

Gibson, William, *Mona Lisa Overdrive,* Bantam Books, New York, 1988.

Green, Mark, and Robert Jacob, "SIGGRAPH '90 Workshop Report: Software Architectures and Metaphors for Non-WIMP User Interfaces," *Computer Graphics,* Vol. 25, No. 3, July 1991, pp. 229-235.

Green, Mark, Chris Shaw, and Randy Pausch, "Virtual Reality and Highly Interactive Three-Dimensional User Interfaces," Tutorial Notes, ACM/SIGCHI Conference (3 May 1992, Monterey, CA), 1992.

Hall, Edward T. Hall and Mildred Reed Hall, *Hidden Differences: Doing Business with the Japanese,* Anchor Books, Doubleday, New York, 1987.

Heiman, Andrea, "Designing a Car a Woman Would Want to Marry," *Jerusalem Post,* 17 August 1992, p. 5 (originally appeared in *Los Angeles Times*).

Hirose, Makoto, "The Role of Metaphor in the Human -Interface,' *Proceedings,* Friend21, 1991 International Symposium on Next Generation Human Interface, 25-27 November 1991, Tokyo, Japan), Institute for Personalized Information Environment, Tokyo, Japan, 1991, Sec. 4-C pp. 1-12.

Iwayama, M., Tokunaga, T. and Tanaka, H., "A Method of Calculating the Measure of Salience in Understanding Metaphors, " *Proceedings,* AAAI-90, 1990, pp. 298-303.

Kimura, Doreen, "Sex Differences in the Brain," *Scientific American,* Vol., 267, No. 3, pp. 118-125.

Kobara, Shiz, *Visual Design with OSF Motif,* Addison-Wesley, Reading, 1992.

Lakoff, George, and Mark Johnson, *Metaphors We Live By,* The University of Chicago Press, Chicago, 1980.

MacKinlay, Jack, George G. Robertson, and Stuart C. Card, "The Perspective Wall: Detail and Context Smoothly Integrated, "Proceedings, ACM/SIGCHI-91 (27 April-2 May 1991, New Orleans, Louisiana), 1991, pp. 173-179.

Marcus, Aaron, "Visual Rhetoric in a Pictographic-Ideographic Narrative," *Semiotics Unfolding,* Proceedings of the Second Congress of the International Association for Semiotic Studies (July 1979, Vienna), ed. Tasso Borbé, Vol. 3, Part 6, Mouton Publishers, Berlin, 1983, ISBN 3-11-009779-6, pp. 1501-1508.

Marcus, Aaron, "Spatial Issues in User Interface Design from a Graphic Design Perspective," in Ellis, Steve, ed., *Proceedings,* "Spatial Displays and Spatial Instruments," NASA Conference (21 August 1987), Publication 10032, 1989, pp. 22.1-22.7.

Marcus, Aaron, "Designing Graphical User Interfaces," *UNIXWorld,* Part 1 of three-part article, Vol. 7, No. 8, August 1990, pp. 107-116.

Marcus, Aaron, and Andries van Dam, "User Interface Developments for the Nineties," *IEEE Computer,* Vol. 24, No. 9, September 1991, pp. 49-57.

Marcus, Aaron, *Graphic Design for Electronic Documents and User Interfaces,* Addison-Wesley, Reading, 1992.

Marcus, Aaron, and N. Gregory Galle, "A Comparison of User Interface Research and Development Centers," in *Proceedings,* Hawaii International Conference on System Sciences, Vol. 2, ed. Bruce D. Shriver, 1992, pp. 741-752.

Marcus, Aaron, Donald A. Norman, Rudy Rucker, Bruce Sterling, and Vernor Vinge, "SCI-Fi at CHI: Cyberpunk Novelists Predict Future User Interfaces," *Proceedings,* ACM SIGCHI Conference (Monterey, CA, 3-7 May 1992), 1992, pp. 435-437.

Marcus, Aaron, N. Gregory Galle, and Grant Letz, "Graphic Design for Advanced User Interfaces," Tutorial Notes, ACM/SIGGRAPH Conference (20 July 1992), Chicago, IL, 1992.

Marcus, Aaron, "Future User Interface Design Issues," *Proceedings of the Ninth TRON Project Symposium (International), 1992,* TRON '92 Conference (November 1992) Tokyo, 1992, pp. 14-21.

Miller, George A. "The Magical Number Seven Plus or Minus Two: Some Limits on Our Capacity for Processing Information, *Psychological Review,* Vol. 63, pp. 81-97, 1956.

Norman, Donald A., *The Design of Everyday Things,* Doubleday, New York, 1990. (Originally published as Norman, Donald A. *The Psychology of Everyday Things,* Basic Books, New York, 1988.)

Nonogaki, Hajime, "Metaware," *Proceedings,* Friend-21 1991 International Symposium on Next Generation Human Interface (25-27 November 1991, Tokyo, Japan), Institute for Personalized Information Environment, 1991, Section 2B, pp. 1-10.

13

Neustupmy, J.V., *Communicating with the Japanese*, The Japan Times, Tokyo, 1987.

Ota, Yukio, *Pictogram Design,* Kashiwashobo, Tokyo, 1987, ISBN 4-7601-0300-7.

Peirce, Charles Sanders, "Existential Graphs" in Hartshorne, Charles and Paul Weiss, eds., *Collected Papers of Charles Sanders Peirce,* Vol. 4: The Simplest Mathematics, Book 2, Chapters 1-7, Harvard University Press, Cambridge, 1933, pp. 293-470.

Roberts, Don D., *The Existential Graphs of Charles S. Peirce*, Mouton, The Hague, Series: Approaches to Semiotics, No. 27, 1973.

Robertson, George A. , Jack D. MacKinlay, and Stuart K. Card, " Cone Trees: Animated Three-D Visualization of Hierarchical Information," *Proceedings,* ACM/SIGCHI-91 (27 April-2 May 1991 New Orleans, Louisiana), 1991, pp. 189-194.

Rowland, Diana, *Japanese Business Etiquette*, Warner Books, New York, 1985.

Rucker, Rudy, *Software,* Avon Books, New York, 1982.

Rucker, Rudy, *Wetware,* Avon Books, New York, 1988.

Snibbe, Scott S., Kenneth P. Herndon, Daniel C. Robbins, D. Brookshire Conner, and Andries van Dam, "Using Deformations to Explore 3D Widget Design," *Proceedings,* 1992 ACM SIGGRAPH Conference (26-31 July 1992), Chicago, IL, issued as *Computer Graphics,* Vol. 26, No. 2, July 1992, pp. 351-360.

Sterling, Bruce, ed., *Mirrorshades,* Arbor House, New York, 1986

Tannen, Deborah, *That's Not What I meant!,* Ballantine Books, New York, 1986.

Tannen, Deborah, *You Just Don't Understand: Women and Men in Conversation,* William Morrow and Company, Inc., New York, 1990.

Thalmann, N. Magnenat, and D. Thalmann, *Synthetic Actors in 3D Computer-Generated Films*, Springer Verlag, New York, 1990.

Thomas, Wes, and the Staff of Desktop Communications "The Future of Computing," *Desktop Communications,* Vol. 4, No. 4, July-August 1992, pp. 29-32.

Ueda, Hirotada, "Agency Model" *Proceedings,* Friend-21 1991 International Symposium on Next Generation Human Interface (25-27 November 1991, Tokyo, Japan), Institute for Personalized Information Environment, Section 2C, pp. 1-7.

Vinge, Vernor, *Grimm's World*, Berkley Medallion Books, New York, 1969.

Vinge, Vernor, *True Names,* Bluejay Books Inc., New York, 1984.

Wall Street Journal, 2 March 1991, p. B1, citing a survey by R. H. Bruskin Associates for Thompson, maker of RCA-brand VCRs.

Winkler, Dean M., "Video," Tutorial Notes, ACM/SIGGRAPH Conference, Chicago, 20 July 1992.

Aaron Marcus is an internationally recognized authority on graphic design for computer graphics, especially chart, form, document, icon, and screen design. He has given knowledge visualization, user interface design, and document design tutorials at SIGCHI, SIGGRAPH, and NCGA conferences in addition to tutorials at companies and conferences in the USA, Australia, Canada, Europe, Israel, Singapore, and Japan.

He and his staff have designed and evaluated knowledge visualization, user interfaces, and electronic publishing/presentations for Apple, Ashton-Tate, Computervision, DEC, DuPont, General Motors, Hewlett-Packard, IBM, Kodak, MCC, McDonnell-Douglas, Microsoft, Motorola, NCR, Pacific Bell, Reuters, Scitex, 3M, Wavefront, and many other organizations. Government clients have included East-West Center, Lawrence Berkeley Laboratory, Lawrence Livermore National Laboratory, Los Alamos National Laboratory, National Endowment for the Arts, National Library of Medicine, New York Department of City Planning, US Department of Defense, and US Department of Labor.

Mr. Marcus has written many articles on graphic design for computer graphics for technical and professional journals. He co-authored *The Computer Image* (1982), for which he wrote the essay "Color: A Tool for Computer Graphics Communication," co-authored *Human Factors and Typography for More Readable Programs* (1990), and authored *Graphic Design for Electronic Documents and User Interfaces* (1991), all published by Addison-Wesley. Mr. Marcus received a B.A. in Physics from Princeton University (1965) and a B.F.A. and M.F.A. in Graphic Design from Yale University Art School (1968). He has taught computer graphics since 1970 and founded AM+A in 1982.

Mr. Aaron Marcus, Principal
Aaron Marcus and Associates
1144 65th Street, Suite F
Emeryville, CA 94608-1109

Using the Whole Hand in the Human-Computer Interface*

David J. Sturman**

Abstract

Sensored gloves allow the user to reach into a virtual environment and manipulate virtual objects as if they were real. However, the use of gloves in VR has not progressed far beyond "point, reach, and grab" interaction, addressing the need for natural user interfaces, but not taking advantage of the full power of using the hand directly in the human-computer interface. This article discusses this problem and presents *whole-hand input* as a distinct study, independent of specific application or interface device. It identifies key components of whole-hand input, outlines potential application areas, discusses the important issues of whole-hand input, and suggests future research for developing the technology.

Keywords: interaction, input devices, VR, gloves, hands

Introduction

One of the technologies synonymous with Virtual Reality (VR) is sensored gloves which allow the user to reach into a virtual environment and manipulate virtual objects as if they were real objects. Most use of these gloves has centered around "point, reach, and grab" interaction or signing. Although this addresses the need for natural user interfaces, it does not explore the full capabilities of the hand as an input device. The dexterity and adaptability of the hand as a tool makes it well suited for a wide range of applications.

This article discusses the full and direct use of the hand's capabilities for VR and the control of computer-mediated tasks in general. It addresses this subject, termed *whole-hand input*, as a distinct study, independent of specific application or interface device. It identifies the key components of whole-hand input, outlines potential areas of application, discusses the important issues of whole-hand input, and suggests future lines of research for developing the technology.

Whole-hand Input

The usefulness of whole-hand input comes specifically from taking advantage of the hand's qualities of *naturalness*, *adaptability*, and *dexterity*. Without these qualities, whole-hand input provides little, if any, advantage over conventional interfaces.

At a functional level, whole-hand input is the information a computer derives from the monitoring of the individual degrees of freedom of the hand. In the fullest sense of the term, this includes the 29 degrees of freedom of the hand and arm as well as forces generated by the hand. In the simplest sense, whole-hand input may be just the monitoring of the position and orientation of the palm or the bends of three or four fingers. *The distinguishing characteristic of*

---

* This work was supported in part by NHK (Japan Broadcasting Company), and Defense Advanced Research Projects Agency–RADC Contract #F30602-89-C-0022

** Author's present address: *MEDIALAB*, 104 av. du Président Kennedy, 75016 Paris France

whole-hand input is that the user does not think in terms of manipulating an input device, as is the case with other haptic forms of input (e.g., mouse, joystick, trackball), but moves his hand to directly affect the task. A functional way to describe the distinction is that whole-hand input is derived from direct measurement of hand motion rather than measurement of the motion of a device manipulated by the hand.

Some examples of whole-hand input are using hand signs to control a teleoperated crane at a construction site; miming the motions of reaching and grabbing to pick and move objects in a computer-simulated scene; flexing different fingers to move the head, arms, and legs of a computer-animated character; tracing space curves with a finger to indicate surgical cuts in a simulated operation; and flexing fingers and moving the hand to modify audio parameters that control the color and tone of a live musical performance.

Features of whole-hand input

The salient features of using the whole hand as an input device can be divided into three principal categories: *naturalness, adaptability,* and *dexterity.* If a task does not need at least one of these three, then another form of user interface is probably more appropriate than whole-hand input.

Naturalness is used to describe a subjective evaluation of interaction. It implies being "free from artificiality, affectation, or constraint," and "obviously suitable for a specific purpose" (Webster's Dictionary, 7th edition). Naturalness is a function of the daily use of the hand for a broad spectrum of tasks using a repertoire of skills that require little thought. Examples include different types of grips, specific finger coordinations, such as those used to turn objects within the grasp, and rhythms used in finger tapping. We should be able to improve the efficiency of performing a task, as well as the time to learn it by basing control schemes on natural and pre-acquired skills. The aspect of using the hand naturally also contributes to an increased sense of presence, an important element in the successful development of teleoperated systems (Sheridan 1989).

Adaptability refers to the hand's ability to quickly and smoothly switch functions. For example, lifting a heavy object into place, carefully aligning it with adjoining supports, and then fitting screws into small holes to secure it. The hand capability that allows all of this enables us to use the same whole-hand input device for a variety of functions, freely switching between modes of control without having to change program modes. Adaptability can be an advantage where physical space is too limited to have different input devices for each task, or transitions between conventional devices are slow and cumbersome.

The adaptability of the hand is a result of its structure and variety of muscles with different ranges of function, strength, and precision. Computer input controls should be coupled with those muscles and motions appropriate for the required task. The ability to dynamically control the impedance of the degrees of freedom of the hand also contributes to the hand's adaptability. Joints can be relaxed or stiffened as needed, manipulating a small flower as easily as a heavy block of wood.

Dexterity can be defined as the integration of movements and senses into higher levels of competence. For example, turning a bolt on a nut is a highly coordinated skill that, once learned, is performed as a single action. The significant aspect of this integration is the ability to draw on known sensorimotor routines and, combining them with practiced sensorimotor control, to manipulate and move the hand in new ways, learning and developing new skills. For example, a Westerner learning to use chopsticks finds the task easier when relying on the already acquired skills for manipulating a pencil. By developing skills, the cognitive load required to accomplish a particular task is reduced.

Application Areas

In many cases, conventional input devices underutilize the dexterity of the hand-arm system. This is not to say that these devices fail; they are very effective for certain tasks. However, when used as generic input devices, they can be inefficient in the many situations where the task requires more or different degrees of freedom than those of the device, or where the task is better suited to a different class of hand shape or muscle control than afforded by the device. Whole-hand input allows all of, or any part of the hand to be used and thus allows input strategies that can appropriately fill the task requirements.

This section discusses six application domains and how whole-hand input can improve user interaction for each. These applications each reflect the importance of a different aspect of whole-hand input. Together they cover a wide range of tasks, control requirements, and user cultures. Prototypes of four of these applications were simulated by Sturman (1992).

Construction Industry

There is a shortage of skilled labor in the construction industry, partly due to long training times for heavy equipment (Kangari and Halpin 1989). The difficulty in crane operation, for instance, is moving a large mass at the end of a long, compliant lever arm, controlled by nonlinear hydraulic actuators, using a single lever per degree of freedom interface. In other words, the task is one of controlling a multi-degree-of-freedom system which has nonlinear response. In addition, the crane operator often cannot see, or has a distant view of the load at the end of the crane and relies on hand signals from an assistant at the load end (fig. 1).

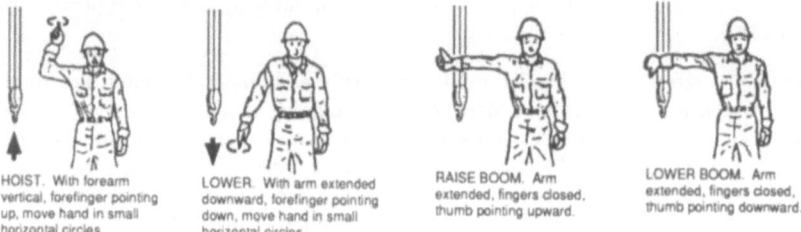

HOIST. With forearm vertical, forefinger pointing up, move hand in small horizontal circles.

LOWER. With arm extended downward, forefinger pointing down, move hand in small horizontal circles.

RAISE BOOM. Arm extended, fingers closed, thumb pointing upward.

LOWER BOOM. Arm extended, fingers closed, thumb pointing downward.

Figure 1: *Hand signals for crane operation* Some of the construction industry hand signals used to communicate to crane operators.

Using electronic processors to handle the non-linearities in the control systems, a whole-hand input solution might allow workers to communicate directly with the equipment using the same hand signals and motions they use now to communicate to the equipment operator, the operator can stand at the load end controlling the crane with natural and familiar hand motions. Other mappings can be developed such as direct control methods, where the angle of a finger controls a degree of freedom of the equipment; the angle of the crane boom, for example. This application is particularly interesting because there is the potential to reduce the training time required to handle this type of machinery, significantly alleviating the problem of the industry's shortage of skilled labor.

Remotely Controlled Vehicles and Manipulators

Remotely controlled robots are used in a variety of environments hazardous to humans. Often the tasks to be performed require a precision and dexterity difficult to achieve with conventional devices. In most cases, special-purpose devices must be built (McKinnon, King, and Runnings 1987; Robotics World 1989).

Whole-hand input is an excellent candidate for use in these situations. An undersea robot vehicle, for example, requires the control of various systems including propulsion, vision (cameras and lights), and manipulators. With whole-hand input, one or two operators might be able to control all of the systems at once. The motions of one hand can be mapped directly to the motions of a robot arm, while the other hand directs a high pressure nozzle, cleaning debris off the object being manipulated. A second person controls the attitude of the vehicle and the position of the cameras and lighting. The naturalness and dexterity of whole-hand input can greatly increase the capabilities and efficiency of each operator.

Puppetry and Computer Animation

In the entertainment industry, remote manipulation is used mainly for puppetry to bring strange and unusual characters to life. The sophisticated puppets used in film production often have many degrees of freedom, and require several puppeteers, each controlling a specific aspect of the character. For each aspect, be it the eyes, cheeks, head position, or other motion, the degrees of freedom are controlled by custom-built devices termed "waldos."

The recent push in the animated entertainment industry towards realism and greater character complexity implies more sophisticated control structures, more puppeteers for interactive control, and greater expensive and difficulty. Whole-hand input improves the ability of performers to manipulate complex puppets by mapping more input channels to coordinated hand motions and allowing more natural control schemes.

Some work already has been done towards coordinated real-time control of computerized characters, both for computer graphics animations and physical puppets. Some of the earliest work was by Ginsberg and Maxwell (1983) who used a body suit mounted with LEDs that allowed a computer-generated figure to follow a performer's motions in real-time. More recently, there has been an emergence of computer graphic performance work based on glove-input and body tracking for television, film, and live performance by companies such as DeGraff/Wharman, Videosystem, Pacific Data Images, Mr. Film, Blue Sky Productions, and SimGraphics (Robertson 1992). Videosystem/Medialab has been using this form of animation for the past three years for a daily French cable-television program and a series of computer animated cartoons.

Musical Performance

Live musical performance requires the simultaneous control of many degrees of freedom with critical time constraints. The standardization of the MIDI (Musical Instrument Digital Interface) protocol and development of FM synthesis has made computer control and synthesis of the musical process a common practice. With MIDI, instruments no longer need to conform to specific shapes or sizes. As a consequence, artists are beginning to use their whole bodies as input to computer synthesized music (Trubitt 1990).

Whole-hand input in music allows many parameters to be controlled at one time and gives the musician the freedom to move expressively, transmitting that expression to the music. At the M.I.T. Media Lab, as part of his "hyperinstument" project, Tod Machover's 1989 musical composition *Bug-Mudra*, used whole-hand input to control the acoustics (and thus color) of the music's performance in real-time via a MIDI controlled audio mixing panel (Machover 1990).

Surgical Simulation and Assistance

Surgeons are beginning to use computer graphics to simulate surgical procedures for training, visual assistance in diagnosis, and prediction of surgical results (Delp and Delp 1989; Pieper 1992). For the simulation to be useful to the surgeon as a training tool or surgical assistant, the surgeon needs to be able to manipulate the graphical representations as if they were real objects.

Surgeons are often reluctant to commit the time or expense to retrain for new tools or procedures. Whole-hand input has an advantage over more conventional input devices since it can ease the transition by allowing surgeons to mimic the methods with which they have been trained and are most comfortable, and allow them to interact with a simulation and simulated tools exactly as they would with real patients and real tools.

Scientific Simulation and Visualization

Scientists developing computer models of complex natural phenomena need to "visualize" their data and interactively modify simulation parameters as the simulation runs. Currently, many complex simulations take so long that "steering" is not an interactive process. However, as computers get faster, many applications that now take hours or days will become real-time interactive simulations. This will require the coordinated manipulation of multi-axes data spaces;[1] a clear application for whole-hand input.

Levit and Bryson (1991) have already used whole-hand input to allow aeronautic researchers to put their hands (and heads) into a simulated fluid flow, adding smoke trails with their finger tips, and peering into the nooks and crannies of the simulated surfaces.

Issues in Whole-hand Input

There are many issues and problems that need to be resolved before whole-hand input becomes a generally useful tool. The most important of these have to do with distinguishing between appropriate and inappropriate uses of whole-hand input. Studying this problem will yield a better understanding of where, when, and how whole-hand input will improve real-time control.

Appropriate Use

Using the hand to manipulate objects and processes is a natural human behavior and so it seems a logical choice for many computer-based tasks. However, not all tasks may be appropriate for whole-hand input. Certainly applications that involve controlling anthropomorphic manipulators, or grabbing, moving, and turning objects (real or graphical)—functions people perform well with their hands—are good choices, but other applications might do better with alternate forms of input. For example, managing a window-based user interface is well suited to mouse and keyboard input because of the application's textual nature and inherent two-dimensionality (or "2.5-dimensionality"); whole-hand input with its extra degrees of freedom may only complicate matters.

Classification efforts extending those of Card, Mackinlay, and Robertson (1990) and Buxton (1990) are needed for whole-hand input. The results must support the classification and dis-

---

[1] For a review of the some of these issues in the field of scientific visualization see (McCormick, DeFanti, and Brown 1987).

cussion of hand positions and motions (*hand actions*), and guide the evaluation of hand actions as input controls to specific applications. Ideally, a well designed classification and evaluation scheme will do not only this, but indicate and reveal novel methods of whole-hand interaction as well.

Classification of whole-hand actions Many of the current user input classification schemes start with the degrees of freedom of the input device or abstract input device[2] (Buxton 1990). With whole-hand input, the hand is essentially the device. The problem is how to usefully describe and quantify the 29 degrees of freedom of the space of the hand, given that these degrees of freedom have assorted grades of interdependency, range of motion, and dynamic capabilities.

A unique aspect of whole-hand input is the separation between hand action and task function, so that although the resulting task output is functional, the hand input can be organized along physiological, symbolic, or functional lines. Different applications and modes of whole-hand input may be best described by one, or a combination of these classifications. The medical field with its physiological classification, the language field with its symbolic classification, and the rehabilitative and robotics fields with their functional classifications, address the problem within the framework of their individual needs. The novel framework of whole-hand input requires a synthesis and evolution of these into a more comprehensive system.

Evaluation of whole-hand actions A classification scheme will allow one to describe a wide variety of hand actions that can be used for whole-hand input. However, the effectiveness of these hand actions must evaluated by experimentation in the application, or by analysis based on knowledge of the hand, hand action, and the application. Experimentation will indicate if the chosen hand action is effective, or if it is better than another tested hand action, but it will not indicate if the hand action is the best choice for the application. A priori analysis is important to be able to pick appropriate candidates for later testing. Unfortunately, the literature provides minimal guidance since it does not analyze the capability to move the hand apart from natural function, whereas in whole-hand input hand motion can be disjoined from function.[3]

To analyze and evaluate whole-hand input methods, more must be known about what actions can and cannot be done with hands; not just *why* ability exists, but *what* ability exists. For example, it is important to know the overall ability of the hand to motion, gesture, and control it's own shape; what makes a hand action difficult or easy; and what are the temporal and spatial limits of hand performance, organized along single degrees of freedom and in combinations of degrees of freedom.

More must be understood about such factors as interfinger coordination, cross-coupling of the degrees of freedom, resolution of joint motion control, speed of joint control (especially in repetition), and endurance (Durlach 1989). These factors have been studied in the literature to evaluate task performance, but not to evaluate hand-motion itself.

Appropriate Control Design

Control designs and implementation eccentricities drastically affect the usefulness of whole-hand input. A well designed mouse, joystick, or tablet interface may easily outperform a poorly designed whole-hand interface. It will be important to know what aspects of tasks are

---

[2]Abstract devices (also called *virtual devices*) are models of input based on logical rather than physical characteristics. For example, a *locator* device locates a position in two- or three-dimensional space, and can be physically implemented with a variety of physical devices such as a mouse, trackball, tablet, or light pen.

[3]See (Jones 1989b) for a review of hand function assessment techniques.

suitable to whole hand control, what schemes and abstractions work best for implementing the hand-space to control-space mapping, and what aspects of the hand and its motion are important to monitor. Some of the more prominent issues are described below.

Distinguishing control motions from personal hand motions One of the issues particular to whole-hand input design is how the interface is able to distinguish between a command in the task domain and an unrelated gesture. The user must be able to disengage from the task, suspend input, or to rest. It is undesirable, for example, for a slaved robot to reorient a power-tool when the operator scratches his nose, or a surgical tool to continue cutting when the surgeon gestures to a nurse. The operator must be able to uncouple periodically from the task to perform non-task related motions or to rest. There are many ways this could be accomplished including foot switches, buttons, and other "dead-man switch" or clutch-like controls. Sturman, Zeltzer, and Pieper (1989) successfully used a rapid flick of the wrist for mode changes. This motion was above the response frequency of the simulation under whole-hand control, but within the tolerances of the monitoring devices.

Skill Whole-hand input designs must take into account the skill necessary for chosen hand motions and probable training times for a particular task. Some applications can afford long training times such as space missions or career tasks, while in others, perhaps with high worker turnover rates, long training times are infeasible. Although there are studies of dexterous skill in the literature (Ervin 1988; Robinette, Ervin, and Zehner 1987), they do not address the dexterous skill of the average population with regard to specific hand motions divorced from particular vocational tasks.

Ergonomics For whole-hand input, ergonomics refers to the comfort of a hand action and the risk of injury with extended use of a hand action. Repetitive motion injuries, such as carpal tunnel syndrome, can be severely debilitating and must be avoided in the design of whole-hand input methods. The medical and rehabilitation fields are replete with discussions of hand motion injuries and are a good source for this information. See Hunter et al. (1984).

Appropriate device

Since there is little collective experience with whole-hand input devices, current designs try to be general and cover many eventualities. As whole-hand input is more carefully studied, general purpose designs may give way to designs based on more carefully collected data. It may be the case that for the majority of successful whole-hand input techniques, only a few select finger joints need to be monitored, or that the spatial and temporal resolution of the devices should be less at some joints and greater at others. This may reduce the cost and increase the usefulness of whole-hand input devices. It also may be that joint measurement is secondary to fingertip placement, or to overall hand shape. For example, Poizner et al. (1983) found that tracking fingertip motion alone is sufficient for human interpretation of American Sign Language.

There are additional trade-offs among sensing technologies and devices. Image-based systems have the advantage of not requiring users to wear anything on their bodies, but have to deal with occlusions and nuances of lighting. Mechanical devices do not suffer these problems, but can be encumbering. Users may reject a device they need to wear, preferring instead a device they can simply hold or touch. Specific designs may be more effective than generic designs, e.g., the Digital Data Entry Glove versus the VPL DataGlove for signed alphabets (Grimes 1983; Zimmerman et al. 1987). Until a method is found to overcome the current limitations of whole-hand monitoring, an analysis of each task's requirements in terms of these trade-offs is needed to determine the most appropriate device for capturing hand motion for that task.

Importance of Constraints on Degrees of Freedom

Conventional input devices, such as mice, trackballs, joysticks, and so on, have helpful physical characteristics that limit range of motion, improve stability, and support unused degrees of freedom. For instance, a tabletop supports the unused degree of freedom of height for mouse input, and joysticks, dials, and sliders usually have a slight amount of damping to facilitate smooth tracking and to avoid overshooting target positions. Likewise, appropriate constraints can benefit whole-hand input methods and devices. For example, a whole-hand input device used for manipulating a slowly moving robot hand might mechanically damp the operator's finger motions to prevent rapid movement and improve stability. None of the current whole-hand input devices provide constraints to the hand; in fact, they avoid constraining the hand in accordance with design goals of being general purpose devices.

Sensory Feedback

Visual feedback is of primary importance and only music systems seem to do well without it. The role of visual feedback is widely studied and well covered in the literature. The issues relevant to whole-hand input include spatial cues (Goldstein 1989), point of view (Ware and Osborne 1990), and spatial and temporal resolution (Rogowitz 1983; Rolfe and Staples 1986).[4]

Tactile and kinesthetic feedback can have an important influence on manual task performance. Sensorimotor actions rely on feedback from cutaneous and musculoskeletal sensors, and reaction time from kinesthetic input is faster than from visual input (Evarts 1974). Studies have shown that kinesthetic feedback can enhance task performance for many applications, but little is known as to what qualities of kinesthetic and tactile feedback affect performance (Brooks et al. 1990; Minsky et al. 1990; Noll 1972; Ouh-young 1990).

In the future, it will be important to know not only what tasks must be performed with and what tasks can be performed without kinesthetic feedback, but what is the nature of the feedback required. In fact, for some applications, costly force and tactile feedback systems may not be necessary. Patrick et al. (1990) have indicated that a just simple vibratory buzz can effectively simulate physical contact.

Auditory feedback is another viable form of sensory feedback for whole-hand input. Auditory feedback is expected in the use of whole-hand input for musical performance, but it is less standard in other applications. The literature comments on the usefulness of everything from clicks and bells, to changes in pitch and volume, to synthesized speech, designed to enhance task performance (Gaver 1986; Jones 1989a). In some situations a simple "click" may be an effective method to indicate the achievement of a target; in others, it may be insufficient or irrelevant. An advantage of auditory feedback is that it does not require shifting attention from visual or other channels of feedback.

The Use of Gestural Languages

The computer interpretation of gestural languages has two aspects. The first is the recognition of gesture, a complex task and an active area of research (Fels 1990; Kramer and Leifer 1989; Rubine 1991; Takahashi and Kishino 1990). At the simplest level is the recognition of static postures, while at the most complex level is the recognition of a rich language such as ASL which has some fifty different grammatical processes that differ along eleven spatial and temporal linguistic domains (Poizner et al. 1983). The second aspect of gestural languages is

---

[4]Rogowitz (1983) and Rolfe and Staples (1986) provide excellent reviews of problems and solutions for visual feedback in computer graphic applications and simulations.

the syntactic parsing of recognized gestures into language. This is a difficult problem that has been extensively studied but not fully solved in the artificial intelligence community (Barr and Feigenbaum 1982).

"Point, Reach, and Grab"

Another aspect of whole-hand input is what can be called the "point, reach, and grab" paradigm, in which a graphic representation of the user's hand appears on the screen, duplicating the user's motions. The graphic hand can interact with other objects on the screen, allowing the user to manipulate those objects as if they had tangible existence in a physical world. Almost all whole-hand input devices currently being used are engaged in this context.[5] As a result, it can be considered "widely used," although it has not been formally studied.

One-handed vs. Two-handed Input

Most manual tasks are done with two hands, often one steadying the work of the other. One can foresee that whole-hand input will be no different, and that by using two hands instead of one, even more work can be accomplished. At least one group, Buxton and Myers (1986), has investigated the role of two hands in computer input.

Recommendations for Future Work

Experimentation and evaluation of hand function

Whole-hand input is not tied to any one application or function. The use of computer-mediated whole-hand input has, for the first time, separated the morphology of hand control from task function. As such, the study of hand capabilities, disjoined from function, is important to the effective design of whole-hand input techniques; particularly as it relates to the intrinsic capabilities of the hand and the statistical variations of abilities across the general population.

Clinical studies evaluating the precision of hand motion are generally performed in specific contexts, such as sensory mechanisms for joint precision (Clark and Horch 1986)[6], range of motion for disability evaluation (Becker and Thakor 1988; Chao et al. 1989; Mesplay and Childress 1988), dexterity studies for evaluating effects of clothing or environment (Ervin 1988; Jones 1989b), or strength and coordination of fingers in work-related tasks (Cole and Abbs 1986). Although many of these studies provide useful data, they tend to address the action of only one or two fingers (usually forefinger and thumb), or treat the hand as a whole entity, performing specific actions. Furthermore, the studies do not correlate different hand action parameters, for instance, range of motion vs. precision, or discriminate precision of task from precision of the hand. These studies need to be expanded to evaluate hand action independent of function, and to evaluate the different parts of the hand in view of appropriately combining individual motions into useful hand actions.

Abstract whole-hand input devices

A distinction can be made between abstract (or virtual) devices and physical devices. The former categorize input behavior with abstractions such as *button*, *pick*, and *valuator*. The latter are physical devices that may behave as one or more abstract devices. Abstract devices

---

[5]VPL Research actually received a patent relating to the use of a computer graphic hand controlled by an instrumented human hand where the graphic hand is capable of interaction with other graphic "virtual" objects (Zimmerman and Lanier 1991). This patent is now held by Thompson-CSF.

[6]Clark and Horch (1986) provide a comprehensive review of kinesthetic testing of the human body.

describe device-independent interface models to which physical devices can be adapted. Current conventions use the GKS set of virtual devices, *pick, choice, locator, valuator, stroke,* and *string.* This set should be extended to encompass the capabilities of the whole hand. For example a *signing device* could be an abstract device which allows the user to specify a number of discrete symbols.

Computational notations for whole-hand input

A notation for whole-hand input could serve as a foundation for the development of the next generation of whole-hand input libraries as well as provide a common basis for the development and communication of whole-hand input techniques. Hand actions could be written in a language that both served as specifications to hand motion interpretation software as well as detailed instructions to a user. With the proper notational conventions, gesture recognition techniques could be developed using the lexical elements of the notation as primitives in the recognition process.

Several systems for movement notation exist in the field of dance, notably Labanotation (Laban 1975) and Benesh notation, in the study of sign language (Cohen, Namir, and Schlesinger 1977; Stokoe 1960), and for hand shape (grips) in robotics (Cutkosky and Wright 1986). Some attempts have been made to implement computer graphic animation systems using dance notations (Calvert and Chapman 1978; Singh et al. 1982), but the notations tend to lack the fine motion specification that is not necessary when directing intelligent humans, but vital when specifying motion to "literal-minded" computers. Nevertheless, the concepts on which the notations are built can serve as basis for the development of movement notations suited for computational use (Badler 1986).

Device improvement

There are many improvements that can be made in whole-hand input device technology. This is not to say that improvements will be technically or economically easy to make, however as more people use whole-hand input the economics of demand will support technological advancements.

Three-space tracking technology The magnetic trackers currently available still exhibit some noise and lag although significant improvements have been made in the past few years. The goal of three-space tracking is to provide noise-free, lag-free, accurate, and unobtrusive, tracking of the position and orientation of the hand at speeds high enough for rapid movement (approximately 100 Hz.). Systems need to have a range equal to that of the human reach envelope (approximately three cubic meters).

Whole-hand input devices also would benefit if they were freed from the electronic umbilical cords necessary in current commercial systems. A small wireless transmitter on the hand or belt could provide the user with greater freedom to move and gesture as well as allow electronic equipment to be placed conveniently in the work area.

Sensor precision, linearity, and calibration Attaching goniometers to the hand in such a way that they are both accurate and comfortable over wide ranges and speeds of motion is a difficult task. The DataGlove is comfortable, but not very accurate. The Dexterous Hand Master is accurate, but not very comfortable. The Cyberglove glove falls in between the two, while the Power Glove has neither quality. Each one fills a niche in the requirements for a whole-hand input device, but none satisfy all needs.

Studies of hand precision and the importance of sensor accuracy should guide the development of future whole-hand input devices. Fidelity (how well the information coming from the sensors reflects the state of the hand) and resolution (the number of bits of information available from the device sensors in tracking the hand) are costly. In some situations, puppetry for instance, fidelity is not as important as resolution. In others, such as clinical analysis, fidelity is more important. Future devices should support a range of accuracies and fidelities (and concomitant costs) commensurate with the application requirements.

Linearity and independence of sensors are also important factors for accurate tracking of the hand and precision control. The DataGlove sensors are non-linear and interdependent. The Dexterous Hand Master sensors are more linear and independent, but require careful calibration in manufacture and need to be recalibrated periodically. Future devices should pay close attention to sensor linearity in the normal range of use and insure that coupling between sensors is avoided. Sensors should be reliably free from drift over long periods of time (years) or easy to recalibrate.

Degrees of freedom   The number of degrees of freedom of general purpose whole-hand input devices should be modular and variable. Different applications require different degrees of freedom. Each degree of freedom has some economic cost and some computational cost. Applications that require few degrees of freedom should be able to take advantage of savings incurred by reducing the degrees of freedom on the devices they use. With a device like the Dexterous Hand Master, the number of degrees of freedom relates to the complexity of the hardware, the comfort of the fit on the hand, and the time it takes to don and doff the device. A whole-hand input device with modular degrees of freedom would reduce these problems to an appropriate level for each application.

Hand to work-space mappings

A ripe area for investigation involves the effect of hand to work-space mappings. Most tasks using direct control do not have one-to-one mappings from hand to task. Thus, controls with linear or non-linear mappings must be used. The ability of humans to adapt to and manage different mappings, and what aids or hinders adaptation is not well understood. Experiments that vary the mapping of hand motion to task motion may reveal optimal paradigms for effective mappings. Rotational scaling is an interesting example. It would be useful to understand how well people can control rotations through linear mappings in which, for instance, 90° rotations of the hand cause 360° rotations in the control space.

Training for whole-hand input

It is not unreasonable for some whole-hand input tasks to require skilled operators. Personal observation indicates that a majority of people have limited general hand and finger dexterity but with training they can improve their hand function. This is certainly true for specific skill-based, dexterity-demanding endeavors such as the playing of musical instruments, dance, and surgery. Many practitioners of these arts regularly perform hand and finger exercises and stretches. Workers using whole-hand input would justifiably benefit from similar regimes.

Conclusion

This article has touched briefly on the use and study of the whole hand in the human-computer interface. The advantages of naturalness, dexterity, and adaptability make whole-hand input an excellent candidate for many, but not all, human-computer interfaces. Future experimentation and analysis will permit more effective use of this new input paradigm. For a more detailed discussion, see Sturman (1992).

Acknowledgements

This article was based on work at the MIT Media Lab under the direction of David Zeltzer. Valuable support and assistance was received from the members of the Computer Graphics and Animation group at the Media Lab between 1988 and 1992.

References

Badler, N. I. (1986), "Animating human figures: Perspectives and directions," *Proceedings Graphics Interface '86 / Vision Interface '86*, Vancouver, B.C., pp. 115–120.

Barr, A. and Feigenbaum, E. A., eds. (1982), *The handbook of artificial intelligence (Vol. 1)*, Addison-Wesley.

Becker, J. C. and Thakor, N. V. (1988), "A study of motion of human fingers with application to anthropomorphic designs," *IEEE Transactions on Biomedical Engineering*, 35(2), pp. 110–117.

Brooks, F. P. ,J., Ouh-Young, M., Batter, J. J., and Kilpatrick, P. J. (1990), "Project GROPE— Haptic displays for scientific visualization," *Computer Graphics*, 24(4), pp. 177–185, Proc. ACM SIGGRAPH '90.

Buxton, W. (1990), "The pragmatics of haptic input," ACM CHI'90 Tutorial Notes #26, Seattle, WA.

Buxton, W. and Myers, B. A. (1986), "A study of two-handed input," *Proceedings of CHI'86*, pp. 321–326.

Calvert, T. W. and Chapman, J. (1978), "Notation of movement with computer assistance," *Proceedings of the ACM Annual Conference*, pp. 731–736.

Card, S. K., Mackinlay, J. D., and Robertson, G. G. (1990), "The design space of input devices," *Proceedings of CHI'90*, Seattle, WA, pp. 117–124.

Chao, E. Y. S., An, K-N., III, W. P. C., and Linscheid, R. L. (1989), *Biomechanics of the hand: A basic research study*, World Scientific Publishing Co., Inc., Teaneck, NJ.

Clark, F. J. and Horch, K. W. (1986), "Kinesthesia," in *Handbook of perception and human performance, v. 1. Sensory processes and perception*, Boff, K. R., Kaufman, L., and Thomas, J. P. (eds.), Wiley, New York, pp. 13.1–13.62.

Cohen, E., Namir, L., and Schlesinger, I. M. (1977), *A new dictionary of sign language: employing the Eshkol-Wachmann movement notation system*, Mouton, The Hague.

Cole, K. J. and Abbs, J. H. (1986), "Coordination of three-joint digit movements for rapid finger-thumb grasp," *Journal of Neurophysiology*, 55(6), pp. 1407–1423.

Cutkosky, M. R. and Wright, P. K. (1986), "Modeling manufacturing grips and correlations with the design of robotic hands," *Proc. IEEE International Conference on Robotics and Automation*, 3, pp. 1533–1539.

Delp, D. and Delp, S. (1989), "Understanding human movement with computer graphics," *SOMA Engineering for the Human Body*, 3(3), pp. 17–25.

Durlach, N. I. (1989), *Research on reduced-capability human hands*, M.I.T. Research Laboratory of Electronics, Proposal to Office of Navel Research, Cambridge, MA.

Ervin, C. A. (1988), "A standardized test battery," in *Performance of protective clothing: Second symposium, ASTM STP 1989*, Mansdorf, S. Z., Sager, R., and Nielsen, A. P. (eds.), American Society for Testing and Materials, Philadelphia, pp. 50–56.

Evarts, E. V. (1974), "Sensorimotor cortex activity associated with movements triggered by visual as compared to somesthetic inputs," in *The neurosciences: Third study program*, Massachusetts Institute of Technology, Cambridge, MA, pp. 327–337.

Fels, S. S. (1990), *Building adaptive interfaces with neural networks: The glove-talk pilot study*, Department of Computer Science, University of Toronto, Technical Report CRG-TR-90-1, Toronto, Canada.

Gaver, W. (1986), "Auditory icons: Using sound in computer interfaces," *Human Computer Interactions*, 2, pp. 167–177.

Ginsberg, C. M. and Maxwell, D. (1983), "Graphical marionette," *Proc. ACM SIG-GRAPH/SIGART Workshop on Motion*, Toronto, Canada, pp. 172–179.

Goldstein, E. B. (1989), *Sensation and perception (3rd ed.)*, Wadsworth Publishing, Belmont, CA.

Grimes, G. J. (1983), *Digital data entry glove interface device*, Bell Telephone Laboratories, United States Patent 4,414,537, Murray Hill, NJ.

Hunter, J. M., Schneider, L. H., Mackin, E. J., and Callahan, A. D., eds. (1984), *Rehabilitation of the hand (2nd ed.)*, CV Mosby, St. Louis.

Jones, D. (1989a), "The sonic interface," in *Work with computers: Organizational, management, stress and health aspects*, Smith, M. J. and Salvendy, G. (eds.), Elsevier Science Publishers B.V., Amsterdam, pp. 383–388, Proceedings of HCI '89, Boston.

Jones, L. A. (1989b), "The assessment of hand function: a critical review of techniques," *Journal of Hand Surgery*, 14A(2, Pt. 1), pp. 221–228.

Kangari, R. and Halpin, D. W. (1989), "Potential robotics utilization in construction," *Journal of Construction Engineering and Management*, 115(1), pp. 126–143.

Kramer, J. and Leifer, L. (1989), *The Talking Glove: An expressive and receptive "verbal" communication aid for the deaf, deaf-blind, and nonvocal*, Stanford University, Department of Electrical Engineering.

Laban, R. (1975), *Laban's principles of dance and movement notation (2nd ed.)*, Plays, Inc., Boston, Published in 1956 and 1970 under the title: *Principles of dance and movement notation*.

Levit, C. and Bryson, S. (1991), "A virtual environment for exploration of three-dimensional flowfields," *SPIE/IS&T Symposium on Electronic Imaging Science and Technology: Conf. 1457 – Stereoscopic Displays and Applications II*, San Jose, CA.

Machover, T. (1990), *Flora*, Bridge Records, compact disc recording.

McCormick, B. H., DeFanti, T. A., and Brown, M. D., eds. (1987), "Visualization in scientific computing," *Computer Graphics*, 21(6), .

McKinnon, G. M., King, M. L., and Runnings, D. (1987), "Multi-axis control of telemanipulators," *Proc. First European In-Orbit Operations Technology Symposium*, Darmstaadt, W. Germany, pp. 487–491.

Mesplay, K. P. and Childress, D. S. (1988), "Capacity of the human operator to move joints as control inputs to prostheses," *Modeling and Control Issues in Biomechanical Systems*, Chicago, IL, pp. 17–25, Presented at the Annual Meeting of the American Society of Mechanical Engineers.

Minsky, M., Ouh-young, M., Steele, O., Brooks, Jr., F. P., and Behensky, M. (1990), "Feeling and seeing: Issues in force display," *Computer Graphics*, 24(2), pp. 235–243, Proc. 1990 Symposium on Interactive 3D Graphics, Snowbird, UT.

Noll, A. M. (1972), "Man-machine tactile communication," *SID Journal (Society for Information Display)*, 1(2), .

Ouh-young, M. (1990), *Force display in molecular docking*, Department of Computer Science, Unpublished doctoral dissertation (TR90-004), University of North Carolina at Chapel Hill.

Patrick, N. J. M., Sheridan, T., Massiminio, M., and Marcus, B. A. (1990), "Design and testing of a non-reactive, fingertip, tactile display for interaction with remote environments," *Proceedings of the SPIE Symposium on Advances in Intelligent Systems*, Boston, MA.

Pieper, S. D. (1992), *CAPS: Computer-aided plastic surgery*, Media Lab, Massachusetts Institute of Technology, PhD Thesis, Cambridge, MA.

Poizner, H., Klima, E. S., Bellugi, U., and Livingston, R. B. (1983), "Motion analysis of grammatical processes in visual-gestural language," *Proc. ACM SIGGRAPH/SIGART Workshop on Motion*, Toronto, Canada, pp. 148–171.

Robertson, B. (1992), "Moving Pictures," *Computer Graphics World*, 15(10), pp. 38–44.

Robinette, K. M., Ervin, C., and Zehner, G. (1987), *Development of a standard dexterity test battery*, Armstrong Aerospace Medical Research Lab, AAMRL-TR-87-034, Wright-Patterson AFB, OH, (NTIS AD-A188314).

Robotics World (1989), "Teleoperated manipulators aid underwater vehicle operation," 7(1), pp. 21–22.

Rogowitz, B. E. (1983), "The human visual system: A guide for the display technologist," *Proceedings of the SID*, 24(3), pp. 235–252.

Rolfe, J. M. and Staples, K. J., eds. (1986), *Flight simulation*, Cambridge University Press, Cambridge, UK.

Rubine, D. (1991), "Specifying gestures by example," *Computer Graphics*, 25(4), pp. 329–337, Proceedings ACM SIGGRAPH '91.

Sheridan, T. B. (1989), "Merging mind and machine," *Technology Review*, pp. 33–40.

Singh, B., Beatty, J. C., Booth, K. S., and Ryman, R. (1982), *A Graphics Editor for Benesh Movement Notation*, University of Waterloo Computer Science Dept., Tech. Report CS-82-41, Waterloo, Ontario, Canada.

Stokoe, W. C. ,J. (1960), *Sign language structure: An outline of the visual communication systems of the American deaf*, Studies in Linguistics: Occasional Papers, 8, University of Buffalo, Department of Anthropology and Linguistics, Buffalo, NY, (Reissued Washington, D.C., Gallaudet College Press).

Sturman, D., Zeltzer, D., and Pieper, S. (1989), "Hands-on interaction with virtual environments," *Proc. UIST '89: ACM SIGGRAPH/SIGCHI Symposium on User Interface Software and Technology*, Williamsburg, VA, pp. 19–24.

Sturman, D. J. (1992), *Whole-hand input*, Media Lab, Massachusetts Institute of Technology, Doctoral dissertation, Cambridge, MA.

Takahashi, T. and Kishino, F. (1990), *Hand gesture coding based on experiments using a hand gesture interface device*, ATR Communication Systems Research Laboratories, Technical Report, Kyoto, Japan.

Trubitt, D. (1990), "Into new worlds; virtual reality and the electronic musician," *Electronic Musician*, pp. 31–40.

Ware, C. and Osborne, S. (1990), "Exploration and virtual camera control in virtual three dimensional environments," *Computer Graphics*, 24(2), pp. 175–183, Proceedings 1990 Symposium on Interactive Graphics.

Zimmerman, T. G., Lanier, J., Blanchard, C., Bryson, S., and Harvill, Y. (1987), "A hand gesture interface device," *Proc. Human Factors in Computing Systems and Graphics Interface (CHI+GI'87)*, Toronto, Canada, pp. 189–192.

Zimmerman, T. G. and Lanier, J. Z. (1991), *Computer Data Entry and Manipulation Apparatus and Method*, VPL Research, Inc., United States Patent 4,988,981, Redwood City, CA.

David Sturman is currently a member of the Research and Development Group of Medialab, a company specializing in high-end computer graphics animation production and custom virtual reality systems. His research interests include real-time computer animation and human-computer interfaces. He completed his Ph.D. at the M.I.T. Media Lab in 1992 where he investigated real-time computer interaction using whole-hand input. Mr. Sturman received a B.S. from MIT in 1979, and an M.S. in computer science from Rutgers University in 1981. He was a member of the technical staff of Bell Laboratories and then the New York Institute of Technology Computer Graphics Lab prior to returning to MIT for his doctorate.

Address: *MEDIALAB*, 104 av. du Président Kennedy, 75016 Paris France

Communicating with Virtual Worlds: Accessing Data, Information, and Knowledge by Multimedia Technologies

Rae A. Earnshaw

ABSTRACT

This paper reviews the current developments and initiatives in multimedia technologies and applications. Video, audio, text and image are increasingly being used in research, teaching developments and applications. Technology is bringing digital media to the workstation desktop at affordable prices, and software facilities enable these media to be integrated into higher level applications. Such facilities offer opportunities for interactive and integrated demonstrations and simulations, and personalized learning via courseware, on the workstation or PC using graphics, audio, and video sequences.

KEYWORDS: computer graphics, visualization, multimedia technologies, digital media, teaching and learning via technology, interactive exploration, virtual reality, virtual worlds, video conferencing, simulation.

1. INTRODUCTION

1.1 Desk-Top Facilities

Video, audio, text and image are increasingly being used in research, teaching developments, and applications. Technology is bringing digital media to the workstation desktop at affordable prices, and software facilities enable these media to be integrated into higher level applications. Such facilities offer opportunities for personalised learning via courseware, and integrated demonstrations and simulations on the workstation or PC using graphics and video sequences.

1.2 Desk-Top Digital Media

A revolution is currently taking place caused by developments in the area of digital media. Simply put, the term refers to the integration in a seamless environment of a variety of entities including, but not limited to, 3D graphics, video, still images, audio and text, all linked in a fashion that allows quick and easy interactivity on the local PC or workstation, across a network, or around the world. A wide range of software tools and facilities is becoming available to enable ordinary users to handle video, animations, and sound just as easily as they have handled lines of text on the PC screen. One author writes: "Over the next decade or two, digital media is likely to to have an impact on nearly every aspect of creative endeavour - an impact that will rival that of the printing press, the telephone, and the motion picture - while incorporating aspects of all of them" (Cruickshank, 1992).

29

1.3 Application Areas

Microsoft's new PC operating system Windows NT is expected in 1993 with increasing capability in the area of digital media. Deliverables for a wide range of application areas (including Teaching and Learning Technology Programmes) will be ported to this environment. Workstation vendors are targetting the area of digital media. Potential applications are video conferencing via the user's local workstation, distributed classrooms, electronic mail with audio and video, training documents, and media composing.

1.4 Video Conferencing

Video conferencing will allow people to participate in a live session without leaving their desks. The workstation will receive the real-time image and voice of the participant and distribute it to the group. At the same time, each participant can refer to displayed text or graphical documents, and show live video sequences or simulations to the group. The whole group can interact with each other and the materials being discussed. The potential use of developments such as this for the national and international collaboration of groups of workers is immense. People can collaborate and interact as if they were meeting in the same office, but they could be physically located on the other side of the world.

1.5 Distributed Classroom Learning

Distributed classroom learning will enable instructional materials and interactive sessions (including video clips) to be stored on a centrally maintained computing/audio/video server. Students can access this material, across the network, from their PC. Because of inter-network communication it is possible for students to access materials at other national or even international centres, given the permission and access to do so.

1.6 Enhanced Electronic Mail

Electronic mail with audio and video will allow some of the disadvantages and limitations of text email to be overcome by providing the capability for more personlised interactions and also the the inclusion of video sequences and simulations.

1.7 Training Manuals and Procedures

Training documents will allow a training manual to be accompanied by an instructional video on a digital media workstation. For a complex area such as a revised procedure for aircraft maintenance, the mechanic can study the detailed visual simulation of the procedure, and practice it, before performing a repair on a real aircraft.

1.8 Desk-top Visualization

Visualization tools are migrating down to the desk top. Application builders such as AVS, Explorer, Data Explorer, and Khoros enable users to set up their requirements by using a visual interface. Icons representing the functions needed are selected from the repertoire available and connected together using a network of pipes. It is possible to run different modules on different systems to take advantage of supercomputers accessed remotely across a communications network. Such tools enable a 3D visualization to be viewed on a desk-top workstation screen. Real-time simulations can be done on higher powered workstations. Virtual reality interfaces allow the user to perform more immersive observations and interactions with the computer model or simulations, and have been particularly effective in the NASA Ames Virtual Wind Tunnel (Bryson 92, Bryson 93) for the study and analysis of

CFD phenomena.

Digital media facilities allow scientific visualization simulations to be transmitted across the network and analysed by a group of workers in different locations. Such developments are likely radically transform the work of groups whose cooperating partners are located in physically separate institutions.

2. TECHNOLOGIES TO SUPPORT MULTIMEDIA APPLICATIONS

2.1 Network Infrastructure

Transmission of data between sites depends on national and international telecomunications networks. Service on these in the past has been slow due to overloading, but plans are being set in place for upgrading the capacity of the major networks. For example, JANET (the academic network in the United Kingdom) is being upgrade from 2Mbps to 140 Mbps (SuperJANET) along with a rolling program for connection to UK Universities. Improving network technologies (e.g. Asynchronous Transfer Mode - ATM) will enable more traffic to be handled on these faster networks. The program for connection to UK sites will link up Cambridge, Edinburgh, Imperial College, Manchester, University College and Rutherford Appleton Laboratory in March 1993, and a further six sites by September 1993.

Multimedia applications are to be used as some of the projects for the evaluation of SuperJANET in 1993. The Joint Network Team in the UK has strong interests in multimedia in the context of developments in SuperJANET, for the areas of distributed functionality, interworking of standards, and the implications for network loadings. Some of the pilot applications expected on SuperJANET by March 93 are in the areas of computer visualization, supercomputer interconnection, medical scanning, and remote teaching. User applications are expected in the areas of distributed hypermedia systems, video conferencing, supercomputer support, and the use of X400 mail with video clips. The latter is likely to overload even a fast network!

The Joint Network Team has a Special Interest Group in Multimedia in order to have effective discussion on the requirements of applications areas (e.g. distributed hypertextual systems, video conferencing, supercomputer support, compound documents, and computer-supported cooperative working (often known simply as CSCW). Multimedia applications may require a store and forward service (e.g. text message with a video clip) or synchronous access (e.g. for pan and zoom across an image across the network).

The JNT also communicates with the RARE Working Group on Multimedia. The RARE Working Group has a number of Work Items including demonstrator projects, document conversion, ISO-VT monitoring, and liaison with X Window organisations.

It is significant that network speeds and bandwidth are increasing significantly exactly at the moment that effective compression techniques via hardware are being realised. It is an excellent opportunity for handling real-time images across networks.

2.2 Video and Compression

Compression is essential because the lowest resolution (VGA) and lowest frame rate saturates an FDDI or high speed line. Compression of still images can be done by non-image compression (e.g. Unix LZW), run-length encoding (can give 20:1 reduction), JPEG, or fractal methods (using area decomposition).

For JPEG, there are lossy and loss-free methods, and software and hardware implementations, with several modes of operation

- sequential encoding
- progressive encoding
- lossy encoding
- hierarchical encoding JPEG is fast and predictable in hardware.

Compression of moving images can use H.261 teleconferencing standard, real time JPEG, MPEG, fractal methods, and DVI (Intel). Further information can be found in Brodlie et al (1992).

Different application areas require different compression systems - no single method is best for all applications. JPEG and MPEG provide symmetric, predictable results for compression.

Digital video is required so that video can be stored with electronic data, transmitted with electronic data, and manipulated on the computer along with electronic data. It is possible that video may be regarded as a data type. However, there is no clear vendor standard as yet; different manufacturers use their own systems (e.g. DVI, Photo-CD, CD-I, MPEG, MPEG11, Quicktime, and Video for Windows).

2.3 Software and Products for the Mass Market

It is clear that the mass consumer electronics market drives the developments in technology. Major advances are expected in 1993 as compression technologies become embodied in the products that are released for the mass market. Major publishing houses are all looking at the potential of multimedia for dissemination of their material, despite the high initial setup costs production on new media.

Developments from the major players in the PC software market are expected in 1993. Power PC and Microsoft Windows NT will become available, with multimedia capabilities.

3. DEVELOPMENTS AND INITIATIVES AT THE UNIVERSITY OF LEEDS

3.1 Overview

The University of Leeds has a well established Scientific Visualization Group which was formed in 1991 to coordinate and develop plans and activities in the University. It coincided with a major upgrade in computing facilities and the procurement of a supercomputer. A report of the work of this group appears in Earnshaw (1992). A Multimedia Group was established in January 1992 to prepare plans, coordinate activities, and initiate developments for what was seen to be an important, strategic, and enabling area for the future. National University bodies in the UK were also concerned to promote and develop areas where teaching and learning could be enhanced by the utilization of modern technology.

These developments in technology have come at a time when the number of students entering Universities in the UK is dramatically increasing. The national funding bodies are therefore concerned to develop infrastructure whereby the additional students can receive tuition without stretching the already overloaded lecturing faculty. This implies the use of automated and computer-based tools.

The following were some of the areas where multimedia tools were regarded as having something useful to contribute to the work of academic institutions -

a) Teaching larger classes more effectively
b) Improving tutorial teaching
c) Benefits in easing lecturer load
d) Perceived benefits from the students' viewpoints in

learning a new subject
e) Teaching concepts or topics not possible by traditional methods

3.2 Multimedia Activities

Initial work at the University of Leeds has concentrated on developing current activities, and the provision of financial support to enable these activities to move forward more quickly. It proved opportune to combine these initiatives into the establishment of a CBL/Multimedia Summer School in the University from July to September 1992. It provided a facilities-rich environment by utilising one of the PC and Workstation Clusters already existing on the University campus (with further equipment and software added for specific multimedia requirements), and also provide a focus for the promotion of interdisciplinary collaboration and exchange in the area of teaching and research.

The initial objectives of the Summer School were therefore to coordinate the current development programme in multimedia in the University; provide a series of Workshops, Demonstrations and Colloquia to disseminate information and stimulate interest; offer a programme of activity to enable staff to produce CBL and related materials; and provide a reference library with a complete set of publications from the Computers in Teaching Initiative (CTI) and the work that has already been done by the existing CTI Centres in the UK.

Current projects in the development programme include 'Teaching for Computer Vision', 'A Library Guidance System', 'Introduction to UNIX', 'Automated Tutorial Teaching', 'Chemistry Experiments', 'Drug Studies', 'Tutorial Aids', 'A Multimedia CAD System Tutorial', 'Application of Mathematica', and 'Understanding Kinematics'.

The emphasis was upon real tools for real users, and more importantly real tools for users who have not been users before, and who wished to produce materials and move applications forward with the minimum of effort in learning how to use and apply the current software tools and facilities available. This was a real and valid test of current tools and the friendliness and usability of the interfaces! Perhaps we can do much to shape future developments and products in this area (provided they conform to agreed standards, of course).

A Medium Term Strategy for Supporting Multimedia and Computer-Based Tools for Learning and Teaching in the University has been drawn up.

3.3 TLTP CBL/Multimedia Unit

On 12 March 1992 the UK Universities Funding Council announced a major £5 million initiative to promote projects in the area of 'Teaching and Learning through Technology' (TLTP) and invited submissions from UK institutions for funds for developments. In August 1992, the University of Leeds was awarded a large grant for a 3 year development program for the University in collaboration with Silicon Graphics Inc. To implement and progress this project a CBL/Multimedia Unit was established in December 1992. Figure 1 illustrates the relationship of this Unit to existing departments, centres, and units in the University. It is evident that the Unit benefits substantially from having strong links to already well-established groups - for the purposes of liaison and support and also for technology transfer. The Unit also benefits from wider links to related work in other UK Universities, and via telecommunication networks to other groups worldwide.

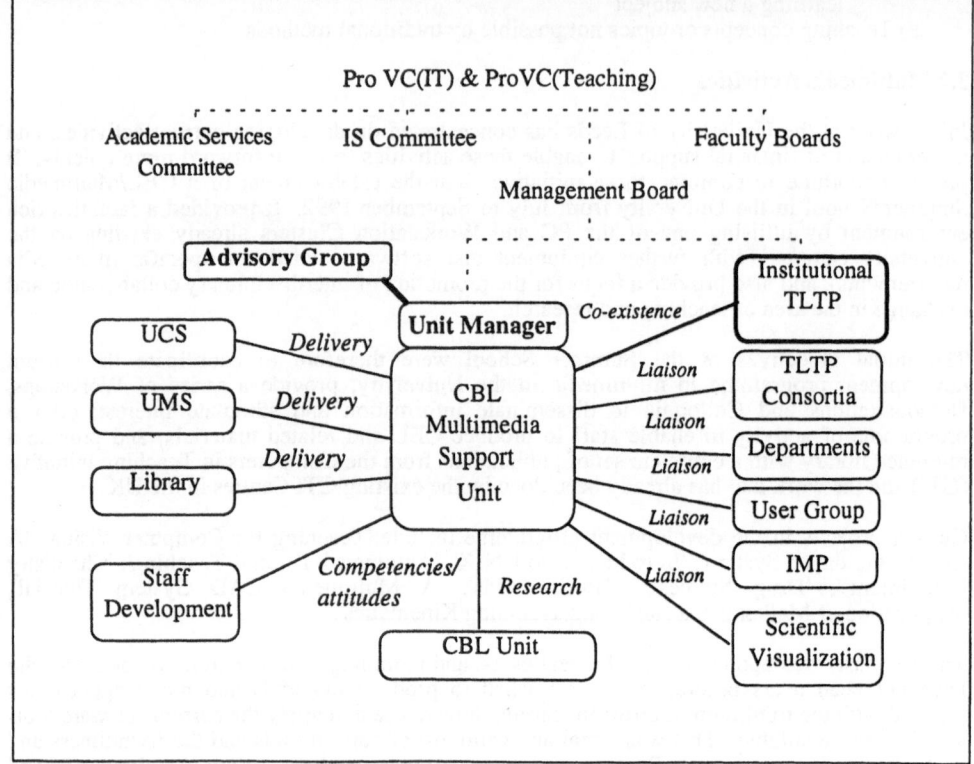

Figure 1. The Relationship of the CBL/Multimedia Support Unit to other Organisations at the University of Leeds

3.4 Network-based Video Facilities

A joint project group between the Graphics and Digital Media Unit, Scientific Visualization, and Computing has been established to draw up plans for the emerging area of digital media and digital video. The objective is to enable any user on the campus network to be able to generate materials on the local workstation then pass them across the network for the generation of slides or videotapes.

4. SOFTWARE, AUTHORING TOOLS, AND STANDARDS

4.1 Overview

Multimedia systems may be classified as follows -
- Presentation systems
- Authoring systems
- Multimedia databases

Presentation systems included Macromind Director (Apple), Media Maker (Apple), Audio Visual Connection (IBM), Animator (IBM), Storyboard Plus (IBM) and Amiga Vision (Commodore).

Authoring systems include PLATO, Ten Core, Top Class, Mentor, Microtext, Avanti,

IconAuthor, Authorware Professional. Hypermedia systems include Guide, Hypercard, Link Way, Super Card, Toolbook, Hyperwriter.

Current generation hypermedia systems such as Hypercard and Toolbook tend to be closed systems with proprietary formats. Applications are limited in size because of the authoring effort required. They are difficult to maintain, update, and extend and are often limited to the original author. There is a lack of integration with other applications. Thus there is a need for more open systems, to utilise source material from sources such as CD-ROM, networks, and databases. A database of links is also needed. Microcosm at Southampton University has been designed to fulfil these objectives.

4.2 HyTime and SGML

SGML is a device-independent standard for producing documents. HyTime is a Hypermedia Time-based Structural Language (ISO standard) for specifying interconnections (hyperlinks) within and between documents and other information objects, and for scheduling multimedia information in time and space. It is parsable as SGML. As a markup language it can describe structural, scheduling, and rendition information which is independent of device, system, and language.

SGML needs a parser, editor, and a translator to a code for output to a printing device, e.g. LaTeX. Similarly, HyTime needs the same as SGML plus a HyTime Engine to process the HyTime markup. HyTime Engines are expected in 1993.

HyTime has been adopted by Apple, IBM, OWL. Current users are US DoD, the Davenport Group, and the Esprit Multimedia Information Presentation System (MIPS) project. The UK ISC Courseware Development Working Party are exploring how such tools can enable personalised materials to be produced, i.e. customised for particular lecturers requirements and contexts.

4.3 Standards

Figure 2 gives an overview of storage and standards, with digital multimedia storage units on the right (usually some kind of optical disk), and linking methods on the left. At the bottom are standards to link together representations, techniques, and networking.

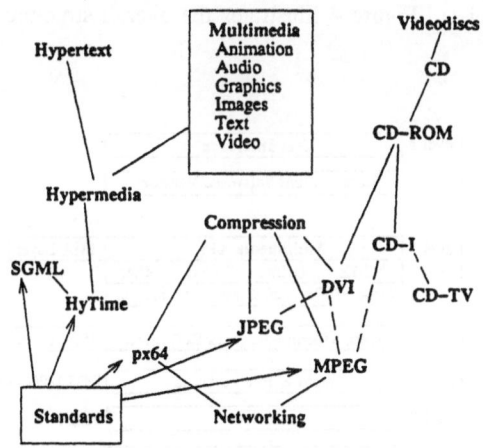

Figure 2: Overview Diagram — Storage, Standards, Technology

(Figure courtesy of Fox (1992))

Developing sophisticated multimedia applications is a time-consuming task. Figure 3 illustrates the authoring process for CD-ROM's.

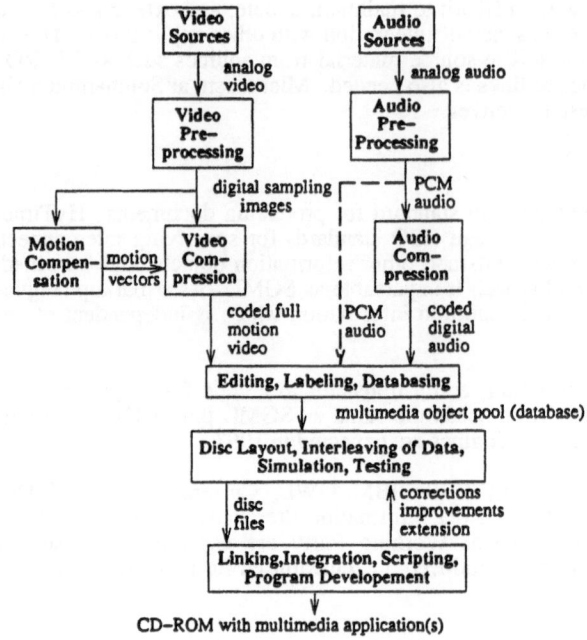

Figure 3   MPEG Based CD-ROM Publishing

(Figure courtesy of Fox (1992))

In order to facilitate interworking the Interactive Multimedia Association are working on the IMA Compatibility Project. Figure 4 illustrates the overall structure and the different layers and standards.

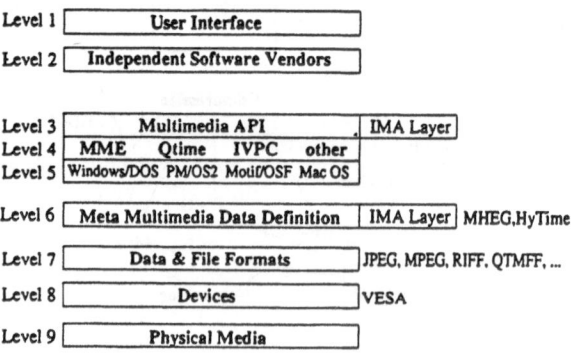

Figure 4: IMA Compatibility Project Architecture
Adapted from [75] p. 90.

(Figure courtesy of Fox (1992))

5. BEYOND MULTIMEDIA

5.1 Retrospective and Overview

Key developments in the areas of computing and graphics from 1945-92 included Sketchpad by Ivan Sutherland (1963), the Virtual Reality Helmet also by Ivan Sutherland (1968), Dynabook in 1968, and the Architecture Machine by Nick Negroponte (1970) - an early example of 'ubiquitous computing' in the sense of matching what humans are good at to what computers are good at (human computer symbiosis). Significant major trends include Main Frame to Desk Top to Anywhere, which coincides with corresponding shifts in control from Procedural (and Data Structures) to Object-Oriented to Agent-Oriented. Recent trends are evidenced by pronounced shifts in the market place, with a number of key computer hardware vendors experiencing severe financial difficulties.

5.2 Interfaces of the Future

Negroponte (1992) outlines two trends accompanying the movement of interface agents. In 1994 he expected that 80% of the human computer interface will be an RF communicating device 'in the pocket', and the important component will be the RF. The second trend is to observe that the desk top metaphor is becoming rapidly out of date and no longer relevant. Desk tops are already full and busy people are not often at their desks anyway. The same will soon apply to computer 'desk tops'.

There is already a world of various kinds of agents - from domestic to electronic. The central question is 'What lives in the network and what lives on the periphery?' Currently 'thin wire' TV could provide information by compression, transmission, and de-compression. The world of agents was the opposite of this. A wide band network will carry vast amounts of information; what is required at the user end is a filter or agent to select the portions required - whether it be personalised TV, tailored newspapers, or technical data. As the amount of information grows, it becomes increasingly difficult for a user to filter this personally. We all see the tip of the ice-berg at the moment in longer and longer email queues - and those who respond quickly soon get known as efficient, which in turn generates longer email queues!

The central issue is one of direct manipulation versus delegation. 90% of business at MIT is currently run by email. This generates vast amounts of electronic folders to contain all the information. How can a particular item be readily accessed? A simple request like 'Fetch the last letter from John Smith' needs to be processed. We should be able to delegate this in a simple way to the computer. Just as a butler would know the relationship between his employer and his colleagues, and arrange things likely to be required accordingly, so an agent should do this for computer-based information. The central idea is shared knowledge between user and machine.

When considering multimedia agents for the 21st century it is essential to have a human computer symbiosis where humans interact kinesthetically with the machine, or can build agents themselves, rather than just treating the computer as a mechanical slave and - like the Roman Empire of old - eventually come to find it has no future. Thus agents with value systems are indispensable to the network systems of the future, and it is of no real consequence whether such agents are anthropomorphic or just metaphors.

If networking was the key to the information revolution of the 1980's, information management will be the key to the information explosion of the 1990's.

6. CONCLUSIONS

6.1 Developments in IT Strategies for Computer-Based Information

Many institutions are have forward plans for IT strategies which have been brought about by the need to implement policies in the areas such as the following -

- o Facilities for Classroom and Lecture room presentations
- o Projection equipment for materials based on PC's
- o Production and copying of colour graphics and OHP's
- o Typsetting and production of reports and books where the material
  originated on a computer

In the past there have isolated success stories in the development and support of multimedia facilities (e.g. Doomsday project) but these had been limited either by dedicated hardware not being general available, or by being discipline-specific. With current trends in technology it is now possible to produce multimedia teaching materials and presentations which can operate on relatively low cost equipment. Thus the end-user level is fairly straighforward. What requires more thought is the complex process of producing multimedia materials and how they integrate into the overall instructional and educational processes. This includes the areas of educational design, graphics design, and computer systems design.

Some questions to consider are: What is the best way to disseminate multimedia instructional materials on campus? Copies of CD's for students? (this has implications for the provision of CD readers and security of the readers). Should the materials be held centrally and be accessed via the campus network? Most sites are bandwidth limited in this area. What kinds of information compression might help in this area?

6.2 The Workstation of the Future

Clark (1992) sees future developments being driven by consumer electronics. The "telecomputer" is one possible scenario, where the home TV set becomes a multi-media player and acts as the visual control centre for many new applications such as television entertainment, virtual reality games, home control systems, interactive books, magazines and newsprint, and telephonic, televideo and data communications.

The workstation of the late nineties is going to be a 3G machine: Gigaops, Gigabyte and Gigabaud. It will handle speech and sound, static and dynamic images, input and output of natural language, and have an intelligent and robust user interface (van Dam, 1992). Thus developments in technology will transform current trends and activities and necessitate a new applications-building environment for the future, of a kind that is appropriate for high-performance, multimedia hardware and software platforms.

7. REFERENCES

Aceves J.J.G.L., A. A. Poggio, "Computer-Based Multimedia Communications" IEEE Computer, Vol 18, No 10, pp 10-14, 1985.

Brodlie K. W., L. A. Carpenter, R. A. Earnshaw, J. R. Gallop, R. J. Hubbold, A. M. Mumford, C. D. Osland, P. Quarendon, "Scientific Visualization - Techniques and Applications" Springer-Verlag, Berlin, Heidelberg, pp 284, Jan 1992

Bryson S. and C. Levit, "The Virtual Wind Tunnel", IEEE Computers Graphics and Applications, Vol 12, No 4, pp 25-34, July 92

Clark J. H., "A TeleComputer", Computer Graphics, Vol 26, No 2 (ACM SIGGRAPH 92), pp 19-23, 1992.

Cruickshank D., "Digital Media", IRIS Universe, No 20, pp 16-21, Spring 1992.

Earnshaw R. A. and N. Wiseman, "An Introductory Guide to Scientific Visualization", Springer-Verlag, pp 156, July 1992

Earnshaw R. A., "Scientific Visualization at the University of Leeds", ACM Computer Graphics, Vol 26, No 3, pp 182-183, August 1992.

Earnshaw R. A. and D. Watson (Eds), "Animation and Scientific Visualization" Academic Press, to be published 1993.

Encarnacao J. L., C. Hornung, H. Kuhlmann, and R. Lindner, "Advancing Interaction, Multi-Media and Visualization - the Enabling Computer Graphics Techniques for Computer-based Distant Education and Industrial Training", in Proceedings of CG International 92 Ed T. L. Kunii, pp 857-868, Springer-Verlag, 1992.

Fox E. A., "Advances in Interactive Digital Multimedia Systems", IEEE Computer, Vol 24, No 10, pp 9-22, 1991.

Fox E.A. "Multimedia: Applications and Practice", EG92, TN6, 1992.

Fuchs H., Foreword to Virtual Reality Systems, "Virtual Reality Systems", Eds R. A. Earnshaw, M. A. Gigante, H. Jones, Academic Press, 1993.

Harrison M. A., "Defining Hypermedia: The Essential Elements", Report No UCB/CSD 92/671, Computer Science Division, University of California at Berkeley, February 1992.

Jobs S. and Gates W. "The Future of the PC", Fortune, pp 26-37, August 26, 1991.

Le Gall D., "MPEG: A Video Compression Standard for Multimedia Applications", Communications of the ACM, Vol 34, No 4, pp 46-58, April 1991.

Myerson T., T Rhyne, "Navigating the Video Maze", ACM Computer Graphics, Vol 26, No 3, pp 190-193, August 1992.

Narasimhalu A. D., S. Christodoulakis, "Multimedia Information Systems: The Unfolding of a Reality", IEEE Computer, Vol 24, No 10, pp 6-7, 1991.

Negroponte N., "The Architecture Machine", MIT Press, Cambridge, MA, 1970.

Poggio A., J. J. G. L. Aceves, E. J. Craighill, D. Moran, L. Aguilar, D. Worthington, J. Hight, "CCWS: A Computer-Based, Multimedia Information System" IEEE Computer, Vol 18, No 10, pp 92-105, 1985.

Reynolds J. K., J. B. Postel, A. R. Katz, G. G. Finn, A. L. DeSchon, "The DARPA Experimental Multimedia Mail System" IEEE Computer, Vol 18, No 10, pp 82-91, 1985.

Ritchie I., "Multimedia versus Reality", The CTISS File, No 14, (Special Issue on Multimedia), pp 6-8, Oct 1992.

Sutherland I. E., "Sketchpad: A Man-Machine Graphical Communication System", SJCC, Spartan Books, Baltimore, MD, 1963.

Sutherland I.E., "A Head-Mounted Three Dimensional Display", FJCC, Thompson Books, Washington DC, 757-764, 1968.

van Dam A., "The 1991 Steven A. Coons Award Lecture", ACM Computer Graphics, Vol 26, No 3, pp 205-206, August 1992.

Wallace G.K., "The JPEG Still Picture Compression Standard", Communications of the ACM, Vol 34, No 4, pp 30-44, April 1991.

Yankelovich N., N. Meyrowitz, A. van Dam, "Reading and Writing the Electronic Book" IEEE Computer, Vol 18, No 10, pp 15-32, 1985.

"The Multimedia Encyclopedia of Mammalian Biology", McGraw Hill, 1992.

Multimedia: Computing with Sound and Motion, EMAP Business and Computer Publications, ISSN 0959 8227

Report on an MIT Media Laboratory Symposium on Interface Agents, "HCI interfaces for the 1990's - Beyond Multimedia", 20 October 1992, Computer Graphics Newsletter, No 28, February 1993.

AGOCG Workshop, 25 November 1992, AGOCG Technical Report No 19. "From Graphics into Multimedia", 1993.

AGOCG Workshop, 12 November 1992, AGOCG Technical Report No 18, "Computing and A/V Services: Managing the Graphics Common Ground", 1993.

AUTHOR BIOGRAPHY

Dr Rae A. Earnshaw, University of Leeds, UK

Rae Earnshaw is Head of Computer Graphics at the University of Leeds, with interests in graphics algorithms, scientific visualization, display technology, CAD/CAM, and human-computer interface issues. He has been a Visiting Professor at Illinois Institute of Technology, Chicago, USA, Northwestern Polytechnical University, China, and George Washington University, Washington DC, USA. He was a Director of the NATO Advanced Study Institute on "Fundamental Algorithms for Computer Graphics" held in Ilkley, England, in 1985, a Co-Chair of the BCS/ACM International Summer Institute on "State of the Art in Computer Graphics" held in Scotland in 1986, and a Director of of the NATO Advanced Study Institute on "Theoretical Foundations of Computer Graphics and CAD" held in Italy in 1987. He is a member of ACM, IEEE, CGS, EG, and a Fellow of the British Computer Society.

Dr Earnshaw has authored and edited 17 books on graphics algorithms, computer graphics, scientific visualization and associated topics.

Dr Earnshaw Chairs the Scientific Visualization Group at the University of Leeds, is a member of the Editorial Board of The Visual Computer, a Committee Member of the Board of the Computer Graphics Society, and Chair of the British Computer Society Computer Graphics and Displays Group.

Address: Head of Graphics, University of Leeds, Leeds LS2 9JT, England.

Distributed, Multi-Person, Physically-Based Interaction in Virtual Worlds

Michael A. Gigante and Robert C. Webb

ABSTRACT

We describe a network-based framework for building virtual environments that incorporate real-time collision detection and physical simulation. This framework allows worlds to be defined and shared by remote, multiple participants. It also provides a conceptually simple and efficient method to build single-person virtual environments.

Keywords: virtual reality, virtual worlds, interactive simulation, collision detection, rigid body motion.

1.0 INTRODUCTION

Two of the primary goals of research in Virtual Reality are to improve performance (increase update rates and complexity, reduce latency) and to make virtual environments more realistic (visual and behavioural).

Increasing performance of VR systems is often driven by hardware developments such as new graphics architectures (Molnar 1992, Silicon Graphics 1992) or improved 3D sensor technology (Ward 1992). While there are obviously enormous benefits from the developments in hardware, there are very significant opportunities to increase performance via algorithmic improvements. Spatial data structures allow significant pre-processing of geometry to improve graphics rendering rates (Funkhouser 1992, Baum 1990) and decrease the cost of collision detection (Webb 1992). The use of predictive filters (Friedmann 1992) can also improve the useable number of 3D sensor updates.

While much of the focus on realism naturally concentrates on visual realism, there is a great deal of work to be done in improving the behavioural fidelity of Virtual Worlds. The goal of more intuitive, natural environments is more accessible if, where appropriate, objects behave in the same manner as their real-world counterparts (Papper 1991, 1992).

2.0 BACKGROUND

2.1 Collision Detection for Simulation/Virtual Environments

There has been considerable research on algorithms for collision detection in both robotic applications (Latombe 1991) and simulation (Zyda 1993). Collision detection algorithms developed by the robotics community are generally characterised by stationary scenes, with single or multiple mobile robotic devices, thus pre-processing can be used to classify regions where collisions will happen. Simulation scenarios can be quite different, with many complex, moving objects or components. If the number of moving objects is not small, then pre-processing does not prove very useful. We developed a technique for very efficient collision detection in complex, dynamic environments (Webb 1992). In that paper we described the use of dynamic automatic bounding volume hierarchies to reduce the cost

of object-object collision detection to $O(N \log N)$ instead of $O(N^2)$. The PIVW system is built around an improved version of the techniques described earlier. In particular, the following changes have been incorporated:

- Support for concave objects
- N-ary trees instead of the original binary trees.
- A subsidiary, static automatic bounding volume hierarchy for the faces defining polygonal objects.

The result of these changes is that for a medium performance workstation (MIPS 33Mhz R3000), 15Hz update can be sustained for approximately 200 polygonal objects of 100 polygons/object.

2.2 Physical Simulation, Rigid Body Motion

There have been two approaches to the use of physics and simulation in computer graphics. The first approach has been to use systems of equations of motion (Baraff 1989), solved by conventional ODE solvers. The simulations can be computationally expensive, typically unsuitable for real-time interaction. The second approach uses gross simplifications or approximations to the laws of physics to allow real-time interaction while still providing some of the benefits of physical realism. Papper (1992) showed that by using simplified, real-time physics, users of both conventional mouse-driven interfaces and virtual environments found the system to be more intuitive than without any physics. In addition, the users were more productive than using the system without any physics.

3.0 ARCHITECTURE

3.1 Overview

This paper describes our research into ways to improve both performance and behavioural realism of virtual worlds. We seek these improvements through the application of spatial data structures to real-time collision detection, selection/picking and the selective use of physical simulation in Virtual Environment applications. The desire to support realistic physical behaviour is tempered by selectively disabling some physical constraints to allow convenient interaction metaphors.

Grasping and extrernal control are integrated with the physical simulation and collision detection so that, for example, grasped objects do not pass through immovable objects (walls, floors) and a grasped object like a bat can be used to impart velocity to a movable object like a ball. Similar to grasping, objects can also be placed under external, programmed control. In the case of conflict (externally controlled object, colliding with an immovable object), the external control or grasp is disabled and the object reverts to simulation control.

The **Physically-based Interaction in Virtual Worlds (PIVW)** framework is built around the notion that Virtual Environment applications are well suited to network distributed computation. This is clearly illustrated by examining our lab setup.

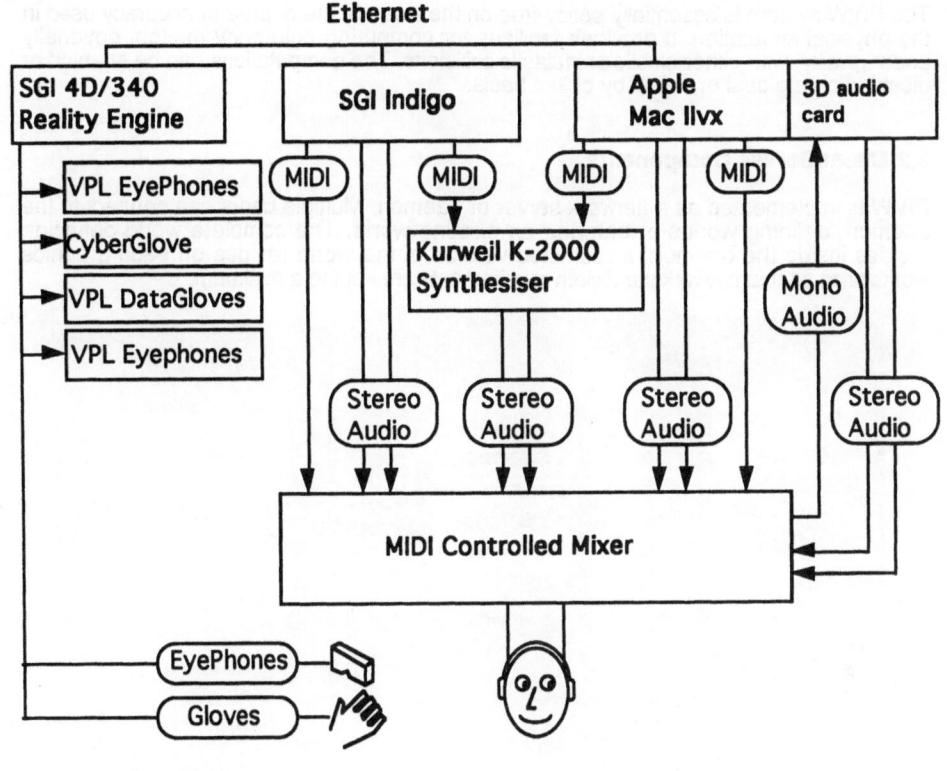

Fig 1 Schematic overview of VR application network

A typical VR application will use the Apple Mac II to generate 3D audio, use the SGI 340 Reality Engine and Head Mounted Display for display, 6 degree of freedom input devices for interaction and the compute server for collision detection and simulation.

In PIVW, all these facilities are available through a single application interface. The application is logically distributed between the compute server, the Audio server(s) and the I/O machine(s). While in our setup, the input devices happen to be located on the display workstation, this is by no means necessary. In our setup, the server executes on the 4D/340, a multiprocessor workstation, thus providing simple and effective parallelism. The server could also run on an available high performance compute machine, increasing the sustainable complexity of the environments.

The PIVW system is essentially policy-free on the issue of the degree of accuracy used in the physical simulation. It provides facilities for computing rigid body motion, optionally under gravity, with either elastic or inelastic collisions. The computations can be enabled or disabled on a global or object by object basis.

3.2 Client/Server Components

PIVW is implemented as a network server or daemon. Multiple users can connect to the daemon, defining worlds or entering an existing world. The complete world definition resides inside the daemon, a restricted version of the world resides on each graphics workstation so that network bandwidth requirements are kept to a minimum.

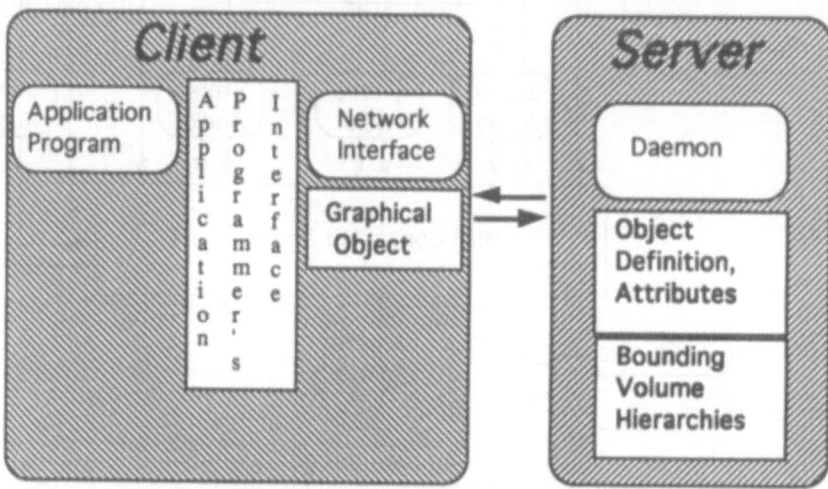

Fig 2 Schematic of an PIVW application

The server maintains the complete world definition, object definitions (including calculated values for mass, centre of mass, moments of inertia, graphics object identifier), object grouping and active attributes (global and object by object flags determining whether, for example, gravity affects the scene/object). The server also computes the collision detection, object selection and rigid body dynamics. The server also provides audio cues on intersection. Currently, the pitch and volume of the sound are simple functions of the collision impulse and the objects' mass. In our facility, MIDI events are sent across the network to a MacIntosh IIvx with a Focal Point 3D audio card connected to a Kurzweil K-2000 sampling synthesiser. In this way, our PIVW applications get 3D sound cues automatically.

The client (graphics) workstation stores the graphical object in some native format. In our case, this is a GL object[1] . The client application is responsible for establishing any required grouping, and for any gesture or command recognition. The application is also responsible for controlling to which objects (if any) the rigid body computations will be applied.

The world is partitioned into 2 parts; static objects and dynamic objects. Each group is stored in a bounding volume hierarchy in the server. The dynamic hierarchy is updated as previously described in Webb (1992). Objects move back and forth between these hierarchies automatically when objects are grasped or released, or when a stationary object is hit by a moving object. The static hierarchy is rebuilt whenever objects are added or

---

[1]GL is the Silicon Graphics native graphics programming library.

deleted. Although rebuilding the hierarchy is an inexpensive operation, for very complex worlds, it is possible to rebuild only the altered branch(es) of the tree.

Object Selection is provided by one of two methods, both of which are made more efficient by using the same bounding volume hierarchies. The first method is containment, i.e. when the grasping hand is inside a leaf node of the bounding volume hierarchy. The second method is by pointing. A ray is traced through the Bounding Volume Hierarchy and intersected with the appropriate leaf node object(s) (Goldsmith 1987).

3.2 Network Communication

The application initiates the connection to the server, and either defines a new world or connects to an existing world. In the latter case, a polygonal description of the world is sent to the client so that local graphics objects (display lists) can be created.

Similarly, when a new world is defined by the client the object definitions are transmitted to the server. The server calculates the necessary object characteristics (mass, volume etc) as each object is defined. The object hierarchies are created when the world definition is complete. In a manner similar to that described above, the polygonal world description is then broadcast back to the client for display purposes.

The complete world is stored on the server, so that it is necessary to broadcast updates to each client. Updates are limited to incremental changes, so that in most cases, a small number of position/orientation updates need to be broadcast to each of the clients. The format for these updates is quite simple as shown in figure 3.

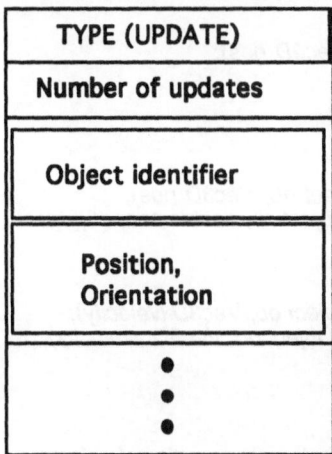

Fig 3 Variable length update packet.

Other packet types include GRASP_ACQUIRE, GRASP_RELEASE, EXTERNAL_UPDATE (an application controlled (i.e. external) object position/orientation change, typically while grasped), EXTERNAL_RELEASE (the server instructing the application to release a grasped object), ENABLE_OBJ_ATTR and DISABLE_OBJ_ATTR (e.g. turning on/off collision detection for a given object), GROUP_CREATE and GROUP_DELETE (allowing a group of objects to be regarded as a single object for the purposes of collision detection and rigid body computations). There are also a number of packet types specifically to define worlds.

Apart from world creation or connection, the communication packets are generally very small, imposing low network load. It is possible that for some types of worlds (e.g. extremely complex examples of the sample application Dodge 'Em!), the number of objects requiring simultaneous updates will cause unacceptable network traffic. We do not have evidence of this so far, but it is possible that the simple network protocol will require revision at some future date.

4.0 PROGRAMMER'S INTERFACE

This section provides an overview of many of the common functions available to the application programmer. This list is by no means complete, but does illustrate the nature of the Application Programmer's Interface.

4.1 Defining and Connecting to Worlds

Creating or connecting to an existing world:

open_world();
close_world();
*connect_to_world(char *name);*

Modifying an existing world:

add_object_to_world(PIVWObject ob);
delete_object_from_world(PIVWObject ob);

Definingg objects:

PIVWObject open_object();
open_face(PIVWObject ob);
set_vertex(PIVWObject ob, Vec3D pos);
close_face(PIVWObject ob);
close_object(PIVWObject ob);

Object transformations:

set_object_position(PIVWObject ob, Vec3D pos);
set_object_orientation(PIVWObject ob, double orient[3][3]);

Object motion:

set_object_linear_vel(PIVWObject ob, Vec3D lvelocity);
set_object_angular_vel(PIVWObject ob, Vec3D avelocity);

4.2 Attribute Control

Setting mass properties or behavioural properties of objects:

set_object_density(PIVWObject ob, double den);
set_object_elasticity(PIVWObject ob, double elas);
set_object_mobile(PIVWObject ob, short mobile);
set_object_collisions(PIVWObject ob, short collisions);

4.3 Interaction

Object selection:

*PIVWObject object_by_name(char *name);*
PIVWObject object_by_point(Vec3D point);
*PIVWObject object_by_ray(Camera *cam, Vec3D origin,*

```
                    Vec3D direction, Vec3D intersection);
PIVWFace face_by_ray(Camera *cam, Vec3D origin,
                    Vec3D direction, Vec3D intersection);
```

Grasping:

```
PIVWGrasp grasp_object(PIVWObject ob);
PIVWGrasp force_grasp_object(PIVWObject ob);
ungrasp_object(PIVWGrasp g);
update_grasp(PIVWGrasp g, Vec3D position, Vec3d orientation);
```

4.4 Miscellaneous

There are a number of convenience functions:

```
read_scene_file(char *filename);
write_scene_file(char *filename);
read_object_file(PIVWObject ob, char *filename);
write_object_file(char *filename, PIVWObject ob);
```

5.0 EXAMPLE APPLICATIONS

5.1 VR Designer

VR Designer is a re-engineered version of VR Cubeworld (Papper 1991, 1992), using the PIVW framework. VR Cubeworld, as an experimental system, only supported simple cuboid objects in very simple environments. These restrictions have been removed in VR Designer. PIVW's support for object grouping has made the support for Papper's conceptual friction (an object will move with any object it is on top of) trivial.

In VR Designer, the user can build, edit and navigate around complex architectural environments. Collision detection, object selection, object grasping and object grouping are integral components of the interaction. Furthermore, VR designer makes heavy use of selective application of both collision detection and rigid body motion. For example, by default collision detection is enabled on a global basis, but for gross changes to the environment, it is often convenient to disable collision detection for a single object. This allows the object to be moved through other objects rather than trying to manually find some collision free path/orientation.

5.2 Dodge 'Em!

Dodge 'Em! is a game that combines elements of billiards, handball and lacrosse in a 3D closed space.

The environment is a random closed volume in which the participants grasp/throw heavy (slow moving) objects with the intent of hitting the "body" of their opponents, whilst avoiding objects thrown by others.

The most successful strategy is to bounce the object off the walls behind the player so that they do not see the object coming. The 3D audio cues therefore play a very important role for the players. The target person can grasp an object, either to throw it at the other object or to hold and deflect the projectile.

In this game, there are potentially a large number of objects in the scene, hence it is fairly demanding of the real-time performance of the system and a heavy tester of the network nature of PIVW.

48

6.0 CONCLUSION

In this paper, we have described an application framework for multi-person Virtual Environment applications that incorporate a high degree of behavioural realism. This framework is built around a network "world" server that supports collision detection and rigid body simulation. It also supports applications where these facilities are only necessary on a selective basis.

PIVW provides a high performance, simple framework to improve the ability to communicate and interact with virtual worlds.

7.0 REFERENCES

Baraff, D., (1989) Analytic Methods for Dynamic Simlation of Non-penetrating Rigid Bodies, Computer Graphics, 23(3): 223-232

Baum, D., Garlick, B., Winget, J. (1990) Interactive Viewing of Large Geometric Databases Using Multiprocessor Graphics Workstations. Proceedings of 1990 Symposium on Interactive 3D Graphics, Snowbird.

Friedmann, M., Starner, T., Pentland, A., (1992) Device Synchronization Using an Optimal Linear Filter. Proceedings of 1992 Symposium on Interactive 3D Graphics, Boston, pp 57-62

Funkhouser, T., Sequin, C., Teller, S., (1992) Management of Large Amounts of Data in Interactive Building Walkthroughs. Proceedings of 1992 Symposium on Interactive 3D Graphics, Boston, pp 11-20

Goldsmith, J., Salmon,J., (1987) Automatic Creation of Object Hierarchies for Ray Tracing", IEEE Computer Graphics and Applications, 7(5)

Latombe,JC (1991) Robot Motion Planning. Kluwer Academic Press, 1991

Molnar, S., Eyles, J., Poulton, J., (1992) PixelFlow: High-Speed Rendering Using Image Composition. Computer Graphics, 26(2): 231-240

Papper, M., Gigante, M., (1992) Using Physical Constraints in a Virtual Environment. In: Earnshaw R.,, Gigante M., Jones H. (eds.), Virtual Reality Systems, Academic Press, London, 1993.

Papper, M. Danaher, J., Baecker, R., (1991) Predictable Modelling Interaction Using High-Level Constraints: Making Objects Behave as They Would in Our Environment. Proceedings of the Association for Computer Aided Design in Architecture (Acadia '91), Los Angeles

Silicon Graphics (1992) Reality Engine Technical Report", Silicon Graphics Computer Systems

Ward, M., AzumaR., Bennett, R., Gottschalk, S., Fuchs, H., (1992) A Demonstrated Optical Tracker With Scalable Work Area for Head Mounted Display Systems. Proceedings of 1992 Symposium on Interactive 3D Graphics, Boston, pp 43-52

Webb, R., Gigante, M., (1992) Using Dynamic Bounding Volume Hierarchies To Improve Efficiency of Rigid Body Simulations.In: Kunii TL (ed.), Visual Computing, Springer Verlag, Tokyo, pp 825-842

Zyda, M., Pratt, D., Osborne, W., Monahan, J., (1993) NPSNET: Real-time Collision Detection and Response. The Journal of Visualization and Computer Animation, 4(1): 13-24

Michael Gigante is the Director of the Advanced Computer Graphics Centre at the Royal Melbourne Institute of Technology

He received a degree in Aeronautical Engineering from the University of Sydney and a degree in Computer Science from the University of Melbourne.

He has been at RMIT since 1985 where he has persued his teaching and research interests in Computer Graphics and CAD. His rsearch areas are Image Synthesis, Real-Time Computer Graphics, Virtual Reality and Computer Graphics in Education.

Mr Gigante has twice served as technical program chair of the Australasian computer graphics conference *Ausgraph*, co-chaired the BCS conference *Virtual Reality Systems*, and is co-chair of *Computer Graphics International 1994*, to be held in Melbourne, Australia.

Address: RMIT Advanced Computer Graphics Centre, Collaborative Information Technology Research Institute, 723 Swanston St., Carlton, Australia 3053

Robert Webb is a research assistant in the Advanced Computer Graphics Centre at the Royal Melbourne Institute of Technology.

He received a 1st class honors degree in Computer Science from the University of Melbourne.

His research interests include Real-Time Computer Graphics and Virtual Reality.

User Guidance in Virtual Worlds

Jürgen Emhardt

ABSTRACT

We introduce a software architecture which supports user guidance in virtual worlds. The user guidance is realized with task-oriented agents communicating with users through a command-based dialogue interface. The agents use an application independent toolbox, the hyper-renderer, for evaluating information that is calculated during the rendering process, but usually not provided for use outside the rendering program. As an application, we describe a prototypical exploration agent which guides visitors of a virtual building to any destination inside the building. The visitor is navigating independently, while the agent presents sign-posts at appropriate locations. In our implementation, we used symbolic visibility preprocessing. Example frames of an interactive walkthrough are included.

Keywords: interactive walkthrough, navigation, visibility preprocessing, hyper-rendering.

1. INTRODUCTION

During the last years, virtual world systems that permit architects and their clients to explore a proposed building have found much attention. The emphasis of these virtual building environments is on high speed performance - the ultimate goal is an interactive walkthrough in real-time with realistically modeled building interiors. As this objective might has been reached in recent time by using sophisticated visibility preprocessing as well as texture mapping in connection with the Reality-Engine from Silicon Graphics, these systems only provide the ability to *navigate* technically, i.e., users can get from one place to another in a large virtual environment and they can look around in order to determine where they are. However, these navigation systems *cannot* be used as information and query systems. In particular, users do not have the ability to conduct a dialogue with the system. For example, an information system which is located in the lobby of a large building must be able to support a user in a wayfinding task. It is not sufficient to offer only a navigation facility, but users must be able to *explore* their virtual environment interactively by asking for information.

In our opinion, the navigation systems described above have three major drawbacks: First, they do not serve as information systems and they do not prevent users from getting lost in a large virtual environment. Second, they are not usable for performing other tasks which are related to the problem of navigation. For example, an architect designing a building would probably like to have a critiquing system available. Another task could be to test whether users can perform their work in the virtual rooms satisfactorily. Tasks like these indicate the third drawback of pure navigation systems: Most of them do not consider any knowledge about the equipment (e.g. furniture) within the building but use textures to perform fast hardware-rendering. As a consequence, it is impossible to critique the furniture placement. For example, Fischer et al. [8] discuss the critiquing approach in building knowledge based interactive systems and describe a critiquing system for the 2D design of kitchens.

In this paper we propose that the usability of navigation systems can be enhanced greatly by defining *task-oriented agents* which communicate with the user and use an application independent *toolbox* for performing their methods. This toolbox is our hyper-rendering software which was introduced in Emhardt and Strothotte [6]. The hyper-renderer makes information about the rendering process explicitly available to other programs. For example, it contains modules determining dynamically the objects which are visible, partially visible or invisible to the user. By using the bidirectional API (Application Program Interface) of the hyper-renderer, it is possible to collect any sequence of hyper-rendering commands into a method which can be used by an agent.

This paper is organized as follows: Previous research is surveyed in Chapter 2. In Chapter 3, we present a new software architecture for navigation systems with task-oriented agents and summarize the capabilities of our hyper-renderer in short. In Chapter 4, we survey the implementation techniques of a prototypical *exploration agent* and give an example. Finally, some other applications and future research are discussed in Chapter 5 and Chapter 6.

2. RELATED WORK

Visibility preprocessing for interactive walkthroughs through complex environments has been done by Teller and Sequin [16] and Airey [2]. Airey also precomputes radiosity. However, the methods applied work on a polygonal basis of the objects and do not use symbolic names. Therefore, equipment like furniture and their functionality is not taken into account. For example, if a mirror is placed at a wall within the view cone of the user in the work of Teller, the PVS (potentially visible set) would be enlarged by polygons which are visible in the mirror.

Besides the research on preprocessing, work is being done on multimedia systems which present 2D and 3D artifacts to users navigating through a virtual environment. De Mey [12] and Tsichritzis and Gibbs [17] describe a Virtual Museum, the software components of which include a navigator, a render server, a modeler, and animators. The virtual museum contains sensitive regions which initiate the presentations of artifacts only when entered by a visitor. Thus, the presentations are triggered statically, i.e. the user cannot interrupt and ask for the way to a particular location. We shall see later that the data flow of this application is similar to the inner circle of Figure 1.

Another topic in this context is the development of knowledge based systems that address the automated design of presentations that explain how to perform simple 3D tasks. These systems generate static and animated graphics (Feiner [7], Seligmann and Feiner [13], and Karp and Feiner [11]) and multimedia presentations (Feiner and McKeown [8]) that satisfy a high-level expression of the information to be communicated. The IBIS system of Seligmann and Feiner has now been extended for the use with a head-mounted see-through display [9]. This virtual world system annotates the real world with knowledge based graphics and has been tested in an equipment maintenance domain (for laser printers).

More flexibility is desirable for human-computer dialogues concerning the virtual scene. Flexibility here refers not only to the viewing specification but also to supplementary information about the objects. In the area of 2D presentations, Strothotte [14] developed a prototypical chemistry explanation system which generates pictorial explanations automatically and is capable of leading a dialogue with the user. For example, as an answer to the question "How is N_2 produced?", several pictures showing the steps of the chemical production are presented. In this system, the user can manipulate the labels on the diagrams to obtain more information.

Our work on agent supported user guidance in virtual environments is intended to bridge the gap between generation-oriented systems, which present "canonical" solutions, and the dialogue-oriented systems, which are able to answer questions. This is especially important in virtual environment applications, as we can interpret virtual reality as an experience technology which relies on *active* users who need the ability to communicate with the virtual world.

3. USER GUIDANCE IN VIRTUAL WORLDS

3.1 A New Architecture

A software architecture which avoids the drawbacks of pure navigation systems as described in the introduction is illustrated in Figure 1. The inner circle depicts the ability of navigation, whereas the outer circle enables an agent-supported exploration. Users can navigate by interactively manipulating the model, i.e., the camera parameters. The result is displayed by a visualization component which performs the rendering of the model. Navigation facilities can be implemented by using the OpenGL or the Graphics Library from Silicon Graphics, for example. However, this API is on a low level and does not support a human-machine dialogue directly.

The agent depicted on the outer circle helps users to explore their virtual environment by conducting a dialogue. It uses the hyper-rendering software as a toolbox, which computes various pieces of information about both the rendering process and the rendered picture, which conventional renderers either throw away or don't bother computing in the first place. This information is transferred back to the agent, which now has information about what the user can see in the picture, and is able to handle the dialogue with the user about the virtual scene, evaluate it under certain criteria or even modify the model of the scene. For example, if a user describes a wayfinding task to an exploration agent (i.e. the user does not know how to get from one place to another), the agent can generate signposts which lead the user towards the destination by making use of the visibility routines of the hyper-renderer which determine the objects the user is looking at dynamically.

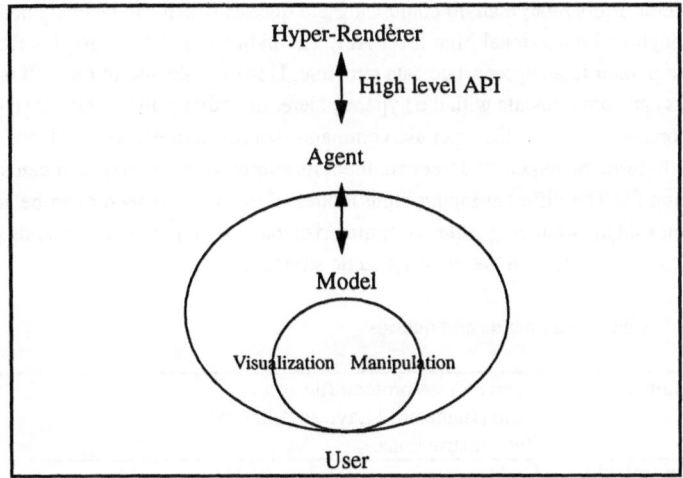

Fig. 1. *A software architecture for agent-supported exploration.* The inner circle depicts the ability of navigation, whereas the outer circle enables users to explore their virtual environment by communicating with a task oriented agent.

3.2 The Hyper-Renderer

Our hyper-renderer is written in about 9k lines of C code on an IRIS 4D35. Input is the scene description file in the format used by the RenderMan. To support maintainability of the scene description file and to facilitate dialogues about the graphics produced by the renderer, we extended its format to include symbolic names of the objects as well as grouping of objects into compound objects.

The hyper-renderer contains typical rendering algorithms which have been enhanced to record information symbolically about the graphics. In particular, an extended z-buffer-algorithm was implemented for hidden-surface removal; however, as opposed to conventional z-buffers, information about hidden surfaces is stored, not thrown away. Our implementation is related to Atherton's implementation of an object-buffer (Atherton [3]). However, while Atherton's three-dimensional display buffer was implemented in the form of a solid object description, we approximated quadric surfaces through polygons. It is important to note that the resolution of the hyper-rendering algorithms need not be the same as the resolution of the actual rendered picture; the resolution is determined dynamically by the application program. A coarser hyper-renderer suffices for many applications. This means that the results of hyper-rendering can be made available significantly before the rendered picture is in fact available.

We also implemented a hyper ray tracer which uses the visibility information supplied by our z-buffer (see therefore the concept of an "item"-buffer as described by Weghorst et al. [18]) and which stores the symbolic name of the object(s) traced. By using this information, the hyper-renderer is able to determine what objects are visible in a mirror, for example.

The hyper-renderer offers more than 40 commands and queries which can be evaluated within any C program through its bidirectional high level API. The bidirectional API supplies for each command or query a pointer to an appropriate data structure. However, the use of the API is *not* recommended as users can communicate with the hyper-renderer directly via the keyboard (if they are not in virtual environment mode) or they can use command sequences (macros) which are stored in an instruction file. In turn, the hyper-renderer can direct its output to the display or it can store it in an image description file.The different input/output modes of the hyper-renderer can be activated via control commands. In the following table, we summarize the most important commands and queries. A slash indicates commands with the same syntactic structure.

Table 1. Hyper-Renderer commands and queries

Control commands	Open / Close protocolfile.
	Load [filename] / Save as [filename].
	Read instructions.
Visualization of objects	Draw.
	Show wires.
	Show [object].
	Show [object] in [other_object].
	Show [object, object, ...] in / through glass.
	Show [object] from [x][y][z].
Navigation commands	Move camera into [object].
	Move camera to [x][y][z].
	Move camera to showing [object].
	Rotate camera [angle] [x][y][z] around origin / [object].
	Redo move.
Scene queries	List names of defined objects.
	What is at [x][y][z] ?
	What is invisible ?
	What is on screen at [x][y] ?
	What is visible ?
Object queries	Centre of [object].
	Is [object] visible ?
	List box of [object].
	What objects are in [direction] of camera / [object] ?
	What surrounds [object] ?
	What is behind [object] ?
	What is in [object] ?
	What is in front of [object] ?
	Where is [object] ?
	Where is [object] from [other_object]?
Help functions	Help.
	Help about [keyword].

In the next section we describe a prototypical exploration agent and demonstrate the usefulness of the above listed commands and queries.

4. A PROTOTYPICAL EXPLORATION AGENT

A major application of the architecture described above is the definition and the implementation of task-oriented agents in a virtual building environment. In this chapter, we describe the design and the implementation of a prototypical exploration agent which supports users in finding a way from one location to another in an unknown virtual building. Users navigate by themselves, and our agent shows them a way towards their destination by presenting sign-posts at appropriate locations. In section 4.1 we describe how the visibility preprocessing of our model is performed and how users can navigate through our virtual environment. The exploration agent is described in detail in section 4.2. Finally, an example is provided in section 4.3.

4.1 Symbolic Visibility Preprocessing and Navigation

In contrast to Teller and Airey we preprocess our model, which obeys the RenderMan Interface specifications on a symbolic level. As we extended the RenderMan specifications to include symbolic names of the objects as well as grouping of objects into compound objects, the virtual building is split according to its components, i.e. its rooms, doors, hallways, etc. The symbolic names and groups are included in the "rib"-file ("rib" stands for RenderMan Interface Bytestream) as comments, and the hyper-renderer parses them appropriately. During an interactive walkthrough, it is sufficient to supply only those "rib"-files the user potentially can see. For example, if the user is inside a room with a closed door, it is sufficient to supply the part of the "rib"-file which contains the model of the walls of the room, its windows, and its furniture. However, the agent has to determine dynamically whether the door is open or not by using the hyper-renderer queries (i.e. by placing the camera in a corner near the door). If the door is open, the model of the hallway and that of other rooms have to be concatenated to the "rib"-file. By using the hyper ray tracer it is possible to predetermine the maximal set of objects which can be seen through the windows by choosing appropriate camera parameters at different positions inside the room. Thus, the API of the hyper-renderer can be used for preprocessing as well.

Users can navigate by using hyper-renderer commands like "move [Camera] to show [Object]" including the symbolic name of an object, and the RenderMan will render the scenes frame by frame. Another possibility is to navigate using the Graphics Library which renders wire-frames or Gouraud-shaded objects based on a triangulation of the corresponding objects in the "rib"-file.

4.2 The Exploration Agent

We consider an agent to be a communicative interactive process. Abowd [1] describes a theory of communicating interactive processes based on the formalisms of CSP and Z (see therefore also Suffrin and He [15]). As the hyper-renderer commands and queries can be interpreted as messages of the agent's *events*, we concentrate here on the description of the *state transitions*. The above described symbolic visibility preprocessing and navigation can be represented by the following *navigation schema* (NS):

Navigation Schema

```
┌──── NS ─────────────────────────────────────────────────────────
│ viewer_location: room(Name) | hallway(Name) | lobby | outside_building
│ camera: (Position, Direction, Roll)
│ model_part: set_of(Parts)
│ door(Room_name): open | closed
│ actual_path: ordered_list((Branching_point, Direction))
```

The parameters beginning with an uppercase letter are variables which are updated in the case a navigation event occurs. For example, if the user moves the camera, the agent has to determine the symbolic name of the location the user is inside ("hallway_1" or "room_5"), the new camera parameters, and the potentially visible part of the scene. The latter parameter is determined by concatenating already preprocessed parts of the model. As mentioned above, the hyper-renderer is also able to determine whether a door is open or closed.

As the agent should present sign-posts which point towards the direction of the destination of our navigating user, we define different *branching points* in the neighborhood of which the walking direction of the user changes potentially. We denote a branching point with "H", if it is at the intersection of one or more hallways, with "R", if it is in the neighborhood of an entrance door of a room, or with "E", if it is in the neighborhood of an entrance of the building (see Figure 2). Usually, the visibility regions of the branching points inside the building are the hallways. As long as the user is inside a visibility region, the agent adds an appropriate sign-post to that (visible) branching point at which the walking direction of the user should change. For the case when the user is *not* looking in the proper direction, our agent presents a stop sign and tells the user the necessary head rotation angle. The agent determines this angle by asking the hyper-renderer what the user is looking at. Note that the user is *not* forced to move on that way the agent proposes. For the case the user moves on another path, the sign-posts are maintained dynamically. The actual path of the user is stored in the navigation schema as an ordered list of branching points and the direction the user has been navigating to.

In addition to the navigation schema, we define the *building schema* (BS) by using the following states:

Building Schema

```
┌──── BS ─────────────────────────────────────────────────────────
│ hallway(Name): ordered_list((Branching_point, Distance_to_successor))
│ entrance(Name): Branching_point
│ lobby: set_of(Branching_points)
│ shortest_path: set_of((H1, H2, Distance, set_of(H, Direction)))
│ connected: set_of((From_object, Towards_object, Branching_point, Direction))
```

A map of the building together with its branching points is represented in the building schema. First of all, the branching points of the hallways and the distance to their successor, as well as the branching points of the entrances and the lobby are defined. Furthermore, all shortest paths from one branching point which is at the intersection of two or more hallways (denoted with "H") to any other branching point "H" are stored. These paths can be preprocessed. Note that it is sufficient to store only those paths as the distance to a particular room can be calculated by using the distance_ to_successor value from the schema.

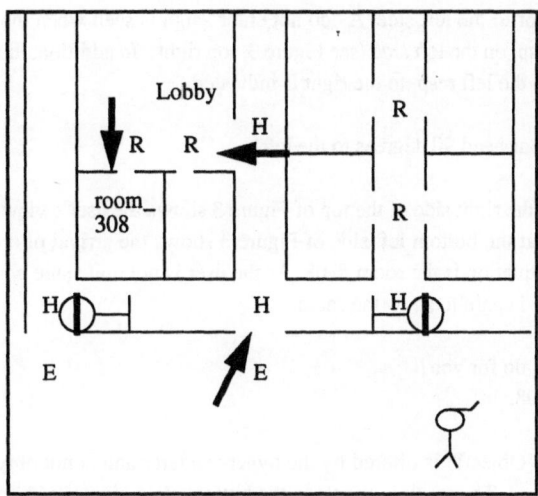

Fig. 2. *Sign-posts for a navigating visitor in a virtual building.* The visitor is standing in front of the building and is guided with signposts towards the destination.

Finally, for each object like a hallway, a room, an entrance, or the lobby we indicate whether they are connected through a path or not. For example, room_308 is connected with the lobby. We now give an example of the topic discussed.

4.3 Example: A Hyperwalk through a Virtual Building

As a case study, we modelled the new building of our department of computer science using the RenderMan and implemented an exploration agent which helps users to navigate by presenting red colored arrows and "do not enter"-signs face on to the user's view. Suppose that the user is standing in front of the building and would like to move to the lobby.

Agent: Please describe task.
User: I'd like to move to the lobby.

First of all, the agent parses the input by using a simple matching algorithm, i.e., the user's activity is to "move", and the destination is the "lobby". The agent then determines the visibility region the user is inside and presents an arrow pointing towards the entrance of the building (see Figure 3, top left).

The user now navigates through the entrance door and has the choice of going straight ahead as well as turning to the right or to the left side. A "do not.enter"-sign is seen when the user looks into the hallway on the right resp. on the left side (see Figure 3, top right). In addition, the agent tells the user that head movement to the left resp. to the right is indicated.

Agent: Please move your head 90 degrees to the left!

The second picture on the right side of the top of Figure 3 shows the user's view towards the proper direction. The picture at the bottom left side of Figure 3 shows the arrival of the user in the lobby. However, the final destination is the room #308. As the user is not quite sure where this room is located, the agent is asked again to show the room.

Agent: What else can I do for you?
User: Show room_308.

The command "Show [Object]" is offered by the hyper-renderer and is not only at the agent's, but also at the user's disposal. The result is shown in the bottom right picture of Figure 3.

5. OTHER APPLICATIONS

In order to demonstrate the flexibility of our architecture with respect to different tasks, we present some other applications which seem to be quite different from the example above. These applications are currently being implemented within the "HyperWalk Project" at the Freie Universität Berlin.

Presentation agent. The architecture presented in this paper can be used for critiquing 3D models. Critiquing systems as introduced by Fisher et al. [10] support users in their problem solving and learning activities. The core task of critics is the recognition of deficiencies in a solution and communication of those observations to users. We are implementing a critics system for the design and investigation of overhead transparencies and slides in a 3D world. Users can prepare a presentation by using a simple editor and then project the resulting overhead transparencies or slides onto a (virtual) wall inside a virtual room. They can choose between virtual rooms of different sizes and locate themselves at different seats. The illumination is done by using a radiosity algorithm. Figure 4 shows a projected overhead transparency in a lecturehall. The presentation title is still legible, whereas the bottom of the slide is *not* legible from the users point of view. The critiquing system determines this deficiency by using rules which can be derived from desktop publishing books like Conover [5]. The knowledge representation uses a constraint formalism similar to that described in Borning et al. [4]. Each parameter is represented by one of five different levels (required, default, prefer, low_risc, high_risc) and a value. For example, a point size of less than 16 pt is at the high_risc level for medium and large rooms. The critiquing system conveys this message to the user who in turn can try to estimate the impression of the slide. Furthermore, it describes the sitting areas within the room from which good legibility is guaranteed.

Tour guide. In contrast to the exploration agent presented in this paper which supports users navigating by themselves, the tour guide guides users through a virtual building by presenting animations and by giving explanations at important locations.

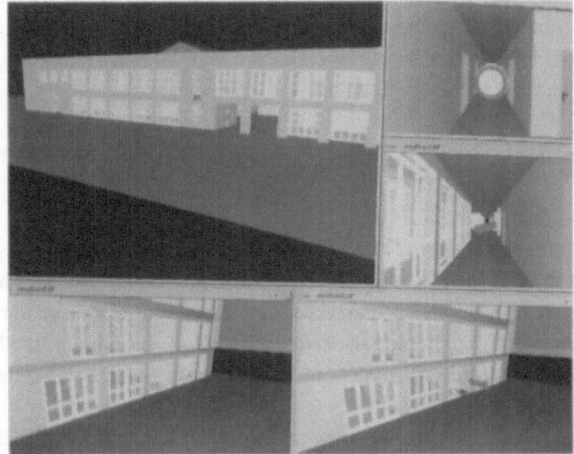

Fig. 3. A hyperwalk through our department of computer science. Top left: The user is standing in front of the entrance. Top right: A view into a wrong hallway. Top middle: A view into the proper direction. Bottom left: The user arrived in the lobby. Bottom right: A particular room is shown by using an arrow.

Fig. 4. A slide presentation in a lecturehall. The presentation title is still legible, whereas the bottom of the slide is *not* legible from the users point of view. The critiquing system recognizes this deficiency and proposes an appropriate solution.

Blind agent. Using the hyper-renderer it is possible to describe an 3D image to blind people. This application is part of the GUIB-project (Graphical User Interfaces for the Blind) within the TIDE program (Technology Initiative for Elderly and Disabled People) of the European Community.

6. CONCLUSION AND FUTURE WORK

We introduced an exploration agent which presents sign-posts to visitors navigating through a virtual building. The agent can be defined formally by using languages like Z and CSP. The implementation is made possible by using a new architecture which in turn makes use of an application independent toolbox, the hyper-renderer. We presented an example as well as a description of other projects under development demonstrating the usefulness of our architecture with respect to different tasks.

Our future work will concentrate on integrating the results of the projects described above and on enhancing the functionality of the equipment in our virtual buildings. Agents should be able to react on and to perform dynamic changes in the environment.

7. ACKNOWLEDGMENTS

I would like to thank Matthias Lehmann and Dirk Krause for implementing the API of the hyper-renderer and the exploration agent. Peter Binner implemented the hyper ray tracer, and Ulrich Scheel implemented the symbolic visibility preprocessing. Andreas Raab and Ralf Preininger prepared the examples discussed in this paper and Debora Weber-Wulff as well as Lars Reichert gave many helpful comments. Finally, I like to thank Prof. Th. Strothotte for some helpful discussions.

8. REFERENCES

1. Abowd GD (1990) Agents: Communicating interactive processes. In: Proc. IFIP TC 13 Third International Conference on Human-Computer Interaction (INTERACT'90), Cambridge, pp 143-148
2. Airey JM, Rohlf JH, Brooks FP (1990) Towards image realism with interactive update rates in complex virtual building environments. Computer Graphics 24(2): 41-50
3. Atherton PR (1981) A method of interactive visualization of CAD surface models on a color video display. Computer Graphics 15(3): 279-287
4. Borning A, Maher M, Martindale A, Wilson M (1989) Constraint hierarchies and logic programming. In: Proc. of the Sixth International Conference on Logic Programming, Lisbon, pp 149-164
5. Conover ThE (1985) Graphic Communication Today, West Publishing Company
6. Emhardt J, Strothotte Th (1992) Hyper-rendering. In: Proc. Graphics Interface'92, Vancouver, pp 37-43

7. Feiner S (1985) APEX: An experiment in the automated creation of pictorial explanations. IEEE Computer Graphics and Applications 5(11): 29-38
8. Feiner S, McKeown K (1991) Automating the generation of coordinated multimedia explanations. IEEE Computer 24(10): 33-41
9. Feiner S, MacIntyre B, Seligmann D (1992) Annotating the real world with knowledge based graphics on a see-through head-mounted display. In: Proc. Graphics Interface'92, Vancouver, pp 78-85
10. Fischer G, Lemke AC, Mastaglio Th (1990) Using Critics to empower users. In: Proc. CHI'90, pp 337-347
11. Karp P, Feiner S (1990) Issues in the automated generation of animated presentations. In: Proc. Graphics Interface'90, Halifax, pp 39-48
12. De Mey V, Breiteneder C, Dami L, Gibbs S, Tsichritzis D (1990) Visual composition and multimedia. In: Proc. EUROGRAPHICS'92, Cambridge.
13. Seligmann DD, Feiner S (1991) Automated generation of intent-based 3D illustrations. Computer Graphics 25(4): 123-132
14. Strothotte Th (1989) Pictures in advice-giving dialog systems: From knowledge representations to the user interface. In: Proc. Graphics Interface'89, London, Ontario, pp 94-99
15. Sufrin B, He J (1990) Specification, refinement and analysis of interactive processes. In: Formal methods in Human Computer Interaction, M.D. Harrison and H.W. Thimbleby, Eds. Cambridge University Press, Cambridge, pp 153-200
16. Teller SJ, Sequin CH (1991) Visibility preprocessing for interactive walkthroughs. Computer Graphics 25(4): 61-69
17. Tsichritzis D, Gibbs S (1991) Virtual museums and virtual realities. In: Proc. of the International Conference on Hypermedia and Interactivity in Museums, pp 17-25
18. Weghorst H, Hooper G, Greenberg DP (1984) Improved computational methods for ray tracing. ACM Transaction on Graphics 3(1): 52-69

Jürgen Emhardt is currently a research staff member in the department of computer science at the Freie Universität Berlin. He is on leave from the Institute of Knowledge Based Systems at the IBM Scientific Center Heidelberg.

His research interests include computer graphics, artificial intelligence, and formal methods in human-computer interaction.

Emhardt received his Diplom degree in mathematics from the Universität Stuttgart in 1985. He has been with IBM Deutschland since 1986.

Address: Freie Universität Berlin, Institut für Informatik, Takustraße 9, D-W-1000 Berlin 33, FRG. E-mail: emhardt @ inf.fu-berlin.de

Computer Aided Color·Coding

A. Della Ventura and R. Schettini

ABSTRACT

In spite of the widespread use of color for coding information, many aspects of color itself and of its use are unknown to both users and system designers. A color coding system based on the fundamental principles of human vision is described here. The system prevents the user from making mistakes in coding, while guaranteeing the possibility of reproducing them on different devices. It allows users to generate unordered or ordered color sets (color scales) for data representation on both screen and paper in a simple and intuitive way. Examples of its application are drawn from remote sensing data analysis. As the basic principles are quite general, applications of a different nature can be easily provided for.

Key-words: color perception, color reference system, color scale, nominal coding, ordinal coding.

1. INTRODUCTION

Color is a basic visual feature, which, together with shape, size, texture, and a few other features, characterizes scenes and pictures (Bertin 1983). Experimental evidence indicates that color or, more exactly, differences in color are directly responsible for the cospicuousness of objects in a scene (Carter 1981). The use of color for encoding information is known to greatly improve the observer's understanding of the information contained in a picture and his capacity for remembering it.
Recent technological developments in color displays and printers have brought a rapid increase in the number of applications in which color is used to convey information. But many aspects of color itself and of its use are not well understood by either users or system designers. In spite of this widespread use of color for coding information, knowledge of color reference systems, of the mechanisms of color production of different devices, of how color is perceived and the user's emotional reaction to color, is not equally diffused. The broad range of variables involved, as well as the interactions and tradeoffs between them, poses difficult problems in selecting specific colors from the gamut of those possible, in predicting their appearance when they are seen in relation to others, and in predicting the observer's interpretation and reaction to them (Della Ventura 1990c), These problems can not be solved without a working knowledge of the results of physiological and psychological research in human color perception (Della Ventura 1992).

This paper describes the development of a computer-aided color coding system. It is based on a device-independent color space for color selection and exploits some basic principles of human vision for the effective use of color. The man-computer dialogue is based on simple visual communication tools, so that the user may concentrate on "what" meaning he wishes to give to colors, rather than on "how" to produce them.

2. USING COLOR EFFECTIVELY

Color is pre-attentively observed and used to divide the visual environment into objects; this makes it particularly effective in coding qualitative information. Associating a set of colors with a set of items to express the significance of each is called "nominal coding". However, there are often more items to represent in an image than easily discriminable colors. Moreover, colors may be used not only to allow recognition or discrimination of information items, but to convey higher-level information at local level (e.g. to evaluate the areas) and/or at global level (apparent conceptual linking between different items) as well (Annoni 1990). Color can also be employed in a quantitative fashion, i.e. to convey information about an ordered data set. When we want to code quantitative information, a compromise must be found between the requisite of correct perception of the single color (so that it can be translated, using the legend, into a numerical value) and that of communicating to the viewer the intrinsic order of the data (Della Ventura 1990b; Ware 1988). This kind of coding is called "ordinal coding".
The problems encountered in using colors to code qualitative or quantitative information fall within the three categories listed in the introduction: they concern the selection of colors, the possibility of predicting their appearance when displayed together, and of predicting the observer's interpretation as well.
The first problem is to select a set of colors. The user may, in theory, select a color among the approximately 16 million available on most commercial monitors and printers. He must therefore navigate in a color space, reasoning preferably in terms of the psychological attributes of colors - hue, saturation, lightness - rather then in terms of blending color components in an additive or subtractive model, such as the RGB or CMY. This color space should not only have psychological dimensions, but, since the color differences the observer assesses may have quantitative connotations, it should be uniform, i.e. present a linear relationship between the physical distances in it and the corresponding differences perceived.
Whatever the color model adopted, the dialogue between the user and the system should be based on a visual language instead of requiring the use of commands or specifying colors by their numerical coordinates. Color selection can be effectively aided by displaying color palettes which are slices of an uniform color space sampled at suitable intervals (Schettini 1992).
In selecting colors for nominal coding another, more serious problem arises because the chosen colors must be displayed together and assigned to regions of different size and morphology. In other terms, while selecting colors one must have in mind the characteristics of the image (the number of classes, any links between them, the geometric and topological features of the regions that correspond to the different classes) so that the association of item with color produces a readable image.

In predicting the color appearance, to have colors remain distin-
guishable and recognizable when associated with the respective image
regions, the relevant phenomena to consider are the simultaneous
contrast, i.e. the shift in perception of a color caused by the
proximity of other colors, and the adaptation, which is a modification of the visual response in relation to the luminance of
stimuli, so that after continued viewing the eye loses its sensitivity to color differences (Della Ventura 1990b; Wyszecky 1982).
While the discriminability of the colors is a basic requisite of
nominal scales, in ordinal scales the colors representing the extremes of the range must remain distinct with a clear and univocal
order of the colors lying within it. If we take, for example, the
color scale from purple to pale green through grey that is created
in the RGB color space, with the Red and Blue values fixed at 50%
and varying the Green from 0 to 100% , a viewer, who is not thor-
oughly familiar with additive color theory, will not perceive the
continuity from purple to grey as a variation in "greenness" and
will not read data encoded in this manner correctly. Hue scales,
moreover, which have no intuitive beginning or end, are not particularly useful in conveying a sense of order in data. Lightness
scales, color scales that increase monotonically in lightness and
saturation, or that increase monotonically in lightness while cy-
cling through a range of hues (short sections of the hue circle may
be perceived as a "continua" e.g. red, orange and yellow) - are more
successfully used for this purpose (Della Ventura 1990b; Robertson
1986; Ware 1988).
Problems related to cognitive aspects of the color impression must
also be considered. While many of these aspects depend strictly on
the application, some expedients remain valid in all cases.
Clusters of colors with an apparent linking or order convey high-
level information and should be used only when there is actually a
corresponding logical link between the associated data. For example
they may be used correctly to evidence a hierarchy among different
classes: if red is chosen to represent urban areas in a map, different kinds of red may be used to represent different kinds of
buildings, all of which belong to the same "urban" class. But if
these different reds form an ordered scale, they may produce an
artifact giving the idea of a "concentration of buildings" (Binaghi
1990).
Many commercial systems include a color coding module which usually
simplifies the color selection task, by proposing a predefined color
palette, or allowing simple manipulation of color attributes. To
facilitate the correct association of colors with image regions,
avoiding artifacts and preserving the intended meaning, the user
has at his disposal numerous guidelines derived from experiments
on human vision (Carter 1981; Cleveland 1983; Della Ventura 1990a,
1990b, 1990c, 1992; MacDonald 1990; Murch 1984; Rice 1991; Robertson
1986; Robertson 1988; Trumbo 1981; Ware 1988). But these guidelines
must be known, understood and translated into operational choices
by the user himself, who is, in general, not really interested in
learning the principles of color perception. This is what suggested
us to code the guidelines into rules and to use them both implicitly
(proposing palettes where the color samples are chosen by appropriate rules) and explicitly (by warnings sent to the user).

3. COMPUTER AIDED COLOR CODING

Our color coding system is structured as in Fig. 1, while the different data handled by the user can be seen in Fig. 2. They are:

i) the color palette ii) the color array; that is a temporary buffer
in which the user can put colors he thinks will be useful for coding
and iii) the image, that is the data set to be colored. In Fig. 1
these data are represented by rectangles. Operations on the data
are managed by controllers which, when an array is created, or an
association color-structure made, apply specific rules and verify
the constraints to which the coding is subjected.

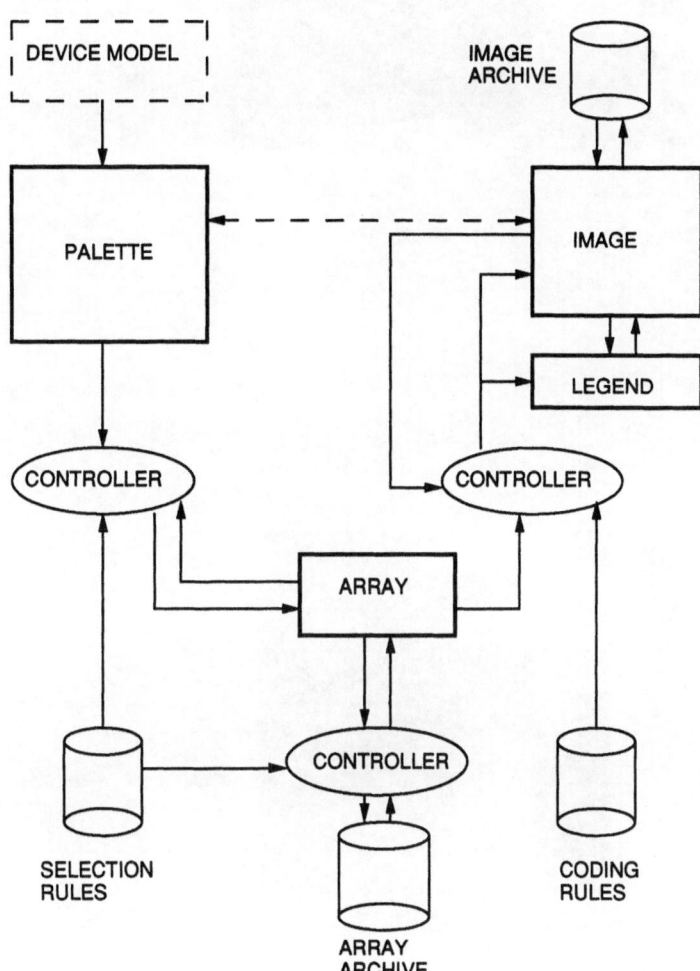

Fig. 1. System architecture.

The device model is transparent for the user and guarantees a
device-independent color specification.
The color coding proceeds as follows: 1) selection of an image in
which the pixel values may be codes representing classes (nominal
coding) or values of the variable to be coded (ordinal coding); 2)
preparation of an array of colors that will be associated with the

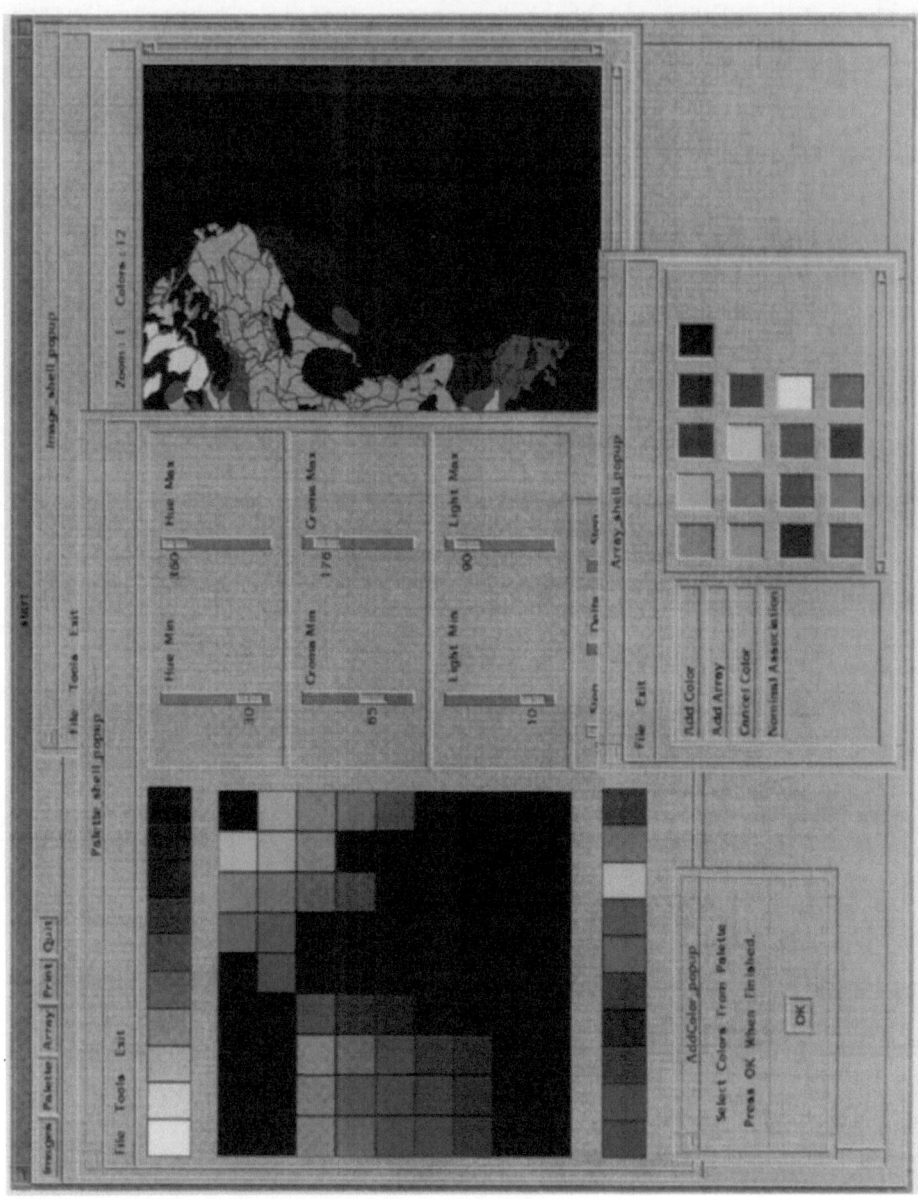

Fig. 2. Interface layout.

image values. The array enables the use of colors chosen interactively in conjunction with existing standard color scales drawn from an archive; 3) association of the colors in the array with the structures of the image and legend editing.

The system is described from the operational point of view here below, starting from the generation of the color palette(s), through the editing of the array up to the association of the colors in the array with the image data. The device modeling and the calibration procedure on which the system is founded conclude the description.

3.1 Generation of the Color Palette

Color scales can be selected from a range of displayed palettes. The dialogue between the user and the system is based on visual interaction. This allows colors to be selected without considering their internal representation, physical qualities, or names.

The color model adopted is just a way of organizing colors that can be produced, in much the same way the user is accustomed to thinking about them, i.e. in terms of the psychological dimensions of hue, saturation (chroma), and brightness (lightness). Correlates of these dimensions can be defined in several color models. The CIELUV color space is adopted here as it seems to closely approximate human perception of color differences (Carter 1983). The CIELUV color space is recommended in additive light source conditions (monitor displays) by the International Commission on Illumination (CIE). It is produced by plotting the quantities L^*, u^*, v^*, which are obtained by a non-linear transformation of the tristimulus values XYZ in a three-dimensional Cartesian space. Lightness L^* is based on perceptual, rather than physical measures of brightness, while u^* and v^* are chromatic coordinates. The difference between two colors, indicated with ΔE, is equal to the Euclidean distance between the two points representing the colors in the space. The variables u^* and v^* make it possible to evaluate correlates of hue (h^*) and chroma (C^*). Surfaces of constant hue-angle are planes having the lightness axis (L^*) at one edge; surfaces of constant chroma are cylinders having as their axis the L^* axis.

The set of colors that can be displayed in the CIELUV color space is represented by an irregularly shaped spheroid. This irregular shape reflects the fact that certain colors have a greater dynamic range than others. The gamut of available colors may be defined as the intersection of the gamut of the display with that of the printer.

The palettes proposed by the system to the user are always composed of three parts: a gray scale, a maximally saturated hue scale of a medium lightness value, and a bidimensional array of colors obtained by intersecting the monitor color solid in the CIELUV space with a cylindrical surface (i.e. at constant chroma), or with a conical surface, and then sampling it.

The default bidimensional color array is composed of 9 lightness scales of constant hue. A color difference interval ΔE of 40 units is used between successive colors in a row, as it appears sufficient to ensure that they will not be confused across images (Carter 1981). while the color interval between successive colors in the lightness scale, is of 20 units.

The user can employ either mouse or keyboard to set the chromas that define a cylinder or cone frustum, the beginning and ending hues, and the beginning and ending lightnesses modifying the default parameters. Variations in hue and lightness of this array are systematic and can be set by the user.

The color palette must be defined according to the meaning of the data to be displayed, considering the expected results of the imaged data (e.g. the presence of small convolute shapes in the image) and the background on which the coded image will be visualized. In some applications, the coded image must be superimposed on the image from which it was derived. The system can exclude those parts of the palette with colors similar to background colors.

3.2 Selection of a Color Scale

The color set can be automatically defined, or the user can interact with the system by selecting some or all of the colors among those displayed.
In nominal coding a reasonably accurate calculation procedure can be used to define high contrast nominal color scale instead of the heuristic approach. The input to the procedure can be either the colors of a displayed palette, or the entire color gamut of the device. In the latter case a (cubic) lattice is defined in the CIELUV space, and intersected with the monitor color gamut. The algorithm selects N high contrast colors among the lattice points taking a distance between them greater than the safe limit of 40 units (in the CIELUV space), and maximizing the smallest color difference between the color pair selected (Della Ventura 1990b, De Corte 1988).
It is possible for the user to switch from the interactive to the automatic mode: once some colors have been interactively selected, the system then completes the number of colors required by automatically assigning those colors remaining in the array that are maximally different from the colors already selected.
Two functions (available on request) support the user in this phase: "warning" and "filter". When the first function is on, the system will warn the user acoustically if any selected color is likely to be insufficiently distinct from the colors already selected. It does so essentially by checking whether the color differences among the selected colors are greater than a given threshold, and whether there is a difference in lightness and hue among the colors (these rules also prevent the creation of undesirable clusters of colors). More formally, let C_i, $i = 1 \ldots n$ be the colors in the array, i.e. the colors already selected, and C_{new} the color (manually or automatically selected) to be added to the array. C_{new} must satisfy the following condition for each C_i :

$$C1: (\Delta E^*(C_i, C_{new}) \geq 40) \text{ AND } (\Delta L^*(C_i, C_{new}) \geq 10) \text{ AND } (\Delta C^*(C_i, C_{new}) \leq 40) \text{ AND}$$

$$(\Delta h^*(C_i, C_{new}) \geq 10) \text{ AND } (\Delta h^*(C_i, C_{new}) \leq 130)$$

The filter function simply prevents the user from selecting these colors by deleting them from those available (since they are not "visible" they can not be selected).
In ordinal coding a color scale can be defined by clicking the extremes of the scale on the color array (unipolar scale), or by combining a number of ordinal color scales (repeating unipolar or bipolar scales). Two or more ordinal color scales are necessary for coding data sets of opposite polarity, such as sea depth and terrain elevation. If part of the designed color scale should stray outside the gamut of available colors (as said above the gamut has an irregular shape) the system will warn the user and propose an appropriate adjustment of the color scale (e.g. desaturating it).
Trumbo's principles are adopted to evaluate the effectiveness of the ordinal color scale selected (Trumbo 1981):

- Principle I (Order). If the data are ordered, then the colors chosen to represent them must be perceived as preserving that order.
- Principle II (Separation) Important differences in data values must be represented by colors clearly perceived as different.

The system checks (and if it is the case warns the user) when the difference in hue between the extremes of scale is larger that 140, to prevent the intrinsic order of the data is altered. Since lightness scales are the most appropriate for signaling data trends the system also checks differences in lightness between the color scale extremes. To comply with the constraint of principle II (separation), the system checks that the difference in color between the extremes of the color scale (O_b, O_e) is large enough for the colors to be clearly perceived as different, i.e:

$$C2:(\Delta E(O_b, O_e) \geq 40) \text{ AND } (\Delta L^*(O_b, O_e) \geq 30) \text{ AND } (\Delta h^*(O_b, O_e) \leq 140)$$

It is worth noting that the color scale should not create boundaries that do not exist in the original data due to the perceptual uniformity of the underlying color space.
Default nominal and ordered color scales (useful for viewers with defective color vision as well as for others) are available upon request, and may be used in conjunction with user-selected scales. In nominal color coding the system can be allowed to check (and if necessary filter) the color scales by employing the same set of rules used to control the selection of single colors.

3.3 Associating the Color Scale to the Data

In this phase the user defines the color coding, setting the colors of the scale in correspondence with the values of the data. The system will (if requested) warn the user if any selected color combination, once associated with the data, is likely to be insufficiently distinct or produce undesirable effects.
The coded rules are formalized in terms of conditional statements, which may also be nested, having the general form:

IF C_1 AND/OR C_2 ... AND/OR C_n THEN D_1 AND D_2 ... AND D_n

where the C_i are propositions denoting conditions that must be satisfied by a color once associated to a region (class) of the image, and the D_i are propositions denoting the actions to be performed which consist in warning and, if required, in explaining the guideline(s) violated. The rules are arranged in a hierarchy to solve conflicts.
In nominal coding an automatic evaluation of the image to be coded obviously requires a description. The data structure used to represent regions and their relationships is the Region Adjacent Graph, in which each node represents a region, and two nodes are joined by an arc if the corresponding regions are adjacent (Rosenfeld 1982). We associate with each node: i) a label which assigns the region on the basis of its area, compactness and elongation (Rosenfeld 1982) to the following classes: Thin, Not Thick, and Thick; ii) a class label which specifies if there are other regions that will share the same color in the image; and iii) a class description which specifies the dominant type of the regions belonging to that class. To each arc linking two nodes (regions) is associated the degree of adjacency of that pair of regions. Descriptions

are evaluated by means of a tool derived by multiple-valued logic theory (Garriba 1985). To use this tool every relevant attribute of a region is first considered as if it were the only one available and a label is assigned to it. A combinatorial function, called Multiple-Valued Logical Tree, is then applied to compute a judgement on the region from its set of labels assigning the region to one of the predefined classes (Della Ventura 1990d). A class description is the label most commonly associated with the regions of that class.

In practice, the rules coded for nominal coding try to avoid local distortions due to interaction between color and shape, and between adjacent colors, which may somewhat alter the coded information.

The phenomenon of simultaneous contrast can be reduced by separating the colors by a thin white or black line (where possible), while adaptation can be contrasted by having the various parts of the image present a significant difference in hue and lightness. Other important guidelines coded are that the edges formed by chromatic differences with little lightness difference are to be avoided, since they are poor guides to accurate focusing (these edges remain fuzzy), and that colors differing only in blue content do not produce a sharp edge (Murch 1984). Since the eye can not maintain its focus on adjacent highly saturated very' bright objects in spectrally extreme hues (eg. blue and red) at the same time (a 3D illusion is produced), these color combinations should be avoided (Murch 1984). As regards interaction between color and shape, the color of a patch is known to affect its perceived area. Saturated colors appear larger than desaturated ones. It has been shown that when highly saturated red and green are used to color a statistical map, the red areas are judged to be larger, even though the regions are actually of the same size. No such consistent distortion occurres when low saturated colors were used (Cleveland 1983). Since the smaller the area, the less discriminable the colors are, the user is encouraged to limit the use of highly saturated and bright colors to render perceivable thin lines and small shapes in the image (Della Ventura 1992).

The following rule regarding the interaction between color and shape exemplifies this approach.

IF $(R_k$ is Thin) AND $((H_g$ is Thin) OR $(H_g$ is Not Thick)) AND

$(L^*(C) \leq 65)$ OR$(C^*(C) \leq 80)$ AND (WARNING is YES)

THEN (SEND WARNING)

in which C is the color associated with the region R_k belonging to the class H_g.

In total, twenty rules have been designed for color association in nominal color coding to depict common situations that might be present in the data. It should be noted, however, that at times some compromises must be made: whatever the color selected for a given class, a guideline may be violated. In the present version of the system it is the user who must resolve this conflict.

In ordinal color coding, given a set of color-value correspondences interactively defined by the user, the range of each perceptual attribute is automatically computed to adjust the color scale to the measured data. When two or more ordinal color scales are used the system checks the polarity of the scales: the direction of lightness and chroma changes must be the same, with the sole exception of the design of a bipolar color scale. The different color scales must, moreover, span different ranges of hue, and the color difference between their extremes must be large enough to prevent

ambiguity in the coded data. An example of bipolar ordinal color coding is depicted in Fig. 3. Nine rules have been designed for color association in ordinal color coding.
When the color scales used are not obvious or standard, the more common errors in interpretation are confusion between the beginnings and the extremes of ordered scales, and memory errors (colors are correctly perceived but badly interpreted). To avoid these errors, a color legend, which may include a narrative description of the image, is created once coding has been performed and associated with the coded image. Robertson (1986) has suggested the use of a movable legend to ensure the correct understanding of the color coding in complex situations. In our system we have preferred to implement a tool by which the user can pinpoint the item in the legend associate to a given color in the image, and easily accentuate the colors associated with a given set of numerical values. This latter function is achieved simply by desaturating all the other colors in the image (which corresponds to increasing the correlation) and increase the lightness and chroma of the selected numerical values. A tool of this type also helps the user to accomodate images with many areas of varying size and shape, since it is likely that the color scale originally selected will have to be partially modified and some color-value correspondences redefined.

3.4 Device Modeling

The system described here includes a semi-automatic monitor calibration procedure to maintain the device independence of color specification so that colors will look the same on every display. The calibration procedure takes into account the monitor black point (the amount by which the monitor gamut has been translated from the origin of the XYZ space), and the ambient light reflected from the screen which is added, in equal proportion, to all the colors (Cowan 1983; Schettini 1992).
The calibration procedure has been tested using 40 test colors taken from Munsell's Atlas (Wyszecky 1982). The difference of tristumulus values of colors displayed compared with the input tristimulus values measured less than 1.5 units in CIELUV color space (Wyszecky 1982).
While it is possible to produce a good color coded image on a screen, obtaining a good print from an image created on a display is not a simple matter (Laihanen 1989). There are two possible printing strategies implemented in the system. Both call for colorimetric calibration of the printer.
This is based on a trilinear interpolation algorithm which is very general, and may be applied to calibrate virtually any color device. To calibrate our printer device 729 lattice points have been used. The difference between the tristimulus values of printed colors and the input tristimulus values averaged less than 3 units in CIELUV color space for the same data set used for testing the display calibration.
Since the gamuts of colors obtainable on displays and color printers overlap but differ (some of the colors displayed can not be reproduced by any printing method), the first strategy allows the user to choose only the colors that lie entirely within the intersection of the color gamuts obtainable by both devices. However, the appearance of a color is not fully described by its CIE tristimulus values. For example, what the visual system perceives as white or black depends on the whole visual scenario. Within the printer gamut, a color with the same chromaticity as the white of the monitor will not seem white, but greenish.

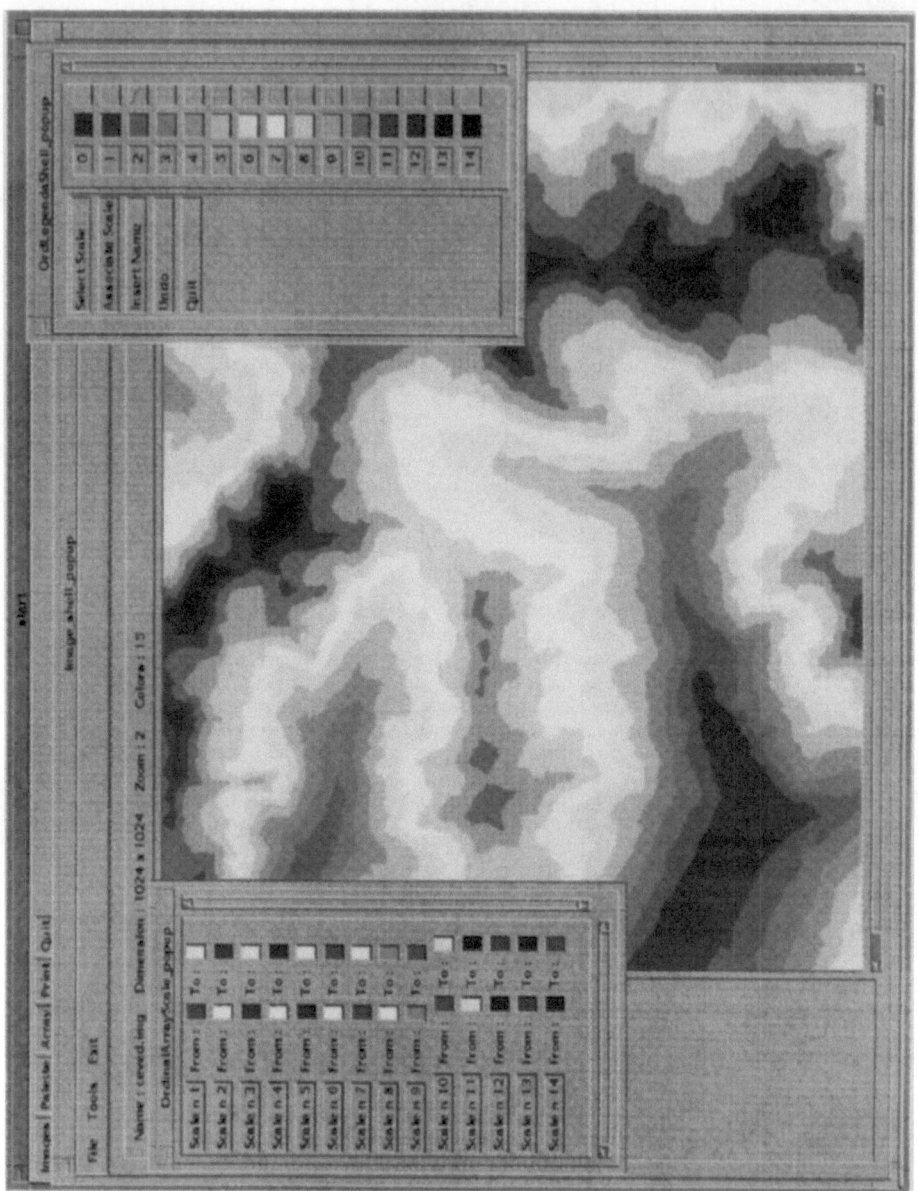

Fig. 3. An example of bipolar ordinal color coding. the coded data
is a digital elevation model that has been sliced to make the image
more readable.

While it is not possible to quantify, objectively the appearance of
a color in an image displayed on the monitor or printer, it is
nevertheless possible to use studies on vision to define a number
of empirical rules which can be translated into programs, to provide
for the satisfactory reproduction of colors on various devices.
The second method which the user can adopt does not limit the gamut
of colors available on the display to those which can be exactly
reproduce on the printer, but consists mainly in compressing and
deforming, in accordance with a given strategy, the three-
dimensional solid that envelops (in the CIELUV space) the colors
of the image displayed on the monitor in the solid that represents
the printer gamut. Given an image on the monitor, the monitor
calibration algorithm is used to to calculate CIE coordinates of
its pixels. The mapping of the gamut transforms, in accordance with
the compression strategy employed, the group of CIE values in the
input, all of which lying within the monitor gamut, into another
group of CIE values, all of which come within the printer's range.
This phase is based on the assumption that it is preferable to apply
a few transformations to the colors of the image, including those
within the printer's gamut, which can be faithfully printed, since
we assume that the appearance of an image depends more on the relationship between the colors present in the scene than on the
colors taken singly. The group of CIE values generated by the gamut
mapping algorithm is then transformed into a printer image, by applying a printer calibration algorithm.
The gamut mapping algorithm generally provides a good match
(heuristically evaluated by experts) between the appearance of a
displayed color image and the corresponding printout.
It is the user who decides which printing method is better suited
for the colored data to be printed. The default method is the one
based on gamut mapping.

4. CONCLUSIONS

In general, all activities related to reading and comparing images
for analysis and interpretation can be facilitated by the use of
color. However, the effective use of color is hampered by the broad
range of variables involved, as well as by interactions and trade-
offs between these.
Concluding a review on the use of color in computer-human interfaces
MacDonald (1990) stated:

"If you have problems in chosing satisfactory combinations of sequences of colors, seek help from an artist or graphic designer.
They have developed skills in the usage of color based on training,
experience, intuition and centuries of tradition. We can learn much
from them".

Our experience is that a computer-aided system designed explicitly
for color coding greatly improves coded image generation and comprehension. Although the system can not emulate the experts and
lacks, therefore, the efficiency necessary for solving complex
situations, satisfactory results (heuristically evaluated by users
themselves) have been achieved in trial applications. The results
demonstrate a drastic reduction of the time required to perform
coding of large and complicated images.
The main features of our system are, in summary:

- Device-independent color description, perceptual addressability, and the capability of representing color differences in a uniform scale is achieved by specifying colors in the CIELUV color space. A device-calibration module builds and maintains mapping between the CIELUV coordinates and the RGB values of the displayed colors, allowing the system to run with different equipment.

- The dialogue between the user and the system is based on visual interaction. This allows colors to be selected and associated with the data to be coded without considering their internal representation, physical qualities, or names.

- Some basic principles have been taken into account in designing the system. It supports the user in color scale selection and association with the data. To this end a set of rules coding physiological, perceptual, and cognitive aspects of human vision system has been drawn up to warn the user if a given color set is likely to be insufficiently distinct or to produce undesirable effects when associated with the data.

REFERENCES

Annoni A, Della Ventura A, Mozzi E, Schettini R (1990) Towards the integration of remote sensing images whitin a cartographic system, Computer-Aided Design 22: 160-166.

Bertin J (1983) Semiology of graphics, Un. of Wisconsin Press, Madison.

Binaghi E, Della Ventura A, Rampini A, Schettini R (1990) A knowledge-based environment for assessment of color similarity. In Proc. International Conference on Tools for Artificial Intelligence, pp 768-775.

Carter RC, Carter EC (1981) Color and conspicuousness, Journal of Optical Society of America 71: 723-729.

Carter RC, Carter EC (1983) CIELUV color difference equations for Self-luminous Displays, Color Research and Applications 8: 252-553.

Cleveland WS, McGill R (1983) A color-caused optical illusion on a statistical graph, The American Statistician 37: 101-105.

Cowan WB (1983) An inexpensive scheme for calibration of a colour monitor in terms of CIE standard coordinates, Computer Graphics 17: 315-321.

De Corte W (1988) Ergonomically optimal CRT colours for nonfixed ambient illumination conditions, Color Research and Applications, 13: 327-331.

Della Ventura A, Schettini R (1990a) Some guidelines for the use and manipulation of colors in visual communication. In: Cantoni V, Cordella LP, Levialdi S, Sanniti di Baja G (eds) Progress in Image Analysis, World Scientific Press, Singapore, pp 165-170.

Della Ventura A, Schettini R (1990b) Perceptual color scales for data display, Automatika 31: A.61-A.71.

Della Ventura A, Padula P, Schettini R, (1990c) Communicating with the help of color: syntactic, semantic and pragmatic aspects, Automatika 31: 5-12.

Della Ventura A, Rampini A, Schettini R (1990d) Image registration by recognition of corresponding structures, IEEE Trans. on Geoscience and Remote Sensing 28: 305-314.

Della Ventura A, Schettini R (1992) Computer-aided color coding for data display. In Proc. 11th International Conference of Pattern Recognition, IEEE Computer Society Press, Los Alamitos III: 29-32.

Garriba S, Guagnini E, Mussio P (1985) Multi-valued logic trees: meaning and prime implicants, IEEE' Trans. on Relaiability R-34: 463-469.

Laihanen P (1989) Optimization of digital color reproduction on the basis of visual assessment of reproduced images, Proceedings of the SID 30: 183-190.

MacDonald LW (1990) Using colour effectively in displays for Computer-human interface, Displays 11: 129-141.

Murch GM (1984) Physiological principles for the effective use of color, IEEE Computer Graphics and Applications 4: 49-54.

Rice JF (1991) Ten rules for color coding, Information Display 3: 12-14.

Robertson PK, O'Callaghan JF (1986) The generation of color sequences for univariate and bivariate mapping, IEEE Computer Graphics and Applications 6: 24-32.

Robertson PK (1988) Visualizing color gamuts: a user interface for the effective use of perceptual color spaces in data displays, IEEE Computer Graphics and Applications 8: 50-64.

Rosenfeld A, Kak AK (1982) Digital picture processing, Academic Press Inc, Orlando, Florida.

Schettini R, Della Ventura A, Artese MT (1992) Color specification by visual interaction, The Visual Computer 9: 143-150.

Trumbo BE (1981) A theory for coloring bivariate statistical maps, The American Statistician 35: 221-227.

Ware C (1988) Color sequences for univariate maps: theory, experiments, and principles, IEEE Computer Graphics and Applications 8: 41-49.

Wyszecky G, Stiles WS (1982) Color science: concepts and methods, quantitative data and formulae, John Wiley & Sons, New York.

Dr. Anna Della Ventura received the Laurea degree in Physics in 1968. She has been working at the National Research Council since 1971 and directs at present the Image Processing Group of the Institute of Cosmic Physics and Related Technologies. Her research areas include image processing and analysis methods, CAD/CAM systems, indexing and retrieval of color images. She has published more than one hundred papers on these subjects.
Address: SIAM IFCTR, CNR, Via Ampere 56, 20131 Milano, Italy

Dr. Raimondo Schettini took his laurea degree in Physics at the University of Studies of Milan. He has been working at the National Research Council of Italy since 1986. In 1989 he joined the Image Processing Group of the Institute of Cosmic Physics and Related Technologies. His current researches include pattern recognition, integration of AI and image processing techniques, and application of color science in scientific data display. He coordinates projects in these areas and has published about forty scientific papers on related subjects.
Address: SIAM IFCTR, CNR, Via Ampere 56, 20131 Milano, Italy

Part II

Rendering Techniques

Solving the Radiosity Linear System

Steven J. Gortler and Michael F. Cohen

Abstract

This paper discusses the various algorithms that have been proposed to solve the linear system arising in the radiosity method for image synthesis. These algorithms are placed within the context of the numerical methods literature. In particular, we show that the progressive radiosity method is equivalent to Southwell iteration, and the hierarchical method can be viewed as a preconditioning method that produces an approximately equivalent sparse system. When integrated with a heuristic predictor of where the significant entries in the sparse system will be, the result is the efficiencies claimed by the hierarchical methods.

The goal in reexamining the radiosity methods is to extend the understanding of current algorithms in the effort of investigating new, more accurate, and efficient techniques.

Keywords: radiosity, progressive radiosity, linear systems, preconditioning, southwell

1 Introduction

One goal of computer graphics is to produce photo-realistic images of non-existent (virtual) environments. To this end, it is necessary to solve global illumination problems characterized by the integral *Rendering Equation* [12]. One approximation of the general rendering equation is derived by assuming all surfaces to be Lambertian diffuse reflectors or emitters. This leads to a set of techniques known as *radiosity methods* [6, 3, 14] that approximately solve the global illumination problem. Recently, many modifications, extensions, and new algorithmic approaches to the radiosity method have been investigated [15, 2, 18, 16, 9, 11].

Many of these algorithms have been inspired by taking an intuitive look at the physical problem we are modeling, namely that of light interreflecting within an environment. On the other hand, it is instructive to have a more formal and mathematical understanding of these algorithms. We can use this understanding to demonstrate that our algorithms produce *correct* answers and to better understand under what circumstances our algorithms work efficiently. Most importantly, we can use this formal understanding to derive algorithmic improvements and generalizations.

The radiosity formulation gives rise to a system of linear equations that must be solved in order to produce an image. In this paper we will describe the formal background behind some of the methods that are used to solve the radiosity linear system. We will discuss the relationship between iterative radiosity methods and relaxation methods. In particular, we will show the correspondence between Progressive Radiosity (PR) [2] and what is called Southwell's relaxation. We will also discuss the relationship between Hierarchical Radiosity [9] and preconditioning. Further details on these topics may be found in [7, 8].

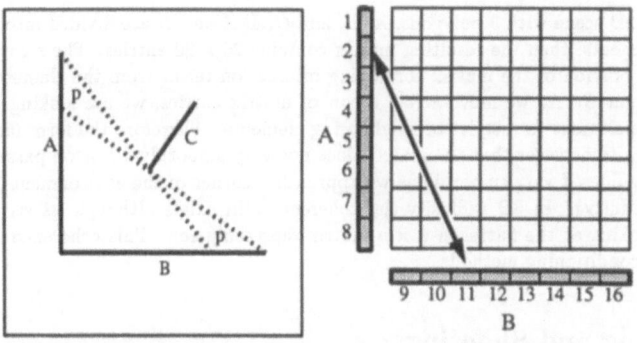

Figure 1: Flatland Radiosity and a Portion of the Matrix

2 The Radiosity Linear System

The radiosity linear system is a system of n linear equations (where n is the number of discrete elements) given by,

$$B_i = E_i + \rho_i \sum_j B_j F_{i,j} \tag{1}$$

or in matrix form, $\mathbf{M\,B} = \mathbf{E}$,:

$$\begin{bmatrix} 1 - \rho_1 F_{1,1} & -\rho_1 F_{1,2} & -\rho_1 F_{1,3} & . & . & -\rho_1 F_{1,n} \\ -\rho_2 F_{2,1} & 1 - \rho_2 F_{2,2} & -\rho_2 F_{2,3} & . & . & -\rho_2 F_{2,n} \\ & . & & & & \\ & . & & & & \\ -\rho_{n-1} F_{n-1,1} & & & . & & B_{n-1} \\ -\rho_n F_{n,1} & & . & & . & . & 1 - \rho_n F_{n,n} \end{bmatrix} \begin{bmatrix} B_1 \\ B_2 \\ . \\ . \\ B_{n-1} \\ B_n \end{bmatrix} = \begin{bmatrix} E_1 \\ E_2 \\ . \\ . \\ E_{n-1} \\ E_n \end{bmatrix}$$

where:

B_i	= the radiosity of the ith element
ρ_i	= the reflectivity of the ith element
E_i	= the emission of the ith element
$F_{i,j}$	= the form factor from element i to element j
	= the fraction of energy leaving element i arriving directly at element j
A_i	the area of the ith element (appears later in the paper)

This linear system can be derived by assuming that, in equilibrium, the light leaving the surfaces of our environment is a piecewise constant function. As explained in [10] the derivation can be more formally understood as a finite element projection of the rendering equation [12]. Using this formal understanding Heckbert [10] and Zatz [19] have been able to extend the radiosity model. By relaxing the assumption that the radiosity function is piecewise constant, they obtain different radiosity linear systems. For the purposes of this paper, these alternative systems can be treated similarly.

A radiosity matrix has some special properties that allow us to solve the system quickly. Firstly it is diagonally dominant; each diagonal element is larger in magnitude than the sum of the off diagonal elements in its row. This allows us to solve the linear system with relaxation methods.

Secondly the matrix is *coherent*. The form factor terms $F_{i,j}$ vary smoothly as we change i (or j) from one element to a neighboring element. For illustration purposes, consider the radiosity matrix for "flatland" radiosity [11] (radiosity in the plane, where instead of surfaces we have curves). Figure 1 depicts a simple 2D scene with 3 polygons, A, B, and C. If A and B are divided into 8 elements each and C into 4 elements, then the resulting matrix contains 20×20 entries. The right side of figure 1 depicts an 8×8 portion of the matrix containing interaction terms from the elements of polygon A to those of polygon B. As we move across a row of matrix entries, we are looking at the the form factor from some element to a series of neighboring elements. Therefore the form factors in the row vary smoothly. Note however that the matrix does not vary smoothly when we pass over a visibility discontinuity, nor does it vary smoothly as we approach a corner of the environment (where the form factor goes to infinity). In 3D radiosity the coherence still exists although its structure is not as obvious when looking at the flattened $n \times n$ matrix representation. This coherence allows us to use Hierarchical/preconditioning methods.

3 Gathering and Shooting

3.1 Gathering

The most obvious approach to solving the radiosity linear system would be to use Gaussian elimination. In fact, this was the original method used in [6]. In [3] Cohen and Greenberg recognized that the matrix was *diagonally dominant*, and suggested the use of Gauss-Seidel (GS) iteration. In [2] Cohen et al. introduced the progressive refinement (PR) approach to obtaining a radiosity solution, presenting a different method for solving the same linear system. The PR method has the advantages of quickly converging to an accurate image, and displaying an approximate image while the computation proceeds.

We will now briefly review and describe the PR and GS methods for solving radiosity problems. Let us begin with the GS method.

```
1   for all i
2       B_i = E_i
3   while not converged
4       for each i in turn
5           B_i = E_i + ρ_i ∑_{j≠i} B_j F_{ij}
6   display the image using B_i as the intensity of element i.
```

There is a simple physical interpretation for this algorithm. In line 5 we obtain a new estimate for the radiosity of element i by adding its emitted radiosity, and all the radiosity that this element reflects from incoming radiosity. We estimate this incoming radiosity by "gathering" the radiosity from the other elements, using the most recent estimates (B_j) as the radiosities of all the other elements.

Each gathering step (line 5) updates the radiosity of only one element, gathering for the elements i in order. A gathering step takes $O(n)$ operations and can be viewed as the dot product of the vector $\mathbf{B}$, with the appropriate row of the radiosity matrix. For all elements to have gathered some radiosity, all rows must be processed. In fact, the solution converges after some number of complete passes through the matrix.

3.2 Shooting

Let us contrast this with the progressive radiosity algorithm.

```
1   for all i
2       B_i = E_i
3       ΔB_i = E_i
4   while not converged
5       pick i, such that ΔB_i * A_i is largest
6       for every element j
7           Δrad = ΔB_i * ρ_j F_{ji}
8           ΔB_j = ΔB_j + Δrad
9           B_j = B_j + Δrad
10      ΔB_i = 0
11  display the image using B_i as the intensity of element i.
```

The above algorithm has the following physical interpretation. All elements i have a value B_i which is the radiosity calculated so far for that element, and ΔB_i which is the portion of that element's radiosity which has yet to be *shot*. During one iteration, the element with the most unshot radiosity is chosen and its radiosity is shot through the environment. As a result of the shooting, the other elements j, may receive some new radiosity, Δrad. This Δrad is added to B_j. Δrad is also added to ΔB_j since this newly received radiosity is unshot. As a result of the shooting, element i has no unshot radiosity so $\Delta B_i = 0$.

In this algorithm one shooting step (lines 6–10) updates all the other elements. We shoot from the element that currently has the most unshot radiosity. One shooting step takes $O(n)$ operations, and can be viewed as multiplying the scalar B_i, by a column of the form factor matrix. Cohen et al.[2] showed that in many cases only a small fraction of n shooting steps is required to closely approximate a solution.

At first glance these two algorithms seem to be very distinct. One gathers, the other shoots. One updates a single element, the other updates all of them. One uses rows of the matrix, the other uses columns. In the next sections (which follow [7]) we will show that in fact these two methods are quite related.

4 Solving Linear Systems

4.1 Neumann Series

It is well known that given a number, m, between 0 and 1, that there is a series equivalent to $1/m$,

$$\frac{1}{m} = \sum_{k=0}^{\infty} (1 - m)^k \tag{2}$$

Similarly, one can invert a *suitable* matrix, $\mathbf{M}$, with an infinite Neumann series,

$$\mathbf{M}^{-1} = \sum_{k=0}^{\infty} (\mathbf{I} - \mathbf{M})^k \tag{3}$$

where $(\mathbf{I} - \mathbf{M})^0 = I$.

In this case a suitable matrix is one with a *norm* of less than one. This is the case with the radiosity system of equations. This provides a solution [12] of the form,

$$B = E + E(I - M) + E(I - M)^2 + E(I - M)^3 + \ldots\ldots \tag{4}$$

where each term represents the contribution of the light after k bounces.

4.2 Iterative Methods and Jacobi Iteration

In the following sections we will briefly review the concept of *relaxation* as it applies to solving linear systems. We will discuss Jacobi iteration and two related relaxation methods, Gauss-Seidel (GS) iteration, and Southwell relaxation. For a more complete discussion see [17, 5].

We wish to solve the linear system

$$M x = b \tag{5}$$

where M is an n by n matrix. Given the approximate solution at the kth step of the algorithm, $x^{(k)}$ we define the kth error as

$$e^{(k)} = x - x^{(k)}, \tag{6}$$

and we define the kth residual as

$$r^{(k)} = b - M x^{(k)}. \tag{7}$$

Notice

$$r^{(k)} = M e^{(k)}. \tag{8}$$

We would like some method of moving from an approximate solution $x^{(k)}$ to an approximation $x^{(k+1)}$ which is closer to the correct solution x. If, when using this method, the residuals $r^{(k)}$ converge to zero, then we have converged to the correct solution.

Jacobi iteration performs a similar series of approximations to the solution as summing the terms in the Neumann series. The Jacobi iteration involves simply adding the residual vector $r^{(k)}$ to the current guess for the solution $x^{(k)}$ to get a new guess $x^{(k+1)}$. In general, a Jacobi iteration takes $O(n^2)$ time to compute the residual vector before the linear time vector addition, however, as we will see below, *if we have a current residual vector in hand* we can simultaneously update all the values of $x^{(k)}$ in $O(n)$ time. We'll call this a *Jacobi sweep*.

4.3 Gauss-Seidel Iteration

Relaxation methods examine a single term of the residual at a time in an attempt to find a solution. Given the approximation x, we pick one of the $x_i^{(k)}$ to change in such a way that $r_i^{(k+1)} = 0$. Of course the other $r_j^{(k)}$ may increase, but we hope that we have made an improvement on the whole.

A little algebra shows that if we wish to relax x_i, we should set

$$x_i^{(k+1)} = (b_i - \sum_{j \neq i} M_{ij} * x_j^{(k)})/M_{ii} \tag{9}$$

Alternatively, since

$$r_i^{(k)} = b_i - \sum_j M_{ij} * x_j^{(k)} \tag{10}$$

we can set

$$x_i^{(k+1)} = x_i^{(k)} + r_i^{(k)}/M_{ii}. \tag{11}$$

This step takes $O(n)$ operations. It involves taking the dot product of x with a row of the matrix.

If we relax the i's in order, we obtain the following algorithm.

```
1  for all i
2     x_i = 0
3  while not converged
4     for each i in turn
5        x_i = (b_i - Σ_{j≠i} x_j M_{ij})/M_{ii}
6  output x
```

This is the GS iteration algorithm. It is easy to see that this is the same as the gathering algorithm presented above. The x_i here corresponds to the radiosities, the b_i here corresponds to the emittances, and the matrix M corresponds to the radiosity matrix defined above. The differences from the Jacobi sweep should also be evident, in that, each term of the vector x is updated in turn and the new value used in the following GS step unlike the Jacobi sweep that updates all entries of x simultaneously.

4.4 Southwell Iteration

Suppose that instead of sweeping the i's in order, we decide to relax the i with the greatest residual r_i. This ordering is called Southwell iteration [5]. At first you might think that we would have to spend $O(n^2)$ operations to compute all the r_i's before picking the greatest one. (The computation of each r_i above involves computing the dot product of x with the row M_i).

Fortunately, there is a better way. If we know, at some step k, $\mathbf{r}^{(k)}$ for a given $\mathbf{x}^{(k)}$, we can express our next approximation as:

$$\mathbf{x}^{(k+1)} = \mathbf{x}^{(k)} + \Delta\mathbf{x}^{(k)} \tag{12}$$

and we can compute the updated residual as:

$$\mathbf{r}^{(k+1)} = \mathbf{b} - \mathbf{M}(\mathbf{x}^{(k)} + \Delta\mathbf{x}^{(k)}) = \mathbf{r}^{(k)} - \mathbf{M}\,\Delta\mathbf{x}^{(k)} \tag{13}$$

since

$$\mathbf{r}^{(k)} = \mathbf{b} - \mathbf{M}\mathbf{x}^{(k)}. \tag{14}$$

In our case $\Delta\mathbf{x}^{(k)}$ is a vector with zeros everywhere except for the ith component which is $r_i^{(k)}/M_{ii}$. Thus,

$$r_j^{(k+1)} = r_j^{(k)} - \frac{M_{ji}}{M_{ii}} * r_i^{(k)}. \tag{15}$$

Updating r takes only $O(n)$ steps. This step involves multiplying a scalar by a column of the matrix.

The only thing we must still show is that we are able to compute $\mathbf{r}^{(0)}$ easily at the start of the algorithm. This is simple. If we choose $\mathbf{x}^{(0)}$ to be 0 (the zero vector), then

$$\mathbf{r}^{(0)} = \mathbf{b} - \mathbf{M}\mathbf{x}^{(0)} = \mathbf{b} - \mathbf{M} * 0 = \mathbf{b}. \tag{16}$$

We can write the Southwell relaxation method as follow.

```
1   for all i
2       x_i = 0
3       r_i = b_i
4   while not converged
5       pick i, such that r_i is largest
6       x_i = x_i + r_i/M_ii
7       temp = r_i
8       for all j
9           r_j = r_j - M_ji/M_ii * temp
10  output x
```

The PR algorithm is similar to Southwell in that both operate with one column of the matrix during one step. The algorithms are different in that PR appears to update all of the variables in one step, whereas Southwell updates only one of the variables per step.

However, we can make equate PR to Southwell by making the following transformation [7]. Define a new variable ∇B_i where $\nabla B_i = B_i - \Delta B_i$. ∇B_i is the amount of *shot* radiosity while ΔB_i is the amount of *unshot* radiosity. PR is then mapped to Southwell by $x \leftarrow \nabla B$ and $r \leftarrow \Delta B$.

At the end of each PR step we output $\nabla B + \Delta B$, which is the variables added to their residuals. This makes sense within our physical interpretation. When the algorithm is finished, we have the "unshot" radiosities stored in ΔB, so adding them to our image should give us a more correct image. This also makes sense from a numerical analysis point of view. By outputting the residuals added to the variables, we are in effect performing one complete Jacobi sweep. In other words, performing m shooting operations is the same as performing m Southwell relaxation steps followed by one complete Jacobi sweep.

By viewing PR as a relaxation method, we can obtain a clearer understanding of the algorithm. We can prove that indeed PR does converge to the correct solution for radiosity problems [7]. We can see why PR works faster than GS for two reasons. PR uses a heuristic ordering for the relaxation steps, and PR includes a full Jacobi sweep at the end. We also can use this point of view to reason about recently presented *overshooting* algorithms [4, 7].

5   Preconditioning the Radiosity Matrix

The radiosity matrix is dense; most of its n^2 elements are non zero. This implies that each relaxation step takes a full $O(n)$ steps. More importantly there are n^2 form factors to compute. Form factor computation is a very costly operation which combines numerical quadrature with visibility testing.

It is sometimes possible to transform a dense matrix into a sparse matrix (a matrix with only $O(n)$ non zero elements) using a preconditioning matrix $\mathbf{P}$. Instead of solving the system

$$\mathbf{Mx} = \mathbf{b}, \tag{17}$$

we solve the equivalent system

$$\mathbf{N}(\mathbf{P}^{-1}\mathbf{x}) = \mathbf{P}^T\mathbf{b} \tag{18}$$

where

$$\mathbf{N} = (\mathbf{P}^T\mathbf{M}\mathbf{P}) \tag{19}$$

is a sparse matrix.

If we can find such a preconditioner, then each relaxation step will take only $O(1)$ steps, and more importantly, if we can predict where the non zero entries in the sparse matrix will occur, we will only have to perform $O(n)$ quadratures (form factor computations) to obtain all of the non zero elements of **N**.

The spatial coherence of the radiosity matrix allows us to use particular preconditioners to obtain matrices with only $O(n)$ large terms. The other terms which are of very small magnitude can be ignored (if we are only interested in finite accuracy) and we are left with a sparse matrix. In the next sections we will sketch the correspondence between Hierarchical Radiosity (HR) [9] and the idea of preconditioning the matrix resulting in an equivalent sparse system. Further details can be found in [8].

5.1 Hierarchical Radiosity

The Hierarchical Radiosity algorithm exploits the coherence of the matrix using the following reasoning. If some element is supposed to gather light from two distant neighboring elements, (or is supposed to shoot light to two distant neighboring elements) the two form factors will be nearly the same. Therefore, the same effect (to within some accuracy) can be achieved by simply gathering their average from some composite bigger element (or shooting to some composite bigger element). This reasoning can be extended to form a multilevel hierarchy of elements. Using this hierarchy, more distant regions interact on a coarser scale.

With this method we are effectively treating the matrix as if it was made up of rectangular blocks with constant magnitude. Since there are far fewer blocks than matrix entries, we have created a *sparse* representation of the matrix operator.

Representing a matrix made up of large constant blocks by a sparse matrix can be achieved by applying a preconditioner such as the one below. Consider the 8 by 8 matrix **P** with the following form:

$$\begin{bmatrix} 1 & & & & 1 & & 1 & 1 \\ -1 & & & & 1 & & 1 & 1 \\ & 1 & & & -1 & & 1 & 1 \\ & -1 & & & -1 & & 1 & 1 \\ & & 1 & & & 1 & -1 & 1 \\ & & -1 & & & 1 & -1 & 1 \\ & & & 1 & & -1 & -1 & 1 \\ & & & -1 & & -1 & -1 & 1 \end{bmatrix} \tag{20}$$

Because of its hierarchical structure, the preconditioning matrix can be multiplied with a vector in linear time using a *pyramid* algorithm [13]. For example, to compute the product of a vector and the preconditioning matrix, $\mathbf{P}^T\mathbf{v}$, we first compute pairwise averages and pairwise differences of the the entries of **v**. We save the computed differences which make up half of the entries in the resulting product vector. We then use the averages to recursively compute pairwise averages and differences on a coarser scale. We continue this process recursively until we have only one average value remaining, (which is the average of the entire vector).

When we multiply the preconditioner by a vector that has large constant runs (for example a column of **M**), the resulting vector will be sparser. If all of the entries of the vector have constant magnitude, the resulting vector will only have one non zero entry. Continuing this reasoning, if the right half and left half of the vector each have constant magnitudes then the corresponding row of the result will only have three non zero entries. This reasoning can be applied to quarters of each row, eights of the vector, etc. If the magnitudes are not exactly constant, but have some small variation, then we will have one large entry in the result, and the remaining entries will be small. We may choose to ignore these small entries to obtain a sparse approximate matrix. This suggests that **P** is a good candidate for a preconditioning matrix.

Computing $\mathbf{N} = (\mathbf{P}^T\mathbf{M}\mathbf{P})$ corresponds to applying the pyramid algorithm on each column of **M**, and then applying the pyramid algorithm on each row of the resulting matrix. Since we are interested in preconditioning a matrix that has rectangular blocks, we would rather precondition the rows and columns together using some two dimensional averaging and differencing pyramid. A two dimensional pyramid would take the pairwise averages and differences of (some parts of) some of the rows, and then take averages and differences on (some parts of) some of the resulting columns, and then recurse on the two dimensional averages. This can be done if we extend our preconditioning context as follows [1]. We write the precondition system like we did above as

$$\mathbf{P}^{-\mathbf{T}}(\mathbf{P}^{\mathbf{T}}\mathbf{M}\mathbf{P})(\mathbf{P}^{-1}\mathbf{x}) = \mathbf{b} \qquad (21)$$

except now we allow $\mathbf{P}^{-\mathbf{T}}$ and $\mathbf{P}^{-1}$ to be fixed *rectangular* matrices. In this case, $\mathbf{P}$ and $\mathbf{P}^{\mathbf{T}}$ are now rectangular and are not unique, as they can be any pseudoinverses of $\mathbf{P}^{-1}$ and $\mathbf{P}^{-\mathbf{T}}$. This will in general allow us to pre and post multiply $\mathbf{M}$ with a series of rectangular matrices while still expressing the same linear system.

In this context let $\mathbf{P}^{-1}$ be the rectangular matrix that performs a pyramid on $\mathbf{x}$ but saves all the averages as it performs the pyramid, and let $\mathbf{P}^{-\mathbf{T}}$ be the matrix that takes averages and differences and reconstructs the original vector. We then have introduced the freedom to perform general two dimensional pyramids on $\mathbf{M}$. Specific details can be found in [8].

As indicated before, it would be very costly to compute the entire matrix, $\mathbf{M}$ to obtain $\mathbf{N}$. Instead we need some oracle that can guess the block structure of $\mathbf{M}$. With this information we can use quadrature to directly compute the non zero entries of $\mathbf{N}$. In radiosity this oracle can be implemented in a top down fashion by a procedure that decides if the interaction between two areas can be characterized using only one form factor value (e.g., they are small and/or far away), or whether they must be subdivided [9]. Using this oracle we can obtain $\mathbf{N}$ in linear time.

Given that our matrix $\mathbf{N}$ is sparse and that we have a linear time pyramid algorithm to operate on vectors, we can apply relaxation techniques to the preconditioned matrix system to quickly arrive at radiosity solutions.

In general there are an infinite number of possibilities for preconditioning matrices. The particular choice will have the effect of creating more and less sparse representations and leading to more and less efficient computation schemes. A particular family of choices based on wavelet theory that improves on HR is discussed in [8]. Note that when we move from flatland to 3D radiosity, the form factor coherence is no longer simply expressed in the matrix as constant rectangular blocks. To derive appropriate preconditioners for these matrices, we must go back and reexamine the multidimensional integral rendering equation as is done in [8].

5.2 Discussion

By understanding HR within the context of a preconditioning operation we can demonstrate that HR produces "correct" solutions; it simply rewrites the linear system to an equivalent system. We can see why the algorithm is efficient; the rewritten system has a sparse matrix. Most importantly we can use this viewpoint to investigate other preconditioners and obtain faster radiosity algorithms.

6 Conclusion

In the above paper, we have tried to place the algorithms that have been developed to solve the linear system arising in the radiosity problem within the context of the numerical methods literature. In particular we have shown that the progressive radiosity method is equivalent to Southwell iteration, and the hierarchical method can be viewed as a preconditioning method (coupled with an appropriate oracle).

We hope this reexamination of the radiosity methods will serve as a means to better understand and extend current algorithms in the continuing research for more accurate and efficient techniques.

7 Acknowledgements

The authors would like to acknowledge the considerable contribution of others to the work in this paper. Pat Hanrahan and Peter Schröder had great input to the sections on preconditioning. Philipp Slusallek was instrumental in the discussion of Progressive Radiosity. We would also like to thank the other members of the graphics group at Princeton University.

References

[1] BEYLKIN, G., COIFMAN, R., AND ROKHLIN, V. Fast wavelet transforms and numerical algorithms I. *Communications on Pure and Applied Mathematics 44* (1991), 141–183.

[2] COHEN, M., CHEN, S. E., WALLACE, J. R., AND GREENBERG, D. P. A progressive refinement approach to fast radiosity image generation. *Computer Graphics 22*, 4 (August 1988), 75–84.

[3] COHEN, M. F., AND GREENBERG, D. P. The hemi-cube: A radiosity solution for complex environments. *Computer Graphics 19*, 3 (July 1985), 31–40.

[4] FEDA, M. Accelerating Radiosity by Overshooting. *1992 Eurographics Rendering Workshop* (June 1992).

[5] GASTINEL, N. *Linear Numerical Analysis*. Academic Press, 1970.

[6] GORAL, C. M., TORRANCE, K. E., GREENBERG, D. P., AND BATTAILE, B. Modelling the interaction of light between diffuse surfaces. *Computer Graphics 18*, 3 (July 1984), 212–222.

[7] GORTLER, S. J., COHEN, M. F., AND SLUSALLEK, P. Radiosity and relaxation methods; progressive refinement is southwell relaxation. Tech. Rep. CS-TR-408-93, Department of Computer Science, Princeton University, February 1993.

[8] GORTLER, S. J., SCHRÖDER, P., COHEN, M. F., AND HANRAHAN, P. M. Wavelet radiosity. Tech. Rep., Department of Computer Science, Princeton University, 1993.

[9] HANRAHAN, P., SALZMAN, D., AND AUPPERLE, L. A rapid hierarchical radiosity algorithm. *Computer Graphics 25*, 4 (July 1991), 197–206.

[10] HECKBERT, P. S. *Simulating Global Illumination Using Adaptive Meshing*. PhD thesis, University of California at Berkeley, January 1991.

[11] HECKBERT, P. S. Radiosity in flatland. *Compute Graphics Forum 2*, 3 (1992), 181–192.

[12] KAJIYA, J. T. The rendering equation. *Computer Graphics 20*, 4 (1986), 143–150.

[13] MALLAT, S. G. A theory for multiresolution signal decomposition: The wavelet representation. *IEEE Transactions on Pattern Analysis and Machine Intelligence 11* (July 1989), 674–693.

[14] NISHITA, T., AND NAKAMAE, E. Continuous tone representation of three-dimensional objects taking account of shadows and interreflection. *Computer Graphics 19*, 3 (July 1985), 23–30.

[15] RUSHMEIER, H. E., AND TORRANCE, K. E. The zonal method for calculating light intensities in the presence of a participating mediuim. *Computer Graphics 21*, 4 (July 1987), 293–302.

[16] SILLION, F., ARVO, J. R., WESTIN, S., AND GREENBERG, D. A global illumination solution for general reflectance distributions. *Computer Graphics 25*, 4 (July 1991), 187–196.

[17] STOER, J., AND BULIRSCH, R. *Introduction to Numerical Analysis*. Springer Verlag, New York, 1980.

[18] WALLACE, J. R., ELMQUIST, K. A., AND HAINES, E. A. A ray tracing algorithm for progressive radiosity. *Computer Graphics 23*, 3 (July 1989), 315–324.

[19] ZATZ, H. R. Galerkin radiosity: A higher order solution method for global illumination. Master's thesis, Cornell University, August 1992.

Biographies

Steven Gortler was born in New York City in 1966. He recieved a B.A. with honors in Computer-Science and Mathematics from Queens College/CUNY in 1989. During his undergraduate studies he held summer and part time positions with the Computer Algebra group at IBM Yorktown. He recieved his M.A. in Computer-Science from Princeton University in 1991. Currently he is a graduate student at Princeton working with Professor Michael Cohen on fast radiosity algorithms. His other interests include applying optimization techniques to Computer Graphics, and dynamical systems.

Prof. Michael F. Cohen is currently an Assistant Professor of Computer Science at Princeton University. He holds a Ph.D. from the University of Utah, an M.S. degree from Cornell University, a B.S. from Rutgers University and a B.A. from Beloit College. Until 1988, he was on the faculty of the Program of Computer Graphics at Cornell University where he conducted research in the area of realistic image synthesis. In particular, he worked on the development of the Radiosity method which has been reported in publications at SIGGRAPH conferences and elsewhere. Prof. Cohen has lectured widely in the are of image synthesis. Current interests include constrained optimization for animation, image synthesis, scientific visualization, and geometric modelling.

email: {sjg,mfc}@cs.princeton.edu

Address: Department of Computer Science
                  Princeton University
                  35 Olden St.
                  Princeton. NJ 08544
                  USA

Lighting Model on Gas and Liquid

Eihachiro Nakamae, Katsumi Tadamura, Hideo Yamashita, Kazufumi Kaneda, and Tomoyuki Nishita

ABSTRACT

A systematic rendering technique for both vapor and liquid those are widely distributed in a 3-D space depending on various conditions is discussed; scattering and absorption in these fields, and reflection and refraction on the boundaries between them are addressed. Photo-realistic images displaying both fog and water illuminated by various light sources and the earth viewed from space are provided to demonstrate the technique.

Keywords: lighting model, photo-realism, water colors, scattering, absorption,

1. INTRODUCTION

Various rendering techniques to realize photo-realistic images have been developed in many fields by numerous pioneers. The discussion in this paper, however, concentrates upon rendering 3-D distributed fields such as vapor and liquid; e.g., dust, smoke, fog, rivers, and pools. The light sources used here are of three types; a point light source with luminous intensity distribution characteristics, direct sunlight, and skylight. The lighting model of illuminated fields including air molecules, aerosols, vapor, water molecules and/or turbid particles, takes into account the following phenomena; scattering and absorption of light in the fields, and reflection and refraction of light on the boundary surfaces between vapor and liquid. Naturally, solid models commonly used in 3-D rendering are also considered in this paper. By using these models, photo-realistic scenes under the following various lighting conditions can be displayed; dry ice lit by spotlights, the beams of head-lights, underwater lights, various water colors which depend on weather conditions, the quality of the water, waves, etc., and the earth viewed from space.

2. PREVIOUS WORK

For rendering lighting effects realistically, both direct light and ambient light, and every object, such as vapor, liquid and solid illuminated by those light sources, should be simulated by using as precise a model as possible. So far, a number of algorithms have been developed for this purpose.

In the 1970s, a parallel light source was usually used for direct light, while for ambient light methods adding either a uniform ambient light or a secondary light source coincident with the viewpoint were used. Concerning direct light, in the early 1980s, various artificial light source models were developed by the authors, namely, point and linear light sources [16], and area light sources [15]. Recently a model taking into account the size of the sun [25] has also been developed by us; it can display penumbrae, unlike a traditional simple model, using a parallel light source. The development of precise models of ambient light inside or outside a room started in the mid 1980s; this is well-known as radiosity or global illumination. Cohen et al.[2] and the authors [17] proposed a method for the modeling of the inter-reflection of light. Using gradual ambient light, the phenomena of color blending can be rendered, that is, the three primary color elements, brightness, hue and saturation, are taken into account. Immel et al.[5] and Kajiya [8] developed a method considering specular reflection. Rushmeier et al.[21] generalized the radiosity method for displaying beams of light visible due to particles in the atmosphere in a room; since then a number of papers have been published in order to compute more precisely to minimize costs.

Simply calculating attenuation as a function of the distance from the viewpoint is a representative of rendering techniques which consider particles in gases such as fog; the farther away the objects, the lower saturation. Blinn [1] developed a method for displaying Saturn's single scattering cloud layers. Kajiya [7] developed a multi-scattering model, in which particle densities are specified at 3-D grid points, and rendered particles with high albedos, even though calculation cost is high. Max [12] proposed an algorithm for the rapid calculation of atmospheric scattering due to particles with an uniform distribution, and in reference [13] he displayed sunbeams shining through the shadow edges. The authors [19] proposed an atmospheric scattering model taking into account both artificial light with luminous intensity distribution characteristics and natural light, i.e. direct sunlight and skylight in reference [18].

Concerning the rendering of water colors, Max [11] created a ray-tracing procedural model to render the reflection of the sky and islands. Ts'o et al.[26] displayed wave surfaces by using texture mapping. Shinya et al.[23] simulated the phenomena of caustics and the focus of light passing through water; in their algorithm, the irradiance of every shade surface is stored as a texture of irradiance and is used in rendering the surfaces. Watt [27] also demonstrated the caustics and focus under parallel light by approximating the water surfaces with triangular patches and applying backward beam tracing to those patches. Furthermore, Kass et al.[10] proposed a method to generate a water surface for animation in which caustic effect can be displayed at a lower calculation cost by assuming the surface and bottom of water to be flat where the rays from the light sources are traced. The authors [9] rendered fairly realistic water colors illuminated by daylight, in which the following is taken into account; refraction and reflection of light on the water surface, radiative transfer in the water, the shapes of the bottom of the water, and shadows on the surface cast by objects. In this paper we discuss the rendering of gases and water distributed in 3-D fields by systematically bringing together our papers [9], [18] and [19].

3. LIGHTING MODEL OF 3-D DISTRIBUTED FIELDS

3.1 Characteristics of lighting effects on vapor and liquid

In almost all atmospheres consisting of air molecules, we find, to a greater or less extents, particles such as fog, dust or smoke, and in those consisting of water molecules, mud or microbes can be found. Lighting phenomena of illuminated fields in both air and water look very similar, at least at a glance; i.e., both of them glow due to the light scattered from particles in those fields, while light traversing them is attenuated by absorption. These effects are modeled as follows: for scattering, particles are considered to be an infinite number of point light sources, and for attenuation, the atmosphere and water are supposed as semi-transparent. Further, the scattering phase functions of both air and water molecules act on the following Rayleigh scattering theory because the size of those molecules is much smaller than the wave length of the light:

$$F(\alpha) = K(1 + \cos^2 \alpha), \tag{1}$$

where K is a constant, and α is the angle between the forward scattering direction and the scattered ray (see Fig.1). In spite of the facts mentioned above, the lighting effect of the atmosphere and natural water differ greatly over the following;

(1) The density of the water can be considered uniform, while that of the atmosphere is a function of the altitude.

(2) Scattering and absorption characteristics including their spectral effects in the atmosphere are quite different from those of natural water, because of the great difference in particle size and density; the effects of scattering and absorption in water cannot be neglected even if the water is very shallow, while those in the atmosphere are often negligible, if the air is very clean and the range of view is close.

(3) The boundary of heterogeneous vapor for example between the ozone layer and the atmosphere is unclear and the refraction of light is usually negligible, while the boundary between vapor and liquid, such as that between the air and water is usually definite, so taking into account boundary conditions, the mirrored reflection and refraction are indispensable when rendering water.

(4) For relatively small particles, such as aerosols in the vapor and various turbid particles in water, the Mie scattering theory is used. The Mie theory is very complicated and much depends on the properties of each particle and its density etc.

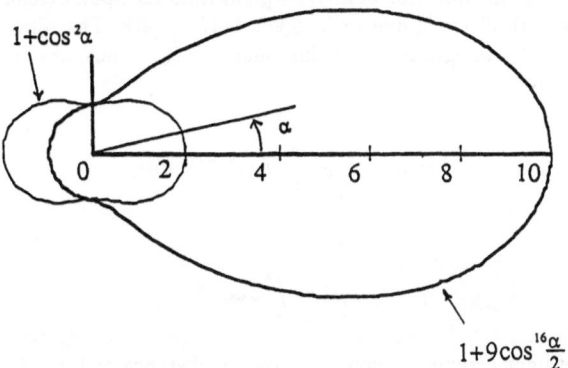

Fig. 1:   Functions of a small particle

Many experimental data and models have been published. For the scattering phase function of vapor, the following simple model [3] is often used for a foggy atmosphere:

$$F(\alpha) = \begin{cases} K_1(1 + 9\cos^{16}(\alpha/2)) \, ; & \text{hazy atmosphere,} \\ K_2(1 + 50\cos^{64}(\alpha/2)) \, ; & \text{murky atmosphere.} \end{cases} \tag{2}$$

Recently William [28] published the following precise model;

$$F(\alpha, g) = \frac{3(1 - g^2)(1 + \cos^2 \alpha)}{2(2 + g^2)(1 + g^2 - 2g \cos \alpha)^{3/2}} , \tag{3}$$

where g is an asymmetry function and is given by

$$g = \frac{5}{9}\mu - (\frac{4}{3} - \frac{25}{81}\mu^2)x^{-1/3} + x^{1/3},$$

$$x = \frac{5}{9}\mu + \frac{125}{729}\mu^3 + (\frac{64}{27} - \frac{325}{243}\mu^2 + \frac{1250}{2187}\mu^4)^{1/2}$$

where if $g = 0$ then this function is equivalent to Rayleigh scattering (Eq. 1), $\mu(0.6 - 0.8)$ is determined by the atmospheric conditions and the wave length. There are a number of papers, for example reference [6].

3.2 Scattering in an uniform field

The density of the air in a room or of seawater is uniform unless something such as smoke or some turbidity exists. Let's discuss the effects of light scattering due to a point light source with luminous intensity distribution characteristics, as shown in Fig. 2. The intensity of light reaching viewpoint P_v from calculation point P_i on an object can be obtained by calculating the sum of the reflected intensity, attenuated by traversing $P_i P_v$ through the absorbing medium, and the intensity scattered in the direction of the viewpoint from each point along $P_i P_v$; attenuation varies exponentially with distance due to Bouger's law(e.g.,[4]). The total contribution from scattering is obtained by integrating all points along $P_i P_v$. Thus, the intensity of light at viewpoint I is given by

$$I = I_i e^{-\tau(L)} + \int_0^L I_p(s)e^{-\tau(s)}\sigma ds, \tag{4}$$

where

$$\tau(s) = \int_0^s \sigma dl, \tag{5}$$

I_i is the intensity of light arriving at point P_i, L is the distance of $P_i P_v$, $I_p(s)$ is the intensity scattered in the direction of the viewpoint at an any point P on $P_i P_v$ at distance s from P_v, $\tau(s)$ is the optical depth of PP_v, and σ is the extinction coefficient per unit length and depends on particle density along the viewing line. If the luminous intensity characteristics of a point light source are expressed by $I(\theta, \varphi)$, where θ is the angle from the illumination axis, φ is the revolution angle, and uniform ambient light is I_a, the intensity of light reaching point P from the point light source is also attenuated due to absorption by particles and subject to the inverse square law of distance. Consequently, I_p is given by

$$I_p(s) = \frac{I(\theta, \varphi)}{r^2}\omega F(\alpha)e^{-\tau(r)} + I_a, \tag{6}$$

where r is the distance between light source Q and point P, ω is degree of reflection, $\tau(r)$ is the optical depth of PQ. In Eq. 4, I_i is also subject to attenuation due to the distance from the light source, as in Eq. 6. Calculation of illuminance due to point light sources with variable angular intensity distributions can be performed by referring to [20]. Thus, Eq. 4 can be expressed by

$$I = I_i e^{-\sigma L} + I_a(1 - e^{-\sigma L}) + \int_0^L \omega I(\theta, \varphi) e^{-\sigma(r+s)} F(\alpha)/r^2 \sigma ds, \qquad (7)$$

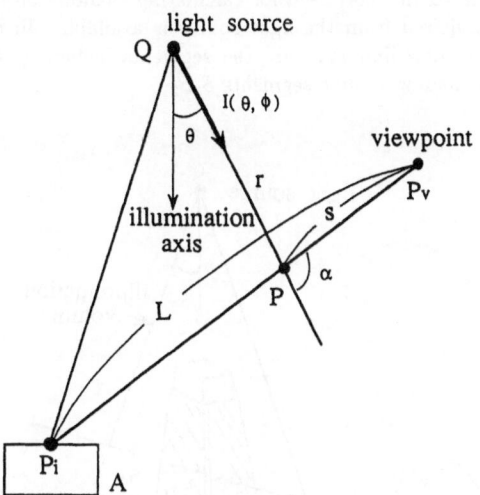

Fig. 2:   Intensity of light reaching a viewpoint from a point P_i on an object.

The following factors should be noted when applying this equation.

1. In the case of multiple light sources, the total intensity is obtained by calculating the sum of the intensities yielded by Eq. 7 for each light source.

2. If the light source is parallel, the direct sunlight, I_p of Eq. 6 becomes:

$$I_p(s) = \omega I_0 F(\alpha) e^{-\tau(r)} + I_a, \qquad (8)$$

where I_o is the intensity of the light and $\tau(r)$ is the optical depth from the reference plane (e.g. a window pane or water surface without waves).

3. The third term refers to the shaft of light. Thus, if the light ray doesn't pass through an illuminated volume, or the air / water is very clean, distance L is quite short, or line segment $P_i P_v$ is far from the light source, the intensity can be expressed by first two terms within a tolerance. For example, those two terms are equivalent to the equation for fog effect in the case of outdoor scenes [14].

4. Even for uniform density, we may consider many types of lamps with various luminous intensity distributions. Thus, numerical integration is useful because of the difficulty of obtaining an analytical solution.

As mentioned above, the third term refers to the shaft of light and its calculation cost is high. Thus, localizing illumination volumes by the following principles should be effective:

1. For a point light source, the direction of radiation is limited by a reflector and a lens.

2. For axisymmetric luminous intensity distribution, such as that of a spot light, the illumination volume, a kind of hull, is defined as a circular cone (see Fig. 3)

3. For a parallel light source such as sunlight entering through a window, the illumination volume should be a prism.

The shadows on each particle in the illumination volume are as important as those on objects. For shading, the shadow volume [14] used for calculating shadows on the object and contour lines [20] of the object viewed from the light source is available. In the case of Fig. 3, the illuminated segments on view line $P_v P_i$ are the segments including the illuminated volume $S_4 S_1$ and excluding the shadow volume segments $S_3 S_2$.

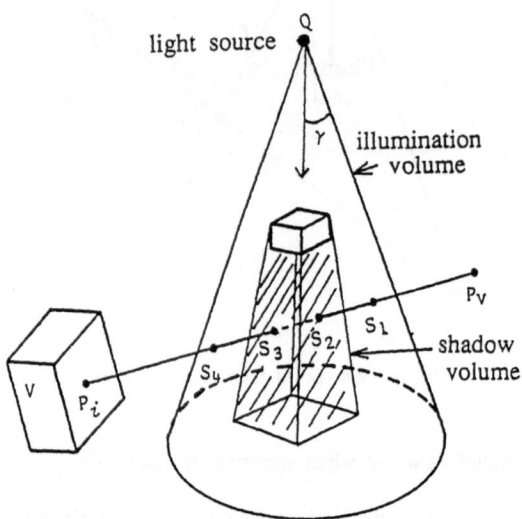

Fig. 3:   Calculation of scattered light using illumination and shadow volumes.

3.3 Scattering in a non-uniform field

For non-uniform fields, the following two cases exist; one field consists of more than two kinds of distributed material, such as dry ice, smoke, clouds in vapor, and turbid river water flowing into the sea, and the other field consists of only one material, but a non-uniform field occurs due to the difference in pressure as in atmospheric pressure. The former has relatively definite boundaries. However, the latter does not have any boundary, but a gradual variation exists.

1)Modeling of density distribution
Rather than to take arbitrary density distribution over the whole space, let's consider the simple case in which certain regions are occupied by smoke or turbidity with uniform density; the distribution of particles is divided into several layers, each with uniform distributed particles. The optical depth in the various layers depends on each extinction coefficient per unit length. Therefore, in Eq. 5 numerical integration along the ray from the viewpoint to the object should be used. Note that when density is sampled only at uniform intervals along the ray, aliasing problems may occur. To overcome this problem, pre-calculation of intersections between the

ray and boundary surface should be executed, and if sampling errors occur in the intervals, intermediate sampling points in those intervals should be added.

2)Modeling of atmosphere

The atmosphere consists of the ozone layer, air molecules and aerosols, but for visible wavelengths of light, absorption in the ozone layer is negligible compared with the others. For air molecules, Rayleigh scattering predominates because of their being much smaller than the wavelength of the light, and for aerosols Mie scattering predominates because of their diameter being almost the same as the wavelength of the light. The density of air molecules exponentially decreases with altitude. The light due to Rayleigh scattering is calculated taking into account the density ratio of air molecules to the standard atmosphere; the molecular density ratio ρ is

$$\rho = exp(-h/H_o), \tag{9}$$

where h is the altitude above sea level and $H_o (= 7,974[m])$ is a scale height. From a viewpoint on a macro-sized object like the earth, the density of aerosols decreases exponentially with altitude, just as the density distribution of air molecules does, even though the rule of decrease is different from that of air molecules. Density can be obtained by setting the scale height H_o of Eq. 9 to $1,200[m]$ [22].

4. LIGHTING MODEL OF THE BOUNDARY BETWEEN VAPOR AND LIQUID

There is a great difference in density between vapor and liquid, and so for rendering to take into account mirrored reflection, refraction, and the critical angle of light on the water surface, this can not be ignored. The forms of water are multifarious, falls, fountains, rivers, ripples, billows, etc. All of these are obedient to the principles of hydrodynamics. So, if we wish to simulate these phenomena precisely, tremendous computation time is required. Actually, even if we were willing to accept such a cost, it would be almost impossible to reach a solution with the computer ability presently available. Despite this, however, the rendering of water is indispensable, especially for attractive animations and so many researchers have been working on this.

4.1 Shapes of Waves

As mentioned in section 2, many papers addressing the shapes of waves have been published. The authors' group is using a bumpmapping technique with data compounding several kinds of waves with different pitches and amplitudes. The amplitude of waves is expressed by the following Stokes wave equations:

$$z(x,t) = \sum_{n=1}^{\infty} a_n \cos nk(x - ct), \tag{10}$$

where $z(x,t)$ expresses the height of water at time t, a_n is a coefficient expressing wave shape, k is the number of waves per unit distance, and c is the wave velocity: Eq. 9 is transformed to the following two dimensional field by specified directional coefficients, p and q:

$$z(x,y,t) = \sum_{n=1}^{\infty} a_n \cos n(px + qy - \omega t), \tag{11}$$

where $p^2 + q^2 = k^2$, $\omega = kc$ and ω is the frequency.

4.2 Lighting for a light source located above the water surface

When a light source is located above the water surface as shown in Fig. 4, the intensity of light I arriving at one's viewing point P_v from calculation point P on the water surface is expressed by

$$I = \alpha(\theta_i, \theta_j)I_r + (1 - \alpha(\theta_i, \theta_j))I_w, \tag{12}$$

where I_r and I_w are the intensity of reflected light arriving on the water surface, and transmitted light from within the water, respectively. Reflectance at point P, $\alpha(\theta_i, \theta_j)$ obeys Fresnel's law expressed by the function of angles θ_i and θ_j, where θ_i is the angle between unit normal vector N of the water surface at point P and the direction of I, and θ_j is the angle between the direction of the refracted ray coming from the viewpoint to point P and the inverse vector of N. θ_i and θ_j obey Snell's law, as is well-known. I_w consists of two factors, I'_Q and I_{PQ}; I'_Q is the attenuated light of the reflected light I_Q at point Q on the bottom of the water, and I_{PQ} is the total amount of the factor of the direction from Q to P of light scattered on the path PQ. Note that in most cases the effects of both attenuation and scattering can not be ignored because in general these factors are much larger in water than that in air. Assuming that the wall including point R (see Fig. 4) is a diffuse reflection surface, and scattering and absorption of light along path RP are negligible because of a very clear atmosphere, I_r is expressed by the function of the degree of irradiance at point R illuminated by both the direct light from light source O and by indirect light, e.g. the reflected light coming from point W_r on the water surface. As for how many factors on indirect light should be taken into account, this rather depends on computation cost and the rendering effects used. In our lighting model, for calculating reflected and refracted light, taking into account cost performance, it is assumed that the water surface is horizontal, except for calculation point P, as shown in Fig. 4.

4.3 Lighting model for a light source located underwater

When a light source is located underwater as shown in Fig. 5, the intensity of light I coming from calculation point P is also expressed by the sum of the functions of I_r and I_w, as directed in the previous section. Concerning I_r a point, which differs from the case of when the light is located above the water, is that incident light at R comes only from light source O through point W_R on the water surface, if global illumination effects are ignored. Note when θ_{WR}, the incident angle from O at W_R, exceeds the critical angle θ_c, incident light is fully reflected because the refractive index of water is larger than that of air. I_w consists of light I_Q from point Q on the bottom of water and light I_s from along the path QP, as described in the previous section. Here, it is important to note that both I_Q and I_w consist of two functions, the direct light from light source O and reflected light at relative points W_Q and W_s on the water surface (see Fig. 5).

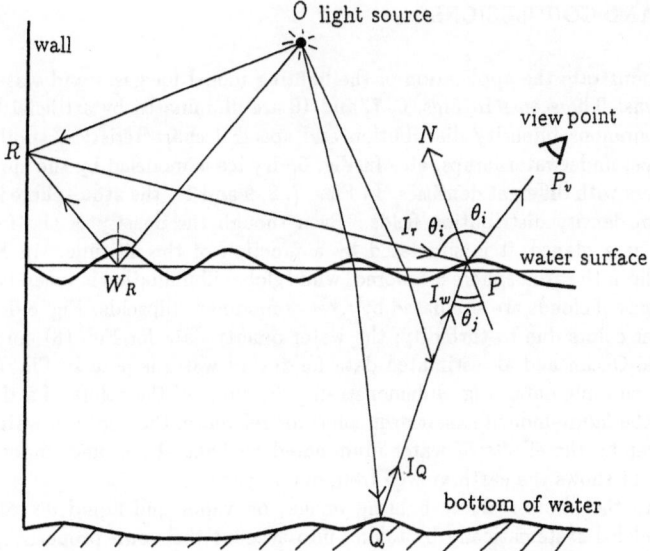

Fig. 4: Lighting model for a light source located above the water surface

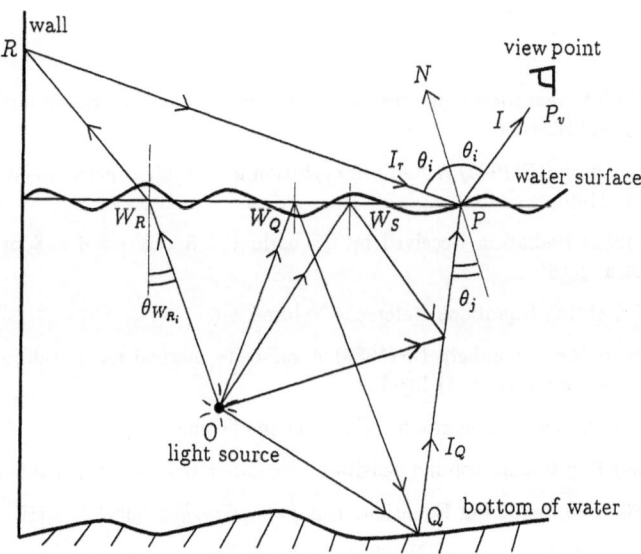

Fig. 5: Lighting model for light source located underwater

5. EXAMPLES AND CONCLUSIONS

Figs. 6 to 11 demonstrate the application of the lighting model for gases and water discussed in previous sections. The scenes in Figs. 6, 7, and 10 are illuminated by artificial light source with their own luminous intensity distribution and spectral characteristics; spotlights, head lights, street lamps, underwater lamps, etc. In Fig. 6, dry ice is modeled by the curved surface boundaries of layers with different densities. In Figs. 7, 8, 9 and 11, the atmosphere is simulated using non-uniform density distribution fields. Even though the density of the fog in Fig. 7 appears uniform at a glance, it is simulated by a function of the altitude. In Fig. 10, the attenuation of light in the atmosphere is ignored, while global illumination is taken into account. In Fig. 9, the shapes of clouds are simulated by a set of modified ellipsoids. Fig. 8 demonstrates the different water colors due to turbidity; the water quality data for Fig. (8) corresponds to the central Pacific Ocean and an estimated data for turbid water is used in Fig. (b) because of a lack of other suitable data. Fig. 9 demonstrates the effect of the colors of a riverbed; the color bars under the figure indicate their own color; for reference, the depth of water is $2.5[m]$. Fig. 10 (a),(b) display the effects of water illuminated by light above, and under the water, respectively. Fig. 11 shows the earth viewed from outer space.

As depicted above the photo-realistic lighting images on vapor and liquid distributing in a 3-D fields are modeled systematically by taking into account their own properties; scattering and absorption in the field, and reflectance and critical angles on the boundaries between the different matters. The preciseness of the images created is proportional to their computation cost. Despite the fact we haven't discussed shadowing at length, because of space limitation, it is very important in rendering techniques but makes cording fairly complicated.

REFERENCES

[1] Blinn JF(1982) Light reflection functions for simulation of clouds and dusty surfaces. *Computer Graphics* 16(3):21-29

[2] Cohen MF, Greenberg DP(1985) A Radiosity solution for complex environment. *Computer Graphics* 19(3):31-40

[3] Gibbons MG(1958) Radiation Received by Uncollimated Receiver a 4 π Source, J. Opt. Soc. of America, 48(8)

[4] IES(1981) IES Lighting Handbook Reference Volume,:6-6

[5] Immel DS, Cohen MF, Greenberg DP(1986) A radiosity method for non-diffuse environments. *Computer Graphics* 20(4):133-142

[6] Jerlov NG(1968) Optical Oceanography. Elservier publishing Co.

[7] Kajiya JT(1984) Ray tracing volume densities. *Computer Graphics* 18(3):165-174

[8] Kajiya JT(1986) The Rendering Equation. *Computer Graphics* 20(4):143-150

[9] Kaneda K, Yuan G, Nakamae E, Nishita(1991) Rendering Visual Simulation of Water Surfaces Taking into Account Radiative Transfer. *The 2nd International Conference on CAD & CG in China*:25-30

[10] Kass M, Miller G(1990) Rapid, Stable Fluid Dynamics for Computer Graphics. *Computer Graphics* 24(4):49-57

[11] Max NL(1981) Vectorized Procedural Models for Natural Terrain: Waves and Islands in the Sunset. *Computer Graphics* 15(3):317-324

[12] Max NL(1986) Light diffusion through clouds and haze. *Computer Vision, Graphics, and Image Processing* 33(3):280-292

[13] Max NL(1986) Atmospheric illumination and shadows. *Computer Graphics* 20(4):117-124

[14] Nakamae E, Harada K, Ishizaki T, Nishita T(1986) A Montage; The Overlaying of the Computer Generated Images onto a Background Photograph. *Computer Graphics* 20(3):207-214

[15] Nishita T, Nakamae E(1983) Half-Tone Representation of 3-D Objects Illuminated by Area Sources or Polyhedron Sources. *Proc. IEEE COMPSAC* :237-242 (1983).

[16] Nishita T, Okamura I, Nakamae E(1985) Shading models for point and linear sources illuminated by area sources or polyhedron sources. *ACM Trans Graph*:4(2):124-146

[17] Nishita T, Nakamae E(1985) Continuous Tone Representation of Three-Dimensional Objects Taking Account of Shadows and Interreflection. *Computer Graphics* 19(3):23-30

[18] Nishita T, Nakamae E(1986) Continuous Tone Representation of Three-Dimensional Objects Illuminated by Sky Light. *Computer Graphics* 20(4):125-132

[19] Nishita T, Miyawaki Y, Nakamae E(1987) A shading model for atmospheric scattering considering distribution of light sources. *Computer Graphics* 21(4):303-310

[20] Nishita T, Okamura I, Nakamae E(1986) Shading Models for Point and Linear Sources. *ACM Trans. on Graphics*:4(2):124-146

[21] Rushmeier HE, Torrance K(1987) The Zonal Method for Calculating Light Intensities in the Presence of a Participating Medium. *Computer Graphics* 21(4):293-302

[22] Sekine S(1987) Optical characteristics of Turbid Atmosphere. *J Illum Eng Int Jpn*:71(6):333

[23] Shinya M, Saito T, Takahashi T(1989) Rendering Techniques for Transparent Objects. *Proceedings of Graphics Interface*, London Ontario: 173-182

[24] Stokes GG(1980) Mathematical and Physical Papers. *Cambridge University Press*,:341

[25] Takita S, Kaneda K, Akinobu T, Iriyama H, Nakamae E, Nishita T(1991) A Simple Rendering for Penumbra Caused by Sunlight. *The Visual Computer* 7(5,6):259-268

[26] Ts'o PY, Barsky BA(1987) Modeling and Rendering Waves: Wave-Tracing Using Beta-Splines and Reflective and Refractive Texture Mapping. *ACM Transactions on Graphics* 6(3):191-214

[27] Watt M(1990) Light-Water Interaction using Backward Beam Tracing. *Computer Graphics* 24(4): 377-385

[28] William M, Cornette, Joseph G, Shanks(1992) Physically Reasonable Analytic Expression for the Single-Scattering Phase function. *APPLIED OPTICS* 31(16):3152-3160

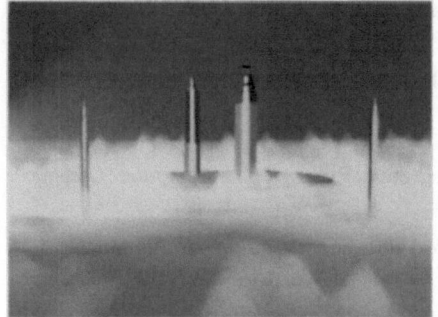

Fig. 6: Effects of multi-layers with different density distribution

Fig. 7: Fog effects

(a) data from the central Pacific Ocean

(b) an estimated data

Fig. 8: Effects of water quality

(a)   (b)

Fig. 9:   Effects of colors of riverbed

(a)   (b)

Fig. 10:   A scene illuminated by lights above and under water

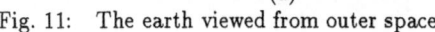

(a)   (b)

Fig. 11:   The earth viewed from outer space

Eihachiro Nakamae received the BE, ME, and DE degrees in 1954, 1956, and 1967 from Waseda University.
He is a professor at Hiroshima Prefectural University from 1992. He was appointed as a research associate at Hiroshima University in 1956 and a professor from 1968 to 1992. He was an associate researcher at Clarkson College of Technology, Potsdam, N. Y., from 1973 to 1974. His research interests include computer graphics and electric machinery. He is a member of IEEE, IEE of Japan, IPS of Japan and IEICE of Japan.
Address: Hiroshima Prefectural University
562 Nanatsuka, Shoubara, 727 Japan.
E-mail: G00234@sinet.ad.jp

Katsumi Tadamura is a research associate in School of Business at Hiroshima Prefectural University. He worked at Hitachi Ltd. from 1986 to 1991. He joined Hiroshima Prefectural University in 1991. His research interests include computer graphics. He received the BE and ME in 1984 and 1986, respectively, from Hiroshima University. He is a member of IPS of Japan.
Address: Hiroshima Prefectural University
562 Nanatsuka, Shoubara, 727 Japan.
E-mail: G00235@sinet.ad.jp

Hideo Yamashita received the B.E. and M.E. degrees in electrical engineering from Hiroshima University, Hiroshima, Japan, in 1964 and 1968, and Dr. of Engineering degree in 1977 from Waseda University, Tokyo, Japan. He was appointed as a Research Assistant in 1968 and Professor in 1992 of the Faculty of Engineering, Hiroshima University. He was an Associate Researcher at Clarkson University, Potsdam, N.Y. in 1981-1982. His research interests lie in the area of the visualization and field analyses by using the Finite Element Method and Boundary Element Method. He is a member of the IEEE, ACM, the IEE of Japan, the IECE of Japan, and the IPS of Japan.
Address: Faculty of Engineering, Hiroshima University
1-4-1 Kagamiyama, Higashihiroshima 724,Japan.
E-mail:yama@eml.hiroshima-u.ac.jp

Kazufumi Kaneda is a reaserch associate in Fuculty of Engineering at Hiroshima University. He worked at the Chugoku Electric Power Company Ltd., Japan from 1984 to 1986. He was a visiting scholarship at Brigham Young University from 1991 to 1992. He joined Hiroshima University in 1986. His research interests include computer graphics and image processing Kaneda received the BE and ME in 1982 and 1984, respectively, from Hiroshima University. He is a member of IEE of Japan, IPS of Japan and IEICE OF Japan.
Address: Faculty of Engineering, Hiroshima University
1-4-1 Kagamiyama, Higashihiroshima 724, Japan.
E-mail: kin@eml.hiroshima-u.ac.jp

Tomoyuki Nishita is an associate professor in the department of Electronic and Electrical Engineering at Fukuyama University, Japan. He was on the research staff at MAZDA from 1973 to 1979 and worked on design and development of computer-controlled vehicle system. He joined Fukuyama University in 1979. He was a visiting professor and research associate in the Engineering Computer Graphics Laboratory at Brigham Young University from 1988 to the end of March, 1989. His reaserch interests involve computer graphics including lighting model, hidden-surface removal, and antialising. Nishita received his BE, ME and Ph.D in Engineering in 1971, 1973, and 1985, respectively, from Hiroshima University. He is a member of ACM, IPS of Japan and IEE of Japan.

Address: Faculty of Engineering, Fukuyama University
Sanzo, Higashimuracho, Fukuyama 729-02 Japan.
E-mail: nis@eml.hiroshima-u.ac.jp

Display of Multi-Isosurfaces by the Volume Rendering Technique from Data Sets in 3D Space*

Zesheng Tang, Jun Yuan, and Jiaguang Sun

ABSTRACT

An algorithm for displaying multi—isosurfaces from data sets in 3D space is presented. The precise locations of isosurfaces or region boundary surfaces are determined by the data values of resampling points on rays cast from each pixel on the screen. The isosurfaces coordinates are the intersection points between the casting rays and the isosurfaces. The local gradients and the shading intensities are only calculated at intersection points rather than at all other resampling points. The final image is generated by composing the shading intensities and opacities along each ray. Two approaches to improve the efficiency of the algorithm are discussed. Several images are shown to illustrate the results.

Key words: Volume Rendering Technique, Multi—isosurface, Data Sets, 3D Space.

1. INTRODUCTION

Visualization of data sets in 3D space is the kernel of scientific and engineering visualizations. There are two approaches to visualizing data sets in 3D space.

The first approach is to create intermediate geometric primitives, such as curved surfaces, and then render them with conventional surface rendering algorithms. The Marching Cubes method (Lorenson 1987) created approximate triangular models for given constant values in cubes of 3D data sets and connected them to generate an isosurface. This method was originally developed for uniform and dense 3D data sets, such as result from Computer Tomography(CT) and Magnetic Resonance(MR). The most important limitation of this method is that the generated result consists of connected triangles which are only an approximate representation of the required isosurface. Akio Doi (1991) created triangle models for given constant values in tetrahedra subdivided from cubes to generate multi—isosurfaces images of electron density field. The results are more precise than those of the Marching Cubes method due to subdivision and quadratic interpolation, however, it requires more computationa effort. R.S.Gallagher (1989) developed an algorithm to create continuous curved surfaces from discrete points of given values using bi—cubic polynomials to generate multi—isosurfaces images of finite element models. This method generates smooth and

---

* This project is supported by the National Natural Science Foundation of China.

non–faceted surfaces but is applicable only to 3D data sets with coarsely spaced points.

The second approach is to generate 2D images directly from 3D data sets without creation of intermediate geometric primitives. J.F. Blinn (1982) proposed an algorithm to generate images of clouds and dusty surfaces. It is based on the statistical simulation of light passing through and being reflected by clouds of similar small particles and is not meant to generate isosurfaces. More recently, the volume rendering algorithm has been developed by several researchers (Drebin 1988; Sabella 1988; Upson 1988). It is based on the reconstruction and the resampling of 3D discrete data sets to generate 2D images directly.

M. Levoy (1988) presented an image order volume rendering algorithm to obtain surfaces from volume data. While his algorithm may be theoretically used to display multi–isosurfaces, the implementation for multi–isosurfaces has not been published. In his algorithm, the opacity assignments for the original data on the isovalue contour surface and on the region boundary surface are defined separately. In addition, the values of resampling points on the ray are interpolated from the shading intensities (or colors) and opacities of the eight data points around each point instead of being interpolated from the original data. Thus, the algorithm requires more memory space to store the shading intensities and opacities of all data points and will inevitably cause blurring in the resulting image because of the non–linear relationship between the original data and the shading intensities

In this paper, an algorithm for displaying multi–isosurfaces from data sets in 3D space is presented. It is based on the image order volume rendering technique with some significant modifications. The precise locations of the isosurfaces or region boundary surfaces are determined from the data values of the resampling points on the rays cast from each pixel on the screen. These locations are actually the intersection points between the casting rays and the isosurfaces. In this algorithm, the local gradients and shading intensities are not calculated at any other resampling points except at intersection points. The final image is obtained by composing the intensities and opacities of intersection points along each ray. Therefore, this algorithm can generate accurate multi–isosurfaces for uniform and dense 3D data sets with moderate computing speed.

The algorithm is described in section 2. In section 3, approaches to improving the efficiency of the algorithm are described. Some results and conclusions are given in section 4.

2. DESCRIPTION OF THE ALGORITHM

In this paper, we assume that the data sets in 3D space are organized logically in 3D arrays and have uniform and rectilinear geometric distributions (Fig. 1a and Fig. 1b). Each element of the data array is called a voxel. Voxels are treated as point samples of a continuous function rather than as volumes having a homogeneous value. The function value of the voxel located at (i,j,k) is represented by $f(i,j,k)$. The spacing between voxels is greater than or equal to the spacing between pixels. It means that minification is not considered. The images represents either the multi–isosurfaces or the region boundary surfaces in miced substances in 3D space.

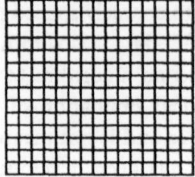 

Fig. 1(a,b)

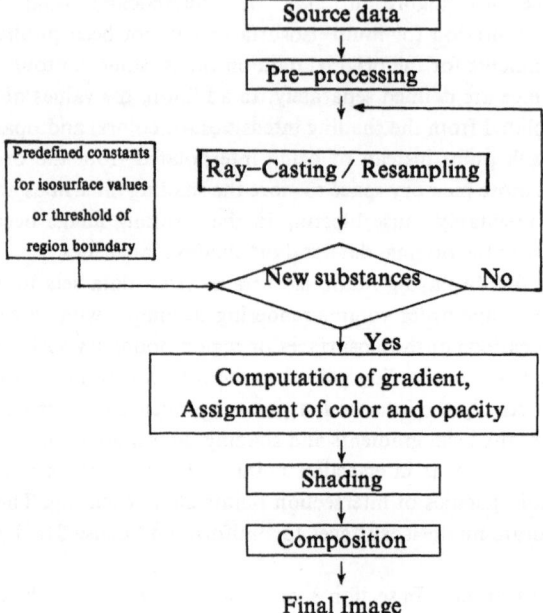

Fig. 2

In our algorithm, creation of intermediate explicit surfaces is not required. The isosurfaces are displayed by locating the resampling points, which have the specified constant values, on the ray cast from each pixel on the screen. The flowchart of the algorithm is shown in Fig. 2.

2.1 Ray–casting and Resampling

In volume rendering, the 2D images are generated directly from 3D discrete data sets in 3D space. The essential part of this process is data resampling and image composition. The image order volume rendering technique is one of several approaches for resampling and composition. According to sampling theory, the first step of the resampling process is to reconstruct

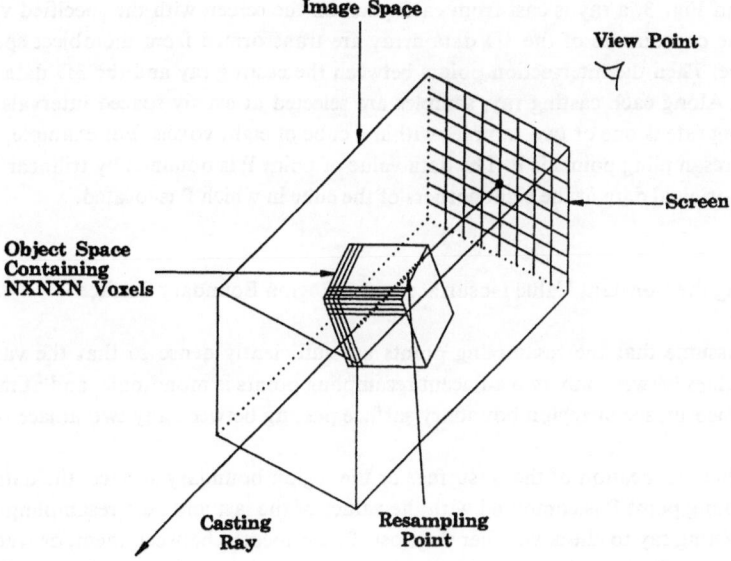

Fig. 3

the continuous function from the input samples by convolving them with a reconstruction filter. The reconstruction step should directly process the original data sets rather than any other data induced from the original ones, such as colors, shading intensities, etc. because the relationships between color values, shading intensities and original data are generally non−linear.

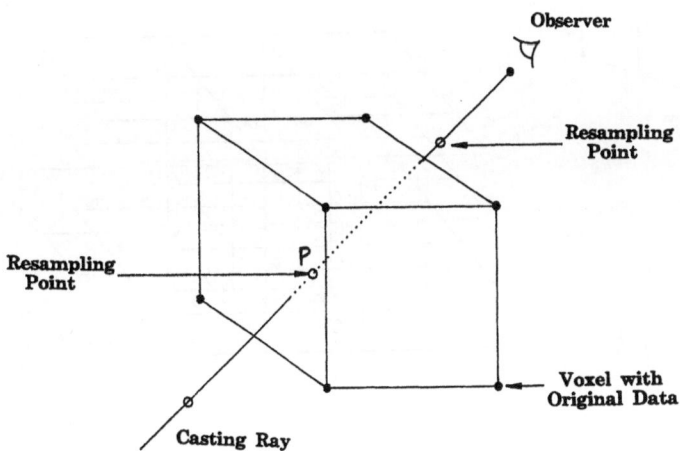

Fig. 4

As shown in Fig. 3, a ray is cast from each pixel on the screen with the specified viewing direction. The coordinates of the 3D data array are transformed from the object space to the image space. Then the intersection points between the casting ray and the 3D data array are calculated. Along each casting ray, samples are selected at evenly spaced intervals. Usually, the sampling rate is one or two samples within a cube of eight voxels. For example, in Fig. 4, one of the resampling points is P. The data value of point P is obtained by trilinear interpolation of the original data at the eight corners of the cube in which P is located.

2.2 Locating the Constant Value Isosurface or the Region Boundary Surface

First, we assume that the resampling points are sufficiently dense so that the variation of function values between any two adjacent resampling points is monotonic, and at most, there is only one isosurface or region boundary surface passing between any two adjacent resampling points.

To determine the location of the isosurface or the region boundary surface, the data value of one resampling point P is compared with the values of the last and next resampling points on the same casting ray to check whether the isosurface is located between them, or whether they belong to two different substances. If either criteria is satisfied, the coordinates of the point on the isosurface are determined by binary search. This point is the intersection of the current casting ray and the isosurface.

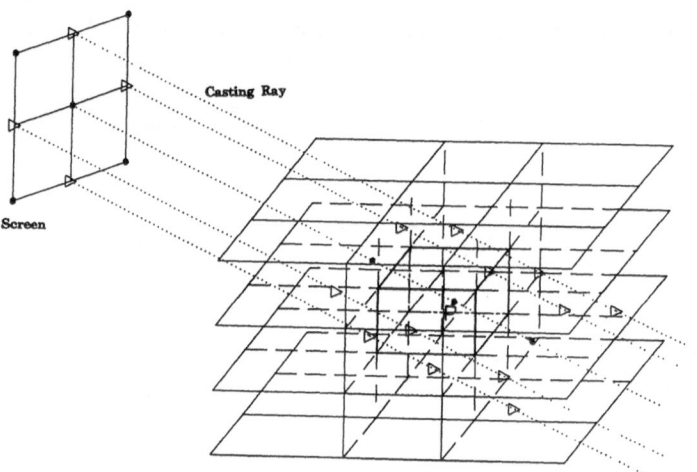

Fig. 5a   Symbol • represents resampling points on the current casting ray, symbol △ represents resampling points on the adjacent rays.

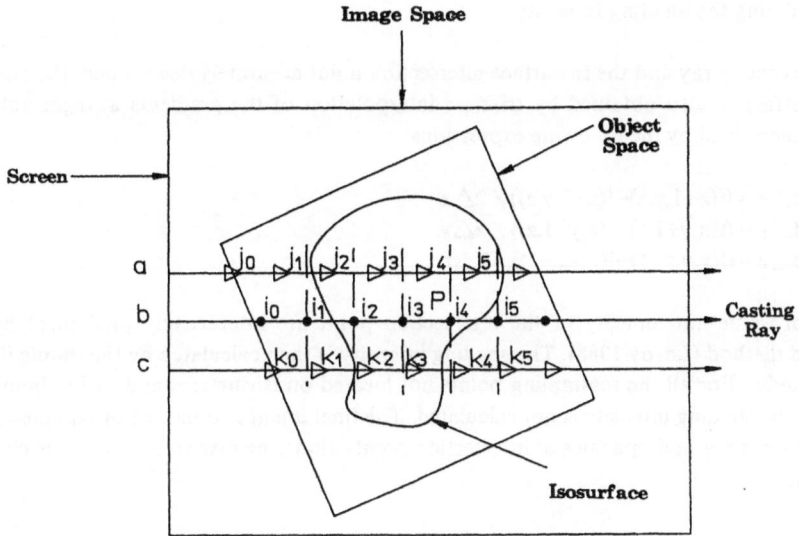

Fig. 5b

If neither of the above criteria is satisfied, the algorithm then seeks to determine the location of the isosurface in the vicinity of the resampling point, P, but not on the casting ray containing P. The vicinity of P is searched by comparing the value at P with the values at resampling points having the same depth as P on eight adjacent casting rays (Fig. 5).For clarity, in Fig. 5a, only the resampling points on five adjacent casting rays are shown in 3D space, and in Fig. 5b, only the top view of three adjacent casting rays are shown. In Fig. 5b, casting ray b is the current casting ray with resampling points i_0, i_1, $\cdots$ evenly spaced on it. The points on casting ray c with the same depth as $P(i_4)$ are located between k_3 and k_4. Therefore, comparisons between the data of i_4 and k_3, k_4 are needed. If $P(i_4)$ and k_4 belong to two different substances, it means there is a region boundary surface between them. If the values of the two points are, respectively, less than and greater than the constant value of the isosurface, then they are located on different sides of the isosurface. In these cases, because we cannot insert an additional casting ray between two adjacent pixels, then we should treat these two resampling points as being in two different substance regions and calculate the shading intensities on both of them seperately.

From this algorithm, one can understand that the multi–isosurfaces generated is based on the surface detection by ray casting method. Because the rays are cast from each pixel of the screen, so that the location of isosurface is the accurate intersection point of the surface and casting ray from each pixel. While in the existing surface construction method, such as Marching Cubes Method, only the intersection points on the edges of cube are on the isusurface. The triangles or curved surfaces passing through intersection points are only approximate representation of the isosurface. Hence, the isosurface generated by this method is more accurate than that generated by existing surface construction method.

2.3 Calculating the Shading Intensity

After the casting ray and the isosurface intersection point accurately determined, the gradient of the surface is also obtained by trilinear interpolation of the gradients at eight adjacent voxels, determined by the following expressions:

$$grad\_x = (f(x+1,y,z)-f(x-1,y,z)) / 2\triangle x$$
$$grad\_y = (f(x,y+1,z)-f(x,y-1,z)) / 2\triangle y$$
$$grad\_z = (f(x,y,z+1)-f(x,y,z-1)) / 2\triangle z$$

The color value and opacity of the intersection point are interactively predefined by the threshold method (Levoy 1988). The shading intensity is then calculated by the Phong illumination model. For all the resampling points not located on isosurfaces and region boundary surfaces, the shading intensity is not calculated. The final image is obtained by composing the shading intensities and opacities of intersection points along the rays from front to back (Porter 1984).

3. ALGORITHM EFFICIENCY ENHANCEMENTS

In the algorithm introduced in Section 2, the data value of the resampling point P will be compared to the last and next resampling points on the same casting ray and to the resampling points on the adjacent casting rays to probe the location of isosurfaces. This leads to numerous duplications of the trilinear calculation and results in a significant degradation of the algorithm's efficiency. The algorithm can be improved in two ways.

3.1 Progressive Refinement Method

This method includes three steps:
Step 1: Only the data value of the resampling point P and the last and next resampling points on the same casting ray are compared to identify the location of an isosurface. This is called single casting ray method. It generates a preliminary image of the multi–isosurfaces.
Step 2: The data value of the resampling point P is compared with the resampling points at the same depth on the four adjacent rays which are cast from the left, right, upper and lower pixels adjacent to the current one. This is called the five casting rays method (see Fig. 5a).
Step 3: The data value of the resampling point P is then compared with additional resampling points at the same depth on other adjacent rays cast from the upper–left, upper–right, lower–left, lower–right adjacent pixels of the current one. This is the called nine casting rays method.
In these three steps, caculated values used in one step can be used in the next step, eliminating duplicate calculations. This method thus includes a global browse process before the final image is generated.

As an example, the isothermal surfaces calculated during a solidification process were displayed using the three steps algorithm. The computing times are given in Table 1 for calculations carried out on a SGI IRIS 4D / 25 workstation using the C language.

Table 1. Computation of temperature isosurfaces in a solidification process for a 512×512 image.

Method	Computing time	Results
Single casting ray	61″	Fig. 6
Five casting rays	143″	Fig. 7
Nine casting rays	212″	Fig. 8

3.2 Shifting Window Method

As described above, the algorithm proceeds line by line across the image. The rays are cast from the pixels scanline by scanline from the top to the bottom of the screen. The resampling point data on each casting ray is compared with the resampling points at the same depth on the rays cast from the pixels of the scanlines above and below the current line. In order to avoid duplication of the trilinear calculation of the resampling points, we need to store the data values of all resampling points on casting rays for further comparson. However, only the resampling data on rays cast from three adjacent scanlines must be stored at any one time. During processing of the resampling points, data for the upper scanline is over-written and new data for the lower scanline is added. A window of three scanlines is shifted from the top to the bottom of the screen. The resulting improvement in the computing time is shown in Table 2.

Table 2. Comparison of computing time for generating four temperature isosurfaces in a solidification process by nine casting rays method.

Methods	Computing time
Computing time without shifting window method	212″
Computing time with shifting window method	118″
Percentages of improvement	44%

4. RESULTS AND CONCLUSIONS

The algorithm has been implemented on a SGI IRIS 4D / 25 workstation using C language. Images generated using the algorthm are shown in Fig. 9, Fig. 10 and Fig. 11. Fig. 9 is an image of three isosurfaces, showing electron density. Fig. 10 illustrates force distribution

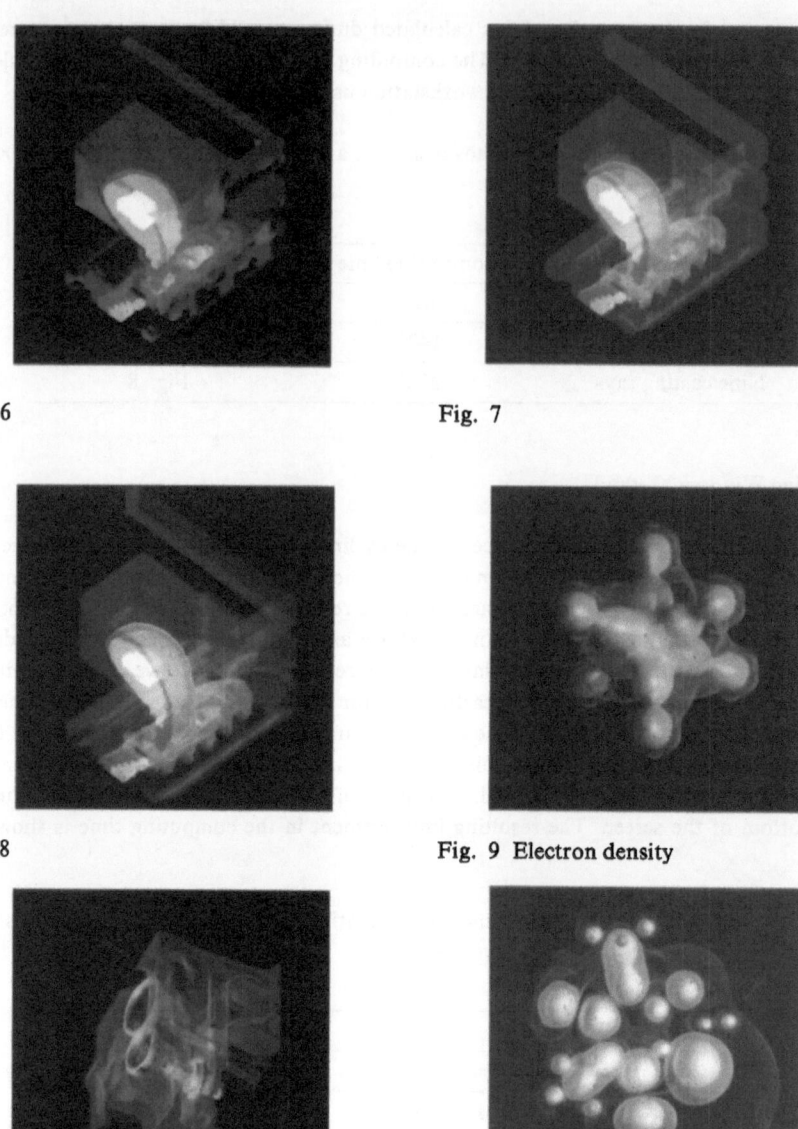

Fig. 6

Fig. 7

Fig. 8

Fig. 9 Electron density

Fig. 10 Mechanical part

Fig. 11 Molecular model

within a mechanical part, using different colors. The structure of a molecular model is shown in Fig. 11.

From these results, we reach the following conclusions:

1) The multi–isosurfaces image generated by the volume rendering technique is more accurate than that generated by existing methods of surface construction.

2) The algorithm to display multi–isosurfaces by volume rendering is especially suitable for dense and uniform data sets in 3D space.

3) This algorithm can easily be integrated with conventional image order and object order volume rendering techniques. The user can then choose the most suitable approach for their need.

ACKNOWLEDGEMENTS

The solidification process temperature data set was provided by Prof. Baichen Liu in the Department of Mechanical Engineering of Tsinghua University. The electron density data set was provided by Prof. Jiye Ximen in the Department of Radio Engineering of Beijing University. The other datasets are courtesy of Vital Image Company. We would like to express appreciation to all of them for their help.

REFERENCES

Akio, Doi and Akio, Koide (1991), An efficient Method of Triangulating Equi–valued Surfaces by Using Tetrahedral Cells, IEICE Transactions, Vol.E74, No.1, Jan. 1991.

Bl inn, James F. (1982), Light Reflection Functions for Simulation of Clouds and Dusty Surfaces, Computer Graphics, Vol.16, No.3, July 1982, pp 21–29.

Drebin, Robert A. , Carpenter, Loren and Hanrahan Pat (1988), Volume Rendering, Computer Graphics, Vol.22, No.4, Aug.1988, pp. 65–74.

Gallagher, Richard S. and Nagtegaal, Joop C. (1989), An Efficient 3D Visualization Technique for Finite Element Models and Other Coarse Volumes, Computer Graphics, Vol.23, No.3, July 1989, pp. 185–194.

Le voy, Marc (1988), Display of Surfaces from Volume Data, IEEE CG&A, May 1988, pp. 148–156.

Lo renson, William E. and Cline Harvey E. (1987), Marching Cubes: A High Resolution 3D Surface Construction Algorithm, Computer Graphics, Vol.21, No.4, July 1987, pp. 38–44.

Po rter, Thomas and Duff Tom (1984), Composition Digital Images, Computer Graphics, Vol.18, No.3, July 1984, pp. 103–109.

Sa bella, Paolo (1988), A Rendering Algorithm for Visualizing 3D Scalar Fields, Computer Graphics, Vol.22, No.4, Aug. 1988, pp. 51–58.

Upson, Craig and Keeler Michael (1988), V–Buffer: Visible Volume Rendering, Computer Graphics, Vol.22, No.4, Aug. 1988, pp. 59–64.

114

Zesheng Tang is a professor in the Department of Computer Science and Technology of Tsinghua University, Beijing, China. In the beginning of the 1980s, Zesheng Tang and his colleagues began education and research work in the field of Computer Graphics. In 1985–1986, he visited the University of Michigan in Ann Arbor, U.S.A. and worked in the Palo Alto Research Center of Xerox Corporation in California. His current research interest includes Volume Visualization, Geometric Modeling and its Application, and Computational Geometry. Zesheng Tang is an executive council member and the vice chairman of the CAD and Computer Graphics Society of the China Computer Federation. He is a senior member and the vice chairman of Computer Engineering and Application Society of China Electronic Institute. He has published more than 50 technical papers in Computer Graphics and CAD Technology.

Jun Yuan recently received M.Sc. from the Department of Computer Science and Technology of Tsinghua University. He received B.Eng. from the University of Science and Technology, Beijing in 1990. His research interests are in scientific visualization, image processing, human–computer interface and parallel processing.

Jiaguang Sun's information can be reached in the paper named "Blending Polyhedra with NURBS".

Address: CAD Center, Dept. of Computer Science and Technology, Tsinghua University, Beijing, 100084, People's Republic of China.

Shadow Volume Generation from Free Form Surfaces*

Gregory Heflin and Gershon Elber

Abstract

The generation of shadows has occupied the computer graphics community for some time. Several approaches have been successfully developed, but many except ray tracing assume a polygonal approximation of the model.

In this paper, an approach is presented that allows one to compute shadow volumes directly from free form models and exploit them for the generation of shadows using a Z-buffer based renderer. A polygonal approximation is not required for either the construction of the shadow volume or for the rendering process.

Key Words: Computer graphics, shadows, shadow volumes, parametric surfaces.

1 Introduction

Classifications of existing shadow rendering techniques have been presented by several authors [Bergeron 1986, Crow 1977, Max 1986]. The techniques can be categorized into the following six categories.

1. **Scan-line shadow generation.** Comparison is done between all models to determine pairs that can interact to produce shadows [Appel 1968, Bouknight 1970, Nishita 1991]. These precomputed relations are used to produce shadows during scan line rendering.

2. **Two-pass model-precision approach.** Models are divided into visible and hidden polygonal regions as viewed from the light source [Atherton 1978]. All the shadowed regions are tagged once and can then be rendered from any desired viewpoint.

3. **Shadow volume approach.** Volumes are generated that enclose shadowed regions of space [Bergeron 1986, Chin 1989, Crow 1977, Fuchs 1985, Max 1986, Nishita 1987]. The boundary surfaces of the shadow volumes are also processed by the Z buffer scan line renderer. Shadow surfaces in the z-list [Atherton 1981] in front of a visible surface are examined to determine if the visible surface is also in shadow. This is a common approach to shadow rendering. Alternatively, the shadow volumes may be used in the first pass of method 2, to classify and tag shadowed regions.

*This work was supported in part by DARPA (N00014-91-J-4123) and the NSF and DARPA Science and Technology Center for Computer Graphics and Scientific Visualization (ASC-89-20219). All opinions, findings, conclusions or recommendations expressed in this document are those of the authors and do not necessarily reflect the views of the sponsoring agencies.

4. **Z-buffer approach.** Depth information is computed and stored in a z-buffer for both the eye and light source viewpoints [Reeves 1987, Williams 1978]. The eye depth values are transformed to the light source view space and depths are compared. If the transformed depth of the point to be rendered is further from the light than the value recorded in the light source z-buffer, then it is in shadow.

5. **Radiosity.** Diffuse light is modeled using techniques from heat transfer theory [Cohen 1985]. Soft shadows are handled particularly well through accurate modeling of diffuse global illumination in polygonal environments.

6. **Ray Tracing.** Rays are traced from the eye through each pixel with shading calculations performed for each surface encountered [Cook 1984, Joy 1988, Kajiya 1982, Nishita 1990, Toth 1985, Whitted 1980, Woodward 1989]. Shadow rays are traced from the surfaces to each light source to determine shadowed regions.

Ray tracing currently provides the most realistic model for shadow generation in environments consisting of free form surfaces, but even direct ray tracing of free form surfaces remains an active and difficult area of research [Joy 1988, Kajiya 1982, Nishita 1990, Toth 1985, Woodward 1989]. In addition, the illumination calculations that ray tracing employs are computationally expensive. Techniques 2 through 5 have an additional computational advantage over ray casting approaches by providing view independent and global shadow representations. This allows one to render scenes from any viewpoint without the need to redetermine the underlying shadow representation, possibly exploiting the use of a hardware renderer. Different approaches for the direct rendering of free from surfaces with shadows, that do not use raytracing, have been examined elsewhere [Nishita 1991, Reeves 1987, Williams 1978].

1.1 Shadow Volume Applications

Shadow volume techniques have been used for near real-time rendering of shadows. Polygonal shadow volumes are represented using BSP trees in many of these approaches to improve performance [Chin 1989, Fuchs 1985]. The shadow volume technique fits well into existing scan line rendering methods and can be implemented with existing hardware approaches. Shadow volumes are also being used in the modeling of atmospheric effects using the notion of a light volume that is the complement of the shadow volume [Max 1986, Nishita 1987].

2 Background

Determining shadow volumes has applications in various fields. In computer graphics, it can make shadow computation a simpler task. In computer aided design and robotics, it can provide cues for accessibility and machinability when the light source direction is considered the direction of access.

A technique for direct generation of shadow volumes from a set of, possibly trimmed, free form surfaces is presented in this paper. A scan line Z buffer was enhanced to support shadow rendering using shadow volumes. All images in this paper were created using this renderer. Methods to render free form surfaces directly, without the need for a polygonal approximations, are under active research, and shadow volumes could easily fit into these approaches [Elber 1992b, Lane 1980, Nishita 1991, Schantz 1988]. In the derivation presented here, light sources are assumed to be point sources at either finite or infinite distances. The following definition of a *model* is used throughout this paper.

Definition 1 *A* model *is a set of, possibly trimmed, parametric surfaces with topological surface adjacency information stored explicitly or implicitly in the representation. Each surface of the model is*

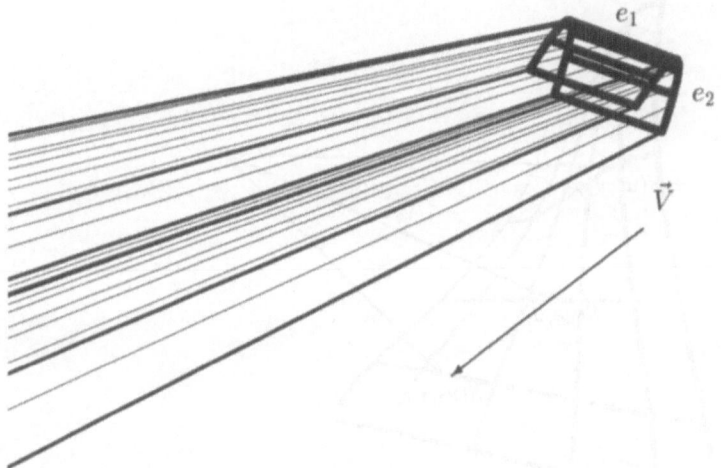

Figure 1: An open model consisting of a single surface with shadow volumes cast from all surface boundaries and silhouette edges. e_1 is a silhouette edge and e_2 is one of four boundary edges.

oriented so that the surface normals point outward. A model is considered closed if it dichotomizes the Euclidean space into regions that are inside and outside the model, and is considered open otherwise.

For example, models used in our implementation were developed within the Alpha_1 geometric modeling environment[EGS 1992] and consist of a set of, possibly trimmed, NURBs surfaces with surface adjacency information stored explicitly as the edges that are shared between two neighboring surfaces.

The addition of shadows to rendered images provides critical cues in determining relative positioning of models within a scene. The top left color image (Fig. 5) gives an example of a chess pawn in a scene rendered with shadows. Generating shadows within a scan line renderer increases the image quality considerably. In addition, the created shadow volumes are view independent as mentioned previously.

Direct generation of shadow volumes without polygonal tessellation has several advantages. It alleviates aliasing effects in the rendered images caused by polygonal approximations, and reduces the sometimes massive memory requirements associated with the polygonal technique. Furthermore, the accuracy of the shadow volume is not bound by a global polygonal approximation and can be adaptively computed. The polygonal shadow volume approach also requires the determination of adjacency information for locating silhouette edges. Surface topological adjacency information is assumed to be stored (Definition 1) in the model and need not be computed.

2.1 Shadow Volume

Our model for *shadow volumes* can now be formally defined.

Definition 2 *A **shadow volume** is a sub-region of the Euclidean space that is occluded from a light source by a model. The volume is delineated by a boundary that partitions the Euclidean space into shadowed and unshadowed regions. The boundary is oriented so that its normals point outward from the shadowed region. The direction opposite the normal is called the **occlusion direction** and is denoted $\vec{O}$.*

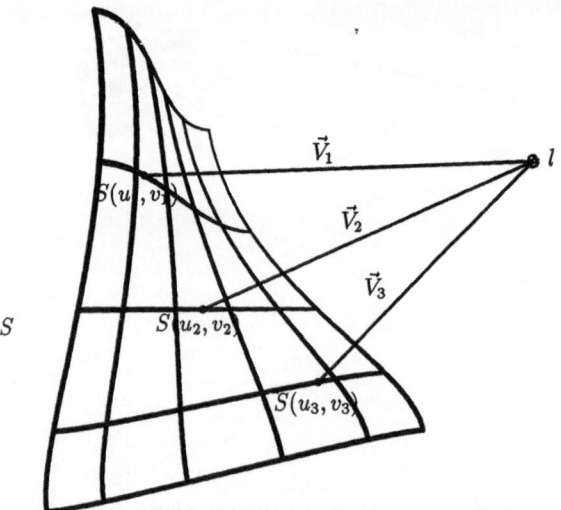

Figure 2: Let l be a point light source at a finite distance from surface S. Then $\vec{V}$, the viewing direction, varies across the surface S or $\vec{V}(u,v) = S(u,v) - l$.

Two types of curves are of interest when attempting to compute shadow volumes, the surface *silhouettes* and the surface boundaries that are not shared by any other surface, the *unshared surface boundary edges*. We refer to these two curve types as the surface *contours*. The shadow volume boundaries correspond directly to the contours of the model cast in the direction opposite the direction of the light source, forming ruled surfaces. The view direction from the light source is referred to as $\vec{V}$. Figure 1 shows an example of an open model consisting of a single surface with shadow volume boundaries cast from a silhouette curve (e_1 in Fig. 1), and from an unshared surface boundary edge (e_2 in Fig. 1). We assume that all surfaces are C^1 continuous. Those that are not can be subdivided in such a way that each resulting surface is C^1 continuous.

Let $S(u,v)$ be a regular [doCarmo 1976] C^1 continuous parametric surface. Then

$$\vec{n}(u,v) = \frac{\partial S}{\partial u} \times \frac{\partial S}{\partial v}, \tag{1}$$

is the unnormalized normal surface of S. The silhouettes of the surface, S, viewed from direction $\vec{V}$ are the solutions to the following equation in two variables,

$$\vec{V} \cdot \vec{n}(u,v) = 0. \tag{2}$$

If the light source is at a finite distance then the view direction varies across the surface and $\vec{V}$ becomes a function of u and v,

$$\vec{V}(u,v) = S(u,v) - l, \tag{3}$$

where l is the location of the light source (see Fig. 2). Equation (2) now becomes

$$\vec{V}(u,v) \cdot \vec{n}(u,v) = 0. \tag{4}$$

Silhouettes may also occur along edges that are shared by two surfaces resulting from a Boolean operation that trims the two intersecting surfaces. A silhouette along the shared edge occurs when one surface sharing the edge is front facing while the other is back facing.

3   Free Form Shadow Volume Computation

Construction of shadow volumes consists of two major tasks, contour extraction and casting. Closed models that partition the Euclidean space into inside and outside regions require only the detection of contours corresponding to silhouettes since surface boundaries are always shared. We first examine the generation of shadow volumes for a single surface and then examine their generation for arbitrary sets of surfaces that include the possibility of silhouettes along shared edges.

3.1   Intra-Surface Contour Extraction

Contours corresponding to silhouettes and surface boundaries must be extracted from the model. Extraction of the surface boundaries is straightforward. Silhouettes that are interior to a surface can be extracted by finding the zero set of Equation (2) or Equation (4) above. One approach [Elber 1992a] determines solutions within a desired tolerance, by symbolically computing the scalar field expressed in these equations and uses root finding techniques to find the zero set. Symbolically computing Equation (2) or (4), results in the need to find the zero set of a bivariate function. The zero sets are computed using a subdivision approach [Elber 1992a]. This approach was found to be extremely robust for silhouette extraction.

The silhouette curves that are extracted do not lie along isoparametric curves of the surface, in general. To extract these silhouettes within a desired tolerance many implementations currently produce piecewise linear curves. This is undesirable since memory requirements can be large and the approximation can again result in aliasing effects in the rendered image. We are currently examining the use of data reduction techniques [Lyche 1987] to increase the order of the extracted silhouettes to significantly reduce their size and alleviate these problems.

The extracted contours are then cast in the view direction to produce ruled surfaces that form the boundaries of the shadow volume. If the light source is at infinity the ruled surfaces degenerate to a simple extrusion. Otherwise, $\vec{V}$ is a function of u and v (Equation (3)) and the casting direction varies along the contours. The resulting cast volume is infinite but can be clipped against the viewing frustum making it representable. The contours of a model always form closed loops. In our implementation contours are extracted from each surface of the model and would need to be connected before casting to yield true shadow volumes. Connecting the contours into closed loops may be necessary in some applications, but for rendering shadows a simpler approach can be taken. The notion of shadow surfaces can be introduced that parallels the use of shadow polygons in the polygonal shadow volume approach. Using this notion, a shadow surface is cast from each extracted contour, without the need to combine the contours into closed loops.

As discussed elsewhere [Bergeron 1986], silhouettes and boundaries produce different occlusion effects. That is, shadow surfaces corresponding to silhouettes delineate regions that are doubly in shadow while those corresponding to boundaries delineate single shadow regions. A 2-D example is shown in Fig. 3. Either each shadow surface corresponding to a silhouette can be dumped twice or it can be tagged with an occlusion count of two. Each shadow surface carries its origin information, including both the geometry surface that it was cast from and the light source to which it is associated.

3.2   Inter-Surface Contour Extraction

Shadow volume generation for geometrically closed models follows closely that of the intra-surface contour extraction discussed above. Contours along unshared surface edges no longer need to be detected since none exist, while contours corresponding to silhouettes along shared edges now need to be detected. Shared edges resulting from the application of boolean operations to free form surfaces are often piecewise linear approximations. This is owing to the complexity of the intersection problem. For example, the

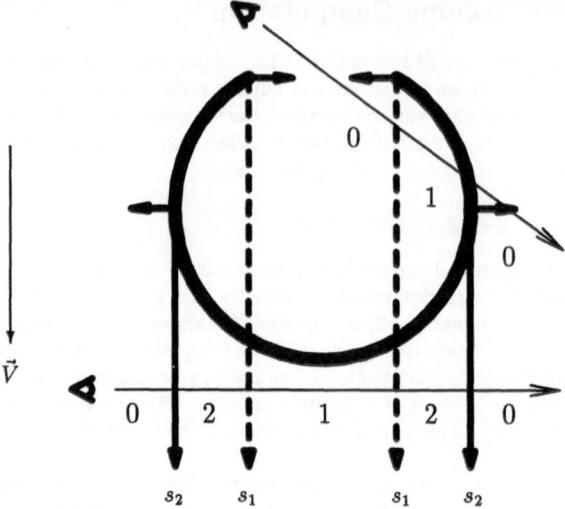

Figure 3: A 2-D example of occlusion counts for shadow surfaces. Shadow surfaces cast from surface unshared edge contours (s_1) delineate regions of space that are in single shadow while those cast from surface silhouette contours (s_2) delineate regions doubly in shadow. The numbers denote shadow occlusion amounts.

curve resulting from the intersection of two bicubic surfaces can be a polynomial with degree as high as 324 [Thomas 1984]. For these piecewise linear shared edges one can step along the vertices of the shared edge examining the normals of the two shared surfaces. Those with one surface normal that is back facing while the other is front facing lie along a silhouette.

Data reduction techniques can significantly reduce the size of the piecewise linear approximation by representing them as higher order curves [Lyche 1987]. Furthermore, special surface–surface intersection cases, such as those for quadric surfaces, have closed form representations as high order curves. Unfortunately, for shared edges represented as higher order curves, one cannot simply step along the curve as done for the piecewise linear case. The following approach has been developed to handle shared edges of arbitrary order. Let $S_1(u, v)$ and $S_2(r, s)$ be two surfaces intersecting along a shared edge e. The edge e can be expressed in the domain of each surface as $e(t) = S_1(u(t), v(t)) = S_2(r(t), s(t))$. Let $\vec{n}_1(u, v)$ and $\vec{n}_2(r, s)$ be the unnormalized normal surfaces of S_1 and S_2 as expressed in Equation (1). Then

$$g(t) = (\vec{n}_1(u(t), v(t)) \cdot \vec{V})(\vec{n}_2(r(t), s(t)) \cdot \vec{V}), \qquad (5)$$

is positive if both normals are front facing or back facing, and is negative if one is front facing and the other is back facing. Since Equation (5) is C^0 continuous if the surfaces S_1 and S_2 are regular C^1 continuous surfaces, the zero set of Equation (5) provides the domain along the shared edge that is a silhouette viewed along $\vec{V}$. $g(t)$ in Equation (5) can be computed symbolically and represented as a single scalar curve [Elber 1992a].

The extracted contours are again cast into ruled shadow surfaces. The approach is summarized in Algorithm 1. We discuss the orientation component of the algorithm in the next section.

4   Shadow Surface Orientation

The shadow surface boundaries must be oriented according to Definition 2. Let p be a point on a silhouette extracted from surface S. The shadow volume cast from the silhouette has a normal at p that is identical

Algorithm 1. Shadow volume generation.

```
For each lightSrc
    For each model in scene
    DO
        contourCrvs = extractContours( model, lightSrcPos )
        shadowSrfs = createRuled( contourCrvs, lightSrcPos )
        orientShadSurfs( shadowSrfs )
    END
```

to the normal of S at p. This is because the orientation of the silhouette is maintained when forming the ruled surface. Somewhat counter intuitively, the shadow surface orientation should sometimes be reversed so that its normals point in the opposite direction. Such a case is now discussed.

4.1 The Torus Anomaly

A torus viewed at a oblique angle is presented in Fig. 4. The star shaped inner silhouette contains four cusps. A cusp in a silhouette can be formed at a point where the tangent of the silhouette curve is collinear with the viewing direction, $\vec{V}$. Inspecting the surface normals of the torus along each of the four regions we see that in two regions the normals point into the silhouette loop while in two others, the normals are pointing outward (see Fig. 4a). Here, it would be impossible to construct a single shadow volume for the star shaped silhouette curve that is orientable [doCarmo 1976]. Two of the shadow surface orientations must be reversed so that their normals point in the direction of $-\vec{O}$ as specified in Definition 2. The correct shadow surface orientations, for the torus example, with shadow surface normals pointing in the direction of $-\vec{O}$, are shown in Fig. 4b. A method for determining $\vec{O}$ and orienting the shadow surfaces is discussed in the following section.

4.2 Occlusion Direction Determination

We now present a method for orienting shadow surfaces cast from silhouettes based on determining $\vec{O}$. Orientation of the other contour types can be performed similarly. Let $p = S(u_0, v_0)$ be a point on a silhouette of surface S. To orient the corresponding shadow surface correctly we compare the shadow surface normal, $\vec{n}(u_0, v_0)$, with $\vec{O}$. If they point in the same direction the shadow surface orientation is reversed to satisfy Definition 2.

The normal of S at p is orthogonal to the view direction, $\vec{V}$, by definition (Equation (2) and Equation (4). The view direction, $\vec{V}$, then lies in the tangent plane of the surface and can be expressed as a linear combination of the surface partial derivatives, provided S is regular,

$$\vec{V} = a\frac{\partial S}{\partial u} + b\frac{\partial S}{\partial v}. \qquad (6)$$

The scalars, a and b, can be determined since Equation (6) is a set of three equations in x, y, and z. It degenerates into two equations and two unknowns (a and b) since $\vec{V}$ is known to lie in the tangent plane spanned by $\frac{\partial S}{\partial u}$ and $\frac{\partial S}{\partial v}$. The values of a and b give the direction in parametric space that corresponds to $\vec{V}$ in Euclidean space, at p. Let $c(t)$ be a curve in S through p such that $c'(t)$ at p is parallel to $\vec{V}$. By examining the component of the second derivative of $c(t)$ at p, in the direction $\vec{n}$, $\vec{O}$ can be expressed

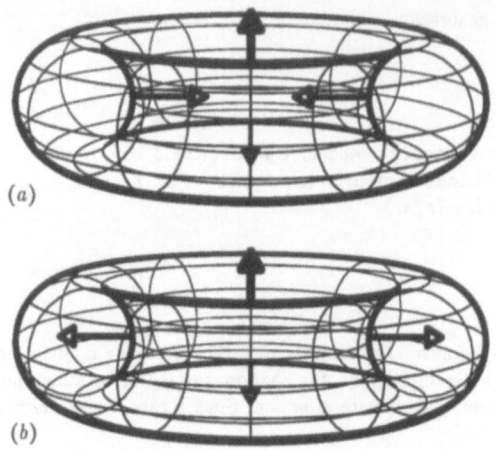

(a)

(b)

Figure 4: View is from the light source. Contours are shown in bold. (a) Shadow surface normals aligned with the normals of the surface (pointing outside the model) from which they were extracted. (b) Shadow surface normals properly oriented to point outside the shadow volume in the direction of $-\vec{O}$.

analytically.

$$c(t) = S(u(t), v(t)), \tag{7}$$

where $u(t) = at + u_0$ and $v(t) = bt + v_0$.

The first derivative of the curve,

$$c'(t) = \frac{\partial S}{\partial u}\frac{du}{dt} + \frac{\partial S}{\partial v}\frac{dv}{dt}, \tag{8}$$

corresponds directly to Equation (6) above, with $a = \frac{du}{dt}$ and $b = \frac{dv}{dt}$. The second derivative is then

$$c''(t) = \frac{\partial^2 S}{\partial u^2}\frac{du}{dt} + \frac{\partial^2 S}{\partial u \partial v}\left(\frac{du}{dt} + \frac{dv}{dt}\right) + \frac{\partial^2 S}{\partial v^2}\frac{dv}{dt} + \frac{\partial S}{\partial u}\frac{d^2 u}{dt^2} + \frac{\partial S}{\partial v}\frac{d^2 v}{dt^2} \tag{9}$$

The component of $c''(t)$ in the direction of $\vec{n}$ can be found by computing the dot product of $c''(t)$ and $\vec{n}$. The last two components of Equation (9) contribute only in the direction of the tangent plane (and are zero when $u(t) = at + u_0$ and $v(t) = bt + v_0$). Taking this into account and substituting $a = \frac{du}{dt}$ and $b = \frac{dv}{dt}$,

$$c''(t) \cdot \vec{n} = \left(\frac{\partial^2 S}{\partial u^2}a + \frac{\partial^2 S}{\partial u \partial v}(a + b) + \frac{\partial^2 S}{\partial v^2}b\right) \cdot \vec{n}. \tag{10}$$

Examining the sign of Equation (10), $\vec{O}$ can be determined. If it is positive then $\vec{O} = \vec{n}$, otherwise $\vec{O} = -\vec{n}$. It is unnecessary to explicitly determine $\vec{O}$ to orient the surface. If Equation (10) is positive then the shadow surface normal, $\vec{n}$, points in the direction of occlusion and the shadow surface orientation must be reversed.

The orientation process is summarized in Algorithm 2. In practice, a finite difference method was found sufficient to approximate $c''(t)$. The remainder of the procedure follows that above. This technique has been found to be robust over a variety of models, including the ones in this papers.

Algorithm 2. Shadow volume orientation.

```
Evaluate shadow surface normal, n̄, at p.
Determine a and b from Equation (6).
If ( c''(t)·n̄ > 0 )
    Reverse shadow surface orientation.
```

5 Rendering

Rendering shadow volumes can be done in two ways. The first technique follows the common scan line approach [Crow 1977]. The shadow surfaces are added to the free form surface database before scan line rendering. These surfaces are not treated as renderable data but are added only to provide shadowing information. Traversing the z-list [Atherton 1981], L, of surfaces at a given pixel of the Z-buffer, we examine the normals of the shadow surfaces that we encounter. While traversing L, occlusion counters for each light source are incremented for each corresponding front facing shadow surface encountered and decremented for each that is back facing. If open surfaces are part of the database, then the counter increments and decrements are by the occlusion count associated with the shadow surface type, with those corresponding to silhouettes having an occlusion count of two. When calculating shading information for a surface, those light sources with a negative occlusion counter are not included in the calculations.

An alternate approach, that corresponds to the two pass model precision approach to shadow generation [Atherton 1978], represents shadows as trimmed regions of the model through a preprocess. The shadow volumes are intersected with models in the scene to trim the model into shadowed and unshadowed regions. This approach provides accurate shadow generation for free form surfaces and the rendering of such models can be done using existing rendering hardware to achieve near real-time shadow generation. The use of Boolean operations requires the grouping of extracted contours curves into closed loops to form true volumes. In addition, data reduction techniques [Lyche 1987] may be needed to decrease the data size and raise the order of the extracted contours to increase the robustness and efficiency of the Boolean operations. The resulting trimmed shadowed and unshadowed regions are desirable if accessibility and visibility is to be explicitly solved.

6 Examples

The included rendered examples were produced by incorporating the above techniques into an existing scan line renderer in the Alpha_1 modeling system [EGS 1992]. The color images show shadow renderings of several free form surface models. The corresponding shadow surfaces for the top left image of the floating torus and sphere (Fig. 6) are shown below it (Fig. 8). Timings of shadow volume generation and rendering are shown in table 1 for the examples.

7 Conclusion

The shadow volume technique we have described provides a method for creating accurate shadow representations directly from free form surface models, without the need for a polygonal approximation. Robust and efficient techniques for trimming the surfaces into shadowed and unshadowed regions using shadow volumes need to be further explored. The regions that result can provide useful accessibility information for manufacturing of parts and robot path planning. Generation of shadow volumes from

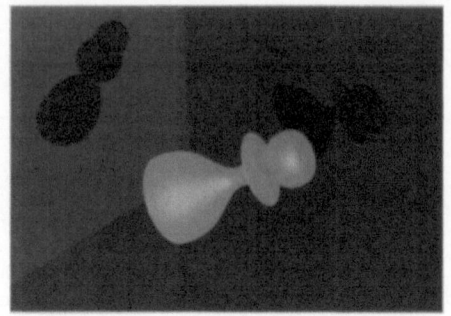

Fig. 5

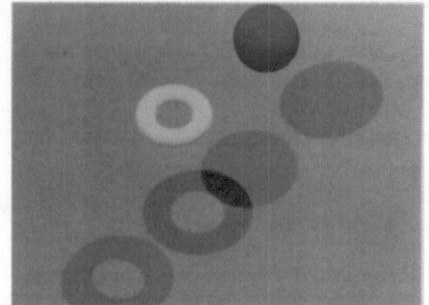

Fig.6

Fig.7

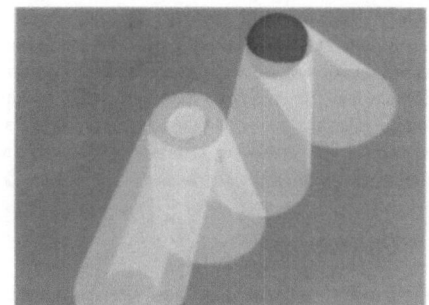

Fig.8

Table 1: Rendering and shadow volume generation times on DEC 5000/240 for 500x350, one sample per pixel, images.

Scene	Without Shadows	Shadow Vol. Generation	With Shadows
Pawn	68 Sec.	23 Sec.	792 Sec.
Torus/sphere	58 Sec.	15 Sec.	625 Sec.
Teapot/mug	94 Sec	38 Sec.	202 Sec.

free form surfaces for area light sources should also be further explored. We plan to investigate the application of shadow volumes in accessibility determination.

8   Acknowledgments

We would like to thank Elaine Cohen, Jamie Painter, and Mike Blum for their valuable comments on the material in this paper.

References

[EGS 1992] Engineering Geometry Systems (1992) *Alpha_1 User's Manual.*

[Appel 1968] Appel A (1968) *Some Techniques for Shading Machine Renderings of Solids.* SJCC Proceedings 1968, Thompson Books, Washington, DC, pp 37-45

[Atherton 1978] Atherton P, Weiler K, Greenberg D (1978) *Polygon Shadow Generation.* SIGGRAPH Proceedings 1978, Computer Graphics 12(3): 275-281

[Atherton 1981] Atherton P (1981) *A Method of Interactive Visualization of CAD Surface Models on a Color Video Display.* SIGGRAPH Proceedings 1981, Computer Graphics 15(3)

[Bergeron 1986] Bergeron P (1986) *A General Version of Crow's Shadow Volumes.* CG&A 6(9): 17-28

[Bouknight 1970] Bouknight J, Kelly K (1970) *An Algorithm for Producing Half-Tone Computer Graphics Presentations with Shadows and Movable Light Sources.* AFIPS Proceedings 1970, AFIPS Press, Reston, VA, 36: 1-10

[Chin 1989] Chin N, Feiner S (1989) *Near Real-Time Shadow Generation Using BSP Trees.* SIGGRAPH Proceedings 1989, Computer Graphics 23(3): 99-106

[Cohen 1985] Cohen M, Greenberg D (1985) *The Hemi-Cube: A Radiosity Solution for Complex Environments.* SIGGRAPH Proceedings 1985, Computer Graphics 19(3): 31-40

[Cook 1984] Cook R, Porter T, Carpenter L (1984) *Distributed Ray Tracing.* SIGGRAPH Proceedings 1984, Computer Graphics 18(3): 137-144

[Crow 1977] Crow F (1977) *Shadow Algorithms for Computer Graphics.* SIGGRAPH Proceedings 1977, Computer Graphics 11(3): 242-248

[doCarmo 1976] doCarmo M (1976) *Differential Geometry of Curves and Surfaces.* Prentice Hall

[Elber 1992a] Elber G (1992) *Free From Surface Analysis using a Hybrid of Symbolic and Numeric Computation.* Ph.D. thesis, University of Utah, Computer Science Department

126

[Elber 1992b] Elber G, Cohen E (1992) *Adaptive Isocurves Based Rendering for Freeform Surfaces.* Technical Report UUCS-92-040, University of Utah

[Fuchs 1985] Fuchs H, Goldfeather J, Hultquist J, Susan S, Austin J, Brooks F, Eyles J Jr., Poulton J (1985) *Fast Spheres, Shadows, Textures, Transparencies, and Image Enhancements in Pixel-Planes.* SIGGRAPH Proceedings 1985, Computer Graphics 19(3): 111-120

[Joy 1988] Joy K, Bhetanabhotla M (1988) *Ray Tracing Parametric Patches Using Numerical Techniques and Ray Coherence.* SIGGRAPH Proceedings 1986, Computer Graphics 20(4): 279-285.

[Kajiya 1982] Kajiya J (1982) *Ray Tracing Parametric Patches.* SIGGRAPH Proceedings 1982, Computer Graphics 16(3): 245-254.

[Lane 1980] Lane J, Carpenter L, Whitted T, Blinn J (1980) *Scan Line Methods for Displaying Parametrically Defined Surfaces.* Communications of the ACM 23(1): 23-34

[Lyche 1987] Lyche T, Morken K (1987) *Knot Removal for Parametric B-spline Curves and Surfaces.* Computer Aided Design 4: 217-230

[Max 1986] Max N (1986) *Atmospheric Illumination and Shadows.* SIGGRAPH Proceedings 1986, Computer Graphics 20(4): 117-124

[Nishita 1987] Nishita T, Miyawaki Y, Nakame E (1987) *A Shading Model for Atmospheric Scattering Considering Luminous Intensity Distribution of Light Sources.* SIGGRAPH Proceedings 1987, Computer Graphics 21(4): 303-310

[Nishita 1990] Nishita T, Sederberg T, Kakimoto M (1990) *Ray Tracing Trimmed Rational Surface Patches.* SIGGRAPH Proceedings 1990, Computer Graphics 24(4): 337-345

[Nishita 1991] Nishita T, Kaneda K, Nakamae E (1991) *A scanline algorithm for displaying trimmed surfaces by using Bézier clipping.* The Visual Computer 7(5-6): 269-279

[Reeves 1987] Reeves W, Salesin D, Cook R (1987) *Rendering Antialiased Shadows with Depth Maps.* SIGGRAPH Proceedings 1987, Computer Graphics 21(4): 283-291

[Schantz 1988] Schantz M, Chang S (1988) *Rendering Trimmed NURBS with adaptive Forward Differencing.* SIGGRAPH Proceedings 1988, Computer Graphics 22(4): 189-198

[Thomas 1984] Thomas S (1984) *Modelling Volumes Bounded by B-Spline Surfaces.* Ph.D. thesis, University of Utah, Computer Science Department, 1984

[Toth 1985] Toth D (1985) *On Ray Tracing Parametric Surfaces.* SIGGRAPH Proceedings 1985, Computer Graphics 19(3): 171-179

[Watt 1992] Watt A, Watt M (1992) *Advanced Animation and Rendering Techniques.* Addison-Wesley Publishers, pp 155-177

[Whitted 1980] Whitted T (1980) *An Improved Illumination Model for Shaded Display.* Communications of the ACM 23(6): 343-349

[Williams 1978] Williams L (1978) *Casting Curved Shadows on Curved Surfaces.* SIGGRAPH Proceedings 1978, Computer Graphics 12(3): 270-274

[Woodward 1989] Woodward C (1989) *Ray Tracing Parametric Surfaces by Subdivision in Viewing Plane.* in *Theory and Practice of Geometric Modeling* Strasser W, Seidel HP editors, Springer-Verlag, pp 273-290

Address: Computer Science Department, University of Utah, Salt Lake City, UT 84112, USA

Fast Analytic Rendering with Accurate Table Integration

Toshimitsu Tanaka and Tokiichiro Takahashi

Abstract

We have proposed two analytic rendering methods: the Area Light Illumination Method and the Precise Rendering Method. Both methods solve the sampling problems and generate high quality, photorealistic images. Unfortunately their image generation speed is slow because their integration operation incurs very long computing times.

To accelerate the integration operation, we develop an adaptive table referencing method. The adaptive table ensures that the sampling degree depends on the variation in reflection intensity; sharp variations are finely sampled. The tables reduce the computing cost of integration by 90% while the image generation cost is 40% to 60% less.

Key Words: Analytic rendering, Accurate and efficient table reference, Area light illumination, Reflection integration on surfaces, Adaptive (irregular interval) tables integration

1 Introduction

Low sampling resolution leads to aliasing problems. Aliasing artifacts appear along object boundaries during hidden surface removal and on tightly curved surfaces during shading. An area light source for illumination causes aliasing if it is roughly approximated by point light sources. Since these aliasing artifacts strongly reduce image quality, eliminating them is an important subject.

Super-sampling techniques can improve image quality in proportion to the degree of over-sampling, however computing cost also increases. The number of points per pixel must be carefully determined to generate high quality images in reasonable computing time. However, determining the optimum number is very difficult because the strength of aliasing artifacts depends on image complexity. Thus image regeneration sometimes occurs because of insufficient sampling. This problem can not be avoided whenever we use super-sampling techniques.

Analytic rendering methods strictly prevent aliasing. We have proposed two analytic rendering methods: the Area Light Illumination Method and the Precise Rendering Method. The Area Light Illumination Method (Tanaka 1991) analytically models the reflection of objects illuminated by area light sources. The method directly integrates illumination intensity, while ordinary methods treat an area light source as point lights (Verbeck 1984). As shown in Plate 1, it can successfully generate dull reflection (Amanatides 1984; Cook 1984).

The Precise Rendering Method (Tanaka 1992) accurately integrates reflected light intensity on curved surfaces. Since the method can exactly generate the highlights that appear on rounded edges and vertices, the method is free from the aliasing artifacts generated in the conventional method (Saito 1989). One example is shown in Plate 2.

Both proposed methods integrate intensity by using the Chebyshev approximation because its error estimation is rather simple. However, since integration incurs long computing times, the methods are not rapid enough. For example, a 6 MIPS computer spent about 1.5 hours to generate Plate 1. Table referencing strongly accelerates the integration process. However,

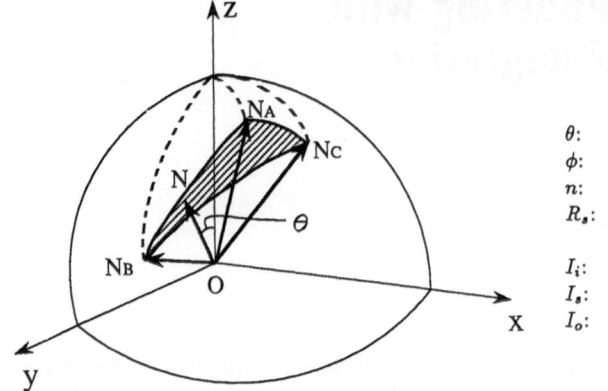

Terminology 1

θ:	Angle from the z axis
ϕ:	Rotation angle around z axis
n:	Index of reflection
R_s:	Specular bidirectional reflectance
I_i:	Intensity of the incident light
I_s:	Intensity of specular reflection
I_o:	Average radiation intensity of the area light

Figure 1: Integration on a curved surface

a simple table, which allocates its sample points at even intervals, is insufficient. For mirror-like surfaces, the reflection intensity rapidly peaks, so the approximation error of the simple table is excessive.

To realize higher accuracy, sample points must be allocated according to the variation in intensity. Such a table can be termed an adaptive table. This paper introduces a method for designing and referencing adaptive tables, then evaluates the adaptive tables in comparison with the simple tables and the Chebyshev approximation.

2 Analytic Rendering

This section briefly introduces results of the Area Light Illumination Method (Tanaka 1991) and the Precise Rendering Method (Tanaka 1992), and shows that integration on the unit sphere is their common principle. Reflection intensity consists of specular and diffuse parts. Since specular intensity is more complex and its computing cost is higher, the integration of specular reflection is discussed.

2.1 Precise Rendering Method

Since the direction of surface normals smoothly varies across curved surfaces, the intensity reflected from an area on a surface is exactly given by integration. For example, if triangle ABC lies on a curved surface and its surface normals are described as N_A, N_B, and N_C, its intensity is given by the integration over Ω as shown in Fig.1 (Tanaka 1992). Here, Ω is the solid angle defined by N_A, N_B, and N_C.

When Blinn's reflection model (1976) is employed, specular reflection can be described by

$$I_s = R_s I_i K_{ABC} \iint_\Omega \cos^n\theta \, \sin\theta \, d\theta \, d\phi. \qquad (1)$$

Here K_{ABC} is the determination of the Jacobian caused by translation to the polar coordinate system. We assume that it is constant. Other symbols in the equation are defined in Terminology 1.

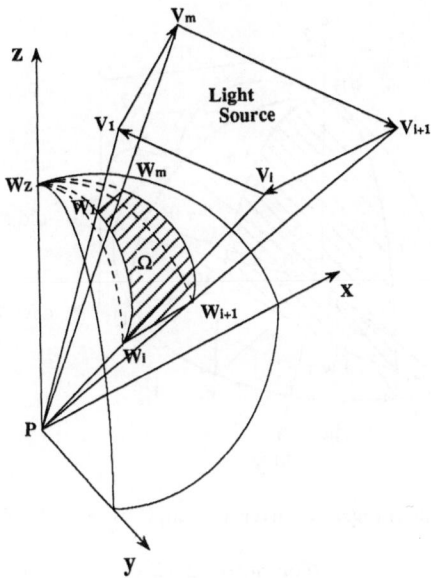

Figure 2: Integration for an area light source

2.2   Area Light Illumination Method

The intensity of light reflected from a surface illuminated by an area light is given by integrating the incident light power. When the emissivity of the light source follows Lambert's law and reflection follows Phong's model (1975), the specular intensity yielded by a polygonal light source is calculated by

$$I_s = R_s I_o \frac{n+1}{2\pi} \int\int_\Omega \cos^n\theta \, \sin\theta \, d\theta \, d\phi. \tag{2}$$

The integral area Ω is the projection of the area light onto the unit sphere as shown in Fig.2. Other symbols are as shown in Terminology 1.

2.3   Integration

We define function $G(n, \Omega)$ as the basis of Equations 1 and 2.

$$G(n, \Omega) = \frac{n+1}{2\pi} \int\int_\Omega \cos^n\theta \, \sin\theta \, d\theta \, d\phi \tag{3}$$

In the following section, we discuss the integration of Equation 3 by using the symbols defined in Fig.2. The integration area, Ω, is defined by points $\{W_i\}_{i=1,\dots,m}$ on the unit sphere and W_z is the intersection of the z axis and the sphere.

Formula transformation was precisely described in the previous papers (Tanaka 1991, 1992). Here, we show it briefly. The area Ω is triangulated using point W_z, and G is described as

$$G(n, \Omega) = \sum_{i=1}^{m} F_i \, G(n, \Delta_i). \tag{4}$$

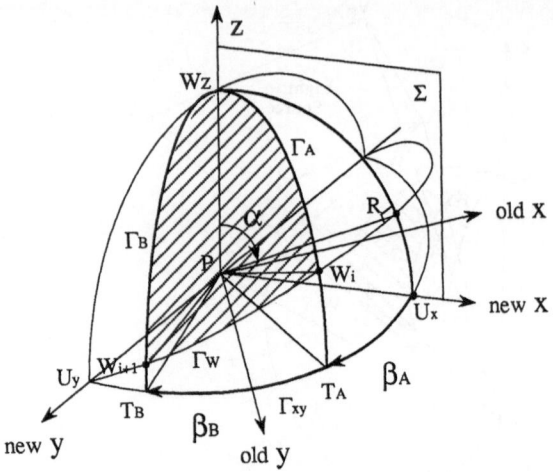

Figure 3: Integration over a triangle on a unit sphere

Terminology 2

Γ Great circle which runs through W_i and W_{i+1}

Σ Plane which includes the origin O and is perpendicular to the vector OU_y

U_y Intersection of Γ and the xy plane

R Intersection of Γ and Σ

T_A Intersection of the xy plane and the great circle which runs through W_z and W_i

T_B Intersection of the xy plane and the great circle which runs through W_z and W_{i+1}

α Angle of the vector OR from the z axis

β_A Rotation angle of OT_A around the z axis from the new x axis

β_B Rotation angle of OT_B around the z axis from the new x axis

In this equation, Δ_i is the triangle $W_z W_i W_{i+1}$ on the unit sphere and F_i is the sign function defined by

$$F_i = \begin{cases} 1 & : W_z, W_i, W_{i+1} \text{ is clockwise when viewed from } P \\ -1 & : \text{Otherwise.} \end{cases} \qquad (5)$$

The integration area of function $G(n, \Delta_i)$ is shown in Fig.3. Symbols in the figure are defined in Terminology 2. To simplify the integration, the coordinate system is rotated around the z axis and the vector PU_y becomes the new y axis. Function G is integrated by θ to yield Equation 6.

$$G(n, \Delta_i) = G(n, \alpha, \beta_A, \beta_B) = \frac{1}{2\pi} \left\{ (\beta_B - \beta_A) - \int_{\beta_A}^{\beta_B} \left(\frac{\cos^2 \phi}{\tan^2 \alpha + \cos^2 \phi} \right)^{\frac{n+1}{2}} d\phi \right\} \qquad (6)$$

2.4   Chebyshev Approximation

Direct integration of Equation 6 is difficult. Our previous methods approximate its integrand by using Chebyshev polynomials (Poulin 1990), and then integrating the equation. Since

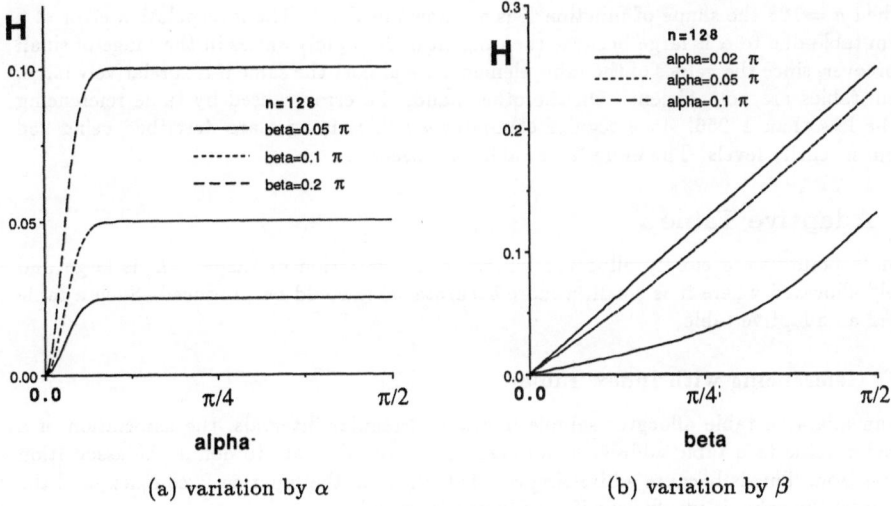

(a) variation by α (b) variation by β

Figure 4: Function H when $n = 128$

the accuracy of the approximation is high enough, the quality of generated images is sufficient. However, since the polynomials include parameters α and n, computation cost of the approximation is very high. Therefore, the methods require long computing times.

3 Accurate Table Integration

3.1 Integration Table

Function H is defined by

$$H(n, \alpha, \beta) = G(n, \alpha, 0, \beta) = \frac{1}{2\pi} \left\{ \beta - \int_0^\beta \left(\frac{\cos^2 \phi}{\tan^2 \alpha + \cos^2 \phi} \right)^{\frac{n+1}{2}} d\phi \right\}, \quad (7)$$

so function G is given as

$$G(n, \alpha, \beta_A, \beta_B) = H(n, \alpha, \beta_B) - H(n, \alpha, \beta_A). \quad (8)$$

Both α and β are continuous in $[0, \pi/2]$, however the reflection index, n, is a natural value. Thus, the values of function $H(n, \alpha, \beta)$ are stored in two dimensional tables of α and β for each n, and described by $T_n(\alpha, \beta)$. A value of the function is given by interpolating 4 table elements to reduce digital error. For example, if $\alpha_i \leq \alpha \leq \alpha_{i+1}$ and $\beta_j \leq \beta \leq \beta_{j+1}$, H is approximated by

$$H(n, \alpha, \beta) = \sum_{k=0}^{1} \sum_{l=0}^{1} \frac{(-1)^{k+l}(\alpha_{i+k} - \alpha)(\beta_{j+l} - \beta)}{(\alpha_{i+1} - \alpha_i)(\beta_{j+1} - \beta_j)} T_n(\alpha_{i+1-k}, \beta_{j+1-l}). \quad (9)$$

3.2 Uniform Table

The set of parameters (α, β) is called a sample point. A simple table which locates the sample points at even intervals is named a uniform table. Uniform tables are commonly used because they are easy to reference. However, accuracy is not sufficient to calculate the function H defined by Equation 7.

When $n = 128$ the shape of function H is as shown in Fig.4. The interpolation error of a uniform table due to α is large because the tangent of H rapidly varies in the range of small α. Moreover, since the values of the table elements are almost the same if α is relatively large, uniform tables are not efficient. On the other hand, the error caused by table referencing must be less than $1/256$, since regular computer graphics images are described using 256 different intensity levels. Therefore large tables are needed.

3.3   Adaptive Table

If sample points were closely allocated wherever the variation of tangent H is large and coarsely allocated where it is small, a more accurate table could be produced. Such a table is called an adaptive table.

3.3.1   Referencing with Index Tables

Since an adaptive table allocates sample points at irregular intervals, the association of a parameter value to a table address is not easy. It is not adequate to define the association by a function. This is because addressing cost is high when the function is complex, and the accuracy of the table is insufficient if the function is simple.

We propose an addressing method that uses index tables. The index table is a one dimensional table and it memorizes parameter values of the sample points. A reference address is determined by using a binary search technique to compare a given parameter value against the saved values. Its computing cost is low because a reference address can be determined with m comparisons for 2^m segments. Thus both free allocation of sample points and quick addressing can be realized.

3.3.2   Allocating Sample Points

Figure 4(b) shows that the interpolation error due to β is small. Our method divides parameter β at even intervals to reduce addressing cost. Therefore, when the number of sample points is m, β sample points are given by $\beta_i = ((i-1)\pi)/(2(m-1))$ for every integer value i in $[1, m]$. For each n, α sample points are determined with the following algorithm to minimize the maximum digital error of $H(n, \alpha, \beta)$.

(1) Many probable values of α sample points are saved in a list L. The number of elements of L is described by N_L. It is initialized to $N_L = m \times r$, where we choose $r = 100$. The i-th element of L is described by L_i which is initialized to $L_i = ((i-1)\pi)/(2(N_L - 1))$ to cover the definition of α; $[0, \pi/2]$.

(2) At each integer value j in $[1, (N_L - 1)/2]$ and k in $[1, m]$, an approximate value, $H_{approx}(n, L_{2j}, \beta_k)$, is calculated by linearly interpolating between $H(n, L_{2j-1}, \beta_k)$ and $H(n, L_{2j+1}, \beta_k)$. Its error, $E_{2j} = \max_{k=1,m} |H_{approx}(n, L_{2j}, \beta_k) - H(n, L_{2j}, \beta_k)|$, is then determined.

(3) The average of the errors is calculated.

(4) Element L_{2j} is removed if E_{2j} is smaller than the average.

(5) Remaining elements are counted. The number of the elements is the new value of N_L.

(6) If N_L is larger than m, the remaining elements are renumbered, and the operation then returns to (2).

(7) If N_L is smaller than m, the $(m - N_L)$ elements that have the largest errors are chosen from the just eliminated elements and reused to achieve m elements.

(8) The remaining elements become samples of α.

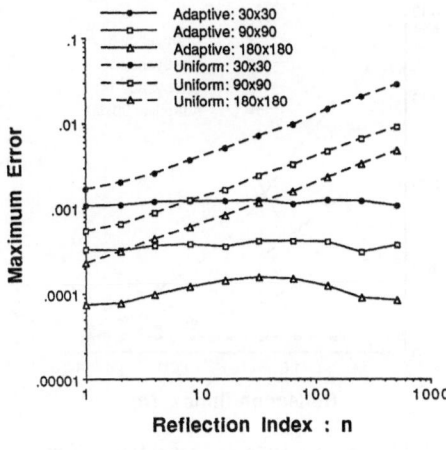

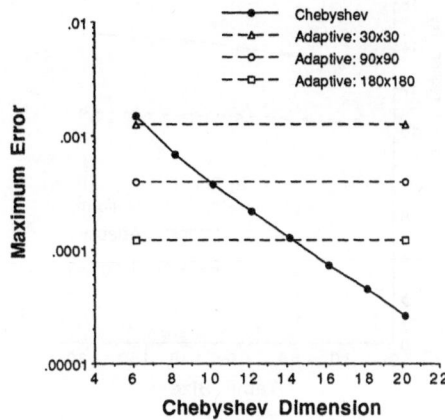

Figure 5: Maximum error vs. reflection index

Figure 6: Average maximum error vs. degree of Chebyshev approximation

Elements $L_1 = 0$ and $L_{N_L} = \pi/2$ are retained in the final list because they were never selected for element reduction in (2). Thus, the list L covers $[0, \pi/2]$.

Accurate calculation of function $H(n, \alpha, \beta)$ is difficult and its numerical integration requires very high cost. As shown in Equation 8, since we have to calculate function G by subtracting two H values obtained by varying β, accuracy of differential H by β is important. Thus, in the place of H, we use its integrand

$$J(n, \alpha) = \left(\frac{\cos^2 \phi}{\tan^2 \alpha + \cos^2 \phi} \right)^{\frac{n+1}{2}}. \tag{10}$$

The suitability of this adaptive table was confirmed by experiments.

4 Experimental Results

Function G was calculated by Equation 6 with the Chebyshev approximation and calculated by Equation 8 and 9 using the uniform or adaptive tables. We used a VAX8800 with a floating point accelerator and G was calculated in single precision (32 bits).

4.1 Approximation Error

Test data, which included 100,000 sets of three angles $(\alpha, \beta_A, \beta_B)$, were generated. Here, α, β_A, β_B are random numbers in $[0, \pi/2]$ and $\beta_A < \beta_B$. The maximum error and computing time of the three methods were measured for 10 reflection indices (n = 1, 2, 4, 8, 16, 32, 64, 128, 256, 512).

We tested 6 table sizes ($\alpha \times \beta = 30 \times 30, 60 \times 60, 90 \times 90, 120 \times 120, 150 \times 150, 180 \times 180$). The maximum errors of the 30×30, 90×90, and 180×180 tables as a function of the reflection index are shown in Fig.5. Since the error of the uniform table increases with n, its accuracy is insufficient. However, the error of the adaptive tables is relatively constant. The adaptive table is much better than the uniform table of comparable size even if n is small.

The maximum errors of the Chebyshev approximation were measured while changing its degree from 6 to 20 in two degree steps. The averages of the 10 indices were calculated for

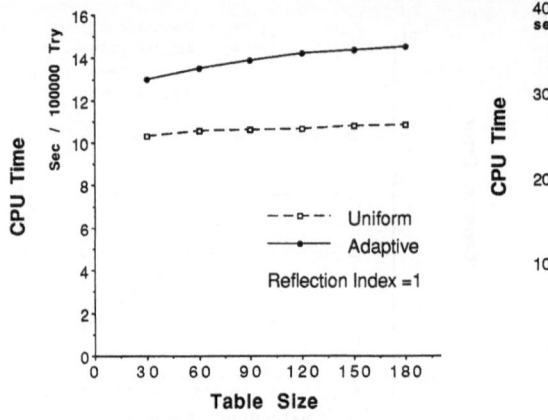

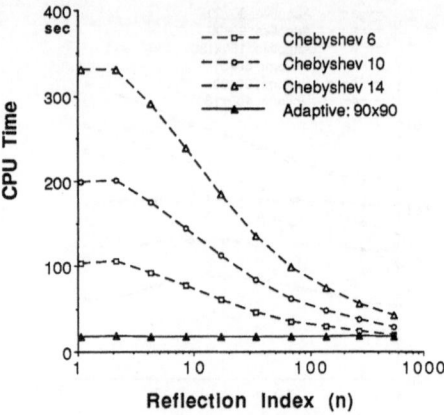

Figure 7: Computing time vs. table size   Figure 8: Computing time vs. reflection index

each degree value. They are shown as the solid line in Fig.6. Horizontal dotted lines are the average errors of the adaptive tables as determined from Fig.5.

The accuracy of pixel intensity should be $1/256 \approx 4 \times 10^{-3}$. Since the intensity is calculated by adding and/or subtracting several G values, the accuracy of function G must be 4×10^{-4} (ten times higher than the final accuracy). Figure 6 shows that the 90×90 adaptive table and the degree 10 Chebyshev approximation achieve the same accuracy. Therefore, they were compared in the following experiments.

4.2   Computing Time

Computing times of the two table reference methods are compared in Fig.7. For each table size, difference of the computing time between the adaptive table and the uniform table is due to the addressing performed through the index tables. Since it increased the total computing cost by about 30%, the addressing method is suitable.

Computing time of the Chebyshev approximation is shown in Fig.8. If the value of integrand in Equation 6 is sufficiently small, the approximation is not used because G can be set to $(\beta_B - \beta_A)/2\pi$. Since the range of α wherein the integrand is small expands with n, the computing time decreases. However, the Chebyshev approximation was slower than the adaptive table in every case. The degree 10 Chebyshev approximation is comparable to the 90×90 adaptive table in accuracy, however, the computational cost is more than 10 times higher than that of the table when n is small.

4.3   Image Quality

The test image was a box ($n = 512$) placed on a plane ($n = 64$) illuminated by a star shaped light source. Plate 3 was generated by the 90×90 adaptive table. The image has no artifacts due to approximation errors. Plate 4 was generated by the 90×90 uniform table. As shown in Fig.5, accuracy of the table is 9×10^{-3} when $n = 512$. Thus, approximation errors cause the bright lines seen in the image. These lines are not eliminated even if the table size is expanded to 180×180.

4.4   Image Generation Speed

Table 1: Image generation time

Test Image		Computing time		Ratio
		Chebyshev	Adaptive Table	
Plate 1	*Pot*	1:35'10"	36'45"	0.39
Plate 3	*Star*	1:04'21"	31'50"	0.49
Plate 5	*Room*	38'37"	13'20"	0.35
Plate 6	*Chessmen*	1:57'59"	1:06'28"	0.56

Four images, Plate 1, 3, 5, and 6, were generated by both the 90 × 90 adaptive table and the degree 10 Chebyshev approximation. Their computing times are shown in Table 1. In this experiment, the adaptive table was 40 ~ 60% faster than the Chebyshev approximation. Image quality of both methods was equivalent.

5 Table Storage Reduction

The experiments should that the 90 × 90 adaptive table is sufficiently accurate to generate high quality images. A 90 × 90 table requires only (90 × 90 × 4 =) 32,400 bytes, however, total memory area will be excessive if tables for every index n are stored.

Since one material has only one reflection index value, an image can be generated with just one table for each material in the image. Fortunately, not many materials appear in one image. Thus, our method loads only those tables related to the materials rendered. This selective loading drastically reduces the memory area needed for table storage. Our method is easily implemented on existing computers because 100 different materials, sufficient to describe most scenes successfully, requires only 3.3 Mbytes of memory area.

6 Conclusion

We previously proposed two analytic methods, the Area Light Illumination Method and the Precise Rendering Method. Their common and basic operation is the integration over a solid angle. In these methods, the integration was calculated by the Chebyshev approximation, however, the computing cost of this is too expensive. This paper proposed a method that uses adaptive tables to improve the integration speed.

An adaptive table closely allocates sample points wherever the reflection intensity varies sharply. We proposed an algorithm for designing and addressing the adaptive tables. Values of a parameter at the sample points are stored in an index table. Reference addresses are determined by using a binary search technique to compare a given parameter value to the stored values. The addressing increased the cost for referencing a simple table by only 30%.

Experiments showed that the accuracy of the adaptive table is much higher than that of a simple table. The accuracy of the 90 × 90 adaptive table was 4×10^{-4}, which is equivalent to that of the degree 10 Chebyshev approximation. Its approximation errors were so small that no artifacts can be seen in the rendered images. The tables reduced the computing cost of integration by 90% while the image generation cost is 40% to 60% less.

Acknowledgment: We would like to thank Dr. Takahiko Kamae, Dr. Rikuo Takano, Mr. Takashi Sakai, and Dr. Kazuyoshi Tateishi for their continuous support. We also would like to thank all members of our research section for their advice and encouragement.

Plate 1: Area Light Illumination Method

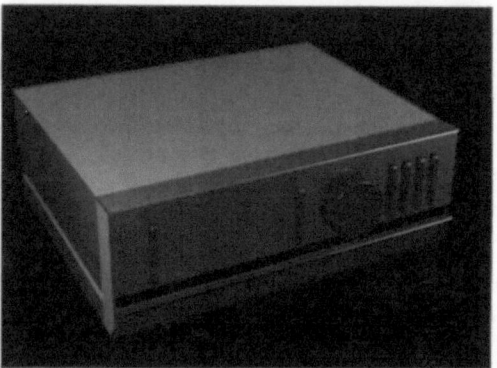

Plate 2: Precise Rendering Method

Plate 3: 90×90 adaptive table

Plate 4: 90×90 uniform table

Plate 5: *Room*

Plate 6: *Chessmen*

References

Tanaka T, Takahashi T (1990) Cross Scanline Algorithm. Proc. Eurographics'90: 63–74

Tanaka T, Takahashi T (1991) Illumination with area light sources. Proc. Eurographics'91: 235–246

Tanaka T, Takahashi T (1992) Precise rendering method for exact anti-aliasing and high-lighting. The Visual Computer 8(5-6): 315–326

Verbeck C, Greenberg D (1984) A comprehensive light-source description for computer graphics. IEEE CG&A 4(7): 66–75

Saito T, Shinya M, Takahashi T (1989) Highlighting Rounded Edges. Proc. CG International'89: 613–629

Poulin P, Amanatides J (1990) Shading and shadowing with linear light sources. Proc. Eurographics'90: 377–386

Blinn J, Newell M (1976) Texture and reflection in computer generated images. Comm. ACM 19(10): 542–547

Phong B (1975) Illumination for computer generated pictures. Comm. ACM 18(6): 311–317

Amanatides J (1984) Ray tracing with cones. Proc. SIGGRAPH'84: 129–135

Cook R, Porter T, Carpenter L (1984) Distributed ray tracing. Proc. SIGGRAPH'84: 137–145

Toshimitsu Tanaka is currently a research engineer of the Autonomous Robot Systems Laboratory, NTT (Nippon Telegraph and Telephone) Human Interface Laboratories. He received the B.E. degree in electrical engineering from Nagoya University in 1982. He also received the M.E. and D.E. degree in information engineering from Nagoya University in 1984 and 1992, respectively. He received the Best Papers Award of The Information Processing Society of Japan (IPSJ) in 1992. He is a member of IPSJ and The Institute of Electronics, Information, and Communication Engineers of Japan.
E-Mail (Internet): toshi@nttarm.ntt.jp

Tokiichiro Takahashi is currently a supervisor and senior research engineer of the Autonomous Robot Systems Laboratory, NTT Human Interface Laboratories. He received the B.E. degree in electronic engineering from Niigata University in 1977. After graduating, he joined NTT and has been doing research into Computer Graphics since 1984. He received the Best Papers Award of The Information Processing Society of Japan (IPSJ) in 1992. He is a member of IEEE, The Institute of Electronics, Information, and Communication Engineers of Japan, The Institution of Image Electronics Engineers of Japan, and NICOGRAPH.
E-Mail (Internet): toki@nttarm.ntt.jp

Address: Autonomous Robot Systems Laboratory, **NTT** Human Interface Laboratories, 3-9-11 Midori-cho, Musashino-shi, Tokyo, 180 Japan.

A Generation Model for Human Skin Texture

Tomomi Ishii, Takami Yasuda, Shigeki Yokoi, and Jun-ichiro Toriwaki

ABSTRACT

This paper describes a generation model of human skin with Computer Graphics. On the basis of the fact that the human skin surface is of fine structure consisting of furrows and ridges, we have established and implemented a geometric model for expressing these features, using hierarchical Voronoi-division process for tile texture pattern, a Bezier cubic curve segment for curved surfaces of ridges, a pseudo-fractal subdivision algorithm for natural fluctuation, and so on. Furthermore, we refer to our own approach to the reflection model and apply our skin-texture generation method to the texture of other objects such as leather from reptile skin.

Keywords:skin, texture synthesis

1 INTRODUCTION

Recently, many researchers in Computer Graphics (CG) field have studied the representation of human body from several points of view. One purpose of these studies is to realize synthetic actors on a graphic screen. Several algorithms about rendering and motion were reported in order to solve difficulties in representing human body itself, that is, body shape, motion, deformation of the body[Komatsu 1988, Magnenat-Thalmann et al. 1987], facial animation[Magnenat-Thalmann et al. 1988, Water 1986], hair[Anjo et al. 1992, Watanabe et al. 1989], and so on. Nevertheless, there are no studies yet to generate realistic human skin texture which is a very important factor to realize computer generated actors. Rendering methods for realistic skin will be useful not only for CG itself, but also for other applications in medicine. Medical imaging technologies have been so improved that even surgical simulations can be realized in the graphic world[Vannier et al. 1983, Yasuda et al. 1990]. In craniofacial or cosmetic surgeries, one should consider patients' skin surface in view of texture pattern match. In order to overcome the problems in synthetic actors and surgical simulation, microscopic skin surface structure should be considered in a rendering method for human skin, because microscopic model of skin surface seems to be a basis of macroscopic model about synthetic actors, and applicable to texture pattern match of skin surface.
Here are some former papers related to realizing skin-like texture:
Miller presented reptile skins[Miller 1988]. He treated the motion dynamics of snakes and worms in his paper in order to generate realistic snakes with skins. Bump mapping and color mapping were used.
Kaufman represented reptile skin pattern by using a high-level language he proposed[Kaufman 1988]. With a texture synthesis language, he showed various patterns, such as honey-comb patterns, French-canvas patterns, and reptile skin patterns.
There have been few papers published about human skin texture itself.

Nahas, et al. described a method for synthetic skin[Nahas et al. 1988]. They obtain the data of skin texture using a laser scanner and use the date directly when human face is rendered. They think it is possible to recreate realistic skin texture using statistical techniques from the given data.

In this paper, we propose a generation model for skin texture by taking notice of features of actual human skin. We generate some texture patterns of other objects such as leather from crocodile or snake using the same generation method for skin texture in order to show our method's potentiality as a general tool for texture generation.

2 GEOMETRY MODEL FOR SKIN SURFACE

2.1 Geometrical features of skin surface

Skin surface consists of four elements such as furrows, ridges, hair holes and sweat holes. Furrows carve the skin surface like a net. A ridge is a area surrounded by furrows. Hair holes exist on the cross-section of furrows, and a hair grows out from this hole. Notice that we pay attention to the skin surface itself, and a hair is ignored in the following description. Sweat holes exist on ridges, and perspiration occurs at these holes[Seiji et al. 1973, The Society of Cosmetic Chemists of Japan 1979]. Among these elements, furrows and ridges have more impressive geometrical features about external appearance than a hair hole and a sweat hole. Not only furrows and ridges but also their global configuration affect the impression of skin surface. On some parts of the human body surface, configuration of furrows and ridges is anisotropic. For example, we can observe it around the wrist. Hierarchical configuration of them can be also seen on various parts of body. That is, recursive structure of elementary patterns can be observed in the skin structure where a parent ridge includes small child ridges.

2.2 Fundamental structure geometry model of skin texture

We now describe geometry model for expressing skin surface based on the elementary structure of furrows and ridges considering their configuration features. The model is derived by considering not only two-dimensional features of texture but also three-dimensional shape of skin surface patterns. The features of our texture generation are as follows:

(1) The tile structure of skin texture is generated with the Voronoi-division process. The anisotropy of tile configuration is controlled in the process.

(2) Natural fluctuation of polygon edges denoting furrows is introduced by a pseudo-fractal subdivision algorithm[Fournier 1982].

(3) Curved surfaces of ridges are defined and controlled with the Bezier curve expression.

(4) Hierarchical structure of polygons in a ridge is described with a recursive description method.

(5) Skin surface image is generated with the bump mapping technique using hierarchical ridge surface description as the bump data.

2.3 Pattern generation

The furrow pattern is generated by the Voronoi-division method[Preparata et al. 1990, Iri 1986]. Voronoi-division divides a two-dimensional plane into mutually exclusive polygons (base polygons) according to some ruled placement of seeds (described in Sec. 2.7). The produced polygons represent base polygons of furrows. To represent natural fluctuation of furrows, the subdivision (used in pseudo-fractal method) is performed for all sides of polygons. This scheme makes a polygon have more natural waving shape. Figure 1

shows the processing flow using Voronoi-division and subdivision method. We
can get various patterns for base polygons by changing some conditions, for
example, seed points' positions in Voronoi-division, intensity of waving
deformation in subdivision method, and so on. Anisotropy of configuration of
base polygons can be represented by expanding or contracting the positions of
vertices along a certain direction.

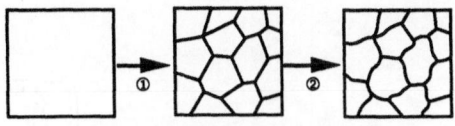

① : Voronoi-division method
② : Subdivision method

Fig.1:Voronoi-division and subdivision.

2.4 Ridge surface definition

A ridge shape is defined by a base polygon and has a curved surface whose
height increases along the direction from the side to the center point (for
example, the center of gravity) of the base polygon (Fig.2).
A Bezier cubic curve segment is used to define the surface shape of the ridge.
Assuming that a base polygon of horizontal section is on the xy plane and
point p1 (x1,y1,0) is included in the polygon, we can determine the height
from p1 to point q1 (x1,y1,z1) on the ridge surface and the normal vector at
q1 as follows (Fig.2).

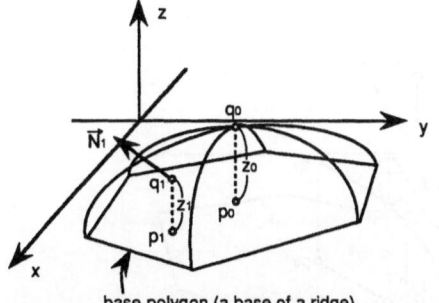

base polygon (a base of a ridge)

Notice :
p_0 : the center point of a polygon
p_1 : a point in a polygon
q_0 : a point on the ridge surface corresponding to p_0
q_1 : a point on the ridge surface corresponding to p_1
z_0 : height from p_0 to q_0
z_1 : height from p_1 to q_1
$\vec{N_1}$: the normal vector at q_1

Fig.2:Three dimensional ridge model.

First, a body coordinate for the ridge is defined by following three steps, 1)
set the origin at the center point p0 of a base polygon, 2) let the x' axis
along the direction from point p0 to point p1, 3) let the z' axis along the
direction which is vertical to the base polygon. Second, in order to represent
the half shape on the vertical ridge section including points q0,p0,q1,p1, we
apply a Bezier cubic curve segment based on pre-defined four control points on

142

the x'z' plane (Fig.3). The four control points are scaled along x' axis in
order to fit the distance d0. The height z1 from the base to the ridge surface
and the normal vector S on the ridge surface can be derived from the defined
Bezier segment curve in the body coordinate. We can then determine the height
z1 and the normal vector N1 in the universal coordinate shown in Fig.4.
We can easily get various shapes of the ridges' surfaces from the same base
polygon by changing conditions, like the location of control points for the
Bezier cubic curve segment.

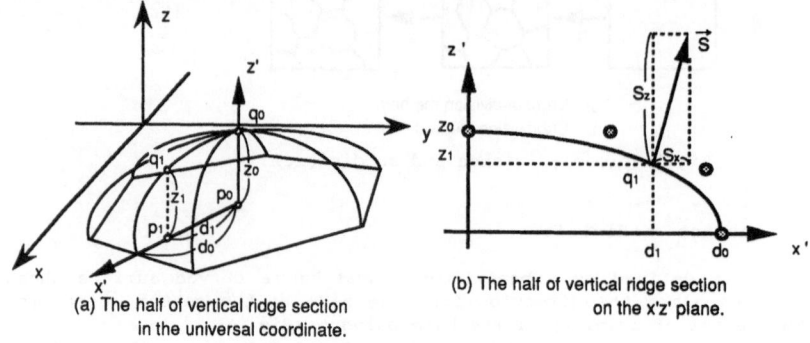

(a) The half of vertical ridge section
in the universal coordinate.

(b) The half of vertical ridge section
on the x'z' plane.

Notice:
    ⊙ : control points for the Bezier curve
    d_0 : distance from p_0 to edge of base polygon
    d_1 : distance from p_0 to p_1
    $\vec{S}=(S_x,S_z)$: unit normal vector at q_1 on x'z' plane

Fig.3:The half of vertical ridge section.

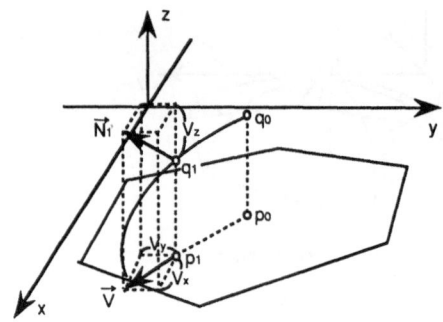

Notice1 :
    $\vec{V}=(V_x,V_y,0)$: vector with direction from p_0 to p_1
    $\vec{N}=(V_x,V_y,V_z)$: normal vector at q_1
Notice2 :
    Next two equations exist about S_x and S_z in Figure 3.
    $$\begin{cases} V_x^2+V_y^2 =S_x^2 \\ V_z = S_z \end{cases}$$

Fig.4:Normal vector on the ridge surface

2.5 Representation of hierarchical structure of skin texture

Ridges have a hierarchical structure. There are small polygons inside a base polygon, and these small polygons have smaller ridges inside them. This hierarchical structure is represented by the following method.

Voronoi-division and subdivision method are applied again to each base polygon in order to generate small polygons in the base one. This process is recursively executed until the desired hierarchical structure is generated. Figure 5 shows base polygons with three hierarchical levels. This hierarchy of base polygons represented with a parent-child relational form is stored. The surface shape of smaller polygons is also defined by the same way as that of base polygons.

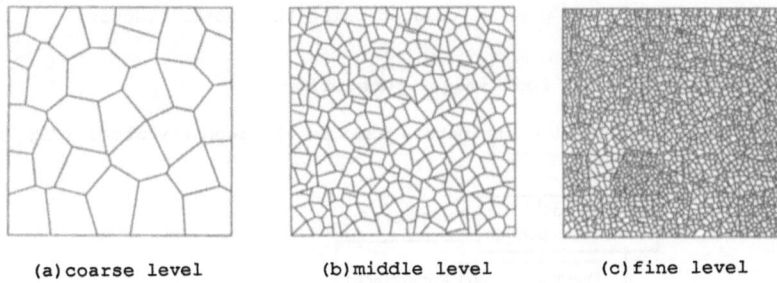

(a) coarse level   (b) middle level   (c) fine level

Fig.5:Base polygons in three hierarchical levels.

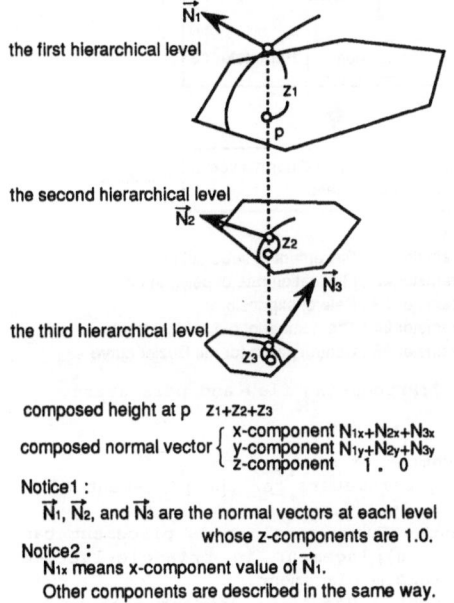

the first hierarchical level

the second hierarchical level

the third hierarchical level

composed height at p $z_1+z_2+z_3$

composed normal vector $\begin{cases} \text{x-component } N_{1x}+N_{2x}+N_{3x} \\ \text{y-component } N_{1y}+N_{2y}+N_{3y} \\ \text{z-component } 1.0 \end{cases}$

Notice1 :
$\vec{N_1}$, $\vec{N_2}$, and $\vec{N_3}$ are the normal vectors at each level whose z-components are 1.0.

Notice2 :
N_{1x} means x-component value of $\vec{N_1}$.
Other components are described in the same way.

Fig.6:The height and the normal vector for the hierarchical ridge structure where three hierarchical levels are involved.

2.6 Image generation algorithm

Basically, we employ the bump mapping technique. Hierarchical structure of polygons express the surface shape of skin. We use this data as the bump pattern to map onto a certain surface. So the shade value of each point on the surface can be computed by estimating its normal vector. The shade of a point in a ridge is computed as follows. First, we determine the base polygons in each hierarchical level which includes this point. The parent-child relational form described in Section 2.5 can be efficiently used in order to find the desired base polygons. Second, for the selected base polygons, we can determine the heights and the normal vectors, respectively, with the scheme used in Section 2.4. Finally, composing these heights and normal vectors, we can determine the height and the normal vector for the hierarchical structure. Figure 6 shows how to calculate the height and the normal vector at point p on the xy plane. The shade of p is calculated using this normal vector.

2.7 Control parameters for image generation

In this section, we summarize parameters used in the geometry model (Fig.7).

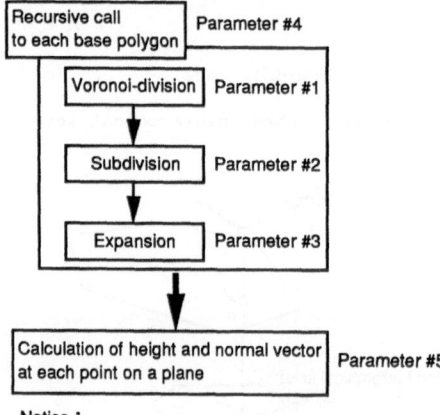

Fig.7:Processing flow and parameters.

(1) Parameter #1 : Placement of seed points
We control the following parameters for the placement of the seed points used in Voronoi-division.
· Fundamental placement : Fundamental seeds placement can be selected from three types, that is, (a)placement in triangle-lattice, (b)placement in square-lattice, and (c)random placement.
· Disturbance of placement : Regular placement such as triangle- or square-lattice can be disturbed by (a)uniform random number or (b)normal random number.
· Rate of disturbance : The intensity of disturbance is determined by this value.

(2) Parameter #2 : Fluctuation rate of polygon edges

In order to make a polygon have wavy shape, the pseudo-fractal subdivision is applied for polygon edges. The degree of fluctuation is controlled by the fluctuation rate defined by the longest distance between a deformed side and a polygonal side.

(3) Parameter #3 : Rate of expansion
In order to express the anisotropic configuration of actual ridges, the vertices of base polygons are transformed. Anisotropy of ridge configuration is controlled by the rate of expansion.

(4) Parameter #4 : The number of hierarchical levels
The number of hierarchical levels is controlled as one of the important factors to express skin texture features.

(5) Parameter #5 : Control points for the Bezier cubic curve segment
In each hierarchical level, the positions of the four control points for the Bezier cubic curve segment is determined by the two terms:
· the number of the Bezier cubic curve segments, and
· placement of four control points for each segment.

2.8 Experimental results of image generation

In this section, we show some typical generated images based on our proposed model. First, we show test images produced by controlling five different parameters. Then, we show some examples of skin surface images generated by adjusting the parameters. These images were generated on a graphic workstation IRIS4D/60G(Silicon graphics Inc.). The program was coded with C language.
Test images are shown in Fig.8 to Fig.12.
Figure 8 shows the effect of controlling parameter #5 (Control points for the Bezier curve). This parameter controls the slope of ridge's surface. Figure 8a, b, and c denote a slope with discontinuous surface derivatives, a steep slope with continuous surface derivatives, and a mild slope, respectively.
Figure 9 shows the effect by changing parameter #1 (Placement of seed points). Rate of disturbance increases from Fig.9a to Fig.9c. Here, the fundamental configuration of seed points is the triangle lattice and the disturbance of placement is given by the uniform random numbers.
The effect of parameter #2 (Fluctuation rate of polygon edges) is shown in Fig.10. Edges of a base polygon have more wavy form as the rate of fluctuation increases. Figure 10a has no wavy edges yet, while Fig.10b has.
Figure 11 shows the effect of parameter #3 (Rate of expansion). Base polygons have anisotropy by controlling the rate of expansion. Figure 11a has an isotropic structure, Fig.11b has been vertically elongated, and Fig.11c has been horizontally elongated.
Figure 12 shows the effect of controlling parameter #4 (The number of hierarchical levels). The number of hierarchical levels in Fig.12a, b, and c is one, two, and three, respectively.
On the basis of the experiments for test images, we generated skin surface images. In Fig.13a, the number of hierarchical levels is three and the polygons are isotropic. Figure 13b and c are the images which have anisotropy vertically and horizontally, respectively. In order to express features of actual skin texture, we employ anisotropy of polygons only in the first hierarchical level in Fig.13d to f.

3 APPROACH TO THE REFLECTION MODEL OF SKIN SURFACE

The reflection model is as important as the geometric model for the appearance of skin surface. We are now trying to construct a reflection model that is based on optical features of microscopic structure inside the skin surface.

Especially, we pay attention to optical features of the horny layer which consists of multiple layers and exists on top of the inside skin. Because whether skin surface seems wet or dry considerably depends on condition of the horny layer, visual appearance of skin surface, such as glossiness and softness, is thought to be highly affected by its condition.

In the condition that the horny layer is assumed to be replaced by alternate parallel layers of two kinds, we examine the reflection model including typical optical phenomena occurred at actual horny layers, that is, absorption, scattering, reflection and refraction at the border between adjacent layers of two kinds, and multiple reflection among parallel layers. Figure 14 shows skin surface images based on the reflection model under examination in addition to the geometric model described in Sec. 2. The left-upper image is an actual photo image of skin surface and the others are generated images which represent visual differences according to parameters of the reflection model about the parallel layers such as refraction index, absorption coefficient, scattering coefficient, thickness, the number of alternate parallel layers, and so on.

This reflection model is not complete considering the point of skin physiology, that is, regarding validity of parameter values, about consideration of color, and so on. So, we only show potentiality of the reflection model.

4 APPLICATION TO TEXTURE PATTERNS OF LEATHERS

We can synthesize leathers of reptiles such as crocodile or snake by using the same generation model for human skin. Since crocodile skin shows rectangular patterns, seed points for Voronoi-division method should be placed in lattice points in the plane before disturbance. Figure 15 shows a generated tile pattern for leather texture. Curved patches are defined for each tile using Bezier curves and the resulting texture data are mapped onto an object surface using the bump mapping technique. Some examples of industrial leather products are shown in Fig.16. A handbag (crocodile) and a belt (snake) are shown in Fig.16a and 16b, respectively.

5 CONCLUSION AND FURTHER WORK

A method to synthesize skin surface with CG has been described. This model is derived by considering the structure of skin surface. The geometric model has the following features. (1) The shape of furrows is produced by Voronoi-division. (2) The surface shape of ridges is produced by using the Bezier curve. Furthermore, (3) we can get a variety of skin textures by controlling features of hierarchical levels, anisotropy, fluctuation of edges, edge roundness and so on. In addition to the description of the geometric model, we described our approach to the reflection model of skin surface. Although our reflection model is not complete, we think we can show its potentiality. Furthermore, we apply our geometric model to generation of texture patterns of other objects such as reptile leathers. This shows our method's potentiality as a general tool for texture generation.

Further work:

We would like to establish a method for evaluating parameter values. For all skin images in this paper, the generated images were evaluated visually after parameter values were changed several times. Values of both geometric features and optical features measured from actual skin are needed in order to develop the method. At the same time, we would like to express the color of skin surface the capability of which our reflection model lacks. Moreover, we would

like to develop our pattern generation method as a general tool of texture
pattern generation, applying it to various textures.

REFERENCES

Anjo K, Usami Y, and Kurihara T (1992) A Simple Method for Extracting the
   Natural Beauty of Hair. Proceedings of SIGGRAPH'92, In Computer Graphics 26,
   2, pp 111-120.
Fournier A, Fussell D, and Carpenter L (1982) Computer rendering of
   Stochastic Models. Communications of the ACM 25, 6, pp 371-384.
Iri M (ED.) (1986) Computational Geometry and Geographic information
   processing(in Japanese). Kyoritsu, Tokyo.
Kaufman A (1988) TSL-a Texture Synthesis Language. The Visual Computer 4, 3,
   pp 148-158.
Komatsu K (1988) Human Skin Model Capable of Natural Shape Variation. The
   Visual Computer 3, 5, pp 265-271.
Magnenat-Thalmann N, Thalmann, D (1987) The Direction of Synthetic Actors in
   the Film Rendezvous a Montreal. IEEE Computer Graphics and Applications 7,
   12, pp 9-19.
Magnenat-Thalmann N, Primeau E, and Thalmann, D (1988) Abstract Muscle
   Action Procedure for Human Face Animation. The Visual Computer 3, 5,
   pp 290-297.
Miller G (1988) The motion Dynamics of Snakes and worms. Proceedings of
   SIGGRAPH'88, In Computer Graphics 22, 4, pp 169-178.
Nahas M, Huitric H, Rioux M, and Domey J (1990) Facial image synthesis using
   skin texture recording. The Visual Computer 6, pp 337-343.
Preparate FP, Shamos MI (1990) Computational Geometry:An Introduction.
   Springer-Verlag GmbH & Co. KG.
Seiji S, Kurosumi K, and Mishima Y (Eds.) (1973) Fundamentals of Dermatology
   (in Japanese). Asakura, Tokyo.
The Society of Cosmetic Chemists of Japan (Ed.) (1979) Cosmetic Science Guide
   Book (in Japanese). Yakuji Nippo, Tokyo.
Vannier MW, Marsh JL, and Warren JO (1983) Three dimensional computer graphics
   for craniofacical surgical planning and evaluation. Proceedings of
   SIGGRAPH'83, In Computer Graphics 17, 4, pp 263-273.
Watanabe Y, Suenaga Y (1989) Drawing Human Hair Using Wisp Model. Proceedings
   of Computer Graphics International, pp 691-700, Springer, Tokyo.
Waters K (1987) A Muscle Model for Animating Three-Dimensional Facial
   Expression. Proceedings of SIGGRAPH'87, In Computer Graphics 21, 4,
   pp 17-24.
Yasuda T, Hashimoto Y, Yokoi S, and Toriwaki J (1990) Computer System for
   Craniofacical Surgical Planning Based on CT Images. IEEE TRANSACTIONS ON
   MEDICAL IMAGING 9, 3, pp 270-290.

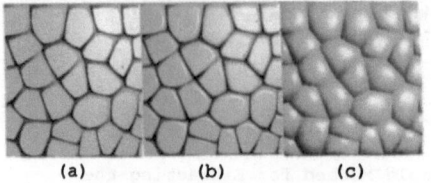

(a)   (b)   (c)

Fig.8:Changes in slope.

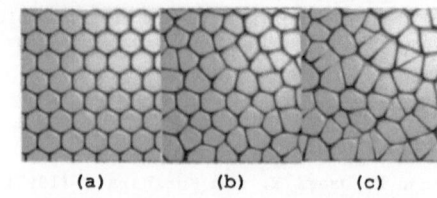

(a)   (b)   (c)

Fig.9:Changes in seed points distribution.

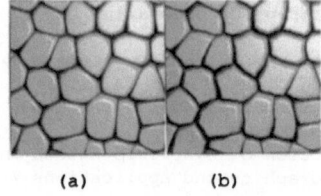

(a)   (b)

Fig.10:Changes in wavy shape.

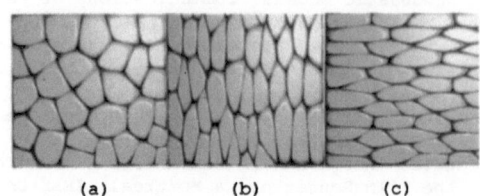

(a)   (b)   (c)

Fig.11:Changes in directional feature.

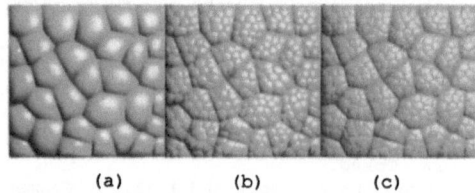

(a)   (b)   (c)

Fig.12:Changes in the number of hierarchical levels.

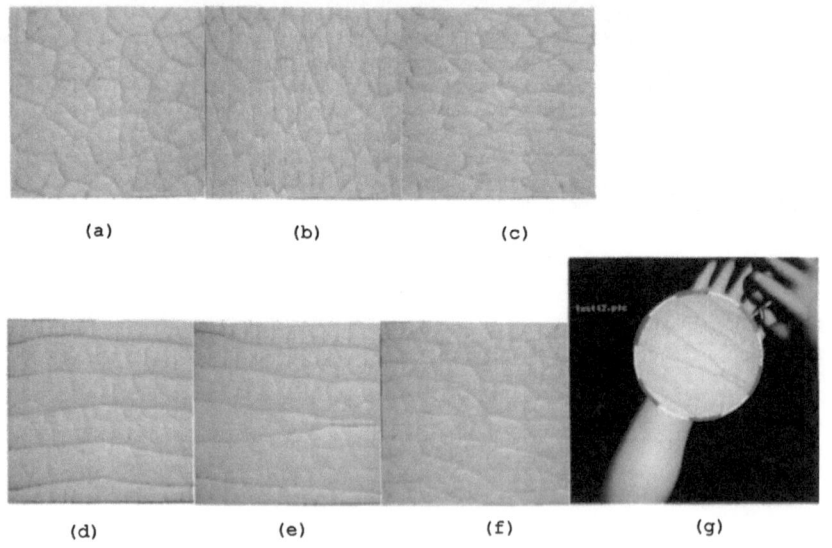

(a)   (b)   (c)

(d)   (e)   (f)   (g)

Fig.13:Examples of skin rendering.

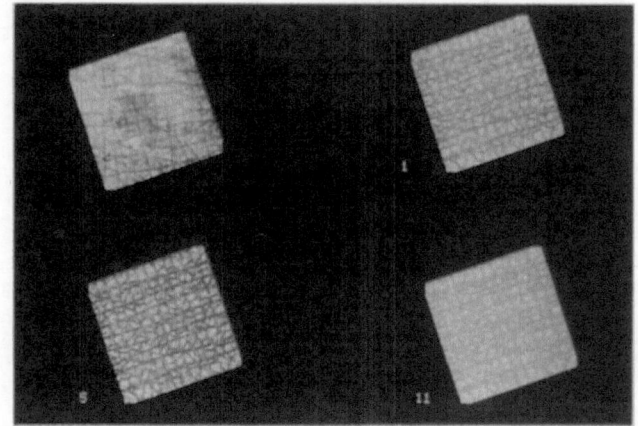

Notice:Left-upper image is actual photo image of skin surface.
The others are computer generated skin images.

Fig.14:Generated skin images based on both the geometric model
and the reflection model.

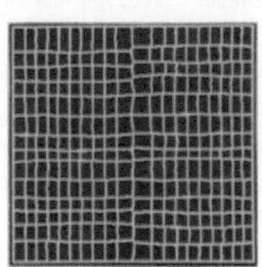 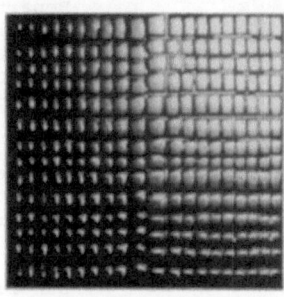

(a) a tile pattern of leather texture. (b) a generated leather texture using
the tile pattern of (a).

Fig.15:A generated leather texture of crocodile.

(a) a handbag (crocodile). (b) a belt (snake).

Fig.16: Examples of industrial leather products.

Tomomi ISHII is a researcher in the Knowledge & Intelligence Science Institute at Kao Corporation. His research interests are computer graphics and CAD. He received BE degree in information science from Tsukuba University. He is a member of the Information Processing Society of Japan.

Address: Knowledge & Intelligence Science Institute, Kao Corporation, 1-3, Bunka, 2-Chome, Sumida-ku, TOKYO, 131 JAPAN

Takami YASUDA is a research associate in the Department of Information Engineering at Nagoya University. His research interests are computer graphics and its applications to medicine. He received BE and ME in electronic engineering from Mie University in 1982 and 1984, respectively. He received a Ph.D. in information engineering from Nagoya University in 1989. He is a member of the Institute of Electronics, Information, and Communication Engineering of Japan, the Information Processing Society of Japan, and the Japan Society of Medical Electronics and Biological Engineering.

Shigeki YOKOI is an associate professor in the Department of information Engineering at Nagoya University. His research involves computer graphics and image processing and their applications to medicine. He received BE, ME, and Ph.D. degrees in electrical engineering from Nagoya University in 1971, 1974, and 1977. He is a member of the Institute of Electronics, Information, and Communication Engineering of Japan, the Information Processing Society of Japan, the Japan Society of Medical Electronics and Biological Engineering, and the Computer Graphics Society.

Jun-ichiro TORIWAKI is a professor in the Department of Information Engineering at Nagoya University, where he teaches and performs research in pictorial pattern recognition, biomedical image processing, and computer graphics and applications. He received his Ph.D. from Nagoya University in 1969. He is a member of the Institute of Electronics, Information, and Communication Engineering of Japan, the Information Processing Society of Japan, and the Japan Society of Medical Electronics and Biological Engineering.

Address: Department of Information Engineering, Faculty of Engineering, Nagoya University, Furo-cho, Chikusa-ku, Nagoya-shi 464-01 JAPAN

A Context Sensitive Texture Nib

Tom Malzbender and Susan Spach

Abstract

Commonly, a "nib" refers to the point of a pen. When used with reference to painting packages, a nib refers to the pattern with which one draws. We introduce a technique for painting with *smart* nibs that draw and blend textures into an existing image. These nibs look in the neighborhood of pixels to be drawn and determine color values that create textures that blend in naturally with what is already in the image. Our technique is based on mimicking second order statistics of samples of scanned textures, typically taken from photographs of real textures occurring in nature. We use Color Co-Occurrence Matrices to capture and optimize these second order statistics. This technique is shown to provide interactive response and good performance over a broad range of stationary textures, from periodic to stochastic.

Keywords:

Texture Synthesis, Modelling, Paint System, Co-occurrence matrix, Image statistics.

1. Introduction

Several manufacturers of high end graphics workstations have recently included hardware support for texture mapping (Martin 90),(Segal 92). These products allow interactive rendering of detailed images by applying texture maps to simple geometric models. These texture maps are usually digitized with some sort of scanning hardware, or are procedurally defined by a function that generates a desired visual effect. One example of the latter approach is the approximation of wood grain by nested concentric cylinders perturbed by a noise function (Lewis 89). We are interested in an intermediate ground between these two approaches that uses parametric texture models measured directly from scanned texture imagery, just as one creates parametric or polygonal models that approximate an object's geometry. This eliminates the need for inventing a clever procedure to generate a texture. In this paper, we present a texture synthesis technique from such a parametric model and show one application of it to painting packages.

Numerous approaches have been applied to the problem of modelling texture. Even a cursory review of the various approaches is beyond the scope of this paper so we refer the reader to (Haralick 79), (Rao 90), (Garber 81). Much of this work concentrates on the analysis of textured regions in images for the purpose of texture classification. This capability is useful in scene understanding and computer vision. Some work has been done on texture synthesis using models derived from acquired images. Unfortunately many of the techniques that have been developed are unsuitable for application in computer graphics, often because they are limited to a single color channel (grey scale) or binary images (black and white). Autoregressive models which allow us to control the autocorrelation function have been used, but we know that the autocorrelation function is insufficient to completely describe a texture (Pratt 78) (Pratt 81). Experimental work has been conducted by Julesz and others (Julesz 62), (Julesz 73), (Julesz 75) on what texture measures the human visual system is sensitive to. This has lead to what is commonly called the Julesz conjecture: the human visual system cannot effortlessly discriminate between textures that are similar in their first and second order statistics, but differ in their third or higher order statistics. Although counter-examples of this have been produced, the claim that much of the information used by the visual system in discriminating textures lies in the first and second order statistics is regarded as valid. For a quantized image with N color levels, $I[x,y] \in \{ L_1 ... L_N \}$, the order of statistics is given by:

$$\text{1st Order:} \quad p[\ I[x_1,y_1] = L_i\ ]$$

$$\text{2nd Order:} \quad p[\ (I[x_1,y_1] = L_i), (I[x_2,y_2] = L_j)\ ]$$

$$\text{3rd Order:} \quad p[\ (I[x_1,y_1] = L_i), (I[x_2,y_2] = L_j), (I[x_3,y_3] = L_k)\ ]$$

where p represents the probability of a pixel or set of pixels being in a certain state. The first order statistics are given by the histogram of the image, whereas the second order statistics are determined by the second order spatial averages, often measured by the Co-Occurrance Matrix defined in the next section.

We will describe the texture nib by first defining Co-Occurrance statistics, then show how to synthesize a field of texture (Gagalowicz 87), and lastly present techniques for extending the synthesis algorithm to interactive drawing with textures.

2. Color Co-Occurrance Statistics and Measurements

A set of texture measures that captures the salient aspects of a large class of textures are the second order spatial averages of that texture. This measure has several names and slight variations, but the fundamental idea was introduced by Haralick in (Haralick 73) under the name of grey-tone spatial dependency matrix. Another name frequently given is the grey-scale co-occurrence matrix. Here we will call its extension from grey-scale into color (Gagalowicz 87) the color co-occurrence matrix, or CCM. Given an image of size (X,Y) consisting of a discrete set of color levels $I[x,y] \in \{ L_1 ... L_N \}$, the CCM is a four dimensional matrix given by:

$$CCM[\Delta x, \Delta y, L_h, L_r] = \frac{1}{K} \sum_{x=0}^{X} \sum_{y=0}^{Y} \delta(\ I[x,y] - L_h) \, \delta(\ I[x+\Delta x, y+\Delta y] - L_r)$$

L_h and L_r are color indices also taken from the set $L_h, L_r \in \{L_1 .. L_N\}$. Typically, these color levels $\{L_1 .. L_N\}$ are indices of a color lookup table where the actual (usually 24 bit) color values are stored. L_h, the home color level, is the color level of the pixel in question and L_r, the remote color level is the color level at offset $(\Delta x, \Delta y)$, δ is the Kronecker delta function which takes a value of 1 if and only if its argument is 0. K is a normalization factor defined as:

$$K = (X - | \Delta x |)(Y - | \Delta y |)$$

which is simply the count of the number of times that a particular offset $(\Delta x, \Delta y)$ appears in the image.

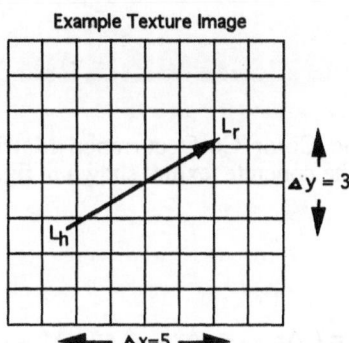

Fig. 1. Collecting Color Co-occurrence Statistics

Figure 1 provides a diagram of these relationships. An entry in the CCM is the probability that a given pixel at some location has value L_h and the pixel at offset $(\Delta x, \Delta y)$ from this pixel has value L_r. This interpretation of a spatial average as a probability is only valid for a stationary texture, ie. a texture whose statistics don't vary across the texture sample and are not a function of position in the sample. Algorithmically, to measure the CCM of a particular image we first clear each entry of the CCM. Then we look at all the pairs of pixels for a given kernel size that occur in the image and increment the CCM entry corresponding to $(\Delta x, \Delta y, L_h, L_r)$. Lastly, all entries of the CCM are normalized by K, the number of pixel pairs available in the image for a given $(\Delta x, \Delta y)$. This procedure, as well as the synthesis procedure described in section 3 has been used in (Gagalowics 87). Figure 2 provides an example of what a typical slice of the co-occurrence matrix looks like. In this case we set $L_h = L_r = 6$, $\Delta x = 0$ and vary Δy to produce a 1 dimensional slice of the 4 dimensional CCM for the digitized concrete image. Notice that the first order statistics are embedded in the CCM as well when $\Delta x = 0$ and $\Delta y = 0$.

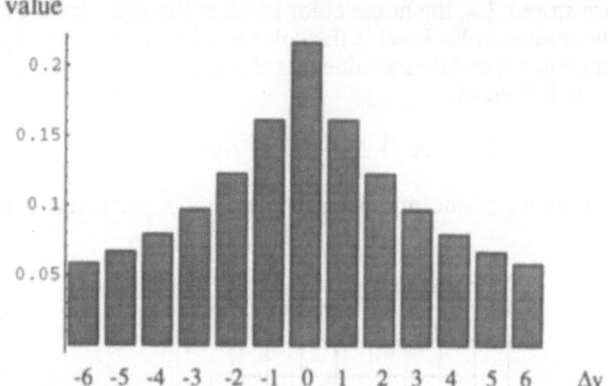

Fig. 2. A slice through the Color Co-Occurrance Matrix produced by holding $L_h = L_r = 6$ and $\Delta x = 0$ for the concrete texture shown in fig. 4.

2.1 Color Quantization

If the CCM offsets span $\Delta x = (-\Delta x_{max} \rightarrow \Delta x_{max},)$ and $\Delta y = (-\Delta y_{max} \rightarrow \Delta y_{max})$ then the CCM will be a four dimensional matrix of size:

$$(2 * \Delta x_{max} + 1) * (2 * \Delta y_{max} + 1) * N * N$$

It is important to keep both the number of color levels N and the size of the offset kernel small to keep the CCM size tractable. For this reason we quantize the original image produced by scanning photographs of real textures from a 24 bit representation down to a low number of color levels, typically 8 in our case. Although at first this may seem a severe truncation of information, one can typically retain excellent texture image quality with this small number of levels. This could be a result of the fact that textures often have high spatial frequency content and that the color sensitivity of the visual system drops with spatial frequency (Granger 73), (Green 68). There are numerous methods in the literature for color quantization (Gervautz 90), (Heckbert 82), (Pratt 78). Many of these, including our method, perform clustering in color space. We choose to use the K-means clustering method described in (Lim 90). It iteratively finds a set of N colors that approximate the centroids of clusters in color space that the texture sample contains. Although we perform this clustering in the (R,G,B) color space for convenience, a perceptually uniform color space such as CIE LUV (Foley 90) might prove more appropriate.

3. Synthesizing a Texture from White Noise

Because the CCM attempts to capture the significant features of a texture that our visual system is sensitive to, we expect that two images with similar CCMs will be visually similar as well. This suggests a texture synthesis procedure first proposed by (Gagalowics 85) and discussed further in (Gagalowics 87). First we measure the CCM of some texture of interest, here referred to as the destination CCM. Also we define a working image, initialize it, and measure its CCM. Each pixel in the working image is then iteratively visited and is changed to the color value that minimizes the euclidean distance between the two CCMs in question. This amounts to minimizing the error function:

$$E = \sum_{\Delta x = -\Delta x_{max}}^{\Delta x_{max}} \sum_{\Delta y = -\Delta y_{max}}^{\Delta y_{max}} \sum_{L_h=1}^{N} \sum_{L_r=1}^{N} (\ CCM_w\ [\Delta x, \Delta y, L_h, L_r] - CCM_d\ [\Delta x, \Delta y, L_h, L_r]\ )^2$$

where CCM_d is the destination co-occurrence matrix of the texture one would like to approximate and CCM_w is the working co-occurrence matrix of the image that is being modified. This can be understood as descending in a discrete error space. Typically we use noise with the same first order statistics (the histogram) to initialize the working image. This starting point is easy to compute, provides an unbiased initial condition in our search space, and yields fast convergence times to a given image quality since the first order constraints are already satisfied.

To find which color level leads to a minimum error for a given pixel, we must test each possible color level. Fortunately, it is not necessary to compute the error, E, for each of these tests. Instead one can compute a delta error, ΔE, that would be introduced by changing the pixel's value from its current level, L_c, to the level being tested, L_t. We then accept the test level yielding the smallest ΔE and proceed to the next pixel. We define CCM_t to be the CCM of our working image with the pixel in question having level L_t instead of L_c. It will differ only slightly from CCM_w. For each offset, $\Delta=[\Delta x, \Delta y]$, there are 4 changes to CCM_w that are caused by changing a pixel from L_c to L_t. If we define

$$L_c = I(x,y)$$

$$L_r^+ = I(\ x + \Delta x, y + \Delta y\ )$$

$$L_r^- = I(\ x - \Delta x, y - \Delta y\ )$$

then these 4 changes are:

1) $CCM_t[\ \Delta x, \Delta y, L_c, L_r^+\ ] = CCM_w[\ \Delta x, \Delta y, L_c, L_r^+\ ] - \frac{1}{K}$

2) $CCM_t[\ \Delta x, \Delta y, L_t, L_r^+\ ] = CCM_w[\ \Delta x, \Delta y, L_t, L_r^+\ ] + \frac{1}{K}$

3) $CCM_t[\ \Delta x, \Delta y, L_r^-, L_c\ ] = CCM_w[\ \Delta x, \Delta y, L_r^-, L_c\ ] - \frac{1}{K}$

4) $CCM_t[\ \Delta x, \Delta y, L_r^-, L_t\ ] = CCM_w[\ \Delta x, \Delta y, L_r^-, L_t\ ] + \frac{1}{K}$.

All other entries in CCM_t are identical to those in CCM_w. Unfortunately, these 4 changes need not refer to independent CCM entries, so in computing ΔE we must keep track of which CCM entries are changed by accepting the test level L_t. We will call this set of changed entries Ω. The differential error ΔE is then:

$$\Delta E = \sum_{\Omega}(CCM_t[\ ] - CCM_d[\ ])^2 - (CCM_w[\ ] - CCM_d[\ ])^2$$

An example of this technique applied iteratively to all pixels in an image starting with white noise is given in Fig. 4. Plots of the error, E, and number of pixels changed in each iteration are given in Fig. 3.

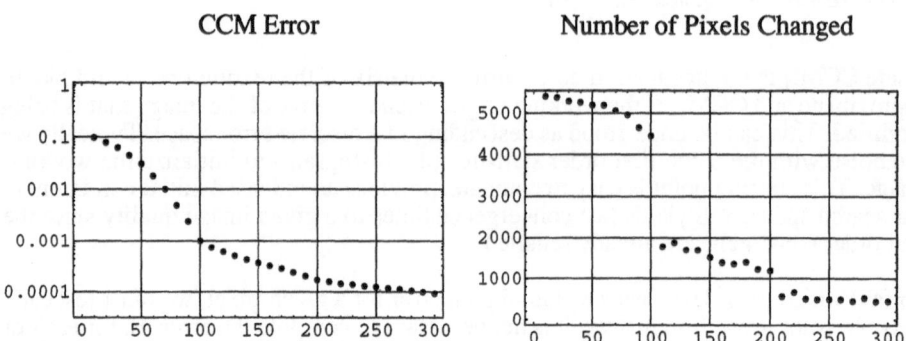

Fig. 3 - Results from a texture synthesis experiment. The left image shows the CCM Error as a function of the percent of pixels visited. The right image shows the number of image pixels changed as we iterate.

4. The Texture Nib

The texture synthesis procedure described above is quite powerful in that contextual information is being used for choosing pixel colors. This suggests application of the technique to illustration, graphics or painting systems ubiquitous on personal computers today. Current advanced painting packages allow areas of texture to be block-copied from one region to another or regions to be filled with particular textures. However, these techniques are not context dependent and don't blend the textures in naturally with surrounding details. The ideas discussed above can be harnessed to provide interactive drawing with predefined textures that use contextual information and provide smooth texture blending. In addition, users may select textured regions of images to define new texture nibs that have these same blending properties.

Figure 5 shows XNib, the texture drawing program. In this example, the working base texture image contains a crushed soda can on a gravel texture. The user selects which nib texture to draw with and is free to vary the size of the nib being drawn with as well as the extent of the CCM, $(\Delta x_{max}, \Delta y_{max})$. The nib cursor (shown in red on the working base texture) is 12x12 pixels, the gravel texture is selected and the CCM extent is $\Delta x_{max} = \Delta y_{max} = 3$. The dotted red line under the working base texture shows the user the CCM extent. As the user draws with the texture nib, the pixels under the nib cursor are changed to the color of the nib texture that minimizes the difference between the measured CCM of the nib texture and the current CCM of the

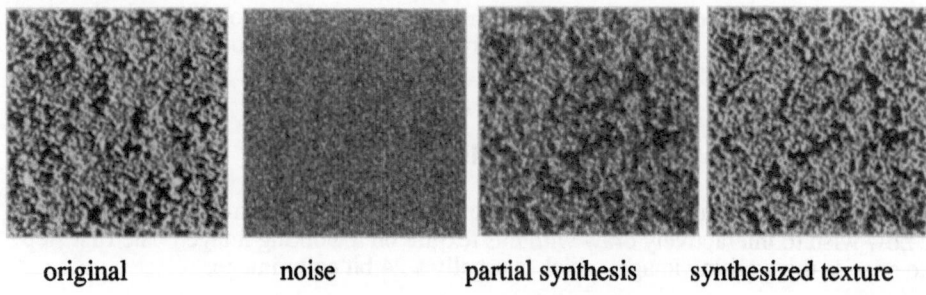

| original | noise | partial synthesis | synthesized texture |

Fig. 4. Full field texture synthesis example.

Fig 5. Xnib texture drawing program

pixels that have been drawn with the texture nib. We will now outline our drawing technique and describe the associated data structures used in the process.

4.1 Data Structures for Interactive Display

As a starting point, assume that we have measured the CCM of some textured area and we now wish to interactively draw with this texture on a working image. The first step is to encode the working image, which is usually a 24 bit color image,

$$\vec{W}[x,y] = (R[x,y], G[x,y], B[x,y])$$

relative to the colors that are used in the texture nib. We call this image *base relative*, B_r, and it is recomputed every time a new texture nib is selected. If the euclidean distance, d, between the working image pixel color and the closest nib color is less than some threshold, φ, we assign that nib color to base relative. Otherwise, a flag is set for the pixel indicating that the color that appears at this location is not relevant to the nib texture statistics collected. More formally:

$$d^2[L_i] = (R[x,y] - C_R[L_i])^2 + (G[x,y] - C_G[L_i])^2 + (B[x,y] - C_B[L_i])^2$$

$$B_r[x,y] = \begin{cases} L_{min} & \text{if } \underset{1<i<N}{\text{Min}}(d^2[L_i]) \le \varphi^2 \\ flag & \text{otherwise} \end{cases}$$

where L_{min} is defined as $d^2[L_{min}] = \underset{1<i<N}{\text{Min}}(d^2[L_i])$ and $(C_R[L_i], C_G[L_i], C_B[L_i])$ are the color values associated with the nib at color index L_i. In the synthesis procedure outlined in section 3 we minimize the difference between our destination and working CCMs. In our interactive drawing program, the destination CCM is that of the nib which is computed either as a preprocess or on the fly. Our working CCM is less straightforward in the interactive case. We build a working CCM from the statistics of the pixels that have been drawn by the current texture nib. Since this set of pixels can be of arbitrary shape, computation of the CCM normalization factors, K_d, is done with the aid of a bitmap called the *occupancy map*, $O[x,y]$, which takes a value of 1 if a pixel has been visited by the nib since the last nib selection, and 0 otherwise. As each pixel is drawn, the map is incremented and an array of dynamic normalization factors, K_d is updated by referencing the map.

$$K_d[\Delta x, \Delta y] = \sum_{x=0}^{X} \sum_{y=0}^{Y} \delta(O[x,y]) \, \delta(O[x-\Delta x, y-\Delta y])$$

An unnormalized working CCM is also updated as each pixel is drawn. We maintain an unnormalized working CCM to avoid having to "unnormalize" repeatedly as the set of drawn pixels changes. This, as well as the array of normalization factors, is cleared when the nib is selected.

4.2 Texture Painting Dynamics

Typically, painting packages allow the user to vary the size of the drawing nib. Providing this capability for our texture painting is more difficult since the computation time for determining an optimal pixel color can be quite long for large $(\Delta x_{max}, \Delta y_{max})$ values. To allow the user to draw with larger nibs and retain smooth mouse performance, we compute how many pixels, η, can be computed in a given time step (eg. say .1 seconds) that ensures interactive response. We then sequence through η pixels of the nib area in a deterministic pseudorandom sequence. The subsequent pseudorandom sequence will start where the previous sequence ended and is designed in such a way that all pixels in the nib are visited once before any pixels are visited twice. In this way, under high computational loads a spray paint pattern of textured pixels is deposited at each cycle of the event loop and a solid area is filled in if the user keeps the nib cursor stationary. The pseudorandom sequence is implemented using an exclusive-or shift-register feedback scheme described in (Press 88).

Our texture nib prototype also allows one to define new texture nibs by outlining a textured region of the current image. The CCM for that region is then measured and can be used to draw with. Depending on the size of the region selected and the color quantization involved, this can typically be done in a matter of a few seconds. We also provide the capability of zooming into arbitrary regions of the image and drawing while pixels are enlarged. In addition, various data structures such as base relative and map can be interactively displayed at any point.

5. Results

We have implemented the texture nib program in C and Motif on a HP 730 workstation, a 76 MIPS machine. On this platform we measure a speed of 450 pixel updates per second in the texture drawing, which allows interactive use. The conditions for this benchmark are N=8 and $\Delta x_{max} = \Delta y_{max} = 2$ pixels, yielding a 5x5 CCM kernel size. Pixel update rates essentially scale inversely with each of these 3 parameters. We limit the minimum drawing speed to 10 frames per second using the spray paint technique.

Figure 6 shows three examples of drawing with the texture nib. Its use for removing unwanted imagery embedded in a texture field is shown. Here we start with an image of a bee on three separate textures. By measuring the statistics of the underlying texture we are able to erase the bee in these images, even though bee is not segmented from the image in any way (no pun intended).

We have realized good performance of this algorithm over a broad range of textures, from stochastic to periodic textures. Textures with long range correlations, such as wood grain, are difficult for our technique since the Δx_{max}, Δy_{max} values must be kept relatively small to keep the CCM size small and pixel optimization time short.

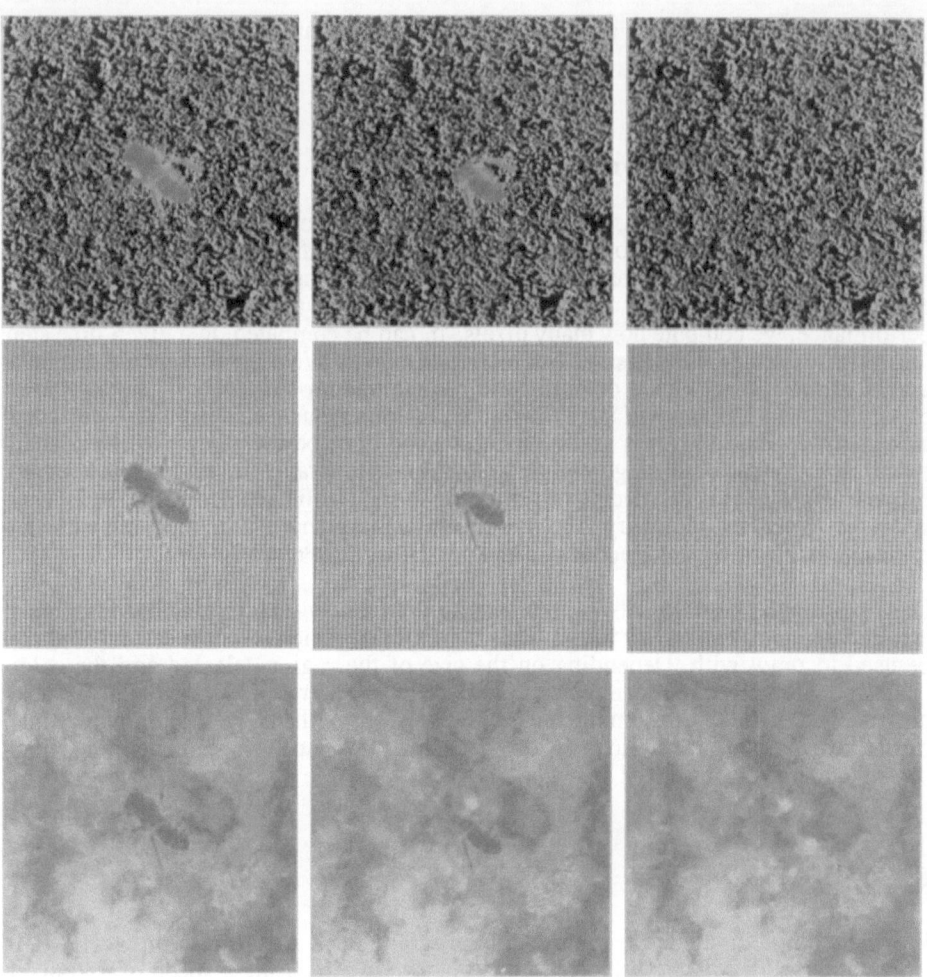

Fig. 6. - Interactive texture synthesis controlled by a nib cursor.

6. Conclusions

We have introduced the capability of interactive drawing with textures that use contextual information in determining which colors to draw with. This is implemented by measuring second order spatial statistics of a desired stationary texture in the form of a four dimensional Color Co-Occurrence Matrix (CCM). Pixels are then drawn with colors that minimize the difference between a CCM representing pixels drawn and the measured, desired CCM. In this way the second order statistics of the pixels drawn approximate the second order statistics of the measured textures and hopefully fool the visual system into regarding the drawn texture as belonging to the same class as the desired texture. There is evidence that these second order statistics are significant for the visual system's perception of texture and this has motivated their use. We have described interactive software that implements this optimization with good performance.

Acknowledgements

We would like to thank Alex Sherstinsky for help with early texture nib prototype software. We also thank Jim Christy for photographing and scanning several of the textures that appear in this paper.

References

Brodatz,P. (1966) "Textures: A Photographic Album", Dover, New York.

Haralick, R.M., Shanmugam,K, Dinstein (1973) "Textural Features for Image Classification", IEEE Transactions on Systems, Man and Cybernetics, SMC-3, pp.610-621.

Gagalowics, A. and De Ma, S. (1985) "Sequential Synthesis of Natural Textures", Computer Vision, Graphics, and Image Processing, 30, pp. 289-315

Gagalowics, A. (1987) "Texture Modelling Applications", The Visual Computer, Vol. 3, pp.186-200.

Garber, D.D. (1991) "Computational Models for Texture Analysis and Texture Synthesis", Phd. Dissertation, University of Southern California, May, 1991.

Gervautz, M. (1990) "A Simple Method for Color Quantization: Octree Quantization", in Graphics Gems, edited by Glassner, A., Acedemic Press, San Diego, pp.287-293.

Gonzalez, R., Woods, R., (1992) "Digital Image Processing", Addison Wesley Publishing Company, Reading, Massachusetts.

Granger, E.M., Heurtley, J.C. (1973) "Visual Chromatic Modulation Transfer Function", Journal of the Optical Society of America, Vol. 63, pp.1173-1174.

Green, D.G. (1968) "The Contrast Sensitivity of the Colour Mechanisms of the Human Eye", Journal of Physiology, Vol. 196, pp.415-429.

Foley, J., Van Dam, A., Feiner, S., Hughes,J, (1990) "Computer Graphics, Principles and Practive, Second Edition", Addison-Wesley Publishing Company, Reading, Massachusetts.

Haralick, R.M., Shanmugam, K., Dinstein, I. (1973) "Textural Features for Image Classification", IEEE Transactions on Systems, Man, and Cybernetics, Vol. SMC-3, No.6, November 1973, pp. 610 - 621.

Haralick, R.M. (1979) "Statistical and Structural Approaches to Texture", Proceedings of the IEEE, Vol. 67, May 1979, pp.786-804.

Heckbert, P.S. (1982) "Color Image Quantization for Frame Buffer Display", Computer Graphics, Vol. 16. No. 3, pp.297-307.

Julesz, B. (1962) "Visual Pattern Discrimination", IRE Transactions on Information Theory, it-8, pp. 84-92.

Julesz, B. (1971) "Foundations of Cyclopean Perception", The University of Chicago Press, Chicago.

Julesz, B. (1973) "Inability of Humans to Discriminate Between Textures With Identical Third Order Statistics Revisited", Perception 2, pp. 391-405.

Julesz, B. (1975) "Experiments in the Visual Perception of Texture", Scientific American, April, 1975, pp.34-43.

Lewis, J.P. (1989) "Algorithms for Solid Noise Synthesis", Computer Graphics, Vol. 23, No. 2, July 1989, pp 263-270.

Lim, J.S. (1990) "Two-Dimensional Signal and Image Processing", Prentice Hall, Edgewood Cliffs, N.J., pp.606, 1990.

Martin, P., Baeverstad, H. (1990) "Turbo VRX: A High Performance Graphics Workstation Architecture", Proceedings of AUSGRAPH 90, September 1990, pp. 107-117.

Pratt, W.K. (1978) "Digital Image Processing", John Wiley and Sons, New York, pp.155- 160.

Pratt,W.K., Faugeras, O.D., Gagalowics, A. (1978) "Visual Discrimination of Stochastic Texture Fields", IEEE Transactions on Systems, Man and Cybernetics, Vol. SMC-8, No,11, November 1978.

Pratt, W.K., Faugeras, O.D., Gagalowics, A. (1981) "Applications of Stochastic Texture field models to image processing", Proceedings of IEEE, Vol. 69, pp.542-551.

Press, W., Flannery, B., Teukolsky, S., Vetterling,W. (1988) "Numerical Recipes in C, the Art of Scientific Computing", Cambridge University Press, Cambridge, pp.224-228.

Roa A.R. (1990) "A Taxonomy for Texture Description and Identification", Springer Verlag, Berlin, Germany.

Segal, M., Korobkin, C., Widenfelt, R.V., Foran, J., Haeberli, P. (1992) "Fast Shadows and Lighting Effects Using Texture Mapping", Computer Graphics, Vol. 26 No. 2., July 1992, pp. 249- 252.

Zucker, S., Terzopoulos, D. (1980) "Finding Structure in Co-Ocuurrence Matrices for Texture Analysis', Computer Graphics and Image Processing, 12, pp. 286-308.

Tom Malzbender is a research engineer in the Media Technology Lab at Hewlett-Packard Laboratories. Tom joined Hewlett-Packard in 1982 and has developed and patented the Permuted Trace Ordering Scheme which is the basis of HP's current line of Graphics Tablets. His research interests include volume rendering, medical imaging, neural modelling and brain functioning. He received a B.S. degree in Electrical Engineering from Cornell University in 1982 and is a member of ACM.

Email: tom_malzbender@hplabs.hp.com

Susan Spach is a member of technical staff in the Media Technology Lab at Hewlett-Packard Laboratories. Her research interests include interactive computer graphics, parallel algorithms for computer graphics and medical imaging. She received her MS in computer science from the University of North Carolina at Chapel Hill in 1981. She is a member of ACM and the IEEE Computer Society.

Email: spach@hplabs.hp.com

Address: Hewlett-Packard Laboratories
1501 Page Mill Rd.
Palo Alto, California
94304, USA

Part III

Geometric Modelling

Geometric Reasoning for the Extraction of Surface Shape Properties

Bianca Falcidieno and Michela Spagnuolo

ABSTRACT

Shape descriptions are essential in computer graphics to provide effective representations of the objects to be modelled. A geometric reasoning approach is here proposed to extract curvature information from a surface approximated by a triangulation. In particular, a curvature measure is defined which is qualitatively similar to the mean curvature. This curvature measure enhances the descriptive power of the shape characterisation previously defined by the authors, based on the decomposition of the surface in its convex, concave, plane and saddle regions.

Keywords: discrete differential geometry, shape decomposition

INTRODUCTION

Representation and description are paradigms common to computer vision and graphics, disciplines which both have to deal with discrete and often incomplete shape data. The *representation* of an object may be regarded as the computational structure needed to define the object in the discrete space handled by computers, while the *description* of an object can be seen as a set of properties which identify the object as a member of some more abstract class, usually mathematically defined.

Descriptions based on shape properties are widely used in computer vision, for example, to perform the difficult task of object recognition in range images (Besl et al. 1986). View-invariant characteristics are also necessary to reconstruct surfaces of unknown shape from range data so that the entire surface can be visualised from any viewpoint with constant accuracy (Tanaka et al. 1992). In computer graphics, effective shape descriptions are essential to provide compact and accurate representations of the objects to be modelled. For example, in (Moccozet et al. 1992) the problem has been addressed of finding good algorithms to reduce the complexity of the representation of synthetic actors and their clothes. In order to perform a simplification without loss of realism, the reduction has to be driven by a suitable shape description which takes into account, for instance, the surface curvature to identify regions with low shape information content.

Several approaches have been proposed in the literature, focusing on the definition of useful shape descriptions and methods to produce them.

Methods based on curvature measurements generally rely on the theory of surfaces developed in the context of differential geometry (Besl et al. 1986, Kasvand 1986, Medioni et al. 1984, Liang et al. 1990). In particular, most of the methods developed for computing surface curvatures directly apply the analytical definitions to a smooth surface which has been locally fitted to a suitable subset of the data points. Beside the

166

occurring numerical errors, the approach is computationally reasonable when the discrete data are regularly distributed, as for range images where the neighbourhood of each pixel is uniquely defined by its position in the grid.

When dealing with scattered data, a triangulation of the samples is generally considered a satisfactory representation of the surface. In this case, however, it is more complex to derive a surface fitting preserving smoothness at vertices, as an arbitrary number of triangles can meet at a vertex. In the context of surfaces represented by a triangulation some methods have been proposed to estimate the curvature at the vertices without resorting to a smooth approximation. Lin and Perry (1982) proposed several formulæ for estimating the Gaussian curvature and other quantities, based on the concept of angle excess which represents the discrete counterpart of the Gaussian curvature (Mortenson 1985). The same approach has been followed by Hinds et al. (1991) to find a development pattern for simple surfaces in terms of Gaussian curvature with applications to 3D garment production. Chen and Schmitt (1992) have also defined a method to compute the surface principal curvatures, which is mainly based on a geometric reasoning which simulates the geometric meaning of the principal curvatures.

Even if intrinsic surface properties have obvious advantages for surface description, estimates of the mean curvature are also needed to characterize the particular embedding of the surface in the space. The authors have proposed a qualitative analysis of the surface shape in (Falcidieno et al. 1992b), which has been used to define a unique surface decomposition in its concave, convex, saddle and plane regions.

In this paper, an extension of the previous work is presented which consists of the definition of a *measure* of curvature along edges and at vertices of a triangulation, which may be regarded as a discrete version of the mean curvature. The proposed definition is useful to enhance the shape description of a triangulation and results from a geometric reasoning which involves only the elements of the triangulation without requiring any smooth approximation. The remainder of this paper is organized as follows. In the next section, the model used to represent discrete surfaces is described, which is based on the Delaunay triangulation of the data points. In the third section, the concept of curvature is explained in the context of polyhedral surfaces, based on the concept of angle excesses. In the fourth section, the proposed measure of curvature is introduced, which has the same information content about the surface shape as the mean curvature for smooth surfaces. Moreover, a measure of curvature density is proposed for the Gaussian and mean curvature. It will also be shown how the quantification of curvature can be used to solve some problems arising in the shape decomposition defined in (Falcidieno et al. 1992b). Finally, some examples are given and conclusions are briefly drawn.

THE DELAUNAY TRIANGULATION AS THE SURFACE GEOMETRIC MODEL

Given a single valued surface S and a set of sampling P_S irregularly distributed on the surface S, a triangulation of P_S is defined as a planar, straight line graph in which pairs of points are joined by line segments, which intersect only at their endpoints. In particular, since S is assumed to be single valued, the problem of finding a triangulation of P_S can be reduced to the problem of finding a triangulation of the projections of P_S onto the plane, which will be then projected back into R^3 (Boissonat 1984). Among all the triangulations feasible, the *Delaunay triangulation* has some important properties which make it a generally accepted standard for surface approximation. The Delaunay triangulation is dual with respect to another fundamental geometric structure, the *Voronoi diagram*, which defines a topology on a set of points, based on the *nearest-neighbour* relationship. Given a set of points $\mathcal{P} = \{P_i \,/\, P_i = (x_i, y_i) \in R^2,\ i=1\ldots n\}$ in the plane, the Voronoi diagram of $\mathcal{P}$ is the partition of the plane into n polygons $\mathcal{V}(P_i)$, $i=1\ldots n$, each associated with its centre P_i, and defined as

$$\mathcal{V}(P_i) = \{Q \in R^2 \,/\, d(Q, P_i) < d(Q, P_j),\ j=1\ldots n,\ i \neq j\}$$

where $d(x,y)$ denotes the Euclidean distance. Thus, the Voronoi polygon associated with P_i denotes the locus of points which are nearer to P_i than to any other P_j in P. Equivalently, the Voronoi polygon can be defined as

$$\mathcal{V}(P_i) = \bigcap_{i \neq j} H(P_i, P_j)$$

where $H(P_i\,P_j)$ denotes the halfspace containing P_i and limited by the perpendicular bisector of $P_i P_j$ (see fig. 1a) The Voronoi diagram has several applications in various disciplines and for a complete overview on this topic see for example (Aurenhammer 1991).

Let us now consider the dual graph of the Voronoi diagram $\mathcal{G}_D(\mathcal{P}) = (\mathcal{P}, \mathcal{E})$, where the set of vertices corresponds to $\mathcal{P}$, while the set of arcs $\mathcal{E}$ is given by pairs of points whose Voronoi polygons share a common edge (Preparata et al. 1985). Provided that no more than three points are cocircular, $\mathcal{G}_D(\mathcal{P})$ is the *Delaunay* triangulation of $\mathcal{P}$, which explicitly represents the nearest-neighbour relationships defined by the Voronoi diagram. In fig.1b, the Delaunay triangulation of the set of points of fig.1a is depicted.

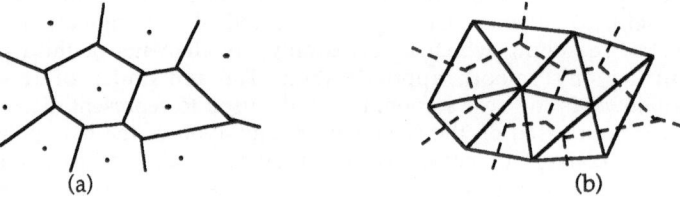

(a)   (b)

Fig.1 The Voronoi diagram of a set of points (a) and the corresponding Delaunay triangulation (b).

Notice that the Delaunay edges are perpendicular to the corresponding Voronoi edges and do not necessarily intersect them. The Delaunay triangulation has several interesting properties, first of all, the max-min angle property: if the diagonal of any strictly convex quadrilateral defined by two adjacent triangles is replaced by the opposite one, the minimum of the six internal angles does not increase. This property assures that most of the triangles are as equiangular as possible, which is desirable in interpolation problems, as it gives bounds for the interpolation errors. The Delaunay triangulation is the only one which satisfy this criteria that particularly shows its uniqueness. Recently, another peculiar property of the Delaunay triangulation has been proved by Rippa (1990) who has shown that this triangulation has minimal roughness over all feasible triangulations. However, even if equiangularity is considered a good property for approximation problems, Dyn et al. (1990) have shown that long thin triangles may give better interpolation results for surfaces which have preferred directions and have introduced the concept of data-dependent triangulations.

We will keep on considering the Delaunay triangulation as the piecewise linear surface approximation, because its connection with the Voronoi diagram furnishes neighbourhood information which may be useful for curvature evaluation. The definition of curvature, however, is independent of the particular triangulation chosen. The Delaunay triangulation is the basis of the geometric model adopted to represent the surface, which is defined as a face-adjacency graph, where each node is defined by one and only one triangular facet in the Delaunay triangulation, while each arc is defined by pairs of triangles being adjacent through one edge (Falcidieno et al. 1991).

THE CONCEPT OF CURVATURE FOR POLYHEDRAL SURFACES

An important aspect of geometry is the study of the properties of a surface which remain invariant under a given class of 1-1 mappings. In particular, a property which is invariant under an isometry (i.e. a length preserving 1-1 mapping) is called an *intrinsic* property of the surface and is independent of the particular embedding of the surface in the space. The Gaussian curvature, whose formal definition can be found for example in (Do Carmo 1977, Lipschutz 1969), is an intrinsic property of a surface and its connection with shape properties can be intuitively explained by the following example. Let us start by considering a disk in the plane, the point $\mathcal{P}$ at the disk centre has a zero Gaussian curvature, that is, the surface represented by the disk is locally flat in a neighbourhood of $\mathcal{P}$ (see fig. 2a). If we imagine to add a sector to the disk, a saddle shaped surface is obtained (see fig. 2b) with a negative Gaussian curvature at $\mathcal{P}$. If, instead, we subtract a sector to the flat disk, a surface is obtained which is shaped as shown in fig. 2c with a positive Gaussian curvature at $\mathcal{P}$. Thus, the Gaussian curvature gives somehow a measure of "how much" a surface locally differs from a flat one and it is positive where the surface is shaped as an ellipsoid, negative where it is shaped, for example, as an hyperboloid.

(a)　　　　　(b)　　　　　(c)

Fig. 2 Intuitive meaning of the Gaussian curvature: (a) has a zero Gaussian curvature, (b) has a negative Gaussian curvature and (c) has a positive Gaussian curvature.

Based on this intuitive notion of Gaussian curvature, the concept of curvature for piecewise flat surfaces can be formally defined as an extension of the theory concerning polygonal subdivisions of curved surfaces. Let us consider a regular surface S and a polygonal path γ, i.e. a closed piecewise regular curve on S, with vertices $\gamma(t_0),...,\gamma(t_k)$. At the vertices of γ, the *external angle* can be defined as the smallest determination of the angle between the normals to the two arcs of γ meeting at a vertex (see fig. 3).

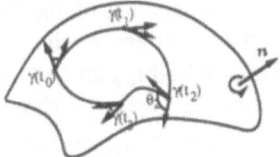

Fig. 3 The external angles of a polygonal path on a surface S.

The next step consists in considering the Gauss-Bonnett theorem, in the local formulation, which states that for a simple region $\mathcal{R}$ of a regular surface S, whose boundary is given by a closed piecewise regular curve γ, the following relation holds:

$$\sum_{i=0}^{k} \int_{t_i}^{t_{i+1}} k_g dt + \iint_R K d\sigma + \sum_{i=0}^{k} \theta_i = 2\pi \tag{1}$$

where k_g denotes the geodesic curvature of the regular arcs of γ, while K denotes the Gaussian curvature of S. See Do Carmo (1977) for more details on this topic. Thus, the Gauss-Bonnett theorem establishes a link between the Gaussian curvature inside a region and the total variation of the orientation along the path defining the boundary of the region on the surface S.

With regard to piecewise flat surfaces, the curvature will be obviously concentrated at the vertices of its polyhedral subdivision and the result (1) leads to the following considerations. Let us consider the region on the surface defined by the triangles incident to a vertex v and bounded by the edges opposite to v (see fig. 4a).

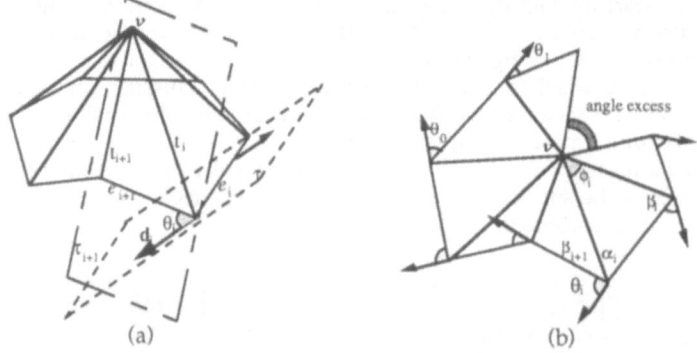

Fig. 4 A polygonal path on a piecewise flat surface (a) and its development onto the plane (b).

First, the geodesic curvature along the boundary of the region will be zero, since the path has straight edges, thus, if the relation (1) is applied to the region, the following quantity results, which can be used to define the total curvature at the triangulation vertex:

$$K = 2\pi - \sum_{i=0}^{k} \theta_i \tag{2}$$

where θ_i correspond to the external angles of the boundary of the region, that is, the changes in orientation occurring when walking along the boundary. With reference to fig. 4a, let us consider two adjacent edges of the region boundary, e_i and e_{i+1}, belonging respectively to the triangles t_i and t_{i+1}, and let us call τ_i and τ_{i+1} respectively the planes defined by the two triangles. Then, the change in orientation between e_i and e_{i+1} is given by the angle on τ_{i+1} formed by e_{i+1} and the intersection d_i between τ_{i+1} and the plane containing e_i and the normal of τ_i. To understand better the geometry of the situation, we can imagine to cut the region along one of the edges incident in v, and to develop the triangles onto the plane, without shrinking the surface. Obviously, each e_i will form an angle of π with the corresponding d_i, as they belong to the same plane in 3D. Finally, it can be observed that $\theta_i = \pi - \alpha_i - \beta_{i+1}$, which derives from trivial geometry considerations. Thus, the quantity defined in (2) becomes:

$$K = 2\pi - \sum_{i=0}^{k} \theta_i = 2\pi - \sum_{i=0}^{k} (\alpha_i + \beta_i) = 2\pi - \sum_{i=0}^{k} \phi_i \qquad (3)$$

where ϕ_i denotes the angle at the vertex v. The result is consistent with the intrinsic nature of the Gaussian curvature since the value of K in (3) only depends on the angles ϕ_i, thus, the curvature does not change if the triangulation is deformed preserving the distance between points, transformation which obviously does not affect the angles at the vertices of the triangulation. Moreover, the computation of (3) can be performed without resorting to any coordinate system, as the angles ϕ_i may be obtained using only the edge length and not the vertices coordinates. This curvature measure has been extensively used, for example, by Lin and Perry (1982) which have proposed many other formulæ to estimates quantities related to the curvature.

CURVATURE MEASURES BASED ON GEOMETRIC REASONING

While the Gaussian curvature is an intrinsic surface property, the mean curvature depends on the embedding of the surface in the space and it is therefore said to be an extrinsic surface property. For example, let us consider a sheet of paper and imagine to bend it in different manners without stretching or cutting it (see fig. 5). While the Gaussian curvature will remain constantly zero in all the different cases, the mean curvature will be, for instance, positive where the bent surface is convex shaped and negative where it is concave shaped. Generally, characterisation methods for smooth surfaces take into account both kinds of curvature to completely classify the surface shape (Besl et al. 1986).

Fig. 5 Different bending of the same surface: the mean curvature changes as the surface assumes a concave, convex or plane shape.

The same difference exists when considering the case of triangulations. As shown in fig. 6, different folding of the triangles around the vertex v may give rise to different shapes even if the angle excess at the vertex remains unchanged.

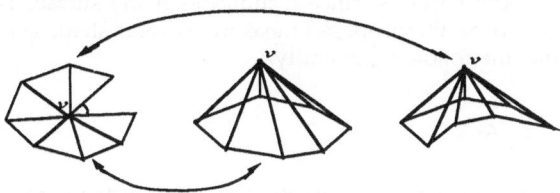

Fig. 6 The same triangle configuration at a vertex can give rise to different shapes when the triangles are folded around the vertex.

By this point of view, the Gaussian type of curvature defined in the previous section

172

is not sufficient to completely characterize the shape of a triangulation, and for this reason it is important to have methods to estimate the behaviour of the mean curvature so that a wider range of shape features can be distinguished.

By a geometric point of view the entity which is responsible of the shape changes in a triangulation is the dihedral angle defined by two adjacent triangles, therefore, this angle will be the basis of the proposed curvature measure (see fig. 7).

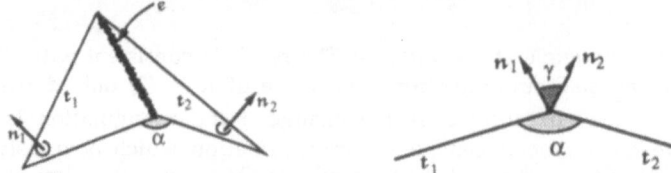

Fig. 7 The angle α between two triangles and the angle γ between their normals.

Given an edge e not belonging to the surface boundary, the idea is to associate a measure with the edge which is negative if the corresponding dihedral angle is concave and positive if it is convex. Moreover, greater measures should be associated with narrow edges, i.e. the measure of curvature should be increasing as the dihedral angle changes from 2π (limit of the possible concave angle) to 0 (limit of the possible convex angle). Thus, it seems natural to choose the angle formed by the normals of the triangles sharing the edge to measure the curvature along that edge. The formal definition of the proposed measure consists of the following two steps.

Definition 1: Let e be an edge shared by two triangles t_1, t_2, the dihedral angle α subtended by e is said to be *convex* (*concave*) if for any two points $p_1 \in t_1$ and $p_2 \in t_2$ the straight line segment $p_1 p_2$ lies completely *below* (*above*) the surface, otherwise it is *plane*.

Definition 2: Let e be an edge shared by two triangles t_1, t_2 and let n_1 and n_2 be the normals respectively to t_1 and t_2. If $\gamma = \sphericalangle(n_1, n_2)$ denotes the unique solution of $\cos\gamma = n_1 \cdot n_2$ then the measure of curvature $m(e)$ is associated with the edge e such that

$$m(e) = \begin{array}{ll} \gamma & \text{if } e \text{ is } convex \\ 0 & \text{if } e \text{ is } plane \\ -\gamma & \text{if } e \text{ is } concave \end{array} \tag{4}$$

This curvature measure locally has the same descriptive power than the mean curvature has for smooth surfaces, since it indicates if the surface is locally convex, concave or plane. Based on the proposed measure, several shape estimators could be defined. For example, the following quantity:

$$m(v) = \sum_{e \in Inc(v)} m(e) \tag{5}$$

has been tested, which represents the curvature at a vertex as the total variation in the orientation of the facets around the vertex. Figures 8 and 9 show the results of the surface characterisation obtained using the operator (5). In the upper left window the triangulated surface is depicted, while in the upper right one the vertices having a positive mean curvature are highlighted in green and those with a negative mean curvature are coloured in light blue. In the lower left window the estimator (5) has been applied and the vertices have been coloured using the same rule than before. Finally, in the lower right window, the vertices depicted in light blue represents the differences between the analytical determination of the mean curvature and the tested estimator. In fig. 8, the chosen surface has been irregularly sampled with 200 points, and in fig.9 the same surface has been sampled with a regular square grid of 500 points. The error rate is around 21% and no great differences have been found approximating the surface with regular or irregular grids. It can be seen that the errors are mainly located where the surface shape changes, where probably the approximation with a triangulation introduces curvature errors in the geometric model.

Some comparisons can be made between the proposed curvature measure and other quantities which have been defined to approximate the curvature. For example, in (Moccozet et al. 1992) cost functions have been proposed which are used to estimate the curvature at the vertices and at the edges of a triangulation. With reference to vertices, the cost function is defined as the sum of the angles between the normals to the triangles incident to the vertex and the average normal vector of the same triangles. As the authors point out in (Moccozet et al. 1992), the closer this sum is to zero, the more the neighbourhood of the point is flat, but there is no precise way to interpret values far from zero. By this point of view, the curvature definition based on the concept of angle excess seems more efficient and precise to recognize those vertices having a flat neighbourhood. The proposed measure of mean curvature would also yield to a more rich knowledge about the shape of the surface as it is able to distinguish a wider range of geometric configurations. Moreover, the cost functions give better results when the angle between normal vectors are explicitly computed, instead of using the cosine value of the same angle which surely does not represent a good approximation of the angle itself.

Beside the defined curvature measure, the utility of a density function for the curvature is currently being studied. The reason for introducing a density function is connected with the fact that the given curvature measure has the meaning of "total" curvature, since the total variation of the facets orientation is estimated along the edges without reference to the area within which this change occurs. The idea is then to associate an area with edges and vertices so that the curvature density can be defined as the curvature divided by the influence area. Since every triangle contributes with three vertices at the curvature of the whole surface, some authors have adopted the criteria to divide the curvature at a vertex by one third of the area of the triangles incident into the vertex (see for example Hinds et al. 1991, Lin et al. 1982). In this manner, it is implicitly assumed that each vertex in a triangle has the same influence independently of the triangle shape.

Our approach, on the contrary, takes into account the spatial distribution of the data points and associates with each vertex an *influence area* defined on the basis of the neighbourhood relationships given by the Voronoi diagram associated with the surface samples. Let us consider the Voronoi diagram of the projection set $\mathcal{P}_S$ of the surface samples onto the xy plane, as defined in the second section, and let us denote with $\mathcal{V}(P_v)$ the Voronoi polygon associated with the projection point on the xy plane of the vertex v. Then, for every edge e in the triangulation, the polygon $I\mathcal{A}(e)$ in the xy plane can be defined as the intersection between the convex hull of $\mathcal{P}_S$ and the quadrilateral obtained by joining the extremes of e with the two Voronoi vertices at the right and at the left of e (see fig. 10a). The *influence area* associated with e is given by the area of the projection of the $I\mathcal{A}(e)$ onto the 3D surface triangulation. With regard to the triangulation vertices, the influence area can be defined in a similar manner. Let us consider for every vertex v the polygon $I\mathcal{A}(v)$ in the plane xy defined by the intersection of $\mathcal{V}(P_v)$ with the convex hull of $\mathcal{P}_S$ (see fig. 10b). The *influence area* associated with v is then given by the area of the projection of the $I\mathcal{A}(v)$ onto the 3D surface triangulation.

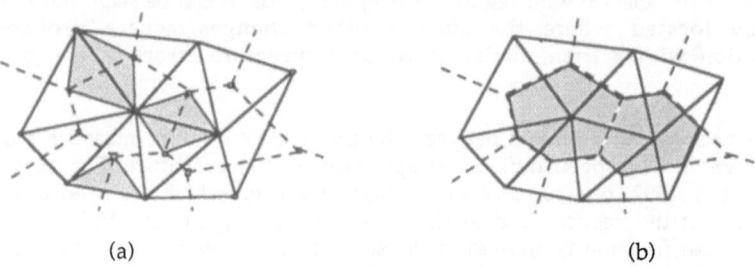

(a)   (b)

Fig. 10 The influence areas associated with edges (a) and with vertices (b).

CONCLUSIONS

In this paper, the potential of geometric reasoning has been highlighted in the context of shape description of discrete surfaces. In particular, some shape descriptors have been presented which are able to extract different kinds of curvature information from the triangulation, without resorting to any smooth surface approximation.

The defined measure of curvature is mainly useful to enhance the results of the surface shape decomposition presented by the authors in (Falcidieno et al. 1991). The decomposition method is based on a qualitative analysis of the surface curvature which yields to the extraction of the convex, concave, plane and saddle regions of the surface. These curvature regions are characterised on the basis of geometric attributes assigned to edges and triangles and consist of maximal sets of triangles having the same label. The surface shape can be described by its curvature regions which provide a *unique* surface decomposition. This method has a natural implementation in sequential and parallel models of computation and the identification of the curvature regions can be performed in parallel with respect to their type, with a linear computational complexity (Falcidieno et al. 1992b).

The problems of the described decomposition method are related to the qualitative and local nature of the curvature analysis which is unable to recognize global shapes. Let us give an example: if a convex area is sampled by a great number of points, the resulting triangles may be adjacent through very smooth convex angles. Within a given tolerance, those edges could be classified as plane and, as a consequence, the triangles would be labelled plane as well. The entire region would be classified as plane, since the triangle labels are inherited by the corresponding region. In other words, the global convex shape has been hidden by the local "flatness" of the surface approximation. The introduction of a curvature measure allow us to solve this problem. After having decomposed the surface into its characteristic regions, a further step can be performed which assigns a total curvature measure to each region, by summing the measure (4) over all the edges belonging to region. Thus, regions being recognised as plane, but having a total curvature greater than a given tolerance could be more precisely characterised as convex or concave according to the sign of the computed curvature.

ACKNOWLEDGEMENTS

This work has been partially supported by the Progetto Strategico: "Metodi e Modelli Matematici per l'Industria". The authors would also like to thank Dr. Paolo Vallebona for the helpful discussions on the topics presented in the paper.

REFERENCES

Aurenhammer, F., (1991) *Voronoi Diagrams - A survey of a fundamental geometric data structure*, ACM Computing Surveys, vol. 23, n° 3, pp

Besl,P.J., Jain,R.C., (1986) *Invariant surface characteristics for 3D object recognition in range images*, Computer Vision, Graphics and Image Processing , n° 33, pp

Boissonnat,J.D., (1984) *Geometric structures for three-dimensional shape representation*, ACM Transactions on Graphics, vol. 3, n°. 4, pp

Chen, X., Schmitt, F., (1992) *Intrinsic surface properties from surface triangulation*, Tech. Rep. TELECOM Paris 92 D 004, Dept. Images, March 1992

Do Carmo, M.P., (1977) *Differential geometry of curves and surfaces*, Prentice-Hall Inc., Englewood Cliffs, New Jersey

Dyn, N., Levin, D., Rippa, S., (1990) *Data dependent triangulations for piecewise linear interpolation*, I.M.A. Journal of Numerical Analysis, vol. 10, n° , pp

Falcidieno,B., Spagnuolo,M., (1991) *A new method for the characterization of topographic surfaces*, International Journal of Geographical Information Systems, vol. 5, n° 4, pp

Falcidieno,B., Pienovi,C., Spagnuolo,M., (1992a) *Discrete surface models: constraint-based generation and understanding*, In: B. Falcidieno, I. Herman, C. Pienovi (eds.) Computer Graphics and Mathematics, EUROGRAPHICS SEMINARS Series, Springer-Verlag

Falcidieno,B., Spagnuolo,M., (1992b) *Polyhedral surface decomposition based on curvature analysis*, In: Kunii, T.L., Shinagawa, Y., (eds.) Modern Geometric Computing for Visualization, Springer-Verlag, Tokyo

Hinds, B.K., McCartney, J.M., Woods, (1991) G. *Pattern development for 3D Surfaces*, Computer-aided Design, vol. 23, n° 8, pp

Kasvand, T., (1986) *Surface curvature in 3D range images*, Proceedings of 8th Int. Conference on Pattern Recognition, 1986

Liang, P. Todhunter, J.S., (1990) *Representation and recognition of surface shapes in range images: a differential geometry approach*, Computer Vision, Graphics and Image Processing, vol. 52, n° , pp

Lin,C., Perry,M.J., (1982) *Surface description using surface triangulation*, Proceedings of the Workshop in Computer Vision: Representation and Control, (Rindge, N.H. August 1982)

Lipschutz, M.M., (1969) *Differential Geometry* , McGraw-Hill, New York

Medioni,G., Nevatia,R., (1985) *Description of 3-D surfaces using curvature properties*, in Proceedings of Image Understanding Workshop, New Orleans, La., October 1984, DARPA

Moccozet L., Magnenat-Thalmann, N., (1992) *Controlling the complexity of objects based on polygonal meshes*, IN: T.L. Kunii (Ed) Visual Computing. Springer-Verlag, Tokyo, pp 763-779

Mortenson,M.E., (1985) *Geometric Modeling* , John Wiley & Sons, New York

Preparata,F.P., Shamos,M.I., (1985) *Computational Geometry*, New York, Springer Verlag

Rippa, S., (1990) *Minimal roughness property of the Delaunay triangulation*, 1990

Tanaka, H., Kishino, F., (1992) *Recovering and visualizing complex shapes from range data*, IN: T.L. Kunii (Ed) Visual Computing. Springer-Verlag, Tokyo, pp 331-347

176

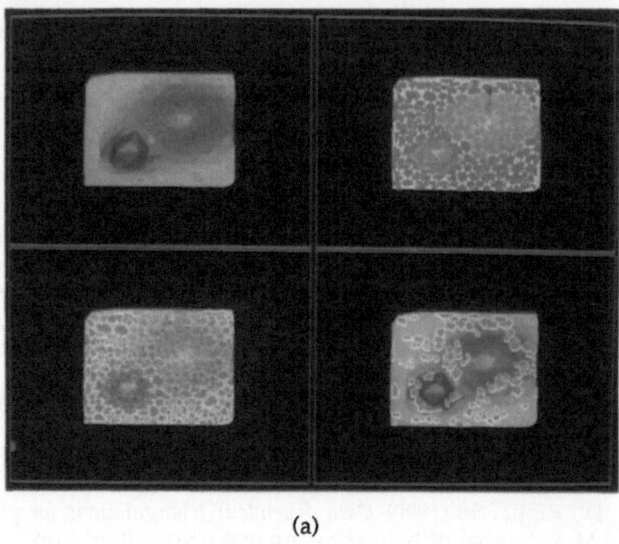

(a)

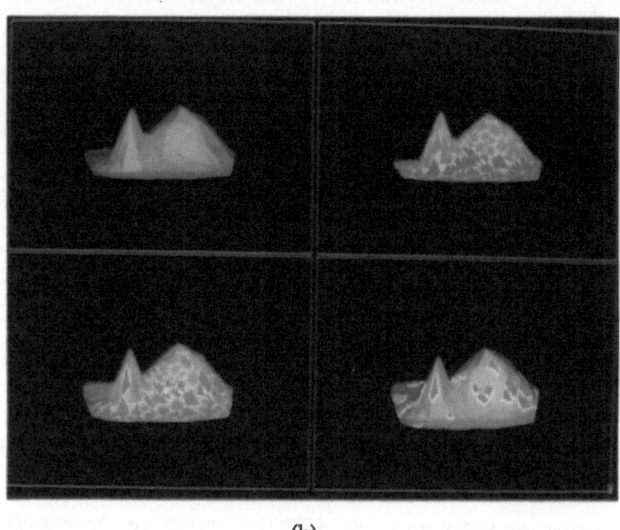

(b)

Fig. 8 The projection onto the xy plane of the characterization results (a) and its perspective view in (b).

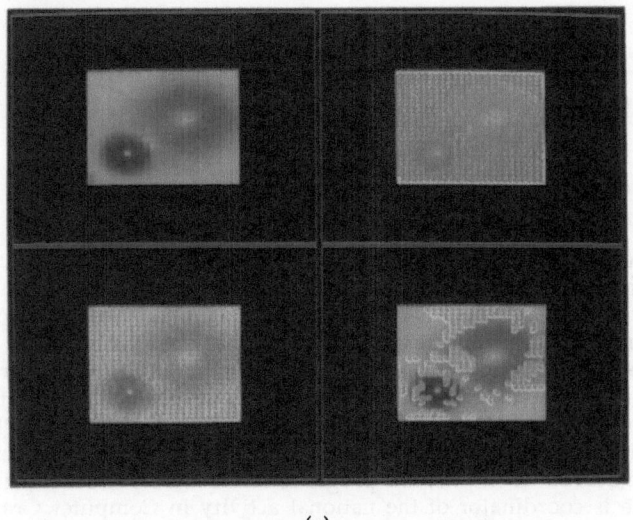

(a)

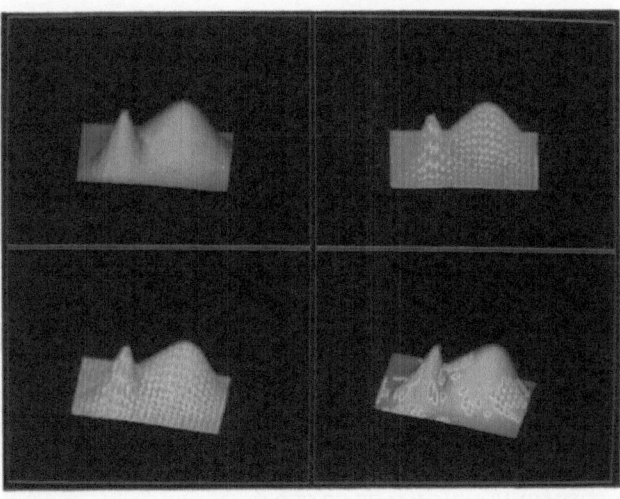

(b)

Fig. 9 The projection onto the xy plane of the characterization results (a) and its perspective view in (b).

Bianca Falcidieno is currently director of research at the Istituto per la Matematica Applicata, an institute belonging to the National Research Council of Italy. She now acts as head of the Computer Graphics Group and as leader of national and international projects on Computer Graphics and its applications. She has written more than 70 refereed technical publications on subjects related to these areas. She is a member of the Editorial Board of Computer and Graphics and Computer Graphics Forum, and coeditor for the Technical Report series in EUROGRAPHICS. As a member of various societies and associations (EUROGRAPHICS, ACM, AICA, IEEE, IFIP, etc...) she served on numerous program committees for several international conferences. She is coordinator of the national activity in Computer Graphics of the Italian Association for Computer Science (AICA) since 1986. Her research interests include Computer Graphics, Geometric Modelling, Computational Geometry.

Michela Spagnuolo graduated from the Department of Mathematics, University of Genova, in 1989.
Since then, she holds a Research Fellowship at the Istituto per la Matematica Applicata of the National Research Council, in Genova.
Her research interests include Surface Modelling and Geometric Modelling for CAD/CAM applications.

Address
Istituto per la Matematica Applicata del C.N.R.
Via L.B. Alberti, 4 - 16132 Genova (Italy)
Phone: +39-10-515510   Fax: +39-10-517801
Email: {FALCIDIENO/SPAGNUOLO}@IMAGE.GE.CNR.IT

Representation of Geophysical Maps with Uncertainty

Séamus T. Tuohy and Nicholas M. Patrikalakis

ABSTRACT

This paper proposes a method for the reconstruction of surfaces from spatially distributed geophysical data with uncertainties. For efficient interrogation and storage and the ability to represent uncertainty, bi-quadratic uniform integral *enveloping* or *interval* B-spline surfaces are fit to uniformly distributed cellular data using linear programming methods. The cellular data function is characterized by an upper and lower bound of the *measured* values for a range (box) of the independent variables. Interior patch boundaries are formed using a quadtree segmentation of the data set and interior knots are placed according to an algorithm for edge detection. C^1 continuity across patch boundaries is maintained by initially fitting auxiliary patches which then define the boundary conditions for the interior patches. A map from measured geophysical data illustrates the method.

Keywords: Image Reconstruction, Spline Approximation, Terrain Modeling, Geophysical Maps

INTRODUCTION

Surface reconstruction is the process of creating a surface from scattered (sometimes sparse) measured data and has applications in: *terrain modeling* - creating a map from elevation data (or from contours); CAD/CAM - creating computer models from measurements of the manu-factured object; *vision* - creating a visual surface (scene) from a variety of visual modalities. In such cases, for a given set of points (x_i, y_i) we have associated values z_i and we wish to construct a surface $Z(x, y)$ that satisfies certain criteria. Furthermore, the data is spatially varying (either uniformly distributed or scattered), requires large amounts of computer memory for storage and is obtained from sensors (e.g. sonar) which introduce uncertainties. For critical applications, methods for surface reconstruction should meet the following criteria: 1) efficient interrogation; 2) compact in storage; 3) able to represent the data to a suitable accuracy (or resolution); 4) able to represent uncertainty.

Previous methods have used techniques from the field of *regularization* (Delingette 1991; Sinha 1991; Terzopoulos 1991) in which a surface is constructed by minimizing an energy functional that characterizes geometric properties of the original surface. The method constructs $Z(x, y)$ such that $z_i = L_i[Z(x, y)] + \varepsilon_i$ for all i where

$$L_i[Z] = \left. \frac{\partial^k Z}{\partial x^j \partial y^{k-j}} \right|_{(x_i, y_i)} \qquad j = 0, 1, 2, \ldots, k \qquad (1)$$

and ε_i is some level of error in the *measured data*. The regularized solution to the surface reconstruction problem seeks a minimum to the Tikhonov general form:

$$|v^2|_k = \int \int_D \sum_{j=0}^{k} \binom{k}{j} \left(L_j(Z) \right)^2 dx \, dy. \qquad (2)$$

179

where D is the 2D rectangular domain of interest.

In a different and more general approach, *homotopy* techniques using continuous deformation based on a toroidal graph allow surface reconstruction from lower-dimensional data, such as contours (Kunii 1991). A toroidal graph represents correspondence between points on adjacent contours in order to prevent unwanted folds or twists in the surface. As an extension of this work, a new type of toroidal graph is used in Ikeda (1992) as a data structure for terrain topology to represent the relationship between multiple contours including critical points where contours split or merge.

Apart from the notable exception of Stewart (1990) in representing uncertainty for measured bathymetry data, *existing smooth surface reconstruction methods do not handle or represent uncertainty of physical data.* In this paper, we introduce the concept of *enveloping* or *interval explicit* B-spline surfaces that not only represent the data, but also the uncertainty of the data resulting from sensor measurement. More specifically, bi-quadratic uniform integral *enveloping* or *interval explicit* (rather than parametric) B-spline surfaces will be fit to data represented by the interval $z_i \in \left[z_i^u, z_i^l\right]$ [1].

For efficient interrogation, robust methods for B-spline surfaces exist (Patrikalakis 1991, 1992). Interrogation efficiency is enhanced by keeping the degree of the surfaces low. Analytic geometric descriptions based on piecewise polynomials can efficiently characterize (with respect to storage vs. accuracy) geophysical parameter variations without the combinatorial explosion that would arise through the use of faceted, linear or decompositional models. Further, uniform spline knot vectors and the use of an explicit rather than a parametric surface formulation limit the storage needed to the height components of the surface control points. The introduction of an *interval* representation for the enveloping surface control points allows uncertainty in both measured data and in interrogation results to be represented and used in critical applications.

In the following sections, it will be shown how to construct maps of a geophysical property (e.g. bathymetry or magnetic field intensity) represented by uniform integral enveloping or interval explicit B-spline surfaces. We begin with a definition of enveloping B-spline surfaces. The following section describes the proposed method beginning with preprocessing the data, then generating the surface equations and finally discussing the results. The paper concludes with some remarks about an application of the surface reconstruction method.

ENVELOPING OR INTERVAL B-SPLINE SURFACE PATCHES

This section is a review of basic B-spline properties with an introduction to enveloping or interval B-spline surfaces. For a more complete review of B-spline properties used here, see Bardis (1988) and DeBoor (1972). An enveloping B-spline surface is defined here as a B-spline with interval coefficients. If we let T be a set of real numbers such that $t_i \leq t_{i+1}, 0 \leq i < k + 2(M-1)$, then a real valued function $f(t)$ in the domain $[t_0, t_{k+2(M-1)}]$ is called a spline of order M or degree $M-1$ if $f(t)$ is a polynomial of degree $M-1$ on each subinterval $[t_i, t_{i+1}]$ and its first $M - p - 1$, where p is the knot multiplicity, derivatives are continuous in the entire interval $[t_0, t_{k+2(M-1)}]$. Moreover, the higher derivatives of a spline function are continuous everywhere except at $t_i, 0 \leq i \leq k + 2(M-1)$. $T = \left\{t_0, t_1, \ldots, t_{k+2(M-1)}\right\}$ is the knot vector and the values $t_{M-1}, t_M, \ldots, t_{k+M-1}$ are the interior knots of the B-spline function. A recursive expression for the B-spline basis functions $B_{i,M}(t)$ is (DeBoor 1972):

$$B_{i,1} = \begin{cases} 1 & \text{if } t_i \leq t < t_{i+1} \\ 0 & \text{otherwise} \end{cases} \qquad B_{i,M}(t) = \frac{t - t_i}{t_{i+M-1} - t_i} B_{i,M-1}(t) + \frac{t_{i+M} - t}{t_{i+M} - t_{i+1}} B_{i+1,M-1}(t) \text{ if } M > 1 \quad (3)$$

The B-spline surface is a tensor product surface defined by a topologically rectangular set

---

[1] The superscripts u and l refer to the upper (or maximum) and lower (or minimum) bounds, respectively, of the measured data.

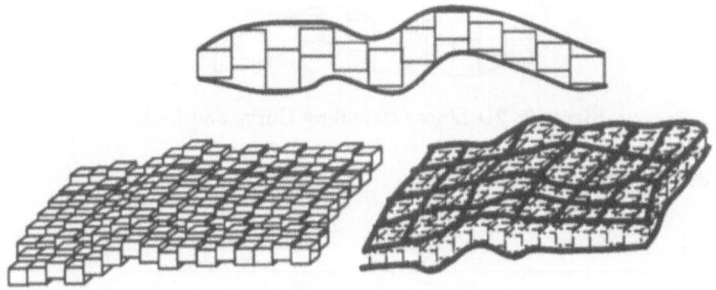

Figure 1: Cell Data and Enveloping Geometry

of control points $Z_{i,j}, 0 \leq i \leq m - 1, 0 \leq j \leq n - 1$ which are the vertices of the control polyhedron, Z, and two knot vectors, T, S, associated with each parameter, u, v. For an interval or enveloping B-spline surface patch, each control point is represented by an interval $Z_{i,j} = \left[Z_{i,j}^l, Z_{i,j}^u \right]$ and the patch definition is

$$Z_{M,N}(u, v) = \left[Z_{M,N}^l(u, v), Z_{M,N}^u(u, v) \right] = \sum_{i=0}^{m-1} \sum_{j=0}^{n-1} Z_{i,j} B_{i,M}(u) B_{j,N}(v) \qquad (4)$$

The support of the basis functions extends over a rectangular area of $M \times N$ adjacent intervals of the parametric space of a B-spline patch. Local control over narrow regions of the patch can be enhanced by knot refinement in both directions. Splitting along parametric lines can be accomplished in the same way.

MAP CONSTRUCTION

The approach for map construction is to represent the range of measured values with an enveloping B-spline surface. In Figure 1 is a 2D example of an enveloping curve, and below is a 3D example of a grid of cellular data, and the enveloping interval surface for this data set. Map construction begins with sorting scattered measured values into a uniformly distributed grid of cells. The cellular data is characterized (in the z direction) by a minimum and maximum *measured* value for a range $[x_i + \Delta_x, y_j + \Delta_y]$. The intersection of the edges of these cells form a lattice of points from which vertices for C^0 piecewise bilinear bounding surfaces are derived. To derive vertices where groupings of empty cells occur, a linear interpolation of a faceted model obtained from a Delaunay triangulation of the vertices derived from non-empty cells is used. Patch boundaries are formed using a quadtree segmentation of the data set and interior knots are placed according to an algorithm based on the evaluation of isoparametric curve inflection points extracted from a smoothed data set. Upper and lower bounding surfaces, in the form of integral uniform biquadratic B-splines, are then fit by minimizing the difference between the bounding B-spline and the corresponding bilinear surface with the constraint that the upper (lower) B-spline surface must lie completely above (below) the upper (lower) bilinear surface. By knot addition and subdivision of auxiliary patches that are fit to junctions (local region of four adjacent patches) and to boundaries (boundary region of two adjacent patches), continuity conditions for the patch boundaries formed by the quadtree segmentation can be obtained so that the resulting enveloping surface is C^1.

The above process is explained in the following sections. For clarification, an example of an upper enveloping surface fit to bathymetry data for a region off the coast of Boston, MA, USA will shown. The data is for the region enclosed by $[42°4'30'', 42°36'18'']$ latitude north by

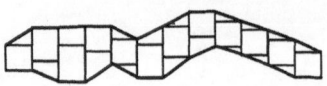

Figure 2: 2D Linear Bounding Curve and Cells

$[70°4'30'', 71°36'18'']$ longitude west [2].

Preprocessing

Input and Sorting

Uniformly distributed cells $c_{q,r}$ consist of the minimum $c_{q,r}^l$ and maximum $c_{q,r}^u$ values of a given set of measured data for a particular region $[x_q + \Delta_x, y_r + \Delta_y]$ where x and y are latitude and longitude, respectively. For scattered data, the sorting procedure $c_{q,r}^u = \max(z_{q,r})$ and $c_{q,r}^l = \min(z_{q,r})$ where $q = \lfloor \frac{x_k}{\Delta_x} \rfloor$, $r = \lfloor \frac{y_k}{\Delta_y} \rfloor$ [3] for $k = 0 \ldots n - 1$ can be used to place the scattered data into the appropriate cells in $O(n)$ time.

For our example, Fig. 8 shows a color level contour [4] for bathymetry data that has been sorted into approximately 128×128 cells of size $15'' \times 15''$. Note the white space signifying empty cells created by the chosen cell size.

Construction of Piecewise Bilinear Bounding Surfaces

C^0 piecewise bilinear bounding surfaces are constructed so that empty cells that are manifestations of the selected cell size can be filled and to enable a discretized linear constraint for the surface fitting method presented later. A 2D example of a C^0 piecewise linear curve bounding a series of cells is shown in Figure 2. The control vertices $g_{q,r}$ for the piecewise bilinear surface are obtained in the following manner for an $n \times m$ number of cells:

1. corner control points

$$g_{0,0}^u = c_{0,0}^u, \ g_{0,0}^l = c_{0,0}^l \qquad g_{n,0}^u = c_{n-1,0}^u, \ g_{n,0}^l = c_{n-1,0}^l$$
$$g_{0,m}^u = c_{0,m-1}^u, \ g_{0,m}^l = c_{0,m-1}^l \qquad g_{n,m}^u = c_{n-1,m-1}^u, \ g_{n,0}^l = c_{n-1,m-1}^l$$

2. interior of boundary control points

$$g_{q,r}^u = \max\left(c_{q-1,r}^u, c_{q,r}^u\right), \ g_{q,r}^l = \min\left(c_{q-1,r}^l, c_{q,r}^l\right), \text{ for } q = 1, \ldots, n - 1, r = 0 \text{ and } m - 1$$
$$g_{q,r}^u = \max\left(c_{q,r-1}^u, c_{q,r}^u\right), \ g_{q,r}^l = \min\left(c_{q,r-1}^l, c_{q,r}^l\right), \text{ for } q = 0 \text{ and } n - 1, r = 1, \ldots m - 1$$

and interior control points found as in Fig. 3. Note that if there are at most three empty cells incident at a point, then g can be computed from the remaining non empty cell(s). To remove outliers during this process, the relative values can be checked and aberrant points removed [5].

Delaunay Triangulation

In order to find the vertices for the bilinear bounding surface that are unknown due to the presence of adjacent empty cells, a linear interpolation surface based on a Delaunay triangulation of the known vertices is used.

Algorithms for triangulation can be found in Cline (1984), Guibas (1985), and Lawson (1977). All algorithms use a sorting procedure of time $O(n \log_2 n)$ to preprocess the data. In the Guibas and Stolfi algorithm, sorting is dominant whereas in the others, there is an additional $O(n^{5/4})$

---

[2] The nomenclature used is $°$ ≡ degree, $'$ ≡ minutes, $''$ ≡ seconds where $1'$ ≡ 1 nautical mile ≈ 1852 meters.
[3] The notation $\lfloor \frac{A}{B} \rfloor$ refers to integer division.
[4] For all color level contours, red denotes shallow, green is transition and blue denotes deep water depth.
[5] Note that aberrant points here is a relative term; in this example they are defined as points which are found to be local maxima (or minima) and also that their value is more than 100 % of the next nearest value.

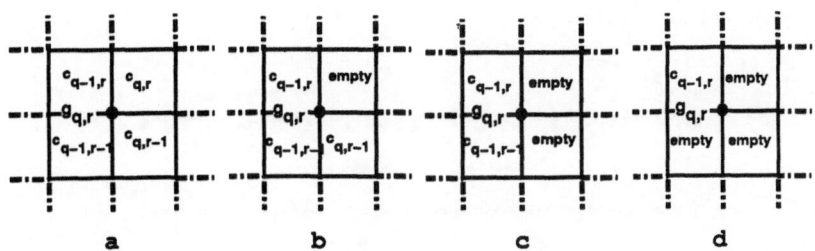

Figure 3: a) $g_{q,r} = \max(c_{q-1,r-1}, c_{q-1,r}, c_{q,r-1}, c_{q,r})$, b) $g_{q,r} = \max(c_{q-1,r-1}, c_{q-1,r}, c_{q,r-1})$, c) $g_{q,r} = \max(c_{q-1,r-1}, c_{q-1,r})$, d) $g_{q,r} = c_{q-1,r}$

time operation. Note however, that if $n \sim 65500$ all methods take essentially the same amount of time [6] and the appropriate method can be selected based on data storage requirements and on the ease of implementation. For example, the algorithm by Cline and Renka (1984) needs only $O(7n)$ integer type data records to record adjacency and ordering information and can be found in the NAG (1992) library.

For our example, Fig. 9 shows the complete bilinear bounding surface (rotated 45° for better viewing) which has 129×129 number of vertices.

Patch Segmentation

A quadtree model provides representation of an object by the discretization of a point set into a number of cellular primitives (Samet 1990). Such models have found application in medical imaging (Kaufman 1991) and underwater visualization (Stewart 1991). The two-dimensional point set of an object is represented by a quadtree where the root node consists of a region that completely bounds the point set. For each node of the tree, the representative region is subdivided into four regions which become nodes for the next level of the quadtree. Each node is classified as either *true* or *false*, or subdivided until it can be classified or until a prescribed depth of the tree is reached.

A quadtree is used here for segmenting the data set into regions forming **patch boundaries** and in which a patch with **uniformly distributed knots** will be fit. In order to achieve data reduction, our goal is to end up with patches possessing the minimum number of internal knots needed to accurately fit the data. For example, a relatively low number of knots should be used in regions that are nearly planar (or in the case of quadratic splines, parabolic) whereas a large number of knots should be used in regions possessing higher order surface features (e.g. oscillations, surface inflections). One added problem for segmentation is that when patches are fit, C^1 continuity across adjacent patch boundaries is required for computational purposes.

Since the surfaces that will be fit are biquadratic tensor product splines, at least one knot in each parametric direction is needed for each *isoparametric curve inflection* point [7]. As an example, if a quadratic B-spline curve is to approximate the data shown in Figure 4 and if the number and location of inflection points (shown by the arrows in the figure) can be computed, then the number of interior knots should equal the number of inflections. Note that in our case, knots and inflection points are located at a subset of the bilinear surface vertex locations.

After initially placing a knot at every vertex of the bilinear bounding patch (this being the worst case), the quadtree segmentation method consists of the following steps: 1) for a region of vertices bounded by a patch with a given set of uniformly distributed knots, approximate the

---

[6] For the approximate value for $n : n \log_2 n = n^{5/4}$.

[7] Isoparametric curves have as control points a row (or column) of vertices from the bilinear bounding surface and are C^0 piecewise linear curves.

184

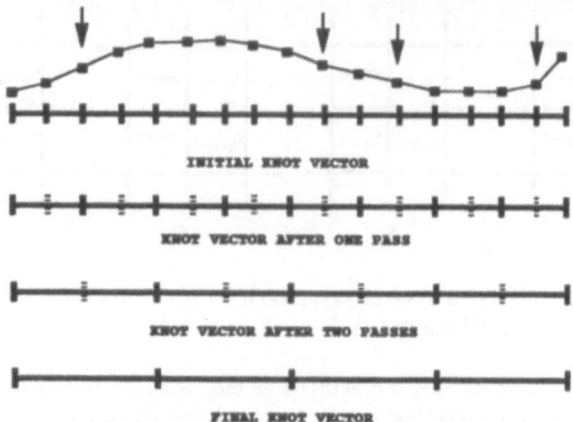

Figure 4: Data and Inflection Points and Knot Vectors

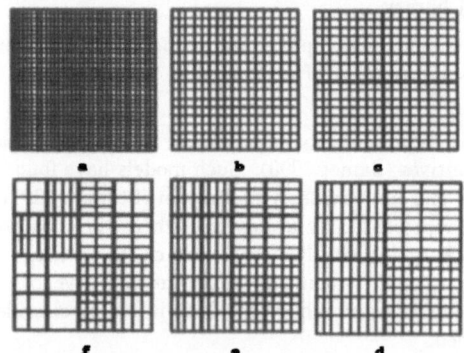

Figure 5: Patch Segmentation

position of isoparametric curve inflection points for each parametric direction; 2) taking one parametric direction at a time, check to see if alternating knots can be removed and still have enough uniformly distributed knots so that in each knot region [8] there is at most one inflection point; 3) subdivide region by quadtree and repeat steps for each subregion.

As an example, Fig. 4 shows the progression of knot removal from an initial knot vector with one knot per vertex, to the removal of alternating knots (shown as dashed lines) until no more knots can be removed and still have at most one inflection point per knot region.

Together with the quadtree subdivision of patch boundaries, the entire process would proceed diagrammatically as shown in Figure 5. Starting from the upper left figure and proceeding clockwise, in a) is the initial placement of knots, in b) some knots are removed, in c) a quadtree subdivision of the patch boundaries is performed (patch boundaries shown in bold), in d) knots are removed from each subpatch, then in e) a quadtree subdivision of each patch is performed, and then finally, in f) each of these patches has knots removed. This continues until a lower limit on knots or an upper limit on subdivision is achieved. The final result of this example would be sixteen patches, each covering a region $\frac{1}{4} \times \frac{1}{4}$ of the original data set.

---

[8]A knot region is defined here as the region extending from the midpoints of two successive knots spans and which includes the knot itself.

In our example, Figure 10 shows the approximate locations of isoparametric curve inflection points (in black) in both the east → west direction and the north → south direction. The computation of the position of isoparametric curve inflection points for each parametric direction is based on edge detection where a central difference method for approximating derivatives is used. In order to overcome the problem of local *noise* in the data and so that segmentation can proceed based on gross features of the data, the bilinear bounding surface vertices are smoothed by iteratively passing over the set of vertices a standard 3×3 Gaussian convolution. Figure 11 shows the resulting patch boundaries and knot locations obtained. Note that we now have (as in the example above) sixteen patches, each covering a region 33×33 number of vertices of the bilinear bounding surfaces.

As a final note, as the quadtree and knot removal algorithms proceed, the number of interior knots is $k = 2 + \sum_{i=0}^{i_{max}} 2^i$, where i_{max} is the maximum allowable number of internal knots, and since the knots are uniformly distributed, continuity across adjacent patch boundaries can be maintained if knot addition and subdivision are used to make control points along the boundary coincident.

Fitting

Once segmentation has been performed, the quadtree data structure provides the **location of patch boundaries** and **number of internal knots** in each parametric direction. In order to maintain C^1 continuity across patch boundaries, two types of *auxiliary* surfaces are fit (in this order): 1) *junction surfaces* which cover a region of the data centered at every point where four patches are incident; and 2) *boundary patches* which cover a region of the data centered along the row (or column) of points where two patches are incident. The method for fitting each patch is similar and is outlined next.

The general goal for the fitting algorithm is to construct a surface $Z = Z(x, y)$ [9] which minimizes the approximation error and still conforms to the shape of the data with a given distribution of control points (which are determined by the knot vectors). For enveloping interval surfaces, upper and lower bounding surfaces, in the form of integral uniform biquadratic B-splines, are fit by minimizing (maximizing) the volume under the B-spline surface with the constraint that the upper (lower) B-spline surface must lie completely above (below) the upper (lower) bilinear surface. If we define $Z(u, v) \in \left[Z^u(u, v), Z^l(u, v) \right]$ as the B-spline bounding surface and $L(x, y) \in \left[L^u(x, y), L^l(x, y) \right]$ as the bilinear bounding surface, then we seek a minimum to:

$$ F = \int_0^1 \int_0^1 \sum_{i=0}^{k^u} \sum_{j=0}^{k^v} Z_{i,j}^u B_i(u) B_j(v) du dv \qquad G = - \int_0^1 \int_0^1 \sum_{i=0}^{k^u} \sum_{j=0}^{k^v} Z_{i,j}^l B_i(u) B_j(v) du dv \qquad (5) $$

where $Z_{i,j}^u$ and $Z_{i,j}^l$ are unknowns, k^u and k^v are the number of interior knots (= number of control points -1) needed for each patch in the u and v parametric directions, respectively, and where (5) is subject to the discretized linear constraint relation

$$ \sum_{i=0}^{k^u} \sum_{j=0}^{k^v} Z_{i,j}^u B_i(u_q) B_j(v_r) \geq g_{q,r}^u \qquad - \sum_{i=0}^{k^u} \sum_{j=0}^{k^v} Z_{i,j}^l B_i(u_q) B_j(v_r) \geq -g_{q,r}^l \qquad (6) $$

where $u_q = A x_q + B$ and $v_r = C y_r + D$ (q and r defined earlier in the section on preprocessing), and $u = 0$, $v = 0$ corresponds to the point (x_{min}, y_{min}) and $u = 1$, $v = 1$ corresponds to the point (x_{max}, y_{max}) so that the constraints are located exactly at the control vertices of the

---

[9]Throughout this work there is an assumed linear relationship, $u = Ax + B$ and $v = Cy + D$ where A, B, C and D are constants defined so that u and v take values in $[0, 1]$.

piecewise bilinear surface. Since the integral of a B-spline surface is (DeBoor 1972):

$$\int_0^1 \int_0^1 \sum_{i=0}^{k^u} \sum_{j=0}^{k^v} P_{i,j} B_i(u) B_j(v) \, du \, dv = \frac{1}{MN} \sum_{i=0}^{k^u} \sum_{j=0}^{k^v} P_{i,j}(t_{i+N} - t_i)(s_{j+M} - s_j) \tag{7}$$

where $M = N = 3$ for biquadratic splines, expanding (5) we get:

$$F = \frac{1}{MN} \sum_{i=0}^{k^u} \sum_{j=0}^{k^v} Z_{i,j}^u(t_{i+N} - t_i)(s_{j+M} - s_j) \qquad G = -\frac{1}{MN} \sum_{i=0}^{k^u} \sum_{j=0}^{k^v} Z_{i,j}^l(t_{i+N} - t_i)(s_{j+M} - s_j). \tag{8}$$

This minimization problem with linear constraints can be solved using techniques for linear programming (Gill 1981 and NAG 1992).

To verify that the enveloping surface satisfies the continuous constraint condition (i.e. for locations other than those satisfied by (6)), a check of the control polygons of the B-spline and bilinear surfaces can be performed using degree elevation, knot addition and the convex hull property as in Bardis (1988). If a surface is found in violation, then the number of discrete constraints can be increased. The added constraints would be located at the midspan(s) between successive vertices of the bilinear surface which bound the point(s) of violation. Indeed, if knots are located at every vertex position, then discrete constraints must be added at all midspans to ensure convergence of the minimization.

Definition of Auxiliary Patches
Auxiliary surfaces are needed to establish boundary conditions for the interior patches so that the resulting surface (which is composed of interior patches) is C^1. Exact boundary conditions are established to prevent invalid constraints that might occur if the interior patches were fit sequentially and tangent plane continuity held through propagation. They are established using a local fitting technique based on the minimization scheme explained above. In each case, interior knots of the auxiliary patches are positioned to lie on the boundaries established by the quadtree segmentation. After fitting, knot addition can be used so that the boundary control points for the interior patches can be extracted.

To fit junction surfaces, if we use the indices i, j to designate association with a particular patch obtained from the quadtree segmentation, then each junction surface will have knot vectors

$$T = \left\{ 0, 0, 0, \frac{\min(k_{i,j}^u, k_{i,j+1}^u) - 1}{\min(k_{i+1,j}^u, k_{i+1,j+1}^u) - 1}, 1, 1, 1 \right\} \qquad S = \left\{ 0, 0, 0, \frac{\min(k_{i,j}^v, k_{i+1,j}^v) - 1}{\min(k_{i,j+1}^v, k_{i+1,j+1}^v) - 1}, 1, 1, 1 \right\} \tag{9}$$

and will be fit to a region

$$\left[x_{ik-\frac{k-1}{\min\left(k_{i,j}^u, k_{i+1,j}^u\right)}}, y_{jl-\frac{l-1}{\min\left(k_{i,j}^v, k_{i,j+1}^v\right)}} \right] \times \left[x_{ik-\frac{k-1}{\min\left(k_{i+1,j}^u, k_{i+1,j+1}^u\right)}}, y_{jl-\frac{l-1}{\min\left(k_{i,j+1}^v, k_{i+1,j+1}^v\right)}} \right] \tag{10}$$

where k and l refer to the number of vertices of the bilinear bounding surface enclosed by a patch (for our example, $l = k = 33$) and k^u and k^v are determined from the quadtree patch segmentation. Figure 12 shows the nine junction surfaces for our example in wireframe with the bilinear surface vertices in depth shaded color contour.

Boundary surfaces of patches that share a common row of data ($y = constant$) have knot vectors T ans S,

$$\left\{ 0, 0, 0, \frac{\min(k_{i,j}^u, k_{i,j+1}^u) - 1}{\min(k_{i+1,j}^u, k_{i+1,j+1}^u) - 1}, 1, 1, 1 \right\} \left\{ 0, 0, 0, \frac{1}{\min(k_{i,j}^v, k_{i+1,j}^v) - 1}, \dots, \frac{\min(k_{i,j}^v, k_{i+1,j}^v) - 2}{\min(k_{i,j}^v, k_{i+1,j}^v) - 1}, 1, 1, 1 \right\} \tag{11}$$

S being a subset of knots common to the adjacent patches. The patches are fit to a region

$$\left[x_{ik-\frac{k-1}{\min\left(k_{i,j}^u, k_{i+1,j}^u\right)}}, y_{jl} \right] \times \left[x_{ik-\frac{k-1}{\min\left(k_{i+1,j}^u, k_{i+1,j+1}^u\right)}}, y_{(j+1)l} \right] \tag{12}$$

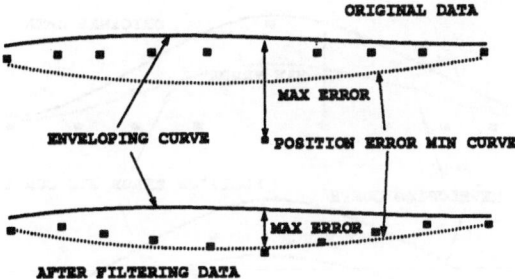

Figure 6: Error, first example, where data are boxes, enveloping curve is shown as a solid line, and the least squares position error minimizing curve is shown as a dashed line.

and have the first two rows of control points on each end coincident with control points obtained from junction surfaces after knot addition and subdivision. For boundary surfaces that run to the edge of the data domain, the ends adjacent to the edge are allowed to be free. Figure 13 shows the boundary surfaces for this direction.

Similarly, boundary surfaces that share a common column of data ($x = constant$) have knot vectors T and S,

$$\left\{0,0,0,\frac{1}{\min\left(k_{i,j}^{u},k_{i,j+1}^{u}\right)-1},\ldots,\frac{\min\left(k_{i,j}^{u},k_{i,j+1}^{u}\right)-2}{\min\left(k_{i,j}^{u},k_{i,j+1}^{u}\right)-1},1,1,1\right\}\left\{0,0,0,\frac{\min\left(k_{i,j}^{v},k_{i+1,j}^{v}\right)-1}{\min\left(k_{i,j+1}^{v},k_{i+1,j+1}^{v}\right)-1},1,1,1\right\} \tag{13}$$

T being a subset of knots common to the adjacent patches. The patches are fit to a region

$$\left[x_{ik},y_{jl-\frac{l-1}{\min\left(k_{i,j}^{v},k_{i,j+1}^{v}\right)}}\right]\times\left[x_{(i+1)k},y_{jl-\frac{l-1}{\min\left(k_{i,j+1}^{v},k_{i+1,j+1}^{v}\right)}}\right] \tag{14}$$

and have the first two rows of control points on each end coincident with control points obtained from junction surfaces after knot addition and subdivision. For boundary surfaces that run to the edge of the data domain, the ends adjacent to the edge are allowed to be free.

Finally, patches are fit by minimization (8) using constraints (6) with the first two rows and columns of control points coincident with control points obtained from boundary surfaces after knot addition and subdivision. For surfaces adjacent to the edges of the data domain, those ends which are adjacent to the edge are allowed to be free. Figures 14 to 19 show different views of the finished map.

Discussion of Example

From our example, have we met our criteria for surface reconstruction stated in the introduction? By definition we are able to represent uncertainty because we use enveloping or interval explicit B-splines. We also have an efficient interrogation capability because the B-splines used are of low order (biquadratic). For compact storage, for the maximum enveloping surface there are 1792 control points for about 90 % reduction in data. For the minimum enveloping surface, there are 1832 control points for about 89 % reduction in data. Data reduction is significant for the application discussed in the conclusion. Resolution is controlled by the selection of cell size; for a smaller cell more resolution is easily achieved at the expense of increased storage.

Finally, a more complicated question is accuracy. For typical surface reconstruction methods that use position error minimization (e.g. least squares or those found in Delingette 1991; Sinha 1991; Terzopoulos 1991), accuracy is usually a measure of the mean and maximum position

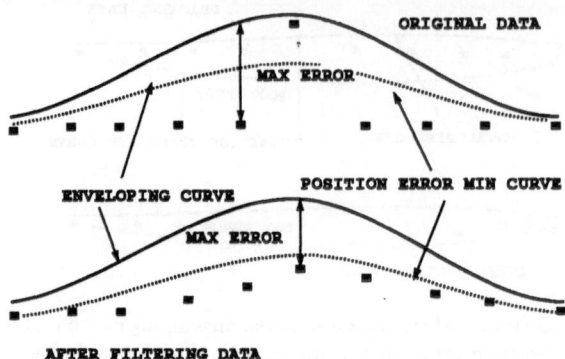

Figure 7: Error, second example, where data are boxes, enveloping curve is shown as a solid line, and the least squares position error minimizing curve is shown as a dashed line.

error. For our example, the maximum enveloping surface has a mean position error of 6.4 meters and maximum position error of 81.8 meters [10]. The minimum enveloping surface has a mean position error of 6.6 meters and maximum position error of 103.5 meters.

What explains such a large maximum position error? Figures 6 and 7 show two examples of data sets that would produce maximum errors that are larger for enveloping curves than for least square position error curves. In each example the maximum position error for the enveloping curve is marked by an arrow. Notice that for the position error minimizing curve, **since it is allowed to pass on either side** of the data, in most instances it can achieve a relatively lower maximum position error. Furthermore, many position minimizing algorithms depend on filtering of the data which would provide even better performance. Is this the same for enveloping curves?

Fitting enveloping curves to filtered data could strictly destroy the enveloping property, therefore we still would fit to unfiltered data. However, what if we use a filtered data set to check accuracy? In the first example, if the enveloping curve fit to the original (unfiltered) data is compared to the data set after filtering, then the maximum position error is indeed lowered. However, in the second example this is not true. In fact, we observed that the maximum position error will at first be lessened, but subsequent passes of the filter can cause the value of the maximum position error to grow again.

In closing this discussion, the application discussed in the conclusion will eventually answer the question of accuracy, but further research is needed in order to quantify the appropriateness of position error analysis.

CONCLUSION

This paper has presented a method for the construction of maps using the concept of enveloping surfaces that enable the representation of data and of the uncertainty of that data due to measurement innaccuracies or to the nature of the cellular data reporting process. An application we are currently investigating is the use of multiple maps of different geophysical properties for autonomous underwater navigation or localization relying on vehicle mounted sensors. In this application, enveloping surfaces are very attractive because, the conservative bounds that are produced ensure that possible solutions are not lost. Since the upper surface is guaranteed

---

[10]Depth ranges in value from 0 to about 200 meters and cell size is about 463 × 463 meters.

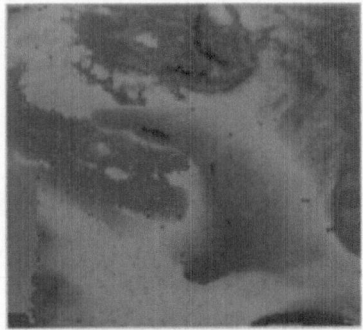

Figure 8: Upper Cell Depth Data

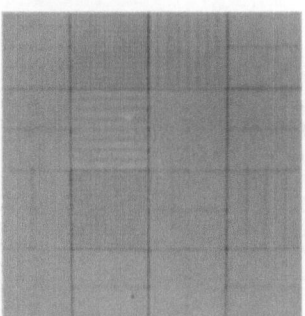

Figure 11: Quadtree Patch Boundaries and Knots for Upper Surface

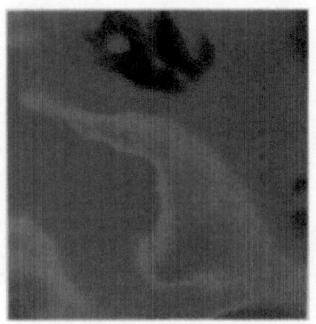

Figure 9: Upper Bilinear Bounding Surface

Figure 12: Junction Patches for Upper Surfaces

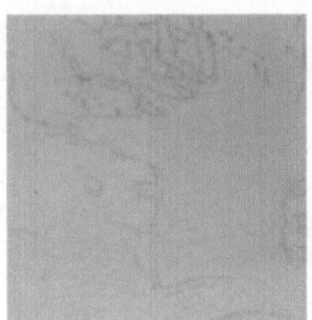

Figure 10: Inflections for Upper Surface

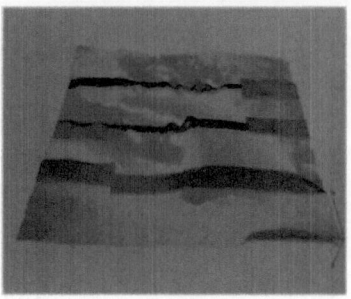

Figure 13: Boundary Patches for Upper Surfaces, x Direction

Figure 14: Upper Enveloping Surface Shaded Image

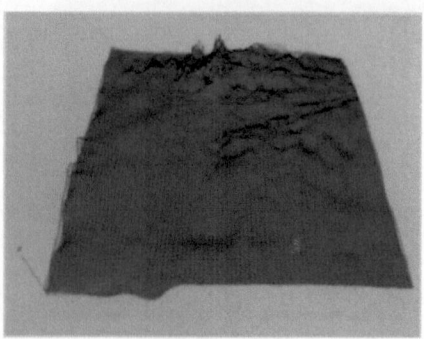

Figure 17: Enveloping Surfaces Shown Together

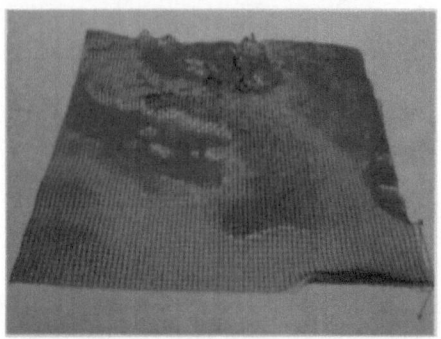

Figure 15: Upper Surface Wireframe Shown with Color Contoured Cell Data

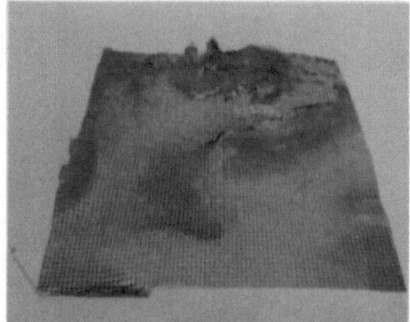

Figure 18: Lower Surface Wireframe Shown with Color Contoured Cell Data

Figure 16: Upper Surface Color Contoured Map Shown with Bilinear Surface Wireframe

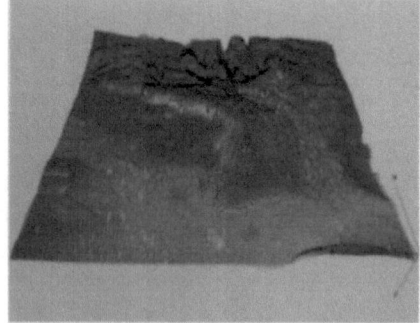

Figure 19: Lower Enveloping Surface Color Contoured Map Shown with Bilinear Surface Wireframe

(at least to the accuracy of the underlying data) to bound the minimum depth, path planning, including obstacle avoidance can be reliably performed. Finally, the interval surface can be used in testing navigation algorithms since a realistic simulation of data acquisition can be performed using *virtual* sensors.

ACKNOWLEDGMENTS

This research was supported in part by the MIT Sea Grant College Program (grant no. NA90AA-D-SG424). We thank Mr. S. L. Abrams, Dr. J. G. Bellingham and Dr. J. J. Leonard for valued assistance.

REFERENCES

L. Bardis and N. M. Patrikalakis (1989) Approximate conversion of rational B-spline patches. *Computer Aided Geometric Design*, 6(3):189–204

A. K. Cline and R. L. Renka (1984) A storage-efficient method for construction of a Thiessen triangulation. *Rocky Mountain Journal of Mathematics*, 14(1):119–139

C. De Boor (1972) On calculating with B-splines. *Journal of Approximation Theory*, 6:50–62

H. Delingette, M. Hebert, and K. Ikeuchi (1991) Energy functions for regularization algorithms. In B. C. Vemuri (ed) *Geometric Methods in Computer Vision*, Volume 1570, SPIE, San Diego, CA, pages 104–115

P. E. Gill, W. Murray, and A. Wright (1981) *Practical Optimization.* Academic Press, NY

L. Guibas and J. Stolfi (1985) Primitives for the manipulation of general subdivisions and the computation of Voronoi diagrams. *ACM Transactions on Graphics*, 4(2):74–123

T. Ikeda, T. L. Kunii, Y. Shinagawa, and M. Ueda (1992) A geographical database system based on the homotopy model. In T. L. Kunii and Y. Shinagawa (eds) *Modern Geometric Computing for Visualization*, Springer-Verlag, Tokyo, pages 193–206

A. Kaufman (1991) Introduction to volume synthesis. In N. M. Patrikalakis (ed) *Scientific Visualization of Physical Phenomena*, pages 25–36

T. L. Kunii and Y. Shinagawa (1991) Visualization: New concepts and techniques to integrate diverse application areas. In N. M. Patrikalakis (ed) *Scientific Visualization of Physical Phenomena*, Springer-Verlag, Tokyo, pages 3–25

C. L. Lawson (1977) Software for C^1 surface interpolation. In J. R. Rice (ed) *Mathematical Software III*, Academic Press, New York, pages 161–194

Numerical Algorithms Group (1990), Oxford, England *NAG Fortran Library Manual, Mark 15, FLSG415D, Silicon Graphics 4D Double Precision User's Notes*

N. M. Patrikalakis, T. Maekawa, E. C. Sherbrooke, and J. Zhou (1992) Computation of singularities for engineering design. In T. L. Kunii and Y. Shinagawa (eds) *Modern Geometric Computing for Visualization*, Springer-Verlag, Tokyo, pages 167–191

N. M. Patrikalakis, P. V. Prakash, H. N. Gursoy, and G. A. Kriezis (1991) Research topics in shape interrogation. In N. Magnenat-Thalmann and D. Thalmann (eds) *Chapter 2 in New Trends in Animation and Visualization*, J. Wiley, London, pages 13–41.

H. Samet (1990) *Applications of Spatial Data Structures: Computer Graphics, Image Processing and GIS.* Addison-Wesley, Reading, MA

S. S. Sinha and B. G. Schunck (1991) Surface approximation using weighted splines. In S. Negahdaripour *et al* (eds) *Proc. of the 1991 IEEE Computer Society Conf. on Computer Vision and Pattern Recognition*, IEEE Computer Society Press, Los Alamitos, CA, pages 44–49,

W. K. Stewart (1990) A model-based approach to 3-d imaging and mapping underwater. *ASME Transactions, Journal of Offshore Mechanics and Arctic Engineering*, 112:352–356

W. K. Stewart (1991) Visualization resources and strategies for remote subsea exploration. In N. M. Patrikalakis (ed) *Scientific Visualization of Physical Phenomena*, Springer-Verlag, Tokyo, pages 85–112.

D. Terzopoulos and M. Vasilescu (1991) Sampling and reconstruction with adaptive meshes. In S. Negahdaripour *et al*, (eds) *Proc. of the 1991 IEEE Computer Society Conf. on Computer Vision and Pattern Recognition*, IEEE Computer Society Press, Los Alamitos, CA, pages 70–75

AUTHORS' BIOGRAPHIES

Séamus T. Tuohy is a doctoral candidate in the Department of Ocean Engineering at MIT. His research interests include geophysical map construction, methods for surface interrogation, navigation for autonomous underwater vehicles and computer aided design for marine applications. He received a B.S. in Naval Architecture and Marine Engineering and an M.S. in Engineering from the University of New Orleans in 1986 and 1988, respectively, and an Ocean Engineer's Degree and S.M. in Mechanical Engineering from MIT in 1992. He is a member of SNAME, ASEE and Sigma Xi.

Nicholas M. Patrikalakis is Associate Professor of Ocean Engineering at MIT. Prof. Patrikalakis' research and teaching focus in the general area of applications of computational geometry in design, analysis, simulation, visualization and fabrication of complex systems. For his work in computer aided design, Dr. Patrikalakis was appointed Doherty Professor of Ocean Utilization (1988-1990). He is a member of ACM, ASME, CGS, IEEE, ISOPE, SIAM, SNAME and TCG. Dr. Patrikalakis has served as consultant to various organizations, has sat on committees of several professional societies, is a member of the board of directors of the Computer Graphics Society, and participates in the editorial boards of several journals. He has recently served as program chair of CG International '91 and as guest editor of The Visual Computer. Prof. Patrikalakis received his Diploma in Naval Architecture and Mechanical Engineering in 1977 from the National Technical University of Athens, Greece, and his Ph.D. in Ocean Engineering in 1983 from MIT.

Address: MIT, Department of Ocean Engineering, 77 Massachusetts Avenue, Cambridge, MA 02139-4307, USA.

Reconstruction of an Object Shape from Multiple Incomplete Range Data Sets Using Convex Hulls

Nobuhiko Wada, Hiroshi Toriyama, Hiromi T. Tanaka, and Fumio Kishino

Abstract

This paper proposes a method of integrating multiple range data sets to be used as a base for accurate 3-D object modeling. This method consists of four parts: reducing each shape data set to its convex hull, matching facets of one convex hull to those of the other, estimating a transformation matrix by correspondences, and putting these data sets together. By using the convex hulls, integration is robust even if the data sets have deficiencies caused by the concave parts of an object. A facet on one convex hull that corresponds to a facet on another can be obtained concisely by utilizing the surface normals of the facets.

Keywords: convex hull, 3-D range data, reconstruction, matching, transformation

1   INTRODUCTION

It is generally said that there can be no range sensor that can acquire an entire the data of surface in one measurement, and such range data sets always include deficiencies. Consequently, it is necessary to put incomplete range data sets together in order to get a complete surface model without deficiencies. Figure 6 shows an example. The shape of the object is usually measured from the pose like Fig. 6(a). The base of the object is hidden by the table, so its shape is unknown. To get the shape of the base, the object needs to be measured in a horizontal pose like Fig. 6(b). The motivation for this study is to obtain integrated data which covers the entire surface, as shown in Fig. 6(c). This integration will also be useful in canceling out errors included in the data.

Estimating the transformation matrix between two range data sets is a classic problem in computer vision (Champleboux et al. 1992). Given two sets consisting of points on the surface of an object in a three-dimensional coordinate system, the problem is to estimate the rigid body transformation matrix T between them.

In this paper, we estimate data-to-data correspondence from the correspondences of convex hulls. Accordingly, we succeeded in matching different data sets of the same object. By using the convex hull of each, integration is robust because almost all objects have concave parts. The correspondences between the facets of convex hulls can be obtained concisely by utilizing the surface normals of the facets.

Generally speaking, the convex hull can be defined for a set of three-dimensional vertices P as the smallest convex boundary that includes P. If P is finite then the convex hull of P is a convex polytope with vertices, edges, and facets making up its boundary. The convex hull has many important applications in commputer-aided design and computer graphics, image generation (Kay and Kajiya 1986) and tomography (Keefe and Chettri 1989). It is also an intermediate stage of processes in several other geometric algorithms, for example, Delaunay triangulations and Voronoi diagram generation (Guibas and Stolfi 1985). The current best output-sensitive algorithm in a 3-D convex hull problem, which takes $O(n \log^2 h)$ time, is by Edelsbrunner and Shi (1991), where n is the number of vertices of P and h is the number of vertices of the convex hull. Clarkson and Shor (1989) give an algorithm running in expected time $O(n \log h)$.

2 ESTIMATING THE 3-D RANGE DATA TRANS-FORMATION

This section first presents the advantages of using convex hulls and formulates the localization problem as the minimization of errors by using convex hulls. We then describe a search method for the rigid transformation T between two convex hulls; the transformation depends on six components.

2.1 Convex Hulls

First, each data set of an object is reduced to a convex hull. It is not important which method is used to get the convex hulls, because the convex hull is uniquely defined.

When we acquire the shape of an object, concave parts of the object tend to be occluded while convex parts are rarely occluded. Consequently, convex hulls from multiple data sets having deficiencies in different concave parts have common shapes. The main advantage of using convex hulls is the elimination of bad effects from concave parts. It is easy to achieve correspondence between convex hulls with a common shape. We can estimate the transformation matrix using very robust characteristics of convex hulls, so that estimated transformation matrix is also accurate.

2.2 Facets Matching

The characteristics of a facet are obtained from the coordinates of its vertices. The errors in the characteristics of each facet depend on the distribution of the vertices. For a larger variance in the distribution of the vertices, the characteristics of the facet become more accurate. These errors that affect the rotational components of the transformation T have greater influence on the gap in the data sets, in parts far from the facet rather than near the facet. Additionally, larger facets depend on the shape of object itself while smaller facets depend on the method measuring precision values and sampling intervals. Reducing the number of facets also reduces the computing cost. Second, M facets are chosen from each convex hull, where the choice is based on the stability of each facet:

$$S_i = \min_j \frac{p_{ij}}{l_{ij}} \tag{1}$$

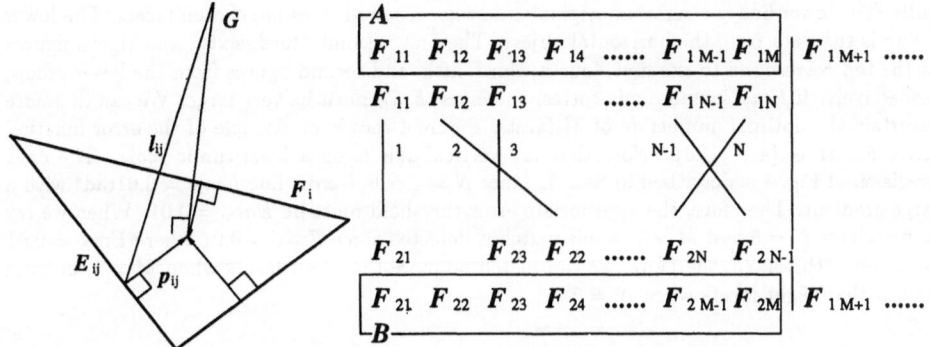

Fig. 1. Definition of stability   Fig. 2. Correspondence of facets

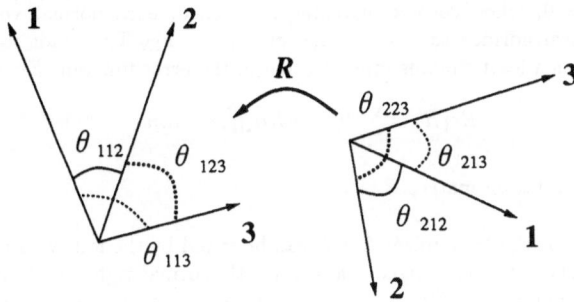

Fig. 3. Facets matching

where l_{ij} is the distance between the center of gravity G of a convex hull (assuming that the inside of each convex hull is homogeneous) and the edge E_{ij} of a facet F_i, and p_{ij} is the distance between the projection of the center of gravity G onto F_i and E_{ij}. The distance p_{ij} is positive when the projection of the center of gravity G is on the inner part of F_i and negative when it is on the outer part (see Fig. 1).

We consider the matching problem of two M facets called A and B. In other words, we construct N combinations of the two facets. In order to simplify the expression of the formulation, we let F_{ij} stand for the facet included in the jth combination (see Fig. 2). The matching problem can be formulated as a least squares minimization of the error function:

$$Em = \sum_{i>j}(\theta_{1ij} - \theta_{2ij})^2 \qquad (2)$$

where θ_{1ij} and θ_{2ij} are the angles between corresponding facets F_{1i}, F_{1j} and F_{2i}, F_{2j}, respectively, and the chosen facets $F_{11}, \ldots, F_{1N}$ correspond to $F_{21}, \ldots, F_{2N}$, respectively (see Fig. 3).

The error function of N corresponding facets that minimizes Em is Em_N. Figure 7 shows an example of the correspondence. The upper group is a series of facets sorted according to their stability from the data measured for the pose in Fig. 6(a). The upper line is a series of convex hulls. The lower line is a series of original data sets. The red faces are chosen facets. The lower group is the data from the horizontal object. The first, second, third, sixth, and eighth figures at the top correspond to the first, fourth, third, fifth, and second figures from the lower group, respectively. If Em_N includes mis-correspondences, Em_N must be very large. We can therefore ascertain the optimal number N of M facets. Figure 4 shows an example of the error function Em_N for $M \in \{4, \ldots, 20\}$. Note that the vertical axis is on a logarithmic scale. The data precision of Fig. 4 is described in Sec. 3. Lines $N = 4, 5, 6, 7$ cross line $Em_N = 0.01 \text{rad}^2$ with a large gradient. Therefore, the appropriate error threshold must be $Em_N = 0.01$. When we try to match for $N = 5$ and $M = 7$, a mis-match is detected since $Em_N > 0.01$ where $Em_N = 0.01$ is the error threshold; therefore, we can match no more than four facets when $M = 7$, or from no less than eight facets when $N = 5$.

2.3   Estimating the Transformation Matrix

First, we assume that the facets $F_{21}, \ldots, F_{2N}$ are transformed to $F_{11}, \ldots, F_{1N}$. In the ideal case, i.e. $Em_N = 0$, when correct matching is reached, each normal vector $n_{21}, \ldots, n_{2N}$ of $F_{21}, \ldots, F_{2N}$ is transformed to $n_{11}, \ldots, n_{1N}$ of $F_{11}, \ldots, F_{1N}$. This leads us to formulate the matching problem as a least squares minimization of the error function $Er(R)$:

$$Er(R) = \sum_i |n_{1i} - Rn_{2i}|^2 \rightarrow min \qquad (3)$$

for the appropriate rotation matrix R.

The rotation matrix R that minimizes $Er(R)$ can be found by the following method (Tsuji and Kanatani 1992). The rotation matrix is a 3×3 orthonormal right-hand system matrix that depends on three components. Given more than two independent vector correspondences, the singular value decomposition $C = Q\Lambda P^t$ of correlation matrix $C = \sum_i n_{1i} n_{2i}^t$ is unique, and the orthonormal solution of the least squares minimization problem can be written with an orthogonal matrix P, Q as

$$R = QP^t. \qquad (4)$$

The normal vector n_{ji} is estimated from the vertices v_{ijk} of facet F_{ji}. Therefore, the error of the normal vector n_{ji} is partially distributed, and the distribution can be regarded as depending on the covarience $V_{ij} = \sum_k v_{ijk} v_{ijk}^t$. Taking the distribution of the error into account, the error function $Er(R)$ is redefined as

$$Er(R) = \sum_i \left(n_{2i}^t R^t V_{1i} R n_{2i} + n_{1i}^t R V_{2i} R^t n_{1i} \right) \rightarrow min. \qquad (5)$$

The new rotation R that is the solution of Eq.(5) can be estimated by perturbation from the R of Eq.(4).

Next, in order to estimate highly accurate translation components, we must use only one component of the center of gravity of the facet that is normal to the corresponding facet of the convex hull.

We make the assumption that points r_{1i} and Rr_{2i} are transformed onto surfaces F_{2i}, and F_{1i}, respectively, where r_{1i} is the center of gravity of facet F_{1i}, and Rr_{2i} is that of facet RF_{2i}.

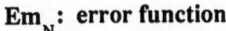

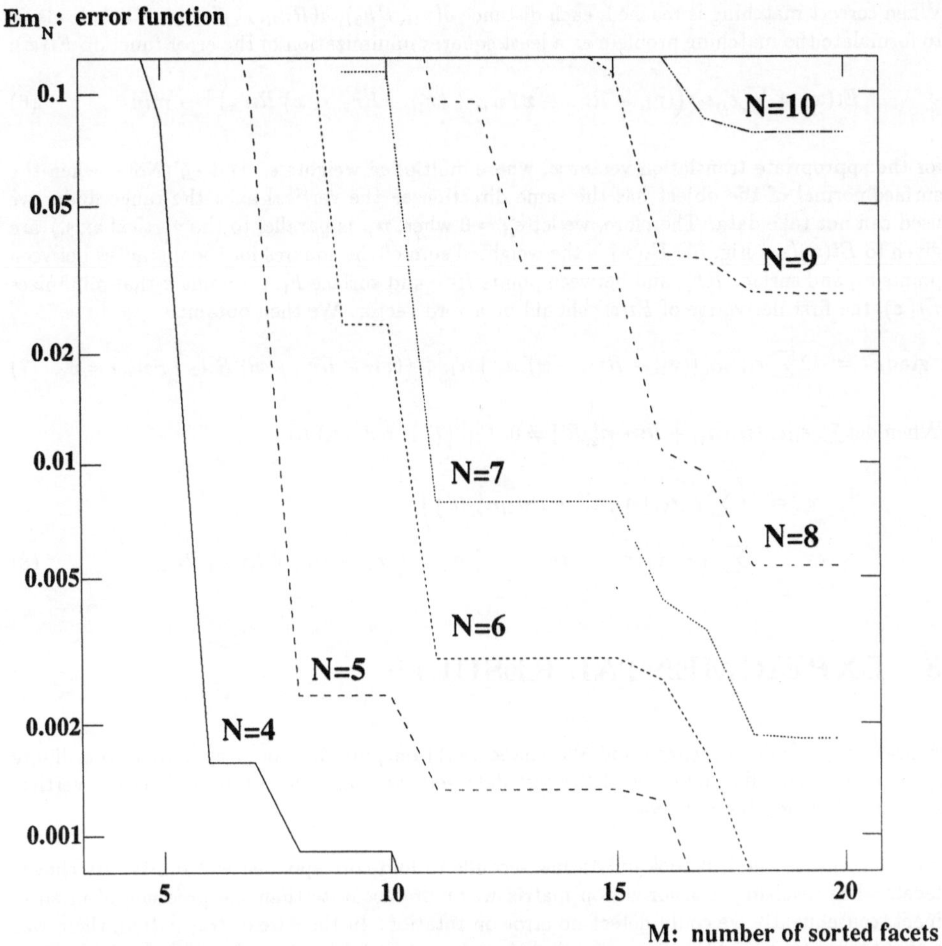

Em_N : error function
0.1
0.05
0.02
0.01
0.005
0.002
0.001
N=10
N=9
N=8
N=7
N=6
N=5
N=4
5
10
15
20
M: number of sorted facets

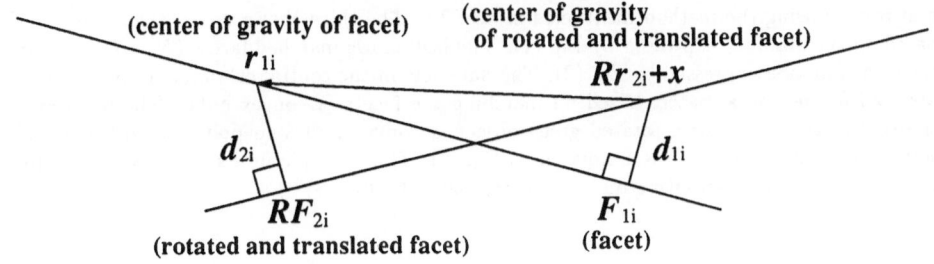

Fig. 4. Error function

(center of gravity of facet)
r 1i
(center of gravity
of rotated and translated facet)
Rr 2i+x
d 2i
d 1i
RF 2i
(rotated and translated facet)
F 1i
(facet)

Fig. 5. Translation

When correct matching is reached, each distançe $d(r_{1i}, RF_2)$, $d(Rr_{2i}, F_1)$ is zero. This leads us to formulate the matching problem as a least squares minimization of the error function $Et(x)$:

$$Et(x) = \sum_i \epsilon_{1i}\epsilon_{2i} \left((r_{1i} - Rr_{2i} - x)^t n_{1i} + (r_{1i} - Rr_{2i} - x)^t Rn_{2i} \right)^2 \rightarrow min \qquad (6)$$

for the appropriate translation vector x, where multiplied weights ϵ_{1i} and ϵ_{2i} (Note: when the surface normal of the object has the same direction as the vertical axis, the range finder we used can not take data. Therefore, we let $\epsilon_{ji} = 0$ when n_{ji} is parallel to the vertical axis.) are given to $Et(x)$(see Fig. 5). $Et(x)$ is the weighted sum of the squares for the distances between points r_{1i} and surface RF_2, and between points Rr_{2i} and surface F_1. At point x that minimizes $Et(x)$, the first derivative of $Et(x)$ should be a zero vector. We then obtain:

$$\mathrm{grad}Et = -2\sum_i \epsilon_{1i}\epsilon_{2i} \left(\left((r_{1i} - Rr_{2i} - x)^t n_{1i}\right) n_{1i} + \left((r_{1i} - Rr_{2i} - x)^t Rn_{2i}\right) Rn_{2i} \right) = 0. \qquad (7)$$

When $\det \sum_i \epsilon_{1i}\epsilon_{2i}(n_{1i}n_{1i}^t + Rn_{2i}n_{2i}^t R^t) \neq 0$, Eq. (7) is reduced to

$$\begin{aligned} x = &\left(\sum_i \epsilon_{1i}\epsilon_{2i} \left(n_{1i}n_{1i}^t + Rn_{2i}n_{2i}^t R^t \right) \right)^{-1} \\ &\sum_i \epsilon_{1i}\epsilon_{2i} \left(\left((r_{1i} - Rr_{2i})^t n_{1i}\right) n_{1i} + \left((r_{1i} - Rr_{2i})^t Rn_{2i}\right) Rn_{2i} \right) \end{aligned} \qquad (8)$$

3   EXPERIMENTAL RESULTS

A laser range finder (Suenaga and Watanabe 1991) outputs data on a cylindrical coordinate system. The sampling intervals of the test data sets we used were 1.6 mm along the vertical axis and $\frac{1}{256}$ along the row axis.

By using this method, it took only a few seconds to find correspondences from twenty chosen facets. The resulting transformation matrix was more accurate than the precision of mesurement, consequently we could detect no error on rotation. In the case of translation, there was a slight error that might have been included in the original data sets. Figure 8 shows two data sets of an object we tested. The red data set is measured for a perpendicular pose which is identical to the pose of the data in Fig. 6(a). The green data set is measured for a horizontal pose which is identical to the pose in Fig. 6(b). In the left column in the first row, each data set is set as it is measured. The second row shows convex hulls reduced from the data sets in the first row by using the method mentioned in Sec. 2.1. The third shows sorted facets ($M = 11$) based on the stability expressed by Eq. (1). The last shows matched facets ($N = 7$) based on the error function expressed by Eq. (2). The data sets in the central column and right column are transformed by a matrix based on matching the facets of convex hulls. The pictures in the central column show a rotated green object, a convex hull, and polygons with red data sets. The rotation matrix was estimated by Eq. (5). The right pictures show translation after rotation, where the translating matrix was estimated by Eq. (8).

4 INTEGRATION OF MULTIPLE IMCOMPLETE RANGE DATA SETS

In order to put the data sets together, it is nessesary to achieve correspondence at the level of the data points. We have already achieved correspondence at the level of the convex hulls. If a polygon of a convex hull has a corresponding polygon in another convex hull, the neighbourhood of the vertices of the polygon must not be deficient in another data set. Consequently, we can always find data points near the vertex of the convex hull if we search for the data point that corresponded to the other convex hull. Thus, we can achieve correspondence between the data points. By reconstructing polygons between the surfaces of the data sets, we can cancel out errors in the data.

Soucy and Laurendeau (1992) proposed a technique to build a non-redundant surface model of an object by using information provided by N registered range views, but they failed to mention why a non-redundant surface model was needed. The data size of a redundant model is at most N times as large as a non-redundant model they built. Such a difference in data size is unimportant only when displaying the shape of a model. In order to get a significantly smaller size of data that can improve the displaying speed, it is essential to use a point reducing technique such as polygonal approximation (Nishino et al. 1989). Figure 6(c) displays the whole data except for the hidden parts.

5 Conclusion

We have proposed a method to integrate multiple range data sets obtained from different view points, which is essential for constructing an accurate and complete surface model. In our method, the matching is achieved between convex hulls; therefore, this step is robust even if the data contains inaccurate concave parts or if the data in concave parts is deficient. Experimental results show that a highly accurate transformation matrix can be recovered using our method.

Acknowledgements

The authors wish to thank Dr. N. Terashima — president of ATR Communication Systems Research Laboratories, and Dr. K. Habara — Exective Vice President of ATR International (Chairman of the Board of ATR Communication Systems Research Laboratories), for their thoughtful advice and encouragement on this research. And the authours also wish to thank their colleagues who voluntarily took part in discussing this study. The authors would also like to thank Dr. Edward Altman for his assistance in reviewing this paper.

References

Champleboux G, Lavallée S, Szeliski R, Brunie L (1992) From accurate range imaging sensor calibration to accurate model-based 3-D object localization. In: *Proc. CVPR'92*. pp 83–89.

Clarkson KL, Shor PW (1989) Applications of random sampling in computational Geometry. *Discrete Comput. Geom.*, II(4):387–421.

Edelsbrunner H, Shi W (1991) An $O(n \log^2 h)$ Time Algorithm for the Three-Dimensional Convex Hull Problem. *SIAM J. Comput.*, 20(2):259–269.

Guibas LJ, Stolfi J (1985) Primitives for the manipulation of general subdivisions and the computation of Boronoi diagrams. *ACM TOG*, 4(2):74–123.

Keefe M, Chettri S (1989) Close-range stereophotogrammetry applied to biological surfaces. In: *Proc. NCGA* Philadelphia, U. S. A.

Kay TL, Kajiya JT (1986) Ray tracing complex scenes. *comput. graph.*, 20(4):269–278.

Nishino H, Akiyama K, Kobayashi Y (1989) Acquisition of 3-Dimensional Object Shape Using Slit-Ray Projection and Reconstruction of Surface Model. *IEICE trans.*, J72-D-II(11):1778–1787 (In Japanese).

Soucy M, Laurendeau D (1992) Surface Modeling from Dynamic Integration of Multiple Range Views. In: *Proc. CVPR'92*, pp 449–452 Champaign, Illinois.

Suenaga Y, Watanabe Y (1991) A Method for the Synchronized Acquisition of Cylindrical Range and Color Data. *IEICE trans.*, E-74(10):3407–3416.

Tsuji H, Kanatani K (1992) Best Estimation of 3-D Rotation and its Applications. Technical Report CV76-14, IPSJ (In Japanese).

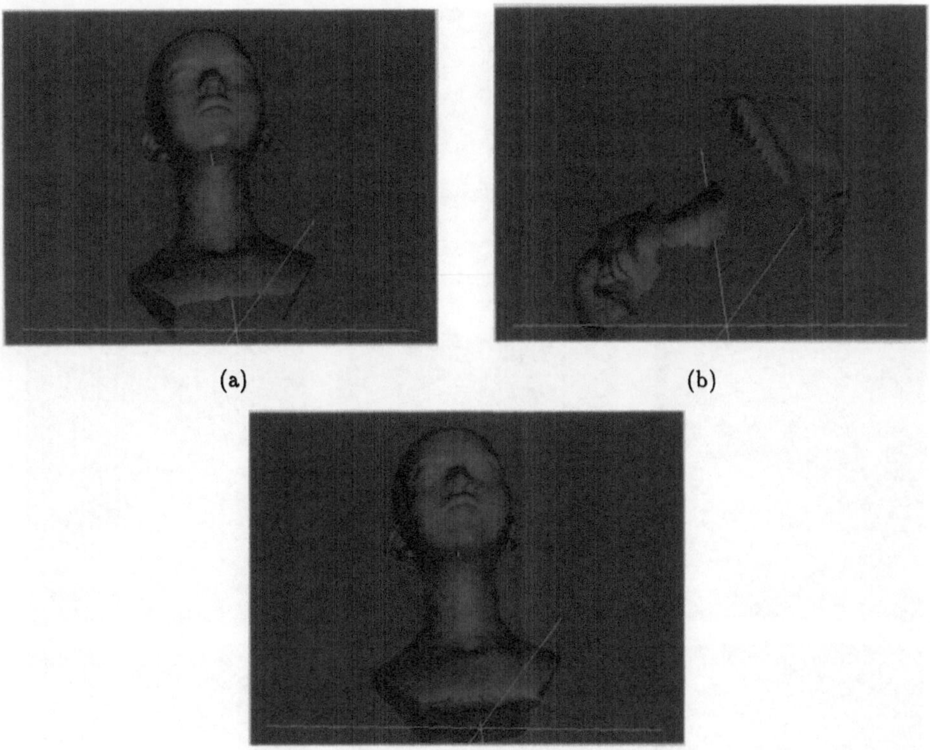

Fig. 6. Range data

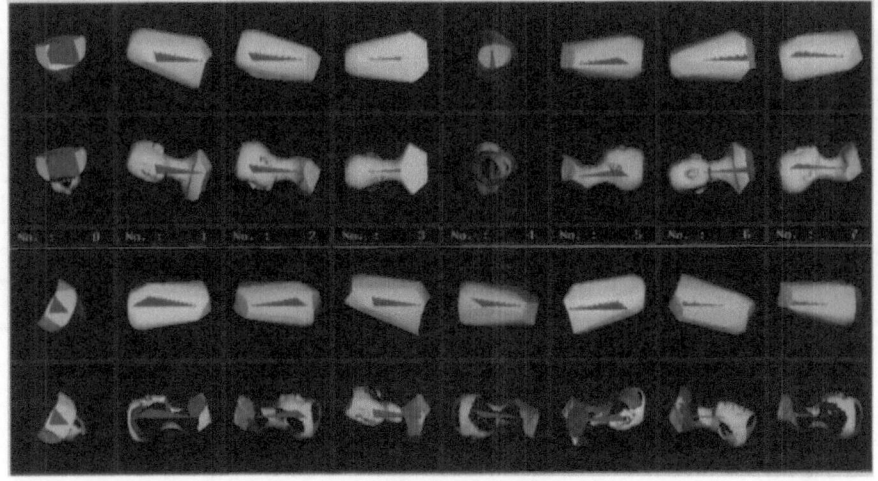

Fig. 7. Sorted facets

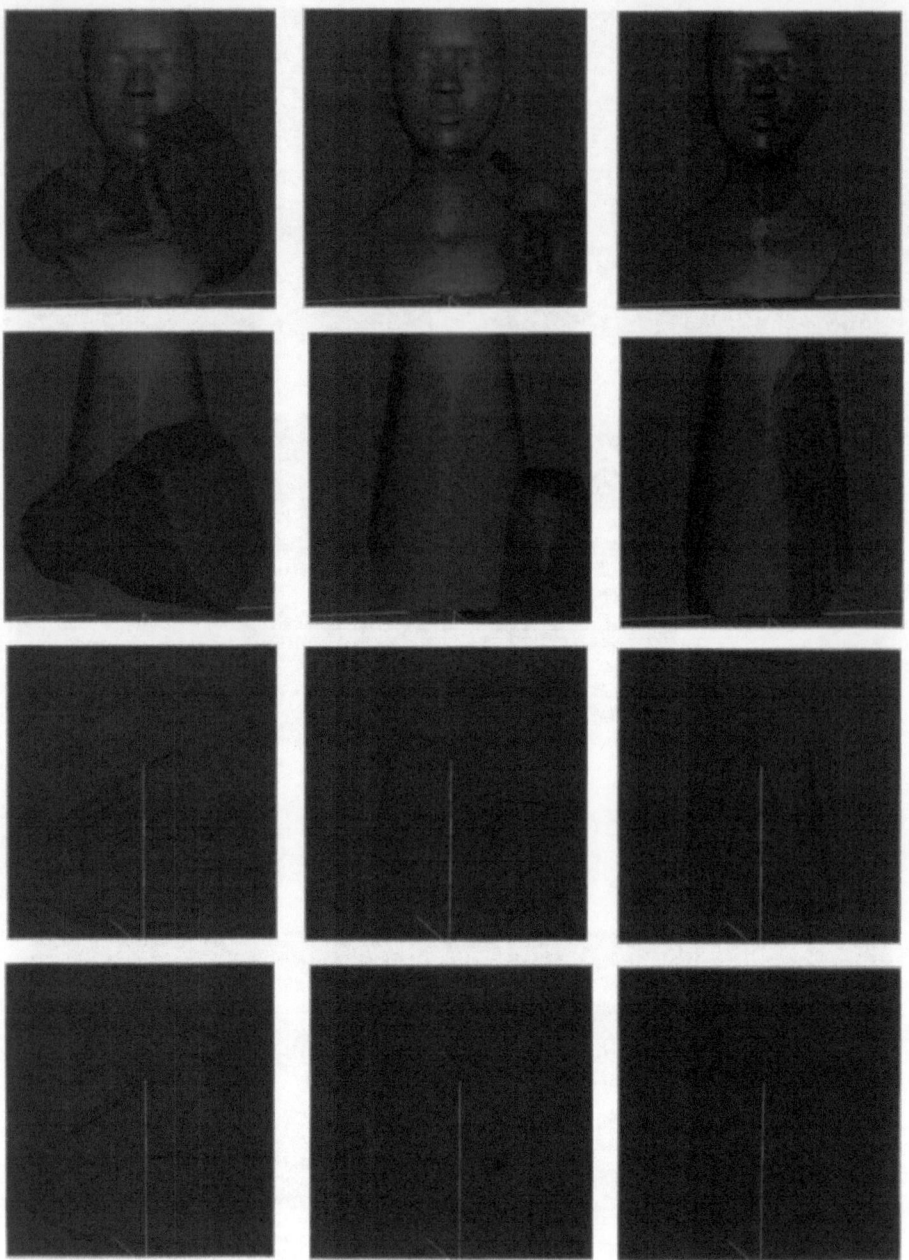

Fig. 8. Localizing

Nobuhiko Wada received the B.E. and M.E. degrees from the University of Osaka Prefecture in 1988 and 1990, respectively. He joined Sumitomo Metal Industry in 1990. In 1991, he became a researcher of ATR Communication Systems Research Laboratories. His research interests include computer vision and visual communication. He is a member of IEICE.

Hiroshi Toriyama received the B.E. degree from Nagoya Institute of Technology in 1981, and the M.E. degree from Nagoya University in 1983. He joined the Communications Research Laboratory, Ministry of Posts and Telecommunications Japan, in 1983. In 1990, he became a researcher of ATR Communication Systems Research Laboratories. His research interests include visual communication, image coding and information theory. He is a member of IEICE, IPSJ and IEEJ.

Hiromi T. Tanaka is a research scientist at the Artificial Intelligence Department of ATR Communication Systems Research Labs, Kyoto, Japan. She is currently engaged in research on 3D curved shape representation, recognition and visualization. She received the B.S. degree in Physics from Ochanomizu Woman University, in 1975, the M.S. degree in Computer Science from the University of Rochester, in 1982, and the Doctor of Engineering degree from Osaka University, Osaka, Japan, in 1988. In 1988 she joined ATR Communication Systems Research Laboratories. Her research interest is in the areas of computer vision, artificial intelligence and 3D visual communication.

Fumio Kishino received the B.E. and M.E. degrees from Nagoya Institute of Technology, Nagoya, Japan, in 1969 and 1971, respectively. In 1971, he joined the Electrical Communication Laboratories, Nippon Telegraph and Telephone Corporation, where he was involved in work on research and development of image processing and visual communications systems. In mid-1989, he joined ATR Communication Systems Research Laboratories, and became the head of the Artificial Intelligence Department. His research interests include image processing, artificial intelligence and communication with realistic sensations. He is a member of IEEE, IEICE and ITEJ.

Address: ATR Communication Systems Research Laboratories. 2-2. Hikaridai, Seika-cho, Soraku-gun. Kyoto. 619-02 Japan.

A New Shape Control and Classification for Cubic Bézier Curves

Shi-Nine Yang and Ming-Liang Huang

ABSTRACT

In this paper, a new shape control method called one-point shape control is proposed for cubic Bézier curves. First, we show that a Bézier curve, with given boundary points and tangent directions, can be uniquely determined by a point called the shape point. Then the advantages of this shape control method are discussed and shape classification with respect to the shape point is also studied. Furthermore, by using this one-point shape control method, we introduce a new offset algorithm for Bézier curves. Empirical tests will be given. It shows that our offset algorithm is not only simple and direct but also effective and efficient.

Keywords: shape control, computer aided design, cubic Bézier spline, offset

1 INTRODUCTION

To design curves and surfaces according to given constraints plays an important role in many science and engineering applications. For example, the graphical description of geological and physical phenomena, the visual representation of experimental or statistical data and the modeling of car bodies, ship hulls, airplane fuselages and etc. Short after the advent of computers, a new discipline called computer aided geometric design – CAGD for short emerged. It is dedicated to the study of designing curves and surfaces. Among various techniques in CAGD, the interpolation is one of the oldest as well as the most useful techniques. Unfortunately, it tends to generate unexpected oscillations (or bumps) that will ruin the shape of curves (or surfaces). It has been found that, in curve design, the piecewise approach by stitching together a succession of curve segments enjoys less number of oscillations and ease of shape control (Bartels, Beatty and Barsky 1987). For example, the interpolation by cubic splines is a typical one (Faux and Pratt 1979). Many methods have been developed to control the shape of interpolating curve segments (Fletcher and McAllister 1986; Harada and Nakamae1982; Harada, Kaneda and Nakamae 1984; Lee and Yang 1989; McLaughlin 1983; Shirman and Séquin 1992). Among them, the notion of shape control through shape parameters is an effective approach for CAGD, since in interactive design, one may modify the curves by varying the shape parameters interactively or in passive plotting, one may preset shape parameters properly to control the fedelity of the interpolation (Fletcher and McAllister 1986; Lee and Yang 1989; Shirman and Séquin 1992).

As possessing some merits for curve design, the Bézier curve is one of the most popular representations in computer aided geometric design (Farin 1988; Faux and Pratt 1979; Lee 1989). In this paper we will confine ourself to the study of shape parameters of cubic Bézier curves. First, the notion of one-point shape control is introduced. It shows that a cubic Bézier curve can be uniquely determined by a point called shape point. Therefore the shape control can be achieved simply by moving the shape point directly with a pick device such as a mouse. Moreover, as the generated Bézier curve will pass through the shape point, the designer can get more intuitive sense visually on how the change of shape parameter – the shape point affects the change of the shape of the curve. Hence, to compare with existing methods, this new control scheme is geometric and it is simpler and more direct. Furthermore, we discuss the shape classification with respect to the shape point. It is known that shape classification will provide a high level shape control in the sense that the intrinsic property of the curve is the major concern, for example, to keep the convex curve from being inflective or having a cusp. To be more precisely, we partition the plane into regions so that each region is associated with a shape type. And the shape type of a curve can be determined by simply checking the whereabout of the shape point. Therefore the shape type of the expecting curve can be well controlled by locating the shape point properly.

In order to demonstrate the capability of our shape control method. We will apply it to the construction of shape preserving interpolation and the approximation of offset curves. For interpolation, we show that most existing shape preserving control schemes can be transformed into the selection of proper shape points. Therefore, the shape preserving interpolation or the visual pleasing interpolation can be realized by adding some extra shape points to the interpolation. For offset curve generation, since the offsetting operator is not closed on polynomials (Tiller and Hanson 1984), most solutions are content with approximated offset curves, preferably in the same function space as the progenitors. In this paper we try to approximate the offset curve of a given cubic Bézier curve by another cubic Bézier curve. Examples and discussions will be given to show that our offset algorithm is simple, direct and easy to be implemented.

The remainder of this paper will be presented in the following order. In Section 2 a new shape control method called one-point shape control is introduced. Besides, the loci of shape points $w.r.t.$ the notions of shape classification are investigated. In Section 3, the application of one point shape control to shape preserving interpolation is discussed. Then based on the control of shape points, a new Bézier offset approximation algorithm is proposed in Section 4. Moreover, examples and empirical tests are given to demonstrate the quality of the proposed algorithms. Finally, the conclusion is presented in Section 5.

2 SHAPE CONTROL AND SHAPE CLASSIFICATION OF BÉZIER CURVES

A cubic Bézier curve is defined by

$$\gamma(u) = (1 - u)^3 \mathbf{r}_0 + 3u(1 - u)^2 \mathbf{r}_1 + 3u^2(1 - u)\mathbf{r}_2 + u^3 \mathbf{r}_3, \tag{1}$$

$0 \leq u \leq 1$, where $\mathbf{r}_0$, $\mathbf{r}_1$, $\mathbf{r}_2$ and $\mathbf{r}_3$ are Bézier points and the polygon formed by $\mathbf{r}_0$, $\mathbf{r}_1$, $\mathbf{r}_2$ and $\mathbf{r}_3$ is called Bézier polygon (Bézier 1972). We refer $\mathbf{r}_1$ and $\mathbf{r}_2$ as interior Bézier points and $\mathbf{r}_0$ and $\mathbf{r}_3$ as boundary Bézier points. From Equation 1, we have the following results.

$$\gamma(0) = \mathbf{r}_0, \quad \gamma(1) = \mathbf{r}_3, \quad \dot{\gamma}(0) = 3(\mathbf{r}_1 - \mathbf{r}_0), \quad \dot{\gamma}(1) = 3(\mathbf{r}_3 - \mathbf{r}_2),$$

where $\dot{\gamma}(u)$ denotes the first derivative of $\gamma(u)$ $w.r.t.$ parameter u. Hence, a Bézier curve passes through its boundary Bézier points. Moreover, vectors $\overrightarrow{\mathbf{r}_0 \mathbf{r}_1}$ and $\overrightarrow{\mathbf{r}_2 \mathbf{r}_3}$ have the same directions as the tangent directions at boundary Bézier points, respectively. The curve is influenced by its interior Bézier points which provide an intuitive means for varying the shape of curve (Faux and Pratt 1979) if the boundary Bézier points are fixed.

Now let us discuss the shape control in the aspect of interpolation. Suppose $\{\mathbf{p}_j | 0 \leq j \leq n\}$ is a set of ordered points. The interpolation problem is to find a set of interior Bézier points $\{\mathbf{r}_1^j, \mathbf{r}_2^j | 0 \leq j \leq n\}$ such that the Bézier spline is a smooth curve passing through the given points. Here, the $j - th$ curve segment is denoted by γ_j. From the above formulation, the boundary Bézier points $\mathbf{r}_0^j$ and $\mathbf{r}_3^j$ are equal to given interpolation points $\mathbf{p}_j$ and $\mathbf{p}_{j+1}$, respectively and therefore they are fixed as far as the interpolation is concerned. In other words, the interpolation requirement implies the C^0 continuity. For smoothness, in this study, we require the interpolating curve to possess at least slope continuity, $i.e.$ G^1 continues (Faux and Pratt 1979). Therefore two adjacent curve segments should have the same tangent direction at the joints $\mathbf{p}_j (1 < j < n)$. As for the choice of tangent directions, several methods have been developed and some good suggestions are given in (Fletcher and McAllister 1986; Shirman and Séquin 1992).

After the tangent directions at boundary Bézier points have been determined, the only shape parameters remain for each curve segment are the magnitudes of tangents, that is velocities, at two boundary Bézier points. Most existing shape control are based on these velocities (Boehm, Farin and Kahmann 1984; Lee and Yang 1989; Piegl 1987; Shirman and Séquin 1992). In the following we will transform these two shape parameters into another parameter domain such that a more simple and direct shape control scheme can be derived.

2.1 One-point Shape Control Method

According to the previous discussions, since an interpolating curve is defined segment by segment, it suffices to study the shape control of a single curve segment. Let $\gamma(u)$ be a cubic Bézier curve with the Bézier control points $\mathbf{r}_i = (x_i, y_i)(i = 0, 1, 2, 3)$. Let $\mathbf{T}_0 = (g_0, h_0)$ and $\mathbf{T}_3 = (g_3, h_3)$ be the unit tangent vectors of γ at $\mathbf{r}_0$ and $\mathbf{r}_3$ respectively. To vary the shape of the curve, one can slide the interior Bézier points $\mathbf{r}_1$ and $\mathbf{r}_2$ along directions of $\mathbf{T}_0$ and $\mathbf{T}_3$, respectively. Because the tangent directions at endpoints are fixed, the following equation holds

$$\mathbf{r}_1 = \frac{\alpha}{3}\mathbf{T}_0 + \mathbf{r}_0, \quad \mathbf{r}_2 = -\frac{\beta}{3}\mathbf{T}_3 + \mathbf{r}_3. \tag{2}$$

Hence, the shape of the curve can be determined by choosing suitable values of α and β, where α and β are known as the shape parameters (Fletcher and McAllister 1986; Foley, Van Dam, Feiner and Hughes 1990; Kochanek and Bartels 1984; Lee and Yang 1989; Shirman and Séquin 1992). From Equation 1 and 2, we have the following.

$$\gamma(u) = (1-u)^2(1+2u)\mathbf{r}_0 + u^2(3-2u)\mathbf{r}_3 + \alpha\ u(1-u)^2\mathbf{T}_0 - \beta\ u^2(1-u)\mathbf{T}_3, \tag{3}$$

that is,

$$x(u) = (1-u)^2(1+2u)x_0 + u^2(3-2u)x_3 + \alpha\ u(1-u)^2 g_0 - \beta\ u^2(1-u)g_3,$$
$$y(u) = (1-u)^2(1+2u)y_0 + u^2(3-2u)y_3 + \alpha\ u(1-u)^2 h_0 - \beta\ u^2(1-u)h_3, \tag{4}$$

where $\gamma(u) = (x(u), y(u))$, $\mathbf{T}_0 = (g_0, h_0)$ and $\mathbf{T}_3 = (g_3, h_3)$.

Let $\Delta = \begin{vmatrix} g_0 & g_3 \\ h_0 & h_3 \end{vmatrix}$, where the notation $| \quad |$ denotes the determinant operator. If $\Delta \neq 0$, that is $\mathbf{T}_0 \nparallel \mathbf{T}_3$, then we have

$$\alpha = \frac{\begin{vmatrix} x(u) - (1-u)^2(1+2u)x_0 - u^2(3-2u)x_3 & g_3 \\ y(u) - (1-u)^2(1+2u)y_0 - u^2(3-2u)y_3 & h_3 \end{vmatrix}}{u(1-u)^2\Delta},$$

$$\beta = \frac{\begin{vmatrix} x(u) - (1-u)^2(1+2u)x_0 - u^2(3-2u)x_3 & g_0 \\ y(u) - (1-u)^2(1+2u)y_0 - u^2(3-2u)y_3 & h_0 \end{vmatrix}}{u^2(1-u)\Delta}, \tag{5}$$

From the above equations, we can find α and β if the point $\mathbf{p} = (x(u), y(u))$ and the value of u are given. That is, if we require γ to pass $\mathbf{p}(x(u_0), y(u_0))$ at $u = u_0$, then γ is uniquely determined. It is obvious that the location of $\mathbf{p}$ will affect the shape of curve, therefore we call the point $\mathbf{p}$ as *the shape point w.r.t.* $u = u_0$. The choice of $u = u_0$ can be arbitrary real in the interval $(0,1)$. But we find that $u_0 = 1/2$ will provide interactive user a better intuition to locate the shape point. Moreover, if $u_0 = 1/2$ then Equation 5 has a simpler form as follows.

$$\alpha = \frac{\begin{vmatrix} 8x_s - 4x_0 - 4x_3 & g_3 \\ 8y_s - 4y_0 - 4y_3 & h_3 \end{vmatrix}}{\Delta}, \quad \beta = \frac{\begin{vmatrix} 8x_s - 4x_0 - 4x_3 & g_0 \\ 8y_s - 4y_0 - 4y_3 & h_0 \end{vmatrix}}{\Delta}, \tag{6}$$

where (x_s, y_s) is the shape point.

From Equation 6, we have established a correspondence between shape points and Bézier curves. Some examples are depicted in Figure 1. In Figure 1(a), the shape point moves upward or downward, the curve will be loosen or tighten accordingly. This effect is called *tension*. It also shows in Figure 1(b), that as the shape point drifts to the right the curve will be biased accordingly. This effect is called *bias*.

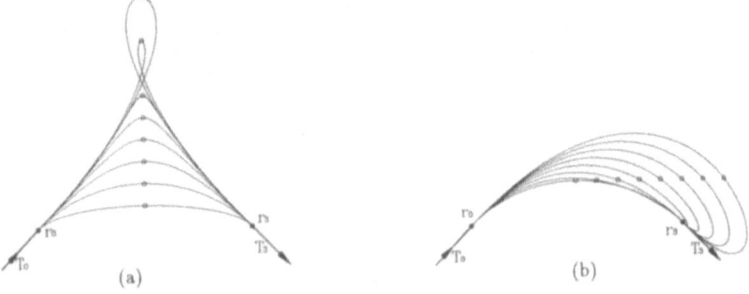

Fig. 1. Shape control by shape points.

The advantage of our shape control scheme is that its shape parameter is a point which is a geometric entity suitable for interactive curve design. In the following sections we will show that our method is good as well in generating interpolation curve passively. Finally we note that, the case $\Delta = 0$, the Bézier curve can not be uniquely determined by a single shape point. Therefore some extra cares must be taken for the degenerate case.

2.2 Shape Classification And Characterization Diagram

In Figure 1(a), we show that if we drag the shape point upward, then beyond certain critical point, the shape of the curve change dramatically – the convex curve becomes concave and a simple curve becomes a loop. It is interesting to know how far the shape point can go without breaking the convexity. More precisely, as far as the shape control is concerned, sometimes we need the ability to fine tune the curve and sometimes we need the ability to prevent the curve from being abnormal. For convenience, we call the former as quantitative control and the latter as the qualitative control. For example, in Figure 1(a), we can perform the quantitative control by move the shape point locally to fine tune the curve but if we want to keep the curve in convex shape then we better know the qualitative changes of the curve. This bring up the study of shape classification (Stone and DeRose 1989; Wang 1981).

For completeness, we introduce the shape classification of Bézier curves in the parametric space $\alpha\beta$–plane, where α and β are defined in Equation 2, a detail study can be found in (Wang 1981). Let $\overleftrightarrow{L}$ be the line with the direction T_0 and passing through the point r_0 and let $\overleftrightarrow{M}$ be the line with the direction T_3 and passing through the point r_3. Since we assume $T_0 \not\parallel T_3$, $\overleftrightarrow{L} \cap \overleftrightarrow{M} \neq \emptyset$. Let s be the intersection point of lines $\overleftrightarrow{L}$ and $\overleftrightarrow{M}$. According to the convex and inflective theorem (Lee and Yang 1989; Wang 1981), we have the following.

Theorem 1: The curve segment γ is a convex one if either $0 \leq \alpha \leq 3l$ and $0 \leq \beta \leq 3m$ or $\alpha \leq 0$ and $\beta \leq 0$, where $l = \|s - r_0\|$ and $m = \|s - r_3\|$. And, the curve segment γ has a single inflection point if either $0 < \alpha < 3l$ and $\beta < 0$ or $\alpha < 0$ and $0 < \beta < 3m$ (see Figure 2(a)).

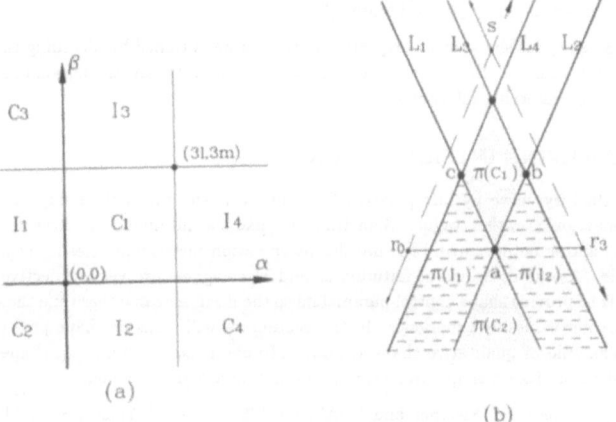

(a)

(b)

Fig. 2. Characterization diagrams of shape parameters (α, β) and shape point $p(x, y)$.

A diagram called the characterization diagram (Stone and DeRose 1989) of Theorem 1 is depicted in Figure 2, where $C_1 \cup C_2$ is the convex region and $I_1 \cup I_2$ is the region having one inflection point (Wang 1981). We note that, from qualitative point of view, there are five shape-types for cubic Bézier curves, namely, convex curve, one inflection point curve, two inflection points curve, loop and cusp (Wang 1981). Since interpolation is our major concern, we prefer that every interpolation curve segment looks nice and simple. Hence we are only interested in regions C_1, C_2, I_1 and I_2. The detail diagram for classifying other shape-types can be found in (Wang 1981).

As we have shown in Equation 6 that there is a correspondence between (α, β) and shape point $p = (x_s, y_s)$. In the following, we will establish an affine transformation such that the characterization diagram in (α, β)

plane is mapped to (x, y) plane to form the characterization diagram of shape point.

Let shape point $\mathbf{p} = (x_s, y_s) = \gamma(1/2)$. Equation 3 can be rewritten as follows.

$$\mathbf{p} = \frac{1}{2}(\mathbf{r}_0 + \mathbf{r}_3) + \frac{1}{8}\alpha\mathbf{T}_0 - \frac{1}{8}\beta\mathbf{T}_3, \tag{7}$$

which has the matrix form as

$$[x_s, y_s] = \frac{1}{8}[\alpha, \beta]\begin{bmatrix} g_0 & h_0 \\ -g_3 & -h_3 \end{bmatrix} + \frac{1}{2}[\mathbf{r}_0 + \mathbf{r}_3] = \pi(\alpha, \beta), \tag{8}$$

where $\mathbf{T}_0 = (g_0, h_0)$ and $\mathbf{T}_3 = (g_3, h_3)$ are two unit tangent vectors of γ at points $\mathbf{r}_0$ and $\mathbf{r}_3$ respectively. Since π can be regarded as a linear transformation plus a translation, it is an affine transformation from (α, β) plane to (x, y) plane.

Under the affine transformation π, lines $\alpha = 0$, $\beta = 0$, $\alpha = 3l$ and $\beta = 3m$ in Figure 2(a) can be transformed easily into lines $\mathbf{L}_1$, $\mathbf{L}_2$, $\mathbf{L}_3$ and $\mathbf{L}_4$ in Figure 2(b) respectively. The equations of these lines are given in the following:

$$L_1 : \vec{\mathbf{P}} = \vec{\mathbf{a}} - \frac{1}{8}t\mathbf{T}_3, \quad L_2 : \vec{\mathbf{P}} = \vec{\mathbf{a}} + \frac{1}{8}t\mathbf{T}_0, \quad L_3 : \vec{\mathbf{P}} = \vec{\mathbf{b}} - \frac{1}{8}t\mathbf{T}_3, \quad L_4 : \vec{\mathbf{P}} = \vec{\mathbf{c}} + \frac{1}{8}t\mathbf{T}_0, \tag{9}$$

where

$$\mathbf{a} = \frac{1}{2}(\mathbf{r}_0 + \mathbf{r}_3), \quad \mathbf{b} = \frac{1}{8}(\mathbf{r}_0 + 3\mathbf{s} + 4\mathbf{r}_3), \quad \mathbf{c} = \frac{1}{8}(4\mathbf{r}_0 + 3\mathbf{s} + \mathbf{r}_3) \tag{10}$$

and t is a parameter.

According to (9), the (x, y) plane is partitioned into regions by these lines. Since (8) is an affine transformation, the correspondence between regions in (α, β) plane and (x, y) plane becomes obvious (see Figure 2). Hence we have the following theorem.

Theorem 2: The curve segment γ is convex if $\mathbf{p} \in \pi(\mathbf{C}_1) \cup \pi(\mathbf{C}_2)$ and the curve segment γ has a single inflection point if $\mathbf{p} \in \pi(\mathbf{I}_1) \cup \pi(\mathbf{I}_2)$ (see Figure 2(b)).

From the above theorems, the shape of the expecting curve can be obtained by identifing the region where the shape point has been located. In the following section, we will illustrate how the notion of shape classification is applied to the shape preserving interpolation.

3   SHAPE PRESERVING INTERPOLATION

To generate a satisfactory curve by interpolation has long been an aim in the study of curve design. But the notion of satisfaction is rather vague. Sometimes we like the interpolation curve to be faithful to the interpolation points and sometimes we prefer that the interpolation curve looks pleasing even it has an irregular interpolation points. As the measures of faithfulness and pleasingness are very subjective, one way to cope with this problem is to provide shape control parameters so the designer can either tune the curve interactively or preset the parameter values by experience. In this section we will focus on shape preserving interpolation and use it as an example of qualitative shape control. Moreover, some interesting shape parameter values which are sufficient to produce a shape preserving interpolation are given explicitly.

The notion of shape preserving (Fletcher and McAllister 1986; Lee and Yang 1989) addresses a high level control of the shape of the interpolation curve. It requires that the turning behavior of the interpolation curve should be in accord with the turning behavior of the polyline obtained by the linear interpolation. Intuitively, a convex (concave) curve segment has its tangent vectors always turn to right (left) and the turning behavior changes at the inflection point. It is known that the turning behavior can be characterized by the curve's intrinsic property (Faux and Pratt 1979). The main concern of shape preserving interpolation is to control the number of inflection points of the interpolation curve to avoid the extraneous oscillations and to prevent the curve from being singular. So it is not the metter of quantitative changes but the qualitative change of the curve.

In (Lee and Yang 1989), a necessary and sufficient condition for shape preserving interpolation with respect to the parameters α and β has been proposed and some parameter values have been suggested to ensure the shape preserving interpolation. We will compute the corresponding shape points for the suggested value in the following.

Let r_0, r_1, r_2 and r_3 be the Bézier points of γ_j and s be the intersection of two lines which contain the vectors $r_1 - r_0$ and $r_3 - r_2$ respectively. Then we have $r_1 - r_0 = t_1(s - r_0)$ and $r_3 - r_2 = t_2(r_3 - s)$. It is obvious that t_1 and t_2 are shape parameters such that $0 \le t_1, t_2 \le 1$. Intuitively, we can increase the tension factor of the shape parameter to avoid the extraneous inflection points. (Fletcher and McAllister 1986) and (Lee and Yang 1989) suggested that $t_1 = t_2 = 1/2$ is a good starting value. To find the corresponding shape point, let $p = (x(1/2), y(1/2))$, then

$$p = \frac{1}{8}(r_0 + 3r_1 + 3r_2 + r_3) = \frac{1}{8}\{r_0 + 3[r_0 + t_1(s - r_0)] + 3[r_3 - t_2(r_3 - s)] + r_3\} = a + \frac{3}{8}(s - a), \quad (11)$$

where $a = (r_0 + r_3)/2$, and $t_1 = t_2 = 1/2$.

Hence for each curve segment if we choose p according to (11), the generated Bézier spline will be shape preserving. In the next section, we will apply the notion of one-point shape control to the construction of offset curves.

4 OFFSETTING BÉZIER CURVES

Offset curve generation is an important application in computer aided design and computer aided manufacturing systems. Recently many research efforts have been devoted to the study of offset construction algorithms (Coquillart 1987; Hoschek 1988; Hoschek and Wissel 1988; Klass 1983; Tiller and Hanson 1984). As the offsetting operator is not closed on function spaces, most existing method are content with approximated curves which preferably belong to the same function space as the progenitors. In this section we will introduce a new offset curve algorithm based on our one-point shape control method. The algorithm was tested on many examples which show that although our algorithm is simple, it perform quit well.

Let $\gamma(u)$ be the given curve. Then the offset curve $\gamma_d(u)$ of $\gamma(u)$ (with offset d) is defined as follows.

$$\gamma_d(u) = \gamma(u) + N(u) \cdot d, \quad (12)$$

where $N(u)$ is the unit normal vector of $\gamma(u)$. For opposite side offset curve, we may choose the offset $(-d)$ in Equation 12. In this paper we assume $\Gamma(u)$ is a cubic Bézier spline. The approximation is to find an approximate offset curve which is also a cubic Bézier spline. First let us consider an arbitrary curve segment $\gamma(u)$ of $\Gamma(u)$. Then by assumption, $\gamma(u)$ is a cubic Bézier curve. Let $r_i = (x_i, y_i)(i = 0, 1, 2, 3)$ be the Bézier control points of $\gamma(u)$ and $T_0 = (g_0, h_0)$ and $T_3 = (g_3, h_3)$ be the unit tangent of γ at r_0 and r_3 respectively. Suppose that the approximated offset curve $\gamma^o(u)$ is another cubic Bézier curve with control points $\bar{r}_i(i = 0, 1, 2, 3)$.

The boundary points of $\gamma^o(u)$ can be determined by

$$\bar{r}_0 = \gamma^o(0) = \gamma(0) + dN(0) = r_0 + dN(0),$$
$$\bar{r}_3 = \gamma^o(1) = \gamma(1) + dN(1) = r_3 + dN(1).$$

Moreover, $\bar{r}_1 = \bar{r}_0 + \alpha T_0$, $\bar{r}_2 = \bar{r}_3 + \beta T_3$, where α, β are parameters introduced in Section 2.

The quality of the approximation is determined by the choice of α and β. In (Hoschek 1988), a least square method was introduced to find proper values of α and β such that the approximation error $w.r.t.$ certain measure can be minimized. In this paper, we introduce a more simple and direct method to determined γ^o by giving a proper shape point which is known on the true offset curve. Note that, like most existing offset algorithm (Coquillart 1987; Hoschek 1988; Hoschek and Wissel 1988; Klass 1983), if the measure of the approximation is not satisfactory, we subdivide the given curve and apply the same algorithm recursively to new subcurves.

4.1 New Offsetting Algorithm

Given a cubic Bézier curve γ with Bézier points $r_i = (x_i, y_i)$, $0 \le i \le 3$, and an offset distance d, the offset problem is to find the corresponding offset cubic Bézier curve γ^o with Bézier points $\bar{r}_0, \bar{r}_1, \bar{r}_0$ and $\bar{r}_3$ which satisfies

$$\bar{r}_0 = r_0 + dN_0, \quad \bar{r}_3 = r_3 + dN_3, \quad \bar{r}_1 = \frac{\bar{\alpha}}{3}T_0 + \bar{r}_0, \quad \bar{r}_2 = -\frac{\bar{\beta}}{3}T_3 + \bar{r}_3, \quad (13)$$

where, $\mathbf{N_0} = ((y_0 - y_1), (x_1 - x_0))/\|\mathbf{r_1} - \mathbf{r_0}\|$ and $\mathbf{N_3} = ((y_2 - y_3), (x_3 - x_2))/\|\mathbf{r_3} - \mathbf{r_2}\|$. Moreover α and β are shape parameters.

From Equation 13, the Bézier points $\bar{\mathbf{r}}_0$ and $\bar{\mathbf{r}}_3$ are easy to be computed. But, the computation of the Bézier points $\bar{\mathbf{r}}_1$ and $\bar{\mathbf{r}}_2$ requires careful thought. The main problem to compute offset is to determine $\bar{\alpha}$ and $\bar{\beta}$ of the offset γ^o with boundary Bézier points $\bar{\mathbf{r}}_0$ and $\bar{\mathbf{r}}_3$. Moreover, the tangent directions at $\bar{\mathbf{r}}_0$ and $\bar{\mathbf{r}}_3$ are given accord with the tangent directions at points $\mathbf{r_0}$ and $\mathbf{r_3}$ respectively.

In what follows, we will give a method that takes the above offset problem as a special case of shape control problem. As discussed in Section 2, the Bézier curve can be determined by its shape point. Therefore to choose a better approximate curve is equivalent to choose its corresponding shape point. So the basic notion of our algorithm is to compute the shape point $\gamma(1/2)$ of the curve γ by using the midpoint subdivision algorithm (Lane and Riesenfeld 1980). Then forces the shape point of γ^o to be

$$\gamma^o(\tfrac{1}{2}) = \begin{cases} \gamma(\tfrac{1}{2}) + d\mathbf{N}_m, & \text{if } \Delta \neq 0, \\ \gamma(\tfrac{1}{2}) + d\mathbf{N}_0, & \text{otherwise,} \end{cases} \tag{14}$$

where $\mathbf{N}_m$ is an unit normal vector of curve γ at point $\gamma(1/2)$.

From the one-point shape control method, the interior Bézier points $\bar{\mathbf{r}}_1$ and $\bar{\mathbf{r}}_2$ can be found by Equation 13. From the above results, the new offset approximation algorithm can be formulated as follows.

Algorithm: Offset;
Input: A parent cubic Bézier curve γ and an offset distance d;
Output: Offset curve γ^o;
Step 1: Find $\bar{\mathbf{r}}_0$, $\bar{\mathbf{r}}_3$ and $\gamma^o(1/2)$ which are discussed in Equation 13 and Equation 14;
Step 2: Calculate the values of shape parameter $\bar{\alpha}$ and $\bar{\beta}$ according to Equation 6 and Equation 13;
Step 3: Compute Bézier interior points $\bar{\mathbf{r}}_1$ and $\bar{\mathbf{r}}_2$ of γ^o and generate offset curve segment γ^o;
Step 4: Check the maximum relative deviation ϵ of γ^o from γ using the following substeps:
    Step 4-1: Select a number k of points $\mathbf{p}_i$, for example $k = 10$;
    Step 4-2: For $i = 1$ to k do the following substeps;
        Step 4-2-1: Compute $\mathbf{p}_i = \gamma(t_i)$ where $t_i = i/k$;
        Step 4-2-2: Project $\mathbf{p}_i$ onto γ^o along the normal direction of γ at $\gamma(t_i)$, denote the projection by $\mathbf{p}_i^o$;
        Step 4-2-3: Compute $\epsilon_i = |\|\mathbf{p}_i - \mathbf{p}_i^o\| - d|/d$;
Step 5: Let $\epsilon = \max\{\epsilon_i | i = 1, \ldots, k\}$;
Step 6: If ϵ is greater than or equal to the precribed tolerance, using the midpoint subdivision algorithm split
    γ into two subcurves γ_1 and γ_2 and apply the above process to each subcurves.
End of offset algorithm.

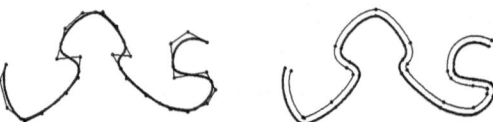

Fig. 3. Offsetting of open Bézier splines.

Figure 3 is an example of our algorithm which offsets one Bézier spline. We note that the discussion of the loop problem caused by the interference of piecewise Bézier offset curve segments is beyond the scope of this paper we will address it elsewhere (Huang and Yang 1992).

4.2 Discussion And Examples

According to our algorithm, the relative error of the approximation is bounded by $\max\{|\|\gamma^o(u) - \gamma(u)\| - d|/d\}$. Since

$$\frac{\gamma^o(u) - \gamma(u)}{d} = (1-u)^2(1+2u)\mathbf{N_0} + u^2(3-2u)\mathbf{N_3} + u(1-u)^2 l_0 \mathbf{T_0} + u^2(u-1) l_3 \mathbf{T_3}, \tag{15}$$

Table 1: Experiment for data set A70 with tolerance 0.001, offset distance 10 and 10 check points. S: number of subdivisions. Time: CPU time (second).

Data	New		Klass		Hosch10		Hosch20		Hosch40		Hosch80	
	S	Time	S	Time	S	Time	S	Time	S	Time	S	Time
a	6	0.66	6	1.26	6	8.24	6	14.06	6	25.70	6	49.05
b	2	0.28	4	0.60	2	2.63	2	3.73	2	6.10	2	10.71
c	3	0.33	4	0.61	3	3.46	3	5.77	3	10.49	3	19.77
d	2	0.22	3	0.38	2	2.48	2	3.68	2	5.99	2	10.66
e	3	0.33	3	0.93	3	3.79	3	6.15	3	10.76	3	20.05
f	4	0.55	4	0.60	6	7.64	4	10.93	4	17.96	4	31.91
g	1	0.05	4	0.61	1	0.11	1	0.16	1	0.11	1	0.16

Table 2: Experiment for data set A15 with tolerance 0.001, offset distance 10 and 10 check points. S: number of subdivisions. Time: CPU time (second).

Data	New		Klass		Hosch10		Hosch20		Hosch40		Hosch80	
	S	Time	S	Time	S	Time	S	Time	S	Time	S	Time
a	5	0.55	5	1.10	9	10.43	8	18.29	5	26.36	5	44.98
b	4	0.49	4	0.66	6	6.70	6	12.47	2	11.87	2	16.54
c	2	0.22	6	1.43	5	5.77	3	9.11	2	9.88	2	14.50
d	1	0.05	2	0.27	3	3.57	1	1.27	1	1.27	1	1.31
e	1	0.06	1	0.11	1	0.60	1	0.60	1	0.60	1	0.61
f	3	0.22	3	0.55	4	4.84	3	6.87	3	11.54	3	20.87
g	1	0.06	1	0.11	1	0.11	1	0.16	1	0.16	1	0.16

where

$$l_0 = 4\frac{2N_m \cdot N_3 - N_0 \cdot N_3 - 1}{T_0 \cdot N_3}, \quad l_3 = 4\frac{2N_m \cdot N_0 - N_0 \cdot N_3 - 1}{T_0 \cdot N_3}, \tag{16}$$

we know that Equation 15 is a Hermite curve with two end points N_0 and N_3 and two tangent vectors l_0T_0 and l_3T_3 (Faux and Pratt 1979). Moreover, two points N_0 and N_3 lie at unit circle and the tangent vectors l_0T_0 and l_3T_3 are tangent vectors w.r.t. the unit circle. Hence if the variation of the curvature on the curve segment is very small, then the Hermite curve is very close to the unit circle, that is, the relative error can be very small. We will not go into the detail study of the convergence of our algorithm in this paper. However, we have implemented our algorithm together with Klass's algorithm (Klass 1983) and Hoschek's algorithm (Hoschek 1988) on IBM compatible PC, with Intel 80386-class CPU and a large number of data set have been tested. We compared their computing time and the number of curve sections caused by the subdivion. According to our experiment, although our algorithm is much more simple, it produces good results for all testing data. In some cases, other methods produce better results in terms of the sections number, the new method is generally very close to those 'best' results. For brief, we only list some of them in Table 1 and 2, where H10, H20, H40 and H80 are stopping criteria of Hoschek's algorithm w.r.t. 10 steps, 20 steps, 40 steps and 80 steps of iterations respectively. Figure 4 and 5 show the corresponding curves.

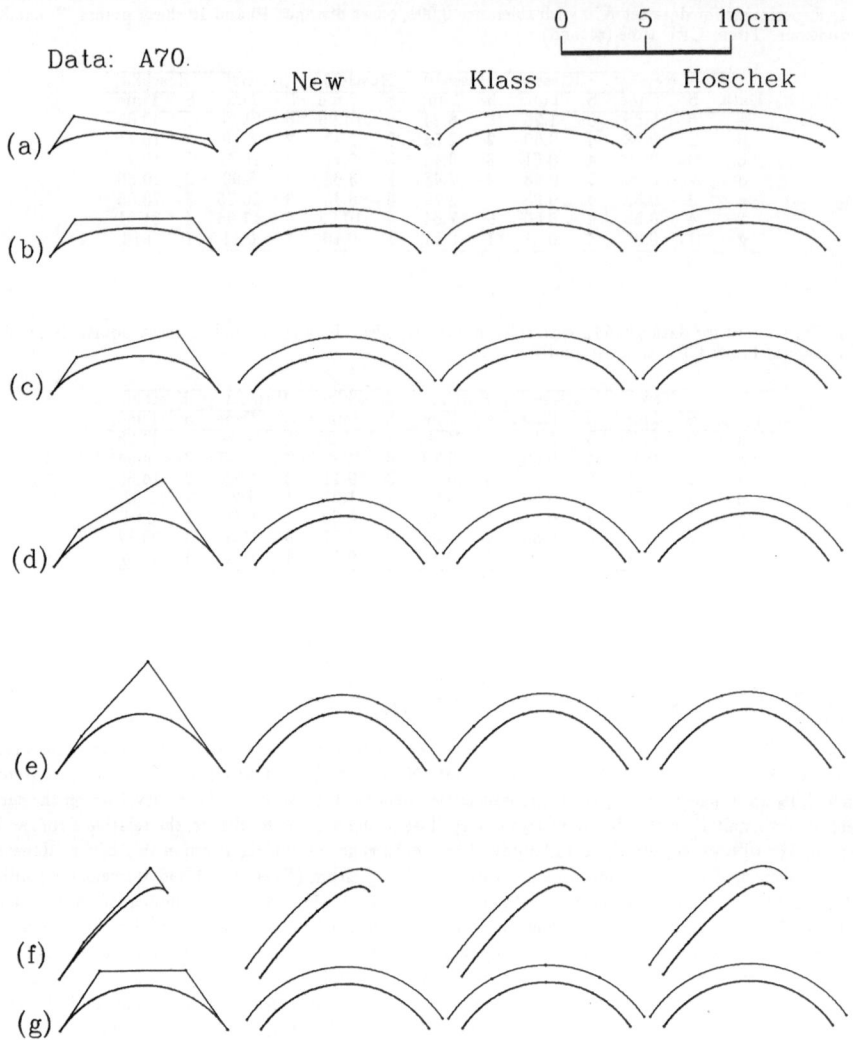

Fig. 4. Figures for data set A70.

213

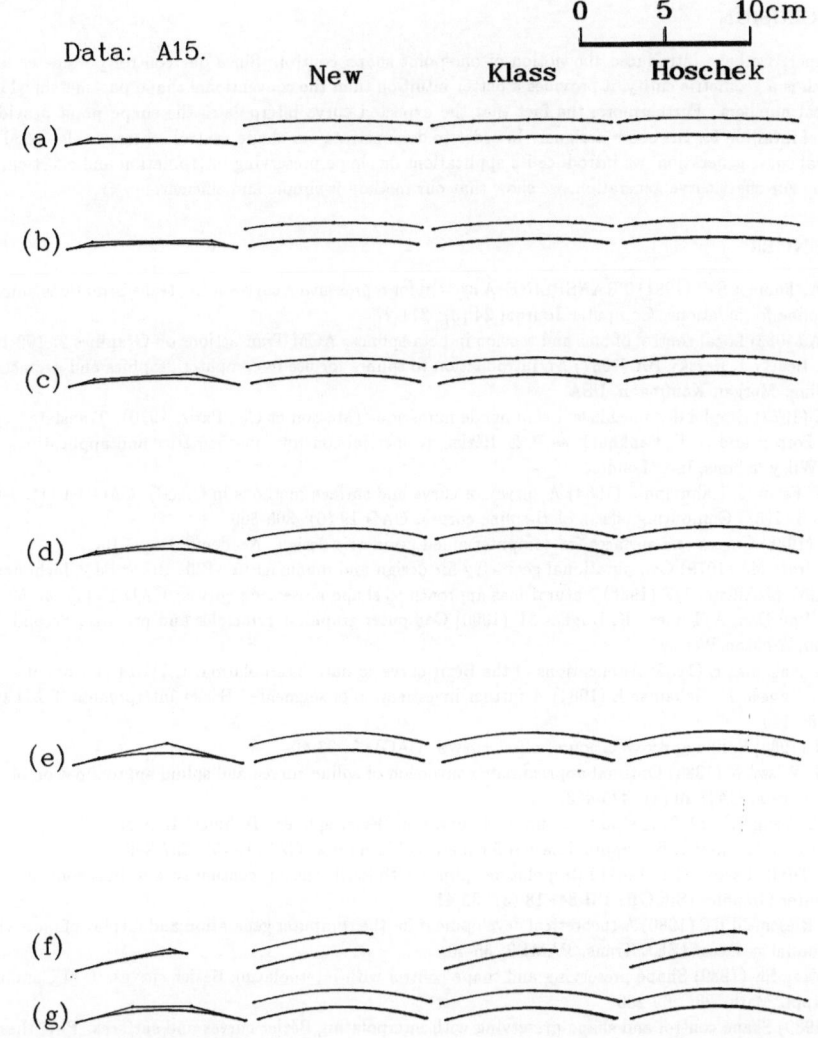

Fig. 5. Figures for data set A15.

5 CONCLUSION

In this paper, we have introduced the notion of one-point shape control. Since our control parameter is a point which is a geometric entity, it provides a better intuition than the conventional shape parameters which are two real numbers. Furthermore, the fact that the expected curve interpolates the shape point provides extra visual intuition for the curve designer. In order to demonstrate our shape control scheme is also good in automatical curve generation, we introduce its applications on shape preserving interpolation and offset curve generation. For offset curve generation, we show that our method is simple and efficient.

REFERENCES

Barsky BA, Thomas SW (1981) TRANSPLINE–A system for representing curves using transformations among four spline formulations. Computer Journal 24 (3): 271-277

Barsky BA (1983) Local control of bias and tension in beta-splines. ACM Transactions on Graphics 2: 109-134

Bartels R, Beatty J, Barsky BA (1987) An introduction to splines for use in computer graphics and geometric modeling. Morgan Kaufmann, USA

Bézier PE (1972) Emploi des machines a commande numérique (Masson et Cie, Paris, 1970). Translated by D. R. Forrest and A. F. Pankhurst as P. E. Bézier, Numerical control – mathematics and applications. John Wiley & Sons, Inc., London

Boehm W, Farin G, Kahmann J (1984) A survey of curve and surface methods in CAGD. CAGD 1 (1): 1-60

Coquillart S (1987) Computing offsets of B-spline curves. CAD 19 (6): 305-309

Farin GE (1988) Curces and surfaces for computer aided geometric design. Academic Press, Inc.

Faux ID, Pratt MJ (1979) Computational geometry for design and manufacture. Ellis Horwood, Chichester

Fletcher GY, McAllister DF (1986) Natural bias approach to shape preserving curves. CAD 18 (1): 48-52

Foley JD, Van Dam A, Feiner SK, Hughes JF (1990) Computer graphics: principles and practice. Second Edition, Addison-Wesley

Harada K, Nakamae E (1982) Applications of the Bézir curve to data interpolation. CAD 14 (1): 55-59

Harada K, Kaneda K, Nakamae E (1984) A further investigation of segmented Bézier interpolants. CAD 16 (4): 186-190

Hoschek J (1988) Spline approximation of offset curves. CAGD 5: 33-40

Hoschek J, Wissel N (1988) Optimal approximate conversion of spline curves and spline approximation of offset curves. CAD 20 (8): 475-483

Huang ML, Yang SN (1992) A study on offsets of curves on Bézier splines. Technical Report

Klass R (1983) An offset spline approximation for plane cubic splines. CAD 15 (5): 297-299

Kochanek DHU, Bartels RH (1984) Interpolating splines with local tension, continuity, and bias control. Computer Graphics (SIGGRAPH'84) 18 (3): 33-41

Lane JM, Riesenfeld RF (1980) A theoretical development for the computer generation and display of piecewise polynomial surfaces. IEEE Trans. PAMI 2: 35-46

Lee JH, Yang SN (1989) Shape preserving and shape control with interpolating Bézier curves. J. of Comput. and Appl. Math. 28: 269-280

Lee JH (1989) Shape control and shape preserving with interpolating Bézier curves and surfaces. PhD thesis, National Tsing Hua Unversity, Taiwan, R.O.C.

McLaughlin HW (1983) Shape-preserving planar interpolation: an algorithm. IEEE computer graphics & Applications: 58-67

Piegl L (1987) Interactive data interpolation by rational Bézier curves. IEEE computer graphics & Applications: 45-58

Shirman LA, Séquin CH (1992) Procedural interpolation with geometrically continuous cubic splines. CAD 24 (5): 267-277

Spiegel MR (1968) Mathematical handbook of formulas and tables. McGraw-Hill Book Company

Stone MC, DeRose TD (1989) A geometric characterization of parametric cubic curves. ACM Transactions on Graphics 8 (3): 147-163

Tiller W, Hanson EG (1984) Offsets of two-dimensional profiles. IEEE computer graphics & Applications: 36-46

Wang CY (1981) Shape classification for the parametric cubic curve and parametric B-spline cubic curve. CAD 13 (4): 199-206

Shi-Nine Yang received the B.S. degree from National Normal University Taiwan in 1967 and the PH.D. degree from SUNY at Buffulo, Buffulo, N.Y. in 1976. During 1976 – 1985 he joined the faculty of Chung Yuan University, Chung-Li, Taiwan. From 1978 – 1984 he was the chairman of the Department of Information Engineering, Chung Yuan University. Currently, he is a professor in the Department of Computer Science, National Tsing Hua University, Hsin-Chu, Taiwan. His research interests include computer graphics, computer aided design and computational geometry. Dr. Yang is a member of the Computer Society of the Republic of China, the Association for Computing Machinery and the IEEE Computer Society.

Ming-Liang Huang received the B.S. degree from Fu Jen Catholic University, Taipei, Taiwan in 1982 and the M.S. degree from National Chung Hsing University, Taichung, Taiwan in 1986. Currently, he is a PH.D. candidate in the Institute of Computer Science, National Tsing Hua University and also a research associate in Department of Computer Science & Engineering, Tatung Institute of Technology, Taipei, Taiwan. His research interests include computer graphics, CAD/CAM and computational geometry.

MAILING ADDRESS: Department of Computer Science, National Tsing Hua University, Hsin-Chu, Taiwan, 30043, R.O.C.

Local and Global Control of Cao En Surfaces

Geoff Wyvill and Dean McRobie

Abstract

A Cao En surface is a closed, parametric surface of arbitrary complexity made in a single piece rather than built from patches. The surface is controlled by manipulating a set of key points that define blending functions, and a set of control points that are blended to form the final shape.

By restricting the effect of each key point to a local region of the parametric space, we gain local control and enable the surface to be computed much more quickly.

An interactive sculpture program based on this principle allows the operator to create and manipulate complicated surfaces directly.

Keywords: geometric modelling, parametric surfaces, direct manipulation, local control.

1 Introduction

Our interest is in the creation and manipulation of surfaces to represent complicated objects like human or animal bodies, or stylised cartoon characters. In particular, we are trying to simplify the task of designing such shapes in 3D.

There is, of course, a considerable literature on parametric surfaces for making free form shapes and a wealth of properties proven for the established methods. Bézier patches have an easily determined convex hull; NURBS can represent cylinders and spheres accurately [Piegl 1991]. In engineering design, there are usually tight constraints on the shape of critical components. A bearing has to be accurately circular or it will not work. A marine screw may look like a free form design but it has to be shaped specially, to do its job. For our purposes, this level of accuracy is not an issue so we have a little more freedom to use a more intuitive approach.

But this does not mean that 'natural' modelling is simpler than engineering. The human ear is a very complicated shape compared with the thigh. We often need to represent a single surface over which the complexity can change widely. We would like to accommodate these changes by adding a minimal number of extra control points.

Hierarchical B-Splines [Forsey 1988] provide an excellent method of variable local control, but at the expense of creating a fairly large number of control points. We would like, where appropriate, to be able to add just one additional point to create a new feature.

The alternative of using blended implicit surfaces has also been explored. See Blinn [1982], Nishimura [1985], Wyvill [1986] and others. Our experience is that implicit surfaces are also rather difficult to work with. Either you use a very large number of control points, or you must choose and place overlapping primitives with great skill in a most non-intuitive way.

We have chosen to use a rational Cao En surface for our experiments. This surface has the advantage that it does not use patches but allows the user to create a complicated shape in a single piece. This avoids the complications of matching boundaries and tangents and it uses a single parametric coordinate system suitable for texture mapping.

2 Definition of the rational Cao En surface

The Cao En surface was described by Wyvill, Cao En and Trotman [1992], but that paper has not yet appeared in English. The following simplified description is given so that this paper can stand alone.

Let $\mathbf{u}$ be a unit vector that represents a point on the surface of a unit sphere.

Let $\mathbf{w}_i$, $1 \leq i \leq n$ be a unit vector that represents one of n *key points*. With each $\mathbf{w}_i$ is associated a blending function F_i.

Let $\mathbf{p}_i$, $1 \leq i \leq n$ be a vector that represents one of n *control points*.

The point $\mathbf{v}$, given by

$$\mathbf{v} = S(\mathbf{u}) = \frac{\sum_{i=1}^{n} \mathbf{p}_i \, F_i(\mathbf{u}, \mathbf{w}_i)}{\sum_{i=1}^{n} F_i(\mathbf{u}, \mathbf{w}_i)} \tag{1}$$

lies on a rational Cao En surface. The surface is defined as the set of points, $\mathbf{v}$, for which a corresponding $\mathbf{u}$ exists on the original sphere.

The rational Cao En surface is thus produced by mapping the surface of a unit sphere to a set of points in 3D space. The surface is continuous and topologically equivalent to the sphere.

In [Wyvill 1992], the definition of the Cao En surface is much broader and describes mapping from a hypersphere and other surfaces into a space with any number of dimensions. For the purpose of this paper, the restricted definition is sufficient and we have limited ourselves to simple, closed surfaces that can be mapped from the sphere.

3 Terminology

We refer to the original sphere on which u is defined, as the *source sphere* or *parametric space*. The *control points*, p_i, correspond to the control points of NURBS or other blended surfaces. The *key points*, w_i, take the place of the knots, but they have a more geometrical interpretation since they are simply points on the source sphere. It is an important feature of the surface that the *key points* can be placed anywhere in the parametric space. Unlike parametric patch surfaces, the Cao En surfaces have no implied controlling grid structure.

The points c_i

$$c_i = S(w_i) \tag{2}$$

are known as the image points. A line connecting a given image c_i to its corresponding p_i is known as a *string*. Intuitively, we can imagine that the point c_i is being dragged towards each p_j by a force proportional to $F_j(c_i, w_j)$. The string represents the principal influence on c_i, balanced by the effect of the other control points.

4 Local control

Every point, v, on the target surface, is a weighted sum of the control points, p_i. For a point, u, close to some w_i, we would expect the corresponding point, v, to be close to p_i. This is achieved if $F_i(u, w_i)$ is large when $u = w_i$ and small when u is reasonably distant from w_i. The original Cao En surface used

$$F_i(u, w_i) = e^{(q_i(u \cdot w_i - 1))} \tag{3}$$

where $u \cdot w_i$ is the dot product of the vectors and q_i is a blending constant. If a high value of q_i is chosen, then the effect of w_i is localised because the exponential function (3) rapidly approaches zero as u moves away from w_i. However, $F_i(u, w_i)$ is still not zero for any u. This means that $F_i(u, w_i)$ has to be calculated for every w_i whenever a point on the surface is drawn.

To handle a large number of key points efficiently, we need to localise the influence of each w_i. It is then only necessary to calculate F_i for a subset of values of i. Also, if we have a large number of key points, then in any small region of the source sphere they are dense and the dot product $u \cdot w_i$ is very close to unity. For these reasons, we have chosen a function F_i calculated from the distance between u and w_i.

$$F_i(u, w_i, r_i) = \begin{array}{ll} C((u - w_i)^2 / r_i^2) & , (u - w_i)^2 < r_i^2 \\ \text{zero} & , (u - w_i)^2 \geq r_i^2 \end{array} \tag{4}$$

where r_i is a new parameter associated with each w_i and $C(x)$ is a polynomial whose value falls to zero at $x = 1$. We have been using

$$C(x) = (1 - x^2)^3 \tag{5}$$

for which the derivatives C', C'' also go to zero at $x = 1$. Fig. 1 compares the original function (3) where $q_i = 100$ with (4) for $r_i = 0.25$. The original function (4) is the upper curve.

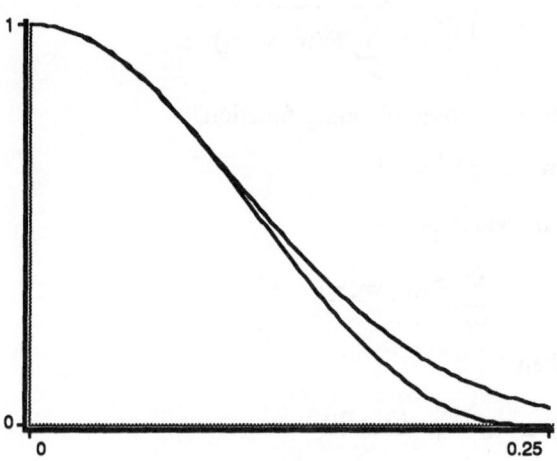

Fig. 1. Blending curves

From this, it is clearly seen that the function (4) is very close to the original but has the desirable property of having no influence beyond a fixed distance, r_i.

Further control can be had by using a different choice of $C(x)$, possibly with parameters to vary the maximum value and decay rate of the curve. So far, we have not experimented with this.

5 Direct manipulation

Several authors, Welch and Witkin [1992] for example, have observed that manipulation of control points is not a good way to adjust curves and surfaces interactively. For this reason, we use the image points, c_i, rather than the control points, p_i, to control the shape. With local control we can write:

$$\mathbf{v} = \frac{\sum_{i=1}^{n} p_i F_i(u, w_i, r_i)}{\sum_{i=1}^{n} F_i(u, w_i, r_i)} \tag{6}$$

and

$$c_j = \frac{\sum_{i=1}^{n} p_i F_i(w_j, w_i, r_i)}{\sum_{i=1}^{n} F_i(w_j, w_i, r_i)} \qquad (7)$$

To move c_j to some desired point, d_j, we need to calculate a new value of p_j. Call this q_j and

$$d_j = c_j + \frac{(q_j - p_j) F_j(w_j, w_j, r_j)}{\sum_{i=1}^{n} F_i(w_j, w_i, r_i)} \qquad (8)$$

Of course, given our chosen blending function,

$$F_j(w_j, w_j, r_j) = 1 \qquad (9)$$

and if we store the value of

$$\sigma_j = \sum_{i=1}^{n} F_i(w_j, w_i, r_i) \qquad (10)$$

for each w_j, then

$$d_j = c_j + \frac{(q_j - p_j)}{\sigma_j} \qquad (11)$$

and we can calculate q_j directly from d_j.

6 Incremental changes

For interactive manipulation, we display a polygonized version of the surface on the workstation screen. After moving an image point, if we don't change the polygonization, we can recalculate all the polygon vertices incrementally without performing the full surface calculation.

Suppose for a particular source point, u, we have stored its image, v, and a corresponding σ where

$$\sigma = \sum_{i=1}^{n} F_i(u, w_i, r_i) \qquad (12)$$

and we have replaced p_j by q_j, w_j by x_j and r_j by s_j. From (6), we see that we can recover the value of

$$\sum_{i=1}^{n} p_i F_i(u, w_i, r_i) = \sigma v \qquad (13)$$

So the new value of $\sigma \mathbf{v}$ is

$$\sigma \mathbf{v} \; := \; q_j F_j(u, x_j, s_j) \; - \; p_j F_j(u, w_j, r_j) \; + \; \sigma \mathbf{v} \tag{14}$$

and the new value of σ is

$$\sigma \; := \; F_j(u, x_j, s_j) \; - \; F_j(u, w_j, r_j) \; + \; \sigma \tag{15}$$

from this we can recalculate $\mathbf{v}$ without performing any of the time-consuming sums.

These incremental calculations are fast enough that we can manipulate a surface with 10,000 control points in real time on a Silicon Graphics 4D/340 VGX workstation. Of course these incremental calculations can also be done with other kinds of parametric surface.

7 Efficiency of local control algorithm

If we have a surface with n control points and represent it with polygonal patches requiring m vertices, in the absence of local control we must calculate 2n sums of m terms. If we first sort the control points, so that each of the m vertices is associated with a list of control points that can affect its calculation, then we calculate 2n sums with k terms where k is the average number of control points to affect each vertex.

Unfortunately, if we want to change one of the w_i or r_i, we have to repeat the sort because that key point may affect a different subset of vertices. We implemented the sorting strategy and got the expected gain, but the full calculation with spatial sorting is still slower than the incremental calculation described above. A better technique of space division is needed here and we are investigating this.

8 Interactive surface editor

We have implemented an interactive surface editor using the principles described here. One or more surfaces are displayed in an editing window and one is selected for editing. A source window displays the source sphere for this surface. Using a mouse or spaceball, the surface can be rotated and shifted in the target space. The shape of the surface can be changed by moving the image points interactively or by moving the key points on the source surface. The radius of influence, r_i, of any key point can also be changed and new key points can be introduced to make local changes and refinements to the surface.

A typical working screen is shown in Fig. 2. The source sphere is shown in the upper left and the blue-grey spots represent the positions of key points. These can be selected and dragged across the image using the mouse cursor. Because these points are constrained to lie on the sphere, it is easy to position them in this way.

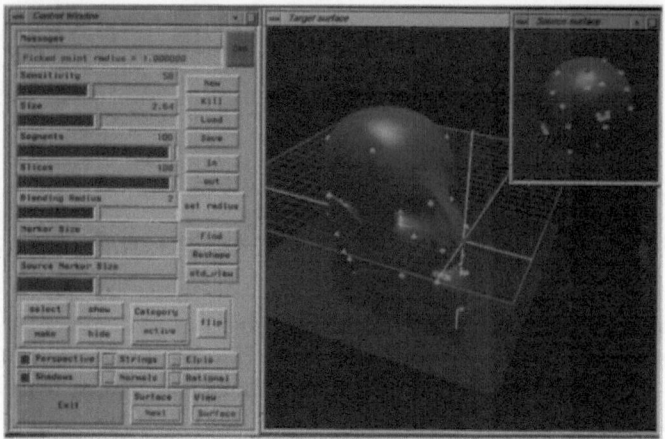

Fig.2. A typical working screen

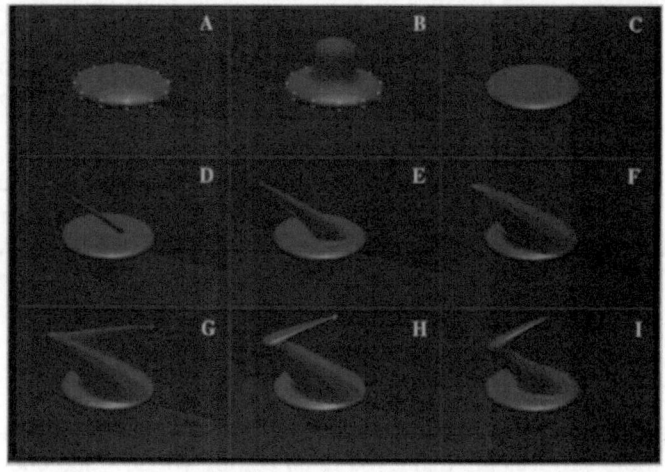

Fig 3. Demonstration of local control

In the target surface window a 3D model is shown being edited. The spots show the position of the image points. One spot is selected and marked in red. Its corresponding key point in the source window is also red. This point can be dragged around in 3D, using the mouse cursor, A 'horizontal' grid is shown in the perspective view and the mouse movements are interpreted to represent movements in the plane of the grid. A mouse movement that is almost exactly vertical can be used to raise or lower the grid. With a little practice, the user can learn to control the image points in 3D from this perspective view. It is also possible to switch to a parallel projection and adjust the image points, more conventionally, in the plane of the screen.

The basic strategy for adding a new feature is to define one or more new key points and move them on the source sphere until their image points are visible in the desired position in the target surface window. The appropriate part of the working surface can then be moved to a new position, by dragging the image points. It is also possible to move existing active key points on the source sphere. This produces wild changes in the surface that are difficult to understand.

The control window on the left contains a representation of buttons, sliders and switches operated by the mouse. The radius of influence of any selected keypoint can be adjusted by means of one of these sliders, shown in blue. Using these controls, the operator can also change the level of polygonization of the surface, switch between perspective and parallel views, display selected source and image points and perform the usual *load file* and *store file* operations expected of an editor. It is also possible to display the *strings* that link the image points to the control points. These are not very useful to the designer. They can change position dramatically even in response to small changes in the positions of the image points. This is an interesting indication of the difficulty of designing surfaces directly using control points.

9 Examples

Fig. 3 illustrates the process of refinement. A shows a button shape defined by 24 control points with radius of influence 2.0. The corresponding image points are represented by grey spots. Twelve new key points are added and their image points are shown as red dots. At this stage they have no effect on the surface shape. In B, the twelve red image points have been raised to make a mushroom shape. The control radius of the new points is 0.5. C shows the mushroom turned over. A single additional image point is placed on the top surface. In D, the new image point has been moved. Its radius is set to 0.125. In E and F the radius of this point is increased, first to 0.5 then to 1.0. In image F a second image point is added to the spike; image G shows the effect of moving it. In H, the second image point has been moved in the parametric space, to coincide with the first. This produces a characteristic bent spike similar to the shapes demonstrated by Forsey and Bartels [1988]. Finally, in I, the radius of the first image point is reduced to 0.6 changing the shape of the spike.

Fig. 4 shows an electric fan blade designed with the surface editor. It is made from four separate surfaces.

Fig. 5 shows an ashtray, a coat hook and a few spoons designed with the surface editor. The three spoons in the foreground are each made with only twelve control points. The different shapes are obtained by varying the radius of selected points.

Fig. 6 shows four stages in the design of a simple human head model. The first approximation has only eight control points. The final one has forty. This model is shown twice. The left hand model includes the visible image points associated with each control point. Using the interactive editor, this model was designed in about three hours.

Fig. 7 shows the head again. Some image points are shifted in the right hand model to create a different face.

10 Discussion

A non-rational Cao En surface is defined by equation (1) with the denominator set to unity. This non-rational surface breaks a basic rule for useful parametric surfaces in that the surface shape is not invariant under transformation of its control points. However, if we think of the control vectors as directions, there is no need to see them as positions in space. They are merely entities from which the surface is calculated. The surface remains invariant under rotation.

The non-rational form of the surface has one great advantage for direct manipulation. A new image point can be added at any point on the surface and associated with a key point and a zero control point. This has no effect at all on the shape of the surface. Local refinements can then be made using this image point. By contrast, the rational surface has all of the usually desired invariant properties, but when you add a new control point, it immediately causes a change in the surrounding surface points. Because of this, the rational surface is harder to manipulate interactively.

Welch [1992] and Fowler [1992] have argued that the user should be presented with a set of surface manipulation tools that are easy to use. They do not have to be related to the surface's underlying definition. We agree, and the problems we have manipulating the rational surface are related to the decision to use only image point position as a control. Even so, the user has to have some notional model for the way he expects the surface to behave. Physical simulation of a block of clay would be complicated and would not necessarily be an improvement. The next stage of this research will be to experiment with some higher level manipulation tools.

The existing software displays the surfaces by creating a simple polygon mesh on the surface of the source sphere and transforming these polygons into the target space. The head models, for example, are displayed using about 10,000 polygons but most of these appear in the large featureless areas on the top and back of the head. We expect to see a dramatic improvement in the representation of detail when we have implemented an adaptive polygonization.

Fig. 4. An electric fan blade made
from four separate surfaces

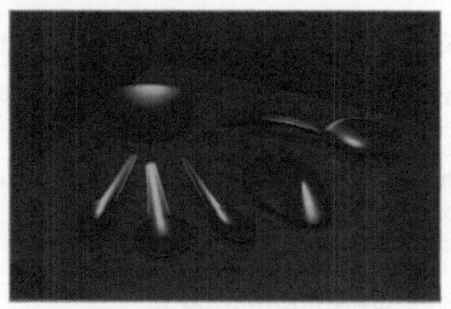

Fig. 5. An ashtray, coat hook and cutlery

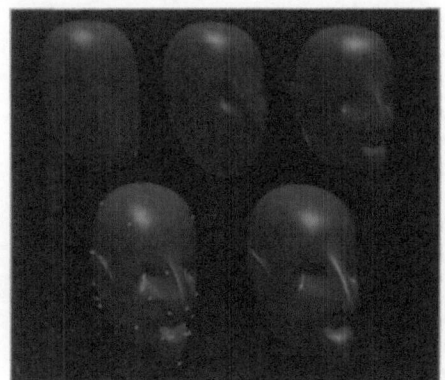

Fig. 6. Design of a simple head model

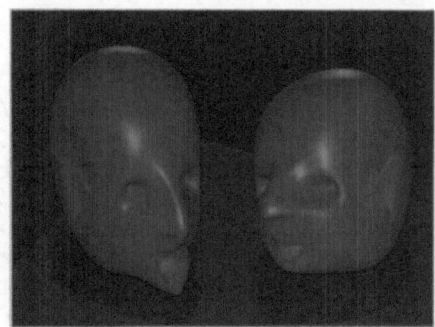

Fig. 7. Two heads

11 Conclusion

One kind of Cao En model has been developed to provide variably local control of the surface.

Efficient algorithms for the generation of these surfaces have been developed.

An interactive surface editor, based on these principles, greatly eases the task of designing free form surfaces.

The ability to introduce new key points anywhere in the parametric space and with control over their locality provides a very simple way to refine a surface definition.

12 Acknowledgements

We wish to thank Professor Daniel Thalmann of EPFL and Professor Nadia Magnenat Thalmann, University of Geneva, for access to their laboratories where the bulk of this development was done and for permission to incorporate the LIG 5D Toolkit [Turner 1990], without which the interactive development would have taken many times longer. Thanks are also due to the assistants at these two laboratories, especially Mr Russell Turner, for useful ideas and practical help. The paper and the examples were all prepared in the Advanced Computer Graphics Centre at RMIT, and we wish to thank Mr Michael Gigante, director of ACGC and Craig McNaughton for photographic and technical assistance.

13 References

Blinn J (1982) A Generalization of Algebraic Surface Drawing. *ACM Transactions on Graphics* 1 : 235 - 256

Forsey DR and Bartels RH (1988) Hierarchical B-Spline Refinement. *Computer Graphics* 22 (4) : 205-212

Fowler B (1992) Geometric Manipulation of Tensor Product Surfaces. *1992 Symposium on Interactive 3D Graphics*, Special Issue of *Computer Graphics:*101-108

Nishimura H, Hirai M, Kawai T, Kawata T, Shirakawa I and Omura K (1985) Object Modeling by Distribution Function and a Method of Image Generation. *Journal of papers given at the Electronics Communication Conference '85* J68-D (4) (in Japanese)

Piegl L (1991) On NURBS: A Survey. *IEEE Computer Graphics and Applications* 11 (1) : 55 -71

Turner R, Gobbetti E, Balaguer F, Mangili A, Thalmann D and Magnenat-Thalmann N (1990) An Object Oriented Methodology Using Dynamic Variables for Animation and Scientific Visualization. *Proceedings of Computer Graphics International 90*, Springer-Verlag : 317-328

Welch W and Witkin A (1992) Variational Surface Modeling. *Computer Graphics*, 26 (2) : 157-166

Wyvill G, McPheeters C and Wyvill BLM (1986) Data Structure for Soft Objects. *The Visual Computer* 2 (4) : 227-234

Wyvill G, Cao En and Trotman A (1992) The Cao En Surface: A new approach to free form geometric models. *Programmirovanie* (4) 1992 (in Russian, but also to be published in English in *Programming and Computer Software*, Plenum Publishing Corporation)

Geoff Wyvill is a senior lecturer in computer science at the University of Otago in New Zealand and a director of Animation Research Limited, a small New Zealand based company which produces computer animation commercially. Although he is best known for his work in free form design software (Soft Objects), his recent research includes lighting and texture models, graphics for engineering design, halftoning, modelling of natural phenomena and the application of computer graphics in art. He is secretary of CGS and a member of ACM, SIGGRAPH and NZCS. He is also on the editorial board of *The Visual Computer* and of *Visualization and Computer Animation*.
Wyvill received his BA from Oxford in 1966 and MSc and PhD degrees from the University of Bradford in 1969 and 1979.

Address:
Department of Computer Science
University of Otago Box 56
Dunedin, New Zealand
e-mail: geoff@otago.ac.nz

Dean McRobie is a graduate student in Computer Science at the University of Otago. He graduated with first class honours from Otago in 1992. He is a senior tutor at Otago and is a student member of the ACM. His research interests include Ray Tracing and Interactive 3D Graphics.

Address:
Department of Computer Science
University of Otago Box 56
Dunedin, New Zealand
e-mail: deano@otago.ac.nz

Interactive Surface Design Using Recursive Subdivision

Tsuneya Kurihara

ABSTRACT

Recursive subdivision methods generate smooth surfaces from arbitrary topological meshes. In this paper, we extend recursive subdivision methods to make them suitable for an interactive design. First, a hierarchical editing method is introduced for surface refinement. This makes it possible to alter large-scale surfaces so that the small-scale surfaces follow the alteration. Second, we present convenient manipulation techniques, such as direct manipulation, to edit a hierarchy of subdivision surfaces. We also discuss display techniques for surfaces that are effective in interactive design. These techniques provide a convenient tool for interactive free-form surface design.

Keywords : recursive subdivision, hierarchy, offset, direct manipulation.

1. INTRODUCTION

Top-down methodology is natural and convenient for interactive surface design in computer graphics: designing large-scale surfaces, and then refining them. In top-down methodology, one quickly defines large-scale surfaces, which are often smooth, with a small number of parameters. Then, details are added to the large-scale surfaces to refine them. To realize this approach, we must address these key issues.

- **Surface Representation:** To design large-scale surfaces, it is desirable that smooth surfaces are represented with a small number of parameters. In addition, arbitrary shapes such as a closed surface or a surface with holes or branches should be represented. These arbitrary topologies often appear in many applications. For example, when we create a human character, the trunk and the arms should be joined. It is also required to be able to describe a wide range of surfaces: from smooth surfaces to irregular surfaces.

- **Refinement:** Details are important for surface design. They must be easily added to a large-scale surface. In addition, it is desirable to combine large-scale and fine-scale manipulation, that is, to alter a large-scale surface without changing the fine details as in hierarchical B-spline refinement (Forsey 1988).

- **Surface Manipulation:** Interactive manipulation is essential for surface design. Easy-to-use and intuitive manipulation techniques, such as a direct manipulation, should be used. Of course, quick response is required.

Polygonal representation of surfaces is currently the most widely used in computer graphics. One reason is that current graphics workstations can rapidly draw polygons. Polygonal representation can describe almost all shapes of arbitrary topology. Additional polygons are easily created where they are needed for refinement. For surface manipulation, free-form deformation (Sederberg 1986), local deformation (Allan et al. 1989) and global deformation methods (Barr 1984) can be applied. However, the main drawback of polygonal descriptions is that many polygons are required to describe curved surfaces.

Parametric surfaces, such as B-spline surfaces or Bézier surfaces, are widely used to represent smooth surfaces. Parametric surfaces represent smooth surfaces with a small number of control points, and are easily manipulated. Knot insertion is generally used for refinement. The hierarchical B-spline technique (Forsey 1988) provides local refinement and *offset referencing* procedures. This technique also provides sufficient tools for surface manipulations. However, one problem about these parametric surfaces is that it is difficult to handle arbitrary topological meshes because a patch of parametric surfaces is in general a deformation of a rectangle. Several techniques have been proposed to overcome this problem (Beeker 1986; Chiyokura and Kimura 1983; Loop and DeRose 1990; van Wijk 1986). These techniques can handle arbitrary topological meshes and are useful for precise surface modeling such as industrial design. However, they are computationally expensive or require complex constraints to maintain the continuity between two patches. Therefore, these methods are not practical or suited for interactive computer graphics where interactive manipulation is essential.

Soft objects (Blinn 1982; Wyvill et al. 1986) represent smooth and closed surfaces with a small number of parameters. When detail is required, one can add a small soft object. One shortcoming is that it requires a great deal of skill to construct complex objects using soft objects. In addition, polygonalization or ray tracing is required to display a soft object, and this can be expensive for interactive manipulation.

Catmull and Clark (1978) and Doo and Sabin (1978) have proposed recursive subdivision methods to generate a smooth surface over a polyhedral mesh of arbitrary topology. This method recursively cuts off the corners of the polyhedron and generates a smooth surface. The faces need not be planar, and the vertices do not have to lie on a topologically rectangular mesh. If the mesh is rectangular, the limit surface is a quadratic B-spline surface. Therefore, this method is an extension of quadratic B-spline surfaces. Although this technique has no parametric forms, it can generate a pleasing surface with very small computation. Thus, this method is very powerful for computer graphics although not for precise geometric modeling. If this method is extended so that refinement and interactive manipulation, such as direct manipulation, are available, then a powerful modeling tool can be realized.

This paper presents an interactive surface design method based on recursive subdivision methods to realize a top-down methodology. Hierarchy is introduced to recursive subdivision methods to refine the surfaces and combine large-scale surfaces with fine-scale surfaces. Efficient interaction techniques such as direct manipulation are then introduced. Effective display methods of surfaces are also introduced.

We briefly review original recursive subdivision methods in Section 2. Section 3 introduces a hierarchy to the recursive subdivision methods. Interaction methods including direct manipulation are presented in Section 4. Section 5 describes display techniques for the surfaces. Section 6 shows several examples.

2. RECURSIVE SUBDIVISION METHOD

Catmull and Clark (1978) and Sabin and Doo (1978) have proposed a quadratic approach for recursive subdivision. We will follow Sabin and Doo's approach because the behavior around a singular vertex is ideal. This method is an extension of the subdivision method for Bézier curve (Chaikin 1974).

This method recursively subdivides the polyhedron by cutting off the corners and edges of the polyhedron. One subdivision procedure is as follows (see Fig. 1):

(1) For every face with n vertices $W_1,...,W_n$ of the original polyhedron, a new (small) face is created. In Fig. 1, a new face $Q_1Q_2Q_4Q_3$ is created from the original face $P_1P_2P_4P_3$. This new face is termed as a *F-face*, and the new vertex as an *image-vertex*.

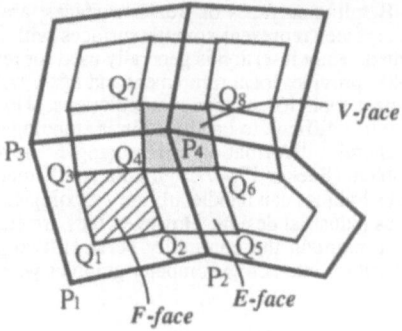

Fig. 1   Recursive subdivision method.

The positions of the image-vertices $V_1,...,V_n$ are determined only by the original face and are specified as

$$V_i = \sum_{j=1}^{n} \alpha_{ij} W_j$$

(1)

where

$$\alpha_{ij} = \frac{n+5}{4n} \qquad \text{for } i = j$$

$$\alpha_{ij} = \frac{3+2\cos(2\pi(i-j)/n)}{4n} \qquad \text{for } i \neq j .$$

(2) For every edge of the original polyhedron shared by two faces, a new 4-sided face is obtained by linking four image vertices. In Fig. 1, a new face $Q_2Q_5Q_6Q_4$ is obtained from edge P_2P_4. This face is termed as an *E-face*.

(3) For each closed vertex of the original polyhedron shared by n faces, a new n-sided face is created by linking n image vertices. In Fig. 1, a new face $Q_4Q_6Q_8Q_7$ is created from vertex P_4. This face is termed as a *V-face*.

By recursively repeating this division process, a smooth (G^1 continuity) surface is obtained (Doo and Sabin 1974). This subdivision process is repeated until the size of the face is sufficient for the required resolution.

Figure 2 shows examples of surfaces created by the recursive subdivision method. In this example, the original polyhedron is a cube. First, second, and third divisions are shown.

This method generates a smooth surface on arbitrary topological meshes: the face need not be four sided or planar, and the vertex need not be shared by four faces. This property is very convenient for creating free-form surfaces. If the original polyhedron is a rectangular mesh, then the resulting surface converges to a quadratic B-spline surface. Therefore, this method is an extension of a B-spline surface. The computation of new faces in the subdivision process consists of very simple linear operations. In addition, the resulting surface is approximated by the polyhedron and can be drawn rapidly with current graphics workstations.

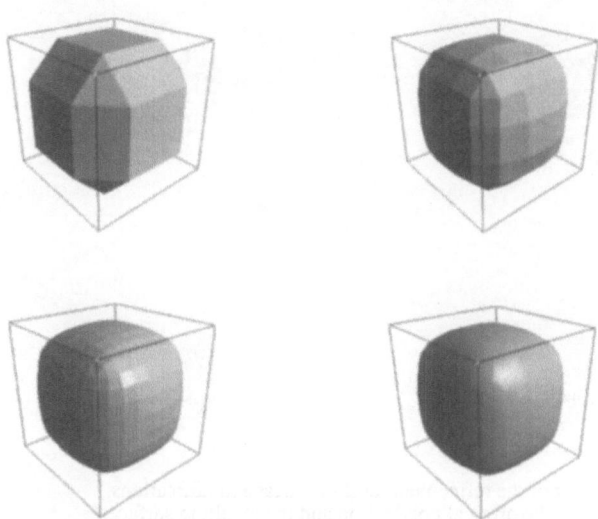

Fig. 2 Surfaces created by recursive subdivision methods.
    (a) Upper left: A cube and its first division.
    (b) Upper right: The second division.
    (c) Lower left: The third division.
    (d) Lower right: The third division with smooth shading.

We can change the division level according to the application. For example, when one deforms the surface globally, he can display the surface with a small subdivision level, so that manipulation is done in real time.

In this method, the limit surface in general does not pass through the original vertices, but rather passes through the centroid of each face. Nasri (1987, 1991a) has extended recursive subdivision methods for the generation of a surface that interpolates the set of vertices of a polyhedron. Brunet (1988) has extended this to cover shape control of the limit surface. Boundary control techniques have been proposed for this method (Nasri 1991b).

One disadvantage of this method is that there are no parametric forms of this surface. In each subdivision, the number of 4-sided faces increases, and for these parts we can use B-spline surfaces. However, around the extraordinary points which do not share 4 faces, the subdivision method is required. Although this is a drawback to create precise surfaces for industrial design, it is sufficient for interactive computer graphics.

3. HIERARCHICAL RECURSIVE SUBDIVISION METHOD

With the recursive subdivision method, more vertices are needed to gain a higher level of detail. Addition of vertices is easy because this method naturally utilizes the division process to generate a smooth surface. Let S_0 be the original polyhedron, and S_n be the polyhedron generated by n-times subdivision. It is obvious that the limit surface created by subdividing S_0 is the same as that created by subdividing S_n. Therefore, S_n is a detailed representation of S_0. This property makes it easy to define details in the subdivision method. That is, when we need global deformation, we manipulate vertices of S_0, and when we need fine-level deformation, we manipulate vertices of S_1, S_2, and so

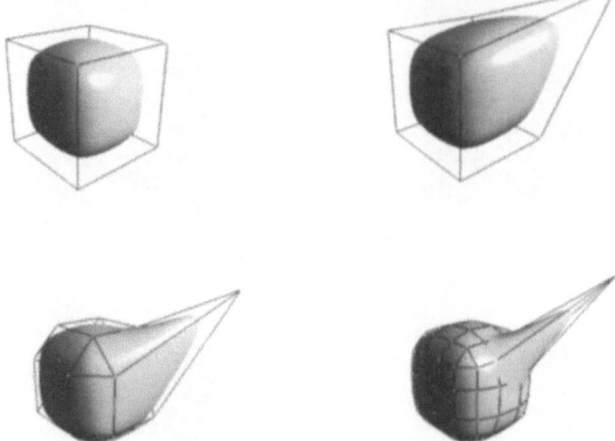

Fig. 3 The effect ot the refinement level on surface modifications.
(a) Upper left: The original polyhedron and the resulting surface.
(b) Upper right: One vertex of the original polyhedron is moved.
(c) Lower left: One vertex of the first level polyhedron is moved.
(d) Lower right: One vertex of the second level polyhedron is moved.

on. Hierarchy is easily introduced because the recursive subdivision method naturally depends on the subdivision process.

In Fig. 3, vertices of different subdivision levels are manipulated. In this example, vertices of S_0, S_1 and S_2 are displaced. Note that the subdivision level determines the influence of deformation.

It is desirable to alter large-scale surfaces without changing the fine-scale detail of the surfaces. Forsey (1988) has proposed the hierarchical B-spline method to solve this problem. We will present a similar method for recursive subdivision.

To have fine details follow the global deformation, the displacement of vertices on a fine-scale surface S_i must be represented in a local coordinate system based on the parent surface S_{i-1}. This method is called *offset referencing* (Forsey 1988). The position of the image-vertex is then defined as

$$V_i = \sum_{j=1}^{n} \alpha_{ij} W_j + O_{i,x} L_x + O_{i,y} L_y + O_{i,z} L_z \qquad (2)$$

where O_i ($O_{i,x}$, $O_{i,y}$, $O_{i,z}$) is the offset vector, and L_x, L_y and L_z correspond to the primary axes of the local coordinate system. Although there are many possibilities to define the local coordinate system, we introduce two methods: one based on the object coordinate system and the other based on the tangent and normal vector.

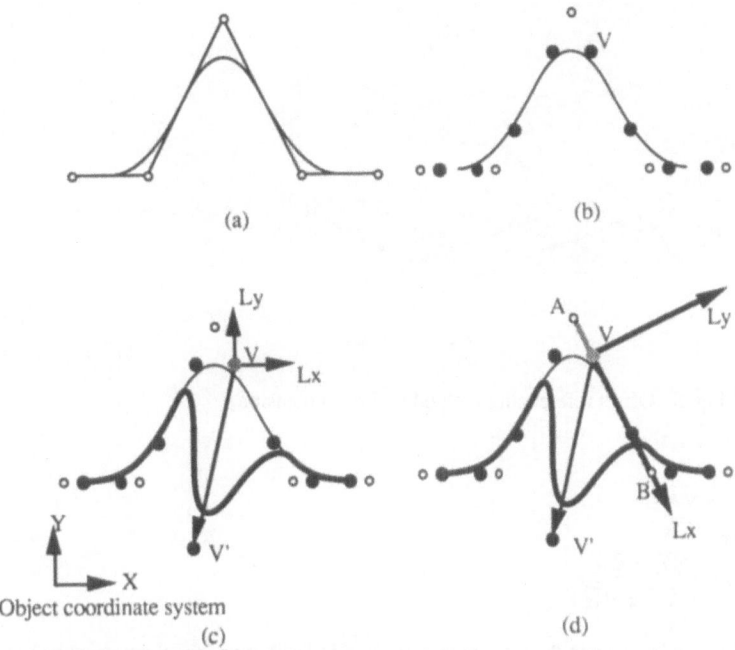

Object coordinate system

(c)   (d)

Figure 4. Hierarchical recursive subdivision methods (in two dimension).
(a) A subdivided line and its control points.
(b) The same subdivided line with subdivided control points (black dots).
(c) An offset referencing method in the object coordinate system.
    One control point is moved along with the displacement vector in the local coordinate
    system that is defined based on the object coordinate system.
(d) An offset referencing method in the coordinate system based on the tangent vector.
    One control point is moved along with the displacement vector in the local coordinate
    system that is defined based on the tangent vector of the curve.

Figure 4 shows these two methods in the two dimensional case. Figure 4a shows the vertices of polyline S_0 and the resulting curve. In Fig. 4b, the black dots are new vertices made by subdivision. In Fig. 4c, one vertex V is displaced. The first method to represent the local coordinate system is quite simple. We describe the displacement as a difference between the original position V and the moved position V' in the object coordinate system. This means that $L_x = (1, 0, 0)$, $L_y = (0, 1, 0)$ and $L_z = (0, 0, 1)$ (Fig. 4c). The second method represents the local coordinate system based on the tangent and normal vector. In Fig. 4d, vertex V is generated by subdividing edge AB. This edge AB is used to define the local coordinate system. That is, $L_x = \vec{AB}$, and L_y is the vector that is perpendicular to L_x and has the same length as L_x (Fig. 4d).

Figure 5 shows the definition of the local coordinate system in the three dimensional case. The first method is obvious so only the second method is explained. In the subdivision process, the image vertices of S_i are generated from one face F of S_{i-1}. Two edges of the original face F are used to define the local coordinate system. In Fig. 5, V, A and B are vertices of S_i, and V', A' and B' are the image vertices of V, A, B, respectively. The local coordinate system is defined by edge VA and edge $\vec{VB}$ as

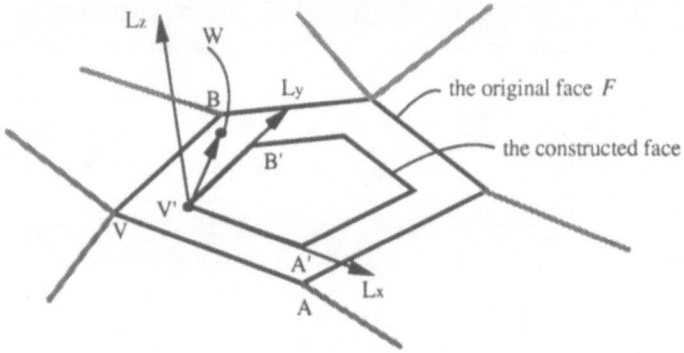

Fig. 5   Offset referencing method in three dimension.

$$L_x = \overrightarrow{VA}$$
$$L_y = \overrightarrow{VB}$$
$$L_z = \frac{\overrightarrow{VA} \times \overrightarrow{VB}}{\sqrt{|\overrightarrow{VA} \times \overrightarrow{VB}|}} \quad ,$$

(3)

where L_x and L_y correspond to the tangent vectors, and L_z corresponds to the normal vector.

These two methods have advantages and disadvantages. The first method is linear, and computationally inexpensive although the detail is not invariant with rotation or scaling. The second method is invariant with rotation and scaling although it is no longer linear and computationally more expensive. In addition, the second method can cause unexpected deformation at the fine level when the large-scale surface is considerably deformed. In the next section, linearity will play an important role for direct manipulation. Therefore, in our prototype editor, the user is allowed to choose which method is applied.

Figure 6 shows the effect of offset referencing using the second method. A simple surface with detail (Character 'T') is deformed. Note that the detail 'T' follows the large-scale deformation.

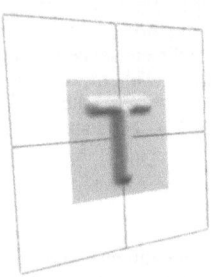
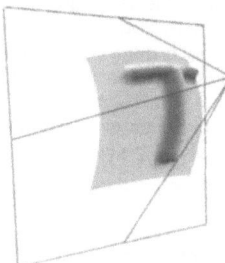

(a) The original surface with detail.   (b) The deformed surface by manipulating
                                                   original polyhedron.

Fig. 6   The effect of offset referencing.

4. MANIPULATION OF SURFACES

4.1 Overview of Interactive Design using Recursive Subdivision

The interactive design process using hierarchical recursive subdivision consists of three steps that are as follows:

Step 1: definition of the original polyhedron
An original polyhedron is defined. It is easy to imagine the resulting surface from the original polyhedron because it is generated by cutting off the corner of the original polyhedron. In addition, there is much flexibility in defining the original polyhedron because arbitrary topological meshes can be used.

Step 2: surface generation by subdivision
The division level n is specified and the subdivided polyhedron is generated. The number of faces after n times subdivision is almost 4^n times that of the original polyhedron (Appendix A). Therefore, from 3 times to 5 times subdivision usually makes a satisfactory surface, although it depends on the application and the original polyhedron. The polyhedron of each level (from S_0 to S_n) is maintained in order to make it possible to manipulate all levels of subdivisions.

Step 3: interactive manipulation of the surface
The surface is manipulated interactively. Because of the hierarchical structure, every level of the polyhedron can be manipulated. We define a global surface by manipulating S_0 at first, and then we refine it by manipulating the higher level polyhedron.

4.2 Manipulation of Control Vertices

Manipulation of control vertices is the most essential operation to deform the surface. It must be performed quickly for interactive use. In this section, we present an efficient deformation technique for vertex manipulation.

The manipulation of vertex $\mathbf{V}$ of S_i moves all the vertices of S_{i+1} created from faces that share vertex $\mathbf{V}$. On the other hand, vertices of S_{i+1} created from faces that do not share vertex $\mathbf{V}$ do not move. Therefore, deformation in the recursive subdivision method is local. This locality brings efficient deformation.

Suppose that vertex $\mathbf{V}$ of polyhedron S_i is edited (moved). The resulting deformation of polyhedron S_{i+1} is obtained as follows:

1. Find all faces F_j of S_i that share vertex $\mathbf{V}$.
2. For each image vertex created from face F_j, update its position using Equation (2).

Manipulation of vertex of S_i moves vertices of S_{i+1}, and successively move vertices of S_{i+2}, and so on. To perform this deformation efficiently each face F of S_i keeps a pointer to the child face of S_{i+1} that is created from F.

4.3 Direct Manipulation

Manipulation of the control vertex is an indirect method. In addition, control vertices are often invisible because they are inside the surface. A natural and easy-to-use manipulation method is direct manipulation: pick one point on the surface, and specify the destination position.

Picking one point on the surface is substituted by picking one vertex on the displayed polyhedron S_n. Suppose that vertex $\mathbf{V}$ of S_n is moved to the new position $\mathbf{V}'$ ($=\mathbf{V}+\Delta\mathbf{V}$) by changing S_i, the polyhedron of division level i. This division level i determines the range of deformation.

The position of vertex **V** is defined by the summation of the offset and linear combination of vertices of S_{n-1} as show in Equation (2). Therefore, the displacement $\Delta \mathbf{V}$ is written as

$$\Delta \mathbf{V} = \sum_{j=1}^{n} \alpha_j \Delta \mathbf{W}_j , \tag{3}$$

where $\Delta \mathbf{W}_j$ is the displacement of the vertex of S_{n-1}. Applying this relationship recursively, the displacement $\Delta \mathbf{V}$ is written as a linear combination of the displacement of the vertex of S_i as

$$\Delta \mathbf{V} = \sum_{j=1}^{m} \beta_j \Delta \mathbf{U}_j, \tag{4}$$

where $\Delta \mathbf{U}_j$ is the displacement of vertex $\mathbf{U}_j$ of S_i. There exist many solutions that satisfy Equation (4). To minimize the changes in position of vertices $\mathbf{U}_j$, displacement $\Delta \mathbf{U}_j$ is determined by (Bartels 1989)

$$\mathbf{U}_j = \frac{\beta_j \, \Delta \mathbf{V}}{\sum\limits_{k=1}^{m} \beta_k^2} . \tag{5}$$

To perform this direct manipulation efficiently, each vertex **V** of S_i keeps a pointer to the parent face and vertex of S_{i-1} that create vertex **V**.

Care must be taken when we use offset referencing based on the tangent and normal vector. In this case, Equation (4) does not hold in general because the local coordinate system is based on the parent polyhedron and linearity is lost. Therefore, the above method does not work precisely. This is undesirable if the vertex **V** is required to move to the precise position **V**.' However, experiments show that the error is often small. Therefore, this error does not pose any serious problems for interactive surface design. If we use offset referencing based on the object coordinate system, Equation (4) holds and precise manipulation is achieved.

5. DISPLAY METHODS

The surface is approximated by a subdivided polyhedron S_n. This approximation is not sufficient for boundary display. This is because the boundary of the limit surface does not pass through the vertices of S_n but rather through the centroid of the boundary faces of S_n (see Fig. 7a). In addition, the error between the boundary of the limit surface and the boundary of S_n changes according to the division level n. Increasing the division level n decreases this error, but results in slower manipulation. This problem is overcome by introducing a new type of polyhedron, *C-polyhedron* (centroid polyhedron) as follows:

For every interior vertex **V**, a new face is obtained by connecting the centroid of all faces that share the vertex **V**. This new face is termed a *C-face*. The new polyhedron, new edge and new vertex are termed the *C-polyhedron*, *C-edge*, *C-vertex*, respectively. Figure 7b and 7c show the C-polyhedron of S_0 and S_1.

In one subdivision process, F-face F' is obtained from the face F of the parent polyhedron. The position of the centroid of F is the same as that of F'. This means that the C-vertex of level i has the corresponding C-vertex of level $i+1$, and the positions of these two C-vertices are identical. A C-edge of level i is subdivided into two C-edges of level $i+1$ where the positions of two end points do not change. An n-sided C-face of level i is subdivided into n C-faces of level $i+1$. Note that C-

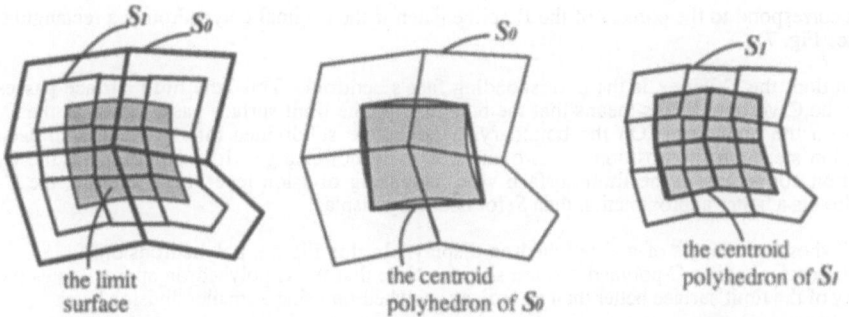

S_1 S_0 S_0 S_1

the limit   the centroid   the centroid
surface   polyhedron of S_0 polyhedron of S_1

(a) polyhedron S_0, S_1 and   (b) the centroid polyhedron of S_0 (c) the centroid polyhedron of
the limit surface.   and the limit surface. S_1 and the limit surface.

Fig. 7   Centroid polyhedron.

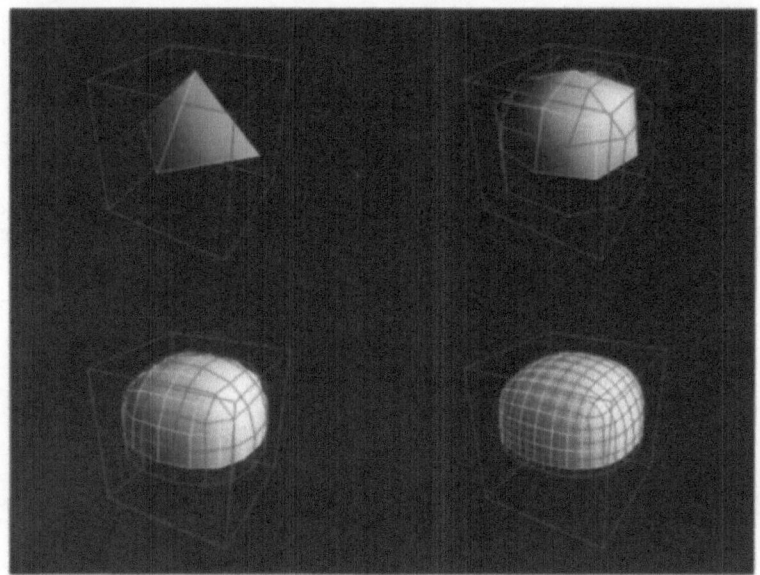

Fig. 8   Display using centroid polyhedron.
(a) Upper left: polyhedron S_0 and its centroid polyhedron.
(b) Upper right: polyhedron S_1 and its centroid polyhedron.
(c) Lower left: polyhedron S_2 and its centroid polyhedron.
(d) Lower right: polyhedron S_3 and its centroid polyhedron.
The magenta lines represent the polyhedron S_i.
The orange lines and shaded surfaces represent the corresponding centroid polyhedrons.

vertices correspond to the corners of the B-spline patch if the original polyhedron is a rectangular mesh (see Fig. 7).

By definition, the C-vertex is the corresponding face's centroid. Thus, the limit surface passes through the C-vertices. This means that the boundary of the limit surface passes through the C-vertices on the boundary. On the boundary, C-edges are subdivided into two edges in each subdivision step, but the positions of two end points do not change. It is obvious that the C-polyhedron converges to the limit surface with increasing division level n. Therefore, the C-polyhedron is a better approximation than S_i for boundary display.

Figure 8 shows examples of a C-polyhedron display. In this Figure, polyhedrons S_0, S_1, S_2, S_3 and their corresponding C-polyhedrons are shown. Note that the C-polyhedron approximates the boundary of the limit surface better than an ordinary polyhedron using a smaller division level.

6. RESULTS

Figure 9 shows the process involved in human body design using the proposed methods. Simple shapes such as boxes or cylinders have been placed and joined around the skeleton of the body (Fig. 9a). The number of vertices of the initial polyhedron is 599. Joints such as the torso and arms are easily represented because the recursive subdivision method handles arbitrary topological meshes. The large scale surface is designed by manipulating vertices of the original polyhedron (Fig. 9b and 9c). Figure 9d shows the surface after manipulating 488 vertices of S_1 (division level 1). Figure 9e shows the resulting surface after manipulating 1046 vertices of S_2 (division level 2). Thus the total number of manipulated vertices is 2133.

Figure 10 illustrates the deformation around the joints. In this example, only the vertices of S_0 around the joints have been interactively manipulated.

Figure 11 shows a face created by the proposed method. The number of vertices of the original polyhedron is 155 and 530 vertices of S_1 are manipulated. In this example, eyes and teeth are modeled by polyhedrons.

In the above examples, the surfaces are assumed symmetric, therefore, the actual number of manipulated vertices is approximately half of that specified above.

7. CONCLUSIONS

We have presented interactive surface design methods using recursive subdivision. Recursive subdivision is a powerful method because it generates smooth surfaces from arbitrary topological meshes. This property makes it easy to create a free-form surface including a closed surface, a surface with joints and handles. Hierarchy and offset reference is introduced as a convenient method to refine the surface. This method supports adding local detail to the surface. Furthermore, this method makes it possible to change the large scale surface without changing the fine-scale details. Interaction techniques, such as direct manipulation, have also been presented.

8. ACKNOWLEDGMENTS

The author would like to thank Russell Turner, Francis Balaguer and Daniel Thalmann for valuable discussions, and Kyoko Kurihara for the design of the human body and face. This research was performed at the Swiss Federal Institute of Technology during the author's stay as a visiting researcher.

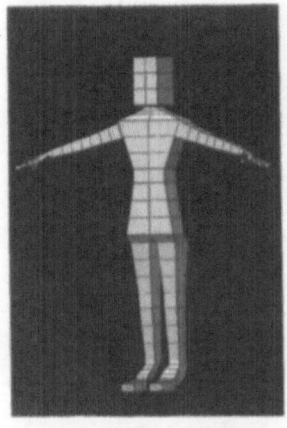

(a) An initial polyhedron
of the human body.

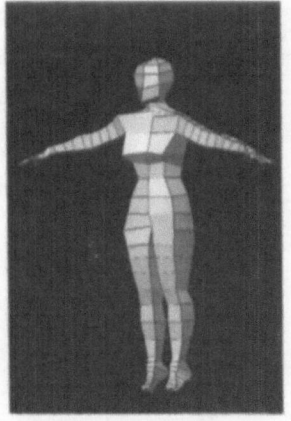

(b) The initial polyhedron
after editing vertices.

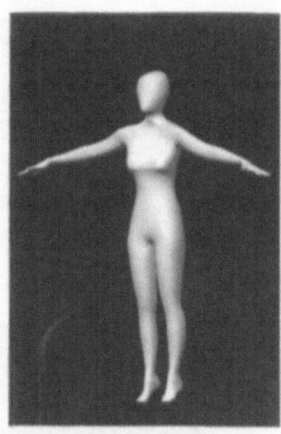

(c) The surface created from
the polyhedron of (b)

(d) Vertices of polyhedron
S1 are edited.

(e) Vertices of polyhedron *S2* are edited.

Fig. 9   The process involved in human body design.

Fig. 9 (f) Details of the resulting surface (e).

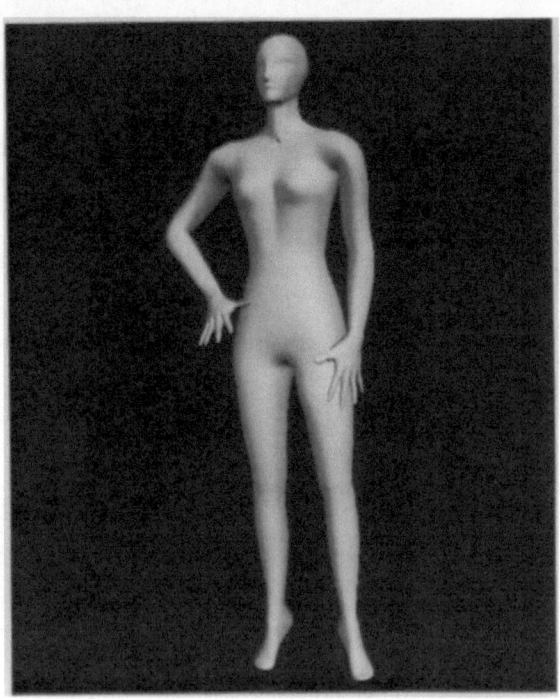

Fig. 10 Deformation
around joints.

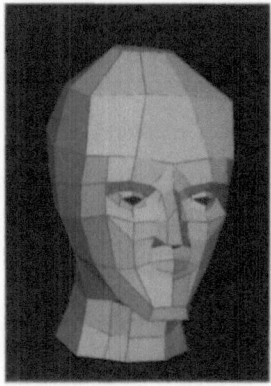

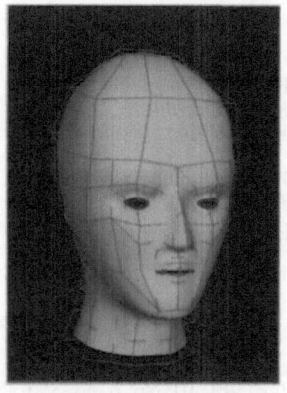

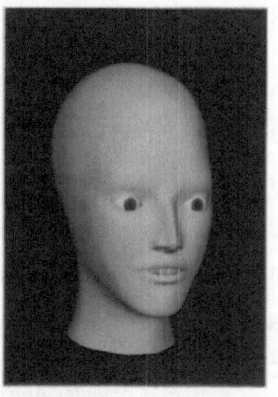

(a) An initial polyhedron of the face.

(b) The face created from the initial polyhedron.

(c) Vertices of polyhedron *S1* are edited.

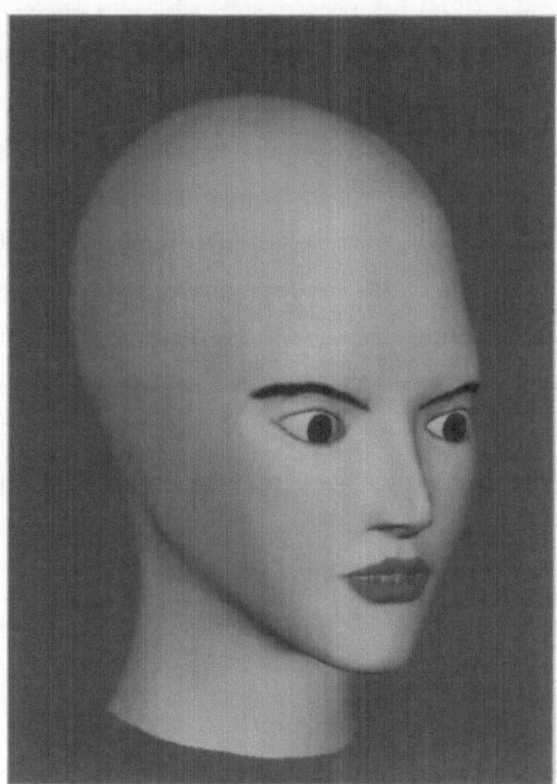

(d) The texture mapped face.

Fig. 11 A face created by recursive subdivision methods.

REFERENCES

Allan J.B., Wyvill B. and Witten I.H. (1989) A methodology for direct manipulation of polygon meshes, *New Advances in Computer Graphics, CGI Proceedings*, pp. 451-469.

Barr A.H. (1984) Global and local deformations of solid primitives, *Computer Graphics*, Vol. 18, No. 3, pp. 21-30.

Bartels R.H. and Beatty J.C. (1989) A technique for the direct manipulation of spline curves, *proceedings of Graphics Interface '89*, pp. 28-39.

Beeker E. (1986) Smoothing of shapes designed with free-form surfaces, *Computer Aided Design*, Vol. 18, No. 4, pp. 224-232.

Blinn J. (1982) A generalization of algebraic surface drawing, *ACM Transactions on Graphics*, Vol. 1, pp. 235-256.

Brunet P. (1988) Including shape handles in recursive subdivision surfaces, *Computer Aided Geometric Design*, Vol. 5, pp. 41-50.

Catmull E. and Clark J. (1974) Recursively generated B-spline surfaces on arbitrary topological meshes, *Computer Aided Design*, Vol. 10, No. 6, pp. 350-355.

Chaikin G.M. (1974) An algorithm for high speed curve generation, *Computer Graphics and Image Processing*, Vol. 3, pp. 346-349.

Chiyokura H. and Kimura F. (1983) Design of solids with free-form surfaces, *Computer Graphics*, Vol. 17, No. 3, pp. 289-298.

Doo D.W.H. and Sabin M.A. (1974) Behavior of recursive subdivision surfaces near extraordinary points, *Computer Aided Design*, Vol. 10, No. 6, pp. 356-360.

Forsey D.R. and Bartels R.H. (1988) Hierarchical B-spline Refinement, *Computer Graphics*, Vol. 22, No. 4, pp. 205-212.

Loop C. and DeRose T., (1990) Generalized B-spline surfaces of arbitrary topology, *Computer Graphics*, Vol. 24, No. 4, pp. 347-356.

Nasri A.H. (1987) Polyhedral subdivision methods for free-form surfaces, *ACM Transactions of Graphics*, Vol. 6, No. 1, pp. 29-73.

Nasri A.H. (1991a) Boundary-corner control in recursive-subdivision surfaces, *Computer Aided Design*, Vol. 23, No. 6, pp. 405-410.

Nasri A. H. (1991b) Surface interpolation on irregular networks with normal conditions, *Computer Aided Geometric Design*, Vol. 8, pp. 89-96.

Sederberg T.W. and Parry S.R. (1986) Free-form deformation of solid geometric models, *Computer Graphics*, Vol. 20, No. 4, pp. 151-160.

van Wijk J. (1986) Bicubic patches for approximating non-rectangular control point meshes, *Computer Aided Geometric Design*, Vol. 3, No. 1, pp. 1-13.

Wyvill G., McPheeters C. and Wyvill B. (1986) Data structure for soft objects, *The Visual Computer*, Vol. 2, No. 4, pp. 227-234.

APPENDIX A: The number of vertices, edges and faces after n times subdivision

For simplicity, we assume that the original polyhedron S_0 is closed. Let n_f^i, n_v^i, n_e^i be the number of faces, vertices and edges of S_i. For each subdivision step, each face, each vertex and each edge generate one F-face, one V-face and one E-face, respectively. Therefore, the number of faces of S_{i+1} is written as

$$n_f^{i+1} = n_f^i + n_v^i + n_e^i .$$
(a1)

Each edge generates two new edges that are shared by an E-face and an F-face. In addition, each edge generates two new edges that are shared by an E-face and V-face. Therefore, the number of edges of S_{i+1} is written as

$$n_e^{i+1} = 4 n_e^i .$$
(a2)

Each n-sided face generates n new vertices. Each n-sided face has n edges and each edge is shared by two faces. Therefore, the number of vertices of S_{i+1} is written as

$$n_v^{i+1} = 2\, n_e^i \ .$$ (a3)

Using Equations (a1), (a2) and (a3), we get

$$
\begin{aligned}
n_f^i &= n_f^0 + \frac{4^i - 1}{2} n_e^0 \\
n_e^i &= 4^i\, n_e^0 \\
n_v^i &= \frac{4^i\, n_e^0}{2}
\end{aligned}
$$ (a4)

Therefore, the number of faces, edges and vertices of S_i is about 4^i times that of S_0.

Tsuneya Kurihara is a researcher at the Central Research Laboratory, Hitachi, Ltd. He received the B.E. and M.E. degrees from the University of Tokyo, Tokyo, Japan, in 1981 and 1983, respectively. His research interests include computer animation, interactive sculpting and physically-based modeling. He is a member of ACM, IEEE CS and IPS of Japan.
Address: Central Research Laboratory, Hitachi, Ltd.,
 1- 280, Higashi-koigakubo, Kokubunji-shi, Tokyo 185 Japan.
E-mail: kurihara@crl.hitachi.co.jp

A Display Algorithm of Brush Strokes Using Bézier Functions

Tomoyuki Nishita, Shinichi Takita, and Eihachiro Nakamae

ABSTRACT

Graphics editors have recently come into wide use. But for displaying high quality images, a more powerful tool has been desired. This paper proposes a useful display method for Chinese calligraphy, traditional Japanese ink painting called *sumie*, and watercolor painting. The method comprises techniques to express the outlines of a brush stroke and to vary shades of color. That is, the outlines of a brush stroke are modeled using piecewise Bézier curves, and the variation of gray shade inside of the outline are defined by Bézier functions. This method provides effective characteristics of a brush stroke such as shade variation, the scratchiness produced by dry brush, and blotchiness caused by the diffusion of ink.

Keywords: Outline fonts, Bézier curves, Brush strokes, Chinese calligraphy, Scan conversion

1   INTRODUCTION

Graphics editors (painting systems) useful in graphic art have recently come into wide use. Due to the increase in users of such systems, a tool able to render such expressions as oil painting and airbrush work has been desired, in order to represent better quality images. This paper proposes a useful method of express the Chinese calligraphy, traditional Japanese ink painting called *sumie*, and watercolor painting. This method provides better quality compared with previous methods which attempt to render such effects as shade variation, scratchiness (produced by a brush with too little ink remaining), blotchiness caused by diffusion of ink, or a stroke with texture; It is made up of the techniques of scan converting an outline of a brush and shade variation; the outline of a brush stroke is described by Bézier curves, the shade variation in the inside of the outline is expressed as Bézier functions, and these regions are scan converted with high accuracy.

In the following sections, the effects of brush strokes, previous work, and the scan conversion method of brush strokes are described. Finally examples of results which prove the usefulness of the proposed method are presented.

2   EFFECTS OF BRUSH STROKES AND PREVIOUS WORK

2.1   Effects of Brush Strokes

Two dimensional painting systems are divided into two types; the painting type giving color information to each pixel, and the drawing type specifying a primitive such as a circle, or a straight line. The representation method discussed here belongs to the latter; both outlines of a stroke and shade variation are described by functions.

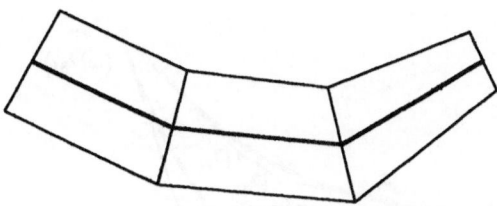

Figure 1: Expression of a brush stroke by quadrilateral approximation.

Sumie can produce not only the shape of curves but also perspective images by using subtle shade variation of ink. The ink density on the brush is uneven. Therefore, the ink density on each part of the brush affects the distribution of shade in a stroke, and the ink quantity varies as the brush moves through the stroke. This produces the effect of fuzzy shade gradation.

When a brush with watery ink moves on absorbent paper, particles of ink diffuse into the paper. This phenomenon is called blotchiness. Meanwhile, when the ink quantity is too little, a part of a brush stroke does not come out clearly. This phenomenon is called scratchiness (dry brush effect). With traditional Chinese calligraphy, depending on the particular character, the brush must be swept up abruptly at the end of the stroke. Such a movement of a brush also gives rise to scratchiness. Change of brush pressure varies the shade and width of a stroke. When drawing *sumie*, the variation of shade has to be taken into consideration. When rendering "Bokusai-painting" (traditional Chinese color painting), variation of color must be considered. Furthermore, outlines of almost all fonts resembling a writing brush style consist of curves. Therefore, a precise scan-conversion method of the closed areas bounded by curves is required.

2.2 Previous Methods for Brush Strokes

Some methods for displaying brush strokes have been developed. Strassmann [11] first attempted to simulate *sumie*. His method uses spline curves to express the trajectory of a stroke, and the area covered by the stroke is approximated by a set of quadrilaterals (see Figure 1). Chua [1] developed the method expressing the outline of a stroke by Bézier curves. This method uses a PostScript equipped printer. As stripes bounded by Bézier curves of a small width with different intensities are arranged to represent shade variation, shade varies discretely. Therefore, the quality of the image produced is not high enough. The effect of blotchiness is not considered in his system. Pham [9] used a B-spline curve to express the trajectory of a brush stroke. The area covered by the stroke is approximated by a set of small quadrilaterals to be filled with ink. Recently a method to simulate the blotchiness caused by the diffusion of ink using microscopic property of paper was proposed by Guo [4], but the area is also approximated by a set of quadrilaterals. As most methods use a set of quadrilaterals as an approximation of the area bounded by curves, the image quality is still open to improvement. The proposed method describing outlines of strokes and shade variation by Bézier functions yields precise and smooth outlines and variation of shade.

The method proposes a scan-conversion method for curved outlines without any polygonal approximation. As direct scan-conversion algorithms of curves, both of the scan-conversion of quadratic splines [8] and the quadratic rational Bézier curve [10] have been developed. In these methods intersections of a scanline and curves are calculated by solving a quadratic equation; intersection points can be obtained analytically. As these methods use quadratic curves, image quality is unsatisfactory. On the other hand, it is difficult to obtain intersections

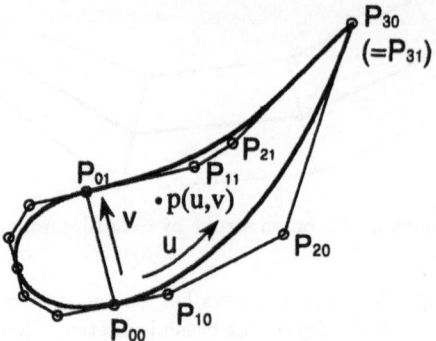

Figure 2: Expression of a brush stroke by Bézie curves.

analytically for curves with a degree of more than two. The Newton method is often used as one of the numerical analysis methods; but it requires a suitable initial guess, and is not robust. It is difficult to guarantee finding all solutions. As far as the authors know, no direct scan-conversion algorithm of curves, which have a degree of more than two, has been published. The advantages of the proposed method are that the intersections of a scanline and a curve can be obtained robustly by employing the convex hull property of Bézier curves, and the high degree Bézier curves are scan converted by iterations using linear equations.

The system which controls the movement of an actual writing brush by a computer like a plotter was proposed [12], though this subject is out of our discussion.

3   BASIC CONCEPT AND OUTLINE OF PROCEDURE

A couple of cubic Bézier curves make up the outline of a stroke. Let's consider Bézier planar patches bounded by curves (see Figure 2). The degree of the Bézier patch is 3×1, and each patch is expressed by two parameters, u and v; u is the parameter along it, and v the parameter across it. A shade value is defined as Bézier functions of u and v. Variation of shade with respect to v is defined as a cubic Bézier function because the distribution of ink across a stroke is uneven.

The outline of a brush stroke is given as Bézier curves of degree three or degree one (i.e., a straight line). A point in the the Bézier patch is denoted by $P(u, v)$, and the shade value at that point is described by function of (u, v).

As a brush stroke is represented by a planar Bézier patch (3×1, or 1×1 degree Bézier patch), point P in the patch is expressed by

$$P(u, v) = \sum_{i=0}^{n} \sum_{j=0}^{1} P_{ij} B_i^n(u) B_j^1(v) \tag{1}$$

where $P_{ij}(x_{ij}, y_{ij})$ $(i = 0, 1, 2, \cdots, n; n = 3 \text{ or } 1, j = 1, 2)$ are the coordinates of the control points, and both curves on $v = 0$ and $v = 1$ give the boundary curves of a stroke. B is the Bernstein polynomial, and is given by $B_i^n(u) = \binom{n}{i} u^i (1 - u)^{n-i}$.

The outline of the procedure is as follows:

(1) A scanline moves from the top to the bottom, and every intersection of the scanline and outline curves is calculated.

(2) For every pixel between these intersections, u and v are evaluated.

(3) The shade is computed using u and v, and is displayed.

In Step (2), in the case of 3×1 degree patch, an equation of degree 6 should be solved to calculate parameters u and v from coordinate (x, y) on a screen (when we use Kajiya's raytracing method[5]). Now we are discussing a painting system, and it is not practical, due to computational expense, to solve such a high degree equation for every pixel. Therefore, we propose an approximation method based on linear equations. That is, the values of u and v for sampling points on the scanline within the patch are obtained as the intersections of iso-parametric curves of the patch (iso-parametric curves of v component are lines) and the scanline.

Data input is performed interactively. Two input methods are available in our system. One of them uses points on the outline of brush stroke, some points on the outline are taken into a computer by mouse, and then Bézier curves are constructed using the data. Another method uses a sequence of points on a center line of a stroke; after inputting these points on the center line, Bézier curves expressing the center line are constructed, then widths are given as offset distances from the control points, and the offset curves are constructed by Bézier curves.

4 SCAN CONVERSION OF BÉZIER PATCHES

4.1 Calculation of Intersections of a Scanline and Curves

The scan-conversion algorithm proposed here is the improved version of calculation of intersections of Bézier curves and a straight line, which has been developed for the ray tracing method [6] of Bézier patches to save on computation time.

To obtain intersection points efficiently the following premises are made. 1)The scanline moves from the top to the bottom, and 2) the curve is monotone decreasing in y component. That is, the curve intersects with the scanline only once. The preprocessing for setting this condition is performed in advance; an original Bézier curve is subdivided at every point where the first derivative is zero.

The algorithm of calculating an intersection point between Bézier curve C of degree n and scanline L is explained using Figure 3 ($n = 3$ in this figure). Coordinates (x, y) of an arbitrary point on C are expressed by using parameter t as follows(e.g., $v = 0$ in equation (2)):

$$
\begin{aligned}
x(t) &= \sum_{i=0}^{n} x_i B_i^n(t), \\
y(t) &= \sum_{i=0}^{n} y_i B_i^n(t).
\end{aligned}
\tag{2}
$$

Let's denote y_s as y coordinate of the scanline, and then the equation of scanline L is expressed by $y - y_s = 0$. The intersection between curve C and straight line L is obtained by substituting y-component of equation (2) in this equation,

$$
\sum_{i=0}^{n} y_i B_i^n(t) - y_s = 0.
\tag{3}
$$

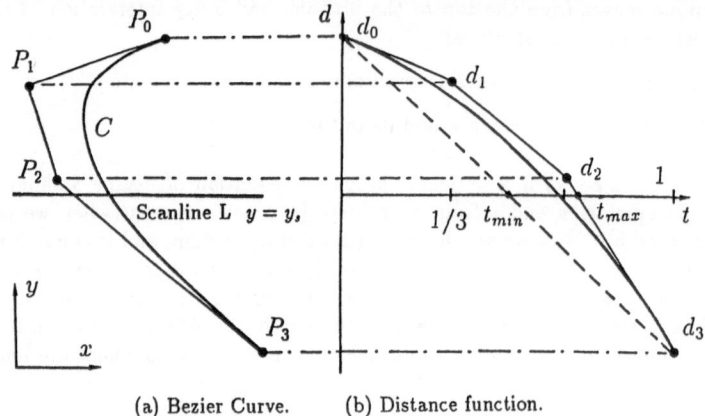

(a) Bezier Curve.　　(b) Distance function.

Figure 3: Intersection between scanline and Bézier curve.

As $\sum_{i=0}^{n} y_s B_i^n(t) = y_s$,

$$\sum_{i=0}^{n} d_i B_i^n(t) = 0. \tag{4}$$

where $d_i = y_i - y_s$.

As shown in Figure 3 (b), equation (4) is equivalent to a non-parametric Bézier curve. Assumed that the function composed of control point $(i/n, d_i)$ is $d(t)$, d is the distance from the scanline to the Bézier curve. Therefore we call equation (4) a distant function. The solutions of equation (4) is obtained by an iteration method (*Bézier clipping* method[6]).

4.2　Scan Conversion Using Coherence between Scanlines

For saving computation time on the iterative method described in the previous sub-section, the coherence between scanlines is utilized. Assume that scanline L decreases by Δy (here $\Delta y = 1$; scanline width). The value of parameter t of curve C is nearly equal to zero at the intersection point of the curve C with the first scanline (i.e., the intersection point is near the starting point P_0 on C). In most cases the intersection interval $[t_{min}, t_{max}]$ between a scanline and the convex hull formed by control points d_is of a distance function is narrow enough (see Figure 4(b)); the solution can be obtained by few iterations. After converging to solution t_{min}, the curve is subdivided at t_{min}; the interval $[0, t_{min}]$ is clipped away, and a new interval $[t_{min}, 1]$ is used for the next scanline as new control points. Then the control points for interval $[t_{min}, 1]$ are used for the next scanline as new control points.

By splitting the curve like this, every intersection point between a new interval and the following(next) scanline (a horizontal chain line shown in the figure) is near the point where $t = 0$ on the new curve. Therefore, the solution is obtained by few iterations. If the difference of t_{min} from that of previous scanline is very small, the Bézier curve is not subdivided as mentioned later. The subdivision of Bézier curves is applied only to y component, rather than to both x and y components. Subdivision is accomplished by the well-known de Casteljau method[2].

Let's denote the minimum and maximum y values of the control points as y_{min} and y_{max}, and the values of t_{min} and t_{max} on the original(i.e., before subdivision) Bézier curve as T_{min}

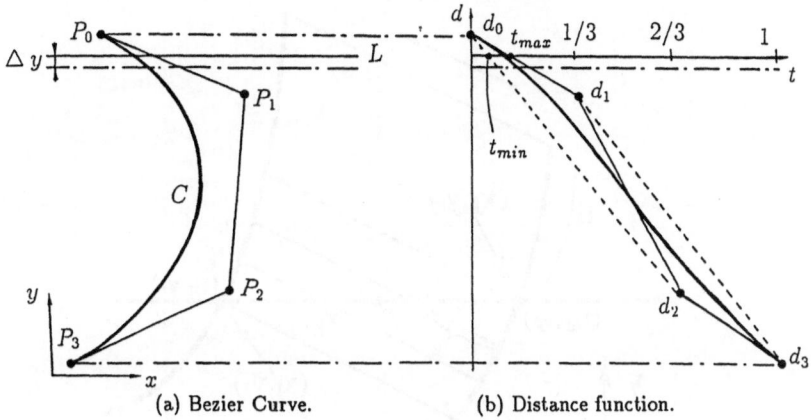

(a) Bezier Curve.   (b) Distance function.

Figure 4: Intersection interval on a scanline.

and T_{max}, respectively. Let *tol* be the tolerance. Then the procedure of scan conversion is as follows:

1) Set $y_s = y_{max}$, $T'_{min} = 0$.

2) Extract the interval $[t_{min}, t_{max}]$ using the control points d_i of the distance function, where $d_i = y_i - y_s$ $(i = 1, 2, \cdots, n)$.

3) If $T_{max} - T_{min} > tol$, extract the distance function of the interval $[t_{min}, t_{max}]$ and go back to 2). Otherwise go to the next step.

4) Calculate $t = (T_{min} + T_{max})/2$, and calculate x coordinate from t(see equation (2)).

5) If $T_{min} - T'_{min} > tol$, extract the interval $[t_{min}, 1]$ on y component of the Bézier curve, and set $T'_{min} = T_{min}$. Otherwise go to the next step.

6) If $y_s > y_{min}$, set $y_s = y_s - \Delta y$ and return to 2). Otherwise terminate the algorithm.

As the tolerance is defined in parameter space, the value of the tolerance has to be given depending on the length of the curve; in order to obtain the same degree of accuracy of the x coordinate of an intersection point, the tolerance may be small for a long curve, and large for a short curve. Therefore, in this paper the inverse of the length of the longer side of the bounding box determined by the control points of the curve is used as the tolerance. Subdivision in step 3) is applied twice, since the left side of t_{min} and the right side of t_{max} should be clipped away. Meanwhile, in step 5) to clip the left side of t_{min} the curve is subdivided once.

In the proposed method the smaller the area of the convex hull composed of the control points of the distance function, the fewer the number of iterations. Namely, as the intervals between y components of the control points approach equidistance, the distance function comes close to a straight line and thus the number of iteration becomes few. For our examples, the proposed method requires only an average of 1.3 iterations to obtain one intersection.

4.3 Inverse Mapping

As stated in the previous sub-section, the intersection points of a scanline and boundary curves can be extracted efficiently by the intersection test using the Bézier clipping method.

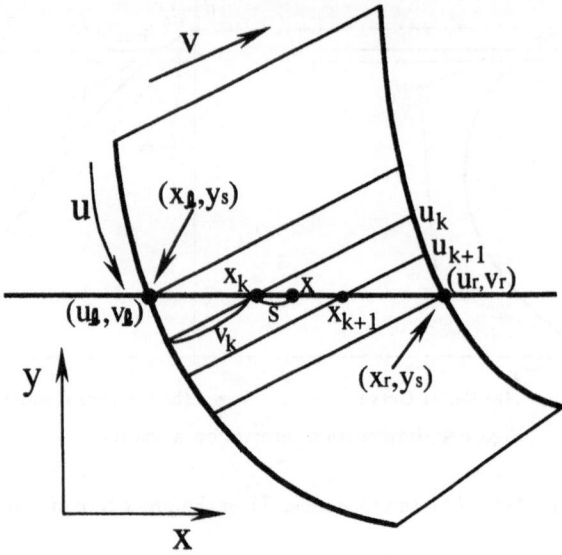

Figure 5: Inverse mapping.

In the next step in order to fill the Bézier patch, inverse mapping calculating values of u and v from coordinate (x, y) is required. For this calculation, as mentioned before, it is necessary to solve equations of degree six. Though the Bézier clipping method .can be used, the following approximation is applied to improve the efficiency.

The intersection points of scanline $y = y_s$ and boundary curves of a Bézier patch are denoted by (x_l, y_s) and (x_r, y_s), and parameters at those points are described by (u_l, v_l) and (u_r, v_r), respectively. After calculation of intersection points (x_l, y_s) and (x_r, y_s) (see Figure 5), (u, v) of every pixel between the intersections are evaluated in the following manner.

As the degree of v component is one, it is guaranteed that an intersection line of the scanline and the Bézier patch is within $[u_l, u_r]$ in the parameter space.

Sampling points are set by dividing the interval $[x_l, x_r]$ by N, where $N = (x_r - x_l)/M$; M is the sampling span (usually it's set to 2 or 3 pixel width). After calculation of (u, v) for every sampling point, the values of the parameters at every pixel between the sampling points are linearly interpolated.

At the k-th sampling point $(k = 1, 2, \cdots, N - 1)$, let (u_k, v_k) denote parameters and x_k express the x-coordinates at the intersections between the scanline and the outline. Then these values are obtained as follows:

1) If $u_r - u_l \geq \epsilon$ $(\epsilon : tolerance)$,

$$
\begin{aligned}
u_k &= u_l + (u_r - u_l)k/N, \\
v_k &= (y(u_k, 0) - y_s)/(y(u_k, 0) - y(u_k, 1)), \\
x_k &= x(u_k, v_k),
\end{aligned}
$$

where functions $x(u, v)$ and $y(u, v)$ are x and y components of the equation, respectively (1). The following equations give the values of (u, v) satisfying the condition $x_k \leq x <$

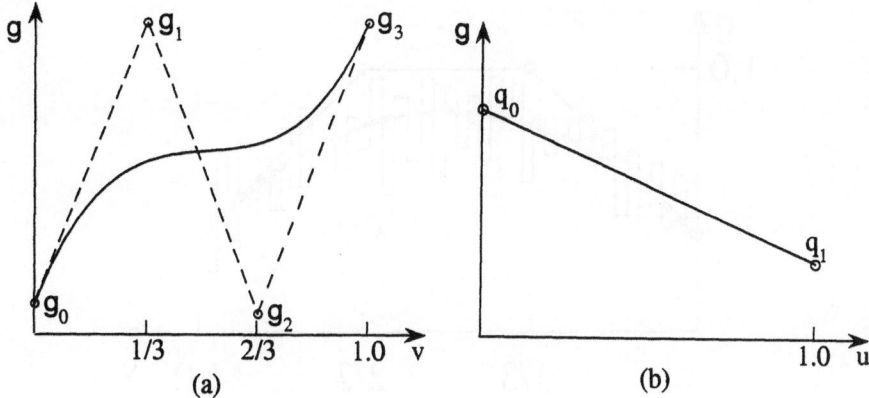

Figure 6: Shade variation by Bézie function.

$x_{k+1}.$

$$
\begin{aligned}
s &= (x - x_k)/(x_{k+1} - x_k), \\
u &= u_k + (u_{k+1} - u_k)s, \\
v &= v_k + (v_{k+1} - v_k)s.
\end{aligned}
\tag{5}
$$

2) If $u_r - u_l < \epsilon$,

$$
\begin{aligned}
s &= (x - x_l)/(x_r - x_l), \\
u &= (u_l + u_r)/2, \\
v &= v_l + (v_r - v_l)s.
\end{aligned}
\tag{6}
$$

5   CALCULATION OF SHADE VARIATIONS

Shade of a brush stroke is given as Bézier functions of u and v (u is the parameter along the stroke and v is the one across the stroke). Shade function g expressed by u and v is shown in Figure 6. This function shows the blending ratio between ink color and paper color. The shade function is defined as

$$
g(u, v) = \sum_{j=0}^{3} g_j B_j^3(v) \sum_{i=0}^{1} q_i B_i^1(u)
\tag{7}
$$

where Bézier functions of u and v are linear and degree 3, respectively, and both g_j and q_i are the control points of Bézier functions for shade variation. It is assumed that the ink decreases linearly along a stroke (with u component), and the distribution of ink across the stroke is not uniform. For example, in case that ink is dense in the center part and thin in the margin, the degree of function should be more than two. Therefore, we use a cubic Bézier function for v component.

Color(or intensity) C at point (x, y) is obtained from ink color C_i and paper color C_p, using shade function g; it is calculated by

$$
C(x, y) = g(u, v)C_i + (1 - g(u, v))C_p(x, y).
\tag{8}
$$

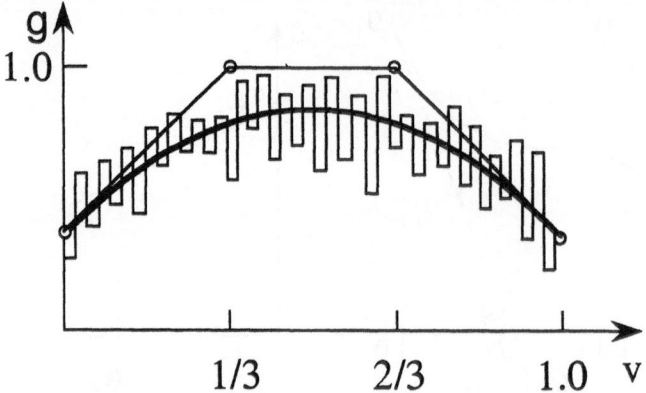

Figure 7: Shade function with dry brush effect.

By treating the color of the colored paper as the color of new paper, it is possible to overlap another stroke.

5.1 Effect of Dry Brush

When the moisture on a brush is too little, a part of a brush stroke does not come out clearly. That is, scratchiness arises; *dry brush* effect. Once this arises, it remains until the ink is replenished. To represent the quantity of each bristle, v component is discretized (e.g., divided into 50 elements). An array is used to memorize the ink quantity of each bristle. Variation of the ink quantity (v component) is given as a cubic Bézier function, and a small amount of variation caused by the application of random numbers is superimposed. Figure 7 shows initial ink quantity at $u = 0$ (User can specify the control points of the Bézier function and the the magnitude of the random numbers). Along the movement of a stroke (in proportion to u), the ink quantity decreases linearly. When the ink quantity of a bristle drops below a given threshold, its locus fades away.

5.2 Effect of Blotchiness

When a sheet of absorbent paper is used, blotchiness (diffusion or *nijimi* in Japanese) arises, and it is noticeable around the boundary of a stroke. The diffusion area is assigned as a function of v component in our system. That is, blotchiness arises in the regions of $0 \le v < dv$ and $1 - dv < v \le 1$, where 0.1 or 0.2 are used as dv. In order to vary shade in these regions, our system uses the Fourier function [3] which is proposed for generating cloud patterns.

The nearer the boundary, the greater the effect of blotchiness. The shade value is weighted by the following equation F which is shown in Figure 8.

$$F(u) = k \sum_{i=0}^{m} c_i \big(\sin(f_i u + p_i) + T\big) \cdot \sum_{i=0}^{m} c_i \big(\sin(g_i v_0 + q_i) + T\big), \qquad (9)$$

where constant k is used to keep the range of F smaller than 1, f_i and g_i are frequencies, c_i is the magnitude for the i-th frequency, and p_i and g_i are phases. Among those constants, there are following relations:

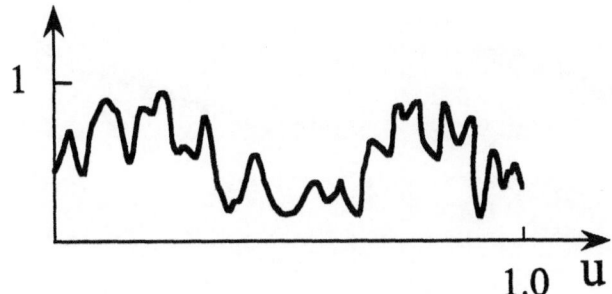

Figure 8: Shade variation by Fourier series.

$f_{i+1} = 2f_i,\ g_{i+1} = 2g_i,\ c_{i+1} = 1/\sqrt{2}c_i, p_i = (\pi/2)\sin(g_i + v_0/2)$ (q_i is given in the similar manner). m ranges from 3 to 6, and T is set to 0.5. v_0 is constant.

For example, when $v < dv$, if $v < Fdv$, the shade function g is set to 0. In the case of $1 - dv < v$, if $v > Fdv/(1 - dv)$, g is set to 0.

Figure 9 shows examples of simple brush strokes; (a) represents shade variation, (b) expresses the effect of dry brush, (c) shows blotchiness, and (d) shows overlapping strokes with different colors.

5.3 Texture Mapping

As (u, v) are calculated for every point in a patch, general texture mapping methods for 3D objects are applicable without any change.

6 EXAMPLES

Figure 10 shows some examples of the proposed method. Figure (a) shows an example of Chinese calligraphy, a character which means heart. Figure (b) demonstrate dry brush effect. Figure (c) represents the effect of blotchiness.

Examples of *sumie* are shown in Figure 11; leaves and branches of a sasanqua camellia branch with a flower is shown in Figure (a), a Japanese nightingale in (b), branches of a tinged Japanese maple tree in (c), and tulips in (d). The number of Bézier curves in these examples are, in order, 232, 212, 633, and 226, respectively. The stamp shown in the bottom left in Figure (a) was the scanned image, and the *sumie* was overlapped. Blotchiness appears in a flower in Figure (a), a part of the leaves in Figure (c), and the flowers of Figure (d). The effect of dry brush is depicted in the leaves in Figure (d). The texture mapped *sumie* is shown in Figure 12; curved surfaces are displayed by the raytracing method [6].

Antialiasing is performed by the multi-scanning method without polygonalization [7].

7 CONCLUSION

We have proposed a powerful display method for Chinese calligraphy, Japanese ink painting, and watercolor painting. The method is composed by the techniques of scan conversion for

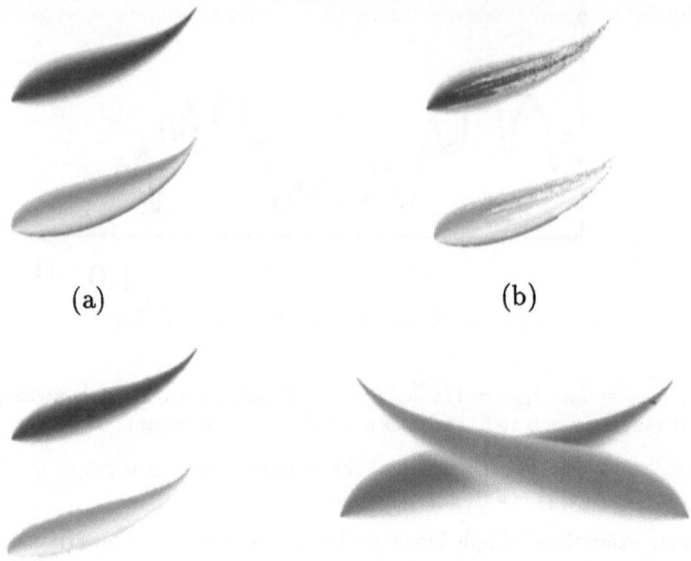

(a) (b)

(c) (d)

Figure 9: Examples of simple strokes.

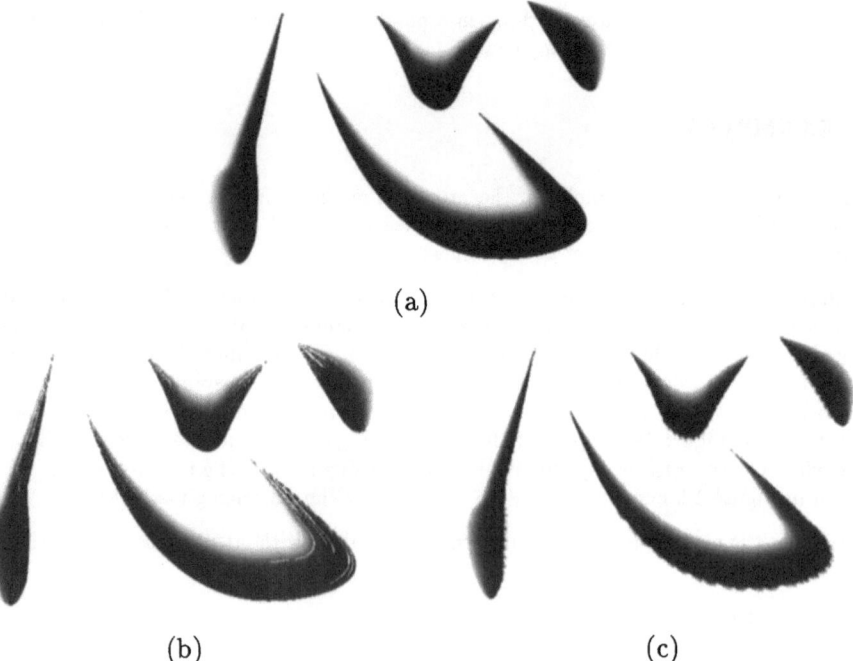

(a)

(b) (c)

Figure 10: Examples of Chinese calligraphy.

(a)

(b)

(c)

(d)

Figure 11: Examples of Japanese ink painting.

Figure 12: An example of texture mapped *sumie*.

an outline of a brush and varying shade; the outline of a brush stroke is described by Bézier curves, and shade variation inside the outline is defined by the Bézier function.

The advantages of the proposed method are as follows:

(1) Scan conversion is performed precisely because the algorithm is without any polygonal approximation of boundary curves. Intersections of scanlines and outlines can be obtained robustly and precisely using the convex hull property of Bézier curves; the proposed method requires only 1.3 times iteration on average to obtain one intersection of a scanline and the Bézier curve.

(2) Subtle shade variations such as fuzzy shade gradation, dry brush, and blotchiness can be displayed.

(3) High quality images can be displayed by performing antialiasing.

Acknowledgment The authors would like to acknowledge Y. Taniguchi and M. Nomura for their help in data creation.

REFERENCES

[1] Chua, Y.S., "Bézier Brushstrokes," CAD, Vol.22, No.9 (1990), pp.550-555.

[2] Farrin, G., "Curves and Surfaces for Computer Aided Geometric Design," Academic Press Inc., (1988), p.25-31.

[3] Gardner, G.W.,"Visual Simulation of Clouds," Computer Graphics, Vol.19, No.4,(1985), pp.229-303.

[4] Guo, Q., Kunii, T., "Modeling the Diffuse Painting of 'Sumie'," Modeling in Computer Graphics (Proc. of the IFIP WG5.10), Springer-Verlag(1991), pp.329-338.

[5] Kajiya, J., "Ray Tracing Parametric Patches," Computer Graphics, Vol.16, No.3,(1982), pp.245-254.

[6] Nishita, T., Sederberg, T.W., Kakimoto, M., "Ray Tracing Rational Trimmed Surface Patches," Computer Graphics, Vol.24, No.4,(1990), pp.337-345.

[7] Nishita, T., Nakamae, E., "Half-Tone Representation of 3D Objects with Smooth Edge by Using a Multi-Scanning Method,"J.Information Processing(in Japanese), Vol.25, No.5,(1984), pp.703-711.

[8] Pavlidis, T., "Scan Conversion of Regions Bounded by Parabolic Splines," IEEE CG & A, 1985,pp.47-53.

[9] Pahm, B.,"Expressive Brush Strokes," Graphical Models and Image Processing, Vol.53, No.1,(1991), pp.1-6.

[10] Saitoh, T., Hosaka, M., "High Quality Outline Fonts by the Extended Rational Quadratic Bézier Curve," J.Information Processing(in Japanese), Vol.31, No.4,pp.562-570.

[11] Strassmann, S., "Hairy Brushes," Computer Graphics, Vol.20, No.4,(1986), pp.225-232.

[12] Yun-Jie, P., Hui-Xiang, Z., "Drawing Chinese Traditional Painting by Computer," Modeling in Computer Graphics (Proc. of the IFIP WG5.10), Springer-Verlag(1991), pp.321-328.

Tomoyuki Nishita is a professor in the department of Electronic and Electrical Engineering at Fukuyama University, Japan. He was on the research staff at Mazda from 1973 to 1979 and worked on design and development of computer-controlled vehicle system. He joined Fukuyama University in 1979. He was an associate researcher in the Engineering Computer Graphics Laboratory at Brigham Young University from 1988 to the end of March, 1989. His research interests involve computer graphics including lighting model, hidden-surface removal, and antialiasing.

Nishita received his BE, ME and Ph. D in Engineering in 1971, 1973, and 1985, respectively, from Hiroshima University. He is a member of ACM, IPS of Japan and IEE of Japan.

Address: Faculty of Engineering, Fukuyama University, Sanzo, Higashimura-cho, Fukuyama, 729-02 Japan.

E-mail: nis@eml.hiroshima-u.ac.jp

Shinichi Takita is a professor in the Department of Education at Kagawa University, Japan. His research interests include computer graphics and CAI.

Takita received his BE and ME degrees in electrical engineering form Hiroshima University in 1964 and 1966, respectively. He is a member of the IEE of Japan, IPS of Japan and the Japan Society of Industrial and Technical Education.

Address: Faculty of Education, Kagawa University,
1-1, Saiwai-cho, Takamatsu, 760 Japan.

E-mail: takita@ed.kagawa-u.ac.jp

Eihachiro Nakamae is a professor at Hiroshima Prefectural University. Previously he worked at Hiroshima University from 1956 to 1992, where he was appointed as research associate in 1956 and a professor in 1968. He joined Hiroshima Prefectural University in 1992. He was an associate researcher at Clarkson College of Technology, Potsdam, N. Y., from 1973 to 1974. His research interests include computer graphics and electric machinery.

Nakamae received the BE, ME, and DE degrees in 1954, 1956, and 1967 from Waseda University. He is a member of IEEE, IEE of Japan, IPS of Japan and IEICE of Japan.

Address: Faculty of Information Science, Hiroshima Prefectural University,
Nanatuka-cho, Shoubara City, Hiroshima Prefecture, 727 Japan.

E-mail: naka@eml.hiroshima-u.ac.jp

Interpolating Solid Orientations with Circular Blending Quaternion Curves*

Myung-Soo Kim and Kee-Won Nam

Abstract

This paper presents a method to smoothly interpolate a sequence of solid orientations using circular blending quaternion curves. We show that, given three solid orientations, there is a circular quaternion curve which interpolates the three orientations. Given four orientations $q_{i-1}, q_i, q_{i+1}, q_{i+2}$, there are two circular quaternion curves C_i and C_{i+1} which interpolate the triples of orientations (q_{i-1}, q_i, q_{i+1}) and (q_i, q_{i+1}, q_{i+2}) respectively. Thus, both the two quaternion curves C_i and C_{i+1} interpolate the two orientations q_i and q_{i+1}.

Using a similar blending method to the parabolic blending of Overhauser [15], we generate a quaternion curve Q_i which interpolates the two orientations q_i and q_{i+1} while smoothly blending the two circular quaternion curves C_i and C_{i+1}. The quaternion curve Q_i has the same tangent direction with C_i at q_i and with C_{i+1} at q_{i+1} respectively. By connecting the quaternion curves Q_i's in a connected sequence, we generate a quaternion path which smoothly interpolates a given sequence of solid orientations.

There are various advantages of this method, in computational complexity as well as in design flexibility, over the previous interpolation methods of solid orientations. Detailed comparisons are made with respect to the Bézier curve of Shoemake [19], the cardinal spline curve of Pletincks [16], and the spherical quadrangle curve of Shoemake [20].

Keywords: Quaternion, rotation, spline, parabolic blending, animation, interpolation, in-betweening

1 Introduction

One of the fundamental problems in computer animation is how to interpolate a sequence of positions and orientations of a rigid body [11]. The interpolation should be smooth and look natural to produce a good animation. For a single solid object, its position and orientation can be uniquely represented with two vectors $v \in R^3$ and $q \in SO(3)$ respectively, where R^3 is the 3-dimensional Euclidean space and $SO(3)$ is the rotation group of R^3 [6, 8, 18]. Thus, the motion of a single solid object can be uniquely represented as a path in the product space $R^3 \times SO(3)$. Given a sequence of position-orientation pairs, i.e., $(p_i, q_i) \in R^3 \times SO(3)$, for $i = 1, \ldots, n$, the motion control problem for a given solid object is how to control the smooth path $\gamma(t) \in R^3 \times SO(3)$ which interpolates the sequence of these n points (p_i, q_i)'s.

$SO(3)$ is a projective space which is constructed from the unit 3-sphere S^3 in R^4 by identifying each pair $[q, -q]$ of two antipodal points $q, -q \in S^3$ as a single point $q \in SO(3)$. Each local neighborhood U of S^3 which contains no antipodal points is in one-to-one correspondence with the same neighborhood U in $SO(3)$. The local geometry of $SO(3)$ is thus identical to that of S^3. By cutting the 3-sphere S^3 by a hyper-plane $L^3 \subset R^4$ which contains the origin of R^4, we get a 2-sphere $S^3 \cap L^3$ which is isomorphic to the standard 2-sphere S^2. That is, by rotating the hyper plane L^3 into the subspace R^3 embedded in R^4, we can rotate the 2-sphere $S^3 \cap L^3$ into the standard 2-sphere S^2. Further, by cutting the sphere S^2 with a plane $L^2 \subset R^3$ which does not necessarily pass through the origin, we generate a circle C on the sphere S^2. By mapping this circle C back to the original 3-sphere S^3, we can generate a circular curve on the 3-sphere S^3. Similar arguments apply to the projective spaces $SO(3)$ and $SO(2)$, too. The circular quaternion curve generation method presented in this paper is based on this simple geometric observation.

Shoemake [19] introduced the quaternion to the computer graphics community for the purpose of interpolating a sequence of solid orientations in keyframe animation. The basic construction tool used in Shoemake [19] is a generalization of de Casteljau algorithm to $SO(3)$. De Casteljau algorithm generates a Bézier curve by a successive subdivision of line segments [2, 12]. Shoemake [19] instead uses *slerp*, the shortest curve segment on $SO(3)$, which is a generalization of the line segment in

*Research supported in part by RIST and KOSEF.

R^3. Each point on a Bézier quaternion curve is generated by computing six slerps. To minimize the number of slerps used in the construction, Shoemake [20] adapted the Boehm quadrangle scheme [3] and generated a cubic quaternion curve on which each curve point can be computed with only three slerps. Both schemes of Shoemake [19, 20] have a local shape control over the constructed quaternion curve by modifying its control points. Shoemake [21] provides a user-friendly interface to manipulate unit quaternions, however, it is cumbersome for a user to manipulate the quaternion control points directly. Duff [9] used an approximate B-spline interpolation scheme to generate a quaternion curve. This scheme generates an extremely smooth quaternion curve with a second degree continuity, however, the constructed curve does not pass through the control points. Nielson and Heiland [14] overcame this drawback by computing the control points for a B-spline quaternion curve which interpolates a given sequence of quaterion points. However, the computation requires a time-consuming interative numerical method to approximate the control points, which may deteriorate the efficiency of the algorithm. Pletincks [16] suggested an algorithm to construct an approximate cardinal spline quaternion curve by recursively generating the middle point of each cardinal spline curve segment. This method is very simple to implement and runs fast. Further, the cardinal spline coefficient c ($0 \leq c \leq 1$) controls the local shape of each quaternion curve segment. A disadvantage of this method is in the recursive construction of the successive middle points, i.e., each curve segment is recursively subdivided into two halves. The total number of middle points generated on the quaternion curve becomes $2^i - 1$ for some positive integer i. In the construction of this scheme, the $2^i + 1$ curve points generated upto the i-th step, i.e., $2^i - 1$ middle points and 2 end points, are stored in an array to generate new 2^i middle points, and the resulting $2^{i+1} + 1$ curve points are stored in a new array. This excessive memory use deteriorates the performance of the algorithm.

Since all the above previous methods [9, 14, 16, 19, 20] are based on the slerp construction, the basic ideas can be easily extended to any complete Riemannian manifold, in which the shorted path, *geodesic*, between any two points can be defined [13]. The rotation group $SO(3)$ is such a complete Riemannian manifold in which the shortest path can be constructed relatively easily as a slerp which is a circular curve segment on a greatest circle of $SO(3)$. In a sense, the above methods [9, 14, 16, 19, 20] are too general. To make them more efficient and flexible on $SO(3)$, one may need to investigate and utilize various simple mathematical structures of $SO(3)$. Compared with the large amount of nice geometric properties known about the various spline curves in R^3, only a few are known about the corresponding quaternion spline curves.

In this paper, we investigate the spherical structures of S^3 and $SO(3)$, and construct relatively simple circular quaternion curves on them. Using these circular curves, we present a new quaternion curve generation method which interpolates a sequence of solid orientations. Our key observation in the development of the new algorithm is based on the circular curve generation method discussed above on the projective space $SO(3)$. Given a sequence of solid orientations $q_i \in SO(3)$, for $i = 1, \ldots, n$, we consider the two circular curve C_i and C_{i+1} which interpolate the two orientations q_i and q_{i+1}, i.e., C_i and C_{i+1} which interpolate the triples (q_{i-1}, q_i, q_{i+1}) and (q_i, q_{i+1}, q_{i+2}) of solid orientations respectively. By blending the two circular curves C_i and C_{i+1} using a similar technique to the Overhauser's parabolic blending [5, 15, 17], we can easily generate a smooth quaternion curve Q_i which interpolates q_i and q_{i+1} while being tangent with C_i at q_i and with C_{i+1} at q_{i+1} respectively on the rotation group $SO(3)$.

Given the two circular frames $C_i(t)$ and $C_{i+1}(t)$ parametrized by t ($0 \leq t \leq 1$), we can generate a spherical ruled surface on $SO(3)$ by taking each slerp connecting $C_i(t)$ and $C_{i+1}(t)$ as the ruling. The circular blending curve Q_i is embedded on this spherical ruled surface. By changing the two parameters $s_i(t)$ and $s_{i+1}(t)$ for the two circular curves $C_i(s_i(t))$ and $C_{i+1}(s_{i+1}(t))$ respectively, one could generate different spherical ruled surfaces on $SO(3)$. Further, the circular blending curve Q_i on the spherical ruled surface would also be deformed according to the deformation of the spherical ruled surface. The parameters $s_i(t)$ and $s_{i+1}(t)$ may be given as polynomials of t, and one could control the local shape of the curve Q_i by changing these two polynomials.

Barr, Currin, Gabriel, and Hughes [1] suggested a method to interpolate the solid orientations smoothly by minimizing the tangential accelerations. They approximated the solution by formulating the problem as a constrained optimization problem for n unit quaternions, where k of them interpolate the given k keyframe quaternions with $k \leq n$. Since each non-keyframe unit quaternion has three degrees of freedom on the 3-dimensional manifold $SO(3)$, the numerical search space for the optimization problem is relatively large. By restricting the intermediate quaternions to the above spherical ruled surfaces which are 2-dimensional submanifolds of $SO(3)$, one could speed up the numerical approximation process.

The rest of this paper is organized as follows. In §2, we present how to generate circular quaternion curves on the space $SO(3)$. In §3, we consider how to blend two circular quaternion curves and construct a quaternion path which smoothly interpolates a sequence of solid orientations. In §4, we analyze the time complexity of the circular blending method. In §5, we give detailed comparisons with some of the previous interpolation methods [16, 19, 20]. Finally, in §6, we conclude this paper and discuss further extensions.

2 Circular Curves in S^3

In this section, we consider the following problem: given three points $p_1, p_2, p_3 \in S^3$, how to generate a circular curve which interpolates the three points.

2.1 Great Circle in S^2

In 3D Euclidean space R^3, given two points $p_1, p_2 \in S^2$, there is always a great circle C which connects these two points. The circle C is the intersection curve between the unit sphere S^2 and the plane L which contains the two points p_1, p_2 and the origin of R^3. Since the two vectors p_1, p_2 are parallel to the plane L, the vector $n_P = p_1 \times p_2$ is normal to the plane L. Let $n_2 = n_P \times p_1$, then the three vectors p_1, n_2, n_P form an orthonormal basis, and the matrix

$$T = [p_1 \ n_2 \ n_P]^t$$

defines a rigid transformation which maps the orthonormal unit vectors p_1, n_2, n_P into the standard unit vectors $e_1 = (1,0,0), e_2 = (0,1,0), e_3 = (0,0,1)$ respectively. Thus, under this rigid transformation, the circle C is transformed into a planar circle of radius 1 in the 2D Euclidean plane R^2. Further, analytic computations become a lot simpler on the standard unit circle S^1 and the computational results can be mapped back to the original curve C in S^2 by using the inverse transformation which is given by

$$T^{-1} = [p_1 \ n_2 \ n_P].$$

2.2 Great Sphere in S^3

Using a conceptual similarity to the great circle on the unit sphere S^2, we consider how to construct a great sphere S which interpolates three points $p_1, p_2, p_3 \in S^3$ in the 4D Euclidean space R^4. First, we construct the hyper-plane $L^3 \subset R^4$ which contains the three points p_1, p_2, p_3 and the origin of R^4. The hyper-plane L^3 is defined in the form

$$a \cdot x + b \cdot y + c \cdot z + d \cdot w = 0,$$

where the 4D normal vector (a, b, c, d) is given by the relation

$$(a, b, c, d) = a \cdot e_1 + b \cdot e_2 + c \cdot e_3 + d \cdot e_4 = \det \begin{bmatrix} e_1 & e_2 & e_3 & e_4 \\ x_1 & y_1 & z_1 & w_1 \\ x_2 & y_2 & z_2 & w_2 \\ x_3 & y_3 & z_3 & w_3 \end{bmatrix}$$

with $e_1 = (1,0,0,0), e_2 = (0,1,0,0), e_3 = (0,0,1,0), e_4 = (0,0,0,1)$, and $p_i = (x_i, y_i, z_i, w_i)$, for $i = 1, 2, 3, 4$. We denote the above ternary operation as $N(p_1, p_2, p_3)$ which computes the 4D normal vector (a, b, c, d) from the given three 4D vectors p_1, p_2, p_3. By normalizing the 4D vector (a, b, c, d), we obtain a unit 4D vector $n_4 = (a, b, c, d)/\|(a, b, c, d)\|$.

Let $n_2 = N(p_3, n_4, p_1)/\|N(p_3, n_4, p_1)\|$ and $n_3 = N(n_4, p_1, n_2)$, then the four 4D vectors p_1, n_4, n_2, n_3 form an orthonormal basis. Note that $N(n_4, p_1, n_2)$ is a unit 4D vector since the three vectors n_4, p_1, n_2 are orthonormal, and thus we do not need to normalize the vector $N(n_4, p_1, n_2)$ to obtain a unit 4D vector n_3. The transformation

$$T = [p_1 \ n_2 \ n_3 \ n_4]^t$$

maps the three points p_1, p_2, p_3 into the 3D Euclidean subspace R^3 which is generated by the first three unit vectors $e_1 = (1,0,0), e_2 = (0,1,0), e_3 = (0,0,1)$. Since the transformation T is an orthogonal matrix, the transformation preserves the lengths and the angles of the vectors [7]. Thus, the transformed three points $\bar{p}_1 = T(p_1), \bar{p}_2 = T(p_2), \bar{p}_3 = T(p_3)$ are on the unit sphere S^2 of R^3. Note that $\bar{p}_1 = e_1 = (1,0,0,0)$. Further, these three points can be mapped back into the original three points p_1, p_2, p_3 under the inverse transformation

$$T^{-1} = [p_1 \ n_2 \ n_3 \ n_4].$$

Let $S = T^{-1}(S^2)$ be the mapping of the unit sphere S^2 into the 3-sphere $S^3 \subset R^4$ under the orthonormal transformation T^{-1}. Then, one can easily show that the greatest sphere S contains the three points p_1, p_2, p_3.

When we restrict the domain of the inverse transformation T^{-1} to R^3, the last column n_4 is redundant. This is because any 4D vector (a, b, c, d) in the subspace R^3 has the last coordinate $d = 0$. Thus, we ignore the last row of T and the last column of T^{-1}, and write

$$T = [p_1 \ n_2 \ n_3]^t,$$

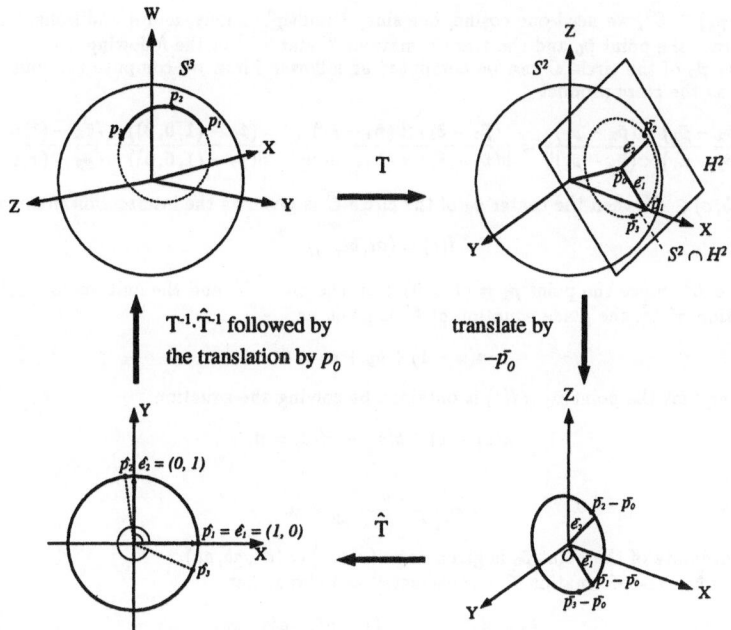

Figure 1: Construction of a Circular Curve Interpolating Three Unit Quaternions.

and

$$T^{-1} = [p_1 \; n_2 \; n_3].$$

2.3 Circular Curve in S^3

The above three points $\bar{p}_1 = \bar{e}_1 = (1,0,0), \bar{p}_2, \bar{p}_3$ on the unit sphere S^2 determines a plane L^2 in R^3 which does not necessarily contain the origin of R^3. The intersection of the plane L^2 with the sphere S^2 determines a circle $\bar{C}$ which interpolates the three points $\bar{p}_1, \bar{p}_2, \bar{p}_3$ on the sphere S^2. The inverse transformed circle $C = T^{-1}(\bar{C})$ generates a circular curve which interpolates the three points $p_1, p_2, p_3 \in S^3$, denoted as $C(p_1, p_2, p_3)$. Note that the circles $\bar{C}$ and C are not centered at the origins of R^3 and R^4 respectively. Let $\bar{p}_0$ be the center of $\bar{C}$, then the translated circle $\bar{C} - \bar{p}_0$ has its center at the origin of R^3 and it is contained in the translated plane $L^2 - \bar{p}_0$. Under the inverse transformation T^{-1}, this circle $\bar{C} - \bar{p}_0$ is transformed back to S^3 as

$$T^{-1} \cdot (\bar{C} - \bar{p}_0) = T^{-1} \cdot \bar{C} - T^{-1} \cdot \bar{p}_0 = C - T^{-1} \cdot \bar{p}_0.$$

Thus, to compute the circular curve C on S^3, we need to add the 4D vector $T^{-1} \cdot \bar{p}_0 \in R^4$ to the inverse transformation $T^{-1} \cdot (\bar{C} - \bar{p}_0)$ of the circle $\bar{C} - \bar{p}_0$ centered at the origin of R^3. Let p_0 denote the vector $T^{-1} \cdot \bar{p}_0$.

Let $\bar{T}$ be the orthogonal transformation which transforms the circle $\bar{C} - \bar{p}_0$ on the plane $L^2 - \bar{p}_0$ into a circle $\hat{C}$ on the 2D plane R^2 which is contained in the 3D space R^3. Further, let S be the scaling of R^2 which expands the circle $\hat{C}$ into the unit circle S^1. Let $\hat{T}$ denote the composition $S \cdot \bar{T}$, then the transformation $\hat{T}$ maps the circle $\bar{C} - \bar{p}_0$ into the unit circle S^1. Let $\hat{p}_i$ denote the transformed 2D vectors $\hat{T} \cdot (\bar{p}_i - \bar{p}_0)$, for $i = 1, 2, 3$. Note that we can easily choose a transformation $\bar{T}$ so that the resulting transformation $\hat{T}$ maps the 3D vector $\bar{p}_1 - \bar{p}_0$ into the unit 2D vector $\hat{p}_1 = \hat{e}_1 = (1,0) \in S^1$. Thus, the unit circle S^1 is transformed back into the circle $C(p_1, p_2, p_3)$ in S^3 under the inverse transformation $T^{-1} \cdot \hat{T}^{-1}$ followed by the translation by p_0. Each point on the unit circle S^1 is represented as $(\cos\theta, \sin\theta) \in R^2$. The composite matrix $T^{-1} \cdot \hat{T}^{-1}$ is a 4×2 matrix. Once the composite matrix $T^{-1} \cdot \hat{T}^{-1}$ and the point p_0 are known, to map each point $\hat{p} \in S^1$ into the corresponding point

$p \in C(p_1, p_2, p_3) \subset S^3$, we need one cosine, one sine, 8 multiplications, and 8 additions. We explain how to construct the point $\bar{p}_0$ and the transformations $\bar{T}$ and $\bar{T}^{-1}$ in the following.

The center $\bar{p}_0$ of the circle $\bar{C}$ can be computed as follows. First, we compute the unit normal of the plane L^2 as the cross product

$$\bar{n}_3 = \frac{(\bar{p}_2 - \bar{p}_1) \times (\bar{p}_3 - \bar{p}_1)}{\|(\bar{p}_2 - \bar{p}_1) \times (\bar{p}_3 - \bar{p}_1)\|} = \frac{(\bar{p}_2 - \bar{e}_1) \times (\bar{p}_3 - \bar{e}_1)}{\|(\bar{p}_2 - \bar{e}_1) \times (\bar{p}_3 - \bar{e}_1)\|} = \frac{(\bar{p}_2 - (1,0,0)) \times (\bar{p}_3 - (1,0,0))}{\|(\bar{p}_2 - (1,0,0)) \times (\bar{p}_3 - (1,0,0))\|}.$$

Let $\bar{n}_3 = (a, b, c) \in R^3$, then the center $\bar{p}_0$ of the circle $\bar{C}$ is given as the intersection point of the line

$$l(t) = (at, bt, ct)$$

with the plane L^2. Since the point $\bar{p}_1 = (1,0,0)$ is on the plane L^2 and the unit vector (a, b, c) is the normal direction of L^2, the plane equation of L^2 is given as

$$a(x - 1) + by + cz = 0.$$

The parameter t for the point $\bar{p}_0 = l(t)$ is obtained by solving the equation

$$a(at - 1) + b(bt) + c(ct) = 0,$$

i.e.,

$$t = \frac{a}{a^2 + b^2 + c^2} = a.$$

Thus, the coordinate of the point $\bar{p}_0$ is given as $a \cdot (a, b, c) = (a^2, ab, ac)$.

The orthogonal transformation $\bar{T}$ is constructed as follows. Let

$$\bar{n}_1 = \frac{\bar{p}_1 - \bar{p}_0}{\|\bar{p}_1 - \bar{p}_0\|} = \frac{(1 - a^2, -ab, -ac)}{\sqrt{(1 - a^2)^2 + a^2 \cdot b^2 + a^2 \cdot c^2}},$$

and

$$\bar{n}_2 = \bar{n}_3 \times \bar{n}_1,$$

where $\bar{n}_3$ is defined as above. Then, the transformation matrix $\bar{T}$ is given as

$$\bar{T} = [\bar{n}_1 \ \bar{n}_2 \ \bar{n}_3]^t,$$

and the inverse transformation matrix $\bar{T}^{-1}$ is given as

$$\bar{T}^{-1} = \bar{T}^t = [\bar{n}_1 \ \bar{n}_2 \ \bar{n}_3].$$

Using a similar argument to the one given at the end of §2.2, we can ignore the last row of $\bar{T}$ and the last column of $\bar{T}^{-1}$, and write

$$\bar{T} = [\bar{n}_1 \ \bar{n}_2]^t,$$

and

$$\bar{T}^{-1} = \bar{T}^t = [\bar{n}_1 \ \bar{n}_2].$$

Let $s = \sqrt{(1 - a^2)^2 + a^2 \cdot b^2 + a^2 \cdot c^2}$, then the scaling transformation S is given as

$$S = \begin{bmatrix} 1/s & 0 \\ 0 & 1/s \end{bmatrix},$$

and the inverse scaling transformation S^{-1} is given as

$$S^{-1} = \begin{bmatrix} s & 0 \\ 0 & s \end{bmatrix}.$$

Thus, the composite transformation matrix $\hat{T} = S \cdot \bar{T}$ is given as

$$\hat{T} = S \cdot \bar{T} = [\frac{1}{s} \cdot \bar{n}_1 \ \frac{1}{s} \cdot \bar{n}_2]^t,$$

and the inverse transformation matrix $\hat{T}^{-1}$ is given as

$$\hat{T}^{-1} = (S \cdot \bar{T})^{-1} = \bar{T}^{-1} \cdot S^{-1} = \bar{T}^t \cdot S^{-1} = [s \cdot \bar{n}_1 \ s \cdot \bar{n}_2] = [\bar{p}_1 - \bar{p}_0 \ \bar{n}_3 \times (\bar{p}_1 - \bar{p}_0)].$$

2.4 Circular Quaternion Curves in $SO(3)$

The above circular curve $C = C(p_1, p_2, p_3)$ in S^3 generates a quaternion curve $QC(p_1, p_2, p_3)$ in $SO(3)$ under the projection which identifies two antipodal points on S^3 as a single point in $SO(3)$. Given three quaternions $q_1, q_2, q_3 \in SO(3)$, there are three pairs of points $[q_1, -q_1], [q_2, -q_2], [q_3, -q_3]$ in S^3 which are identified with q_1, q_2, q_3 respectively. There are eight different circular curves in S^3 which interpolate the sequence of three points $\pm q_1, \pm q_2, \pm q_3$ on S^3. Among these eight circular curves, there are four pairs of circular curves which are point-symmetric with respect to the origin of the sphere S^3. Each pair of the point-symmetric circular curves are identified into a single circular quaternion curve in $SO(3)$ under the projection.

3 Circular Blending Quaternion Curves in $SO(3)$

In this section, we consider how to smoothly blend the two circular quaternion curves C_i and C_{i+1} which interpolate the two quaternions q_i and q_{i+1} into a quaternion curve Q_i so that Q_i is tangent to C_i at q_i and to C_{i+1} at q_{i+1}. In this section, we use the parabolic blending method which was first suggested by Overhauser [15] and later simplified by Brewer and Anderson [5]. Since it is not easy to construct parabolic curves embedded in $SO(3)$, we use the circular quaternions curves C_i and C_{i+1} in $SO(3)$. In §3.1, by smoothly blending the two circular quaternion curves C_i and C_{i+1} using a similar method to the parabolic blending, we generate a circular blending quaternion curve Q_i which interpolates the two quaternions q_i and q_{i+1} in $SO(3)$.

3.1 Circular Blending Quaternion Curves in $SO(3)$

Given two circular quaternion curves C_i and C_{i+1} which interpolate two quaternions q_i and q_{i+1}, we can parametrize the two circular curves $C_i(t)$ and $C_{i+1}(t)$ so that

$$C_i(0) = C_{i+1}(0) = q_i \quad \text{and} \quad C_i(1) = C_{i+1}(1) = q_{i+1}.$$

We define the circular blending quaternion curve $Q_i(t)$ of $C_i(t)$ and $C_{i+1}(t)$ as

$$Q_i(t) = Slerp(C_i(t), C_{i+1}(t), t),$$

where $Slerp$ is the spherical linear interpolation [19, 20]. Using the quaternion differentiation [20], one can easily show that

$$Q_i'(0) = C_i'(0) \quad \text{and} \quad Q_i'(1) = C_{i+1}'(1).$$

Thus, the blending quaternion curve Q_i is tangent with C_i at q_i and with C_{i+1} at q_{i+1}.

Let C_i^1 (resp. C_i^2) be the subsegment of C_i which connects the two quaternions q_{i-1} and q_i (resp. q_i and q_{i+1}). For the two blending quaternion curve segments Q_{i-1} and Q_i to join smoothly at the quaternion q_i with a C^1-continuity, we need to parametrize the two curve segments $C_i^1(t)$, for $t_{i-1} \leq t \leq t_i$, and $C_i^2(t)$, for $t_i \leq t \leq t_{i+1}$, in a compatible way so that

$$\frac{\partial}{\partial t} Q_{i-1}(t) = \frac{\partial}{\partial t} C_i^1(t) = \frac{\partial}{\partial t} C_i^2(t) = \frac{\partial}{\partial t} Q_i(t)$$

at $t = t_i$. We can easily enforce this condition by parametrizing the two subcurves C_i^1 and C_i^2 as $C_i^1(t) = C_i(t)$, for $t_{i-1} \leq t \leq t_i$, and $C_i^2(t) = C_i(t)$, for $t_i \leq t \leq t_{i+1}$, for a curve C_i which is parametrized with a single parameter t, for $t_{i-1} \leq t \leq t_{i+1}$. Thus, we consider how to parametrize the whole curve $C_i(t)$ so that

$$C_i(t_{i-1}) = q_{i-1}, \; C_i(t_i) = q_i, \text{ and } C_i(t_{i+1}) = q_{i+1},$$

for $t_{i-1} < t_i < t_{i+1}$.

Suppose the angular domains of the circular curve segments C_i^1 and C_i^2 are the angular intervals $[0, \theta_i^1]$ and $[\theta_i^1, \theta_i^1 + \theta_i^2]$ respectively. By linearly rescaling the angular domains of C_i^1 and C_i^2, we may assume

$$0 \leq \theta_i^1 \leq \theta_i^1 + \theta_i^2 = 1.$$

Further, by reparametrizing t, we may assume $t_{i-1} = 0$ and $t_{i+1} = 1$. Thus, we have

$$C_i(0) = q_{i-1}, \; C_i(t_i) = q_i, \text{ and } C_i(1) = q_{i+1},$$

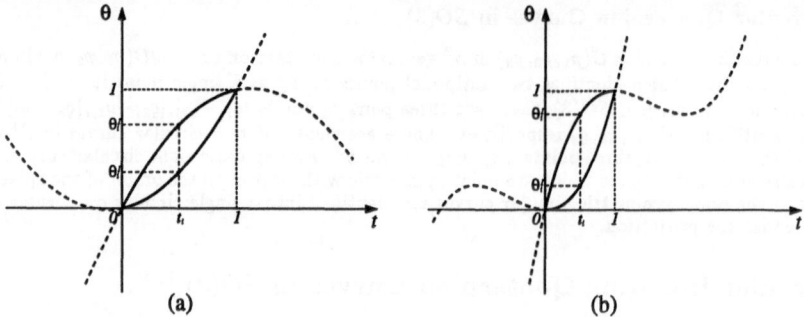

Figure 2: Low Degree Polynomials (a) $\theta_i(t) = at^2 + (1-a)t$, and (b) $\theta_i(t) = at^3 + (1-a)t^2$.

where $0 < t_i < 1$. When we subdivide the two circular curves C_i^1 and C_i^2 into m_i^1 and m_i^2 in-between subsegments respectively, a smooth monotonically increasing angular function $\theta(t)$, for $0 \le t \le 1$, which satifies the condition

$$\theta(0) = 0, \ \theta(t_i) = \theta_i^1, \ \text{and} \ \theta(1) = 1,$$

is given as

$$\theta(t) = t^k,$$

where the constant $k > 0$ is determined by the condition

$$\theta(\frac{m_i^1}{m_i^1 + m_i^2}) = (\frac{m_i^1}{m_i^1 + m_i^2})^k = \theta_i^1.$$

Thus, we have

$$k = \log(\theta_i^1)/\log(\frac{m_i^1}{m_i^1 + m_i^2}).$$

Each value $\theta(t) = t^k$ is computed as

$$\theta(t) = \exp(k \cdot \ln t).$$

Since the computation of $\theta(t)$ as an exponential function t^k requires $(m_i^1 + m_i^2 + 2)$ log and $(m_i^1 + m_i^2)$ exp computations which are quite expensive, we replace it with a low degree polynomial, mostly with a degree 2 or 3 polynomial, for reasonable ranges of $0 < t_i < 1$ and $0 < \theta_i < 1$ values. Consider a quadratic polynomial

$$\theta(t) = at^2 + bt + c,$$

which satisfies

$$\theta(0) = 0, \ \theta(t_i) = \theta_i^1, \ \text{and} \ \theta(1) = 1.$$

For this polynomial, we have

$$c = \theta(0) = 0, \ a + b = \theta(1) = 1,$$

and

$$\theta_i^1 = \theta(t_i) = at_i^2 + (1-a)t_i = (t_i^2 - t_i)a + t_i.$$

Thus, we have

$$a = \frac{\theta_i^1 - t_i}{t_i^2 - t_i}, \quad \text{and} \quad a - 1 = \frac{\theta_i^1 - t_i^2}{t_i^2 - t_i}.$$

In the degenerate case $a = 0$, i.e., $\theta_i^1 = t_i$, the polynomial $\theta(t)$ becomes a linear polynomial $\theta(t) = t$. The quadratic polynomial

$$\theta(t) = at^2 + (1-a)t$$

has its derivative

$$\theta'(t) = 2at + (1-a).$$

For the polynomial $\theta(t)$ to be monotonically increasing, for $0 \le t \le 1$, the root of the derivative $\theta'(t) = 2at + (1-a)$ should be ≤ 0 or ≥ 1 (see Figure 2(a)). That is, we should have

$$\frac{a-1}{2a} \le 0, \quad \text{or} \quad \frac{a-1}{2a} \ge 1,$$

	add	sub	mul	div	sin	cos	asin	acos	sqrt
Steps 1 ~ 5	73	84	197	20	-	-	2	2	8
Step 6	$9m$	-	$12m$	m	m	m	-	-	-
Total	$9m+73$	84	$12m+197$	$m+20$	m	m	2	2	8
$m = 8$	145	84	293	28	8	8	2	2	8
$m = 16$	217	84	389	36	16	16	2	2	8
$m = 32$	361	84	581	52	32	32	2	2	8
$m = 64$	649	84	965	84	64	64	2	2	8

Table 1: Time Complexity for Circular Quaternion Curve.

and equivalently,

$$\frac{a-1}{2a} = \frac{\theta_i^1 - t_i^2}{2(\theta_i^1 - t_i)} \le 0, \quad \text{or} \quad \frac{\theta_i^1 - t_i^2}{2(\theta_i^1 - t_i)} \ge 1.$$

Thus, we have

$$t_i^2 \le \theta_i^1 \le 2t_i - t_i^2.$$

When $0 < \theta_i^1 < t_i^2$, for a certain range of θ_i^1, we may use the polynomial

$$\theta(t) = at^3 + (1-a)t^2,$$

which satisfies the conditions

$$\theta(0) = 0, \ \theta'(0) = 0, \ \theta(1) = 1, \ \text{and} \ \theta(t_i) = \theta_i^1.$$

For the polynomial to be monotonically increasing, the root of the second derivative $\theta''(t) = 6at + 2a(1-a)$ should be ≤ 0 (see Figure 2(b)). The root of $\theta''(t)$ gives the t value for an inflection point. Using a similar argument as above, we can easily show that the range of θ_i^1 should be

$$t_i^3 \le \theta_i^1 \le t_i^2.$$

Using a symmetry, the polynomial

$$\theta(t) = a(t-1)^3 + (a-1)(t-1)^2 + 1$$

satisfies the conditions

$$\theta(0) = 0, \ \theta(1) = 1, \ \text{and} \ \theta'(1) = 0.$$

For the polynomial to be monotonically increasing and further to satisfy the condition

$$\theta(t_i) = \theta_i^1,$$

the range of θ_i^1 should be

$$2t_i - t_i^2 < \theta_i^1 < 2t_i - t_i^3.$$

We can continue the same procedure to even higher degree polynomials, however, the cases which require high degree polynomials are quite rare. For these rare cases, we can use the exponential function $\theta_i(t) = t^k$ without affecting the overall performance of the algorithm significantly.

4   Computational Complexity

A pseudo-code is given in Appendix A for the circular curve generation algorithm. There are six steps in the algorithm. The details of each step are explained in §2. The presentations in §2 are mainly for the underlying mathematical structures of the algorithm which are useful in understanding the basic ideas of the algorithm. In the implementation of the algorithm, various computational shortcuts are made to make the algorithm more efficient.

Table 1 shows the time complexity for the generation of a single circular curve approximated with m unit quaternions. Table 2 shows the time complexity for the generation of a circular blending curve which blends two circular curves each approximated with m unit quaternion curves. Table 3, Table 4, and Table 5 show the time complexities for the Bézier curve method of Shoemake [19], the spherical quadrangle method of Shoemake [20], and the cardinal spline method of Pletincks [16]. The complexity analyses for the previous methods [16, 19, 20] are based on the pseudo-codes given in Shoemake [20] and Pletincks [16]. Since these pseudo-code are extremely simple, it is hard to over-estimate their complexities.

	add	sub	mul	div	sin	cos	asin	acos	sqrt
Steps 1 ~ 5	73	84	197	20	-	-	2	2	8
Step 6 × 2	18m	-	24m	2m	2m	2m	-	-	-
slerp	8m	2m	14m	2m	3m	-	-	m	-
Total	26m+73	2m+84	38m+197	4m+20	5m	2m	2	m+2	8
m = 8	281	100	501	52	40	16	2	10	8
m = 16	489	116	805	84	80	32	2	18	8
m = 32	905	148	1413	148	160	64	2	34	8
m = 64	1737	212	2629	276	320	128	2	66	8

Table 2: Time Complexity for Circular Blending Curve.

	add	sub	mul	div	sin	cos	asin	acos	sqrt
Double × 3	9	12	27	-	-	-	-	-	-
Bisect × 2	14	-	8	8	-	-	-	-	-
slerp × 6	48m	12m	84m	12m	18m	-	-	6m	-
Total	48m+23	12m+12	84m+35	12m+8	18m	-	-	6m	-
m = 8	407	108	707	104	144	0	0	48	0
m = 16	791	204	1379	200	288	0	0	96	0
m = 32	1559	396	2723	392	576	0	0	192	0
m = 64	3095	780	5411	776	1152	0	0	384	0

Table 3: Time Complexity for Bézier Curve.

	add	sub	mul	div	sin	cos	asin	acos	sqrt	atan2
inverse	3	-	8	1	-	-	-	-	-	-
mult × 3	18	18	48	-	-	-	-	-	-	-
add	4	-	-	-	-	-	-	-	-	-
div by scalar	-	-	-	4	-	-	-	-	-	-
exp	2	-	6	1	1	1	-	-	1	-
log × 2	4	-	12	2	-	-	-	-	2	2
slerp × 3	24m	6m	42m	6m	9m	-	-	3m	-	-
Total	24m+31	6m+18	42m+74	6m+8	9m+1	1	-	3m	3	2
m = 8	223	66	410	56	73	1	0	24	3	2
m = 16	415	114	746	104	145	1	0	48	3	2
m = 32	799	210	1418	200	289	1	0	96	3	2
m = 64	1567	402	2762	392	577	1	0	192	3	2

Table 4: Time Complexity for Spherical Quadrangle Curve.

	add	sub	mul	div	sin	cos	asin	acos	sqrt
smid × 2	16m	-	18m	2m	-	-	-	-	2m
slerp	8m	2m	14m	2m	3m	-	-	m	-
Total	24m	2m	32m	4m	3m	-	-	m	2m
m = 8	192	16	256	32	24	0	0	8	16
m = 16	384	32	512	64	48	0	0	16	32
m = 32	768	64	1024	128	96	0	0	32	64
m = 64	1536	128	2048	256	192	0	0	64	128

Table 5: Time Complexity for Cardinal Spline Curve.

Machine	m	methods & time (μsec)			
		Circular	Bézier	Squad	Cardinal
SGI Crimson/Elan	8	3700	7300	4300	2600
	16	6400	13100	7800	5700
	32	11700	24700	14800	11300
	64	22400	47000	28600	20000
SGI Indigo/XS24	8	7300	14700	9000	4300
	16	12400	26600	16300	9300
	32	23200	50400	30800	18800
	64	44400	97600	59500	34200
SGI 4D/35TG	8	6400	13600	8200	3900
	16	11100	24300	14700	8400
	32	20800	45800	27700	17100
	64	40100	88900	53700	31000

Table 6: Computational Results.

5 Experimental Results

We implemented four different methods to interpolate a sequence of solid orientations, i.e., the circular blending curve method presented in this paper, the Bézier curve method of Shoemake [19], the spherical quadrangle curve method of Shoemake [20], and the cardinal spline curve method of Pletincks [16]. The test runs were made on the 16 input solid orientations. Table 6 shows the computational results of the four methods with four different values of $m = 8, 16, 32, 64$, on three different machines, i.e., SGI Crimson/Elan with 50MHz R4000 CPU and 64MB main memory, SGI INDIGO/XS24 with 33MHz R3000 CPU and 32MB main memory, and SGI 4D/35TG with 36MHz R3000 CPU and 48MB main memory. The computation times were measured using the UNIX system call clock().

On the test run of the circular blending curve generation method, all but two of the monotonically increasing angular functions $\theta_i(t)$'s are quadratic polynomials. The exceptions are cubic polynomials. The animation results show that the spherical quadrangle curve of Shoemake [20] does not give a motion as smooth as the other three methods. The cardinal spline curve of Pletincks [16] is very simple and the most efficient one among all the methods, however, the cardinal spline requires the number of in-betweens to be a power of 2, which can be a drawback when the number of in-betweens are not given as a power of 2. The computer animation systems generate 24 frames/second for films and 30 frames/second for videos. Thus, it would be quite cumbersome to specify the key frames so that the distance between any two adjacent key frames becomes a power of 2. This drawback might be quite serious. Though the circular blending curve has a relatively high preprocessing time, as the number of m increases, the processing time becomes relatively insignificant. The circular blending curve has a lower time complexity than the previous methods, except the cardinal spline curve.

6 Conclusions

We have described an efficient algorithm to construct a circular quaternion curve which interpolates a given triple (q_{i-1}, q_i, q_{i+1}) of solid orientations. Using a generalization of the parabolic blending curve generation method of Overhauser [15], we constructed a quaternion curve Q_i which smoothly blends the two circular curves C_i and C_{i+1} which interpolate the two solid orientations q_i and q_{i+1}. By connecting the curves Q_i's in a sequence, we constructed a C^1-continuous quaternion curve on $SO(3)$ which smoothly interpolates a sequence of solid orientations.

Though there are some preprocessing costs to set up the circular parametrization from the unit circle $S^1 \subset R^2$ into the circular quaternion curve in $SO(3)$, each quaternion point on the circular curve can be generated quite efficiently using a 4×2 transformation matrix which realizes a linear transformation from R^2 into R^4. The construction of each quaternion point on the circular quaternion curve takes a slightly less computation time than that of a slerp computation. Thus, except the preprocessing time, the computational complexity of the suggested method is slightly better than that of the quaternion curve generation method which uses only three slerp computations. The squad quaternion curve of Shoemake [20] uses only three slerp computations which is an optimal number of slerp computations which is required to obtain the smoothness of the quaternion curve interpolating the solid orientations. The circular blending curve has a higher time complexity than the cardinal spline curve, however, it has much higher flexibilities than the cardinal spline curve.

As far as the computational efficiency is concerned, it is very hard to expect to significantly improve upon the previous methods. This is because two previous methods [16, 20] are already almost optimal algorithms. Though rather complicated mathematical details are involved, the relative efficiency of the circular curve method depends on these details. Thus, the technical merits of the circular blending curve should be found in the mathematical structures we have investigated in this paper. Using these nice geometric structures, we may expect more effective algorithms would be further developed in future researches, which would give more design flexibilities on the interpolating quaternion curves.

References

[1] Barr, A., Currin, B., Gabriel, S., and Hughes, J., "Smooth Interpolation of Orientations with Angular Velocity Constraints using Quaternions," *Computer Graphics (Proc. of SIGGRAPH '92)*, Vol. 26, No. 2, pp. 313–320, 1992.

[2] Barry, P., and Goldman, R., "De Casteljau-type Subdivision is Peculiar to Bézier Curves," *Computer Aided Design*, Vol. 20, No. 3, pp. 114–116, 1988.

[3] Boehm, W., "On Cubics: A Survey," *Computer Vision, Graphics, and Image Processing*, Vol. 19, pp. 201–226, 1982.

[4] Brady, et al., *Robot Motion: Planning and Control*, The MIT Press, Mass., 1982.

[5] Brewer, J., and Anderson, D., "Visual Interaction with Overhauser Curves and Surfaces," *Computer Graphics (Proc. of SIGGRAPH '77)*, Vol. 11, pp. 132–137, 1978.

[6] Canny, J., *The Complexity of Robot Motion Planning*, The MIT Press, Mass., 1988.

[7] Curtis, M., *Matrix Groups*, Springer-Verlag, New York, 1979.

[8] Donald, B., "Motion Planning with Six Degrees of Freedom," A.I. Technical Report 791, MIT, 1984.

[9] Duff, T., "Splines in Animation and Modeling," *State of the Art in Image Synthesis (ACM SIGGRAPH '86 Course Notes #15)*, 1986.

[10] Farin, G., *Curves and Surfaces for Computer Aided Geometric Design: A Practical Guide*, Academic Press, Boston, 1988.

[11] Foley, J., van Dam, A., Feiner, S., and Hughes, J., *Computer Graphics: Principles and Practice*, Addison-Wesley, Reading, Mass., 1990.

[12] Fomenko, A., *Symplectic Geometry*, Gordon and Breach Science Pub., New York, 1988.

[13] Milnor, J., *Morse Theory*, Princeton University Press, Princeton, 1969.

[14] Nielson, G., and Heiland, R., "Animated Rotations using Quaternions and Splines on a 4D Sphere," *Programmirovanie* (Russia), July–August 1992, No. 4, pp. 17–27. English edition, *Programming and Computer Software*, Plenum Pub., New York.

[15] Overhauser, A., "Analytic Definition of Curves and Surfaces by Parabolic Blending," Tech. Rep. No. SL68-40, Ford Motor Company Scientific Laboratory, May 8, 1968.

[16] Pletincks, D., "The Use of Quaternions for Animation, Modelling and Rendering," *New Trends in Computer Graphics (Proc. of CG International '88)*, Magnenat-Thalmann and Thalmann (Eds.), Springer-Verlag, pp. 44–53, 1988.

[17] Rogers, D., and Adams, J., *Mathematical Elements for Computer Graphics*, 2ed, McGraw-Hill, 1990.

[18] Sattinger, D., and Weaver, O., *Lie Groups and Algebras with Applications to Physics, Geometry, and Mechanics*, Springer-Verlag, New York, 1986.

[19] Shoemake, K., "Animating Rotation with Quaternion Curves," *Computer Graphics (Proc. of SIGGRAPH '85)*, Vol. 19, No. 3, pp. 245–254, 1985.

[20] Shoemake, K., "Quaternion Calculus for Animation," *Math for SIGGRAPH (ACM SIGGRAPH '91 Course Notes #2)*, 1991.

[21] Shoemake, K., "ARCBALL: A User Interface for Specifying Three-Dimensional Orientation Using a Mouse," *Proc. of Graphics Interface '92*, pp. 151–156, 1992.

A Pseudo Code for a Circular Quaternion Curve

```
Algorithm CircularCurve(p1, p2, p3, m1, m2)
   begin
   { Step 1: Initial setup }
   n4 ← compute the normal N(p1,p2,p3);   n4 ← normalize n4;
   n2 ← compute the normal N(p1,p3,n4);   n2 ← normalize n2;
   n3 ← compute the normal N(p1,n4,n2);
```

$$\{ \text{Step 2: Project } p1, p2, p3 \text{ into the 2-sphere } S^2. \}$$

```
   T⁻¹ ← the matrix [p1, n2, n3, n4];   T ← the transpose of T⁻¹;
   p̄1 ← T (1,0,0);   p̄2 ← T · p2;   p̄3 ← T · p3;
```

```
   { Step 3: Determine the circle which contains p̄1, p̄2, and p̄3. }
   n̄3 ← (p̄2 − (1,0,0)) × (p̄3 − (1,0,0));   n̄3 ← normalize n̄3;
   p̄0 ← the center of the circle;   n̄1 ← normalize p̄1 − p̄0;   n̄2 ← n̄3 × n̄1;
```

```
   { Step 4 }
   p0 ← T⁻¹ · p̄0;   e1 ← T⁻¹ · n̄1;   e2 ← T⁻¹ · n̄2;
```

```
   { Step 5 }
   a1 ← the angle between n̄1 and n̄2;   a2 ← the angle between n̄2 and n̄3;
```

```
   { Step 6: Generate points on the circular curve. }
   output(p1);
   for i := 1 to m1+m2 do
      begin;
      a ← GetNextAngle(i, a1, a2, m1, m2);
      p ← p0 + cos(a) · e1 + sin(a) · e2;
      output(p);
      end;
   end
```

Myung-Soo Kim is an assitant professor in the Department of Computer Science, POSTECH, Korea. He received the B.S. and M.S. degrees in Mathematics from Seoul National University, Korea, in 1980 and 1982 respectively. He continued his graduate studies at Purdue University, U.S.A., where he received the M.S. degree in Applied Mathematics in 1985, and the M.S. and Ph.D degrees in Computer Science in 1987 and 1988 respectively. His research interests are in Computer Graphics, Computational Geometry, and Robot Motion Planning.
Address: Department of Computer Science, POSTECH, P.O. Box 125, Pohang 790-600, Korea.
Electronic mail: mskim@vision.postech.ac.kr

Kee-Won Nam received the B.S. degree in Computer Science from POSTECH, Korea, in 1992. He is currently a M.S. student in the Department of Computer Science, POSTECH. His research interests include Computer Graphics and Computer Animation.
Address: Department of Computer Science, POSTECH, P.O. Box 125, Pohang 790-600, Korea.
Electronic mail: namkw@vision.postech.ac.kr

G² Continuous Interpolation over Rational Curve Meshes

Kenjiro Takai Miura

ABSTRACT

This paper introduces a new type of free-form surface patches named rational bondary C^2 Gregory patch(RBC²G patch). It can be said an extension of C^2 Gregory patch developed by Miura and Wang, which gives users the capability of designing curvature-continuous(G^2 continuous) surfaces with reasonable flexibilities, and also that of rational boundary Gregory patch proposed by Chiyokura et al., which is surrounded by rational Bézier curves and can be interpolated with the continuity of tangent plane(G^1 continuity). As the name of the patch implies, its boundary consists of rational Bézier curves. Its derivation is explained and methods for G^2 continuity are proposed to connect it with a rational Bézier patch and with another RBC²G patch. Finally, a G^2 continuous interpolation method based such patches over rational curve meshes is discussed.

Key word: computer-aided geometric design, C^2 Gregory patch, rational boundary C^2 Gregory patch, continuity of curvature, rational Bézier curve

1 INTRODUCTION

In Computer-Aided Geometric Design, especially design of mechanical products whose shapes include free-form surfaces, the continuity of curvature(G^2 continuity) is often required when two surface patches are connected. To guarantee G^2 continuity between two patches means they should have coincident tangent planes and identical normal curvature in every direction at every point of their common boundary curve. G^2 continuity is sometimes necessary for the purpose of both aesthetic and functional requirements in engineering design. For example, although tangent-continuous surfaces look smooth, reflection lines generally have been broken at the points where curvature is not continuous. In cam design, in order to avoid creating abrupt changes in acceleration, the cam surfaces must be connected without G^2 discontinuity. In other applications, such as the wing and body of an aircraft, or the bow and hull of a ship or submarine, there should be G^2 continuity to minimize flow separation and turbulence.

Miura and Wang (1991) proposed the C^2 Gregory-patch formulation, which can be easily connected with the continuity of curvature on its boundary. This formulation is similar to a bi-quintic Bézier patch, but like Gregory patch, each of its interior control points $P_{ij}(i, j = 1, ..., 4)$ is specified by two points and it moves on the line segment connecting these two points according to its parameters. As they showed, it can be derived by extending the idea of Gregory patch for G^2 continuity or by restricting the degrees of the boundary curves and the first and second partial derivatives of the C^2 Gregory Square (Barnhill 1983) to be quintic. They studied a method to connect it with a Bézier patch G^2-continuously (Miura 1991; Miura and Wang 1991), a connection of two C^2G patches (Miura 1991; Miura and

Wang 1991) and a removal of the singularity at its four corner points (Miura 1991; Miura and Wang 1992).

On the other hand, a Gregory patch is surrounded by polynomial curves(Bézier curves) and it is not allowed to use rational Bézier curves like arcs of circles or ellipses as its boundary. Chiyokura et al. (1991) developed a new type of free-form surface patch whose boundary consists of rational Bézier curves. They called it rational boundary Gregory patch. They showed an interpolation method of this type of patches in order to guarantee the continuity of tangent plane.

Therefore, since quadric curves are very important for design of mechanical parts, we have proposed a new type of free-form surface patches named rational boundary C^2 Gregory patch, whose boundary consists of four rational Bézier curves and can be easily connected with G^2 continuity. In particular, we show properties of the RBC^{2}G patch and the connections between Bézier and RBC^{2}G patches as well as a G^2 continuous interpolation method based upon such patches.

2 RATIONAL BOUNDARY C^2 GREGORY PATCH

2.1 Formulation of a Rational Boundary C^2 Gregory Patch

The formulation of a bi-n-th($n \geq 5$) degree rational boundary C^2 Gregory patch is defined as follows(see Fig.1):

$$\mathbf{S}(u,v) = \frac{\sum_{i=0}^{n} \sum_{j=0}^{n} B_i^n(u) B_j^n(v) \mathbf{Q}_{ij}(u,v)}{\sum_{i=0}^{n} \sum_{j=0}^{n} B_i^n(u) B_j^n(v) w_{ij}(u,v)}, \qquad 0 \leq u,v \leq 1 \tag{1}$$

where $B_i^n (i = 0, ..., n)$ are Bernstein basis functions defined by

$$B_i^n(t) = \binom{n}{i} t^i (1-t)^{n-i}. \tag{2}$$

The control points of the patch $\mathbf{Q}_{ij}(u,v)$ and its weight $w_{ij}(u,v)$ $(i = 0, ..., n, j = 0, ..., n)$ are

a) $i = 0, 1, 2$ and $j = 0, 1, 2$

$$\mathbf{Q}_{ij}(u,v) = \frac{u^3 \mathbf{P}_{ij0} w_{ij0} + v^3 \mathbf{P}_{ij1} w_{ij1}}{u^3 + v^3}$$

$$w_{ij}(u,v) = \frac{u^3 w_{ij0} + v^3 w_{ij1}}{u^3 + v^3} \tag{3}$$

b) $i = n-2, n-1, n$ and $j = 0, 1, 2$

$$\mathbf{Q}_{ij}(u,v) = \frac{(1-u)^3 \mathbf{P}_{ij0} w_{ij0} + v^3 \mathbf{P}_{ij1} w_{ij1}}{(1-u)^3 + v^3}$$

$$w_{ij}(u,v) = \frac{(1-u)^3 w_{ij0} + v^3 w_{ij1}}{(1-u)^3 + v^3} \tag{4}$$

c) $i = 0, 1, 2$ and $j = n-2, n-1, n$

$$\mathbf{Q}_{ij}(u,v) = \frac{u^3 \mathbf{P}_{ij0} w_{ij0} + (1-v)^3 \mathbf{P}_{ij1} w_{ij1}}{u^3 + (1-v)^3}$$

$$w_{ij}(u,v) = \frac{u^3 w_{ij0} + (1-v)^3 w_{ij1}}{u^3 + (1-v)^3} \tag{5}$$

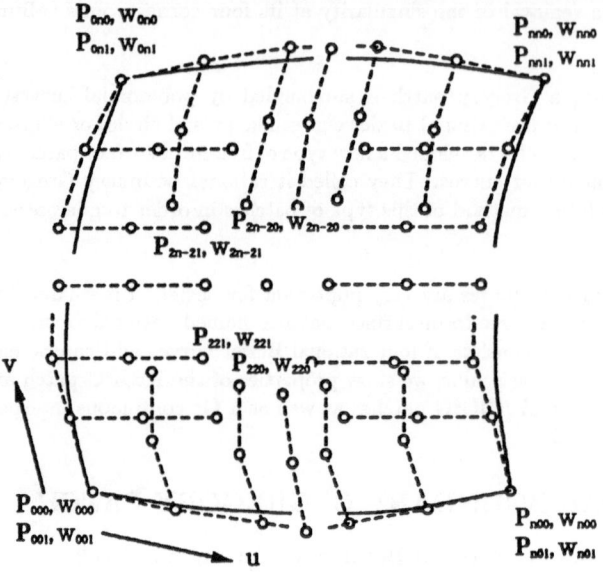

Figure 1: A rational boundary C^2 Gregory patch

d) $i = n - 2, n - 1, n$ and $j = n - 2, n - 1, n$

$$\mathbf{Q}_{ij}(u, v) = \frac{(1-u)^3 \mathbf{P}_{ij0} w_{ij0} + (1-v)^3 \mathbf{P}_{ij1} w_{ij1}}{(1-u)^3 + (1-v)^3}$$

$$w_{ij}(u, v) = \frac{(1-u)^3 w_{ij0} + (1-v)^3 w_{ij1}}{(1-u)^3 + (1-v)^3}. \tag{6}$$

Other control points and their weights do not depend on parameters and they are constant.

Points $\mathbf{P}_{ij0}$ and $\mathbf{P}_{ij1}$ which define a control points $\mathbf{Q}_{ij}$ of the boundary are identical, i.e.

$$\mathbf{P}_{ij0} = \mathbf{P}_{ij1} \qquad (i = 0, ..., n, j = 0, n) \ \ or \ \ (i = 0, n, j = 0, ..., n). \tag{7}$$

Furthermore, the following conditions are given to the weights:

$$
\begin{aligned}
w_{i,0,0} &= w_{i,1,0} &= w_{i,2,0} & \quad (i = 0, ..., n) \\
w_{i,n-2,0} &= w_{i,n-1,0} &= w_{i,n,0} & \quad (i = 0, ..., n) \\
w_{0,j,1} &= w_{1,j,1} &= w_{2,j,1} & \quad (j = 0, ..., n) \\
w_{n-2,j,1} &= w_{n-1,j,1} &= w_{n,j,1} & \quad (j = 0, ..., n).
\end{aligned} \tag{8}
$$

The above definition is different from that of a bi-n-th degree rational boundary Gregory patch (Chiyokura et al. 1991) in the following two points:

1. The power of parameters u, v, (1-u) or (1-v) in the definition of the control points and weights is 3 instead of 2.

2. The conditions on the weights expressed by equation (8) are added to the second rows as well as the first rows from the boundary.

The modifications on the definition are carried out in order not to make the second partial derivatives of the patch as well as the first ones too complicated similar to the definition of a RBG patch which makes its first partial derivatives relatively simple. In the next subsection, these derivatives will be expressed explicitly.

2.2 Properties of a Rational Boundary C^2 Gregory Patch

A bi-n-th degree RBC^{2}G patch degenerates to a bi-n-th degree rational Bézier patch like a RBG patch when all pairs of the interior control points and their weights are identical, i.e. if equations $\mathbf{P}_{ij0} = \mathbf{P}_{ij1}$ and $w_{ij0} = w_{ij1}(i,j = 0,...,n)$ are satisfied.

If all weights w_{ij0} and w_{ij1} are not less than 0, the RBC^{2}G patch has a convex hull property like a Bézier patch, i.e. it lies inside the convex hull defined by all of its control points $\mathbf{P}_{ij0}$ and $\mathbf{P}_{ij1}$.

Along the boundary, the first and second derivatives across the boundary curves (cross-boundary derivatives) are simpler than those of a rational Bézier patch. For example, on the boundary curve where parameter u is equal to 0, they are given by the following expressions:

$$\frac{\partial \mathbf{S}(0,v)}{\partial u} = \frac{n \sum_{i=0}^{n} B_i^n(v) w_{0i0}(\mathbf{P}_{1i0} - \mathbf{P}_{0i0})}{\sum_{i=0}^{n} B_i^n(v) w_{0i0}} \tag{9}$$

$$\frac{\partial^2 \mathbf{S}(0,v)}{\partial u^2} = \frac{n(n-1) \sum_{i=0}^{n} B_i^n(v) w_{0i0}(\mathbf{P}_{2i0} - 2\mathbf{P}_{1i0} + \mathbf{P}_{0i0})}{\sum_{i=0}^{n} B_i^n(v) w_{0i0}}. \tag{10}$$

3 G^1 CONTINUITY AND G^2 CONTINUITY

3.1   Conditions for G^1 Continuity

The conditions for G^1 continuity(continuity of tangent plane) are formulated as follows (Kahmann 1983):as figure 2 shows, let $\mathbf{A}(u,v)$ and $\mathbf{B}(u,v)$ $(0\leq u,v\leq 1)$ be two vector-valued functions which represent two patches, let their common boundary curve be given by

$$\mathbf{A}(1,v) = \mathbf{B}(0,v) \qquad 0\leq v\leq 1. \tag{11}$$

Both patches have coincident tangent planes at every point of their common boundary curve if three vectors $\partial \mathbf{A}(1,v)/\partial u, \partial \mathbf{A}(1,v)/\partial v$ and $\partial \mathbf{B}(0,v)/\partial u$ are coplanar for $0\leq v\leq 1$. Hence the relation

$$\frac{\partial \mathbf{B}(0,v)}{\partial u} = p(v)\frac{\partial \mathbf{A}(1,v)}{\partial u} + q(v)\frac{\partial \mathbf{A}(1,v)}{\partial v} \tag{12}$$

with some functions $p(v) > 0$ and $q(v)$ ensures G^1 continuity.

3.2   Conditions for G^2 Continuity

G^2 continuity between two patches means the continuity in the tangent plane and normal curvature across the common boundary curve. Kahmann (1983) showed that the conditions for G^2 continuity are equation (12) and one more condition expressed by the equation

$$\frac{\partial^2 \mathbf{B}(0,v)}{\partial u^2} = p(v)^2\frac{\partial^2 \mathbf{A}(1,v)}{\partial u^2} + 2p(v)q(v)\frac{\partial^2 \mathbf{A}(1,v)}{\partial u\partial v} + q(v)^2\frac{\partial^2 \mathbf{A}(1,v)}{\partial v^2}$$
$$+r(v)\frac{\partial \mathbf{A}(1,v)}{\partial u} + s(v)\frac{\partial \mathbf{A}(1,v)}{\partial v} \qquad 0\leq v\leq 1 \tag{13}$$

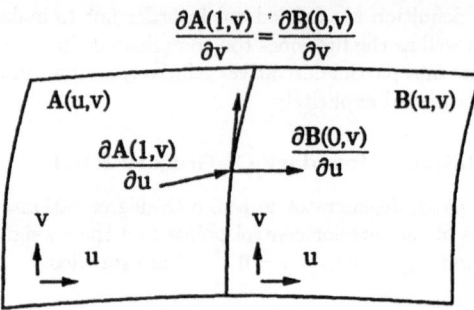

Figure 2: Two surface pathces with a common bondary curve

in which some functions $r(v)$ and $s(v)$ hold along the common boundary curves.

Similar to a C^2 Gregory patch, a RBC^{2}G patch has a singularity at its four corner points of the patch where $((u,v) = (0,0),(1,0),(0,1),(1,1))$ and neither its second partial derivatives nor curvature can be generally decided(see Miura (1991); Miura and Wang (1992) about the singularity of a C^2 Gregory patch). We therefore remove the end points from the domain of parameter v and the continuity of curvature will be discussed for $0 < v < 1$ in the next sections.

4 CONNECTION WITH PATCHES

In this section, we will discuss connections of a RBC^{2}G patch with a given rational Bézier patch and with another RBC^{2}G patch to guarantee G^1 and G^2 continuities. Mainly we will make an analysis of these patches' degrees in order to guarantee these continuities.

4.1 Connection with a Rational Bézier Patch

In Fig.2, let $\mathbf{A}(u,v)$ be a bi-m-th degree rational Bézier patch and $\mathbf{B}(u,v)$ be a bi-n-th degree RBC^{2}G patch. The first and second partial derivatives with respect to u at $u = 1$ of patch $\mathbf{A}(u,v)$ are given by the following expressions:

$$\frac{\partial A(1,v)}{\partial u} = \frac{\partial}{\partial u}\left(\frac{\mathbf{A}_n}{A_d}\right)\Big|_{u=1} = \left\{\frac{\frac{\partial \mathbf{A}_n}{\partial u}A_d - \mathbf{A}_n\frac{\partial A_d}{\partial u}}{(A_d)^2}\right\}_{u=1}$$

$$= \frac{\mathbf{g}(v)}{f(v)^2} \tag{14}$$

$$\frac{\partial A(1,v)}{\partial v} = \left\{\frac{\frac{\partial \mathbf{A}_n}{\partial v}A_d - \mathbf{A}_n\frac{\partial A_d}{\partial v}}{(A_d)^2}\right\}_{u=1} = \frac{\mathbf{h}(v)}{f(v)^2} \tag{15}$$

$$\frac{\partial^2 A(1,v)}{\partial u^2} = \frac{\mathbf{x}(v)}{f(v)^3} \tag{16}$$

$$\frac{\partial^2 A(1,v)}{\partial u \partial v} = \frac{\mathbf{y}(v)}{f(v)^3} \tag{17}$$

$$\frac{\partial^2 A(1,v)}{\partial v^2} = \frac{\mathbf{z}(v)}{f(v)^3} \tag{18}$$

where $\mathbf{A}_n$ and A_d are the numerator and denominator of $\mathbf{A}$, $f(v) = \sum_{i=0}^{m} B_i^m(v)w_i$, $w_i(i = 0, ..., m)$ are weights of the control points of the common boundary curve. See the appendix about equations (16), (17) and (18). The degrees of functions of v in the above equations, $f(v), \mathbf{g}(v), \mathbf{h}(v), \mathbf{x}(v), \mathbf{y}(v)$ and $\mathbf{z}(v)$ are m, 2m, 2m-1, 3m, 3m-1, 3m-2, respectively. As you can see from equations (9) and (10), the first and second partial derivatives at $u = 0$, which are necessary for equations (12) and (13) are

$$\frac{\partial \mathbf{B}(0, v)}{\partial u} = \frac{\partial}{\partial u}\left(\frac{\mathbf{B}_n}{B_d}\right)\bigg|_{u=0} = \frac{\frac{\partial \mathbf{B}_n}{\partial u}}{A_d}\bigg|_{u=0} = \frac{\mathbf{k}(v)}{f(v)} \tag{19}$$

$$\frac{\partial^2 \mathbf{B}(0, v)}{\partial u^2} = \frac{\frac{\partial^2 \mathbf{B}_n}{\partial u^2}}{B_d}\bigg|_{u=0} = \frac{\mathbf{l}(v)}{f(v)}. \tag{20}$$

Note that since patches $\mathbf{A}$ and $\mathbf{B}$ have the common boundary curve and have the same weights for their control points, $A_d = B_d$. We can substitute function $f(v)$ for each of them. Both $\mathbf{k}(v)$ and $\mathbf{l}(v)$ are of degree n.

Assume that constants p_0, p_1, q_0 and q_1 satisfy the following two equations:

$$\mathbf{k}(0) = p_0\mathbf{g}(0) + q_0\mathbf{h}(0) \tag{21}$$
$$\mathbf{k}(1) = p_1\mathbf{g}(1) + q_1\mathbf{h}(1), \tag{22}$$

i.e. the shape of these patches' boundaries satisfies the conditions expressed by the above equations. Furthermore, we assume $p(v)$ and $q(v)$ are given by

$$p(v) = \{(1 - v)p_0 + vp_1\}f(v) \tag{23}$$
$$q(v) = \{(1 - v)q_0 + vq_1\}f(v). \tag{24}$$

Then, after multiplying both sides of equation (12) by $f(v)$, the left side will become a n-th degree polynomial of v and the right side will be a (2m+1)-th polynomial of v. Since the boundary curve has already been given and weights $w_{1j1}(j = 1, ..., n - 1)$ are determined by equation (8), the coordinates of the control points $\mathbf{P}_{1j1}(j = 1, ..., n - 1)$ can be determined by solving equation (12). Namely we can connect these two patches with $\mathbf{G}^1$ continuity if conditions (21) and (22) are satisfied and $n \geq 2m + 1$.

Furthermore, assume constants r_0, r_1, s_0 and s_1 satisfy the following equations:

$$\mathbf{l}(0) = p_0^2\mathbf{x}(0) + 2p_0q_0\mathbf{y}(0) + q_0^2\mathbf{z}(0) + r_0\mathbf{g}(0) + s_0\mathbf{h}(0) \tag{25}$$
$$\mathbf{l}(1) = p_1^2\mathbf{x}(1) + 2p_1q_1\mathbf{y}(1) + q_1^2\mathbf{z}(1) + r_1\mathbf{g}(1) + s_1\mathbf{h}(1), \tag{26}$$

i.e. the shape of the boundaries and the result of the interpolation for $\mathbf{G}^1$ continuity satisfy the above conditions. In addition, assume functions $r(v)$ and $s(v)$ are given by

$$r(v) = \{(1 - v)r_0 + vr_1\}f(v) \tag{27}$$
$$s(v) = \{(1 - v)s_0 + vs_1\}f(v). \tag{28}$$

Then, after multiplying both sides of equation (13) by $f(v)$, the left side will become a n-th degree polynomial of v and the right side will be a (3m+2)-th polynomial of v. Since weights $w_{2j1}(j = 1, ..., n - 1)$ are determined by equation (8), the coordinates of the control points $\mathbf{P}_{2j1}(j = 1, ..., n - 1)$ can be determined by solving equation (13). Namely we can join these two patches with $\mathbf{G}^2$ continuity if conditions (25) and (26) are satisfied and $n \geq 3m + 2$.

4.2 Connection with a Rational Boundary C² Gregory Patch

At this time, in Fig.2, let $\mathbf{A}(u,v)$ be a bi-m-th degree RBC²G patch and $\mathbf{B}(u,v)$ be a bi-n-th degree RBC²G patch. The first and second partial derivatives with respect to u at $u=1$ of patch $\mathbf{A}(u,v)$ are given by the following expressions:

$$\frac{\partial \mathbf{A}(1,v)}{\partial u} = \frac{\frac{\partial \mathbf{A}_n}{\partial u}}{A_d}\bigg|_{u=1} = \frac{\mathbf{g}_R(v)}{f(v)} \tag{29}$$

$$\frac{\partial^2 \mathbf{A}(1,v)}{\partial u^2} = \frac{\frac{\partial^2 \mathbf{A}_n}{\partial u^2}}{A_d}\bigg|_{u=1} = \frac{\mathbf{x}_R(v)}{f(v)} \tag{30}$$

$$\frac{\partial^2 \mathbf{A}(1,v)}{\partial u \partial v} = \frac{\mathbf{y}_R(v)}{f(v)^2}. \tag{31}$$

(See the appendix about equation (31).) Since the derivatives coresponding equations (15) and (18) depend on only the shape of the common boundary curve, these expressions can be used without modifications. The degrees of functions, $\mathbf{g}_R, \mathbf{x}_R(v)$ and $\mathbf{y}_R(v)$ are m, m, 2m-1, respectively.

Similar to the case of the RBC²G patch, assume that on the shape of the boundaries, there are constants p_i, q_i, r_i and s_i $(i=0,1)$ which satisfy

$$\mathbf{k}(0) = p_0 \mathbf{g}_R(0) + q_0 \mathbf{h}(0) \tag{32}$$

$$\mathbf{k}(1) = p_1 \mathbf{g}_R(1) + q_1 \mathbf{h}(1) \tag{33}$$

$$\mathbf{l}(0) = p_0^2 \mathbf{x}_R(0) + 2p_0 q_0 \mathbf{y}_R(0) + q_0^2 \mathbf{z}(0) + r_0 \mathbf{g}_R(0) + s_0 \mathbf{h}(0) \tag{34}$$

$$\mathbf{l}(1) = p_1^2 \mathbf{x}_R(1) + 2p_1 q_1 \mathbf{y}_R(1) + q_1^2 \mathbf{z}(1) + r_1 \mathbf{g}_R(1) + s_1 \mathbf{h}(1). \tag{35}$$

Here, assume that $p(v), q(v), r(v)$ and $s(v)$ are given by

$$p(v) = (1-v)p_0 + vp_1 \tag{36}$$

$$q(v) = \{(1-v)q_0 + vq_1\}f(v) \tag{37}$$

$$r(v) = (1-v)r_0 + vr_1 \tag{38}$$

$$s(v) = \{(1-v)s_0 + vs_1\}f(v), \tag{39}$$

then if $n \geq 2m$, G¹ continuity can be guaranteed. If $n \geq 3m$, G² continuity can be guaranteed.

5 INTERPOLATION OF RBC²G PATCHES

As shown in the previous section, a n-th degree rational Bézier patch and a 3n-th RBC²G patch can be connected with G² continuity if the conditions at the end points of the common boudary curve are satisfied. We will therefore interpolate a bi-3n-th degree RBC²G patch surrounded by four rational Bézier curves of degree n by thinking the connection with a virtual n-th degree RBC²G patch as a base patch (Miura 1991; Miura and Wang 1991) at each of its boundary curve. Here, similar to the interpolation method of a C² Gregory patch (Miura 1991; Miura and Wang 1991), at first, the coordinates of the control points in the first rows from the boundary curves will be determined so as to guarantee the continuity of tangent plane. Next, the second rows will be determined to do the continuity of curvature. The weights of the control points in the first and second rows will be determined by equation (8).

5.1 Determination of the First Rows

In order to determine the coordinates of the control points in the first row, we have to specify the first partial derivatives $\partial A/\partial u$ and $\partial A/\partial v$ of a virtual n-th RBC^2G patch $A(u,v)$ along the common boundary curve. Since the shape of the boundary curve has already been given, it is enough to specify only $\partial A/\partial u$. In Fig.3, let a'_0 and a'_n be vectors defined by the differences of two contol points of the boundary, i.e. $a'_0 = P_{n,0} - P_{n-1,0}$ and $a'_n = P_{n,n} - P_{n-1,n}$ where P_{ij} are control points of patch A. We specify them as

$$a'_0 = \frac{b_{b0} - b_{a0}}{|b_{b0} - b_{a0}|} \tag{40}$$

$$a'_n = \frac{b_{bn} - b_{an}}{|b_{bn} - b_{an}|} \tag{41}$$

where b_{a0}, b_{an}, b_{b0} and b_{bn} are vectors defined by the differences of two control points of the boundaries of two patches to be connected. In order to make the patch as smooth as possible, function $g_R(v)$ is specified as a linear interpolation of these vectors with weights w_i of the common boundary curve, i.e.

$$g_R(v) = \sum_{i=0}^{n} B_i^n w_i a'_n. \tag{42}$$

where $a'_i = \{(n-i)a'_0 + ia'_n\}/n \ (i = 1, ..., n-1)$. By using this $g_R(v)$, the coordinates of the control points in the first row are determined.

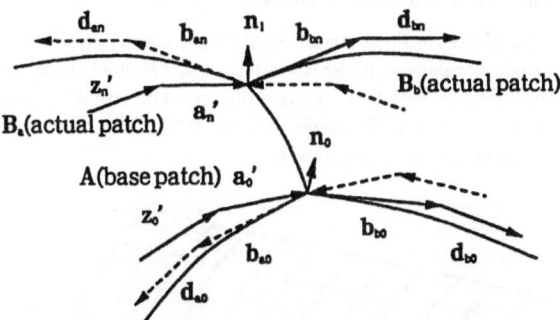

The base patch A is connected with B_b.

Figure 3: Interpolation of RBC^2G patch

5.2 Determination of the Second Rows

We will use equation (13) to determine the coordinates of the control points in the second rows. For that sake, we have to specify the second partial derivative $\partial^2 A/\partial u^2$ of a virtual patch $A(u,v)$(it is not necessary to specify other second partial derivatives $\partial^2 A/\partial u\partial v$ and $\partial^2 A/\partial v^2$ because of the specification of $\partial A/\partial u$ and the shape of the boundary curve, respectively).

In Fig.3, assume z_0' and z_n' are vectors which define the shape of the boundary given by

$$z_0' = a_0' + \beta_0 n_0 \tag{43}$$
$$z_n' = a_n' + \beta_1 n_1 \tag{44}$$

where β_0 and β_1 are constants and vectors n_0 and n_1 are unit vectors which are normal at the end points of the common boundary curve. By these assumptions, β_0 and β_1 can be determined by makeing interior products of both sides of equations (34) and (35), respectively.

Similar to function $g_R(v)$, we define function $x_R(v)$ with a linear interpolation of two vectors $a_0' - z_0'$ and $a_n' - z_n'$ and weights w_i $(i = 0, ..., n)$ of the common boundary curve. By using this $x_R(v)$ in equation (13), the second rows will be determined.

The above procedures are applied to each of the boundary curves and the first and second rows are determined. After that, if there may be some undetermined control points which have no effects on G^1 and G^2 continuity, other methods like one developed by Forrest (1972) are used to determine their positions.

We show several examples of RBC^2G patches in Fig.(4)~(6) generated by the interpolation method described above. The boundaries of the paches in these figures consist of quadratic rational Bézier curves and the patches are of degree 6×6. By using our method, rational curve meshes can be interpolated with RBC^2G patches G^2-continuously except for the four corner points of the patches.

5.3 Modification of Patch Boundary Curves

Depending on the results of the determinations of the first rows, equation (34) or (35) might not be satisfied. In such a case, in order to guarantee G^2 continuity, the shape of the boundary has to be modified to satisfy these conditions. For equation (34), similar to the modification of the bounday of a C^2G patch (Miura 1991; Miura and Wang 1991), it is possible to think about modifications as follows:

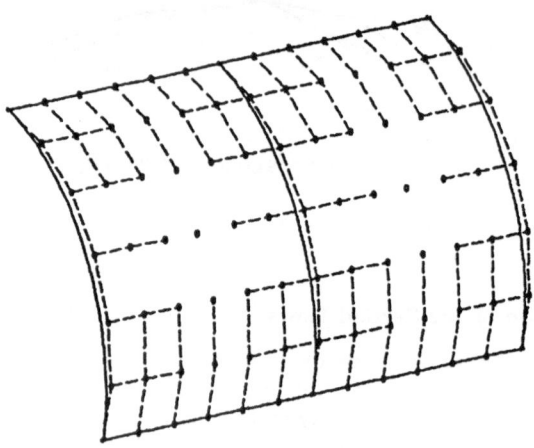

Figure 4: Example No.1

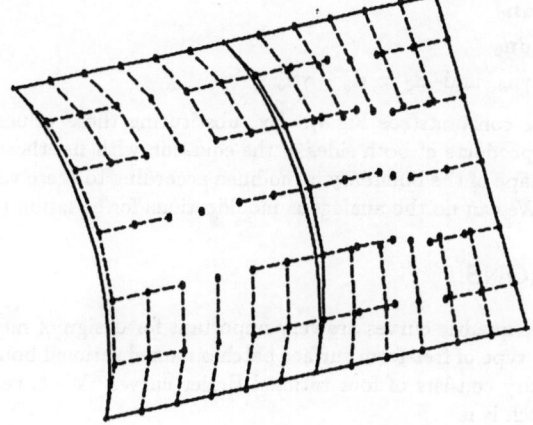

Figure 5: Example No.2

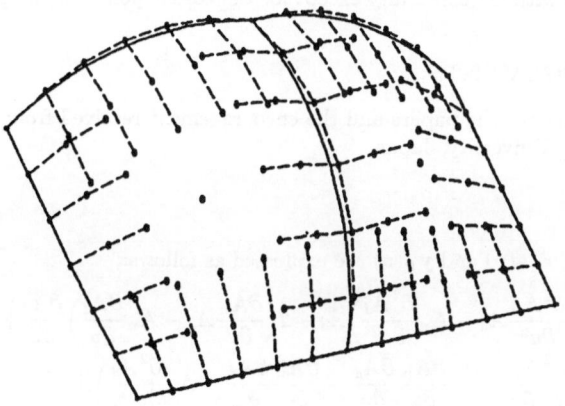

Figure 6: Example No.3

(a) $\mathbf{z}_0$ $\Rightarrow$ $\mathbf{z}_0 - \alpha\mathbf{n}_0$

(b) $\mathbf{d}_0$ $\Rightarrow$ $\mathbf{d}_0 - \beta\mathbf{n}_0$

(c) $\mathbf{z}_0$ $\Rightarrow$ $\mathbf{z}_0 - \gamma\mathbf{n}_0$ and $\mathbf{d}_0 \Rightarrow \mathbf{d}_0 - \gamma\mathbf{n}_0$

where α, β and γ are constants(see Fig.3). By substituting these values in equation (34) and making interior products of both sides of the equation with $\mathbf{n}_0$, these constants can be determined. If the shape of the boundary is modified according to these value, G^2 continuity can be guaranteed. We can do the analogous modifications for equation (35).

6   CONCLUSIONS

In this research, since quadric curves are very important for design of mechanical parts, we have proposed a new type of free-form surface patches named rational boundary C^2 Gregory patch, whose boundary consists of four rational Bézier curves. We have shown that when the degree of the patch is n,

1. With a m-th degree rational Bézier patch, if equations (21) and (22) are satisfied and $n \geq 2m + 1$, it can be connected with G^1 continuity. If equations (25) and (26) are satisfied and $n \geq 3m + 2$, it can be connected with G^2 continuity.

2. With a m-th degree RBC^{2}G patch, if equations (32) and (33) are satisfied and $n \geq 2m$, it can be connected with G^1 continuity. If equations (34) and (35) are satisfied and $n \geq 3m$, it can be connected with G^2 continuity.

Furthermore, we have developed a method to interpolate a RBC^{2}G patch by connecting it with virtual low-degree RBC^{2}G patches as base ones. By this interpolation method, free-form surfaces with G^2 continuity except for the corner points of the patches can be gererated.

ACKNOWLEDGEMENTS

The author appreciates the papers and the encouragement received from Professor Hiroaki Chiyokura of Keio University, Japan.

APPENDIX

Functions $\mathbf{x}(v), \mathbf{y}(v), \mathbf{z}(v)$ and $\mathbf{y}_R(v)$ are expressed as follows:

$$\mathbf{x}(v) = \left\{ \left(\frac{\partial^2 \mathbf{A}_n}{\partial u^2} A_d - \mathbf{A}_n \frac{\partial^2 A_d}{\partial u^2} \right) A_d - 2 \left(\frac{\partial \mathbf{A}_n}{\partial u} A_d - \mathbf{A}_n \frac{\partial A_d}{\partial u} \right) \frac{\partial A_d}{\partial u} \right\}_{u=1}$$

$$\mathbf{y}(v) = \left\{ \left(\frac{\partial^2 \mathbf{A}_n}{\partial u \partial v} A_d - \frac{\partial \mathbf{A}_n}{\partial u} \frac{\partial A_d}{\partial v} - \frac{\partial \mathbf{A}_n}{\partial v} \frac{\partial A_d}{\partial u} - \mathbf{A}_n \frac{\partial^2 A_d}{\partial u \partial v} \right) A_d \right.$$
$$\left. + 2\mathbf{A}_n \frac{\partial A_d}{\partial u} \frac{\partial A_d}{\partial v} \right\}_{u=1}$$

$$\mathbf{z}(v) = \left\{ \left(\frac{\partial^2 \mathbf{A}_n}{\partial v^2} A_d - \mathbf{A}_n \frac{\partial^2 A_d}{\partial v^2} \right) A_d - 2 \left(\frac{\partial \mathbf{A}_n}{\partial v} A_d - \mathbf{A}_n \frac{\partial A_d}{\partial v} \right) \frac{\partial A_d}{\partial v} \right\}_{u=1}$$

$$\mathbf{y}_R(v) = \left(\frac{\partial^2 \mathbf{A}_n}{\partial u \partial v} A_d - \frac{\partial \mathbf{A}_n}{\partial u} \frac{\partial A_d}{\partial v} \right)_{u=1}.$$

$$(45)$$

REFERENCES

Barnhill RE (1983) Computer aided surface representation and design. In: Barnhill RE, Boehm W (ed) Surfaces in CAGD. North-Holland Publishing, Amsterdam, pp 1-24

Boehm W (1988) Visual continuity. CAD 20: 307-311

Chiyokura H, Takamura T, Konno K, Harada T (1991) G^1 surface interpolation over irregular meshes with rational curves. In: Farin G (ed) NURBS for curves and surface design. SIAM, Philadelphia PA, pp 15-34

Forrest AF (1972) On Coons and other methods for the representation of curved surfaces. Computer Graphics and Image Processing 1: 341-359

Kahmann J (1983) Continuity of curvature between adjacent Bézier patches. In: Barnhill RE, Boehm W (ed) Surfaces in CAGD. North-Holland Publshing, Amsterdam, pp 65-75

Miura KT (1991) C^2 Gregory patch and its applications in computer-aided geometric design. Ph.D. dissertation. Cornell University, Ithaca NY

Miura KT, Wang KK (1991) C^2 Gregory patch. Proc. Eurographics'91, Vienna, pp 481-492

Miura KT, Wang KK (1992) Everywhere-G^2-continuous interpolation with C^2 Gregory patches. Proc. CGInternational'92, Tokyo, pp 497-516

Kenjiro Takai Miura is an associate professor of Department of Computer Software at the University of Aizu, Japan. He worked for Canon Inc., Japan as a research engineer from 1984 to 1992. His research interests include computer-aided geometric design, computer graphics, robotics, especially computer vision, and auto mesh generation.

He received his BEng and MEng in precision machinery engineering from the University of Tokyo in 1982 and 1984, respectively and his PhD in mechanical engineering from Cornell University in 1991. He is a member of ACM and ASME.

Address: Department of Computer Software, School of Computer Science and Engineering, the University of Aizu, Aza Kami-iawase 90, Oaza Tsuruga, Ikki-machi, Aizu-Wakamatsu-shi, Fukushima, 965 Japan.

Blending Polyhedra with NURBS

Xuefu Wang, Jiaguang Sun, and Kaihuai Qin

ABSTRACT

An approach of blending edges and vertices of a polyhedron using NURBS surfaces with C^1 continuity along their common boundaries is presented in this paper.The approach presented can unify the transaction of these two cases. Compare with other methods published, first , NURBS surface can represent the blending edge surface precisely;second, when blending the vertex, we depart the blending surfaces of its adjacent edges, so the surfaces don't need to join with each other, then "supplementary surfaces" are stitched together with C^1 contonuity to blend the vertex. We produce the blending surfaces by constructing boundary curve networks with C^1 continuity, then according to the continuity rule to generate the NURBS surfaces.

Keywords: blending surface, NURBS, Polyhedra, boundary curve networks, continuity.

1. INTRODUCTION

In CAD / CAM, blending of the edges and the vertices of the polyhedra is of great importance. Several methods about blending polyhedron have been published. Doo and Sabin(1978) and Catmull(1978) use a subdivision algorithm and that costs much. Chiyokura(1983,1987)first generates a curve mesh, after that, Gregory patches are chosen to blend the edge and vertex. Szilvasi(1991) uses bicubic Fergusion patches, but these patches have only C^0 continuity along their common boundary curves,and they can't represent the blending edge surface precisely. Hartmann(1990) and Jinggong(1990) adopt functional splines to blend a polyhedra, the blending surface is represented in an implicit form, however, to get high order continuity of the blending surface, the order of the blending surface is high too.In Wang(1992), sweeping surfaces are generated to replace the edges and vertices and have C^1 continuity (even along their common boundary).However, some properties of sweeping surface is difficult to calculate and it doesn't tally with the industry standard, e.g. IGES, STEP. Since NURBS surface has become industry standard in representing 3D objects in surface modeling and solid modeling and has many fine properties such as continuity and shape controllability etc, it is necessary to develop efficient blending polyhedra techniques using NURBS surface.In this paper, NURBS surfaces are generated to blend a polyhedron.In blending the edge of the polyhedron, NURBS surfaces can present the blending surface (constant radius or variable radius) precisely. In blending the vertex of the polyhedron, we introduce the concept of "supplementary surfaces". In most algorithm ever published , when blending the vertex, the surfaces used to blend its adjacent edges meet with each other at some points, this makes it difficult to get higher continuity at these places.But in our algorithm , we depart these surfaces, and a C^1 continuous curve is generated to link them, then a C^1 continuous boundary curve network is generated. After that "supplementary surfaces " are generated to form the blending surface for the vertex together with other surfaces.

This paper is categorized as follows:section 2 and 3 introduce the basic concept about blending polyhedron and NURBS surface. Section 4 gives detail in applying the NURBS surface to blend the edge of a polyhedron.The continuity rules about the blending surfaces are described in section 5.Section 6 explains how to blend the vertex of a ployhedron using NURBS surface,while section 7 shows some examples.

2. BLENDING OPERATION FOR POLYHEDRA

The two basic blending operations,i.e.,blending the edge and vertex of the polyhedra, used by most geometric modelers are shown in Fig.1 to Fig.4.In blending the edge, constant radius and variable radius blending can be offered. Fig. 1 depicts a constant radius blending for the edge e which is replaced by a constant radius cylindrical surface. Fig.2 shows a variable radius blending for the edge e that is blended by a variable radius cylindrical surface.These two kinds of blending surfaces all satisfy: (1) has C^1 continuity with its two adjacent planes.(2) The cross section curves at the two ends are circular arcs with radius r1 and r2 respectively. Where the cross section curve is the intersection curve between the cross section plane and the blending surface.The plane is vertical with the edge to be blended . (3) Any cross−section curve is a circular arc(the cross−section plane is perpendicular to the edge to be blended).

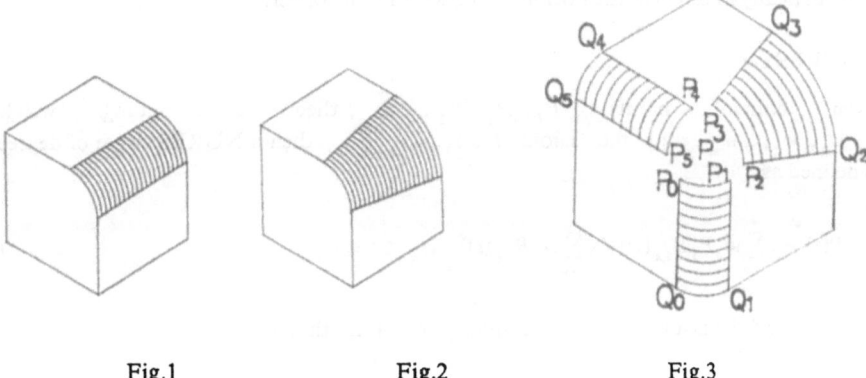

Fig.1   Fig.2   Fig.3

As our discussion continues , we will see that these two kinds of surfaces can all be represented precisely using NURBS, but in other algorithms described in section 1, they can not present the two kinds of surfaces precisely. Those blending surfaces only satisfy with (1) Blending the vertex of a polyhedron is relevant with the blending of its adjacent edges. The blending surface of a vertex must only intersect with its adjacent planes tangentially,but also have a C^1 continuity along the common boundary curve with the blending surfaces of its adjacent edges. These conditions are not easy to be met, but in some special cases, they can be easily met.For example,a vertex of a cube is to be blended,if its three adjacent edges are replaced by equally constant radius cylindrical surface,a 1 / 8 spherical surface can be used to blend the vertex(see Fig. 12) . This surface can easily be constructed using NURBS technique as shown in Tiller(1983) and Piegl (1987). But in general,this is not true for all cases.For a polyhedron with arbitrary topologies,the adjacent edges of a vertex are not necessarily vertical with each other, and the blending radius of each edge is different.The blending surface in the neighbourhood of a vertex where several convex and concave edges meet(Fig. 4) or where several edges with different blending radii meet(Fig.3). All these make the blending operation for the vertex P more difficult.

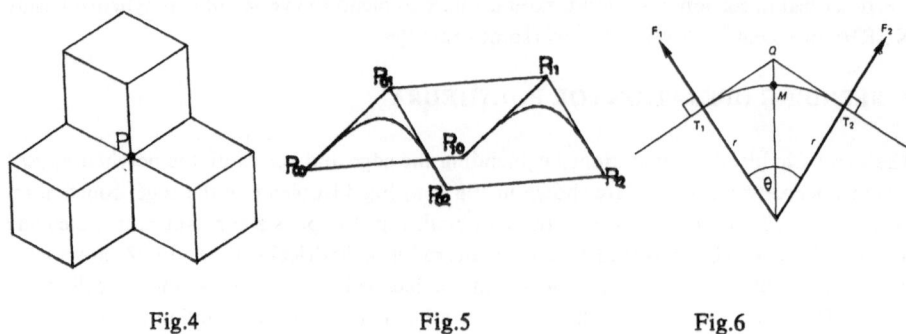

Fig.4   Fig.5   Fig.6

3. NURBS TECHNIQUE

The semantics of blending the edge and / or vertex of the polyhedra is defined mathematically in terms of the notion of NURBS in this paper.

3.1 NURBS curve

Given control points P_0, P_1, P_2,..., P_m, their corresponding weights w_0, w_1, w_2,...,w_m, and the knots t_0, t_1,...,t_{m+k+1}, then a NURBS curve of degree k is defined as:

$$P(t) = (\sum_{i=0}^{m} w_i P_i B_{i,k}(t)) / (\sum_{i=0}^{m} w_i B_{i,k}(t)) \quad (t_k \leqslant t \leqslant t_m) \tag{1}$$

If the first and the last knots have multiplicity of $k + 1$, that is

$$t_0 = t_1 = ... = t_k = 0.0$$
$$t_{m+1} = ... = t_{m+k+1} = 1.0$$

then the NURBS curve passes through the first and the last control points. At these two points,we have the following theorem about the derivatives of the NURBS curve.

Theorem 1.

The derivatives of a NURBS curve of degree k(its first and last knots have multiplicity of $k + 1$) at its two both ends are as follows:

$$P'(0) = (w_1 / w_0) * (k / (t_{k+1} - t_0)) * (P_1 - P_0)$$

$$P'(1) = (w_{m-1} / w_m) * (k / (t_{m+k+1} - t_m)) * (P_m - P_{m-1})$$

Proof:

Let $A(t) = \sum_{i=0}^{m} w_i * B_{i,k}(t),\qquad B(t) = \sum_{i=0}^{m} w_i * P_i * B_{i,k}(t)$

then $P(t) = B(t) / A(t)$

Since

$$B'_{i,k}(t) = k(t_{i+k} - t_i) * B_{i,k-1}(t) + k / (t_{i+k+1} - t_{i+1}) * B_{i+1,k-1}(t)$$

then

$$A'(t) = \sum_{i=1}^{m} k(w_i - w_{i-1}) / (t_{i+k} - t_i) * B_{i,k-1}(t)$$

$$A'(t) = \sum_{i=1}^{m} k(w_i P_i - w_{i+1}) / (t_{i+k} - t_i) * B_{i,k-1}(t)$$

$P'(t) = 1 / A^2(t) * (B'(t) * A(t) - A'(t) * B(t))$ and its two end knots are with multiplicity of $k + 1$, then

$$P'(0) = w_1 / w_0 * k / (t_{k+1} - t_0) * (P_1 - P_0) \tag{2}$$

similarly

$$P'(1) = w_{m-1} / w_m * k / (t_{m+k+1} - t_m) * (P_n - P_{n-1}) \tag{3}$$

By theorem 1, one can decide if C^1 continuity exists when two NURBS curves are connected end by end.

3.2 NURBS surface

Given control points net $\{P_{ij}\}(i = 0,1,\cdots,m; j = 0,1,\cdots,n)$, their corresponding weights $\{w_{ij}\}$ and the knots $\{u_i\}(i = 0,1,\cdots,m + k + 1)$ and $\{v_j\}(j = 0,1,\cdots,n + l + 1)$ then a NURBS surface of degree $k * l$ is defined as followes:

$$p(u,v) = \frac{\sum_{i=0}^{m}\sum_{j=0}^{n} w_{ij} P_{ij} B_{i,k}(u) B_{j,l}(v)}{= \sum_{i=0}^{m}\sum_{j=0}^{n} w_{ij} P_{ij} B_{i,k}(u) B_{j,l}(v)} \qquad u_k \leq u \leq u_m,\ v_l \leq v \leq v_n \tag{4}$$

4. BLENDING THE EDGE WITH NURBS SURFACE

L.Piegl has shown that NURBS curve of degree two can represent conics precisely. Let the two end knots of a NURBS curve have multiplicity of three, weights of its two end control points be 1. 0, then the weight of the middle control point determines what kind of conics represented by the NURBS curve is, if $0.0 < w_1 < 1.0$, then the NURBS curve represents an elliptic arc; if $w_1 = 1.0$, a parabola; if $w1 > 1.0$, a hyperbola.

Theorem 2.
A NURBS curve of degree two has the first and last knots with multiplicity of three,if its control triangle is an equilateral one and the weight $w_0 = w_2 = 1.0$, $0.0 < w_1 < 1.0$ then the radius of the circular arc represented by the NURBS curve is:

$$r = 2 * w_1^2 * \frac{|P_1 - P_0|^3}{|(P_2 - P_1) * (P_1 - P_0)|} \tag{5}$$

Proof:
Since the NURBS curve can represent a circular arc, so its curvature is constant everywhere.Without loss of generality, we calculate the curve's curvature at $t = 0.0$.
Let $P(t)$ be a NURBS curve of degree two with respect to control points P_0, P_1, P_2 and weights w_0, w_1, and w_2,then

$$P(t) = \frac{P_0 B_{0,2} + w_1 P_1 B_{1,2}(t) + P_2 B_{2,2}(t)}{B_{0,2}(t) + w_1 * B_{1,2}(t) + B_{2,2}(t)}$$

the knot vector is $(0.0,0.0,0.0,1.0,1.0,1.0)$, then we have:

$$P'(0) = 2 * w_1 * (P_1 - P_0), \qquad P''(0) = 2 * (P_2 - P_0)$$

so the curvaturous radius of the curve is:

$$\rho = \frac{|P'(t)|^3}{|P'(t) * P''(t)|}$$
$$= 2w_1^2 \frac{|P_1 - P_0|^3}{|(P_2 - P_1) * (P_1 - P_0)|}$$

This completes the proof of Theorem 2.

Theorem 3.
Suppose P_{00}, P_{01}, P_{02} be the control points of NURBS curve $c_1(t)$, P_{10}, P_{11}, P_{12} be the control points of NURBS curve $c_2(t)$, the two NURBS curves are of degree two,and they all represent circular arcs, their equilateral control triangles are parallel(the planes that they lie in are parallel).Line $P_{01} P_{11}$ is vertical with the plane that each triangle lies in, line $P_{00} P_{01}$ and line $P_{10} P_{11}$ are parallel,line $P_{01} P_{02}$ and $P_{11} P_{12}$ are parallel too.Then, the rule surface constructed by $c_1(t)$ and $c_2(t)$ is a cylindrical surface S,that is,any cross section curve of S (the cross section plane is perpendicular to Line $P_{01} P_{11}$) is a circular arc.(see Fig. 5).

Proof:
According to the definition of a rule surface,we know that the rule surface formed by $c_1(t)$ and $c_2(t)$ can be represented in NURBS. Its control net and corresponding weights are:

$$\begin{bmatrix} P_{00} & P_{01} & P_{02} \\ P_{10} & P_{11} & P_{12} \end{bmatrix} \qquad \begin{bmatrix} 1.0 & w_1 & 1.0 \\ 1.0 & w_2 & 1.0 \end{bmatrix}$$

u knots are $(0.0,0.0,0.0,1.0,1.0,1.0)$ and v knots are $(0.0,0.0,1.0,1.0)$

Next we will prove that: any v parametric curve is a cross section curve and this cross section curve is a circular arc. By the calculating method of a NURBS surface, we know that the control points of v parametric curve are: $vP_{00} + (1.0 - v)P_{10}$, $vP_{01} + (1.0 - v)P_{11}$, and $vP_{02} + (1.0-v)P_{12}$. Their corresponding weights are $1.0, vw_1 + (1.0-v)w_2, 1.0$ respectively. Its knot vector is $(0.0,0.0,0.0,1.0,1.0,1.0)$. Because the plane which P_{00}, P_{01} and P_{02} lie in and the plane which P_{10}, P_{11}, P_{12} lie in are parallel, then the plane which the three control points of the v parametric curve lie in is parallel with them, and these planes are vertical with $P_{01}P_{11}$. So the v parametric curve is a cross section curve and vice versa.

Since $0 < w_1$, $w_2 < 1.0$, and $0.0 \leqslant v \leqslant 1.0$, then $0 < vw_1 + (1.0 - v) * w_2 < 1.0$

Let

$$Q_0 = vP_{00} + (1-v)P_{10}$$
$$Q_1 = vP_{01} + (1-v)P_{11}$$
$$Q_2 = vP_{02} + (1-v)P_{12}$$

then

$$Q_1 - Q_0 = v(P_{01} - P_{00}) + (1-v)(P_{11} - P_{10})$$
$$Q_2 - Q_1 = v(P_{02} - P_{01}) + (1-v)(P_{12} - P_{11})$$

Since $P_{01}P_{00}$ is parallel with $P_{11}P_{10}$, $P_{02}P_{01}$ is parallel with $P_{12}P_{11}$, and $|P_{01}P_{00}| = |P_{02}P_{01}|$, $|P_{11}P_{10}| = |P_{12}P_{11}|$ then $|Q_0Q_1| = |Q_2Q_1|$, this means that the control triangle is an equilateral one. Based on Theorem 2, the v parametric curve is a circular arc as shown in Fig.5. This completes the proof of Theorem 3.

Specify two points on the edge to be blended, the two points are positions where the two end cross section planes intersect with the edge. The cross section plane is vertical with the edge, the radius of the two end cross section curves (they are circular arcs) can be given by the user (if they are equal, then the blending suface is a constant radius one, if they are different, the blending surface is a variable radius one). The control triangle of each curve can be calculated, their relevant positions of the triangle are illustrated in Fig.6.

According to Theorem 2, let the weight of the two end points be 1.0, we can calculate the weight of the middle point w_1. After the two end cross section curves have been constructed, a NURBS surface that is the surface of blending the edge of the polyhedron can be formed precisely according to Theorem 3. It is straightforward to verify that the surface is tangent with its adjacent planes.

5. CONTINUITY RULE ABOUT STITCHING TOGETHER OF TWO NURBS PATCHES

Gregory (1987) describes the sufficient conditions for joining the two patches with C^2 continuity, we here only introduce the conditions in the case of a C^1 join.

Theorem 4

Suppose Ωp and Ωq are domains of the patches p and q, map $e_q:[0,1] - > R^2$ be a parametric representation of a boundary segment of q. This boundary curve is shared by p and q. There exists a diffemorphism $\Phi:R^2 \to R^2$ defined in the neighbourhood of Ω_q, then

if the following conditions hold, the patches p and q will have a C^1 join:
(1) (Domain continuity) $e_p = \Phi e_q$ is a boundary segment of Ωp and is such that interior points of Ωp are mapped from exterior points of Ωq.
(2) (patch continuity) for all $s \in [0,1]$

$$q(e_q(s)) = p(\Phi(e_q(s))) \quad (C^0 \text{ continuity})$$

$$\partial q|eq(S) = \partial(p\Phi)|_{(\Phi(eq(S)))} \quad (C^1 \text{ continuity})$$

This theorem gives the sufficient conditions for two patches to have a c^1 join. According to it, we can know the sufficient conditions for two NURBS patches with c1 join.

Lemma 1

Suppose p and q are two NURBS patches, p join q along one of their common boundary curves. If, at any point on their common boundary curve, r_u and r_v of p and q are all equal, then p and q have C^1 join.

Consider a NURBS surface $p(u,v)$ of degree $k * l$, its control net is $\{p_{ij}\}(i = 0,1,...,m; j = 0,1,...,n)$ u knot and v knot all have multiplicity of $k+1$ and $l+1$ at their first and last knots respectively, their weights are $\{w_{ij}\}(i = 0,1,...,m; j = 0,1,...,n)$, which satisfy:

$$w_{i,0} = w_{i,n} = 1.0 \quad (i = 0,1,...,m) \tag{7}$$

$$w_{i,1} = w_{j,1} \quad (i,j = 0,1,...,m) \tag{8}$$

$$w_{i,n-1} = w_{j,n-1} \quad (i,j = 0,1,...,m) \tag{9}$$

Let's analyze its derivatives along one boundary curve. Without loss of generality, we will calculate r_u along the boundary curve $u = 0$ defined as $P'_u|_{u=0}$ their r_v are equal).
Suppose

$$A = \sum_{i=0}^{m} \sum_{j=0}^{n} w_{ij} B_{i,k}(u) B_{j,1}(v)$$

$$B = \sum_{i=0}^{m} \sum_{j=0}^{n} w_{ij} P_{ij} B_{i,k}(u) B_{j,1}(v)$$

then

$$P_u(u,v) = (B'_u A - A'_u B) / A^2$$

Since u knots have multiplicity of $k+1$ at its two end knots and (7), so when $u = 0.0$, $A = 1$, then we have a simplified form:

$$P'_u(u,v)|_{u=0} = B'_u - A'_u B$$

$$= \sum_{j=0}^{n} k * w_{j1} (P_{j1} - P_{j0}) B_{j,1}(v) / (u_{k+1} - u_0)$$

Similarly, along the parametric curve $u = 1$, we have:

$$P_u(u,v) = \sum_{j=0}^{n} k * w_{j,n-1} (P_{j,n} - P_{j,n-1}) B_{j,1}(v) / (u_{m+k+1} - u_k)$$

According to the above analysis, we have the following Theorem:

Theorem 5:

Suppose two NURBS patches p and q with the degree $k1 * l1$, and $k2 * l2$ respectively join along their common boundary, for p the common boundary is the parameter curve $u = 1$, for q it is the parameter curve $u = 0$, and the two patches satisfy:

(1) the u knot at its first and last knots with multiplicity of k+1 ,k is the degree of the v parametric curve of the surface(k1 and k2 respectively).

(2) $w_{i0} = w_{im} = 1.0 \qquad (i = 0,1,...,n)$

$\qquad w_{i1} = w_{j1} \qquad\qquad (i,j = 0,1,...,n)$

$\qquad w_{i,n-1} = w_{j,n-1} \qquad (i,j = 0,1,...,n)$

(3) $k_1 / (u_{k1+m+1} - u_m) * w_{j,n-1} * (P_{jn} - P_{j,n-1}) = k_2 / (uu_{k2+1} - uu_0) * ww_{j0} * (Q_{j1} - Q_{j0})$

where u_i, uu_i, w_{ij}, ww_{ij}, P_{ij}, Q_{ij} are the v knots, weights and control points of the two surfaces respectvely.

If the above conditions are held, then p and q have a C^1 join.

6. BLENDING THE VERTEX OF A POLYHEDRON WITH NURBS

In this section, we will blend the vertex of a polyhedron with C^1 continuous NURBS surfaces based on Theorem 5.The blending of a vertex of a polyhedron is relevant with that of its adjacent edges. The blending operation can be divided into the following steps:(1) Construct the boundary curves of the blending surface . (2)Construct the NURBS surface according to Theorem 5. We will illustrate the algorithm in detail by blending the vertex P in Fig. 3.

P is the vertex to be blended, the edges i,j and k are its adjacent edges, the plane a,b and c are its adjacent planes, NURBS surface R_1, R_2, and R_3 are the blending surface for the edges i,j and k respectively(constant radius blending or variable radius blending). Circular arc P_0P_1, P_2P_3 and P_4P_5 are the cross−section curves of R_1, R_2 and R_3, where the cross section plane is vertical with i, j and k respectively. The position of the end cross section plane must satisfy:$|PP_0| = |PP_1| = ... = |PP_5|$

This can easily be done. Fig. 7 shows their relevant positions.

From Fig.7, we see that P_1 and P_2, P_3 and P_4, P_5 and P_0 don't coincide. However,they are coincident in most algorithms ever published. If they are coincident, it is difficult for the blending surface to achieve high order continuity at these places, but if they are away from each other, we can link them with a C^1 continuous curve segment and make it possible to construct a blending surface with C^1 continuity at these places.

We have constructed the NURBS representation for the circular arc P_0P_1, P_2P_3 and P_4P_5 in section 4. In Fig.7 for the points P_1, P_2, the tangent vector has been determined, so according to Therorem 1, we can construct a NURBS curve of degree three that joins arc P_0P_1, and $P_2 P_3$ with C^1 continutiy. As shown in Fig.8, the weight of P_0, P_1, P_2, P_3 are all 1.0, the weights of M_0 and M_3 are w_0 and w_3 respectively, w_0 and w_3 have been calculated using Theorem 2, (In fact, these three curve segments don't lie in the same plane, we do so just for simplicity). According to theorem 1, we can get:

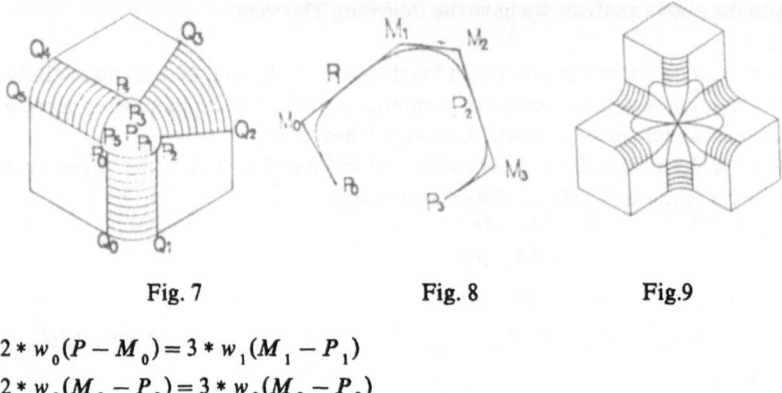

Fig. 7   Fig. 8   Fig.9

$$2 * w_0(P - M_0) = 3 * w_1(M_1 - P_1)$$
$$2 * w_3(M_3 - P_2) = 3 * w_2(M_2 - P_2)$$

so we can determine w_1, w_2 and M_1, M_2. Similarly, curve $P_3 P_4$ and $P_5 P_0$ can all be generated.

At point P we construct a plane A, it is the tangent plane of the blending surface at this point. We can generate another group of boundary curves in the following way: construct a NURBS curve that have P_1 and P be its two end points, and join $Q_i P_i$ with C_1 continuity. Its tangent vector at P lie in the plane A. The direction of this vector is defined, yet its length is to be defined. Later we will show how to define the length of this vector. In this way we can construct all the six curve segments. Fig.9 shows the boundary curve networks that are used to blend the vertex P in Fig.4.

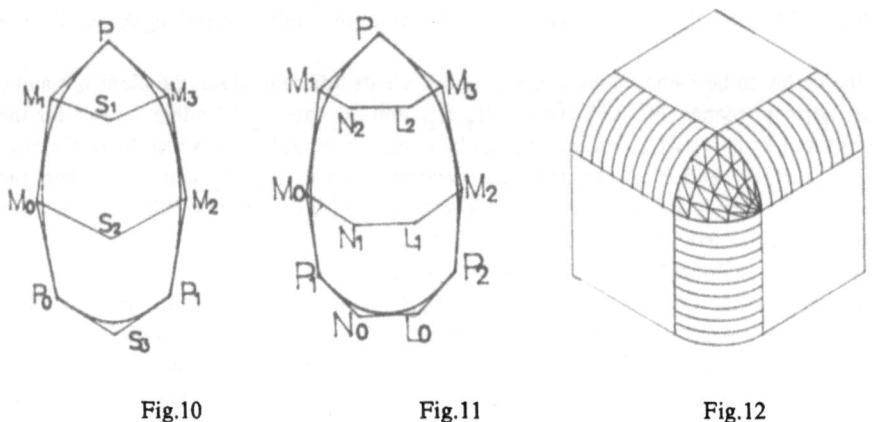

Fig.10   Fig.11   Fig.12

We set all the weights of the control points of the NURBS curve $P_i P$ $(i = 0, 1, ..., 5)$ to be 1.0. Suppose the curve $P_i P$ is a three order NURBS curve, four control points of the $P_0 P$ are P_0, M_0, M_1, P, but the control points of $P_1 P$ are P_1, M_2, M_3, P. Let M_1 and M_3, M_0 and M_2 lie in a plane that is parallel to the cross section plane as illustrated in Fig.10. In this way we have defined the length of the vector. Without loss of generality, we will construct the NURBS surface bounded by the curve P_0P, P_1P, and P_0P_1, then construct another NURBS surface bounded by curve P_1P, P_2P, and P_1P_2 as shown in Fig.11.

As shown in Fig.10, circular are P_0P_1 is represented in NURBS, since M_0 and M_2 lie in the plane that is parallel with the cross–section plane, we can set the tangent vectors at M_0 and M_2 which are parallel to that of arc P_0P_1 at P_0 and P_1 respectively. Then, point S_2 can be determined. Similarly, points S_1 can also be determined and their weights are equal to that of S_3. In this way we construct the control points and their weights of a NURBS surface S_0 of degree 2 * 3, their u knot is $\{0,0,0,1,1,1\}$, v knot is $\{0,0,0,0,1,1,1,1\}$. In the same way, we can construct NURBS surface S_1 bounded by the curve P_2P_3, P_2P, P_3P, and surface S_2 bounded by P_4P_5, P_4P, and P_5P.

In the published algorithms, P_0 and P_2,P_3 and P_4,P_5 and P_0 are coincident, so surface S_0,S_1, and S_2 together form the blending surface of vertex P. It is difficult for them to get higher continuity along their boundary curves. In our algorithm, we will construct the "supplementary surfaces" to make C^1 continuity between them.

As shown in Fig.11, we can construct the 3 * 3 NURBS surface bounded by the curve P_1P_2,P_1P and P_2P. We have calculated the positions of M_0,M_1, M_2 and M_3, and the positions of N_0 and L_0, the weights of M_0,M_1,M_2 and M_3 are all 1.0, the weights of N_0 and L_0 are w_1 and w_2 respectively. They have been calculated in section 4. Since this NURBS surface have a C^1 join with the NURBS surface bounded by the cruve P_0P_1,P_1P and P_2P and the surface bounded by the curve P_1P_2,P_1P and P_2P based on Theroem 5, we can calculate the position of N_1 and N_2, their weights are equal to w_1. Similarly, the position of L_2 and L_1 and their weights can also be determined. In the same way, the NURBS surface bounded by the curve P_3P_4,P_2P and P_4P and the surface bounded by the curve P_5P_0,P_5P, and P_0P can all be solved out. These three NURBS surfaces are called as "supplementary surfaces". Now, we have constructed the NURBS surfaces that can be used to blend the vertex P. Since they are generated according to Theroem 5, so they should have a C^1 join. It is easy to verify that the cylindrical surfaces R_1,R_2 and R_3 have a C^1 join with their adjacent NURBS surfaces constructed above. From the description above, we see that this approach can be used to blend any polyhedra with arbitrary topologies.

7. EXAMPLES

For the vextex P of a cube, a constant radius blending is applied to its adjacent edges, then a 1 / 8 spherical surface is used to round the vertex P,this surface is constructed using NURBS illustrated in Fig.12. For the example depicted in Fig. 4, NURBS surfaces are used to blend the edges and vertex shown in Fig. 13.

For the vertex P in a polyhedron with arbitrary topologies, NURBS surfaces are used to blend the point P, this case is illustrated by two examples shown in Fig. 14 and 15, 16 and 17.

8 CONCLUSION

An approach using NURBS surface to blend polyhedra is presented in this paper. By using NURBS, we can represent the blending surface for the edge precisely.By using "supplementary surfaces", we can construct a C^1 continuous surface to blend the vertex of a polyhedra. This algorithm is simple and easy to be implemented and can blend any polyhedra with arbitrary topologies.

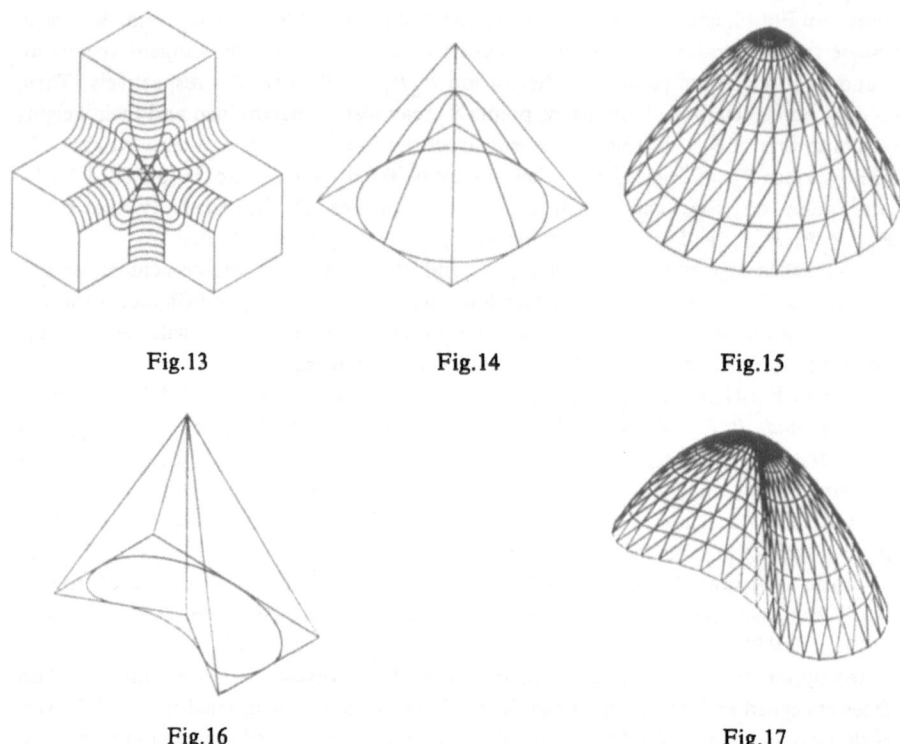

Fig.13   Fig.14   Fig.15

Fig.16   Fig.17

REFERENCES

Catmull E E and Clark J H(1978) Recursively generated B spline surfaces on arbitrary topological meshes. CAD 10:350–355.

Chiyokura H and Kimura F(1983) Design of solids with free form surfaces. Comput. Graph. 17(3):289–298.n

Chiyokura H(1987) An extended rounding operation for modelling solids with free–form surfaces. IEEE CG&A 7(12):27–36.

Doo D and Sabin M(1978) Behavior of recursive division surfaces near extraordinary points.CAD 10:356–360.

Floater MS(1992) Derivarives of Rational Bezier curves.CAGD 9:161–164.

Gregory J A and Hahn J M(1987) Geometric continuity and convex combination patches, CAGD 4(1):79–90.

Hartmann E(1990) Blending of implicit surfaces with functional splines. CAD 22(8):500–506.

Jinggong Li, Josef Hoschenk and E. Hartmann(1990) G^{n-1} functional splines for interpolation and approximation of curves, surfaces and solids. CAGD,22(7):209–220.

Moreton,H and Sequin,C(1991) Surface Design with Minimum Energy Networks.

293

In:Rossignac J and Turner J(ed) Proc. of Symposium on Solid Modeling Foundations and CAD / CAM Applications.ACM Press,Austin,Texas, pp291–302.

Piegl L(1991) On NURBS:A Survey,IEEE CG&A,11(1):55–71.

Piegl L and Tiller W(1987) Curve and Surface Constructions using rational B–splines.CAD 19(9):485–498.

Szilvasi Nagy M(1991) Flexible rounding operation for polyhedra, CAD 23(9):629–633.

Tiller W(1983) Rational B splines for Curve and Surface Representation. IEEE CG& A 3(6):61–69.

Wang Xuefu,Sun Jiaguang,Qin KaiHuai(1992) Blending Polyhedra with Sweeping.to be submitted.

Wang Xuefu is a PHD candidate in Department of Computer Science, Tsinghua University.He received his BS in 1991. His research interests are Computer Graphics and Geometric Modeling.

Sun Jiaguang is professor of Computer Science, and director of Computer Aided Design Center at Tsinghua University.Professor Sun received a B S in Computer Science from Tsinghua University in 1970. His research interests are in Computer Graphics, Computational Geometry, Computer Aided Geometric Design , Geometric Modeling , Engineering DataBase Management System and CAD / CAM system.
Address:Department of Computer Science, Tsinghua University, Beijing100084,China.

Kaihuai Qin is an associate professor in Computer Science at Tsinghua University, Beijing, China. He obtained his PhD degree in 1990 and MS in 1984 in Computer Integrated Manufacturing from Huazhong University of Science and Technology and BS in 1982 from South China University of Tecnology. His research interests include computer graphics, geometric modelling, computational geometry, surface NC machining and integrated intelligent CAD / CAM systems. He has written more than thirty technical papers in the areas of research.

Direct Manipulation Devices for the Design of Geometric Constraint Networks

Ari Rappoport

ABSTRACT

Geometric constraints play an important role in the parameterization and design of geometric models. We describe an application of the *Direct Manipulation Device (Dmd)* concept to interactive specification and editing of geometric constraint networks. A Dmd is a virtual interactive device for visualizing an instance of an abstract data type and for performing operations on the data using direct manipulation. We present a methodology for using Dmds in geometric applications and demonstrate Dmds for numerous constraints. We consider many common constraint types, such as distances and angles between points, and also a *probabilistic position* constraint, which treats the position of a point as a suitably distributed random variable. The Dmd for this constraint specifies the random variable's mean vector and covariance matrix. The underlying representation of a constraint network is a labeled bi-partite graph having object nodes, constraint nodes, and arcs that connect constraint nodes to object nodes. The arcs are labeled to distinguish the a-symmetric role that points possess relative to the constraints.

Keywords: Direct Manipulation Device (Dmd), geometric constraints, parametric design, probabilistic constraints.

1   INTRODUCTION

Usage of geometric constraints is becoming increasingly common in geometric modeling applications. Specification of relations that must hold between geometric objects provides a higher level interface than directly specifying the degrees of freedom (DOFs) of the model. When using constraints the DOFs can automatically be computed using numerical or symbolic constraint solvers, thereby reducing the user's efforts and increasing the flexibility of the resulting design. The importance of constraints can be seen in the field of mechanical computer-aided design, where parametric modeling is one of the most influential commercial developments of the last few years.

The success of any application depends on the quality of its user interface. It is widely accepted that for most applications the quality of the user interface can be greatly improved via *direct manipulation* (Shneiderman 1983). Direct manipulation means operating on visual representations of the application objects rather than through command languages or scripts. Most people recognize a direct manipulation interface when they see it, but direct manipulation principles and techniques have not yet been categorized to the extent that they can be encapsulated and implemented in general user interface toolkits. A coherent user input model is presented in (Myers 1990), but it is not suited for geometric applications with several different types of direct manipulation. A few recent attempts in the computer graphics field are the *3D widgets* described in (Conner 1992), the *Manipulators* of Iris Inventor (SGI 1992) and the *Direct Manipulation Device (Dmd)* (Rappoport 1993, Emmerik 1992).

Several constraint-based systems have been described in the computer graphics and CAD literature. Prominent systems include Sketchpad (Sutherland 1963), CONSTRAINTS (Sussman 1980), Juno (Nelson 1985) and ThingLab (Borning 1981). The emphasis in those systems was more on enforcing constraints than on the user interface for constructing constrained models.

More recently, a few researchers have started dealing with graphical constraint specification (Borning 1986, Sistare 1991) and representation of constraints (Rossignac 1986, Kalra 1990, Emmerik 1991, Gleicher 1992). (Olsen 1990) described the usage of constraints for creating direct manipulation techniques. Icons for visualizing graphs and relations are described in (Chen 1992). None of these has substantively addressed the concepts and principles underlying the design of direct manipulation interfaces for geometric constraint networks.

In this paper we present direct manipulation devices for constructing and editing geometric constraint networks. We discuss the general principles of designing Dmds for such networks and the considerations that should be addressed when specifying and implementing the user interface to such systems. The discussion is presented in the context of a novel approach to constraints, which we call *probabilistic constraints* (Hel-Or 1993). The focus of the present paper is on the direct manipulation interface, not on the semantics and mathematics of systems of probabilistic constraints. However, these will be discussed where relevant to the interface issue.

Section 2 presents the definition of a Dmd and a discussion on the principles relating to its usage in interactive systems. Section 3 describes the application domain, which includes the types of objects and constraints we use and the data structure used for representing them. Section 4 describes the design of specific constraint Dmds. Finally, Section 5 briefly discusses our prototype implementation.

2 THE DIRECT MANIPULATION DEVICE (DMD)

In this section we briefly summarize the concept of a Dmd, as described in (Emmerik 1992, Rappoport 1993). The Dmd is based on the notion of an abstract data type (ADT) and consists of the following:

- A symbolic data type,

- A data vector (also called the internal representation),

- A visual representation,

- A set of operations invoked by manipulation of the visual representation.

A Dmd is, then, an ADT augmented with a visual representation and an interactive, direct manipulation interface to the operations defined for the ADT.

When used by an interactive application, an instance of a Dmd is *bound* to an application object with the same data type. For example, a local coordinate system can be represented by a Dmd. An application may use this Dmd by binding a specific instance of it to the location and orientation of a rigid body. The well-known 3-D cursor of (Nielson 1986) can be regarded as a Dmd for specifying a 3-D position. When a Dmd is manipulated, a new value of its data vector is determined according to the operation performed. The application then needs to update any bound object.

There are three distinct dimensionalities associated with a Dmd. The most important is the dimensionality of the data vector, i.e., the number of independent parameters needed to uniquely specify a single data instance of the ADT's type. We call this dimensionality the *data dimension*. A second dimensionality is the apparent dimension of the Dmds visual representation and the interactive operations, referred to as the *visual dimension*. Usually, this dimension is two or three. The third associated dimensionality is this of the application object bound to the Dmd, referred to as the *object dimension*. All of these dimensionalities can be different: a Dmd representing a 2-D local coordinate system has a data dimension of at least six (a scaling, rotation and translation matrix), possibly a 3-D visual dimension, and a 2-D object dimension,

To use the Dmd concept in an application, the designer should first identify the types of application entities which are to be controlled by the user. A Dmd should be defined for each such entity type. For each desired Dmd type, the required operations should next be determined. A Dmd representing an ADT does not have to supply an interactive interface to all the operations supported by the ADT. For example, a Dmd representing an affine transformation may choose not to supply a direct manipulation interface to the shearing operation if this operation is not required by the specific application.

The Dmd type and operations guide the next step, that of visual design. The visual design should provide feedback regarding the current value of the ADT. Even if no direct manipulation operations are provided by the Dmd, it can still be of great advantage. We refer to a Dmd that serves only for visual feedback as a *Visual Feedback Device (VFD)*.

The next step is the design of ways in which the user interactively selects one of the available operations. In most cases there is more than a single operation and a simple graphics pick does not suffice. There are two main tools to use for this purpose: *handles* and *gestures*. A *handle* is a hot spot on a Dmd's visual representation that corresponds to a particular operation. Clicking on the Dmd inside the handle area using the pointing device (usually a mouse) serves two purposes at once: making the Dmd the active object and selecting one of the operations that it provides. An alternative to handles are *gestures*. The Dmd is made the active object by ordinary picking, and the desired operation is determined by a gesture that the user performs with the pointing device. One simple gesture, for example, is the direction of motion.

Naturally, handles and gestures can be combined when desired or necessary, as when there is a large number of supported operations. Picking a handle serves for choosing a particular family of operations, while a specific one is chosen according to a gesture.

Many operations need parameters. The parameters to an operation are usually determined as a function of the current and previous mouse positions. For example, a 2-D rotation angle can be determined from the vectors between the current and previous mouse positions and a reference center of rotation.

An important issue regarding the design of Dmds is that of visual degeneracies. During the design of the visual representation care should be taken that all desired handles and gestures are always selectable. For example, it may happen with a 3-D visual dimension that a particular handle is hidden by the rest of the Dmd, in which case the operation associated with that handle is not available. If this cannot be prevented, at least a reset option should be supplied. A convenient feature of a Dmd is provision of special user events for expressing exact parameter values. For example, if the left mouse button is the one used for ordinary pick and manipulation, the middle button (or a combination of the left button and a control key) can be used to cycle through exact, useful parameter values, such as a 90 degree angle or a unit vector.

Another important issue regarding design of Dmds is customization. Since a Dmd possesses a visual representation, the user should be given ways of customizing it, e.g. change its colors, overall size, font and so on.

3 GEOMETRIC CONSTRAINT NETWORKS

In this section we analyze our application domain, geometric constraint networks. We discuss the constructed geometric model and explain the labeled bi-partite graph representation of the network.

3.1 Geometric Model

The purpose of a modeling application is to construct a model comprised of geometric objects. An object is represented by a finite number of degrees of freedom (DOFs) that uniquely determine it. In most cases the DOFs can be represented as the coordinates of points in an appropriate space. For example, a circle can be represented by its center and radius but also by its center point and an arbitrary point on its boundary or by three points on the boundary. Representing all DOFs by coordinates of points is sometimes redundant (i.e., uses more data items than necessary), as in the circle example, but it serves to simplify the data structures and algorithms used. In the following we assume that all the degrees of freedom of the constructed model can be represented as coordinates of points in R^k. If the total number of points is n, the total number of DOFs is kn. This assumption is only made to simplify the exposition. Note that the assumption is common in parametric design (Lin 1981).

3.2 Constraints

Constraints relating model points are called *first order constraints*. A first order constraint is characterized by three parameters: the type of the constraint, the number of points that it constrains, and the types and numbers of parameters that it depends upon. We say that a constraint is $C_{i,k}$ when it relates i points and depends on k parameters. For example, the PointDistance constraint, which fixes the distance between two points, is $C_{2,1}$.

Second order constraints are constraints which relate first order constraints. For example, assume two PointDistance constraints that constrain the distances P_1, P_2 and P_3, P_4 to be d_1 and d_2, respectively. A constraint that relates d_1 and d_2, say using their ratio ($\frac{d_1}{d_2} = r$), is a second order constraint. In effect, a second order constraint adds variables to the system of equations that must be solved to satisfy the constraints. In the example, d_1 and d_2 are the additional variables. Second order constraints can usually be expressed as first order ones by 'substituting in' the first order constraints they involve.

3.3 Labeled Bi-Partite Graph Representation

The representation we use for a constraint network is a labeled bi-partite graph. The graph has two node types, point nodes and constraint nodes. A constraint node is connected by arcs to the point nodes representing the points attached to it. There are no other arcs in the graph. The point parameters of a constraint are not necessarily symmetric. For example, the ThreePointAngle constraint fixes the angle formed by three points; the role of the middle point is different from the roles of the two other points. Arcs labels are used to denote the role of a point relative to a constraint. Note that due to this a-symmetry a hyper-graph is not a suitable representation. The parameters on which a constraint depends are stored inside the node representing it.

The labeled bi-partite graph representation is a low-level one, since it does not take into account the existence of different types of objects. This follows from our assumption that an object is represented by a set of points. The set of points representing the same object should be associated; We will not discuss the association scheme since it is irrelevant from the point of view of the constraint solver.

4 DMDS FOR CONSTRAINT NETWORKS

In this section, we describe principles and considerations in the application of the Dmd concept to interactive specification and editing of constraint networks. We will describe the decisions made for a particular 2-D prototype implementation. We restricted our implementation to two dimensions since our purpose was to study the conceptual issues related to Dmds and constraint networks. The principles we elucidate are valid for other dimensions and other applications as well.

4.1 General Considerations

As discussed in Section 2, the first step in designing an application interface that uses Dmds is to decide on the application entities which are bound to Dmds. In our constraint networks application there are two kinds of entities: model points and constraints. Interactive manipulation of both kinds is-desired. Note that we could have dealt with three entities: two node types and arcs. Arcs denote attachment of a point node to a constraint node. We decided that direct manipulation is not needed for this simple binary variable, but the opposite decision could also have been taken. The treatment of attachment is described at the end of this section.

The visual representation chosen for 2-D model points is an empty square. The only operation needed for a point is translation, which is easily achieved by picking the point and dragging it to the desired location. In most 2-D systems translation by dragging can be directly supported by the system's architecture and a Dmd is not needed. However, strictly speaking this does describe a Dmd, since there is a visual representation which is directly manipulated by the user. Note that a 3-D application would probably need a more elaborate Dmd for moving a point in 3-D space (Nielson 1986).

The constraint Dmds are all of the same type, a fact which should be reflected by their visual and behavioural design. The most obvious way to associate a family of objects is through a common set of colors. All model points are drawn using one color while constraint Dmds use a different color. Three additional colors are used for the current picked object, current picked Dmd handle and the attachment of a point to a Dmd (see below).

Many Dmds use fixed points. The visual representation chosen for a fixed point is a full square. Fixed points are distinguished from model points both by the fact that they are full, not empty, and by their color, which is the Dmd color and not the object color. All Dmd handles are shown by a small filled square, so that the user recognizes the hot spots sensitive to direct manipulation. The left mouse button is used for ordinary manipulation while the middle button is used for special, extreme values of constraint parameters. In addition, all Dmds can be moved as a single rigid unit by picking them in any area which is not a handle and then dragging.

Attachment between a model point and a constraint Dmd is depicted by a line segment connecting the point and some area of the Dmd. In many cases this area is a Dmd handle, but not necessarily. Recall that the segment is drawn in a color reserved for attachment.

A central guideline in the design of constraint Dmds is that they serve to visualize the *distance from a solution*. Constraint systems do not always admit a solution, and even when one exists it is not always discovered by numerical solvers. The rationale behind this guideline is to have each Dmd also convey a feeling regarding the amount by which the represented constraint is met. This way, one brief look of the user suffices to get an impression regarding the quality of the solution and its deviation from the desired model.

We adopted a technique which we refer to as *hard-wired visual constraints* for visualizing solution quality and emphasizing the Dmd-point attachment relation. When possible, a Dmd's position and orientation is modified according to the location of the points attached to it. The constraints on the location of the Dmd as a function of the location of attached points are hard-wired into the Dmd display routine. When a point is dragged by the user, the Dmds attached to it are moved accordingly, serving as an easy way of identifying all the constraints attached to a point.

4.2 Specific Dmds

Following is a description of each constraint type and the Dmd implemented for it. For each Dmd we describe its visual design, hard-wired visual constraints when attached to model points, handles and interactive behaviour. The Dmd of a constraint `Name` is called `DmdName`.

Distance

`Distance` constrains a point to be at a certain distance from a fixed point. `Distance` is $C_{1,k+1}$ since it constrains a single point and depends on the k coordinates of the fixed point and on an additional scalar distance. `Distance` actually specifies that a point lies on a circle. `DmdDistance`'s visual representation is a line segment originating at the fixed point and whose length is the required distance (Fig. 1).

`DmdDistance` supports operations for setting the distance and the location of the fixed point. Two handles are provided, one at the fixed point and one at the other end of the distance segment. Both handles can be picked and dragged. When the fixed point handle is dragged the length of the line segment remains constant, while dragging the other end modifies the length and leaves the fixed point in place.

Attachment between a model point and `DmdDistance` is depicted by a line segment connecting the non-fixed end of `DmdDistance` and the point. Recall that this segment is drawn in a color reserved for attachment. When a point is attached to the Dmd, a hard-wired visual constraint is invoked which moves the free end of the Dmd to be collinear with its fixed point and the attached point. This hard-wired constraint is kept also when the user manipulates the free end. When there is an attached point, this has the effect that the free end can only slide along the line connecting the fixed end and the attached point. This behaviour does not constitute any limitation on the user, since the free end is a handle that is only used to specify the desired distance.

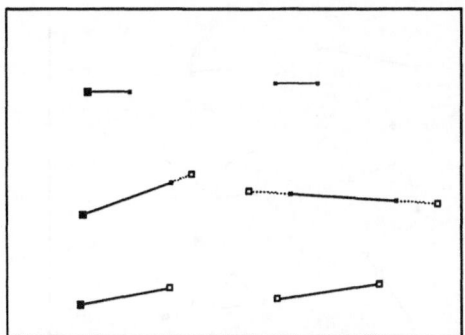

Figure 1: The `Distance` (left) and `PointDistance` (right) constraints. Top: with no points attached; middle: with points attached, not satisfied; bottom: satisfied.

When attached to a point, `DmdDistance` looks like a line segment composed of two segments having two different colors, the usual Dmd color and the attachment color. The length of the attachment segment is inversely related to the amount by which the constraint is satisfied. When it is completely satisfied the attachment segment is not seen at all. A brief look at the Dmd shows if and to which extent the constraint is satisfied.

PointDistance

`PointDistance` constrains two points to lie at a certain distance from each other. It is $C_{2,1}$ since it constrains two points and depends only on a single distance parameter. Distance is again visualized by a line segment whose length equals the distance (Fig. 1). Two handles, one at each end of the segment, are provided for modifying the segment's length. Their appearance and behaviour are completely symmetric. A hard-wired visual constraint ensures that the two attached points and the Dmd are collinear. Two line segments drawn in the attachment color connect the attached points, one to each end of the Dmd. Again, the amount by which the constraint is satisfied is visualized through the lengths of the attachment segments: the constraint is completely satisfied when their color does not show.

PointOnLine

`PointOnLine` constrains a point to lie on a fixed line. `PointOnLine` is $C_{1,m}$ where m is the number of parameters needed to specify a fixed line. A redundant but convenient representation for a line is by two distinct points that lie on it, in which case $m = 4$. The fixed line is visualized by two fixed points (full squares) connected by a line segment (Fig. 2).
Both fixed points serve as handles for modifying the location and slope of the line. Attachment is visualized by a line segment connecting the attached point and its projection on the line. If the projection falls outside the segment between the two fixed points, the nearer of them is moved to coincide with the projection. For `DmdDistance` the hard-wired constraints only affect the visualization of attachment (by computing the projection when the attached point is moved) since the parameters to the constraint are fixed.
The middle mouse button is used to cycle between a vertical and a horizontal line slope. These are very common, especially in mechanical design, and it is very convenient to be able to express them using a single mouse click.

ThreePointAngle

`ThreePointAngle` fixes the angle formed by three points. `ThreePointAngle` is $C_{3,1}$ since it

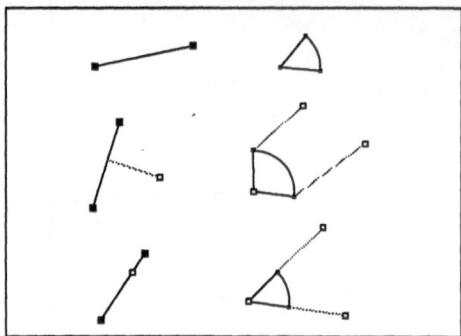

Figure 2: The `PointOnLine` (left) and `ThreePointAngle` (right) constraints. Top: with no points attached; middle: with points attached, not satisfied; bottom: satisfied.

depends only on the angle. `DmdThreePointAngle` looks like a circular arc whose angle is the desired angle (Fig. 2). It has three handles, one at the center of the circle and two on the two ends of the arc. The first handle only serves for translating the Dmd as a single rigid unit. The other two handles are manipulated to modify the angle. The radius of the arc remains constant during interactive modification, since it does not mean anything. The constant is automatically determined so that its size is large enough to see and manipulate but not too large.

Denote the center by C, the two other handles by H_1, H_2 and the points attached to them by P_1, P_2. Hard-wired constraints keep the center of the circular arc incident on the point attached to it and orient the arc such that the angles CH_1P_1 and CH_2P_2 are identical. When the constraint is satisfied, both CH_1P_1 and CH_2P_2 are straight lines. It is easy to see the extent by which the constraint is satisfied.

The middle mouse button is used to cycle between an angle of 0, 90, 180 and 270 degrees. The exact set of angles to cycle through should be determined by the application. In some applications 30 and 45 degrees would be also useful.

ThreePointsOnLine

`ThreePointsOnLine` constrains three points to be collinear. `ThreePointsOnLine` is $C_{3,0}$ since it constrains three points and does not depend on any numerical parameter. `ThreePointsOnLine` is a special case of `ThreePointAngle` with a 0 or 180 degrees angle, but it is so common that we provided a special Dmd for it. `DmdThreePointsOnLine` looks like a line segment with three handles, two at each end and one in the middle. Attachment segments connect the handles to the points attached to them (Fig. 3).

A hard-wired constraint positions and orients the segment so that the middle handle lies in the center of mass of the three attached points and the segment's slope is an average of the line slopes defined by the two other points. When the constraint is satisfied all points and handles are collinear. The length of `DmdThreePointsOnLine` remains constant. Since `ThreePointsOnLine` is a $C_{3,0}$ constraint (i.e., it has no parameters), once attached its visual representation cannot be modified by the user.

ProbabilisticPosition

`ProbabilisticPosition` Specifies a probabilistic location for a point. The location of a point is viewed as a normally distributed random variable. A probabilistic location is represented by the mean vector and covariance matrix of the distribution. The covariance matrix determines

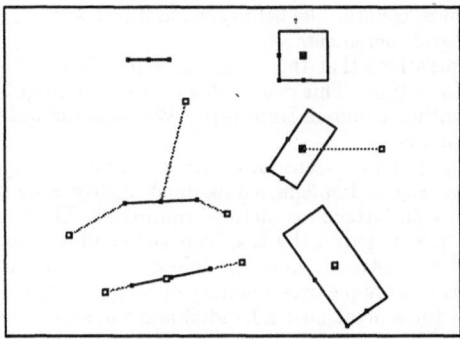

Figure 3: The `ThreePointsOnLine` (left) and `ProbabilisticPosition` (right) constraints. Top: with no points attached; middle: with points attached, not satisfied; bottom: satisfied. Note that the `ProbabilisticPosition` constraint is always satisfied, since there is a non-zero probablility for a point to be everywhere. However, the highest probability is at the center of the rectangle.

the direction of the principal axes of the Gaussian and the standard deviation along each axis. It could be represented symbolically by two points for the axes' directions and two scalars for the standard deviations. Another possible representation is by a scaling and rotation matrix, whose scale factors are the standard deviations and whose rotation parameters rotate the global coordinate system to coincide with the principal Gaussian axes. We use the second representation since it was easier for the implementation of the Dmd. This representation can be easily converted to a covariance matrix, which is the representation required by the numerical solver we use to solve the resulting system of probabilistic constraints. A model point can be fixed in some space location using `ProbabilisticPosition` with a zero covariance matrix. `ProbabilisticPosition` is visualized by a rectangle whose center is located at the desired position, rotated and scaled according to the principal directions and standard deviation of the desired covariance (Fig. 3). The operations that `DmdProbabilisticPosition` supports are translation, rotation and scale along two axes. We used four handles, one for each operation. The handle for translation is located at the middle of the rectangle. The two scale handles are located at the middle of two of the rectangle edges. The amount of scaling is determined such that the the edge follows the mouse. The rotation handle is located at the vertex connecting the two edges on which the scale handles lie. The amount of rotation is determined so that the rotation vertex lies on the line connecting the center and the mouse.

When the middle mouse button is pressed on the center handle, the Dmd toggles between a zero-width and height rectangle (a point) and the previous rectangle. This way an exact position (not a probabilistic one) can be expressed. When the middle button is pressed on a scaling handle, the corresponding scale factor toggles between zero and the previous one. A zero scale factor collapses the rectangle into a line segment, which is another way of expressing the `PointOnLine` constraint.

4.3 Summary

All of the constraints described above except `ProbabilisticPosition` are standard in geometric constraint systems. Note that we could have defined two more angle-type constraints, relating two model points and one fixed point. These were omitted for simplicity. There are cases in which exact values for the constraint parameters are required. In such cases exact numbers can be expressed using the special user interface device for number specification described in (Rappoport 1992a). The device enables typing directly using the keyboard, single digit manipulation using the mouse, counter-like behaviour, and fast and exact navigation through a slider and programmable grid increments.

There are three essential operations that the system user interface should support. It should enable choosing a specific Dmd type. This can be done using a pop-up or pop-down menu, or through icons, each representing a unique Dmd type. We took the latter approach, which is common in 2-D drawing systems.

The user interface should also provide means for attaching and detaching a model point to and from a constraint. The easy way to implement this functionality is by picking a point and a constraint handle and issuing an 'attach' or 'detach' command. The command can be issued using a software button, a menu item or by a special key-combination. Note that it is not enough to pick a point and a constraint, since the role of handles in some constraints is not symmetric. A more attractive technique uses a variant of 'snap-dragging' (Bier 1990): the user drags a handle near a point (or a point near a handle) and the system snaps them together if the mouse button is released when they are in close proximity to each other.

5 IMPLEMENTATION

Our prototype 2-D system was implemented in C under Unix using the X/Motif user interface toolkit and X or SGI/GL for graphics. The system enables the definition of constrained models using the set of constraints described previously. The standard operations of cut, copy, read, write etc are supported. Statistics regarding the solution process are gathered. The system provides an option to produce a postscript representation of the visual appearance of the model, using which the figures in this paper were created.

The Dmd concept was implemented as an encapsulated C object, supporting the operations Init, End, Read, Write, Display, ReactToEvent, AttachPoint, DetachPoint, Pick, UpdateData, HardWiredConstraint. The Pick operation decides whether or not the Dmd is picked according to a user event. If the answer is yes, it also returns the picked handle, since user events are interpreted differently according to the manipulated handle.

The data structure used for the constructed model is a labeled bi-partite graph as described in Section 3. Every constraint node in the graph has an associated Dmd object through which it is visualized and manipulated. Point nodes are visualized and manipulated by squares as described above. The arcs in the graph correspond to attachment segments; they are only visualized, not manipulated directly.

The data in the graph are updated when the user manipulates a Dmd, and then all Dmds are updated. It is necessary to update them since an operation done using one Dmd can cause another one to change due to the hard-wired constraints. The Dmd update operation is coupled with the model display operation, since the hard-wired constraints are very fast and their execution has not caused noticeable performance problems.

Figures 4 and 5 show a simple model with various constraints before and after a solution. The constraints relating each point and the amount by which they are satisfied are clearly seen. The model is comprised of five points, four of them constrained to lie on vertical lines on the right and on the left (two on each line). A probabilistic position is defined for three of them, serving as a soft guideline for their desired location. Distances between two of the points and between another and a fixed point are specified; three points should be collinear.

Exposing the process of expressing and solving the system of probabilistic equations needed to satisfy the model is outside the scope of this paper. A complete discussion of the solution process is given in (Hel-Or 1993). That paper also introduced the relaxed parametric design modeling paradigm, which utilizes 'soft' constraints (constraints which do not have to be met exactly) to express guidelines that can later change during other stages of the design (or manufacturing) process. Probabilistic constraints are one way of implementing relaxed parametric design.

6 CONCLUSION

In this paper we discussed the usage of the Direct Manipulation Device (Dmd) concept in the context of specifying and editing geometric constraint networks. We explained the general

303

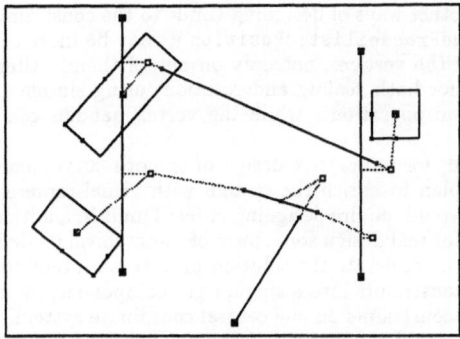

Figure 4: A simple model with several constraints before solution.

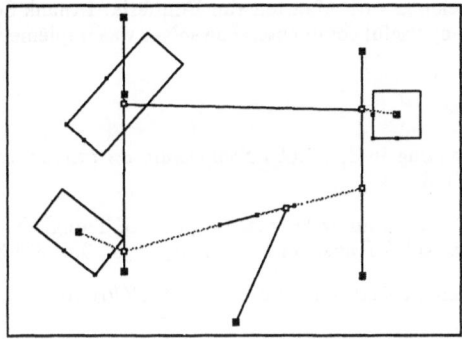

Figure 5: The model after the solution.

model of a constraint network, reviewed the definition of a Dmd and guidelines for its usage in real systems, and presented detailed examples for the design and implementation of numerous Dmds representing 2-D geometric constraints.

The prototype system implemented to test our ideas is novel both in its usage of Dmds for geometric constraint networks and in the usage of probabilistic constraints.

The Dmd was shown to be an extremely valuable design technique for producing high quality direct manipulation interfaces. Users of the system have expressed their appreciation to the interface. Dmds provide: a visualization of the relations between points and of the degree by which they are satisfied; interactive means for expressing these relations; and interactive means for manipulating the parameters of the relations, all using the same mechanism.

There are two potential difficulties with the Dmd approach. First, in some cases there may be no obvious visual representation for a given constraint. In this case a visual icon may actually confuse the user, who will have to exert mental effort to learn the meaning of the icon. Second, the display of the model can become very cluttered in the presence of many constraints, especially if model objects are shown explicitly rather than using only points. The user should be supplied with filters that cause only some of the Dmds to be displayed, e.g. only those attached to certain points or lying in a certain part of space.

Naturally, there are many other ways of designing Dmds to the constraints we discussed in this paper. For example, for `DmdProbabilisticPosition` it may be more convenient to provide a rotation handle on each of the vertices, not only on one of them. Alternatively, the handles on the edges can be used for both scaling and rotation, using simple directional gestures to distinguish between the two operations, while the vertex handles can be used for uniform scaling.

We have already used Dmds for interactive design of smooth curves and surfaces (Rappoport 1992b). In the future we plan to enrich the system with visual representations of the model objects themselves, which would require designing object Dmds in addition to constraint Dmds. In order to use the system for real design some form of hierarchical modeling must be provided. For this purpose and also to accelerate the solution process we intend to provide an option of freezing a combination of constraints into a single rigid component, by translating constraints on its comprising points to constraints on one central coordinate system. Direct representation of second order constraints would enhance the expressive power of our constraint networks. All of the above should also be done in 3-D. We feel that a Dmd interface can significantly enhance the applicability of constraints in 3-D modeling.

ACKNOWLEDGEMENTS

The Dmd concept was developed with Maarten van Emmerik. I thank Seth Teller for reading the paper and providing many useful comments. The solver was implemented by Yacov Hel-Or.

REFERENCES

Bier, EA, (1990) Snap-dragging in 3D, *ACM Symposium on Interactive 3D Graphics, Computer Graphics* 24(4):193-204.

Borning, AH, (1981) The programming language aspects of ThingLab, a constraint-oriented simulation laboratory, *ACM Trans. on Prog. Lang. Sys.*, 3(4):353-387.

Borning, AH, (1986) Defining constraints graphically, *SIGCHI Bulletin*, 17(4):137-143, (CHI '86).

Chen, M, Townsend, P, Wang, CY, (1992) A development environment for constructing graph-based editing tools, *Computer Graphics Forum* 11(3):345-355 (*Eurographics '92*).

Brookshire Conner, D, Snibbe, SS, Herndon, KP, Robbins, DC, Zeleznik, RC, van Dam, A, (1992) Three-dimensional widgets, *ACM Symposium on Interactive 3D Graphics, ACM Symposium on Interactive 3D Graphics, Computer Graphics* 24(4).

Emmerik, MJGM van, (1991) Interactive design of 3D models with geometric constraints, *The Visual Computer* 7:309-325.

Emmerik, MJGM van, Rappoport, A, Rossignac, J, (1992) Simplifying interactive design of solid models: a multiview, hypertext approach, to be published in *The Visual Computer*.

Gleicher, M, (1992) Integrating constraints and direct manipulation, *ACM Symposium on Interactive 3D Graphics, Computer Graphics* 24(4):171-174.

Hel-Or, Y, Rappoport, A, Werman, M, (1993) Relaxed parametric design with probabilistic constraints, *2nd ACM/SIGGRAPH Symposium on Solid Modeling and Applications*, Montreal.

Kalra, D, Barr, AH, (1990) A constraint-based figure maker, *Eurographics '90*, pp. 413-424.

Lin, VC, Gossard, DC, Light, RA, (1981) Variational geometry in computer aided-design, *Computer Graphics*, 15(3):117-126 (SIGGRAPH '81).

Myers, BA, (1990) A new model for handling input, *ACM Trans. Info. Sys.*, 8(3):289-320.

Nelson, G, (1985) Juno: a constraint-based graphics system, *Computer Graphics*, 19(3):235-243, (SIGGRAPH '85).

Nielson GM, Olsen DR, (1986) Direct manipulation techniques for 3D objects using 2D locator devices, *ACM Symposium on Interactive 3D Graphics*, ACM Press, pp. 175-182.

Olsen, D, Allan, K, (1990) Creating interactive techniques by symbolically solving geometric constraints, *ACM Symposium on User Interface Software*, pp. 102-107.

Rappoport A, Emmerik MJGM van, (1992a) User interface devices for fast and exact number specification, submitted.

Rappoport A, (1992b) Interactive design of smooth objects using probabilistic point constraints, submitted.

Rappoport A, Emmerik MJGM van, (1993) The Direct Manipulation Device (Dmd): Definition and Implementation, in preparation.

Rossignac, JR, (1986) Constraints in constructive solid geometry, *ACM Symposium on Interactive 3D Graphics*, ACM Press, pp. 93-110.

SGI (1992) IRIS Inventor Technical Report, Silicon Graphics, Inc.

Shneiderman B, (1983) Direct manipulation, a step beyond programming languages, *IEEE Computer* 16(8), pp. 57-69.

Sistare, S, (1991) Graphical interaction techniques in constraint-based geometric modeling, *Graphics Interface '91*, pp. 85-92.

Sussman, GJ, Steele, GL, (1980) CONSTRAINTS – a language for expressing almost hierarchical descriptions, *Artificial Intelligence,* 14:1-39.

Sutherland, IE, (1963) Sketchpad: a man-machine graphical communication system, *Proceedings of the Spring Joint Computer Conference,* IFIPS, pp. 329-345.

Ari Rappoport received his Ph.D. in computer graphics from the Institute of Computer Science, The Hebrew University of Jerusalem, Israel, in 1990. He afterwards visited the Interactive Geometric Modeling group at the IBM T.J. Watson Research Center, Yorktown Heights, New York. Currently he conducts research in geometric modeling and computer graphics at the Institute of Computer Science, The Hebrew University. His research interests include representations and algorithms for geometric objects, interaction techniques, constraints and parameterizations in modeling, applications of image processing and computer vision to computer graphics, and scientific visualization.

His address is: Institute of Computer Science, The Hebrew University, Jerusalem 91904, Israel, email: arir@cs.huji.ac.il, phone: +972-2-585867, FAX : +972-2-585439.

A Methodology for Geometric Algorithm Development

Seth J. Teller

ABSTRACT

Much current development of geometric algorithms is performed in a batch fashion, even though the algorithms themselves are often intended for highly interactive and visual applications. This predominance of batch techniques has resulted in lessened intuition about, experimentation with, and productivity of geometric algorithms.

We describe a methodology for the development of robust geometric algorithms. First, we propose that algorithm development should be, and can be, performed in a visually and interactively rich environment, and that this environment facilitates robustness, intuition, and pedagogy. We relate some experience that bolsters our claims of increased robustness. Second, we argue that geometric computations should be designed to "prove" the validity of their conclusions to the practitioner via data objects called *geometric witnesses* that have direct visual representations. Third, we show that an interactive "template" program for algorithm development is easy to construct on currently available workstations, and that it is well worth it to do so. Finally, we enumerate several other development principles, touching on interaction techniques and the use of temporal coherence to detect subtle algorithmic flaws.

Key Words: Algorithm visualization, geometric computation, robustness, interaction techniques, geometric witnesses.

1 INTRODUCTION

Practitioners of computer graphics, computational geometry, computer-aided geometric design, and related fields routinely design, implement and use sophisticated geometric algorithms. In contrast to the eventual ways in which these algorithms are *used* (typically in complex modeling or geometric visualization or simulation applications), the environments in which such algorithms are *implemented* are often relatively unsophisticated. One reason for this phenomenon may be that interaction techniques are widely (and erroneously) thought to be "expensive;" that is, to require many person-hours of implementation effort and an expensive hardware platform. Thus the activities of implementing the components of the system, and of using the system, tend to remain separate in practice.

Geometric Algorithms Are Often Developed in Batch Mode

A specific example of the problem might be a computational geometry practitioner developing a convex hull algorithm. The practitioner writes an algorithm that reads a file of input points, computes the convex hull, and writes a textual representation of it to another file. This file is then read by another program that displays the points and the hull described in the file. If a problem is observed, the code is modified, and another iteration of execution and inspection begun.

This procedure is essentially a batch computation, since it runs from start to finish with no interaction. The convex hull algorithm has no access to the graphical environment in which the algorithm is "used" (i.e., its output displayed). This separation tends to have at least two deleterious effects. First, the slowness and rigidity of the development process tends to discourage experimentation and intuition. Second, algorithms developed in this manner tend to have bugs that show up "later" than is desirable (e.g., after the algorithm is subsumed into some larger application), for the simple reasons that relatively few test inputs to the algorithms are generated and exercised, and the algorithm is not tested in the fashion in which it will be used (i.e., repeatedly). Since exhaustive enumeration of all inputs is computationally infeasible, even if systematic or randomized testing is performed, there is no reason to suppose that it will find troublesome input cases. In short, batch computations discourage intuition and experimentation.

A New Way of Developing and Testing Geometric Algorithms

In this paper we propose that the design and use of geometric algorithms be combined in a single interactive environment. By this, we do not mean that development and application tools be combined into one monolithic application, but rather that algorithm development should be, and can be, performed in a visually and interactively rich environment. Moreover, the availability of such an environment makes possible a novel methodology for algorithm development. We have constructed an algorithm visualization system in which the practitioner interacts with visual representations of the input and output of a geometric algorithm, which is re-invoked whenever the input is modified (Figure 1). The environment was straightforwardly constructed on an existing workstation, and is a "template"; it can be easily reused whenever a new geometric algorithm is to be developed.

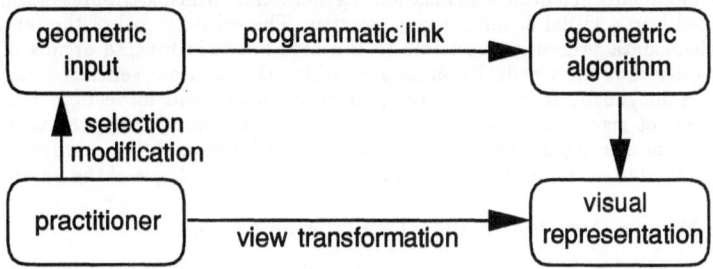

Figure 1: The interaction model. The practitioner modifies the geometric inputs through selection and direct manipulation. The visual representations of both inputs and outputs are displayed and inspected via directly-manipulable viewing transformations.

Specific Recommendations for Practitioners

Interactive operation allows efficient, high-level directed search of a many-dimensional input space, and (with suitable techniques such as alignment and snapping (Bier 1990) allows easy generation of highly degenerate input. The combination of these techniques probably bests stochastic or (non-exhaustive) systematic search of the input space, since it can be interactively directed by the practitioner.

In addition to our recommendation that batch techniques be replaced by interactive methods, we make the following recommendations:

- **Geometric Witnesses.** Geometric computations should be designed to prove their conclusions with visually representable data objects. These objects should be computationally verifiable by some agent other than the original algorithm.

- **Integrated Development and Use.** While under development, The algorithm inputs should be manipulated with a user interface at least as sophisticated as that of the algorithm's intended application.

- **Interaction techniques.** All geometric inputs should be mapped to a directly observable and manipulable representation. Moreover, the *space* embedding the problem instance should be directly manipulable (i.e., via viewing transformations). Interaction should be direct and non-modal to the extent possible. This allows any aspect of the input to be examined, regardless of scale or position.

- **Data Invariants.** Valid properties of data should be checked at input and enforced by all subsequent operations to maintain a correctness invariant.

- **Temporal Coherence.** A rapid succession of interactively generated images allows the visual system to detect errors that are almost impossible to notice in single-frame renderings.

We argue that the construction of a simple, but powerful, interactive environment, and the adoption of these principles regarding algorithm design, visualization, and interaction techniques, will substantially improve the practitioner's intuition about geometric algorithms, and the robustness of the algorithms themselves. Moreover, we argue that the general opinion of interactive environments as "too hard" to construct is in error, and perhaps due more to the enormous amount of bad system software than to reality.

Geometric Algorithm Development is Analogous to Scientific Visualization

Other investigators have developed interactive systems that are used, for example, to visualize scientific data. A strong analogy can be made between scientific visualization and interactive algorithm development. Scientific visualization is a method by which attributes of complex data are transformed into a visual or aural representation. The primary goal of the representation is to make these data primarily accessible to the high-bandwidth sense organs of a human observer, in order that the physical *processes* by which the data are generated can be better understood. Analogously, interactive algorithm development and inspection is a technique in which a space of algorithm *inputs* is navigated and continuously subjected to a geometric computation – the algorithmic process. The goal of the interaction is to understand, verify, and perhaps extend the computation. The computation is the analogue of the physical process.

Motivation From a Real-World Visual Simulation System

Our need for robust geometric algorithms operating on real-world data arose as part of a group development effort of a system for constructing and simulating extremely complex architectural models (described extensively in Teller, 1991; Khorramabadi, 1991; Funkhouser, 1992; Teller, 1992b). The system, based on a techniques for three-dimensional spatial subdivision, visibility computation and database management, achieves interactive display rates for models that, without such techniques, would require several seconds or even minutes to render even on the fastest workstations currently available. The fact that the algorithms are in daily use for actual design, evaluation, modification, and visual simulation of a complex architectural model served as a strong incentive to make the algorithms quite robust.

This paper presents several examples of the use of the proposed methodology during the conception, development, and verification of complex geometric algorithms. Throughout, the examples illustrate the value of a graphical environment in visualizing the operation of an interactive geometric algorithm, and how this visualization affords verification that the algorithm is operating correctly.

Geometric Witnesses

The notion of "geometric witnesses" is central to the methodology that we propose. The term "witness" has long been used among computational geometers to connote a data object that evinces the outcome of a geometric computation. These computations are typically *existence* computations, in that they determine (for a given input) whether or not there exists a geometric datum satisfying some collection of constraints. Perhaps the simplest example of a geometric witness occurs for the computation of an intersection between two line segments in the plane. If the segments intersect, a witness to their intersection is a point lying on both segments. If the segments do not intersect, a witness to this fact is a line separating the two input segments. In either case, the witness serves as visual "proof" that the answer computed by the algorithm is correct. Moreover, the witness can be computationally verified by an agent other than the intersection routine: the witness point can be compared against the interiors of the input line segments, or the two halfspaces of the witness separating line can be compared against the segment endpoints.

Many of the details of the geometric algorithms developed for the walkthrough system are outside the scope of this paper. However, the algorithms can be characterized by the fact that they require geometric input and produce geometric output. The geometric libraries were developed using an interactive graphics environment that supplies a uniform interface for algorithm inspection. A template graphics program operates solely in terms of a "region of interest" (typically a 3D bounding box), and arranges this area as the graphical center of attention, by default. To be useable in this template, a data object need only be able to report its bounding region. At run time, this region appears centered in the window, scaled to a reasonable window-filling size, with reasonable perspective, and preserved aspect ratio. The environment then enters a standard command loop in which the area of interest can be scaled, rotated, and translated via mouse actions. The command loop also supports selection and modification actions, which depend on the dimensionality and type of the input.

2 THE WALKTHROUGH SYSTEM

The architectural simulation system takes as input a building model consisting of a set of large planar polygonal *occluders*, and a set of bounding volumes of complex *detail objects* (Khorramabadi 1991; Teller 1991; Funkhouser 1992; Teller 1992b). The occluders represent the gross structural detail of the building, whereas the detail objects represent complex entities such as personal items and furnishings, which typically cause little occlusion. The space of the model is then partitioned into convex *cells*, and any non-opaque portions of shared cell boundaries are explicitly represented as convex *portals* (Figures 2 and 3). Each portal stores with it an identifier for the cell to which the portal leads. We call a spatial subdivision with explicitly enumerated portals a *conforming* spatial subdivision.

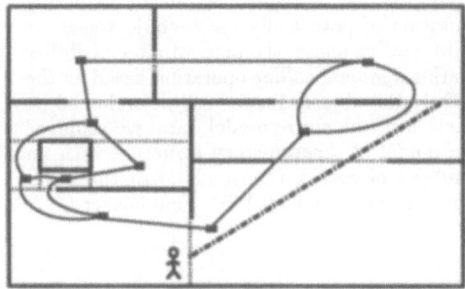 

Figure 2: A conforming spatial subdivision in 2D, and its corresponding adjacency graph. Portals are (dashed) line segments. An observer is schematically represented at the lower left, and a sightline (broken) stabs a portal sequence of length three.

Figure 3: A conforming spatial subdivision with five convex cells in 3D. Occluders are rendered as gray polygons. Four convex polygonal portals (the white central areas in each subdivision plane) are shown.

The cell and portal abstraction for the spatial subdivision is effectively a directed graph whose vertices are cells, and whose edges are portals. A number of useful static (observer-independent) and dynamic (observer-dependent) visibility computations can be framed as constrained *depth-first searches* (DFS) of this graph. For example, if a given portal is treated as a light source, then the region illuminated by this light source in the remainder of the subdivision constitutes an upper bound on the visibility of an observer situated on or behind the plane of the portal. This "antipenumbral" region (Teller 1992a) is exactly the bundle of lines that *stabs*, or pierces, all portal sequences originating at the light source (Figure 4).

Data Invariants

Note that the construction of a valid spatial subdivision amounts to enforcing a *data invariant* on the input model, in that during construction, all overlapping and interpenetrating polygons are found, as are any gaps or cracks between polygons. Errors found at this stage can be reported and/or corrected; the "correctness" (manifold properties) of the model can therefore be ensured at the beginning of the program, and assumed by all further operations.

Figure 4: The regions visible to an observer constrained to the leftmost cell.

Since the illuminated region is an upper bound on visibility, only objects whose bounding volumes are spatially incident on this region can possibly be visible to an observer known to be in the source cell. In sufficiently occluded environments, therefore, significant rendering accelerations can be achieved by an offline computation of potentially visible object sets for each cell of the spatial subdivision. During a later interactive phase, the precomputed visibility data is retrieved and subjected to a more discriminating *dynamic culling* operation based on the known position and field of view of the observer. Only the objects surviving this cull need be rendered. These objects typically form a small fraction of the entire model data; we achieved rendering speedups of about one hundred using a model of a seven-story structure with an atrium, terraced balconies, scores of hallways, hundreds of rooms, thousands of textures and detail objects, and nearly a million individual polygons (Khorramabadi 1991; Funkhouser 1992; Teller 1992b).

3   A CASE STUDY

Our development environment consisted of Silicon Graphics workstations with varied computing and graphics capabilities. A shared repository of geometric libraries comprised routines for manipulating: points, vectors, planes, hyperplanes, etc.; linear programs of general dimension; planar convex polygons; convex polytopes of general dimension; spatial subdivisions; stabbing problems; and visibility data structures. Routines were designed and implemented for two-, three-, and higher-dimensional operands as needed. This paper is concerned with the development of spatial subdivision abstractions and dynamic visibility computations, which are discussed below.

The hardware platform provided a C-language interface, the "SGI GL" or graphics library, for operations such as: specification of perspective and modeling view transformations; simulated point light sources; immediate-mode issuance of drawing commands for such primitive objects as points, wires, and polygons. Rendering is typically double-buffered for smooth animation, although single-buffering and immediate-mode graphics are sometimes useful. The hardware and software also support a graphical selection operation in which objects rendered near the mouse position could be reported to the application.

Dynamic Eye-Based Culling

The dynamic culling operation is an interactive and highly geometric computation. Given a model and spatial subdivision, and an instantaneous observer position and field of view, the dynamic culling operation must compute the set of cells and detail objects potentially visible to the observer. Moreover, the dynamic culling operation must complete in time comparable to interactive frame rates: about one twentieth of a second. In the remainder of this paper, the dynamic culling algorithm is used as an illustrative vehicle for our recommendations about algorithm development.

The precomputation of antipenumbral bundles has only approximate knowledge of the observer position, and can therefore produce only gross upper bounds on the visibility of any particular observer. During the real-time walkthrough phase, however, the simulation system tracks the precise instantaneous position and field of view of the observer. The observer variables can be modeled as an eye-centered view pyramid, defined as the common interior of four halfspaces in three dimensions (Figure 5). In the context of algorithm inspection, the observer variables form the algorithm input; the set of potentially visible objects form the algorithm output.

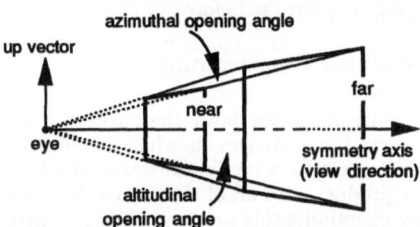

Figure 5: The observer variables in three dimensions.

Linear Programming

The dynamic culling operation employs a constrained depth-first search of the subdivision graph. A list of constraints is initialized to the four halfspaces whose intersection is the view frustum. The source cell is placed on a stack, and a recursive search begins. Each portal leading out of the current cell is considered in turn. Each portal edge encountered contributes a single linear constraint to the sightline specification; the edge and the eye span a plane, whose orientation is chosen so that its positive halfspace contains the interior of the associated portal (Figure 6). The DFS advances recursively only as long as the current portal sequence admits a sightline through the eye.

These constraints are cast as a two-dimensional linear program as follows. If the kth plane constraint has normal $\mathbf{n}_k$, any stabbing line through the eye and the active portal sequence must have a direction vector $\mathbf{v}$ such that

$$\mathbf{n}_k \cdot \mathbf{v} \geq 0, \qquad \text{for all } k.$$

Note that the linear program is two-dimensional since all of the planes contain the eyepoint; therefore, we need only compute a *vector* that has a non-negative dot product with each

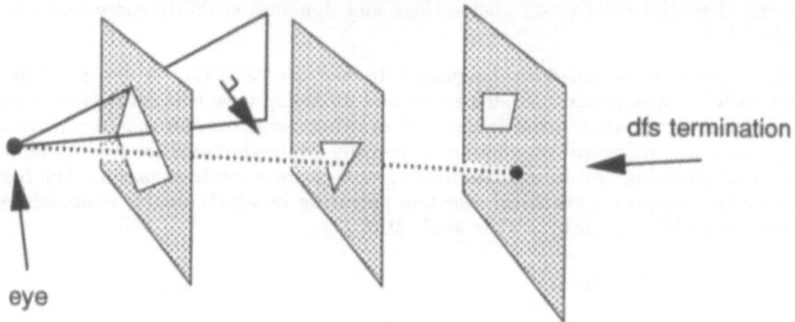

Figure 6: Encountering a portal in the eye-to-cell DFS.

of the plane normals. We examine this collection of three-coefficient linear constraints for a feasible solution in linear time using a linear programming algorithm (Seidel 1991). If the linear program fails to find a stabbing line through the eye, the most recent portal is impassable, the reached cell is not visible through the current portal sequence, and the active branch of the DFS terminates.

Otherwise, the cell is at least partially visible; its contents (the incident detail objects) are then examined for sightlines. Recall that only the axial bounding boxes of objects are retained. Convex objects always have convex silhouettes; in the case of axial boxes, the silhouette edges are easily obtained via a table-lookup of the eye position. Generically, a cube has a hexagonal silhouette; again, each silhouette edge spans a plane with the eye, oriented so as to contain the object centroid in its positive halfspace. The augmented set of linear constraints is examined for a sightline using linear programming, as before.

Geometric Witnesses for Linear Programming

We wish to define geometric witnesses for both the success and failure cases in the DFS; i.e., geometric "proof" data for the instances in which eye-based sightlines do and do not exist. The witness for the success case is straightforward: the linear program computes and returns a vector whose inner product with all of the active constraints is positive (this can be straightforwardly checked by examining this product for each active constraint). The witness in this case has an obvious visual representation: a line segment, originating at the eye, and ending at the plane of the newly encountered portal (Figure 10).

The witness for the failure case is slightly more complex. We must consider the linear programming algorithm (the discussion here follows that of Seidel 1991). The algorithm is given a set h_k of halfspaces, and a linear objective function to minimize. Recursively, the algorithm removes a halfspace H from the set, and computes the optimum with respect to the remaining halfspaces. The removed halfspace is then replaced, and the computed optimum is examined with respect to this halfspace. If the optimum is in the halfspace, we are done. If it is not, then, if there is any feasible solution, there must be a solution on h, the bounding hyperplane of H (this is true by convexity of the feasible region). Thus, the algorithm projects the active constraints onto h and solve the $d - 1$-dimensional linear program there. Infeasibility is established when the algorithm projects to a one-dimensional problem instance and the active constraints are found to be infeasible. For our problem, this means that three constraints are necessary: one that is the current subspace, and two that together produce an infeasible region in this space.

Visual Representations and Visual Correctness

Figure 7 depicts the dynamic eye-based culling operation as seen from "outside" of the model, i.e., above the room containing the observer (backfacing polygons have been removed so that we can see through the ordinarily opaque walls and ceiling). Note the visual representations of the observer, a one-eyed stick-figure, and the instantaneous view frustum, emanating from the center of the observer's head. Portals are depicted as × shapes. The window portal is successfully stabbed by a sightline through the eye and inside the view frustum. The object bounding boxes shown are those surviving the eye-based visibility cull (the objects' many constituent polygons are not displayed as they are irrelevant to the culling operation).

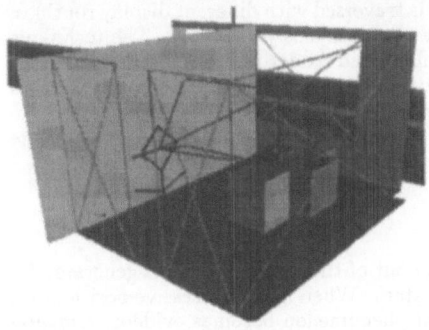

Figure 7: An outside view of the point observer.

Figure 8: The point observer's view. Note contracted view frustum.

Figure 8 shows the same situation, from the point of view of the observer. The window portal, and the object bounding boxes shown, are clearly incident on the view frustum. However, the view frustum is displayed so that it does *not* fill the display window. This is so that, from the inside view, we can ascertain visually that A) portals and objects outside the view frustum are discarded, as desired, and B) no portals or objects outside the view frustum are traversed. This is difficult to do from the outside view, and would be impossible from the observer's view if the frustum were to fill the display window (as it does in the intended application).

Figure 9: Objects failing the cull are drawn in wireframe.

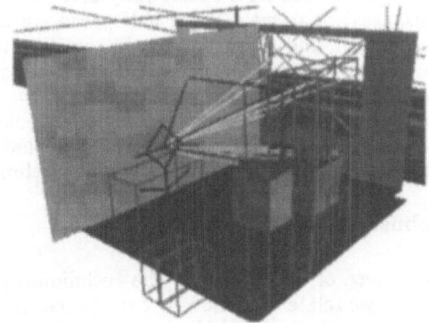

Figure 10: The outside view, with witness object sightlines.

Figure 9 illustrates the utility of the contracted view frustum. Objects surviving the visibility cull are drawn as solid parallelepipeds, whereas objects failing the visibility cull are drawn in wireframe. The witness for the failure case is three edges, where one edge defines an extremal edge of the visible region, and two further edges show that there are no feasible points on that edge. One such witness is shown for the wireframe object at the lower left; the leftmost edge of the view frustum is constraint on which the recursive linear programming algorithm "bottomed out," and the oppositely directed (horizontal) edges clearly exclude any feasible points on this edge. The three witness edges are rendered as thick white line segments.

The correctness of the visibility cull is evident; all wireframe objects are outside of the view frustum. Finally, Figure 10 shows the outside view of the same situation. The wireframe objects are again seen (the witness from the previous figure is visible as a white line segment on the top of the wireframe object at lower left). For each object surviving the cull, a witness *sightline* is drawn from the observer to some point on the object (in Figure 9, each sightline appears as a single pixel, since it necessarily contains the eye).

We distinguish the technique of outside/inside views presented above from traditional "multi-view" systems. In traditional systems, some dataset is traversed with different display routines, and the resulting differing visual representations are simultaneously displayed. The technique above is subtly different, in that the traversal (i.e., culling and rendering) routine that generates the pictures is *exactly identical* in both cases; only the viewing transformations differ. This means that the resulting visual representations *must* agree. This ensures consistency of representations in a somewhat stronger sense than does a traditional system, which must arrange that differing traversal codes produce isomorphic representations of the traversed data.

Temporal Coherence

The above figures represent a single observer position out of the many thousands generated by a typical interaction session with the walkthrough system. When many successive positions on the observer's path are considered, a new and useful phenomenon becomes evident: *temporal coherence*. The human visual system is extremely sensitive to sudden changes in the visual field. In ordinary human experience, objects tend to change position and appearance slowly and smoothly. Therefore, we are well-equipped to detect transient or rarely-occurring errors in geometric algorithms, simply by changing the input smoothly, and watching the output for non-smooth behavior. We found several important errors in exactly this manner, when a user of the system noticed objects within the view frustum "flashing" on and off in the visual field. Moreover, scripting of the user's path allowed the error to be reliably reproduced.

During the constrained depth-first search, each portal edge encountered gives rise to a halfspace spanned by that edge and the eye (cf. Figure 6). These halfspaces can be drawn explicitly, for example as shaded triangles. However, there is a more effective way to visualize their aggregate effect. When the DFS successfully arrives at a cell, a single portal sequence (and thus set of halfspaces) is active. These halfspaces are appended to the list of halfspaces bounding the reached cell, and their common intersection is computed (using a standard three-dimensional convex hull algorithm). The result is a necessarily convex volume that bounds the region of the reached cell potentially visible to the observer through the active portal sequence (Figure 11). Computing and drawing these convex regions in real time gives a powerful visual confirmation that the DFS is operating correctly, and that the correct potentially visible regions are being enumerated by the dynamic culling algorithm.

Robustness

As a piece of evidence that the techniques proposed here actually help to make code more robust, we relate the following experience. In our system, there are several versions of libraries to compute the convex hull of a set of points in three dimensions. Each of the libraries functions differently, but is encapsulated by a code "wrapper" that presents a uniform interface to the calling code. This wrapper code also performs consistency checks on the hull data structure, checking for example that it satisfies Euler's relation ($V - E + F = 2$), that every edge is shared by two faces, that every vertex is used (referenced) by at least three faces, etc. If the computed data structure does not pass all of these tests, an error bit is set in the hull data structure. When the hull is later drawn, its color is overridden and set to bright red to indicate the existence of the error. This visual cue alarms the practitioner, and the problem can be isolated.

After (an estimated) several hundred thousand interactive invocations of the convex hull code, a list processing bug became apparent, in code that had been used by "fifty people around the world" and was said to be "bug-free," i.e., to handle all possible inputs correctly (O'Rourke

Figure 11: The polyhedral regions potentially visible to the observer.

1992a); this was a reasonable statement to make, because the algorithm operates in integer coordinates. The author of the code explained:

> Found the bug and fixed it. It was.... a basic list-processing bug, which I wonder if now is not elsewhere in the code. The vertex list at a certain point consists of (0,6,5,4,3,2,1), and 0 and 6 are marked for deletion. The loop deletes 0, but since 0 is the head, the head gets changed to 6, and the loop [terminates].... so 6 never gets deleted.

This bug turned out to be very subtle, and had gone undetected by scores of other users of the code. We claim that it was found largely because of the particular interactive fashion in which the code was exercised.

Interaction Techniques

Finally, it is worthwhile to examine the method by which the algorithm developer generates observer positions from the "outside" view. Figures 12 through 14 show three successive observer positions, fields of view, and dynamic cull results. The observer is depicted as a stick-figure and frustum as before. The observer's position in the architectural model is derived from the mouse position by intersecting a line from the eye to the mouse (in model coordinates) with a horizontal plane containing the last-known observer position (the graphics library makes the aggregate viewing transformation constantly available, so the conversion of the line to model coordinates requires a 4 × 4 matrix inversion). The observer's field of view is derived by computing a weighted average of the mouse-motion vector with the current view-direction, using a small adjustable coefficient (usually about 0.05) for the mouse term. Thus the observer's view direction smoothly and exponentially relaxes to the predominant direction of mouse motion, and the observer can be directed anywhere in the model by the developer. Finally, the interface is slightly modal in that, when an interesting user position is found, it can be "frozen" with a key-press; further mouse motion does not change the observer position, and can be used, for example, to effect view transformations. This freeze technique was used to generate Figures 7 through 10; the inside/outside views were toggled via a key-press, or they can be simultaneously displayed.

Figure 12: Frame A.   Figure 13: Frame B.   Figure 14: Frame C.

CONCLUSION

Practitioners can develop robust geometric algorithms more effectively by transferring interactive functionality typically found only in applications to graphical environments used for
algorithm development and inspection. We discussed some simple but important elements of
a successful algorithm visualization framework, and presented some examples of the use of
each element. This system was used to develop a robust architectural simulation application
that depends on the correct operation of many non-trivial complex geometric algorithms. We
maintain that these algorithms were much easier to develop and verify using the proposed interaction techniques than they would have been otherwise, and that the interaction techniques
were employed for little incremental effort over that needed to develop the geometric algorithms
themselves.

ACKNOWLEDGMENTS

The author is grateful to Carlo Séquin and to Ari Rappoport for their encouragement and
helpful comments.

The general-dimensional linear programming code was supplied by Michael Hohmeyer of U.C.
Berkeley from a description in (Seidel 1991). The fast three-dimensional convex hull code was
adapted from integer code supplied by Joe O'Rourke of Smith College (O'Rourke 1992).

BIBLIOGRAPHY

Bier, E (1990) Snap-dragging in three dimensions. In: *ACM Symposium on Interactive 3D
Graphics*, pp 193–204.

Funkhouser, T, Séquin, CH, Teller, SJ (1992) Management of large amounts of data in interactive building walkthroughs. In: *Proc. 1992 Workshop on Interactive 3D Graphics*, pp
11–20.

Khorramabadi, D (1991) A walk through the planned CS building. Technical Report UCB/CSD
91/652, Computer Science Department, U.C. Berkeley.

O'Rourke, J (1992a) Personal Communication, November 1992.

O'Rourke, J (1992b) Computational geometry in C: Chapters 3 & 4 convex hulls. Technical
Report TR # 017, Department of Computer Science, Smith College.

Seidel, R (1991) Small-dimensional linear programming and convex hulls made easy. In:
Discrete and Computational Geometry, pp 423–434.

Teller, SJ (1992a) Computing the antipenumbra cast by an area light source. In: *Computer Graphics (Proc. SIGGRAPH '92)*, 26(2):139–148.

Teller, SJ (1992b) *Visibility Computations in Densely Occluded Polyhedral Environments.* PhD thesis, Computer Sciences Department, U.C. Berkeley.

Teller, SJ and Séquin, CH (1991) Visibility preprocessing for interactive walkthroughs. *Computer Graphics (Proc. SIGGRAPH '91)*, 25(4):61–69.

Seth J. Teller is currently a postdoctoral researcher in the Institute of Computer Science at the Hebrew University of Jerusalem. His research interests include computer graphics and computational geometry. Teller received his BA in Physics from Wesleyan University in 1985, and his MSc and PhD in Computer Science from the University of California at Berkeley in 1990 and 1992, respectively. He has also been a part-time member of the Research and Development group at Silicon Graphics since 1988.

Address: Institute of Computer Science, Hebrew University of Jerusalem, Givat Ram, Jerusalem, 91904, Israel. Phone: +972-585867; Fax: +972-585439.

A Fast Incremental Algorithm for Computing the Voronoi Diagram of a Planar Shape

Martin Held

We present an incremental algorithm for the generation of Voronoi diagrams of simply-connected planar areas bounded by straight lines and circular arcs. For so-called monotonous areas – which are a generalization of convex areas – bounded by n contour segments, the algorithm needs only $O(n)$ steps in the worst case in addition to up to $O(n \log n)$ time devoted to the maintenance of a priority queue. In more detail, if k is the number of bisectors in the final Voronoi diagram only k bisectors are generated in total and the number of computationally expensive arithmetic floating-point operations is bound by $O(k)$. For general shapes these worst-case complexities have to be multiplied by a shape-dependent factor, which is small in all except perhaps very few practically relevant applications. Extensive practical tests gave evidence that this incremental algorithm is nearly always (much) faster than Lee's conventional divide&conquer algorithm, with savings of CPU-time going up to about 60%.

Keywords: Voronoi diagram, internal skeleton, medial axis, incremental construction.

1 INTRODUCTION

Consider a planar, bounded, and closed area $\mathcal{A}$ which is simply-connected, and suppose that its boundary $\mathcal{C}$ consists of n straight lines and circular arcs. For every point $p \in \mathcal{A}$, the *(contour) clearance* $d(p, \mathcal{C})$ is defined as the minimum Euclidean distance $d(p, q)$, where q is on the boundary $\mathcal{C}$. The *clearance disk* is the disk with radius $d(p, \mathcal{C})$ centered at p.

Figure 1: Medial Axis.

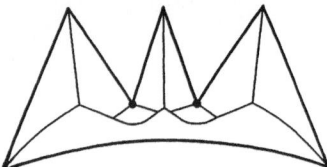

Figure 2: Voronoi Diagram.

The *internal skeleton* with respect to $\mathcal{C}$ and $\mathcal{A}$ is the set of points of the interior of $\mathcal{A}$ whose clearance disks touch $\mathcal{C}$ in at least two disjoint points, cf. Fig. 1. From this structure the *Voronoi diagram* $\mathcal{VD}(\mathcal{C})$ is derived by adding straight line segments at the reflex vertices of $\mathcal{C}$ (normal to the incident boundary segments), cf. Fig. 2. In order to help understanding, imagine that a prairie fire is started simultaneously at all boundary segments. The points where the fire fronts meet form the Voronoi diagram – supposing that the fire propagates at uniform speed.

The Voronoi diagram partitions $\mathcal{A}$ into mutually disjoint subareas, where every subarea is associated with exactly one boundary segment. Essentially, such a subarea is the nearest neighborhood of its defining boundary segment[1]. The boundary shared by two adjacent subareas is the locus of points equidistant from the areas' defining segments; it is called a *bisector*.

---

[1]This statement has to be refined in the presence of reflex vertices, cf. (Yap 1987, Held 1991).

Voronoi diagrams turned out to be useful in a variety of diverse applications. Well-known applications comprise, for instance, planar point location (Kirkpatrick 1983) and path-finding (O'Dunlaing 1985). Recently, Gürsoy and Patrikalakis (1992) and Srinivasan et al. (1992) successfully applied Voronoi diagrams to the automatic generation of meshes for finite element analysis. Our own investigations of offsetting and path-finding by means of Voronoi diagrams are documented in (Held 1991, Held 1992).

It is well-known that Voronoi diagrams can be constructed in worst-case optimal time $O(n \log n)$, cf. Lee (1982), Fortune (1987), Yap (1987). Lee applies a divide&conquer algorithm to the generation of Voronoi diagrams of simple polygons. Fortune uses an elegant plan-sweep algorithm for computing (transformations of) Voronoi diagrams defined by disjoint points and line segments. Yap proposes a divide&conquer algorithm for computing the Voronoi diagram of a set of disjoint points, line segments, and circular arcs.

From a theoretical as well as practical point of view, it is interesting to investigate whether the knowledge of some specific properties of an area can be exploited for circumventing the $O(n \log n)$ lower bound for the construction of Voronoi diagrams. For the special case of convex polygons this question has been settled in the affirmative by a fine $O(n)$ algorithm, cf. Aggarwal et al. (1987a). Unfortunately, for similar specializations to star-shaped or monotone polygons a lower bound of $O(n \log n)$ could be proved, cf. Aggarwal et al. (1987b).

In the following, we describe and analyze an incremental algorithm for computing the Voronoi diagram of a Jordan curve C consisting of straight lines and circular arcs. The underlying incremental construction scheme is due to a landmark paper by Persson (1978), who applied it to the generation of Voroni diagrams of simply-shaped contours C. However, his paper does not give any details nor does it contain an analysis of the correctness or complexity of his scheme.

From a purely theoretical point of view, this incremental algorithm fails to extend the class of polygons for which $O(n)$ Voronoi algorithms are known. From a practical point of view, the algorithm achieves a major extension because it requires only $O(n)$ arithmetic floating-point operations for the generation of Voronoi diagrams of so-called monotonous areas, which are a generalization of convex areas; in addition to up to $O(n \log h)$ computationally less expensive comparisons and assignments of floating-point values spent on maintaining a priority queue of size $h \leq n$. This linear bound on the number of arithmetic floating-point operations also applies to a specific further generalization of monotonous areas to arbitrary areas bounded by Jordan curves consisting of straight lines and circular arcs. According to our own experience, this generalization is sufficient for all (except perhaps very few) practical applications.

The rest of this paper is organized as follows: The next section contains an informal description of the algorithm, an introduction to the concept of monotonous areas, and a review of the major complexity results obtained. A more formal algorithmic description together with sketches of the correctness and complexity proofs is presented in Section 3. We conclude our paper in Section 4 with a review of results obtained experimentally.

2 INCREMENTAL ALGORITHM

2.1 Outline of the Algorithm

In the first step of the algorithm a bisector $b(s_1, s_2)$ between every pair of consecutive contour segments (s_1, s_2) is computed. We call these bisectors *contour bisectors* because they originate at the boundary contour, cf. Fig. 3. Of course, contour bisectors incident at reflex vertices extend to infinity, i.e., they are rays.

Although we are not interested in technical details in this section we remark that all bisectors are restricted to the so-called cones of influence of their defining segments. As illustrated in Fig. 4, the *cone of influence* of a circular arc is the closure of the cone bounded by the pair of rays originating in the arc's center and extending through its endpoints. Similarly, for a straight line segment the cone of influence is given by the closure of the strip bounded by the normals through its endpoints. For a point, the cone of influence is the whole plane. Restricting

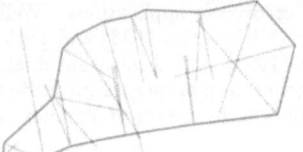  

Figure 3: Contour Bisectors.   Figure 4: Cones of Influence.

the bisectors to the cones of influence of their defining entities abolishes some problems arising when a formal definition of Voronoi diagrams is sought, cf. (Held 1991). From a practical point of view it has the beneficial side-effect of shortening bisectors which results in less dummy intersections between bisectors which are to be discarded lateron, anyway.

Secondly, for every triple (s_1, s_2, s_3) of consecutive contour segments, the corresponding contour bisectors $b(s_1, s_2)$ and $b(s_2, s_3)$ are intersected. If an intersection exists then both bisectors are terminated at the point of intersection and the intersection is associated with both bisectors.

In the third step, a subset of all intersections is selected as possible candidates for the subsequent incremental merging. An intersection between two bisectors is a suitable *candidate* if and only if no other intersection with a smaller contour clearance is associated with any of the two bisectors. All candidates are stored in a priority queue whose elements are ordered according to increasing clearance; i.e., the front end of the queue represents the intersection with smallest clearance. In Fig. 5, the candidate intersections are denoted by small bullets.

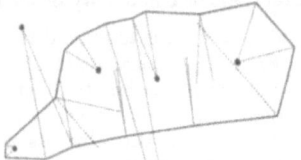 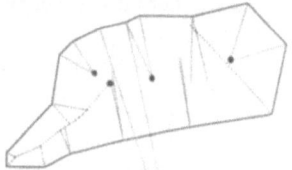

Figure 5: Candidate Intersections.   Figure 6: After First Run.

After the priority queue has been initialized the actual incremental construction starts. The front element is deleted from the queue and the corresponding intersection is *accepted* as a valid bisector intersection. Accepting a bisector intersection means that this point is used as a start point for the next merge bisector to be computed. This new merge bisector is defined by those contour segments defining the intersecting bisectors which do not define both of them; i.e., if the intersection between $b(s_1, s_2)$ and $b(s_2, s_3)$ is accepted, then the new merge bisector is defined by (s_1, s_3). Similarly to the divide&conquer algorithms, the new merge bisector $b(s_1, s_3)$ is intersected with the chains of bisectors incident in s_1 and s_3. If one intersection exists then this intersection is stored in the priority queue. If two intersections exist then the intersection encountered first when moving away from the start point (along the merge bisector) is stored.

An intersection needs only be stored if the actual front end of the queue corresponds to an intersection which has a smaller clearance than the new intersection. Otherwise, the new intersection can be accepted without any further manipulation of the queue. This subsequent accepting and computing of intersections until an insert into the queue is inevitable is called a *run*. Fig. 6 depicts the actual status of the Voronoi diagram after the end of the first run.

Individual runs are carried out until the total Voronoi diagram is eventually constructed. In our example, Fig. 7 and Fig. 8 depict the situations after the end of the second respectively third run. Of course, at the start of a new run an intersection fetched from the priority queue may only be accepted if it still constitutes a *valid intersection*. Otherwise, it can be discarded and the next intersection has to be fetched from the priority queue. For instance, an intersection stored has become invalid if lateron one of its associated bisectors has been discarded or shortened by an intersection with another bisector encountered during the construction process.

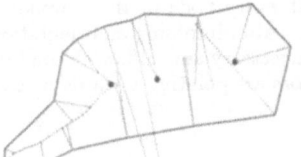

Figure 7: After Second Run.

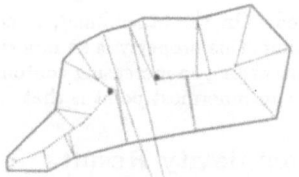

Figure 8: After Third Run.

In order to set up a termination condition it is sufficient to check the defining contour segments intersected by the merge bisector: the construction process is finished if two coinciding intersections exist and if the bisectors intersected by the merge bisector share a defining contour segment. Fig. 9 depicts the completed Voronoi diagram after the final run.

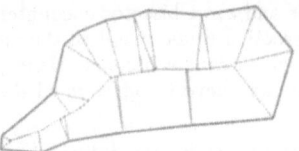

Figure 9: After Final Run.

Figure 10: Three Monotonous Areas.

2.2 Voronoi Diagrams and the Concept of Monotonous Areas

The concept of monotonous areas was originally developed by the author a number of years ago when dealing with the automatic generation of tool paths for pocket machining. As monotonous areas play a key role in the analysis of the algorithm presented we include a short review of monotonous areas. For a more detailed introduction we refer to (Held 1991).

As illustrated in Fig. 10, we call a simply-connected and bounded area a *monotonous area* if its closed boundary contour can continuously and uniformly be shrunk to a point without splitting the area into separate subareas. Convex areas are also monotonous, but monotonous areas need not be convex-shaped – just think of a banana-shaped area. We call those points of a monotonous area which have maximal clearance *innermost points*.

An arbitrary multiply-connected planar area $\mathcal{A}$ can be partitioned into its monotonous subareas in time linear in the number n of its boundary segments, provided that the Voronoi diagram of its boundary is available. Fig. 11 depicts a simply-connected area subdivided into three monotonous areas; innermost points are depicted by bullets, straits between adjacent monotonous areas are depicted by dashed lines.

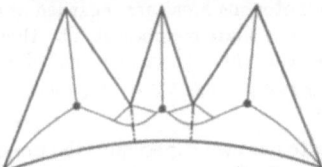

Figure 11: Innermost Points and Straits.

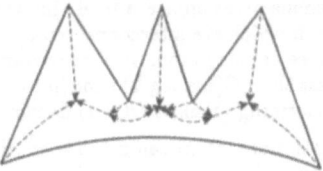

Figure 12: Bisector Orientations.

It is easy to prove that, for any monotonous area A of $\mathcal{A}$, all innermost points of A are located on the Voronoi diagram. Furthermore, at least one innermost point of A is a node of the diagram, cf. Fig. 11. Now, imagine sitting at a Voronoi node which corresponds to an innermost point of A. Moving away from this node along any incident bisector of the Voronoi diagram causes the clearance to decrease monotonously[2] until the boundary or the midpoint of a strait is

---

[2]Due to this property we speak of 'monotonous' areas.

encountered. On the other hand, it can be shown that every node of the Voronoi diagram which exhibits this property is an innermost point. Hence, after imposing an orientation on the bisectors according to increasing contour clearance, the necessary and sufficient condition for a node to be an innermost point is that all incident bisectors are pointing towards it, cf. Fig. 12.

2.3 Complexity Results

What is the worst-case complexity of this incremental scheme? Assume that all nodes of $\mathcal{VD}(\mathcal{C})$ are of degree three and let us start with considering the boundary $\mathcal{C}$ of a monotonous area. It can be proved for monotonous areas that no bisector intersection accepted during the incremental merge process will be discarded by a latter merge step. In other words, any bisector ever constructed, or at least a portion of it, is guaranteed to be part of the final Voronoi diagram.

As a consequence, it is not necessary to scan more than two bisectors – one on the left-hand side and one on the right-hand side of the merge bisector – when looking for intersections: Suppose that an intersection between the merge bisector and some bisector encountered after repeated scanning would exist. The existence of an intersection would result in the discarding of at least one bisector intersection accepted previously, which cannot happen. Hence, if there are k bisectors in the final Voronoi diagram, only k bisectors have to be handled during the entire construction process.

Handling a bisector means accepting its start point, computing it, and intersecting it with exactly two other bisectors, and in addition possibly storing a new intersection point in the priority queue. Obviously, the arithmetic bisector operations can be carried out in constant time. As far as the complexity of the queue manipulations – deletion of the intersection to be accepted and insertion of a new intersection – is concerned, one should observe that the size of the queue does not increase during the merge process: for each accepted intersection at most one new intersection is stored in the queue. As priority queues can be implemented as heaps, for instance, every queue manipulation takes $O(\log h)$ time, where h denotes the number of intersections originally stored in the queue during the initialization stage.

Hence, we conclude that our incremental algorithm computes all k bisectors of the Voronoi diagram of a monotonous area in time $O(k + r \log h)$, where r denotes the number of runs. In particular, only $O(k)$ computationally expensive floating-point operations associated with the handling of bisectors have to be executed. The number[3] k ranges between n and $4n - 3$. Since $r \leq k - n$ and $h \leq \lfloor n/3 \rfloor$, we get an overall worst-case complexity of $O(n \log n)$.

What about the complexity of applying this incremental algorithm to a general simply-connected area $\mathcal{A}$? One should observe that in the case of general areas it is no longer valid that no accepted bisector intersections will ever be discarded during subsequent runs. Rather, as in the case of the divide&conquer algorithm the Lee/Drysdale scanning scheme – cf. (Lee 1982, Held 1991) – has to be applied when looking for intersections in order avoid a re-scanning of bisectors.

Now suppose that, for all monotonous areas A of $\mathcal{A}$, m is an upper bound on the number of monotonous areas adjacent to A. In other words, if the monotonous areas are regarded as nodes of a graph which are interconnected by edges if and only if they share common straits, then m is the degree of this graph. It is proved in the subsequent section that the incremental algorithm takes less than $O(mn \log h)$ time in the worst case, thereby computing at most $O(mn)$ bisectors and performing at most $O(mn)$ floating-point operations.

As a matter of fact, m can go up to n. However, according to our own experience, the worst case $m = O(n)$ will occur very rarely in practical applications. Furthermore, there exists another fact which makes the case of $O(mn)$ bisectors being generated most unlikely: This worst-case upper bound can only be attained, if at all, in case that the clearance distances of the innermost points of all m monotonous areas adjacent to the area A are greater than the clearance distance of the innermost point of A. Otherwise, the number of adjacent areas which have innermost points with smaller clearance can be subtracted from m. Usually, m is much smaller than n.

---

[3]Readers familiar with bounds on the number of Voronoi edges should observe that the number of reflex vertices has to be added to n, resulting in the bound $4n - 3$ instead of the well-known bound $2n - 3$.

Unfortunately, up to now we have not succeed in carrying out a full-scale average-case analysis. However, the term $O(n \log h \log m)$ serves as a very rough upper bound on the average-case complexity, with at most $O(n \log m)$ bisectors being constructed and with at most $O(n \log m)$ floating-point operations being performed. As witnessed by our practical tests this bound still seems to be too crude for most practical applications.

3 DETAILED DESCRIPTION AND ANALYSIS

3.1 Definitions

For non-convex areas $\mathcal{A}$, all reflex vertices – i.e., vertices of the boundary contour with interior angle greater than π – have to be inserted as individual contour elements at their proper places. In the sequel we will speak of *contour segments* when we consider only the lines and arcs forming the boundary; lines, arcs, and reflex vertices will be addressed as *contour objects*. A collection of consecutive contour objects of $\mathcal{C}$ is called a *profile*, usually denoted by P.

Before we can start with a more formal description and analysis of the algorithm we need some definitions. The following definition relies on the fact that the Voronoi diagram $\mathcal{VD}(\mathcal{C})$ of a Jordan curve $\mathcal{C}$ can be regarded as a tree rooted at any of the nodes of $\mathcal{VD}(\mathcal{C})$.

Definition 3.1 For a profile P and a bisector $b \in \mathcal{VD}(P)$, the subtrees of $\mathcal{VD}(P)$ containing b and rooted in either the start or end node of b are called *Voronoi trees* w.r.t. b, $\mathcal{VT}(b)$.

It will always be clear out of the context in which subtree we are interested, so there is no need for a more complicated formalism. As a rule of thumb, we are always interested in that subtree whose leaves correspond to contour bisectors. In Fig. 13, $\mathcal{VT}(b)$ is depicted by dashed lines.

Definition 3.2 For $b \in \mathcal{VD}(P)$, the *profile spanned* by b, $P(b)$, is the counter-clockwise sequence of contour objects between the left defining object of the left-most leaf bisector of $\mathcal{VT}(b)$ and the right defining object of the right-most leaf bisector of $\mathcal{VT}(b)$.

Obviously, the Voronoi tree $\mathcal{VT}(b)$ of a contour bisector b is b itself, and $P(b)$ only consists of its defining contour objects.

Definition 3.3 For an object o and a profile P, we call the nearest neighbourhood of o w.r.t. P the *Voronoi area* $\mathcal{VA}(o, P)$ of o w.r.t. P. That portion of the boundary of $\mathcal{VA}(o, P)$ which is in the interior of $\mathcal{A}$ is called the *Voronoi polygon* of o w.r.t. P and is denoted by $\mathcal{VP}(o, P)$.

3.2 Algorithmic Description

We start with describing the initialization of the set of candidate intersections CI. The following algorithm determines a suitable initial set CI. Within this algorithm all tuples $o_1, \ldots, o_i$ denote i consecutive objects of $\mathcal{C}$.

1. $CI := \emptyset$.

2. For all pairs o_1, o_2, compute the contour bisector $b(o_1, o_2)$.

3. For all quadruples o_0, o_1, o_2, o_3:

   (a) Intersect $b(o_1, o_2)$ with $b(o_0, o_1)$ and with $b(o_2, o_3)$.

   (b) If there exist intersections then adjoin that intersection ν to CI which has the smaller clearance, and associate ν with $b(o_1, o_2)$.

4. For all pairs o_1, o_2, if $b(o_1, o_2)$ is associated with an intersection ν then terminate it at ν.

5. Arrange CI as a priority queue such that the front end is the intersection with smallest contour clearance.

Let us now turn to the main part of the incremental algorithm. The following algorithm incrementally computes the Voronoi diagram of a contour C. In Step 2 an intersection ν is accepted. When searching for intersections in Step 3(a) the well-known Lee/Drysdale scanning scheme (Lee 1982, Held 1991) is applied.

1. Fetch and delete the front end ν of CI until ν is acceptable as a valid bisector intersection.

2. (a) Let $b(o_L, o_M)$ and $b(o_M, o_R)$ be the left and right bisectors ν is associated with.

    (b) Compute the new merge bisector $b := b(o_L, o_R)$.

    (c) Let P_L be the maximal profile ending in o_L such that there exists a bisector[4] b_L spanning P_L; let P_R be the maximal profile starting in o_R such that there exists a bisector b_R spanning P_R.

3. (a) Intersect b with $\mathcal{VP}(o_L, P_L)$ and with $\mathcal{VP}(o_R, P_R)$.

    (b) If two intersections exist, then select that intersection ν which is first encountered when moving along b away from the start of b; and associate the two bisectors intersecting at ν with ν. If both intersections coincide then associate ν randomly with b and any one of the two other bisectors intersecting at ν.

4. If no intersection exists then go to Step 1.

5. If two coinciding intersections exist and if the bisectors intersected by b share a defining contour object, then go to Step 7.

6. If the contour clearance of the new intersection ν is larger than the contour clearance of the front end of CI, then:

    (a) Insert ν into CI.

    (b) Go to Step 1.

    Else:

    (a) Go to Step 2.

7. Report 'finished' and stop.

3.3 Formal Analysis

We start with a sketch of the correctness proof of the algorithm. For the sake of simplicity we assume[5] that no node of $\mathcal{VD}(C)$ has a degree greater than three. The following lemma already captures the main correctness aspects of the algorithm proposed.

Lemma 3.1 (Loop Invariant) After all steps of the incremental algorithm, the following conjecture holds: If b is a bisector of the diagram constructed so far and if $\mathcal{VT}(b)$ is completely contained in the interior of $\mathcal{A}$, then $\mathcal{VT}(b) = \mathcal{VD}(P(b))$, except for a possibly too short b.

Proof: For the Steps 2 and 3, the conjecture follows from Lemma 3.2 and Lemma 3.3. Furthermore, the conjecture trivially holds after all the other steps and also before Step 1.   □

In the subsequent lemma we will make use of term 'clearance ray'.

Definition 3.4 The *clearance ray* w.r.t. to a segment s and a point p out of the cone of influence of s is the ray originating at p that is perpendicular on s. If p is the center of the circular arc s then any ray originating at p and passing through an interior point of s qualifies. The clearance ray w.r.t. p and a reflex vertex of C is the ray orginating at p that passes through this vertex.

---

[4]For every contour object, pointers to the correct bisectors b_L and b_R are maintained throughout the execution of the algorithm; thus, b_L and b_R can be determined in constant time.

[5]This restriction can be waived if Lemma 3.5 is properly reformulated by allowing i additional bisectors to be generated for a node of degree $3 + i$.

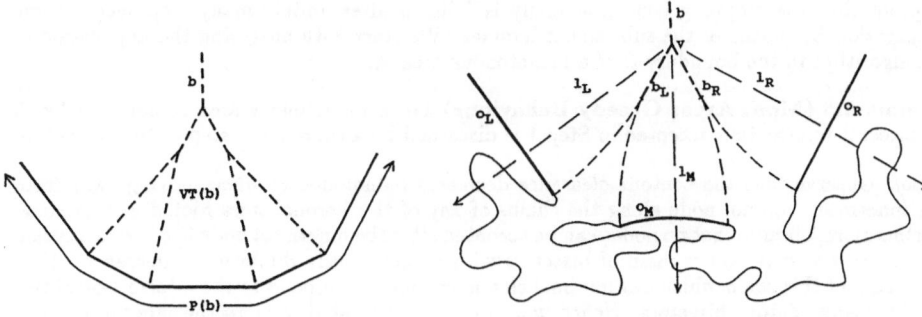

Figure 13: $\mathcal{VT}(b)$ and $P(b)$. Figure 14: Situation after Step 2(b).

Lemma 3.2 (Correctness of Step 2) The conjecture stated in Lemma 3.1 is invariant under the application of Step 2.

Proof: We concentrate on the situation after substep (b) has been executed, as depicted in Fig. 14, because all the other substeps cannot do any harm. Let $b_L := b(o_L, o_M)$ and $b_R := b(o_M, o_R)$, and let P_L be the profile spanned by b_L; similarly, P_R is the profile spanned by b_R. First of all, we note that the generation of b does not affect any of the Voronoi trees existing before its generation. In particular, the equalities $\mathcal{VT}(b_L) = \mathcal{VD}(P_L)$ and $\mathcal{VT}(b_R) = \mathcal{VD}(P_R)$ still hold provided that they were fulfilled before carrying out substep (b). Now consider the clearance rays ℓ_L, ℓ_M, and ℓ_R of ν w.r.t. o_L, o_M, and o_R. Since $\nu \in \mathcal{VA}(o_L, P_L)$, the portion of ℓ_L between ν and the intersection of ℓ_L with o_L is completely contained in $\mathcal{VA}(o_L, P_L)$. In particular, the left-most chain of $\mathcal{VT}(b_L)$ intersects ℓ_L only at ν. Similar arguments apply to ℓ_M w.r.t. $\mathcal{VA}(o_M, P_L)$ and $\mathcal{VA}(o_M, P_R)$, and to ℓ_R w.r.t. $\mathcal{VA}(o_R, P_R)$. Hence, $\mathcal{VT}(b_L)$ is completely contained in the union of the cone defined by ℓ_L, ℓ_M and some parts of $\mathcal{A}$ to the left of ℓ_L (resp. to the right of ℓ_R) bounded by portions of ℓ_L and P_L (resp. by portions of ℓ_M and P_L). The region containing $\mathcal{VT}(b_R)$ is obtained symmetrically. By assumption, $\mathcal{VT}(b_L)$ and $\mathcal{VT}(b_R)$ are completely contained in $\mathcal{A}$. We conclude that $\mathcal{VT}(b_L)$ and $\mathcal{VT}(b_R)$ do not intersect except at ν. By similar arguments, b does not intersect $\mathcal{VT}(b_L)$ or $\mathcal{VT}(b_R)$ except at ν. If $\mathcal{VT}(b) \neq \mathcal{VD}(P(b))$, then a second intersection among $\mathcal{VT}(b_L)$, $\mathcal{VT}(b_R)$ or b must exist, in contradiction to what we have just proved. Hence, $\mathcal{VT}(b) = \mathcal{VD}(P(b))$. $\qquad\square$

Lemma 3.3 (Correctness of Step 3) The conjecture stated in Lemma 3.1 is invariant under the application of Step 3.

Proof: Let b_L, b_R, P_L, P_R as defined by the algorithm in Step 2. Observe that $\mathcal{VP}(o_L, P_L)$ is the right-most chain of the Voronoi tree $\mathcal{VT}(b_L)$ rooted at that bisector b_L which spans P_L. If any bisector of the right-most chain is discarded due to the application of the Lee/Drysdale scan, then all bisectors of this chain up to b_L are discarded. Hence, a discarding of bisectors of $\mathcal{VP}(o_L, P_L)$ results in a split-up of $\mathcal{VT}(b_L)$ into several subtrees. Obviously, if $\mathcal{VT}(b_L) = \mathcal{VD}(P_L)$ holds before the application of the Lee/Drysdale scan, then similar equalities hold for its subtrees, before and after the application of the Lee/Drysdale scan. Symmetric arguments can be applied to $\mathcal{VP}(o_R, P_R)$. Since no other parts of the Voronoi diagram under construction are effected by Step 3, we conclude that the conjecture is invariant under Step 3. $\qquad\square$

Lemma 3.4 (Correctness at Step 7) The Voronoi diagram $\mathcal{VD}(\mathcal{C})$ has been successfully computed as soon as the stopping condition is fulfilled.

Proof: Similar to the proof of Lemma 3.2. $\qquad\square$

A proof that the stopping condition really is fulfilled after finitely many steps needs some preparation by means of the subsequent lemmas. We start with analyzing the application of the algorithm to the boundary C of a monotonous area A.

Lemma 3.5 (Mon. Area: Greedy Behaviour) For a monotonous area A bounded by C, no bisector intersection accepted in Step 1 is discarded by a subsequent step of the algorithm.

Proof: Observe that the contour clearance decreases monotonously when moving away from the innermost Voronoi node along the chains of any of the Voronoi trees rooted at this node. Furthermore, observe that no nodes can be accepted after the innermost node has been accepted: Otherwise we would get a chain of bisectors with monotonously diminishing clearance. That node ν_{min} of this chain which has minimal clearance must correspond to the intersection of two neighbouring contour bisectors. Hence, ν_{min} would be accepted prior to the innermost node, thus reversing the process. Now consider Fig. 14 and assume that ν has been accepted, but b_R is intersected by some bisector b_{new} at ν_{new}. As the clearance of ν_{new} must be less than the clearance of ν, and as the clearance of the start of b_{new} must be less than or equal to the clearance of ν_{new}, we get a chain of bisectors with monotonous contour clearance. Again we get an intersection of two neighbouring contour bisectors with smaller clearance than ν. □

Lemma 3.6 (Mon. Area: Termination) For a monotonous area A bounded by C, the algorithm terminates after generating k bisectors, where k is the number of bisectors of $\mathcal{VD}(C)$.

Proof: Observe that every time an intersection is accepted the Voronoi area of an contour object has been 'closed'. Since no Voronoi nodes are discarded in subsequent steps of the algorithm, Voronoi areas that were closed are not 'reopened' again. Thus, after a finite number of steps the algorithm must get to a situation where only three remaining contour objects still have open Voronoi areas. Let b_1, b_2, b_3 be the loose ends of the corresponding Voronoi polygons. Obviously, these bisectors are defined by the three remaining contour objects. W.l.o.g. assume that b_1 and b_2 intersect at ν but that b_3 does not intersect with b_1 or b_2 at ν. In this case ν would be accepted and a new merge bisector originating at ν and identical to b_3 would be generated, which yields a contradiction. The bound on the number of bisectors immediately follows from the fact that no bisectors are discarded during the construction process. □

The previous lemma settles the termination of the algorithm applied to the boundary of a monotonous area and it also establishes the worst-case complexity of the construction process. We summarize the results obtained so far in the following theorem.

Theorem 3.1 (Monotonous Area) For a monotonous area A bounded by C, the incremental algorithm computes $\mathcal{VD}(C)$ thereby generating k bisectors. In the worst case the computation takes $O(n \log h)$ time, where n is the number of contour segments of C, k is the number of bisectors of $\mathcal{VD}(C)$, and where h is the initial size of CI.

Proof: The termination together with the complexity bound follows from the previous lemma; the correctness is implied by Lemma 3.1 and Lemma 3.4. Note that the initialization phase does not consume more than $O(n)$ time because CI can be initialized in time $O(n + h)$. □

Corollary 3.1 For a monotonous area A bounded by C, suppose that the Voronoi diagrams (resp. Voronoi trees) of m disjoint profiles of C are available. Let CI only contain those intersections of neighbouring contour bisectors that are not both contained in the same Voronoi tree. Then the incremental algorithm computes $\mathcal{VD}(C)$ and takes at most $O(n \log h)$ time, where n is the number of contour segments of C, and where h is the initial size of CI.

Corollary 3.2 For a monotonous area A bounded by C, when restricted to $P \subset C$ the algorithm computes $\mathcal{VD}(P)$ in time $O(n_P \log h)$, where n_P is the number of segments of P, and where h is the initial size of CI.

We now consider the boundary C of a general area $\mathcal{A}$ and turn our attention to monotonous subareas that have more than one adjacent monotonous subarea. In graph-theoretic parlance this means that we are interested in nodes of the graph of monotonous areas that have degree $m > 1$. For shorthand, we call such a monotonous subarea a subarea of degree m. An area which itself is monotonous has degree 0. The previous corollary settles the complexity for computing the Voronoi diagram of a monotonous subarea of degree 1.

Observe that a monotonous subarea $A \subset \mathcal{A}$ of degree $m > 1$ is bounded by m disjoint profiles $P_i \subset C$ and by m straits. In the best case, all m bisectors at the straits bounding A are available prior to the acception of any intersection inside A. By regarding the bisectors at straits as conventional contour bisectors the complexity bounds of Theorem 3.1 would be fully applicable. What might happen in the worst case is analyzed in the following lemmas. We start with guaranteeing the termination and the correctness of the algorithm.

Lemma 3.7 (General Termination and Correctness) For a general area $\mathcal{A}$ bounded by C, the incremental algorithm terminates and correctly computes $\mathcal{VD}(C)$.

Proof: We note that the algorithm computes $\mathcal{VD}(C) \cap A$ for all monotonous subareas A of degree 1 in a finite number of steps. After all subareas of degree 1 have been handled the bisectors at the straits bounding these subareas are available. By regarding these bisectors as contour bisectors we may safely reduce the degree of all those monotonous subareas by 1 which are adjacent to these previously handled subareas. Let us call the processing of all degree-1 subareas a round. It is a simple graph-theoretic exercise to prove that after each round there exist monotonous subareas of (new) degree 1. Due to Corollary 3.1, these subareas are processed correctly provided that all (except possibly one) bisectors at their straits are available. $\square$

Lemma 3.8 (Mon. Area of Degree $m > 1$) For a monotonous subarea $A \subset \mathcal{A}$ of degree m bounded by $P_1, \ldots, P_m \subset C$, the algorithm spends at most $O((m + 1)n_A \log h)$ time on the computation of $\mathcal{VD}(C) \cap A$ during computing $\mathcal{VD}(C)$, where n_A is the total number of segments of $P_1, \ldots, P_m$, and where h is the initial size of CI.

Proof: We note that at most $O(n_A \log h)$ time is spent on computing $\mathcal{VD}(P_1), \ldots, \mathcal{VD}(P_m)$ prior to the availability of the first bisector at a strait. In the worst case, the Voronoi diagram $\mathcal{VD}(C) \cap A$ is generated by incrementally merging $\mathcal{VD}(P_{i+1})$ with $\mathcal{VD}(P_1 \cup \ldots \cup P_i)$, thereby generating the entire diagram $\mathcal{VD}(P_1 \cup \ldots \cup P_{i+1})$. Such a merger takes at most $O(n_A \log h)$ time. Since there are exactly m mergers, the claimed complexity bound follows. $\square$

Theorem 3.2 (Worst-Case Complexity) For a general area $\mathcal{A}$ bounded by C, the incremental algorithm takes at most $O((m + 1)n \log h)$ time for the computation of the Voronoi diagram $\mathcal{VD}(C)$, where n is the total number of segments of C, h is the initial size of CI, and where m is the maximal degree of a monotonous subarea of $\mathcal{A}$.

Proof: The correctness follows from Lemma 3.7, the complexity is implied by Lemma 3.8. $\square$

What about the average case? The following lemma establishes a crude upper bound on the average-case complexity. More precisely, it is an upper bound on the 'average-case complexity of the worst case', because it only assumes a somewhat more balanced distribution of the indices i governing the merger of profiles and their associated Voronoi diagrams in the proof of Lemma 3.8. The proof of the following lemma is carried out under the unrealistic worst-case assumption that $\mathcal{VD}(P_i \cup \ldots \cup P_j)$ is fully computed prior to the start of a merger at the beginning of P_i or at the end of P_j.

Lemma 3.9 (Upper Bound on Average-Case Complexity) For a monotonous subarea $A \subset \mathcal{A}$ of degree $m > 1$ bounded by $P_1, \ldots, P_m \subset C$, when computing $\mathcal{VD}(C)$ the algorithm on the average spends at most $O(n_A \log m \log h)$ time on the computation of $\mathcal{VD}(C) \cap A$, where n_A is the total number of segments of $P_1, \ldots, P_m$, and where h is the initial size of CI. Furthermore, at most $O(n_A \log m)$ bisectors are generated on the average.

Proof: For $1 \leq i \leq j \leq m$, denote the average-case complexity of computing $\mathcal{VD}(P_i \cup \ldots \cup P_j)$ by $T(i, j)$. Thus, $T(1, m)$ is the complexity we are looking for. Similarly to the partition step of the 'QuickSort' sorting algorithm, we observe that

$$T(1, m) = O(n_A \log h) + \frac{1}{m} \sum_{k=1}^{m-1} (T(1, k) + T(k+1, m)),$$

which yields $T(1, m) = O(n_A \log m \log h)$. □

Theorem 3.3 (Average-Case Complexity) For a general area $\mathcal{A}$ bounded by $\mathcal{C}$, the incremental algorithm on the average takes at most $O(n \log m \log h)$ time for the computation of the Voronoi diagram $\mathcal{VD}(\mathcal{C})$, where n is the total number of segments of $\mathcal{C}$, h is the initial size of CI, and where $m > 1$ is the maximal degree of a monotonous subarea of $\mathcal{A}$.

Proof: The complexity bound is implied by Lemma 3.9. □

4 CONCLUDING REMARKS

4.1 Summary

We have presented a simple incremental algorithm for the computation of the Voronoi diagram of a planar shape. If the shape is a monotonous area then the algorithm works according to the greedy paradigm: based on a careful selection of contour objects to be processed it is guaranteed that at least a portion of every bisector ever generated is part of the final diagram.

For monotonous areas $\mathcal{A}$, the worst-case complexity of the algorithm is $O(k + r \log h)$, where $r \leq k - n$ denotes the number of runs and where $h < \lfloor n/3 \rfloor$ is the shape-dependent initial size of the set CI of candidate intersections; k denotes the number of bisectors in the final Voronoi diagram. Furthermore, only $O(k)$ computationally expensive arithmetic floating-point operations have to be performed.

For general areas $\mathcal{A}$, the incremental algorithm takes at most $O((m + 1)n \log h)$ time, where m is the maximal degree of a monotonous subarea of $\mathcal{A}$. Furthermore, at most $O(nm)$ computationally expensive arithmetic floating-point operations have to be performed. We remark that increasing n usually does not result in an increase of m, provided that the overall shape of the area under consideration is preserved. Furthermore, the term $O(n \log h \log m)$ serves as a crude upper bound on the average-case complexity. Similarly, $O(n \log m)$ is an average-case upper bound on the number of bisectors generated and floating-point operations performed.

4.2 Practical Evaluation

The incremental algorithm presented and a version of Lee's (1982) divide&conquer algorithm, cf. (Held 1991), have been implemented and extensively tested. During our work on pocket machining this divide&conquer algorithm formed the algorithmic basis for the generation of offset curves. Except for the procedure governing the overall strategy of the algorithms – either divide&conquer or incremental – both algorithms rely on exactly the same code.

Our practical tests gave evidence of a significant advantage of the incremental over the divide&conquer algorithm, with savings of CPU-time reaching up to about 60 percent. For monotonous areas the incremental algorithm always was significantly faster than the divide&conquer algorithm. For general areas our tests supported the conjectured bounds on the number of bisectors ever generated and on the average-case complexity. With the single exception of one out of several contours which were specifically designed as worst-case examples for the incremental algorithm, all other contours tested were processed faster by the incremental than by the divide&conquer algorithm. In particular, for the incremental algorithm the ratio between

n and the CPU-time consumed remained roughly constant when increasing n. This is a clear indication that a roughly linear growth of the CPU-consumption can be expected for practical applications of the incremental algorithm! The divide&conquer algorithm, however, usually showed a non-linear growth. For a detailed survey of test results we refer to (Held 1993).

Anyway, our extensive practical tests gave clear evidence that the worst-case and the average-case upper bounds are much too crude for most practical applications, even in the case of $m \gg 0$. It remains an open problem to improve any of the two bounds, as far as possible.

REFERENCES

Aggarwal A, Guibas LJ, Saxe J, Shor PW (1987a) A Linear Time Algorithm for Computing the Voronoi Diagram of a Convex Polygon. In: Proc. 19th Ann. Symp. of the Theory of Computing (STOC), pp. 39–45

Aggarwal A, Raghavan P, Tiwari P (1987b) Lower Bounds for Closest Pair and Related Problems in Simple Polygons. Technical report, IBM Thomas J. Watson Research Center, Yorktown Heights, NY 10598, USA

Fortune S (1987) A Sweepline Algorithm for Voronoi Diagrams. Algorithmica 2(2):153–174

Gürsoy HN, Patrikalakis NM (1992) An Automatic Coarse and Fine Surface Mesh Generation Scheme Based on Medial Axis Transform: Part I. Engineering with Computers 8:121–137

Held M (1991) On the Computational Geometry of Pocket Machining. Vol. 500 of Lecture Notes in Computer Science. Springer, Berlin Heidelberg New York

Held M (1992) A Versatile Geometric Data Structure for Handling Clearance Problems of CAD/CAM and Robotics. In: Ko NWM, Tan ST (eds.) Proc. Int. Conf. on Manufacturing Automation. Hong Kong, pages 11–18

Held M (1993) Incremental Computation of Voronoi Diagrams of Planar Shapes. Technical Report CS-93-1.0, U. Salzburg, CS Dept., A-5020 Salzburg, Austria

Kirkpatrick DG (1983) Optimal Search in Planar Subdivisions. SIAM J. Comput. 12(1):28–35

Lee DT (1982) Medial Axis Transformation of a Planar Shape. IEEE Trans. Pattern Analysis and Machine Intelligence PAMI-4(4):363–369

O'Dunlaing C, Yap CK (1985) A Retraction Method for Planning the Motion of a Disc. J. Algorithms 6:104–111

Persson H (1978) NC Machining of Arbitrarily Shaped Pockets. CAD 10(3):169–174

Srinivasan V, Nackman LR, Tang JM, Meshkat S (1992) Automatic Mesh Generation Using the Symmetric Axis Transform of Polygonal Domains. Proc. IEEE 80(9):1485–1501

Yap CK (1987) An $O(n * \log n)$ Algorithm for the Voronoi Diagram of a Set of Simple Curve Segments. Discrete Comput. Geom. 2(4):365–393

Martin Held studied Technical Mathematics at the University of Linz, Austria, where he received his Dipl.-Ing. degree in 1987. In 1991, he obtained the doctorate from the Departments of Mathematics and Computer Science at the University of Salzburg, Austria. He currently is a staff member and lecturer at the University of Salzburg's Department of Computer Science. Prior, he was a research assistant at the Research Institute for Symbolic Computation (RISC), Linz, Austria. His research interests include computational geometry, geometric modeling, and computer graphics, with particular emphasis on the handling of geometric and non-numerical data by means of conventional and distributed algorithms.

Address: Univ. Salzburg, Inst. für Computerwissenschaften, Jakob-Haringer Str. 5, A-5020 Salzburg, Austria; E-mail: held@cosy.sbg.ac.at.

Part IV

Modelling and Animation

Abstract and Natural Forms from Iterated Function Systems

Huw Jones and Aurelio Campa

ABSTRACT

Iterated Function Systems are used to generate a variety of regular and irregular fractal objects.within two dimensional and three dimensional spaces. Visualization of the latter types is enabled using depth cueing and z-buffer algorithms. Of particular interest is a family based on the regular polyhedra and associated cube-based forms. Fractal dimensions of these new objects are calculated. The visualization method is also used to shown similarly generated simulations of natural phenomena, such as clouds and plants.

KEY WORDS
Depth cueing, Fractal dimension, Iterated Function Systems (IFS), Platonic solids, z-buffer.

INTRODUCTION: ITERATED FUNCTION SYSTEMS

Michael Barnsley (1988) has popularised the technique of iterated function systems (IFSs). An IFS is a set of contracting affine transformations which, when recursively applied to an original region of space, generates an object whose image under the transforms is itself, called the attractor of the IFS. Within a two dimensional Cartesian space, an affine transformation changes the point (x, y) to the point (x', y') using

$$x' = ax + by + e$$
$$y' = cx + dy + f,$$

where the six constants a, b, c, d, e, and f define the transformation. The determinant (ad - bc) is numerically less than one when the transformation is a contraction, giving an area reduction.

Fig. 1 A set of tiles and the associated IFS

The transformations can be represented as a set of 'tiles' covering the object to be depicted with affine copies of itself. Figure 1 shows a set of four tiles and the associated IFS. Here the tiles can be associated with specific features of the tree like image, such as the lower trunk, lower branches and upper structure. Skill is needed to devise the forms of transformations or tiles needed to generated a specified image. Interactive systems, such as that developed by Horn (1991), can aid a designer in this process . It can be seen, from the above simple example, that a relatively complex image can be defined by a small data set. This image compression feature is one of the main reasons for interest in IFSs (Bown 1992).

Barnsley's 'Chaos game' method is a special case of an IFS, where the forms of transformations are restricted to translations and scalings of factor $\frac{1}{2}$. The ith of n transformations can be represented a single point, (x_i, y_i) say, so that an original point (x, y) is transformed into its 'image' (x', y') using

$$x' = \frac{1}{2}(x + x_i)$$
$$y' = \frac{1}{2}(y + y_i).$$

In simple terms, (x', y') is the mid point of the line joining (x, y) to (x_i, y_i). Given an arbitrary starting point, an IFS image can be produced by repeatedly entering the current point into a randomly selected transformation, plotting the image point at each stage. Figure 2 shows the classical 'Sierpinski gasket' (Sierpinski 1916), created using the vertices of an equilateral triangle to define three such transformations. Using this technique a few stray points may be plotted before the sequence falls into the attractor of the Sierpinski gasket. If the first twenty, say, generated points are not plotted, this problem is eliminated. The object contains three exact copies of itself at scale $\frac{1}{3}$.

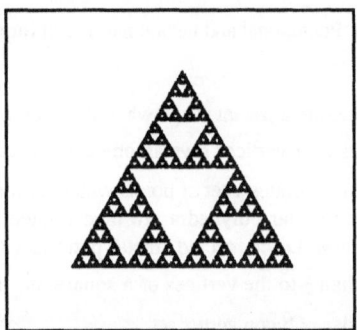

Fig 2 Chaos game depiction of a Sierpinski triangle

The fractal dimension of such exactly replicating forms is evaluated as (Voss 1988, Mandelbrot 1977)

$$D = \frac{\log(N)}{\log(1/f)}$$

where N is the number of exact copies and f is the linear scale of the copies. For the Sierpinski gasket, this gives D as 1.585, correct to three decimal places.

This method has been extended by operating on larger sets of differently located vertices and plotting new points a given fraction f of the distance between the randomly selected vertex and the current point (Jones 1991a). This fraction is equivalent to the scaling of a uniform contraction used within an IFS transformation, so is referred to as a 'shrink factor'. A family of fractal objects has been generated from the vertices of the regular polygons; this includes the Sierpinski gasket, based on the vertices of an equilateral triangle and a shrink factor of $\frac{1}{2}$.

This fractal family can also be generated by recursively redrawing scaled down copies of the original polygon, but the IFS method is a purer technique for depiction of such objects. Figure 3 shows the result of applying it to the vertices of a pentagon and hexagon respectively. The boundaries of these are fractal curves (the hexagon has interior and exterior boundaries in the form of standard Koch curves) which do not have well defined tangents. Any form of depiction using line segments would impose tangent information where none should exist.

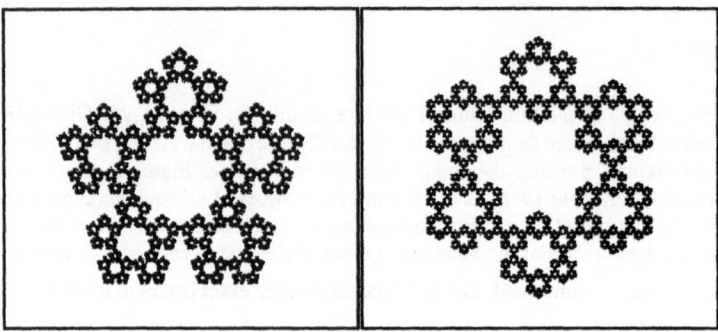

Fig 3 Pentagonal and hexagonal fractal forms

One regular polygon does not generate a fractal shape when this method is applied. For a square, the calculated shrink factor is $\frac{1}{2}$, so its four vertices give an object with fractal dimension $\log(4)/\log(2)$, which reduces to 2. The algorithm generates a set of points which uniformly fills the two dimensional square (Jarrett 1990). When the regular polyhedra are investigated below, a similar situation is discovered with respect to the cube. Disconnected fractal patterns can, however, be generated by applying a shrink factor of less than $\frac{1}{2}$ to the vertices of a square, or, indeed, applying less than the standard shrink factor to any regular polygon vertex set.

IFSs WITHIN A THREE DIMENSIONAL SPACE

Without changing the method described above, the vertices used and points generated can be interpreted as three dimensional Cartesian coordinate triads, (x, y, z), with formulae being applied to each of these coordinates in turn. Objects generated in this way can be rendered using depth cueing and z-buffering. Initially, the frame store is filled with a background colour and the z-buffer is uniformly filled with a large background distance. The perspective projection of each newly generated point occupies a specific pixel which will remain unchanged if the pixel is already 'occupied' by a point closer to the view position. Otherwise, the z-buffer is updated and the pixel's intensity is linearly related to the distance of the point from the observer, brighter intensities lying closer to the observer. The method can be used without a z-buffer, as the depth of a displayed point can be computed from its pixel intensity, making implementation possible on relatively modest platforms (Scott 1992).

Fractals Based on the Platonic Solids

This technique has been applied to the vertices of four of the five Platonic solids or regular polyhedra to generate another family of fractals. The four faced tetrahedron yields the well known 'Sierpinski tetrahedron', the eight faced octahedral form was described by Jones (1991b). The twelve faced dodecahedron and the twenty faced icosahedron also produce fractal forms. The special case of the cube is considered below. Shrink factors are calculated so that the shrunken versions of the polyhedron concerned will just touch each other when fitted inside the original polyhedron. Considerations of solid geometry give shrink factors of $\frac{1}{2}$ for the tetrahedron and octahedron, $\frac{1}{(2 + \rho)}$ for the dodecahedron and $\frac{1}{(1 + \rho)}$ for the icosahedron, where $\rho = \frac{1}{2}(1 + \sqrt{5})$ is the 'golden ratio' (Cundy 1961). Some of the objects produced have almost organic forms (plate 1). The fractal dimensions of these forms are easily calculated. The number N of self similar copies is equal to the number of vertices and the shrink factors are given above, so the fractal dimension formula $D = \log(N)/\log(1/f)$ gives 2.000, 2.585, 2.330 and 2.582 (to 3 decimal places) for the tetrahedral, octahedral, dodecahedral and icosahedral forms respectively.

It is worth noting that the well known Sierpinski tetrahedron is an object that exists within a three dimensional space, but has dimension 2. The generation method used here gives a one-to-one mapping between points within a 2 dimensional square and the Sierpinski tetrahedron. As mentioned above, if the algorithm is applied, with shrink factor of $\frac{1}{2}$, to the vertices of a square, the square is uniformly filled. Exactly the same algorithm applied to the vertices of a regular tetrahedron will generate points within the Sierpinski tetrahedron. If the vertices of both forms are equivalently numbered 1, 2, 3, 4 and the starting point in both cases is taken to be, say, vertex 1, then any point within the square and any point within the Sierpinski tetrahedron can be equivalently labelled as a sequence of the characters 1, 2, 3, 4, giving the orders in which the vertices were chosen in the point generation sequence.

The method of generation and depiction used here is purer than the normally used technique for drawing a Sierpinski tetrahedron. This recursive method ends by drawing small tetrahedra, which impose surface normals on the fractal object where none should exist (unless the subdivision is continued so that the sub-polyhedra depicted occupy less than the space of a single pixel in image space). The IFS method shows the object to the full precision of the display device without imposing any incorrect surface information.

Varying the location of near and far planes when points are generated enables the generation of slices through the objects. These produce a variety of fractal forms, some of which show a surprising richness of symmetries. As an example, plate 2 shows a collection of slices through an octahedral fractal, occupying about one tenth of the original object's thickness. Depth cueing is still enabled, so sections to front and back of the central slicing plane are indicated with higher and lower intensity respectively. Some slices are asymmetric, others display hexagonal, triangular or square based symmetries. The square based form in the upper central position of the plate displays the classical 'space filling' Sierpinski curve.

The algorithm does not generate a fractal object from the vertices of a cube or hexahedron when the natural shrink factor of $\frac{1}{2}$ is applied. Eight half scale cubes, one for each vertex of an original cube, exactly fill that original cube, so the algorithm generates a cloud of points that also fills the cube, having fractal dimension 3. This is analogous to the filled square generated for the two dimensional form of the algorithm. This observation shows that it is possible to use the technique to produce images of solid objects. Another apparently solid form can be produced by using the algorithm with shrink factor $\frac{1}{2}$ on eight vertices consisting of the four vertices of a tetrahedron and its four edge mid points. This creates a tetrahedron with a continuous surface, although slices through the object reveal it to have interior cavities. The vertices of regular prisms with shrink factor $\frac{1}{2}$ can also be used to generate continuous surfaced objects. Other forms of polyhedrally based vertex sets produce fractal forms. A family of pylon like objects is based on the vertices of regular pyramids, when shrink factors are allowed to differ for different Cartesian coordinate directions. If an n-gon based regular pyramid has its base in the (x, y) plane, using the n-gon shrink factor described by Jones (1991a) for the x and y coordinate transformations and a shrink factor of $\frac{1}{2}$ for the z coordinate transformation gives a 'pylon' form.

The Menger or Sierpinski sponge and a related object

The Menger sponge is a well known fractal based within three dimensional space. Imagine a cube subdivided into 27 sub-cubes, each scaled by a linear factor $\frac{1}{3}$ of the original cube's size. Now remove seven sub-cubes, one from the centre of each face plus the sub-cube that lies at the original cube's centre (the only one that is totally interior to the original). Those familiar with Rubik's cube may find its shape useful in visualizing this process. By recursively applying the same procedure to the 20 remaining sub-cubes, the Menger sponge is generated. This is an exactly self similar fractal containing 20 self similar copies of itself, each at a scale of $\frac{1}{3}$ of the original. It thus has fractal dimension log(20)/log(3) or 2.727 to three decimal places.

An IFS based in 3D space using 20 projective transformations with scalings by a factor of $\frac{1}{3}$ and ·uitable translations can be used to generate the object. This can be effected using the same algorithm as used to generate the family of objects described above. A set of twenty attracting points V_1 to V_{20} is formed from the eight vertices of a cube and the twelve mid-points of the cube's edges. The object is generated using a shrink factor of $\frac{1}{3}$ (plate 3, left part). Each separate transformation of the IFS corresponds to one of the sub-cubes in the Menger sponge. It is interesting to note how the linear depth cueing used in this illustration and in earlier figures enables co-planar points to be interpreted as such by the observer.

In experimenting with this method, the authors generated a related object using a shrink factor of $\frac{1}{3}$, and a vertex set V_1 to V_{32} formed from the eight vertices of the cube and the 24 points of tri-section of each of its edges. The object so generated (plate 3, right part) is superficially similar to the Menger sponge. Although the central axial holes are similarly located, the sub-cubes are not similarly subdivided. There are clearly four holes of $\frac{1}{9}$ scale across the top row of sub-cubes, rather than three as in the Sierpinski sponge. Lansdown (1991) has named this object the 'Jones/Campa cake'. A family of similar objects can be generated by increasing the numbers of evenly spaced attracting points along the cube edges and adjusting the shrink factor accordingly. Taking slices through this object also reveals fascinating patterns. Plate 4 shows such a slice, with points colour coded to appear yellow if last attracted towards a vertex, red if last attracted towards an edge trisection point.

Fractal dimension of the Jones/Campa cake

The transformations for this object generate overlapping parts, so the simple formula used above for calculation of the fractal dimension is not appropriate. The new object contains two types of sub-cube compared to the one self similar form in the Sierpinski sponge. Eight sub-cubes of type A are similar to the Jones/Campa cake itself and appear as $\frac{1}{3}$ linear scale copies of the original shape, adjacent to its eight vertices. Twelve B type sub-cubes form links between the type A sub-cubes and are adjacent to the mid sections of the twelve edges of the original cube. Type A and type B sub-cubes can themselves be subdivided into smaller copies of type A and type B forms (fig 4). Each type A cube contains eight $\frac{1}{3}$ scale type A cubes and twelve $\frac{1}{3}$ scale type B cubes, whereas a type B cube contains four $\frac{1}{3}$ scale type A cubes and twelve $\frac{1}{3}$ scale type B cubes.

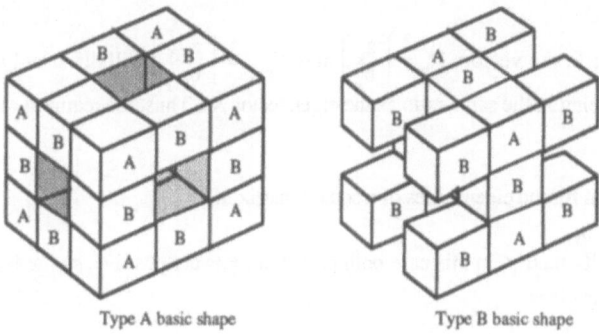

Type A basic shape   Type B basic shape

Fig. 4 Constituents of type A and B sub-cubes

The initial stage consists of one cube of type A. Suppose that there are a_{k-1} cubes of type A and b_{k-1} cubes of type B at the $(k-1)^{th}$ stage of scaling. At the next or k^{th} stage, there will be

$$a_k = 8a_{k-1} + 4b_{k-1} \quad \text{sub-cubes of type A}$$

and $$b_k = 12a_{k-1} + 12b_{k-1} \quad \text{sub-cubes of type B,}$$

each of these sub-cubes being linearly scaled by factor $\frac{1}{3}$ compared to the equivalent form in the previous stage. This can be expressed in matrix form as

$$N_k = M N_{k-1} = M^k N_0$$

where $$N_k = \begin{bmatrix} a_k \\ b_k \end{bmatrix}, M = \begin{bmatrix} 8 & 4 \\ 12 & 12 \end{bmatrix} \text{ and } N_0 = \begin{bmatrix} 1 \\ 0 \end{bmatrix}.$$

In order to find the fractal dimension of the Jones/Campa cake, we must use to the definition based on Hausdorff's neighbourhood principle (Voss 1988). The evaluation involves finding the limiting ratio R of occupied cubes at one sub-cube level to the number of occupied cubes at the previous sub-cube level, in other words,

$$R = \lim_{k \to \infty} \left\{ \frac{a_k + b_k}{a_{k-1} + b_{k-1}} \right\}.$$

A result from matrix eigenvalue theory enables us to find this limiting ratio. A numerical technique for finding the 'dominant eigenvalue' λ_1 of a square matrix M and its eigenvector X_1, uses the result that

$$M^k X = \lambda_1^{\ k} X \approx c\lambda_1^{\ k} X_1,$$

where c is some constant and X is any column vector which is not orthogonal to X_1 (Wilkinson 1965). The approximation improves as k increases. Thus,

$$N_k = M^k N_0 \approx c\lambda_1^{\ k} X_1,$$

and $\quad N_{k-1} = M^{k-1} N_0 \approx c\lambda_1^{\ k-1} X_1.$

For large values of k, the vectors $N_k = \begin{bmatrix} a_k \\ b_k \end{bmatrix}$ and $N_{k-1} = \begin{bmatrix} a_{k-1} \\ b_{k-1} \end{bmatrix}$ will differ only by the factor λ_1 their components being in the same ratio as the eigenvector X_1. Thus, the required ratio R is the value λ_1.

The general equation for the eigenvalues of a square matrix M is
$$|M - \lambda I| = 0,$$
where I is the identity matrix. In this case both potential roots are positive, so the larger of the two is the required λ_1. This gives

$$(8 - \lambda)(12 - \lambda) - 48 = 0$$
or $\quad \lambda^2 - 20\lambda + 48 = 0,$

which has roots

$$\lambda = 10 - 2\sqrt{13} \text{ or } \lambda = 10 + 2\sqrt{13}.$$

The dominant eigenvalue is the larger of these, so

$$\lambda_1 = 10 + 2\sqrt{13}. = 17.211 \text{ (to 3 decimal places)}.$$

Note that as the ratio of the two eigenvalues is relatively large (6.171 to 3 decimal places), repeated multiplication will reduce N_k to be approximately parallel to X_1 for relatively low values of k. The equation for finding the associated eigenvector for λ_1

$$(M - \lambda_1 I)X_1 = 0$$
gives
$$X_1 = \begin{bmatrix} 1.000 \\ 2.303 \end{bmatrix} \text{ (to 3 decimal places)}.$$

This means that for fairly small scalings of sub-cubes, there will be about 2.303 times as many type B sub-cubes as there are type A sub-cubes.

In order to find the fractal dimension of the Jones/Campa cake, we return to the Hausdorff definition of dimension. If the object can be covered by n_1 neighbourhoods of one size or by n_2 neighbourhoods a fraction f of that size, the dimension of the object is the limiting value of the ratio

$$\frac{\log(n_2/n_1)}{\log(1/f)}$$

as the size of the neighbourhoods involved becomes small. Covering neighbourhoods can be represented by filled cubes in this example, so we have shown that

$$\lim_{k \to \infty} \left\{ \frac{n_2}{n_1} \right\} = \lim_{k \to \infty} \left\{ \frac{a_k + b_k}{a_{k-1} + b_{k-1}} \right\} = \lambda_1 \, ,$$

where the ratio of the sizes of the neighbourhoods is $\frac{1}{3}$. Thus, we can evaluate the fractal dimension of the object as

$$D = \frac{\log(\lambda_1)}{\log(3)} = \frac{\log(10 + 2\sqrt{13})}{\log(3)} = 2.590 \text{ (to 3 decimal places)}.$$

SIMULATION OF NATURALLY OCCURRING FORMS

Clouds

Less regular structures, designed to simulating naturally occurring forms, can be generated from IFSs. For example, by using the algorithm used in the above sections with an initial set of points distributed randomly on the surface of and within an ellipsoid, cloud like images can be generated. These may initially appear convincing, but when viewed at particular angles, regular artefacts such as Koch curve like outlines, are often observed. More 'fuzzy' outlines can be created by amending the algorithm so that the shrink factor f for each generated point is allowed itself to vary randomly about a given mean. This new system does not constitute a genuine IFS, but it generates convincing cloud like objects. In plate 5, shrink factors of form $\frac{1}{r}$, where r varies uniformly between 2.5 and 3.5, were used on a set of 32 attracting points. The clouds generated are unlike many examples of clouds shown in Computer Graphic images, as they exist within a three dimensional space, rather than taking the form of a painted backdrop. An observer could 'fly' around and through them convincingly. The method has considerable potential for use in flight simulators, when trainee pilots could experience the visual sensation of flying through cloud formations. By varying the locations and numbers of the vertices and changing the mean shrink factor, animation of cloud forms is possible.

Simulation of trees and plants

Through his illustration of the Spleenwort fern, Barnsley (1988) showed the power of general iterated function systems for generating models of repetitive branching processes. The original images shown were in a two dimensional space, although similar forms within a three dimensional space can be generated. The tilings that generate trunk, lower branches and upper portion of a tree form, shown as rectangles in fig. 1, can be replaced by rectangular blocks in the three dimensional equivalent. More general forms use rotations, so the simple method of the sections above, restricted to translations and scalings, is too limited for such object generation. However, the method of depiction described above, using depth cueing and a z-buffer, produces convincing images of such forms.

Suppose we have n contractive affine transformations T_1, T_2, ... T_n and an associated set of probabilities π_1, π_2, ... π_n which sum to unity. Given an initial point, select a transformation T_i with probability π_i, apply it to the initial point, plot the resulting image point and repetitively apply randomly selected transformations to the latest point created. If the probabilities are proportional to the contraction ratios of their corresponding transformations (now representing the volume reduction of an object under the transformation), the object created will be evenly filled with points. Varying these probabilities can be used to the advantage of the image generator.

Plate 6 shows an example of a plant like form generated using two passes through such a system, using only four transformations. The green 'foliage' parts of the image are produced in the first pass, with very low probability given to the 'trunk' transformation. The trunk and branches are then created in a second pass, allocating a different basic colour to the points generated. By varying the locations and numbers of transformations and introducing more passes through the system with varying probabilities and base colours, a wide variety of plant like forms can be created. Greater sophistication can be introduced by generating shapes such as blossoms or leaf images as sub-features, but this would reduce the simplicity of the system that is part of its charm.

CONCLUSION

A number of objects generated by Iterated Function Systems has been described, lying within two dimensional and three dimensional spaces. A simple combination of depth cueing and z-buffer algorithms is shown to be adequate for depiction of the latter forms. The shapes generated include familiar and novel abstract forms based on regular geometric shapes, but can be easily adapted to generate models of irregularly surfaced naturally occurring phenomena, such as clouds and plants. The three dimensional basis of such objects make them potentially useful in a range of visualization systems.

ACKNOWLEDGMENTS

The authors would like to thank their colleagues and friends who have discussed the ideas underlying this paper. These include Allan Findlay, David Jarrett and, particularly, Professor John Lansdown, who has been most supportive.

REFERENCES

Barnsley MF (1988) Fractals everywhere, Academic Press, San Diego

Bown W (1992) Fractal maths adds up to a clearer vision, New Scientist 1824: 20

Cundy HM, Rollett AP (1961) Mathematical models (2 ed), Oxford University Press, Oxford, 1961

Horn AN (1991) IFSs and the interactive design of tiling structures, In: Crilly AJ, Earnshaw RA, Jones H (eds) Fractals and chaos, Springer-Verlag, New York, pp 119 – 144

Jarrett D (1990) Personal correspondence, Middlesex University, London

Jones H (1991a) Dürer, gaskets and the chaos game, Computer Graphics Forum 9 (3): 327 – 332

Jones H, Campa A (1991b) Fractals based on regular polygons and polyhedra, In: Patrikalakis NM (ed) Scientific visualization of physical phenomena, Springer-Verlag, Tokyo, pp 299 – 314

Lansdown RJ (1991) Serendipity, not only computing – also art, The Computer Bulletin 3(7): 12–13

Mandelbrot BB (1977) The fractal geometry of nature, W.H.Freeman, New York

Scott D (1992) 3D IFS generation and rendering of botanical images, MSc Applied Computing Technology Dissertation, Middlesex University

Sierpinski W (1916, re-published 1975) Sur une courbe dont tout point est un point de ramification, in W Sierpinski: oeuvres choisis (Tome II) PWN - Polish Scientific Publishers, Warsaw, Poland

Voss RF (1988) Fractals in nature: from characterisation to simulation, In: Peitgen H-O, Saupe D (eds) The science of fractal images, Springer-Verlag, New York

Wilkinson JH (1965) The algebraic eigenvalue problem, Clarendon Press, Oxford, 1965

PLATE CAPTIONS, JONES & CAMPA

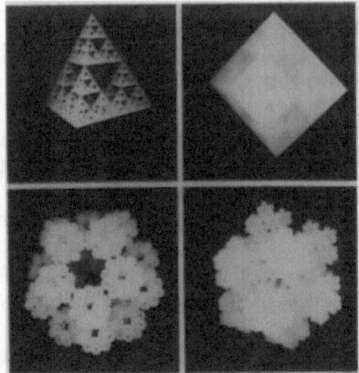

Plate 1 Clockwise, from top left, tetrahedral, octahedral, icosahedral and dodecahedral fractal forms

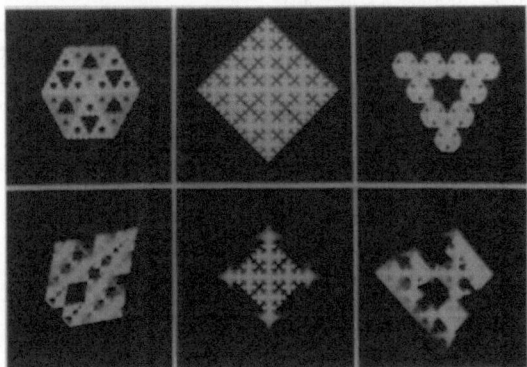

Plate 2 Slices through an octahedral fractal form

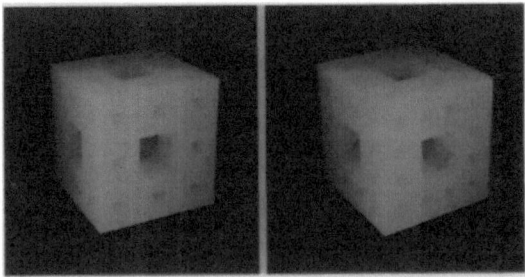

Plate 3 A Menger sponge and a Jones/Campa cake

Plate 4 A colour coded slice through the Jones/Campa cake

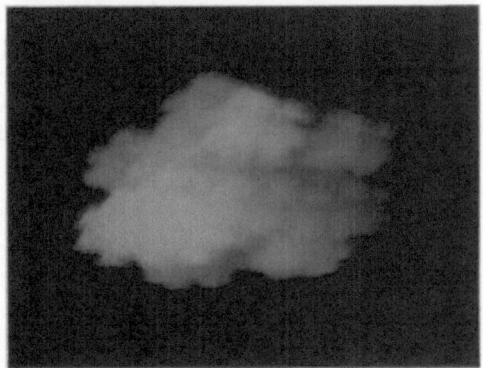

Plate 5 A cloud generated from a data set of 32 points

Plate 6 A tree like form generated from a four transformation IFS

THE AUTHORS

Huw Jones graduated from University College, Swansea with a BSc in Applied Mathematics in 1966 and a Post Graduate Diploma in Education in 1967. In 1976, he obtained an MSc in Statistics from Brunel University and has worked in Higher Education for over 20 years. He is currently Principal Lecturer in Computer Graphics at Middlesex Polytechnic, where he is leader of the MSc Computer Graphics course. He is a Fellow of the Royal Statistical Society, a Member of the British Computer Society and of Eurographics and is vice-Chair of the British Computer Society's Computer Graphics and Displays Group. He has co-authored or co-edited four books on Computer Graphics related topics. His wife, Judy, teaches Mathematics and his son, Rhodri, and daughter, Ceri, study, all in Secondary Schools in North London. Address: Computer Graphics Section, Middlesex University, Bounds Green Road, London N11 2NQ, UK.
(huw1@uk.ac.mdx.cluster)

Aurelio Campa graduated from University College London with a BSc in Computer Science and Electronic Engineering. In 1991, he obtained an MSc in Computer Graphics from Middlesex University, where he now works at the Centre for Advanced Studies in Computer Aided Art and Design. Address: CASCAAD, Faculty of Art and Design, Middlesex University, Cat Hill, Barnet, EN4 8HT, UK.
(aurelio1@uk.ac.mdx.cluster)

Verification of Visual Characteristics of Complex Functions $f_{\alpha,c}(z) = z^\alpha + c$

Young Bong Kim, Hyoung Seok Kim, Ho Kyung Kim, Hwang Soo Kim, Hong Oh Kim, and Sung Yong Shin

ABSTRACT

A self-squared function, $f(z) = z^2 + c$, provides typical fractal images such as the Mandelbrot set and Julia sets. As an extension of this function, polynomials whose degree is a positive integer have been used to generate fractal images. Recently, it has been attempted to extend their degree into a real number, i.e., the family of functions $f_{\alpha,c}(z) = z^\alpha + c$ where α is a real number. Gujar et al. [Guja91, Guja92, Vang90] conjectured nice graphical features by observing fractal images generated from this family of functions. In this paper, we characterize the behavioral pattern of $f_{\alpha,c}(z)$ depending on the value of α to verify these conjectures.

Keywords: Fractal Geometry, Complex Functions, Iterative Function Systems.

1. INTRODUCTION

The self-squared function, $f(z) = z^2 + c$, has been attracting much attention for fractal image generation. Its chaotic behavior provides two kinds of typical fractal images such as the Mandelbrot set and Julia sets [Barn88, Deva89, Mand82]. A Julia set classifies a point z_0 depending on its stability [Mand82, Peit88]. If the orbit of a point z_0 behaves together with those of its neighbors, then the point z_0 is said to be a stable point. Otherwise, the point is an unstable point. The behavior of the orbit of each point z_0 divides the domain of the variable z into two sets, that is, the set of stable points and the set of unstable points called a Julia set [Entw89, Peit86].

The Mandelbrot set classifies a parameter value c depending on whether the orbit of a critical point 0 of $f(z) = z^2 + c$ tends to ∞ or not. The Mandelbrot set acts as a guide map of Julia sets. For example, if the parameter c is contained in the Mandelbrot set, then its corresponding Julia set is connected. Otherwise, the Julia set is totally disconnected [Blan84, Peit88].

As an extension of the self-squared function, a family of polynomials, $z^p + c$ where p is a positive integer, have been investigated [Blan84]. These polynomials give another interesting fractal images visualizing their Mandelbrot set and Julia sets.

Recently, Gujar et al. [Guja91, Guja92, Vang90] made an attempt to investigate the behavior of a family of functions, $f_{\alpha,c}(z) = z^\alpha + c$, where α is a real number. These functions provide $c-$plane fractal images and $z-$plane fractal images by varying the parameter c and the variable z, respectively, which are analogues of the Mandelbrot set and Julia sets. Fractal images resulting from this family of functions exhibit various lobular structures for $\alpha > 1$ and satellite structures for $\alpha < 0$ as shown in Figure 1. They made twelve conjectures about the visual characteristics of these fractal images such as the number of lobular (satellite) structures, their shapes, and their symmetry about the real axis. However, such characteristics have not yet been proven.

In this paper, we characterize the behavioral pattern of $f_{\alpha,c}(z)$ depending upon the value of α and thus verify these conjectures. In section 2, we derive a bound of $c-$plane fractal images, which gives

345

(a) $\alpha = 6.0$ (b) $\alpha = -5.0$

Fig. 1. Lobular and Satellite structures from fractal images resulting from $f_{\alpha,c}(z) = z^{\alpha} + c$

a condition for testing the unboundedness of an orbit. A bound of $z-$plane fractal images will also be given. Section 3 gives a number of results that can verify the six conjectures about $c-$plane fractal images [Guja91]. Section 4 provides a theorem which can explain the other six conjectures on $z-$plane fractal images [Guja92, Vang90]. Concluding remarks are given in Section 5.

2. PRELIMINARIES

Consider a complex function $f_{\alpha,c}(z) = z^{\alpha} + c$ for a given α and c. In the polar coordinate system, a complex number z has representations such as $z = re^{i(\theta+2k\pi)}$ for all integer k. Therefore, $z^{\alpha} = r^{\alpha}e^{i\alpha(\theta+2k\pi)}$, which gives a unique point $r^{\alpha}e^{i\alpha\theta}$ for an integral value of α. However, for a non-integral value of α, z^{α} represents finitely or infinitely many points depending on whether α is rational or not, respectively. In order to assign a unique point for z^{α}, we restrict the representation of z in the polar coordinate system so that z^{α} indicates a unique point in the complex plane [Barn88]. We choose a representation of z such that

$$z = re^{i\theta} \quad for \ r \geq 0 \ and \ \phi_0 \leq \theta < \phi_0 + 2\pi \tag{1}$$

for a fixed ϕ_0. A different choice of ϕ_0 gives a different fractal image of $f_{\alpha,c}(z)$. The image for a non-integral real number of α has the discontinuity at the ray of angle ϕ_0. Unless otherwise stated, we choose $\phi_0 = -\pi$ as assumed in [Guja91, Guja92, Vang90] although this is not explicitly mentioned in [Guja91, Vang90].

For a real parameter α, the $c-$plane fractal of $f_{\alpha,c}(z)$ is defined as the set $M(\alpha)$ of all c for which the sequence $\{f_{\alpha,c}^n(c)\}_{n=0}^{\infty}$ is bounded, i.e., the orbit of c

$$c \mapsto c^{\alpha} + c \mapsto (c^{\alpha} + c)^{\alpha} + c \mapsto \cdots \tag{2}$$

is bounded. The sequence (2) is well-defined in representation (1). Notice that we take the orbit of c rather than the orbit of a critical point. However, it does not lose the mathematical essence since the point at ∞ is the critical point when $\alpha < 0$. For $\alpha = 2$, sequence (2) is the orbit of the critical point 0 for the quadratic polynomial $z^2 + c$, and hence $M(2)$ is the famous Mandelbrot set.

As an analogue of the filled-in Julia set for the familiar quadratic polynomial $z^2 + c$, the $z-$plane fractal of $f_{\alpha,c}(z)$ is defined as the set $K(\alpha, c)$ of all z_0 for which the sequence $\{f_{\alpha,c}^n(z_0)\}_{n=0}^{\infty}$ is bounded. Thus $K(2, c)$ is the usual filled-in Julia set for $z^2 + c$.

2.1 A Bound for $c-$plane Fractal Images

In this section, we compute a bound of the $c-$plane fractal $M(\alpha)$. This bound gives a condition to test the unboundedness of the orbit starting from a value of c. It is also helpful in determining the size of a window where $c-$plane fractal images are contained. There are four cases depending on α.

Case 1: $\alpha > 1$. We show that the $M(\alpha)$ lies in the disk of radius $2^{\frac{1}{\alpha-1}}$ centered at the origin. For $|z| \geq |c| > 1$, we see that

$$\begin{aligned}
|f_{\alpha,c}(z)| &\geq |z|^\alpha - |c| \\
&\geq |z|(|c|^{\alpha-1} - 1) \\
&= \gamma|z|
\end{aligned}$$

where $\gamma = |c|^{\alpha-1} - 1$. If $\gamma > 1$, or if $|c| > 2^{\frac{1}{\alpha-1}}$, then $|f_{\alpha,c}(z)| > |c|$. Therefore, we can inductively show that

$$\begin{aligned}
|f_{\alpha,c}^n(c)| &\geq \gamma|f_{\alpha,c}^{n-1}(c)| \geq \cdots \\
&\geq \gamma^n|f_{\alpha,c}^0(c)| \\
&= \gamma^n|c|.
\end{aligned} \tag{3}$$

From inequality (3), we see that $f_{\alpha,c}^n(c) \to \infty$ as $n \to \infty$. Therefore, $M(\alpha)$ is contained in the disk of radius $2^{\frac{1}{\alpha-1}}$ centered at the origin.

Case 2: $\alpha = 1$. In this case, the orbit, $c \mapsto 2c \mapsto 3c \mapsto \cdots$, obviously diverges to infinity unless $c = 0$. Thus $M(1)$ is $\{0\}$.

Case 3 : $0 \leq \alpha < 1$. For $|c| > 1$, we note that

$$\begin{aligned}
|f_{\alpha,c}(c)| &\leq |c|^\alpha + |c| \\
&\leq 2|c|.
\end{aligned}$$

Suppose that $|f_{\alpha,c}^i(c)| \leq 2|c|$ is true for some $i \geq 1$. If $2^\alpha|c|^\alpha < |c|$, or $|c| \geq 2^{\frac{\alpha}{1-\alpha}}$, then

$$\begin{aligned}
|f_{\alpha,c}^{i+1}(c)| &\leq |f_{\alpha,c}^i(c)|^\alpha + |c| \\
&\leq 2^\alpha|c|^\alpha + |c| \\
&\leq 2|c|.
\end{aligned}$$

Therefore, the orbit $\{f_{\alpha,c}^n(c)\}_{n=0}^\infty$ is bounded by $2|c|$ for $|c| \geq 2^{\frac{\alpha}{1-\alpha}}$. For $|c| < 2^{\frac{\alpha}{1-\alpha}}$, we also show that the orbit $\{f_{\alpha,c}^n(c)\}_{n=0}^\infty$ is bounded. Suppose for contradiction that it is not bounded. We can choose m so that $|f_{\alpha,c}^m(c)| \geq 2^{\frac{1}{1-\alpha}}$ and set $\gamma = |f_{\alpha,c}^m(c)|$. Then

$$\begin{aligned}
|f_{\alpha,c}^{m+1}(c)| &\leq |f_{\alpha,c}^m(c)|^\alpha + |c| \\
&\leq \gamma^\alpha + \gamma \\
&= f_{\alpha,\gamma}(\gamma).
\end{aligned}$$

Continuing this process, we see that

$$|f_{\alpha,c}^{m+j}(c)| \leq f_{\alpha,\gamma}^j(\gamma).$$

Since $\gamma \geq 2^{\frac{\alpha}{1-\alpha}}$, the orbit $\{f_{\alpha,\gamma}^j(\gamma)\}_{j=0}^\infty$ is bounded by 2γ by the previous argument. Hence, $\{f_{\alpha,c}^{m+j}(c)\}_{j=0}^\infty$ is also bounded. This is a contradiction to the assumption that $\{f_{\alpha,c}^n(c)\}_{n=0}^\infty$ is not bounded. Therefore, the orbit $\{f_{\alpha,c}^n(c)\}_{n=0}^\infty$ is also bounded for $|c| \leq 2^{\frac{1}{\alpha-1}}$. Hence, $M(\alpha)$ is the whole complex plane.

Case 4 : $\alpha < 0$. For $|c| > 2$ and $|z_0| > 1$, we note that

$$|c| - 1 \leq |c| - |z_0|^\alpha \leq |f_{\alpha,c}(z_0)| \leq |c| + |z_0|^\alpha \leq |c| + 1.$$

In particular, $|c| - 1 \leq |f_{\alpha,c}(c)| \leq |c| + 1$. Suppose that $|c| - 1 \leq |f_{\alpha,c}^i(c)| \leq |c| + 1$ is true for some $i \geq 1$. Since $|f_{\alpha,c}^i(c)| > 1$,

$$|c| - 1 \leq |c| - |f_{\alpha,c}^i(c)|^\alpha \leq |f_{\alpha,c}^{i+1}(c)| \leq |c| + |f_{\alpha,c}^i(c)|^\alpha \leq |c| + 1.$$

Hence, we can inductively obtain that $|c| - 1 \leq |f_{\alpha,c}^n(c)| \leq |c| + 1$ for all n. Therefore, $M(\alpha)$ contains all points outside the disk of radius 2 centered at the origin.

In cases 2 and 3, $M(\alpha)$ is either $\{0\}$ or the whole complex plane. Therefore, $f_{\alpha,c}(z)$ does not give any interesting fractal images for $0 \leq \alpha \leq 1$. Thus we concentrate on cases 1 and 4 in which $\alpha < 0$ and $\alpha > 1$. For $\alpha > 1$, $M(\alpha)$ is contained in the disk of radius $2^{\frac{1}{\alpha-1}}$ centered at origin. However, for $\alpha < 0$, $M(\alpha)$ contains all points lying outside the disk of radius 2 centered at the origin. In either case, the most interesting part of a $c-$plane fractal image is contained in a disk centered at origin although its radius depends on α. Therefore, the size of a window for containing $c-$plane fractal images can be accordingly determined.

In order to generate an image, we first need to establish a condition for testing the unboundedness of an orbit $\{f_{\alpha,c}^n(c)\}_{n=0}^\infty$. That is, it is necessary to determine the number of iterations N and a threshold $L(\alpha)$ such that

$$\{f_{\alpha,c}^n(c)\}_{n=0}^\infty \text{ is unbounded if } f_{\alpha,c}^j(c) \geq L(\alpha) \text{ for some } j \leq N.$$

For $\alpha > 1$, it is reasonable to set $L(\alpha) = 2^{\frac{1}{\alpha-1}}$. If $\alpha < 0$, then it is hard, if not impossible, to find $L(\alpha)$ although all points outside the disk of radius 2 centered at the origin are guaranteed to be contained in $M(\alpha)$. It seems apparent that most of points near the origin in the disk are oscillating. In fact, Gujar et al. [Guja91] chose $L(\alpha) = 10$ regardless of α. We thus set $L(\alpha) = 10$ if $\alpha < 0$. Hence,

$$L(\alpha) = \begin{cases} 2^{\frac{1}{\alpha-1}} & \text{if } \alpha > 1 \\ 10, & \text{if } \alpha < 0. \end{cases}$$

However, for $\alpha < 0$ such $L(\alpha)$ does not result in an image which exactly reflects $M(\alpha)$. Therefore, a different combination of $L(\alpha)$ and N gives a different image in this case. For consistency, we set $N = 100$ as suggested in [Guja91].

2.2 A Bound for $z-$plane Fractal Images

We compute a bound of the $z-$plane fractal $K(\alpha, c)$ depending on α. This bound can be used as a condition for testing the unboundedness of an orbit for generating the graphical image of $K(\alpha, c)$. It also helps computing the size of a window in which $z-$plane fractal images are contained.

Case 1 : $\alpha > 1$. For $|z_0| \geq |c|$ and $|z_0| > 1$, we note that

$$\begin{aligned} |f_{\alpha,c}(z_0)| &\geq |z_0|^\alpha - |c| \\ &\geq |z_0|^\alpha - |z_0| \\ &= \gamma|z_0|. \end{aligned} \tag{4}$$

where $\gamma = |z_0|^{\alpha-1} - 1$. If $\gamma > 1$, or $|z_0| > 2^{\frac{1}{\alpha-1}}$, then $|f_{\alpha,c}(z_0)| > |c|$ and also $|f_{\alpha,c}(z_0)| > 1$. From inequality (4), we can inductively obtain that $|f_{\alpha,c}^n(z_0)| \geq \gamma^n|z_0|$ for all n. Therefore, the orbit $\{f_{\alpha,c}^n(z_0)\}_{n=0}^\infty$ is unbounded when $|z_0| > |c|$ and $|z_0| > 2^{\frac{1}{\alpha-1}}$. That is, $K(\alpha, c)$ is contained in the disk of radius $r = \max\{|c|, 2^{\frac{1}{\alpha-1}}\}$ centered at the origin.

Case 2 : $\alpha = 1$. In this case, the orbit of every point z_0 becomes $\{z_0 + nc\}_{n=0}^\infty$ because $f_{\alpha,c}^{j+1}(z_0) = f_{\alpha,c}^j(z_0) + c$ for all $j \geq 1$. Thus, it goes to infinity unless $c = 0$. If $c = 0$, the orbit starting from a point z_0 stays at z_0. Therefore, $K(1, c)$ is either the whole complex plane or empty according as c is 0 or not, respectively.

Case 3 : $0 \leq \alpha < 1$. For $|z_0| \geq |c|$, we note that

$$\begin{aligned} |f_{\alpha,c}(z_0)| &\leq |z_0|^\alpha + |c| \\ &\leq |z_0|^\alpha + |z_0| \\ &\leq 2|z_0|. \end{aligned}$$

Suppose that $|f_{\alpha,c}^i(z_0)| \le 2|z_0|$ is true for some $i \ge 1$. If $2^\alpha |z_0|^\alpha \le |z_0|$, or $|z_0| \ge 2^{\frac{\alpha}{1-\alpha}}$, then

$$
\begin{aligned}
|f_{\alpha,c}^{i+1}(z_0)| &\le |f_{\alpha,c}^i(z_0)|^\alpha + |c| \\
&\le 2^\alpha |z_0|^\alpha + |z_0| \\
&\le 2|z_0|.
\end{aligned} \tag{5}
$$

Therefore, the orbit $\{f_{\alpha,c}^n(z_0)\}_{n=0}^\infty$ is bounded by $2|z_0|$ for $|z_0| \ge \max\{2^{\frac{\alpha}{1-\alpha}}, |c|\}$.

We will show that it is also bounded for $|z_0| < \max\{2^{\frac{\alpha}{1-\alpha}}\}$. Suppose for contradiction that $\{f_{\alpha,c}^n(z_0)\}_{n=0}^\infty$ is not bounded. We can choose m so that $|f_{\alpha,c}^m(z_0)| \ge \max\{2^{\frac{\alpha}{1-\alpha}}, |c|\}$, and set $\gamma = |f_{\alpha,c}^m(z_0)|$. Then,

$$
\begin{aligned}
|f_{\alpha,c}^{m+1}(z_0)| &\le |f_{\alpha,c}^m(z_0)|^\alpha + |c| \\
&\le \gamma^\alpha + \gamma \\
&= f_{\alpha,\gamma}(\gamma).
\end{aligned}
$$

Continuing this process, we have $|f_{\alpha,c}^{m+j}(z_0)| \le f_{\alpha,\gamma}^j(\gamma)$ for all $j \ge 1$. But $\{f_{\alpha,\gamma}^j(\gamma)\}_{j=0}^\infty$ is bounded by 2γ according to inequality (5) because $\gamma \ge \max\{2^{\frac{\alpha}{1-\alpha}}, |c|\}$. This is a contradiction to the assumption that $\{f_{\alpha,c}^n(z_0)\}_{n=0}^\infty$ is not bounded. Therefore, the orbit $\{f_{\alpha,c}^n(z_0)\}_{n=0}^\infty$ is also bounded. Hence, $K(\alpha,c)$ is the whole complex plane.

Case 4 : $\alpha < 0$. For $|z_0| > 1$ and $|c| \ge 2$, we note that

$$
|c| - 1 \le |c| - |z_0|^\alpha \le |f_{\alpha,c}(z_0)| \le |c| + |z_0|^\alpha \le |c| + 1.
$$

In particular, $|f_{\alpha,c}(z_0)| > 1$. By induction, $|c| - 1 \le |f_{\alpha,c}^n(z_0)| \le |c| + 1$ for all n. Therefore, when $|c| \ge 2$, $K(\alpha,c)$ contains all points outside the disk of radius 1 centered at the origin.

In cases 2 and 3, $K(\alpha,c)$ is either empty or the whole complex plane as $M(\alpha)$ is. Therefore, we focus on cases 1 and 4 in which $\alpha > 1$ and $\alpha < 0$, respectively. For $\alpha > 1$, let $r = \max\{|c|, 2^{\frac{1}{\alpha-1}}\}$. Then, $K(\alpha,c)$ is contained in the disk of radius r centered at the origin. Therefore, the size of a window can accordingly be determined. However, the bound of $K(\alpha,c)$ is hard to obtain for $\alpha < 0$ although all points outside the disk of radius 1 centered at the origin are guaranteed to lie in $K(\alpha,c)$ when $|c| \ge 2$. Thus, we locate a fixed-size window around the origin for $\alpha < 0$.

We set the number of iterations N and the threshold $L(\alpha)$ in the similar way as those for $M(\alpha)$ in section 2.1, i.e.,

$$
N = 100, \quad \text{and}
$$
$$
L(\alpha) = \begin{cases} \max\{|c|, 2^{\frac{1}{\alpha-1}}\}, & \text{if } \alpha > 1 \\ 10, & \text{if } \alpha < 0 \end{cases}
$$

mainly for consistency with the results in [Guja91]. We again note that a different combination of $L(\alpha)$ and N gives a different image for $\alpha < 0$.

3. CHARACTERISTICS OF C−PLANE FRACTAL IMAGES

In this section, we characterize the behavioral pattern of $f_{\alpha,c}(z)$ to obtain three theorems and two corollaries. Using these results we verify six conjectures on c−plane fractal images [Guja91].

We first investigate the behavior of an orbit $\{f_{\alpha,c}^n(c)\}_{n=0}^\infty$ depending on θ for $c = re^{i\theta}$.

Theorem 1 Let $\alpha \ne 1$. Suppose c_1 and c_2 have the same modulus and let $c_j = re^{i\theta_j}$ for $j = 1,2$ with $-\pi \le \theta_j < \pi$. Then, $|f_{\alpha,c_1}^n(c_1)| = |f_{\alpha,c_2}^n(c_2)|$ for all n if and only if $\theta_1 \pm \theta_2 = \frac{2k\pi}{\alpha-1}$ for some integer k.

Proof. Let $z_n^{(j)} = f_{\alpha,c_j}^n(c_j)$ for $j = 1,2$ and suppose that $|z_n^{(1)}| = |z_n^{(2)}|$ for all n. In particular,

$$
\begin{aligned}
|r^\alpha e^{i\alpha\theta_1} + re^{i\theta_1}| &= |r^\alpha e^{i\alpha\theta_2} + re^{i\theta_2}|, \quad \text{or} \\
|r^\alpha e^{i(\alpha-1)\theta_1} + r| &= |r^\alpha e^{i(\alpha-1)\theta_2} + r|.
\end{aligned}
$$

This implies that either $(\alpha - 1)\theta_1 = (\alpha - 1)\theta_2 + 2k\pi$ or $(\alpha - 1)\theta_1 = 2k\pi - (\alpha - 1)\theta_2$, where k is an integer. That is, either $\theta_1 - \theta_2 = \frac{2k\pi}{\alpha-1}$ or $\theta_1 + \theta_2 = \frac{2k\pi}{\alpha-1}$.

Conversely, assume that $\theta_1 \mp \theta_2 = \frac{2k\pi}{\alpha-1}$ for some integer k. For $\theta_1 - \theta_2 = \frac{2k\pi}{\alpha-1}$, we have

$$
\begin{aligned}
z_1^{(1)} &= c_1^\alpha + c_1 \\
&= r^\alpha e^{i\alpha\theta_1} + re^{i\theta_1} \\
&= r^\alpha e^{i\alpha(\theta_2 + \frac{2k\pi}{\alpha-1})} + re^{i(\theta_2 + \frac{2k\pi}{\alpha-1})} \\
&= e^{i\frac{2k\pi}{\alpha-1}}(r^\alpha e^{i\alpha\theta_2} + re^{i\theta_2}) \\
&= e^{i\frac{2k\pi}{\alpha-1}} z_1^{(2)}.
\end{aligned}
$$

Similarly, for $\theta_1 + \theta_2 = \frac{2k\pi}{\alpha-1}$, we obtain $z_1^{(1)} = e^{i\frac{2k\pi}{\alpha-1}} \bar{z}_1^{(2)}$. For induction, assume that

$$
z_n^{(1)} = e^{i\frac{2k\pi}{\alpha-1}} z_n^{(2)}, \quad \text{or} \quad z_n^{(1)} = e^{i\frac{2k\pi}{\alpha-1}} \bar{z}_n^{(2)}.
$$

Since $e^{i\frac{2k\pi}{\alpha-1}\alpha} = e^{i\frac{2k\pi}{\alpha-1}}$,

$$
\begin{aligned}
z_{n+1}^{(1)} &= (z_n^{(1)})^\alpha + c_1 \\
&= e^{i\frac{2k\pi}{\alpha-1}\alpha}(z_n^{(2)})^\alpha + e^{i\frac{2k\pi}{\alpha-1}} c_2, \\
&= e^{i\frac{2k\pi}{\alpha-1}}[(z_n^{(2)})^\alpha + c_2], \\
&= e^{i\frac{2k\pi}{\alpha-1}} z_{n+1}^{(2)}.
\end{aligned}
$$

for $z_n^{(1)} = e^{i\frac{2k\pi}{\alpha-1}} z_n^{(2)}$. Similarly, if $z_n^{(1)} = e^{i\frac{2k\pi}{\alpha-1}} \bar{z}_n^{(2)}$, then $z_{n+1}^{(1)} = e^{i\frac{2k\pi}{\alpha-1}} \bar{z}_{n+1}^{(2)}$. Thus, $|z_n^{(1)}| = |z_n^{(2)}|$ for all n. $\square$

From Theorem 1, we obtain the following results on the structure of $M(\alpha)$. For a complex number $c \neq 0$, let $\arg(c) = \theta$, where $c = re^{i\theta}$ with $-\pi \leq \theta < \pi$.

Corollary 2 *A c−plane fractal image for $M(\alpha)$ is symmetric about real axis. The same structure repeats around the origin by an angle $\frac{2\pi}{|\alpha-1|}$ for $-\pi \leq \arg(c) < \pi$.*

Proof. By Theorem 1, $|f_{\alpha,c}^n(c)| = |f_{\alpha,\bar{c}}^n(\bar{c})|$ for all n. Therefore, $M(\alpha)$ has the symmetry about real axis. Now take any pair of points c_1 and c_2 such that $\arg(c_1) - \arg(c_2) = \frac{2\pi}{\alpha-1}$ and $|c_1| = |c_2|$. From Theorem 1, $|f_{\alpha,c_1}^n(c_1)| = |f_{\alpha,c_2}^n(c_2)|$ for all n. Therefore, the same structure repeats by an angle $\frac{2\pi}{|\alpha-1|}$ in the graphic image of $M(\alpha)$. $\square$

Corollary 3 *For $-\pi \leq \arg(c) < \pi$, the portion of a c−plane fractal image for $M(\alpha)$ in the angular space $0 \leq \theta \leq \frac{\pi}{|\alpha-1|}$ is symmetric about the ray $\theta = \frac{\pi}{|\alpha-1|}$ and repeatedly appears by an angle of a multiple of $\frac{2\pi}{|\alpha-1|}$.*

Proof. Let c_1 and c_2 be symmetrically located about the ray $\theta = \frac{\pi}{|\alpha-1|}$ in the angular space $0 \leq \theta \leq \frac{2\pi}{|\alpha-1|}$. Then $c_1 = re^{i(\frac{\pi}{\alpha-1}+\psi)}$ and $c_2 = re^{i(\frac{\pi}{\alpha-1}-\psi)}$ for some ψ. By Theorem 1, $|f_{\alpha,c_1}^n(c_1)| = |f_{\alpha,c_2}^n(c_2)|$ for all n. Therefore, $M(\alpha)$ has the symmetry about the ray $\theta = \frac{\pi}{|\alpha-1|}$. By Corollary 2, the portion of $M(\alpha)$ in the angular space $0 \leq \theta \leq \frac{\pi}{|\alpha-1|}$ repeatedly appears by an angle $\frac{2\pi}{|\alpha-1|}$. $\square$

The characteristic pattern of a repeating structure, stated in Corollary 3, can better be visualized by properly characterizing its bounding rays. The following two theorems give natural ways for identifying these rays.

Theorem 4 *Let $\alpha > 1$. The portion of a ray of angle θ lying in $M(\alpha)$ is shortest if $\theta = \frac{2k\pi}{\alpha-1}$, where k is an integer so that $-\pi \leq \theta < \pi$.*

Proof. Letting $c = re^{i\theta}$, we can easily see by the triangle inequality that

$$|f_{\alpha,c}^n(c)| \le f_{\alpha,r}^n(r) \tag{6}$$

for all natural numbers n. We claim that the equality holds if and only if $\theta = \frac{2k\pi}{\alpha-1}$ for some integer k. For $c = re^{i\theta}$, $c^\alpha + c = e^{i\theta}(r^\alpha e^{i\theta(\alpha-1)} + r)$. Therefore, $|c^\alpha + c| = r^\alpha + r$ if $\theta = \frac{2k\pi}{\alpha-1}$, and its converse is also true. Setting $\theta = \frac{2k\pi}{\alpha-1}$,

$$
\begin{aligned}
f_{\alpha,c}(c) &= c^\alpha + c = (r^\alpha + r)e^{i\frac{2k\pi}{\alpha-1}} = f_{\alpha,r}(r)e^{i\frac{2k\pi}{\alpha-1}}, \quad \text{or} \\
f_{\alpha,c}(c) &= f_{\alpha,r}(r)e^{i\frac{2k\pi}{\alpha-1}}.
\end{aligned}
$$

We can inductively obtain

$$f_{\alpha,c}^n(c) = f_{\alpha,r}^n(r)e^{i\frac{2k\pi}{\alpha-1}} \quad \text{for all } n.$$

Therefore, our claim holds true. From the definition of $M(\alpha)$, the portion of a ray of angle θ lying in $M(\alpha)$ is shortest when $\theta = \frac{2k\pi}{\alpha-1}$. □

Theorem 5 *If $\alpha < 0$, then the ray of angle $\theta = \frac{2k\pi}{\alpha-1}$ is contained in $M(\alpha)$ where k is an integer so that $-\pi \le \theta < \pi$,*

Proof. Let $c = re^{i\theta}$ where $r > 0$ and $\theta = \frac{2k\pi}{\alpha-1}$. By the similar argument as in the proof of Theorem 4,

$$f_{\alpha,c}^n(c) = f_{\alpha,r}^n(r)e^{i\frac{2k\pi}{\alpha-1}}$$

for all n. Now, by induction, we will show that

$$r \le f_{\alpha,r}^n(r) \le r^\alpha + r \tag{7}$$

for all natural number n. We note $r \le f_\alpha(r) \le r^\alpha + r$. For induction we suppose that $r \le f_{\alpha,r}^i(r) \le r^\alpha + r$ is true for some $i \ge 1$. Then,

$$r \le (r^\alpha + r)^\alpha + r \le f_{\alpha,r}^{i+1}(r) = (f_{\alpha,r}^i(r))^\alpha + r \le r^\alpha + r.$$

Therefore, inequality (7) is true for all natural number n. In particular, $\{f_{\alpha,r}^n(r)\}_{n=0}^\infty$ is bounded by $r^\alpha + r$. Thus, the orbit $\{f_{\alpha,c}^n(c)\}_{n=0}^\infty$ is also bounded. Therefore, $M(\alpha)$ contains all points on the ray of $c = re^{i\theta}$ where $r > 0$ and $\theta = \frac{2k\pi}{\alpha-1}$ for some integer k so that $-\pi \le \theta < \pi$. □

From Corollary 3, the portion of a c−plane fractal image for $M(\alpha)$ in the angular space $0 \le \theta \le \frac{2\pi}{|\alpha-1|}$ repeats around the origin. That is, a c−plane fractal image can be obtained by rotating this portion $|\alpha - 1|$ times by angle $\frac{2\pi}{|\alpha-1|}$ for an integer α if $\alpha < 0$ or $\alpha > 1$. Therefore, for $\alpha > 1$, a ray of angle $\theta = \frac{2k\pi}{\alpha-1}$ for an integer k is a bounding ray of this repeating pattern. Furthermore, Theorems 4 and 5 provide a way to visually identify such a ray since its intersection with $M(\alpha)$ is shortest, i.e., the intersection point of a bounding ray with the boundary of $M(\alpha)$ is closer to the origin than any point on the boundary.

A graphical representation of $M(\alpha)$ exhibits nice repeating patterns such as lobular and satellite structures [Guja91]. For $\alpha > 1$, a c−plane fractal image consists of a number of lobe-shaped patterns called lobes, and thus is said to have a lobular structure (see Figure 1(a)). On the other hand, if $\alpha < 0$, it looks like a constellation. That is, it consists of a main planet and a number of planetary arrangements each with a central planet surrounded by clusters of satellites, which is called a satellite structure (see Figure 1(b)).

Gujar et al. [Guja91] made six conjectures on these structures, which can be summarized as follows: as $|\alpha|$ increases, the number of such structures also increases; a c−plane fractal image is symmetric about the real axis; an embryonic (incomplete) structure emerges around the negative real axis for non-integral α. For detail, refer to [Guja91].

Now, we are ready to verify these conjectures. The lobular (satellite) structures are separated by the rays of argument $\theta = \frac{2k\pi}{\alpha - 1}$ by Theorems 4 and 5 where k is an integer so that $-\pi \leq \theta < \pi$. These rays are shown as red lines in Figures 2 and 3. For example, see Figure 2(b) with $\alpha = 4.33$. The lobular structure in the angular space $0 \leq \theta \leq \frac{2\pi}{3.33}$ also appears in the angular space $-\frac{2\pi}{3.33} \leq \theta \leq 0$. Thus two structures are obtained, and the remaining part in the angular spaces $-\pi \leq \theta < -\frac{2\pi}{3.33}$ and $\frac{2\pi}{3.33} < \theta < \pi$ shows incomplete lobular structures, called embryonic lobular structures. Figure 3(c) with $\alpha = -3.77$ shows four complete satellite structures in angular spaces $-\frac{4\pi}{4.77} \leq \theta \leq -\frac{2\pi}{4.77}$, $-\frac{2\pi}{4.77} \leq \theta \leq 0$, $0 \leq \theta \leq \frac{2\pi}{4.77}$, and $\frac{2\pi}{4.77} \leq \theta \leq \frac{4\pi}{4.77}$. The embryonic structures are located in the angular spaces $-\pi \leq \theta < -\frac{4\pi}{4.77}$, and $\frac{4\pi}{4.77} < \theta < \pi$. It is interesting to observe that an embryonic structure grows to be a complete one as α increases to approach an integer.

For a general exponent, we see that each lobular (satellite) structure occupies an angular space of angle $\frac{2\pi}{|\alpha - 1|}$. If $k(\alpha)$ is the largest natural number such that $\frac{2k(\alpha)}{|\alpha - 1|}\pi \leq \pi$ (or $2k(\alpha) \leq |\alpha - 1|$), then a computer-generated image for $M(\alpha)$ has $2k(\alpha)$ complete lobular (satellite) structures if $\alpha > 1$ (resp. $\alpha < 0$). The embryonic structure occupies an angular space of angle $2\pi - 2k(\alpha)\frac{2\pi}{|\alpha - 1|}$ about the negative real axis. Figure 2(b) with $\alpha = 4.33$ illustrates two complete structures and Figure 3(b) with $\alpha = -3.33$ also shows four complete structures. If α is an even integer, these embryonic structures are merged into one complete structure because of the symmetry of a structure described in Corollary 3. Its example is shown in Figures 2(a) and 3(d) with $\alpha = 4$ and -4, respectively. Figures 2(d) and 3(a) each have four complete structures, and Figure 3(d) shows five complete structures. When α is an odd integer, the symmetry about the imaginary axis can also be observed in Figures 2(d) and 3(a). It can be explained using the angular symmetry about the rays of angle $\frac{\pi}{2}$ and $-\frac{\pi}{2}$ given by Corollary 3. These facts verify the six conjectures [Guja91].

We note that the choice of the starting point z_0 of an orbit $\{f_{\alpha,c}^n(z_0)\}_{n=0}^{\infty}$ is very important for $\alpha < 0$. Differently from [Guja91], we choose $z_0 = c$ regardless of α as explained in section 2. As illustrated in Figure 4, resulting images look cleaner and also better reflects visual characteristics which are proved in this section.

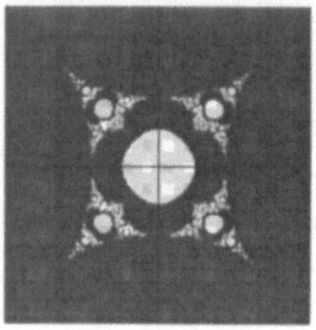 

(a) $\alpha = -3.0$ and $z_0 = c$ (b) $\alpha = -3.0$ and $z_0 = 0.5 + 0.5i$

Fig. 4. The dependency of a $c-$plane fractal image on starting points z_0

Instead of setting $\phi_0 = -\pi$ in representation (1), we can choose other values for ϕ_0. In this case, the visual characteristics of $M(\alpha)$ is little different from that for $\phi_0 = -\pi$ as illustrated in Figure 5. In particular, the symmetry about the real axis may not be satisfied.

4. CHARACTERISTICS OF $Z-$PLANE FRACTAL IMAGES

In this section, we first derive a theorem on the behavior of an orbit $\{f_{\alpha,c}^n(z)\}_{n=0}^{\infty}$ and then explain six conjectures on $z-$plane fractal images using this theorem.

 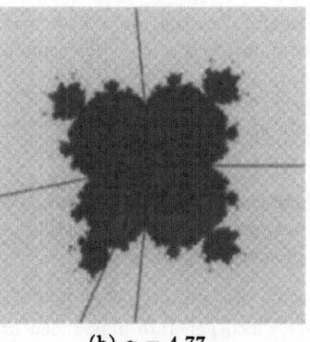

(a) $\alpha = 4.0$ (b) $\alpha = 4.77$

Fig. 5. $C-$plane fractal images when $\phi_0 = -2$

Theorem 6 *Let two points $z_0^{(1)}$ and $z_0^{(2)}$ have the same modulus, i.e., $z_0^{(j)} = re^{i\theta_j}$ for $j = 1,2$. Then, $|f_{\alpha,c}^n(z_0^{(1)})| = |f_{\alpha,c}^n(z_0^{(2)})|$ for all n and for all c if and only if $\theta_1 - \theta_2 = \frac{2k\pi}{\alpha}$ for some integer k.*

Proof. Suppose that $|f_{\alpha,c}^n(z_0^{(1)})| = |f_{\alpha,c}^n(z_0^{(2)})|$ for all n and for all $c = \rho e^{i\phi}$. Since

$$f_{\alpha,c}(z_0^{(j)}) = r^\alpha e^{i\alpha\theta_j} + \rho e^{i\phi}$$
$$= e^{i\phi}(r^\alpha e^{i(\alpha\theta_j - \phi)} + \rho),$$

the condition $|f_{\alpha,c}(z_0^{(1)})| = |f_{\alpha,c}(z_0^{(2)})|$ for $\rho > 0$ implies that either the points $r^\alpha e^{i(\alpha\theta_j - \phi)}$ for $j = 1, 2$ coincide or they are located symmetrically about the real axis. Therefore, either

$$(\alpha\theta_1 - \phi) - (\alpha\theta_2 - \phi) = 2k\pi, \quad \text{or} \tag{8}$$
$$(\alpha\theta_1 - \phi) + (\alpha\theta_2 - \phi) = 2k\pi, \tag{9}$$

where k is an integer. Since equation (9) cannot be satisfied for all ϕ, we must have $\alpha(\theta_1 - \theta_2) = 2k\pi$. Conversely if $\theta_1 - \theta_2 = \frac{2k\pi}{\alpha}$ for some integer k, then we actually have $f_{\alpha,c}^n(z_0^{(1)}) = f_{\alpha,c}^n(z_0^{(2)})$ for any n and for all c. $\square$

A $z-$plane fractal image for $K(\alpha,c)$ also exhibits the similar repeating structures such as lobular and satellite structures as explained for $M(\alpha)$ in section 3. Gujar et al. [Guja92, Vang90] raised another six conjectures on these structures. Since these conjectures are almost the same as those for $c-$plane images except for the symmetry about the real axis, we do not repeat their summary as in the previous section.

From Theorem 6, we see that $K(\alpha,c)$ consists of a repeating pattern occupying the angular space of angle $\frac{2\pi}{|\alpha|}$. A complete lobular (satellite) structure is originally assumed to lie in the angular spaces $\pi - \frac{2\pi}{|\alpha|} \leq \theta \leq \pi$ or $-\pi \leq \theta \leq -\pi + \frac{2\pi}{|\alpha|}$ depending on the integer part of the value of α [Guja92, Vang90]. However, this distinction does not look much meaningful. Thus, we assume that a repeating lobular (satellite) structure lies in the angular space $\pi - \frac{2\pi}{|\alpha|} \leq \theta \leq \pi$ regardless of α. We note that the same result can be obtained even for the other case. A computer-generated image for $K(\alpha,c)$ has a number of structures with one incomplete structure below the negative real axis. As an example, Figure 6(c) with $\alpha = 4.77$ and $c = 0.5 + 0.5i$ gives four complete lobular structures in angular spaces $\pi - \frac{2\pi}{4.77} \leq \theta < \pi, \pi - \frac{4\pi}{4.77} \leq \theta \leq \pi - \frac{2\pi}{4.77}, \pi - \frac{6\pi}{4.77} \leq \theta \leq \pi - \frac{4\pi}{4.77}$, and $\pi - \frac{8\pi}{4.77} \leq \theta \leq \pi - \frac{6\pi}{4.77}$, respectively. The remaining angular space $-\pi \leq \theta \leq \pi - \frac{8\pi}{4.77}$ contains an embryonic structure. Similarly, Figure 7(a) with $\alpha = -3.33$ and $c = 0.5 + 0.5i$ shows three satellite structures with an embryonic one below the negative real axis. Figure 7(d) exhibits one more complete structure since $\alpha = -4.5$. In general, it is easy to see that a $z-$plane fractal image has $k(\alpha)$ complete and one embryonic structures, where $k(\alpha)$ is a largest natural number such that $\pi - \frac{2k(\alpha)\pi}{|\alpha|} \geq -\pi$ (or $k(\alpha) \leq |\alpha|$). This property can easily be observed in other images in Figures 6 and 7. Hence, we verify the six conjectures on $z-$plane fractal images [Guja92, Vang90]. As a final comment, a repeating structure is not so visually natural in a z-plane fractal image as it is in a c-plane fractal image since the analogues of Theorem 4 and 5 do not hold true.

5. CONCLUDING REMARKS

The family of a function $f_{\alpha,c}(z) = z^{\alpha} + c$ provide two kind of fractal images, c-plane fractal images and z-plane fractal images, depending on whether a fractal image is defined on the domain of parameter c or the domain of complex variable z.

$M(\alpha)$ is bounded in the disk of radius $2^{\frac{1}{\alpha-1}}$ centered at the origin for $\alpha > 1$. When $\alpha < 0$ and $|c| > 2$, all points which generate unbounded orbits are contained in the disk of radius 1 centered at the origin. The orbit behavior of $\{f_{\alpha,c}^n(c)\}_{n=0}^{\infty}$ is characterized and results in three theorems and two corollaries. For two points c_1 and c_2 having the same modulus, $|f_{\alpha,c_1}^n(c_1)| = |f_{\alpha,c_1}^n(c_1)|$ for all n whenever $\arg(c_1) \pm \arg(c_2) = \frac{2k\pi}{\alpha-1}$ for an integer k. The portion of $M(\alpha)$ for $\alpha > 1$ lying in the ray of $\arg(c) = \frac{2k\pi}{\alpha-1}$ for an integer k is shortest. We also show that $M(\alpha)$ is symmetric about the ray of angle $\frac{k\pi}{\alpha-1}$ for an integer k and contains several lobular (satellite) structures each having the angular space of $\frac{2\pi}{|\alpha-1|}$. These results verify the conjectures on c-plane fractal images.

$K(\alpha,c)$ is also bounded in the disk of radius $r = \max\{2^{\frac{1}{\alpha-1}}, |c|\}$ centered at the origin for $\alpha > 1$. When $\alpha < 0$ and $|c| \geq 2$, all points outside the disk of radius 1 centered at the origin are guaranteed to lie in $K(\alpha,c)$. An image for $K(\alpha,c)$ consists of several lobular (satellite) structures each having the angular space of angle $\frac{2\pi}{|\alpha|}$ and one embryonic structure below the negative real axis. When a complete structure is defined as a shape lying in the angular space $\pi - \frac{2\pi}{|\alpha|} \leq \arg(c) \leq \pi$, the number of complete structures is $\lfloor |\alpha| \rfloor$. Hence, the conjectures on z-plane fractal images can be verified.

ACKNOWLEDGEMENTS

This research was partially supported by TGRC.

REFERENCES

[Barn88] M. Barnsley (1988), *Fractals Everywhere*, Academic Press, New York.

[Blan84] P. Blanchard, Complex Analytic Dynamics on the Rieman Sphere, *Bull. Amer. Math. Soc.*, Vol. 11, pp. 85-141.

[Deva89] R.L. Devaney (1989), *An Introduction to Chaotic Dynamical Systems*, Addison-Wesley, Menlo Park.

[Entw89] I.D. Entwistle (1989), Julia Set art and Fractals in the Complex Plane, *Computer & Graphics* 13(3), pp. 389-392.

[Guja91] U.G. Gujar, and V.C. Bhavsar, Fractals from $z \leftarrow z^{\alpha} + c$ in the Complex Plane, *Computer & Graphics* 15(3), pp. 441-449.

[Guja92] U.G. Gujar, V.C. Bhavsar, and N. Vangala (1992), Fractal Images from $z \leftarrow z^{\alpha} + c$ in the Complex z-Plane, *Computer & Graphics* 16(1), pp. 45-49.

[Mand82] B.B. Mandelbrot (1982), *The Fractal Geometry of Nature*, W.H. Freeman and Co., New York.

[Peit86] H.-O. Peitgen and P.H. Richter (1986), *The Beauty of Fractals*, Springer Verlag, New York.

[Peit88] H.-O. Peitgen and D. Saupe (Eds) (1988), *The Science of Fractal Images*, Springer Verlag, New York.

[Vang90] N. Vangala, U.G. Gujar, and V.C. Bhavsar (1990), Julia Sets of $z \leftarrow z^{\alpha} + c$, *Computer Graphics International '90*, pp. 133-145.

355

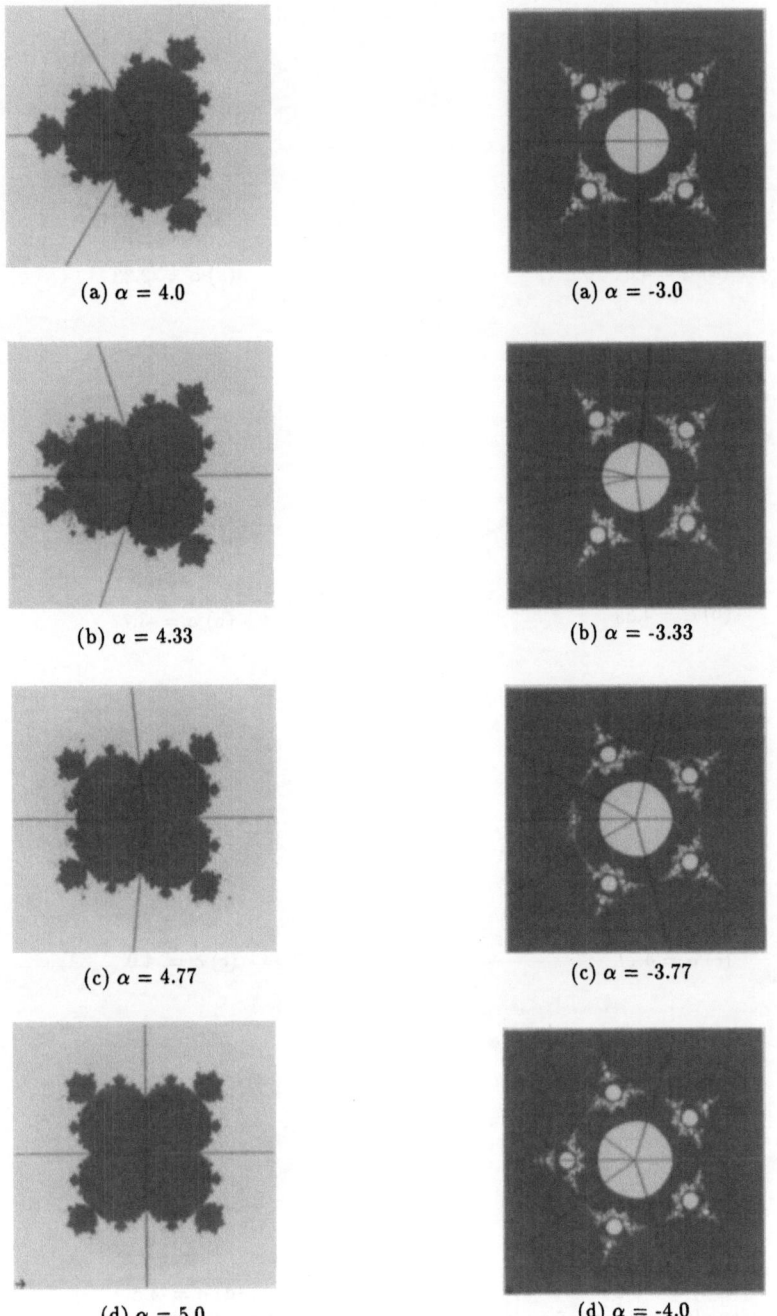

(a) $\alpha = 4.0$

(a) $\alpha = -3.0$

(b) $\alpha = 4.33$

(b) $\alpha = -3.33$

(c) $\alpha = 4.77$

(c) $\alpha = -3.77$

(d) $\alpha = 5.0$

(d) $\alpha = -4.0$

Fig. 2. c−plane fractal images for $\alpha > 1$

Fig. 3. c−plane fractal images for $\alpha < 0$

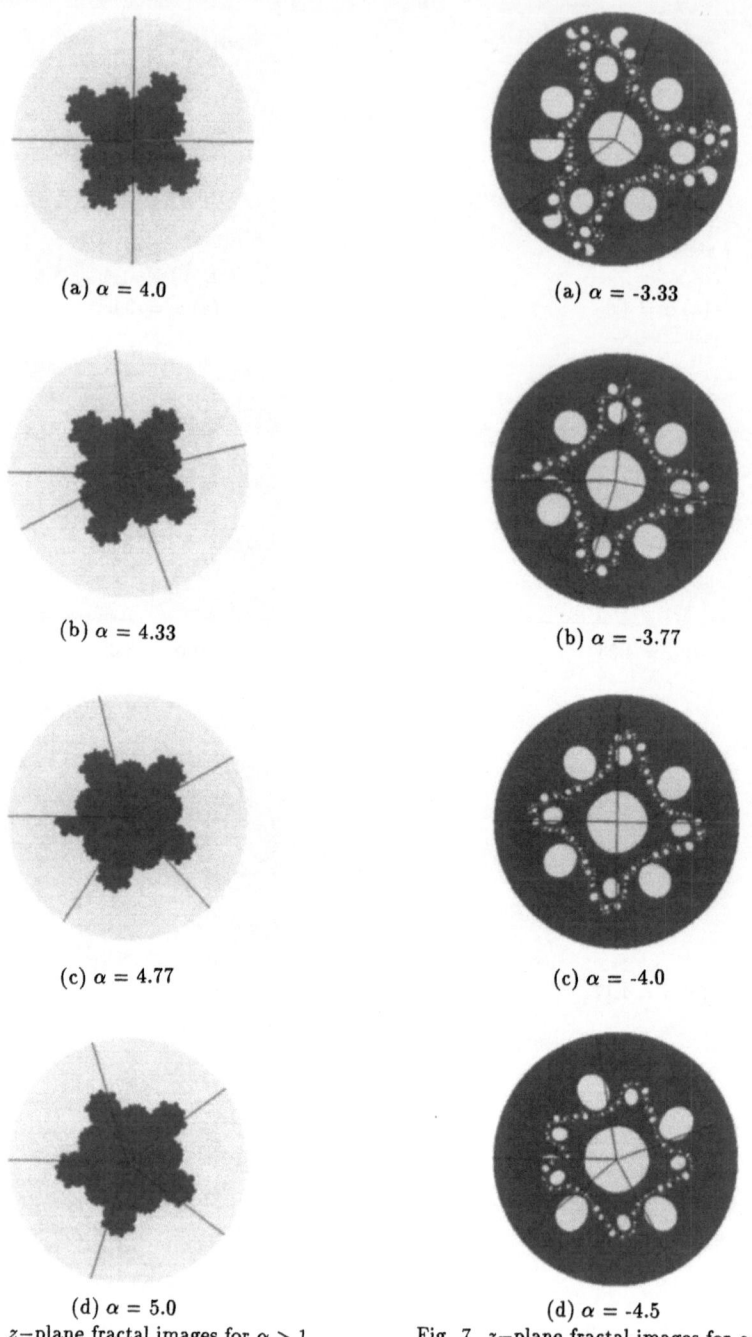

(a) $\alpha = 4.0$

(a) $\alpha = -3.33$

(b) $\alpha = 4.33$

(b) $\alpha = -3.77$

(c) $\alpha = 4.77$

(c) $\alpha = -4.0$

(d) $\alpha = 5.0$
Fig. 6. z-plane fractal images for $\alpha > 1$
and $c = 0.5 + 0.5i$

(d) $\alpha = -4.5$
Fig. 7. z-plane fractal images for $\alpha < 0$
and $c = 0.5 + 0.5i$

Young Bong Kim received the B.S. degree in Computer & Statistics from the Seoul National University in 1987, and the M.S. degree in Computer Science from the Korea Advanced Institute of Science and Technology. He is currently pursuing his Ph.D. degree at KAIST. His research interests include computer animation, geometric modeling and user-interface.

Hyoung Seok Kim received the B.S. degree in Mathematics from the Yonsei University in 1990 and the M.S. degree in Mathematics from the KAIST in 1992, respectively. He is currently pursuing his Ph.D. degree in Mathematics at KAIST. His research interests include geometric modeling and complex analysis.

Ho Kyung Kim received her B.S. degree in Computer Science from Ewha Womans University in 1992. She is currently a M.S. student at KAIST. Her research interests include computer animation and human-body modeling.

Hwang Soo Kim received the B.S. degree in electrical engineering from the Seoul National University in 1975, and the M.S. and Ph.D. degrees in electrical engineering and computer science from the University of Michigan at Ann Arbor in 1982 and 1988, respectively. He is now an assistant professor in Department of Computer Science at the Kyung Pook National University. His interests include computer vision, neural networks, and computer graphics.
Address: Department of Computer Science, Kyung Pook National University, Taegu 702-701, Korea.

Hong Oh Kim is currently a professor in Department of Mathematics at KAIST of Korea. He received his Ph.D. degree in Mathematics from the University of Wisconsin in 1982. His research interests include complex analysis, iteration theory and applied analysis.
Address: Department of Mathematics, Korea Advanced Institute of Science and Technology, 373-1, Kusong-dong, Yusung-gu, Taejon 305-701, Korea.

Sung Yong Shin received the B.S. degree in industrial engineering in 1970 from Hanyang University, Seoul, Korea, and the M.S. and Ph.D. degrees in industrial and operations engineering from the University of Michigan, Ann arbor, USA, in 1983 and 1986, respectively. He is presently an associate professor in Department of Computer Science at KAIST. His research interests include computer graphics and computational geometry.
Address: Department of Computer Science, Korea Advanced Institute of Science and Technology, 373-1, Kusong-dong, Yusung-gu, Taejon 305-701, Korea.

Creating Virtual Fur and Hair Styles for Synthetic Actors

Agnes Daldegan and Nadia Magnenat Thalmann

ABSTRACT

In this paper, we discuss both the aesthetic and technical concerns involved in the creation of synthetic hair and fur using our Styler and Hair Rendering software. Both pieces of software described in this paper were originally conceived for creating any kind of hair and rendering images of natural-looking hair. Taking advantage of the impressive realism of these images, we present in this paper an exploration of the software's capacity to improve the appearence and quality of hair in synthetic human images, one of our main research areas.

In Section 2. we summarize some of the approaches to creating synthetic hairstyles. In the two following sections we describe the basic processes of the Styler and Hair Rendering programs for modeling and rendering hair, their technical improvements and aesthetics related to the main interface's limitations. In the last section we present all the steps involved in making hair styles, beards, moustaches, furs, hair rendering with facial texture mapping, and hair growth animation. The images resulting from this interactive work are shown on their corresponding section.

1. INTRODUCTION

In synthetic human performance animation, any research attempting to reach the corresponding realism of physical and biological human features also faces the problem of aesthetics. In synthetic human animation, traditional research is basically oriented towards the following subjects: physical characteristics of the human body and personal physical features; physical-movement related to skin deformations in walk and grasping; facial expressions; and behavioral movement. In these research areas, all plans of creating a "look" in terms of cloths and hair styles are equally addressed. Hence, the natural aesthetic aspects of the human being require not only meeting the challenge of synthesis and animation of clothes or hair styles, but also allowing the variety and originality of the different physical effects and their appearance observed in nature.

Originally, our program was conceived to reach principally good and realistic effects in rendering hair. Its first satisfying results led to efforts in hair style elaboration, moustaches and beards and diversified application: cloths and actor's limbs, rather than a synthetic human's scalp or face. For these purposes some basic modifications were made to facilitate artistic design. Although, as frequently happens, the creative characteristics of the aesthetic experience often overcomes the technical resources of the means itself (Nadin, 1991). However this important remark must be understood, since the aesthetic experiment can effectively contribute to software technology evolution and development as it poses new problems which require new approaches.

This paper describes, in fact, the most recent stages of the evolution of our **Styler** and **Hair Rendering** programs after scores of design challenges and modifications.

2. APPROACHES TO CREATING SYNTHETIC FUR AND HAIR STYLES

Creating fur and hair styles even in artificial beards, moustaches and furs is a complex and meticulous task involving the treatment of numerous segments of hair, their placement on the surface, form, material features and their dynamic aspects.

The first works in synthetic hairs were conceived to render fur-like volumes (Csuri et al. 1979) and furry animals (Miller 1988). Concerning the synthesis of human hair, some recent models were developed to create and animate hair styles.

Watanabe and Suenaga (Watanabe et al. 1992) presented a trigonal prism model of human hair. Each individual hair is a series of short trigonal prisms. Several kinds of hair can be created changing the parameters of length, direction vector, thickness, twist angle, and number of trigonal prisms. In order to facilitate the design work, hairs are grouped in wisps. To make the desired hair style, the user can change parameters and assign values to the wisp model. The rendering method is based on sellecting areas for the backlighting effect and using a doble z-buffer.The animation is determined by defining a parabola trajectory of wisps in order to approximate their location according to the initial velocities and acceleration. As an example of their model, they present various images of hair styles with varied wisp parameters, as well as a sequence of hair animation.

Rosenblum, Carlson and Tripp III (Rosenblum et al. 1991) developed a technique to simulate human hair structure and dynamics. The hair structure is defined by connected straight cylindrical segments with a fixed width and it is modeled as a linear series of masses, springs and hinges. Hairs are rendered using z-buffers and animated by a simple dynamic simulation with a physically-based approach. As examples they present colored furry doughnuts, cylinders covered with strands, sequences of long hair animation on spheres, and moustashes with different modeling parameters on parallelepipeds.

Anjyo, Usami and Kurihara (Anjyo et al. 1992) improved a physically based modeling approach to compute the dynamic behavior of hair. For this purpose their hairstyle model consists of three basic steps. The definition of an ellipsoidal hull for the head model. The calculation of hair bending. Finally, the adjustment of the hair style by cutting and modifying hair. This methodology offers satisfactory tools to make different hairstyles based on constraints like gravity and hair collision detection. As examples of design work they present some styles of straight hair.

LeBlanc, Turner and Thalmann (Leblanc et al. 1991b) developed a system to create synthetic hair and fur styles, which consists of two independent modules for modeling and rendering hair: the **Styler** and **Hair Rendering** programs. Descriptions and the design work are presented in the following sections.

3. HAIR MODELING PROCESS

To create realistic images of hair styles and furry objects it is necessary to define an appropriate file of all individual hair curves, containing their hair segment geometry and material aspects. In the hair modeler program **Styler**, the elaboration of such file characteristics follows two main steps:

- hair curve creation
- hair style definition

The hair segment data base generated by these designing steps will be used in the rendering process. The rendering program will generate realistic hair shadows on the surface and among the hairs themselves.

3.1. Designing Types of Hair Curves

To create images of human hair a complex modeler is need, given the fact that human hair styles are much more complex than furry balls and require more modeling flexibility. The hair modeling program **Styler** was originated from the SurfMan surface generator (LeBlanc et al. 1991b). The **Styler** program assigns to every polygon of an SM surface the information of the type of hair, the basic curve or hair segment, its orientation, and many stochastic parameters.

Each polygon has a curve identifier created by cylindrical straight segments joined by defining a sequence of points in the 3D space. The three dimensional definition of the hair curve gives the designer more flexibility and control to the final configuration of the hair style.

The process of designing hair curves to create a style:

- start the hair curve set by selecting "new" from the interface panel;
- create each curve by defining its number identifier and selecting the option "add curve."
- create straight segments, with the option "insert point." The segments of these in-between points can be moved, split or deleted when a new hair segment or curve is created or modified. These facilities allow the creation of any kind of hair format. Fig. 1 shows some steps of defining hair curves.

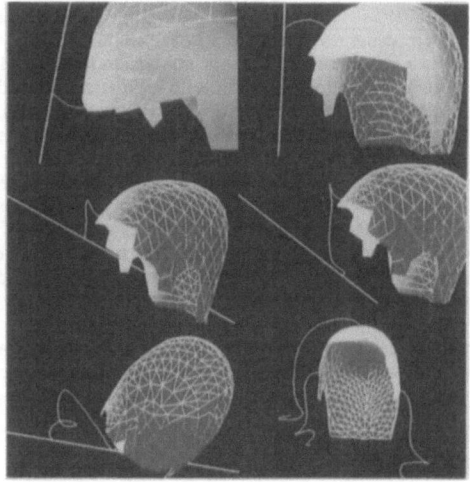

Fig.1 The creation of a hair curve by defining points in 3D space.

3.2. Creating Furry Objects and Human Hair Styles

The **Styler's** modeling flexibility offers the designer the possibility to create a wide range of hair styles by assigning some specific information to the selected polygons (LeBlanc et al. 1991). The hair curves are distributed on the surface's triangular mesh, conforming the hair style idealized by the designer. By *default*, the program assigns to each polygon of the mesh a regular hair configuration. The final hair style is reached by changing the *default* value of the following parameters for the selected polygons:

- material;
- jitter;
- hair orientation;
- scale value;
- density;
- angle variation;
- a seed for the random generator.

The material parameter is a color identifier for the hair set of each polygon. The jitter parameter defines a random base location for the hair on the polygon. Angle variation assigns a random angle applied to the tangent vector to the set of hair on the polygon. The scale value gives a random scale for each segment of hair in the selected set. The density value means the number of hairs per unit area; generally a human hair style has approximately 100,000 to 150,000 hairs. Fig. 2 shows the employment of the last five parameters. Finally the seed generator defines the final size for the hair style (fig. 3).

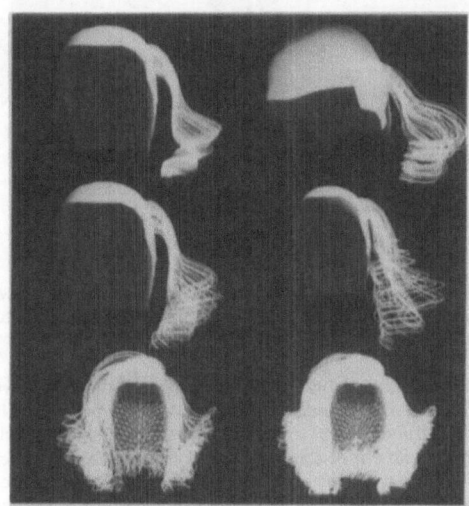

Fig. 2 The employment of different parameter values in a hair style.

The surface for hair modelling should only contain polygons where the hair will grow. The surface for the new hair file should be first prepared using the SurfMan sculpting software. Once started, the surface can't be modified or moved, otherwise the hairs may not follow along as expected. It happens because each polygon of the SM surface has a database, as described above, that parameterizes hair growth, and a change in the number or orientation of the polygons will cause the drawing order to change and random values for each hair will differ.

To solve the problem of movement of the SM surface after the hair style is ready, we calculate the binormal vector equal to the cross vector of the new triangle normal and the old tangent vector, and calculate a new tangent vector as the cross vector of the normal and binormal. This method was used to solve the constraint of rendering more than one ready hair style placed differently.

To give the designer flexibility for modeling hair for any kind of object and in order to create different kinds of styles, all synthetic objects can be converted to the SM format and later used in **Styler** for modelling the respective hair file segment.

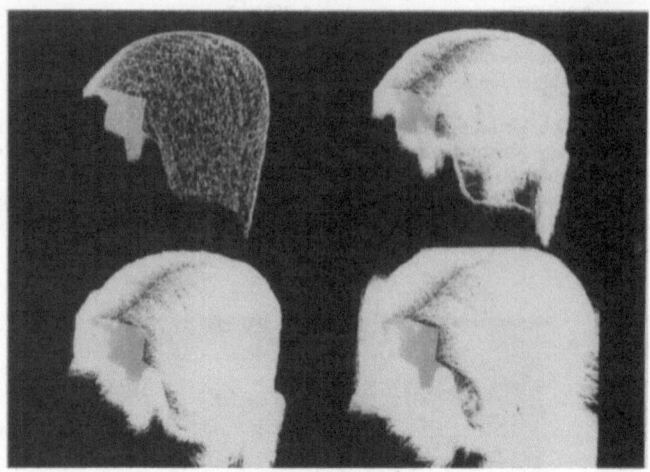

Fig. 3 Growing hair.

3.3. Design Resolutions to the Technical Limitations

Although some structural problems were solved in order to facilitate the design work, and the new modeler version gives more flexibility to the designer, there are still some functional constraints to be solved in order to achieve a better design performance in terms of quality and time.

The most significant constraints are the problems of hair curve creation and growth. The creation of a curve is directly related to the tangent of the assigned polygon, in other words, the direction of a curve follows the curvature of the surface. If the designer wants to create a straight hair style, for example, he or she should pay attention to the assignment of the curves and respective parameters to the polygons of the scalp surface. The same curve cannot be assigned to a polygon at the end of the scalp surface, near to the neck, as the same way as at the top of the head, otherwise it will grow inside. If the designer wants to create a curly hair curve, he or she will need to define several points in order to construct a round curve as desired, which means several straight segments for the hair segment data base.

However, in design work, the designer's aesthetic judgement can creatively solve these problems by adding intermediate curves, making a smooth variation for the hair style around the surface curvature, or making the layers of polygons grow with the same hair curve identifier at the different times on the whole surface.

Some simple technical solutions for the **Styler** interface could include, allowing the designer to select bigger regions on the surface, in order to substitute the curve assignment to a polygon unity, or creating of specific hair curves for a spline by defining control points for each extremity of these regions. The program would automatically interpolate the format, direction and size of all these spline curves in order to obtain the final hair style, with a determined hair density choosen by the designer. In this way the program could save memory allocation and clarify the hair curve format by the definition of the control points, and also save time design by the automatic interpolation of hair curves.

Other possibilities for providing the integration between technical and aesthetic research would be a powerful interface modeler for the specialized designer. It means, a hair design interface that could emulate real tools like brushes and scissors with physical aspect constraints of hair gravity (Watanabe et al. 1989), (Anjyo et al. 1992), hair thickness, hair resistance and specific type. These tools could at once integrate direct and realistic interaction manipulation and designer creativity in real time, for the creation of furry objects and synthetic actor hair styles.

4. HAIR RENDERING PROCESS

The **Hair Rendering** module presents a more complex program structure of image rendering control and some secondary tools for aiding the design work in rendering scenes with furry objects and hair styles. In the program "each individual cylindrical hair is rendered by the technique of pixel blending combined with Z-buffer and shadow buffer information from the scene to yield a final anti-aliased image with soft shadows" (LeBlanc et al. 1991b).

The render process encompasses two main parts:

- The hairless scene, where the shadows of normal objects are calculated by a modified version of the shadow buffer algorithm of **Rayshade** (by Craig Kolb). First, the new raytracing version generates the shadow buffers from light sources and then generates an intermediate step of the scene with full shadows coming also from the hair.

- The hair blending on the hairless scene, calculated by the special hair rendering program to manipulate all shadow buffers for the scene.

These two parts of the rendering process involve the following gradual steps:

- Create a data base hair segments in the hair modeler **Styler**.

- Define all shadows for the scene from shadow buffers:
  - create one scene shadow buffer for each light source projected on the scene model description;
  - create one hair shadow buffer for each light source projected on the hair model;
  - create one single composite shadow buffer for each light source from the composition of the depth maps for the scene shadow buffer and hair shadow buffer;

- Render hairless objects with **Rayshade** using all shadow buffers by generating the scene image and it's Z-buffer.

- Compose the hair on the hairless image by blending the hair segments into the scene image.

As some undesirable effects of shadow rendering can appear sometimes from the incorrect definition of light source parameters, some secondary tools address this kind of problem. These tools allow the designer to control the visibility and the composed shadow buffers, in order to determine shadow quality when defining light source, yielding final images with hair and full shadows.

Another useful adaptation of the rendering software is the possibility of rendering in the same scene various hair styles with their own rendering features, which facilitates their independent elaboration and combination.

5. AESTHETIC INVESTIGATION IN HAIR AND FUR INTEGRATING SYNTHETIC ACTOR'S RESEARCH

The last two sections described the basic working of the **Styler** and **Hair Rendering** software, the principal commands and their problems, technical solution and creative design resolution. However creating hair styles or fur for different types of object means dealing with several particularities that remain on the relation of the software possibilities and each design project's characteristics.

Creating hair styles, beards, moustaches, and fur clothes for instance, requires different care in data treatment; we follow the general methodology:

- Prepare the object and its corresponding surfaces for hair generation:
  All changes on the surface must be done at this step. Objects are modified in **SurfMan** software. This includes deleting or sharing triangles and changing its direction or position. If objects are created in other programs they must be converted to SM format (see section 3.1).

- Create individual hair segment files:
  The hair styles or fur should be created separately on their respective surface in the **Styler** module. In this way the designer can have more flexibility and combine hair files creatively.

- Mix hair segment files:
  The **Hair Rendering** software accepts the designation of only one file of hair segments, as mentioned above in section 4. After all necessary hair files are created correctly, they can be mixed in a unique hair segment file.

- Render the final scene:
  Suitable files containing parameters for the camera, lights and material must be created in this step. As the rendering software is not interactive in the sense that there is not an interface for visualising the effect of the chosen parameters, many tests should be made taking into account the correct shadow buffer's area, in order to obtain the desired visual effects.

5.1. Making Human Hair Styles

The scalp surface has a curved configuration that implies special care in creating hair styles, because of the software's special constraints for defining hair curves and growth (see section 3.3). Two kinds of hair style creation were tried, and each one required different data treatment.

- The synthetic actress' hair style

  - The actress' old polygonal hair was substituted by a flat scalp, that was adapted to her head using **SurfMan**.
  - Basically four curves were created and distributed on the scalp. As the hair curve is defined by straight cylindrical segments (see section 3.1), several points were defined to give a curly configuration to the hair. For this reason each hair curve had about 30 to 40 cylindrical segments, which increasedconsiderably the size of the hair segment file for a density of 100,000 hairs.
  - The camera parameters focus only on the actress' bust. The position of the lights were determined in such a manner as to square all shadow buffers (see section 4). The actress' hair material was defined for 4 different specular colours. Even if the hair style is the same, the different materials give the actress different looks. Plate 1 shows this experiment with different materials.

- The synthetic actor's hair style

  - The actor's scalp was adapted from the actress' scalp, and applied to the actor's head using the **SurfMan** program.
  - Fourteen curves were created for the actor's style. As the actor's style has a different configuration, it basically following the head structure format. For that reason many curves should be defined with an average of 10 cylindrical segments. In spite of the greater number of the hair curves, the 10 segments for each hair did not increase the size of the hair segment file as much as the actress' curves did.
  - The eyebrows and eyelashes were defined separately and then combined with the hair style.
  - A similar process for rendering the synthetic actress' hair style was used. Plate 2 shows the synthetic actor with eyebrows and eyelashes using a hair style.

Because of the discrepancy in size of the two hair segment files, they had different rendering times. In order to rendering calculations for the actress' style, its density was decreased by 1/4 and its hair thickness increased a little.

5.2. Making Beards and Moustaches

Basically, beards and moustaches require as surface structure the chin, the cheeks and the region between the nose and the upper lip. The polygon tangents for those regions are relatively constant, varying their directions only on the chin. This topology facilitates the application of the same curve almost in all polygons. When creating several beard and moustache styles, variations are made by changing the hair parameters appropriately (see section 3.2).

- The process:

    - Using the SurfMan program, some polygons between the cheeks and chin surfaces were spliced in order to generate a curved line among the polygons for differentiation.
    - Basically four curves of approximately 5 segments were created and suitably distributed on the beard and moustache regions. The hair parameters were changed to create 13 beard styles.
    - All the beard and moustache styles were individually mixed with the hair style, eyebrows and eyelashes defined before.
    - Plate 3 shows several images of the actor using a single hair style and different moustaches and beards.

As hair can be placed on any part of the body, a hair segment file was generated also for the synthetic actor's chest (see Plate 4).

5.3. Making Fur Clothes and Rendering Three-dimensional Textures

Because of the functionality of the Styler Program in applying hair on polygonal mesh structures, this important facility integrates, in this way, important research on synthetic actor animation, like cloths.

Making furs is a complex task since it includes not only the cloth model of the coat itself, but also more than hundreds of thousands of individual hairs to be rendered along the lenght of the coat.

An example of application can be seen in Plate 5. In this picture two different objects, the synthetic actress and her cloth (Magnenat-Thalmann et al. 1991), are used to render different hair data files: the synthetic hair and fur coat. Meanwhile, another important and difficult goal of computer graphics can be noticed in those pictures: three-dimensional texture. In the Styler program, depending on the density and hair length chosen, the fur rendered object is in fact a three dimensional texture surface made by concentrated segments of curves, reflecting rays of light in different directions with shadows and highlight effects.

- The process:

    - The initial position of the actress' body was designed using a human free-walking model (Boulic et al. 1991). The new position was converted to the clothes software format to generate the long coat. This coat was then converted to SM format to be used in the Styler program.
    - Just one hair of one segment was created and distributed on the coat surface. Two types of fur coats were generated using different parameters of material, density, distribution and growth.
    - The two coats' segment files were separately mixed with the actress' hair style.
    - The camera parameters were determined to focus the entire actress body. The materials of the synthetic actress' coats were defined for four different specular and diffuse colors, one pair of two gradual tones of grey and one of brown for each coat.

Looking for different appearances of the coats' materials, several tests were made with lights and shadow parameters. Plate 6 shows these final results. The coats on the left have an opaque reflection of the light giving the coats the appearance of a real fur. The other ones have a high degree of reflectance and their appearance is like a bright fur coat made from synthetic material like acrylic.

5.4. Rendering Fur and Hair Styles With Facial Texture Mapping

In order to obtain a more natural look for synthetic actors with realistic hair styles, another concentrated effort was made to integrate facial texture mapping research into the hair rendering process.

The skin texture mapping process for synthetic actors, as described in (Kalra et al. 1993), is done by a plane or cylinder projection of a real face's photograph by use of few control points selected on the 3D facial model.

Plate 7 shows the synthetic actress with a skin texture, hair style and fur coat, and Plate 8 shows the synthetic actor with a skin texture, hair style, beard and moustache. Both pictures were rendered as described above, with just the texture mapping information added to the actors' body files. The visual quality of synthetic actors' facial look shown on these plates can be compared with Plates 5 and 2, respectively.

5.5. Hair Design: Possibilities of Elementary, Creative and Particular Hair Animation

One of the first objectives of our research on hair was the rendering of realistic hair, as we have described above. The challenge was render "not only the individual hairs but also a continuous image consisting of regions of hair colour, shadow, specular highlights and, under backlight conditions, hallooing" (LeBlanc et al. 1991b).

After satisfactory image results, some efforts were made to improve the modelling part for better quality of design and also the software compatibility with other important research in the domain of synthetic actors as skin texture mapping and synthetic clothes.

The new version, as it is at the present, allows the designer to create a wide range of hair styles and furry objects according to his or her creative objective. As the basic program's output is an image of three dimensional hair rendered, a classical desire would visualize the entire hair style, to see it from different angles. Plate 9 shows some frames, extracts from the film "Fashion Show," of the camera moving around the synthetic actress hair style. However Styler can animate the hair growth on a synthetic actor's head.

To create the final hair styles, the Styler program offers the option to make grow the hair on the surface in order to do the adaptation hair length to the curve surface as a scalp, for example (see section 3.2). However, this facility can be used in a creative way to make hair grow slowly enough to be seen in a continuous sequence.

- The growing hair animation process:

    - The actor's scalp and facial expression were modified using the SurfMan program.
    - The hair style was made by the applying on the entire scalp using just one type of hair of one segment. For the animation sequence, 25 hair segment files were generated using different parameters to make hair grow gradually for each segment file.
    - Each hair segment file of growing hair was mixed with hair files for the eyelashes and eyebrows, the beard, and furry chest.
    - Plate 10 shows pictures from a sequence of a growing hair on the synthetic actor's head.

The Hair Rendering software was not optimized for this kind parameter use. To generate sequences like that, it requires a lot of space in memory for each frame's hair segment file. Deppending on the hair file's complexity, also a considerable amount of time is required to rendering the entire sequence. However, the visual effect shown in these images is interesting for its uniqueness.

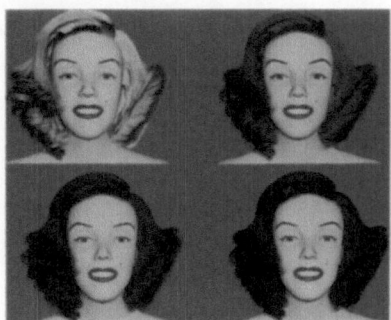

Plate 1. Material variations
for the synthetic actress' hair style.

Plate 2. The synthetic actor's hair style.

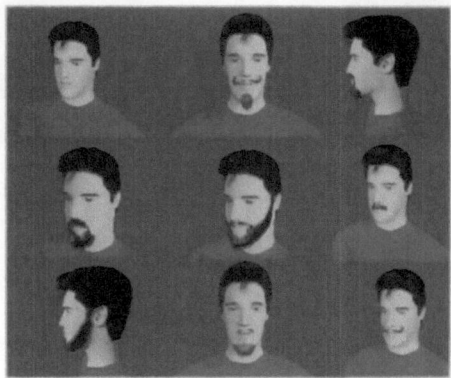

Plate 3. The synthetic actor using
a hair style with different moustaches and beards.

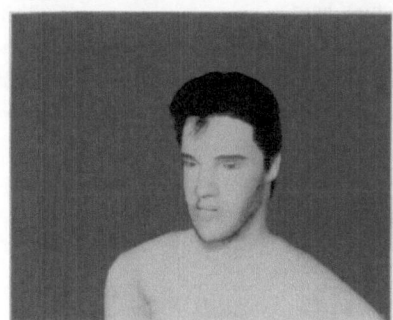

Plate 4. The synthetic actor using
hair and beard styles with furry chest.

Plate 5. A detail of the synthetic actress
with a hair style and fur coat

Plate 6. Different visual effects
for the synthetic actress fur coats

Plate 7. The synthetic actress using hair style
and fur coat with facial skin texture mapped.

Plate 8. The synthetic actor using hair
style and beard with facial skin texture mapped.

Plate 9. Some frames of a camera animation
sequence around the synthetic actress' head.

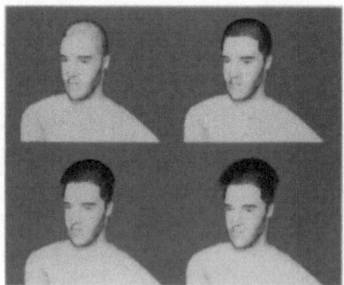

Plate 10. Some frames of hair growing on
the synthetic actor's head, with a beard and furry chest.

6. CONCLUSION AND FUTURE WORKS

Aesthetic challenges led to important technical modifications and adaptations in **Styler and Hair Rendering** programs during the last four years, which permited considerable improvement of design work possibilities for synthetic hair visual products. These final rendered images not only show interesting and realistic results, but also represent the integration of other main topics of our research in the field of synthesizing human actors on more realistic natural look.

Some efforts will be made in the future to solve the software's problem of placing hair in 3D interactively, without regenerating hair segment files for each new position. The importance of this new improvement will be to preserve the rendering quality of the hair details such as hair density, shadows and highlight effects, to allowing save design time and memory allocation, and to permit new hair design employment in simple animation, like in walking and speaking sequences with body and head movements.

7. ACKNOWLEDGEMENT

This project has been sponsored by the "Fonds National Suisse de la Recherche Scientifique". The authors would like to thank Hans Martin Werner for improving the English text.

REFERENCES

Anjyo K, Usami Y, Kurihara T (1992), A Simple Method for Extracting The Natural Beauty of Hair, Computer Graphics, Vol. 26 N0. 2, pp. 11-120.

Boulic R, Magnenat-Thalmann,N.; Thalmann D.(1991), A Global Human Walking Model with Real-Time Kinematic Personification. The Visual Computer, Vol 6, No 6, 1991.

Csuri C, Hakathorn R, Parent R, Carlson W, Howard M (1979) Twoards an Interactive High Visual Complexity Animation System. Computer Graphics, Vol.13, No 2, pp 289-299.

Kalra P,Magnenat-Thalmann N. (1993) Simulation of Facial Skin Using Texture Mapping and Coloration. International Conference on Computer Graphics ICCG'93, proceedings, Bombay, India 1993.

LeBlanc A.; Kalra P.; Magnenat-Thalmann N.; Thalmann D. (1991a) "Sculping With the Ball & Mouse" Metaphor". Proc. Graphics Interface '91, Calgary, Canada.

LeBlanc A; Turner R.: Thalmann D. (1991b) "Rendering Hair using Pixel Blending and Shadow Buffers". The Journal of Visualization and Computer Animation 2, 3 - pp 92-27.

Magnenat-Thalmann N.; Yang Y, Thalmann D. (1991) The Problematics of Cloth Modeling and Animation. Second Conference on Cad and CG, proceedings, Hangzhou, China, September 1991.

Miller G. S.P. (1988) From Wire-Frame to furry Animals, Proc. Graphics Interface'88, pp. 138-146.

Nadin M. "Science and Beauty: Aesthetic Structuring of Knowledge" Leonardo, vol. 24, no. 1 pp 67-72, 1991.

Rosenblum R.E., Carlson W.E. and Trip III E. (1991) Simulating the structure and Dynamics of Human Hair: Modelling, Rendering and Animation. The Journal of Visualization and Computer Animation vol.2: pp 141- 148 (1991).

Watanabe Y, Suenaga Y (1989) Drawing Human Hair Using Wisp Model, Proc. Computer Graphics International '89, pp. 691 - 700.

Agnes Daldegan is a PhD student in the Computer Graphics Lab at the University of Geneva sponsored by the National Council of the Scientific and Technological Development CNPq - Brazil. Her research interests are in facial synthesis and animation. She studied Fine Arts in the Department of Visual Arts of the Art Institute of the University of Brasilia followed by some post-grad work in computer science in the Department of Computer Science, UnB.

Adress:	MIRALab, CUI, University of Geneva
	24 rue Général Dufour, 1211 Geneva,
	Switzerland
E-mail:	daldegan@uni2a.unige.ch

Nadia Magnenat Thalmann is currently full Professor of Computer Science at the University of Geneva, Switzerland and Adjunct Professor at HEC Montreal, Canada. She has served on a variety of goverment advisory boards and program committees in Canada. She has received several awards, including the 1985 Communications Award from the Government of Quebec and the Moebius Award from the European Community in 1992. Dr. Magnenat Thalmann received a BS in psychology, an MS in biochemistry, and a Ph.D in quantum chemistry and computer graphics from the university of Geneva. She has written and edited several books and research papers in image synthesis and computer animation and was codirector of the computer-generated films *Dream Flight, Englantine, Rendez-vous à Montréal, Galaxy Sweetheart, IAD, Flashback, Still Walking* and *Fashion Show*. She served as chairperson of Graphics Interface '85, CGI '88, and the annual workshop on Computer Animation.

Adress:	MIRALab, CUI, University of Geneva
	24 rue Général Dufour, 1211 Geneva,
	Switzerland
E-mail:	thalmann@uni2a.unige.ch

Modeling Blades of Simple Leaves

Masa Inakage and Hiro Inakage

ABSTRACT

This paper describes modeling techniques of simple leaf blades of vegetal trees. The techniques are based on leaf morphology. A leaf blade is assumed to be symmetrical. A blade consists of the midrib, the blade surface, and veins. The general shape of a leaf blade is determined by the outline and the margin. Both outline and margin are defined by vectors. Main and secondary veins are "pressed" onto the blade surface to create semi-cylindrical bumpiness on the blade surface. Displacement, bump, and texture mapping techniques are used to "press" the venation pattern onto the blade surface, depending on the level of detail. To curl the blade, we parametrically deform the surface. Surface attributes are determined by the surface property of the blade. If the surface is waxed, specular components of the blade surface is increased. For hairy surface, the specular roughness parameter is adjusted for dull reflections. Procedural textures are used to generate speckle patterns of the blade.

Keywords: blade, curl, hairy surface, leaf, margin, morphology, procedural textures, speckle, vein, venation

1. INTRODUCTION

Trees and plants always fascinate our eyes. They have complex shapes with ample textures. Closer scrutiny of trees and plants reveals amazing rules in their structure. Computer generated trees have focused on simulating the rules to model realistic trees.

Various modeling techniques on trees and plants have been proposed in the past few years. There are several different approaches to modeling trees. Aono and Kunii [1], Bloomenthal [3], Kawaguchi [9], Oppenheimer [11], and Reeves and Blau [14] applied modeling techniques that are geometrically defined branching mechanisms. Prusink-iewicz et al. [12] and Smith [16] introduced formal languages to generate the tree topology. de Reffye et al. [15] introduced empirically based growth model of plants.

371

Greene [6],[7] proposed a voxel-based technique to describe growth model capable of sensing environment.

Unfortunately, modeling techniques of leaves have received very little attention by the computer graphics community despite of their complexity. In many of the computer generated leaves, they are crudely approximated by small number of polygons. Bloomenthal [3] combined texture and transparency mapping techniques of digitized photograph. Viennot et al. [17] showed a fast leaf drawing method with an assumption of the leaves to be flat. In this paper, the leaf modeling adopted a topological approach. Demko et al. [4] generated flat leaves using stochastic technique called the iterated function systems. Similarly, Oppenheimer [11] used fractal model to grow internal veins. Lienhardt [10] proposed a technique to define the topology of leaves by modular maps. Prusinkiewicz and Lindenmayer[13, chapter 5] presents L-system to model leaves. However, it does not account for venation patterns and speckles. Recently, Hammel et al.[8] used implicit surfaces to model compound leaves.

The techniques above suffer from accurate modeling of leaves. Many models assume leaves to be flat, and they do not discuss leaf morphology. Although leaves apprear to be flat from a distance, they are twisted and bent in three dimensions. Furthermore, leaves have variety of shapes and textures. It is for this reason that we present a method to model leaf blade which is the prominent part of the leaves.

2. LEAF FUNDAMENTALS

There are variety kinds of leaves. It is important to study the basic structure of leaves from botany.[2][18] **Figure 1** illustrates different parts of leaves. A leaf consists of a flat blade or lamina, a stalk or petiole, a leaf base, and stipules. A leaf that has all of these parts is called a complete leaf, but some leaves have missing parts. A leaf with a single blade is called a simple leaf, while a leaf with multiple blade-like structure is called a compound leaf. In this paper, we focus on the modeling techniques of blades in a single leaf.

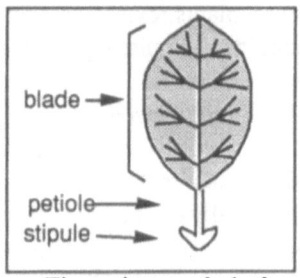

Figure 1 parts of a leaf

The shape of a leaf is determined by the outline of the blade, the edge of the leaf blade, and the surface features of the blade. Common outlines of a blade is depicted in **figure 2**. The blade edge is called its margin. Common margins are shown in **figure 3**. The combination of a leaf outline and margin provides the general shape of a blade.

A blade is composed of veins or vascular bundles and soft tissue between. A pattern of veins is called the venation, and venation characterizes plant species or groups. There are 3 types of venation patterns: dichotomous or forked venation, netted or reticulate venation, and parallel or nerved venation, as illustrated in **figure 4**.

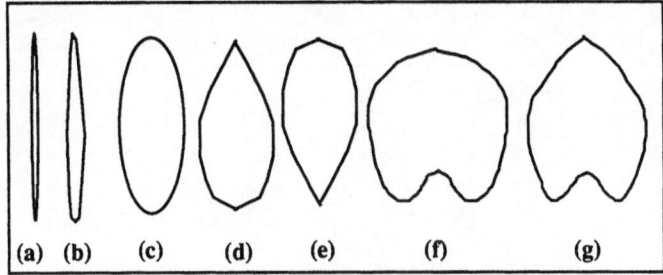

Figure 2 Types of blade outlines: (a)needle; (b)linear; (c)elliptic; (d)ovate; (e)obovate; (f)reniform; (g)sagittate.

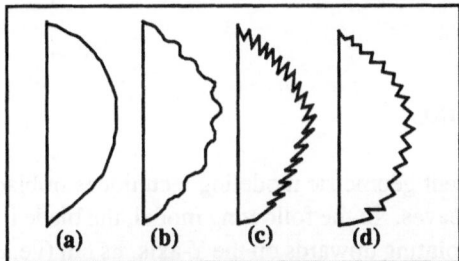

Figure 3 Types of blade margins: (a)entire; (b)repand; (c)serrate; (d)dentate.

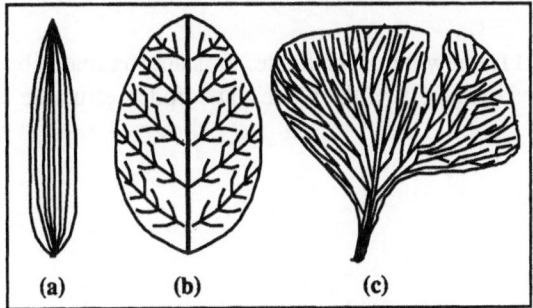

Figure 4 Types of venations: (a)parallel; (b)netted; (c)forked.

Veins are categorized into primary veins, secondary veins, and smaller veins. The primary or central vein is called the midrib. Soft tissues occupy areas between the venation. Soft tissues and venation cause the bumpy surface of the blade. Soft tissues have semi-cylindrically curved surfaces.

Another important features of the epidermis are wax coating. In some leaves, blades are covered by waxes, causing specular surface characterisctics of the blade. In addition, some leaves have hairy surfaces. This causes the surface reflection characteristics to be dull. Some blade surfaces have speckles due to lack of chlorophyls. Typical speckle patterns are illustrated in **figure 5**.

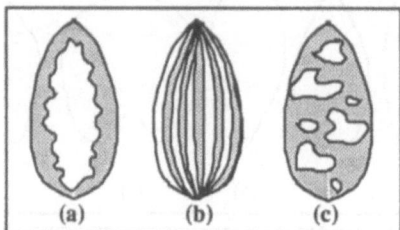

Figure5 Types of blade speckles:
(a)ring; (b)stripes; (c)spots.

3. THE BLADE MODEL

In this section, we present geometric modeling techniques of blades. The blades are assumed to be simple leaves. In the following model, the blade is defined on the XY-plane, and the midrib pointing upwards on the Y-axis, its tail (i.e. closer to the base) is located at $y=0$.

3-1. The Midrib
Midrib is the central framework of the blade. It is approximated by a long cone, and its length determines the length of the blade. The midrib structure is defined as

```
struct Midrib {
    double radius;
    double length;
    }
```

3-2. The Shape

The shape of a blade is modeled by the combination of outline data and margin data. We first define the outline expressed in vectors, then replace the margin vectors to each of the outline vectors, as shown in **figure 6**. The outline and margin data structures are:

```
struct Outline {
    int out_num;
    struct Vectors out_vec[];
}

struct Margin {
    int mgn_num;
    struct Vector mar_vec[];
}

struct Vector {
    double x;
    double y;
}
```

where the parameters *out_num* and *mgn_num* defines the number of vectors in the outline and margin structures respectively. Note that both outline and margin vectors are assumed to lie on the XY plane, thus they only have (x,y) coordinates. Sinusoidal, sawtooth, and triangular wave functions are used to generate repand, serrate, and dentate margin vectors respectively. These vectors are scaled to match the length of the midri, so that the blade surface is attached to the midrib. Blades have front and back surfaces to account for different surface properties.

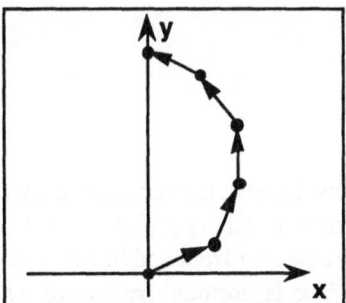

Figure 6 Vector representation of an outline.

3-3. Veins

The venation patterns have similar appearance as growth models of vegetal trees, except the patterns are two dimensional. We can apply the graftals [14] to define the rules of the venation patterns. In general, only primary and secondary veins are noticeable. The venation pattern must be "pressed" onto the blade surface to create the semi-cylindrical bumps. In order to simulate this bumpiness, we propose 3 models dependent on the level of detail. At the largest level, actual bumpy surface is required. Instead of generating geometrical model with complex bumpy surfaces, we suggest to use the displacement mapping. At the medium level, the bumpiness may be simulated by bump mapping technique. At the smallest scale, simple texture mapping of the venation pattern is sufficient.

3-4. Surface Attributes

Surface attributes for the blade include color and reflectivity of the blade surface.

```
struct Surface {
    struct Color front;
    struct Color back;
    struct Reflectivity front_coating;
    struct Reflectivity back_coating;
}

struct Color {
    double red;
    double green;
    double blue;
}

struct Reflectivity {
    double diffuse;
    double specular;
    double roughness;
}
```

If the blade surface is coated by the wax, the surface becomes very specular. However, the specularity becomes dull in case of hairy surface. Note that the data structure allows one to define the surface attributes for front and back surfaces independently. This is important because front surface is normally reflective while back surface is non-reflective.

4. CURLS AND SPECKLES

We allow horizontal and vertical blade deformations to simulate the curls. A grid is first projected onto the blade surface. The blade surface is subdivided into a mesh that corresponds to the projected grid. In order to deform the blade, we manipulate each grid line which corresponds to the blade mesh. Hence, the deformation of the grid successfully curls the blade. Leaf morphology suggests that curls are generally a class of spirals.[2] Hence, for a given point $p(x,y)$, the spiral function for a horizontal and vertical curl is

$$p'(x,y) = \mathbf{spiral}(d, w)$$

where d is $\mathbf{abs}(x)$ for horizontal curl and $\mathbf{abs}(y)$ for vertical curl, and w is the weight of a curliness. The parameter w is adjusted for each grid line so that maximum freedom for blade deformation can be achieved.

Speckles are procedurally defined. Speckles have distinct border, thus a high contrast function or a binary thresholding function are applied to the output value of procedural textures. Ring and stripe speckle functions are simple thresholding functions. Spot speckle can be generated by a band-limited **noise** function. More complex functions may provide interesting speckle patterns.

Figure 7 is an example of Chlorophytum with stripe speckles. **Figure 8** is an example of blades with netted venation and sawtooth margin. These examples are rendered by PRISMS ray tracing rendering software (Side Effects Software Inc.) on Silicon Graphics 4D-30 workstation.

5. CONCLUSIONS

We have described a method to model simple leaf blades. In our model, the overall shape of the leaf blades are defined by an outline and a margin. The venation patterns are generated procedurally, and mapped onto the blade surface. We propose displacement, bump, and texture mapping techniques for different level of detail. Speckles are added to the blades using procedural textures. Future research interests include the growth model of leaf blades including dead leaves, modeling of the whole leaf structures, consideration of external parameters such as temperature and water, and extensions to modeling flowers.

Figure 7 Synthetic Chlorophytum

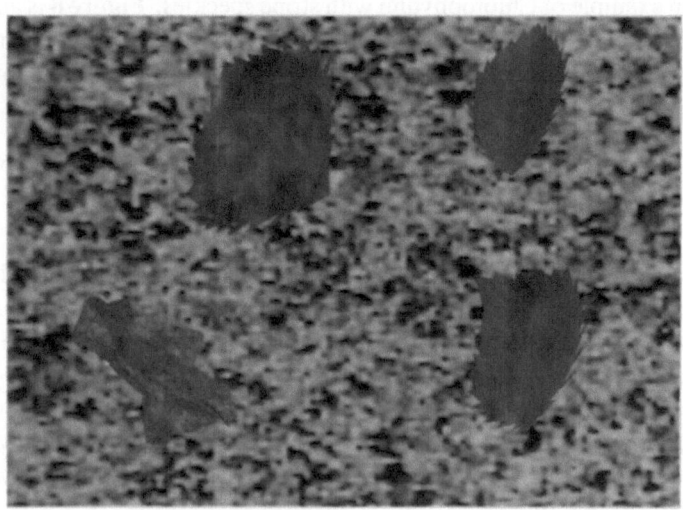

Figure 8 Leaf blades with sawtooth margins

REFERENCES

[1] Aono,M. and Kunii,T.: "Botanical Tree Image Generation," *IEEE Computer Graphics and Applications*, May 1984, pp.10-34

[2] Bell,A.D.: *Plant Form*, Oxford University Press, Oxford, 1991.

[3] Bloomenthal,J.: "Modeling the Mighty Maple," *Computer Graphics, 19*, 3, 1985, pp.305-311

[4] Demko,S., Hodges,L. and Naylor,B.: "Construction of Fractal Objects," *Computer Graphics*,
19, 3, 1985, pp.271-278

[5] Fournier,A.: *The Modeling of Natural Phenomena*, SIGGRAPH course notes #16, 1987

[6] Greene,N.: "Voxel Space Automata: Modeling with Stochastic Growth Processes in Voxel Space," *Computer Graphics, 23*, 3, 1989, pp.175-184

[7] Greene,N.: "Detailing Tree Skeletons with Voxel Automata," *SIGGRAPH course notes #27*, 1991

[8] Hammel,M.S., Prusinkiewicz,P. and Wyvill, B., "Modelling Compound Leaves Using Implicit Contours," *proceedings of CG International '92*, pp.199-212

[9] Kawaguchi,Y.: "A Morphological Study of the Form of Nature," *Computer Graphics, 16*, 3, 1982, pp.223-232

[10] Lienhardt,P.: "Free-Form Surfaces Modeling by Evolution Simulation," *proceedings of EUROGRAPHICS '88*, pp.327-341

[11] Oppenheimer,P.E.: "Real Time Design and Animation of Fractal Plants and Trees," *Computer Graphics, 20*, 4, 1986, pp.55-64

[12] Prusinkiewicz,P., Lindenmayer,A., and Hanan,J.: "Developmental Models of Herbaceous Plants for Computer Imagery Purposes," *Computer Graphics, 22*, 4, 1988, pp.141-150

[13] Prusinkiewicz,P. and Lindenmayer,A., The Algorithmic Beauty of Plants, Sprin-ger Verlag, New York, 1990.

[14] Reeves,W.T. and Blau,R.: "Approximate and Probablistic Algorithms for Shading and Rendering Structured Particle Systems," *Computer Graphics, 19*, 3, 1985, pp.313-322

[15] Reffye (de) P., Edelin,C., Francon,J., Jaeger,M., and Puech,C.: "Plant Models Faithful to Botanical Structure and Development," *Computer Graphics, 22*, 4, 1988, pp.151-158

[16] Smith,A.R.: "Plants, Fractals, and Formal Languages," *Computer Graphics, 18*, 3, 1984, pp.1-10

[17] Viennot,X.G., Eyrolles,G., Janey,N., and Arques,D.: "Combinational Analysis of Ramified Patterns and Computer Imagery of Trees," *Computer Graphics, 23*, 3, 1989, pp.31-40

[18] Woodland,D.W.: *Contemporary Plant Systematics*, Prentice Hall, Englewood Cliffs, New Jersey, 1991.

Masa Inakage is currently president of The Media Studio, Inc. in Kanagawa, Japan. He received a B.A. from Oberlin College, Ohio, and M.F.A. from California College of Arts and Crafts. He has been developing ray tracing algorithms, animation systems, and various image syntheses techniques at the Media Laboratory, MIT. His research interests include volume modeling and rendering techniques, natural phenomena, and artistic image synthesis techniques. He is a member of Computer Graphics Society, ACM SIGGRAPH, EUROGRAPHICS, and Japanese Society for Science of Design.

address:The Media Studio, Inc., 2-24-7 Shichirigahama-Higashi, Kamakura, Kanagawa 248 Japan

Hiro Inakage is currently a lecturer at Women's College of Fine Arts and Tokyo School of Arts. Her research interests include the use of computer graphics as a medium for fine arts. She has received B.A. from Women's College of Fine Arts and M.A. from Tsukuba University. She is a member of Computer Graphics Society, ACM SIGGRAPH, and Japanese Society for Science of Design.

address:Women's College of Fine Arts, 1900 Asamizodai, Sagamihara, Kanagawa 228 Japan

A Model of Hands and Arms Based on Manifold Mappings

Tosiyasu L. Kunii, Yukinobu Tsuchida, Yasuhiro Arai, Hiroshi Matsuda, Masahiro Shirahama, and Shinya Miura

ABSTRACT

A multibody model of hands and arms is presented. Representative points of contact are considered as the end-effectors. The configuration space and the workspace are modeled as manifolds, and the task feasibility is defined using the notions of manifold mappings and Jacobian matrices. Joint rotation limits and dependencies between the joints are considered in the configuration space. A procedure to check the task feasibility is presented. The causes which lead to the infeasible task are classified into singular configuration, boundary transgression, and disharmony. Finally, a technique of martial arts, *Shorinji Kempo*, is analyzed to demonstrate the usefulness of the model.

Keywords: multibody, model of hands and arms, manifold, task feasibility, singular configuration

1. INTRODUCTION

Hands and arms are extremely important tools that we, human beings, are endowed with. They can perform various motions, for instance, pinching, seizing, grasping, pressing, scooping, wrenching, and slapping. This dexterity primarily comes from a large number of joints.

Many researchers (Gourret 1989, Lee 1990, Rijpkema 1991, Monheit 1991) have investigated the various motions of human body, including the hand and the arm. Generally speaking, they used the statistical average data or the intuitive imaginary geometric data. As a result, though the animations they produced look sufficiently realistic, if we want to analyze the real motion of a person, the models they developed are powerless.

This paper is concerned with the analysis of the real motions of specific persons. The result obtained through the analysis can be interpreted in the words of the real world. Hands and arms can be modeled as a multibody system, which is a system of rigid bodies connected by joints. In this paper, the contact surface of a body with other bodies is approximated by a finite set of representative points of contact through which the representative forces are applied. We view the representative points of contact as the end-effectors, through which the hand or the arm can influence the other bodies.

A multibody model of hands and arms which can decide whether a given task can be performed or not is presented. In order to analyze the real motion of specific persons, we develop a system to acquire the real geometric data of these persons. The data required for our model are (1) the relative position and orientation of the adjoining joint axes, (2) the joint rotation limits, and (3) the dependencies between the joint angles (Landsmeer 1963). Evidently, these data are different from person to person, so we have to acquire the real data of a specific person in order to analyze the motion of this person. Statistic average data are meaningless. The procedure to acquire the data is as follows:

1. For each joint of the hand and the arm, L-shaped sticks are attached to the two segments connected to the joint as marks, and the images of the hand and arm revolving around the joint are taken using multiple video cameras. In this way, we can find out the joint axes of the hand and the arm, and determine the relative position and orientation of the adjoining joint axes.

2. The model constructed up to this point has only the concept of the joint axes. That is, the segments connected to a joint may revolve around the joint beyond the natural limits. To avoid this, we acquire the data of the joint rotation limits by fitting the model to the images of the hand and arm bending or flexing to the maximum angle of each joint.

3. We take the images of the hand and arm in the postures where the joint angles are dependent on each other, and acquire the data concerning the dependencies between the joint angles.

381

Using the data acquired with this procedure, we can compute the degrees of freedom that a certain part of the hand and arm has in a configuration. The joint angles of the configuration in some real motion of a person can be acquired using the images taken with multiple video cameras.

The configuration space and workspace are modeled as manifolds. Forward kinematic functions which map the configuration space manifold to the workspace manifold and their Jacobian matrices are derived. The joint rotation limits and the dependencies between the joints are considered in the configuration space.

Given a task to the end-effectors, the task feasibility is defined to express whether the task is feasible or not. A procedure to check the task feasibility based on the model is presented. The causes which lead to the infeasible task are classified into three situations: *singular configuration, boundary transgression,* and *disharmony.* Finally, by using the model of hands and arms, the masterly performance of an expert of *Shorinji Kempo* is analyzed to demonstrate the usefulness of the model. It is shown that the technique of the *Shorinji Kempo* takes advantage of the joint rotation limits, the dependencies between the joints, and the singular configuration of hands and arms.

Section 2 presents the basic multibody model of hands and arms. Section 3 extends the model so that the task feasibility can be determined. Section 4 describes the results of testing and validating the model against a technique of martial arts, the *Shorinji Kempo.* Section 5 summarizes this paper and gives the future work.

2. MODEL BASIS

2.1. Multibody Kinematics

2.1.1. Multibody Modeling of Hands and Arms
A hand and an arm can be modeled as a multibody system (Huston 1990), which is a system of bodies. In this paper, the multibody system of the hand and arm is supposed to be connected, rigid, and open. The multibody system of such a class is often called an open-chain system or an open-tree system. We use the term an open-tree system for the name of a class of the multibody system consisting of a hand and an arm.

The root body of the open-tree system of a hand and an arm is defined to be the upper arm in this paper. The position and orientation of the root body represent those of the whole system.

2.1.2. Point of Contact as an End-Effector
When a body comes into contact with another body which either belongs to the same or different multibody, it receives the force through the contact surface and its motion is restricted. Conversely, a body applies the force to another body through the contact surface. It is possible to view the contact surface as an infinite set of the points of contact. Moreover, since the forces which apply or are applied through a vicinity of a certain point are almost same in the magnitude and directions, they can be approximated by a single force which applies or is applied through a single point. In this way, the contact surface can be approximated by a finite set of the representative points of contact through which the representative forces apply or are applied.

In this paper, we view the representative points of contact as end-effectors, through which a hand or an arm can influence the other bodies. The position of the end-effector coincides with the position of the representative point of contact, and its orientation is aligned with the normal vector of the tangent plane at the point. It is important to evaluate the manipulability or effectiveness of a configuration of the hand and arm using the degrees of freedom and the movable space of the end-effectors.

2.1.3. A Manifold Mapping Formulation of Multibody Kinematics
When there are m representative points of contact, we have the same number of end-effectors. Let x_i describe the state of the i-th end-effector, usually the position and orientation of the end-effector. The i-th forward kinematic function, f_i, relates a set of variables representing the joint angles and the position and orientation of the root body, q, to x_i:

$$x_i = f_i(q), \tag{1}$$

where $\mathbf{f}_i$ is represented as a nonlinear vector algebraic expression.

From a mapping perspective, the forward kinematic function maps points in one space, called the "configuration space," which contains all possible values of the variables representing the joint angles and the position and orientation of the root body, to points in another space, called the "workspace," which contains all possible positions and orientations of the end-effector.

Let us look how a multibody configuration space is interpreted as a manifold with boundary. Let θ_j denote the joint angle for the j-th joint. In the case of a hand and an arm, joints have the rotation limits, which limit the domain of θ_j to an interval of the real line, $I_j = [min_j, max_j]$, which is a compact manifold with boundary.

If there is no dependency between joints, the configuration space manifold with boundary, denoted by the symbol $\mathcal{C}$, is represented as follows:

$$\mathcal{C} = I_1 \times I_2 \times ... \times I_n \times \mathbf{R}^3 \times SO(3), \tag{2}$$

where $\mathbf{R}^3$ is the 3-dimensional Euclidean space, which is also a manifold, though not compact, and $SO(3)$ is the group of 3-parameter (spatial) rigid body rotations. $\mathcal{C}$ is a manifold with boundary.

Now consider the manifold representation of the workspace. Suppose a multibody has m representative points of contact. Attach a Euclidean frame to the i-th representative point of contact of the multibody. Then the i-th workspace manifold, denoted by the symbol $\mathcal{W}_i$, is expressed as follows:

$$\mathcal{W}_i = \mathbf{f}_i(\mathcal{C}). \tag{3}$$

The forward kinematic function (1) can be viewed as an algebraic mapping of points from the configuration space to the workspace.

The workspace manifold is contained in a larger space, termed the "output space," which is the ambient space of smallest dimensions that contains the workspace. The output space is also a manifold. The workspace is therefore a manifold which is a subset of the output space manifold. Let $\mathcal{O}$ denote the output space manifold. In the case of the point of contact of a hand and an arm, the type of the output space is generally spatial:

$$\mathcal{O} = \mathbf{R}^3 \times SO(3). \tag{4}$$

In summary, if there is no dependency between joints, the multibody kinematics can be viewed as a set of the mappings of the configuration space manifold with boundary, $\mathcal{C}$, to the set of the workspace manifolds, $\{\mathcal{W}_i\}$, under the action of the set of the forward kinematic maps, $\{\mathbf{f}_i\}$:

$$\mathbf{f}_i : \mathcal{C} \to \mathcal{W}_i \subset \mathcal{O} \qquad (i = 1, ..., m). \tag{5}$$

2.1.4. Denavit-Hartenberg Kinematic Parameters for Open-Tree Multibody Systems

We extend the Denavit-Hartenberg notation (Craig 1986, Burdick 1988) for the case of the serial chain manipulators to that of the open-tree multibody systems. Here, we focus on the revolute joints, because our hands and arms can be considered to have the revolute joints rather than the prismatic or helical joints which are common in the areas of mechanics and robotics.

A set of four parameters $\{\alpha, d, a, \theta\}$ to describe the relative position and orientation of a multibody are defined as follows(Fig.1):

1. Starting from a single root body of the open-tree multibody system, label the joint axes $1, 2, 3, ..., n$ in the depth-first tree traverse order. Let $[j, k]$ denote a link connected to both joint axes j and k, $[j, \phi]$ a virtual link connected to only the joint axis j at a leaf body, and $[\phi, 1]$ a virtual link at the root body.

2. For the link $[j, k]$, let $\mathcal{F}_{[j,k]}$ denote a frame, which is composed of a triad of coordinate directions (represented by orthogonal unit vectors $\mathbf{x}_{[j,k]}$, $\mathbf{y}_{[j,k]}$, and $\mathbf{z}_{[j,k]}$) and a triad of scalars representing the frame origin.

3. Attach the frame $\mathcal{F}_{[j,k]}$ to the link $[j, k]$ such that $\mathbf{z}_{[j,k]}$ is aligned with the joint axis j. Note that this is not a unique description, since there are two ways to orient $\mathbf{z}_{[j,k]}$ along the joint axis. The orientation is defined in step 5. The choice of $\mathbf{z}_{[\phi,1]}$ of the root body frame is arbitrary.

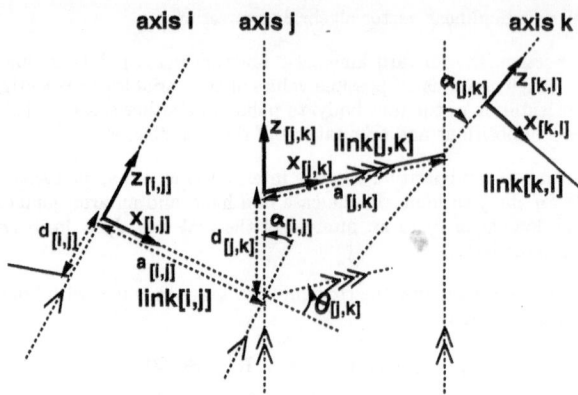

Figure 1: Parameters $\{\alpha, d, a, \theta\}$

4. After $\mathbf{z}_{[j,k]}$ has been aligned along the joint axis j, align $\mathbf{x}_{[j,k]}$ along the mutually orthogonal line from the joint axis j to the joint axis k. If axes j and k intersect, there are two equally valid ways to choose $\mathbf{x}_{[j,k]}$ to be orthogonal to both $\mathbf{z}_{[j,k]}$ and $\mathbf{z}_{[k,l]}$. The choice of $\mathbf{x}_{[j,\phi]}$ of the leaf body frame is arbitrary.

5. $\mathbf{z}_{[j,k]}$ is oriented to the direction of the vector from the point of intersection of $\mathbf{z}_{[j,k]}$ with $\mathbf{x}_{[i,j]}$ to the origin of the frame $\mathcal{F}_{[j,k]}$ which is determined as the point of intersection of $\mathbf{z}_{[j,k]}$ with $\mathbf{x}_{[j,k]}$. If the vector is zero, either of the two ways to orient $\mathbf{z}_{[j,k]}$ along the joint axis is valid. The length parameter, $d_{[j,k]}$, is defined as the length of the vector.

6. The length parameter, $a_{[i,j]}$, is defined as the distance between $\mathbf{z}_{[i,j]}$ and $\mathbf{z}_{[j,k]}$ along the mutually orthogonal line.

7. The twist angle, $\alpha_{[i,j]}$, is defined as the angle between $\mathbf{z}_{[i,j]}$ and $\mathbf{z}_{[j,k]}$, as measured using the right hand rule with thumb along $\mathbf{x}_{[i,j]}$.

8. The angle $\theta_{[j,k]}$ is defined as the angle between $\mathbf{x}_{[i,j]}$ and $\mathbf{x}_{[j,k]}$, measured using the right hand rule with thumb along $\mathbf{z}_{[j,k]}$.

An example of an open-tree multibody system with the revolute joints is shown in Fig.2. In this example, there are 7 joint axes, 6 real links, and 4 virtual links.

Suppose that two links $[j, k]$ and $[j, l]$ are connected to the same joint axis j. Then, evidently, the angles $\theta_{[j,k]}$ and $\theta_{[j,l]}$ represent the same joint angle. Thus the following equation holds:

$$\theta_{[j,l]} - \theta_{[j,k]} = constant. \tag{6}$$

2.1.5. Partial Translational Velocities and Partial Angular Velocities
Let N denote the number of the variables which describe the joint angles and the position and orientation of the whole system of a hand and an arm, thus:

$$N = n + 6, \tag{7}$$

where n is the number of the joint axes, and 6 is the degrees of freedom of the root body.

Suppose, relative to the global coordinate system, the velocity of the origin of the i-th end-effector frame and the angular velocity of the i-th end-effector frame are denoted by the 3×1 vectors $\mathbf{V}^i$ and $\mathbf{w}^i$, respectively. The end-effector frame velocities are expressed in terms of the individual joint velocities and root body velocities as:

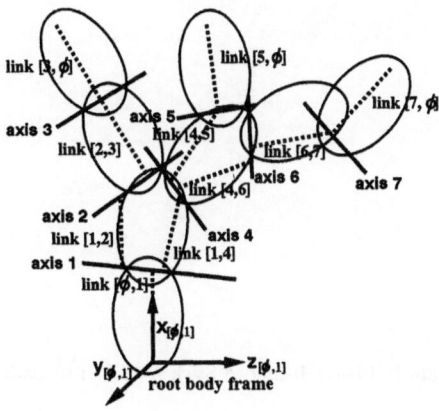

Figure 2: An Example of Open-tree Multibody System with Revolute Joints

$$\mathbf{V}^i = \sum_{j=0}^{N} \tilde{\mathbf{V}}_j^i \dot{q}_j, \text{ and} \tag{8}$$

$$\mathbf{w}^i = \sum_{j=0}^{N} \tilde{\mathbf{w}}_j^i \dot{q}_j, \tag{9}$$

Where $\tilde{\mathbf{V}}_j^i$ and $\tilde{\mathbf{w}}_j^i$ $(j = 1, ..., N)$ are 3×1 vectors that are termed *partial translational velocity* and *partial angular velocity* vectors. As their names indicate, the partial translational velocity and partial angular velocity vectors are computed as partial derivatives of the i-th end-effector frame velocity and the angular velocity with respect to the individual joint velocities or the root body translational or angular velocities (Kane 1983):

$$\tilde{\mathbf{V}}_j^i = \frac{\partial \mathbf{V}^i}{\partial \dot{q}_j}, \text{ and} \tag{10}$$

Where

$$\tilde{\mathbf{w}}_j^i = \frac{\partial \mathbf{w}^i}{\partial \dot{q}_j}. \tag{11}$$

A partial translational velocity is, therefore, a measure of the contribution to the linear motion of the i-th end-effector frame due to one particular joint or one parameter, describing the position or the orientation of the root body. Similarly, a partial angular velocity is the contribution of one joint or one parameter of the root body to the angular velocity of the i-th end-effector frame.

2.2. Experiment for Finding out Joint Axes

In order to acquire the Denavit-Hartenberg parameters of the hand and the arm of a specific person, the relative position and orientation of the joint rotation axes must be measured. As the relative position and orientation of the adjacent joint axes have no relation with the joint angles, the position and orientation of the joint axes can be measured separately, and the relative position and orientation of the adjacent axes can be computed in the local coordinate system common to the adjacent axes.

We use a plastic L-shaped stick which is attached to a body by a magic tape(Fig.3). The two lines forming the L-shape almost make a right angle so that they can be the first and second axes of the local coordinate system, and that the third can be the external product of them.

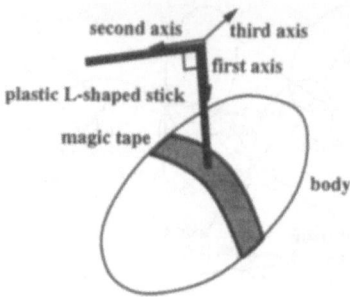

Figure 3: Plastic L-shaped Stick Attached to Body

When finding an axis of a joint, two L-shaped sticks are needed for the two adjacent bodies connected to the joint. We find out the joint axes one by one, starting from the elbow joint, in the depth-first order of the tree structure of our model.

Two frames are taken for each joint axis. These frames contain the postures where the joint angles are different from each other. The two dimensional positions of the L-shaped sticks in the frames are input interactively using the mouse. From the multiple images taken by the multiple video cameras, three dimensional position and orientation of the L-shaped sticks are determined. Then the motion of one stick attached to one body relative to the other stick attached to the adjacent body is extracted and the axis of rotation is determined.

Using the position and orientation of the two adjacent joint axes, the relative position and orientation of the two axes can be computed. In this way, the Denavit-Hartenberg parameters of the hand and the arm of a specific person can be acquired.

3. ADVANCED MODEL

3.1. Model Extension

In this subsection, the concept of *task feasibility* is introduced in the frame of the manifold mappings. Firstly, the joint limits and the dependencies are considered in the configuration space manifold. The configuration space manifold can be decomposed into the direct product of manifolds where the variables of a manifold are independent of those of other manifolds. Secondly, a *task* is specified in terms of the velocities, the angular velocities, or both the velocities and the angular velocities of the end-effectors, depending on whether the task is positional, spherical, or spatial, respectively. Thirdly, the Jacobian matrix of the forward kinematic function is considered. Regular and singular configurations are defined using the submatrices extracted from the Jacobian matrix. The task feasibility is then defined to express whether the system can perform the given task or not. And finally, the method to check the task feasibility is presented using the concepts of the configuration space manifold and singular configurations.

3.1.1. Joint Rotation Limits and Dependencies between Joints

The variable which represents the rotation angle of the j-th joint axis takes the domain of the form $I_j = [min_j, max_j]$, which is a topological space homeomorphic to a 1-disk, D^1.

Let us consider the two joint angle variables q_j and q_k ($j \neq k$). If there is no dependency between the j-th and k-th joint axes, a pair of the two variables (q_j, q_k) take the domain which is the Cartesian product of the domains of q_j and q_k:

$$I_j \times I_k = [min_j, max_j] \times [min_k, max_k], \qquad (12)$$

which is homeomorphic to a circular disk, D^2.

Now consider that there is dependency between the rotation angles of these two joint axes. There are two cases distinguished from each other topologically.

Case 1. The domain that a pair of the two variables (q_j, q_k) takes is homeomorphic to a circular disk, D^2(Fig.4(a)).

Case 2. The domain that a pair of the two variables (q_j, q_k) takes is homeomorphic to a 1-disk, D^1(Fig.4(b)).

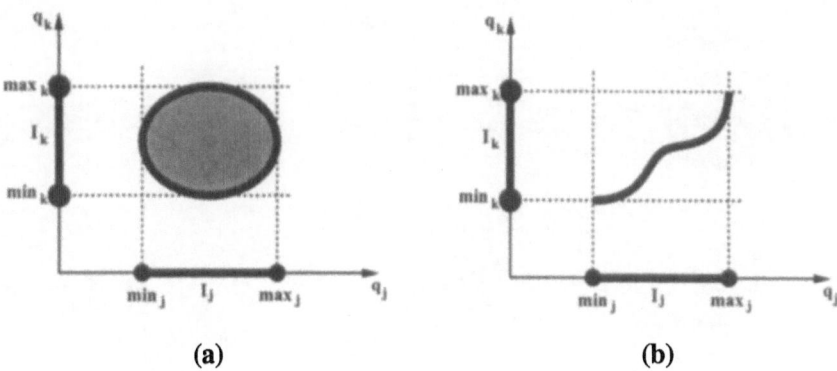

(a)   (b)

Figure 4: Two Cases of Dependency between Two Joint Axes

Case 1 dependency occurs, for example, between the two axes of a wrist joint. Case 2 dependency may occur, for example, between the two distal joints of any finger except for the thumb. Of course, these dependencies differ from person to person. There exist people who can, for example, move the two distal joints of a finger independently.

Now let us consider a system with an arbitrary degree of freedom. Let N be the minimum number of variables which describe the state of the system. Dependency which is related to more than two variables can be handled in the same way as the case of two variables. There exist l cases of dependencies which are related to l variables, depending on the dimension of the disk to which the domain of the l variables is homeomorphic. That is, the domain of the l variables is homeomorphic to D^1, D^2, ..., or D^l.

If there are dependencies, the domain $\mathcal{D}$, in which the variables $\mathbf{q}$ can take a value, becomes a subset of $\mathcal{C}$:

$$\mathcal{D} \subset \mathcal{C}. \tag{13}$$

If there is no dependency, a configuration $\mathbf{q}(t)$ is considered as a point in the configuration space $\mathcal{C}$. If there are dependencies between the joints in the system, $\mathbf{q}(t)$ cannot take all the possible values in $\mathcal{C}$, and takes the values in the domain $\mathcal{D} \subset \mathcal{C}$. If there is no dependency between the joints, the domain $\mathcal{D}$ is equal to $\mathcal{C}$.

In the case where dependencies between joints exist, we view the domain $\mathcal{D}$ as the *configuration space*. $\mathcal{D}$ can also be considered as a manifold. Let us consider p sets of joint axes, $\mathcal{L}_1, \mathcal{L}_2, ..., \mathcal{L}_p$, which satisfy the following:

$$
\begin{aligned}
j_1, j_2 \in \mathcal{L}_k &\implies \text{joints } j_1 \text{ and } j_2 \text{ are dependent on each other} \\
j_1 \in \mathcal{L}_k, j_2 \in \mathcal{L}_i, (k \neq i) &\implies \text{joints } j_1 \text{ and } j_2 \text{ are independent of each other}
\end{aligned}
\tag{14}
$$

The configuration space, $\mathcal{D}$, can be viewed as the direct product of manifolds representing the domains of variables for the mutually dependent sets of the joint axes and $\mathbf{R}^3 \times SO(3)$:

$$\mathcal{D} = \mathcal{D}_{\mathcal{L}_1} \times \mathcal{D}_{\mathcal{L}_2} \times ... \times \mathcal{D}_{\mathcal{L}_p} \times \mathbf{R}^3 \times SO(3). \tag{15}$$

388

where $\mathcal{D}_{\mathcal{L}_k}, (1 \leq k \leq p)$, denotes the domain of variables for the joint axes in the set $\mathcal{L}_k$. $\mathcal{D}_{\mathcal{L}_k}$ can also be viewed as the manifold.

For example, suppose that $\mathcal{L}_1 = \{1\}, \mathcal{L}_2 = \{2,3\}, \mathcal{L}_3 = \{4,5\}, \mathcal{L}_4 = \{6,7,8\}$ and that joints 4 and 5 are completely dependent on each other. Then, the configuration space $\mathcal{D}$ is expressed as follows(Fig.5):

$$\mathcal{D} = \mathcal{D}_{\mathcal{L}_1} \times \mathcal{D}_{\mathcal{L}_2} \times \mathcal{D}_{\mathcal{L}_3} \times \mathcal{D}_{\mathcal{L}_4} \times \mathbf{R}^3 \times SO(3). \tag{16}$$

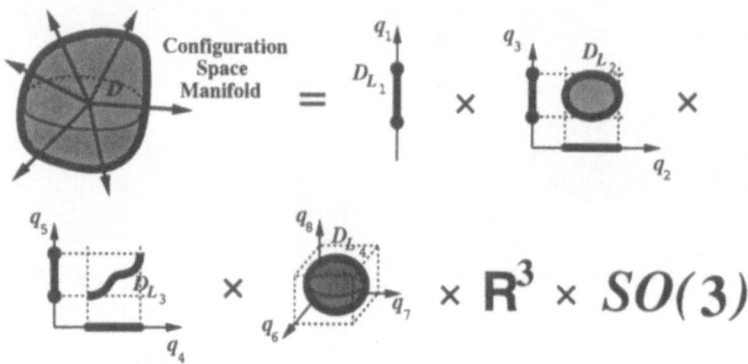

Figure 5: Example: Decomposition of Configuration Space $\mathcal{D}$

3.1.2. Task Feasibility
Jacobian Matrices
When we are interested in only the translational motion of an end-effector, we call the end-effector *positional.* When the rotation of an end-effector is of concern, we call the end-effector *spherical.* When we are interested in both the translation and rotation of an end-effector, we call the end-effector *spatial.*

Using the partial translational velocity and the partial angular velocity vectors, the Jacobian matrix for the i-th end-effector can be written according to the class of the end-effector as follows:

Jacobian matrix for a positional end-effector

$$\mathbf{J}_i = \begin{pmatrix} \check{\mathbf{V}}_1^i & \check{\mathbf{V}}_2^i & \cdots & \check{\mathbf{V}}_N^i \end{pmatrix}. \tag{17}$$

Jacobian matrix for a spherical end-effector

$$\mathbf{J}_i = \begin{pmatrix} \tilde{\mathbf{w}}_1^i & \tilde{\mathbf{w}}_2^i & \cdots & \tilde{\mathbf{w}}_N^i \end{pmatrix}. \tag{18}$$

Jacobian matrix for a spatial end-effector

$$\mathbf{J}_i = \begin{pmatrix} \check{\mathbf{V}}_1^i & \check{\mathbf{V}}_2^i & \cdots & \check{\mathbf{V}}_N^i \\ \tilde{\mathbf{w}}_1^i & \tilde{\mathbf{w}}_2^i & \cdots & \tilde{\mathbf{w}}_N^i \end{pmatrix}. \tag{19}$$

The Jacobian matrix is $3 \times N$ if the end-effector is positional or spherical. The Jacobian matrix is $6 \times N$ if the end-effector is spatial. The columns of the Jacobian matrix for the spatial end-effector can also be interpreted as *partial screw* vectors, since they express the contribution of each joint rotation and the position and orientation of the whole system to the screw motion of the output frame.

Singular Configurations
In order to consider the singularity, a square matrix is extracted from the Jacobian matrix. In the case of the positional or spherical end-effector, we extract arbitrary 3 column vectors from the Jacobian matrix. In the case of the spatial end-effector, we extract arbitrary 6 column vectors from the Jacobian matrix. We call the joint axes corresponding to the extracted column vectors the *extracted joint axes.*

Also, we call the extracted 3×3 or 6×6 square matrix the *extracted submatrix* for the extracted joint axes. If the extracted submatrix is regular, then we say that the extracted joint axes are in a *regular configuration*. In a regular configuration, the determinant of the extracted submatrix is not zero. If the extracted submatrix is *not* regular, then we say that the extracted joint axes are in a *singular configuration*. In a singular configuration, the determinant of the extracted submatrix becomes zero.

Similarly, in the case of the positional or spherical end-effector, we can extract arbitrary 1 or 2 column vectors from the Jacobian matrix. In the case of the spatial end-effector, we can extract arbitrary 1, 2, 3, 4, or 5 column vectors form the Jacobian matrix. Again, we call the joint axes corresponding to the extracted column vectors the *extracted joint axes*, and the extracted matrix, which is not square, the *extracted submatrix* for the extracted joint axes. If the rank of the extracted submatrix is equal to the number of the column vectors of the extracted submatrix, then we say that the extracted joint axes are in a *regular configuration*. Otherwise, we say that the extracted joint axes are in a *singular configuration*.

Singular configurations of the extracted joints can be studied in a more geometric fashion by considering the dimension of the space spanned by the column vectors in the extracted submatrices. In fact, the rank of the extracted submatrix is equivalent to the number of the linearly independent column vectors of the matrix. If the dimension of the space spanned by the column vectors is less than the number of the column vectors, the system is in a singular configuration. In other words, in a singular configuration, the column vectors become dependent and form a space with dimension less than the number of the column vectors.

Tasks

A *task* is conceptually an instantaneous motion given to an end-effector. A task is classified into a *positional*, *spherical*, or *spatial* task. A positional task requires only the translation of an end-effector. A spherical task requires only the rotation of an end-effector. A spatial task requires both the translation and rotation of an end-effector. Therefore, a task is given in the form of $\mathbf{V}^i$, $\bar{w}^i$, or $\$^i$.

Let $\mathbf{A}^i(t)$ denote the task for the i-th end-effector at time t. $\mathbf{A}^i(t)$ is $\mathbf{V}^i(t)$ if the i-th end-effector is positional, $\bar{w}^i(t)$ if spherical, or $\$^i(t)$ if spatial.

Movable Space of One End-Effector

Let $\mathcal{Q}(t)$ denote a set of all the values $\dot{\mathbf{q}}(t)$ can take at time t. The *movable space* of the i-th end-effector at time t, $\mathcal{M}_i(t)$, is defined as the following:

$$\mathcal{M}_i(t) = \{\mathbf{m} \mid \mathbf{m} = \mathbf{J}_i(t)\dot{\mathbf{q}}(t), \ \dot{\mathbf{q}}(t) \in \mathcal{Q}(t)\}, \tag{20}$$

where $\mathbf{J}_i(t)$ is the Jacobian matrix for the i-th end-effector at time t. The movable space represents a set of all the possible instantaneous motions of the i-th end-effector.

Task Feasibility of One End-effector

In order to determine the feasibility for the i-th end-effector to perform a given task at time t, it is necessary to check whether the task is included in the movable space of the i-th end-effector. *Task feasibility* of the i-th end-effector at t can be expressed as follows:

$$\mathbf{A}^i(t) \in \mathcal{M}_i(t). \tag{21}$$

If this task feasibility is true, the i-th end-effector can perform the task at time t. If false, it cannot perform the task. This task feasibility becomes false in the following two cases:

Case 1. The task is *not* contained in the space spanned by the column vectors in the Jacobian matrix $\mathbf{J}_i(t)$.

Case 2. $\mathbf{q}(t)$ is at the boundary of the configuration space manifold $\mathcal{D}$, and $\dot{\mathbf{q}}(t)$ which satisfies $\mathbf{A}^i(t) = \mathbf{J}_i(t)\dot{\mathbf{q}}(t)$ is directed to the outside of $\mathcal{D}$.

Case 2 will not appear if we neglect the joint rotation limits and the dependencies between the joints.

Movable Space

Let us consider a task which requires the simultaneous (cooperative) motions of two or more end-effectors. Let $\mathcal{E}(t)$ denote the set of end-effectors which are required to execute the task at time t. The *movable space*, $\mathcal{M}(t)$, is expressed as follows:

$$\mathcal{M}(t) = \{(..., \mathbf{m}_i, ...)_{i \in \mathcal{E}(t)} \mid \mathbf{m}_i = \mathbf{J}_i(t)\dot{\mathbf{q}}(t), \ \dot{\mathbf{q}}(t) \in \mathcal{Q}(t)\}. \tag{22}$$

Task Feasibility

The *task feasibility* at time t can be expressed as follows:

$$(..., \mathbf{A}^i(t), ...)_{i \in \mathcal{E}(t)} \in \mathcal{M}(t). \tag{23}$$

Given a continuous task $\mathcal{T}$ which requires, at time t ($t_{start} \leq t \leq t_{end}$), the end-effectors in the set $\mathcal{E}(t)$ to perform an instantaneous motion $\mathbf{A}^i(t)$, the *feasibility* of the continuous task is expressed as follows:

$$(..., \mathbf{A}^i(t), ...)_{i \in \mathcal{E}(t)} \in \mathcal{M}(t), \ \text{for } \forall t(t_{start} \leq t \leq t_{end}). \tag{24}$$

3.1.3. Task Feasibility Check

A task, in general, requires the simultaneous motions of multiple end-effectors. The methodology to check the task feasibility presented below first checks the task feasibility of each end-effector separately. Then it checks the possibility that the motions of all the end-effectors required for the task can be performed simultaneously. Finally, if the configuration is at the boundary of the configuration space manifold, the the methodology checks if the possible solution is directed to the interior of the configuration space manifold. This check is performed by checking one by one the projection of the vector representing the solution on the manifolds representing the domains of variables for mutually independent sets of the joint axes.

First step: Task feasibility check for individual end-effectors

Check the task feasibility of individual end-effectors one by one. Consider the i-th end-effector. Solve the following system of linear equations in order to find out the possible $\dot{\mathbf{q}}(t)$:

$$\mathbf{A}^i(t) = \mathbf{J}_i(t)\dot{\mathbf{q}}(t). \tag{25}$$

If this system of linear equations has no solution, the task feasibility in terms of the i-th end-effector becomes false, and consequently the task feasibility of the given task is also false.

If this system of linear equations has a single solution or a set of solutions, record the constraints which determine the single solution or the set of solutions as $\mathbf{Co}_i(t)$.

Second step: Task feasibility check for all end-effectors

Check if all the end-effectors can perform the given tasks concurrently. There exists the possibility that the end-effectors can perform the tasks only sequentially, not concurrently.

For each i there exists the constraint $\mathbf{Co}_i(t)$. As a whole, the constraints form a system of linear equations. If this system of linear equations has no solution, the simultaneous motions of the end-effectors cannot be performed, thus the task feasibility becomes false.

If it has a single solution or a set of solutions, remember the constraints which determine the single solution or the set of solutions as $\mathbf{Co}(t)$.

Third step: Boundary check

If the configuration $\mathbf{q}(t)$ is in the interior of the configuration space manifold $\mathcal{D}$, then the task is feasible.

If the configuration $\mathbf{q}(t)$ is at the boundary of $\mathcal{D}$, check if there exists a solution which satisfies the constraint $\mathbf{Co}(t)$ obtained in the second step, and is directed to the interior of the configuration space manifold. This check is performed by checking one by one the projection of the vector representing the solution on the manifolds, $\mathcal{D}_{\mathcal{L}_k}, (1 \leq k \leq p)$, representing the domains of variables for mutually independent sets of the joint axes. If such a solution exists, the task is feasible. Otherwise, the task is infeasible.

In summary, let us describe the relationships between various notations introduced in the above discussions:

$$\begin{aligned}
\mathbf{f}_i &: \mathbf{q}(t) \in \mathcal{D} \longmapsto \mathbf{x}_i(t) \in \mathcal{W}_i \\
\mathbf{J}_i(t) &: \dot{\mathbf{q}}(t) \in \mathcal{Q}(t) \longmapsto \mathbf{A}^i(t) \in \mathcal{M}_i(t)
\end{aligned} \quad (i \in \mathcal{E}(t)). \quad (26)$$

Given a task $\mathbf{A}_i(t)$ to the i-th end-effector, $\dot{\mathbf{q}}(t)$ which performs $\mathbf{A}_i(t)$ is computed in the first step. In the second step, the $\dot{\mathbf{q}}(t)$ which performs all $\mathbf{A}_i(t)$, $(i \in \mathcal{E}(t))$ is computed. In the last step, if $\mathbf{q}(t)$ is at the boundary of $\mathcal{D}$, $\dot{\mathbf{q}}(t)$ is checked whether it is directed to the interior of $\mathcal{D}$ or to the exterior of $\mathcal{D}$.

3.1.4. Infeasible Task: Singular Configuration, Boundary Transgression, and Disharmony
When the given task is infeasible, the cause is one or some combination of the three situations: singular configuration, boundary transgression, and disharmony.

Singular Configuration
Extract arbitrary 3 joint axes from the joint axes which can influence the i-th end-effector, if this end-effector is positional or spherical. Extract arbitrary 6 joint axes, if the end-effector is spatial. If the extracted joint axes are in a *singular configuration*, the extracted column vectors span the space whose dimension is less than the number of the extracted column vectors. If the vector representing the task is not contained in this space, the task is not feasible in terms of the extracted joint axes. Infeasible tasks due to the singular configuration can be detected during the first step of the task feasibility check.

Boundary Transgression
Even if the vector representing the task is in the space spanned by all the column vectors in Jacobian matrix, when the system configuration is at the boundary of the configuration space, the motions which are directed to the outside of the configuration space manifold cannot be performed. We call this case the *boundary transgression*. Infeasible tasks due to the boundary transgression can be detected during the third step of the task feasibility check.

Disharmony
When the given task requires the (cooperative) simultaneous motions of the multiple end-effectors, there are the situations where the simultaneous motions are impossible even if the tasks given to the end-effectors could be performed separately. We call this case the *disharmony*. Infeasible tasks due to the disharmony can be detected during the second step of the task feasibility check.

3.1.5. The Choice of Root Body Frame
The choice of the root body frame is arbitrary. So we choose here the root body frame such that the origin of the root body frame coincides with the location of the shoulder joint. If we permit the free translation of the shoulder, the task feasibility will always be true. In practice, however, there are many cases where the shoulder is not permitted to move freely or the motion of the shoulder is not desirable. In this case, it is often necessary to consider the position of the shoulder as fixed.

In the case of the *Shorinji Kempo*, the meaning of the task for the performer of a technique is different from for the receiver of the technique. For the performer, the task is to move the end-effectors to throw the opponent. On the other hand, the task for the receiver is classified into two types depending on the condition. While the receiver is able to resist, the task will be to move the end-effectors in order not to be thrown by the performer. Once the receiver is not able to resist any more, the task will now be to move the end-effectors just as the performer forces to. At this point, if the receiver can move the end-effectors without the shoulder motion, the receiver has not be thrown yet. If the receiver cannot, the shoulder must be moved and consequently the receiver is being thrown at last.

3.1.6. Boundary of Manifold
The boundary of D^l is the $(l-1)$-sphere, S^{l-1}. At the boundary point p of the domain as the topological space, the neighborhood of p, $U(p)$, is homeomorphic to the open set of H^l, where H^l denotes the half space of $\mathbf{R}^l$, $\{(x_1, x_2, ..., x_l) \in \mathbf{R}^l \mid x_l \geq 0\}$.

Let us consider the peculiarity of the boundary point in the configuration space. We can distinguish between the type $\mathbf{R}^N$ and the type H^N of $\mathcal{Q}(t)$ as follows (N is the degree of freedom of the configuration space):

Type $\mathbf{R}^N$
  $\exists h : \mathbf{R}^N \to \mathbf{R}^N, h :$ homeomorphism, and $h(\dot{\mathbf{0}}) = \mathbf{0}$,

$$h(\mathcal{Q}(t)) = \begin{cases} \mathbf{R}^N, & \text{ideally, or} \\ D^N, & \text{practically.} \end{cases} \tag{27}$$

Type H^N
  $\exists h : \mathbf{R}^N \to \mathbf{R}^N, h :$ homeomorphism, and $h(\mathbf{0}) = \mathbf{0}$,

$$h(\mathcal{Q}(t)) = \begin{cases} H^N, & \text{ideally, or} \\ D^N \cap H^N, & \text{practically.} \end{cases} \tag{28}$$

The type $\mathbf{R}^N$ occurs when $\mathbf{q}(t)$ is in the interior, $\mathcal{D}_0 = \mathcal{D} - \partial\mathcal{D}$, and the type H^N in the boundary $\partial\mathcal{D}$.

3.2. Measurement of Joint Limits and Dependencies Using Model Fitting System

3.2.1. Model Fitting System Overview
We developed a system with which we can fit interactively the model of the hand and arm to the multiple images of the actual hand and arm taken by the multiple video cameras (Sun 1989, Kunii 1990, Wang 1992). The system can also fit the model automatically using inverse kinematics to help the tiresome work of the manual fitting. The user can choose both the manual and automatic fitting scheme according to the situation. Normally, the user first lets the system fit the model automatically, and then manually corrects the errors.

The automatic fitting process uses the two dimensional position of the center of gravity of each segment in the image and compute the three dimensional position of the center of gravity of the segment using the principle of stereo. Then, using inverse kinematics, the system computes the joint angles which yields the position of the center of gravity of the model best matched with the position of the center of gravity acquired from the images.

Let us follow the fitting process. First, the five images are drawn in the background of the multiple windows. Then the user lets the system fit the model to the images. Though the result of automatic fitting suffers from the error and is not completely acceptable yet, this automatic fitting process saves the user considerable time to fit the model roughly. Then the user manually fits the model accurately. The user can either input the correct position of the center of gravity of the segment in the images and let the system fit the model again, or fit manually by changing the joint angles directly using the slider.

After this model fitting process, the joint angles are saved. In this way, the configuration of various postures of the hand and arm can be measured. In the first place, we measured the joint rotation limits and added the acquired data of the limits to the model. Then, we measured the dependencies between the joints and also added the acquired date of the dependencies to the model to make the model complete. The following two subsections show the result of the experiment for finding out the maxima and minima of the joint rotation angles and the experiment for finding out the dependencies between the joints.

3.2.2. Experiments
The experiments for finding out the joint rotation limits and the dependencies between the joints were carried out using the model fitting system.

The result of the experiment for finding out the joint rotation limits of the forearm rotation about the principal axis acquired in this way is shown in Fig.6.

Fig.7 shows the result of the experiment for finding out the dependency between the two axes of the wrist joint. The horizontal axis represents the angle of rotation toward back and forth, and the vertical axis right and left. There exists the dependency between these two axes of rotation of the wrist joint. The six extreme postures were taken by a person and the model of the person was fitted to the images of the postures. The angles of rotation acquired by the fitting process are plotted as the black dots and the six dots are connected. The region surrounded by the lines can be considered the domain in which a pair of the two variables describing the rotation angles around the wrist axes can take a value.

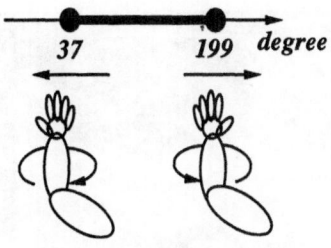

Figure 6: Result of an Experiment for Finding out the Maximum and Minimum Rotation Angles of the Forearm about the Principal Axis

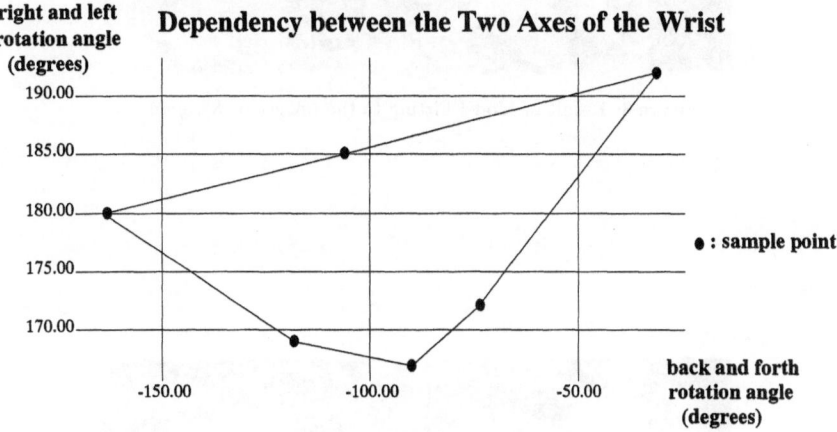

Figure 7: Result of an Experiment for Finding out Dependency between the Two Axes of the Wrist

This kind of relationship between the two variables describing the joint rotation angles could not have been easily acquired, if there had not been the model with the kinematic parameters measured for a specific person and the model fitting system with which the model can be fitted to the images of the hand and arm postures.

4. TESTING AND VALIDATION OF THE MODEL AGAINST A TECHNIQUE OF MARTIAL ARTS, THE SHORINJI KEMPO

In this section, our model of hands and arms is applied to the example of martial arts, the *Shorinji Kempo*. One of the techniques, *Kirigote*, is analyzed using the concept of the task feasibility.

The images of the techniques of the *Shorinji Kempo* were taken by five video cameras, three from the upper, and the rest two from the lower positions. The scene containing the moment when the opponent starts to be thrown down was extracted. Fig.8 shows the result of the fitting of the model to the person who is thrown down.

Suppose that two representative points of contact of the opponent are chosen and the forces applied at the points are given as shown in Fig.9. Green dots indicate the representative points of contact and the lines originating from the dots indicate the task given to the end-effectors. We consider that the tasks are positional. Thus the lines indicate the velocities required for the end-effectors to perform

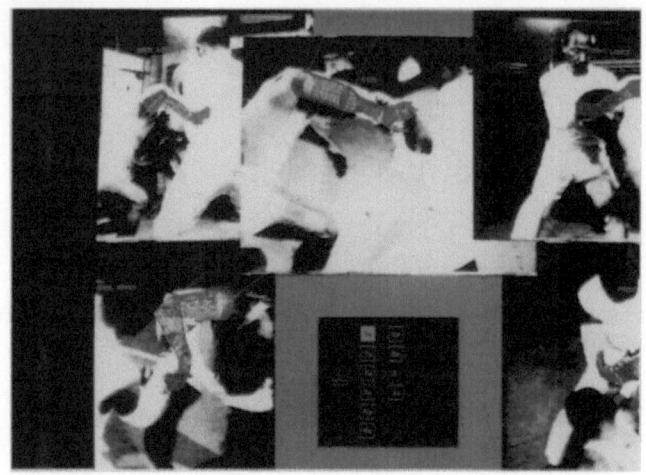

Figure 8: Result of Model Fitting to the Images of *Kirigote*

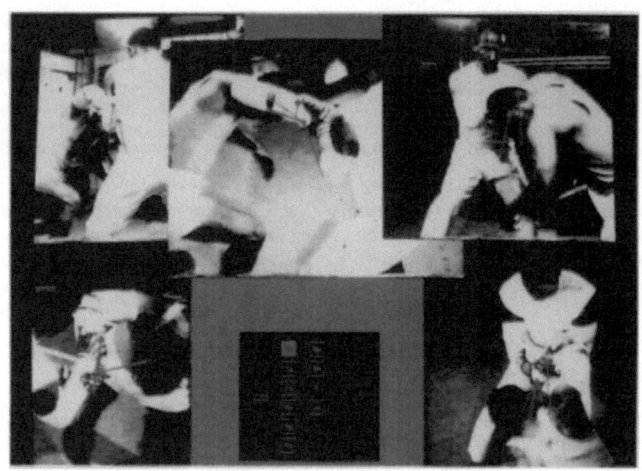

Figure 9: Tasks and Singular Configuration in *Kirigote*

the given tasks. Because the opponent loses the balance and cannot resist the forces applied at the representative points, the task given to him is to perform the motion which results from the applied forces.

Using the task feasibility check procedure presented in Section 3, it is shown that this task is infeasible without the shoulder translation. Let us analyze the reasons why this task is infeasible.

Singular Configuration
First of all, consider the end-effector which is farther from the body. Then the extracted three joint axes, the elbow axis, the principal axis of the forearm, and the back and forth rotation axis of the wrist, are in a *singular configuration*. The absolute value of the determinant of the normalized extracted submatrix in terms of the extracted joint axes are computed:

$$|\text{Determinant}| = 0.007895. \tag{29}$$

In general, the absolute value of the determinant of a normalized square matrix takes the value between 0 and 1:

$$0 \leq |\text{Determinant}| \leq 1. \tag{30}$$

If the matrix is orthogonal, the absolute value of the determinant is 1, whereas if the matrix is singular, the value is 0. Thus the value 0.007895 means the matrix is almost singular. The column vectors are the partial velocity vectors. They are shown as the red lines originating from the end-effector in Fig.9. This figure shows that the partial velocity vectors in terms of the three axes span almost 2-dimensional space. The task velocity vector is *not* contained in this 2-dimensional space. Thus the rotation about the shoulder joint is needed in order to perform the task.

Disharmony
Suppose that end-effector 1 is the end-effector which is nearer to the body and end-effector 2 the farther one.

Solving $\mathbf{A}^1(t) = \mathbf{J}_1(t)\dot{\mathbf{q}}(t)$ yields the solution: angular velocity 4.599256 about the shoulder joint axis $(0.466886, 0.260193, -0.845173)$.

Solving $\mathbf{A}^2(t) = \mathbf{J}_2(t)\dot{\mathbf{q}}(t)$ yields a possible solution: angular velocity 1.294783 about the shoulder joint axis $(0.097477, 0.247768, -0.963903)$.

Disharmony occurs because the shoulder rotation is insufficient to satisfy these tasks concurrently.

Boundary Transgression
Solving simultaneously the above two systems of equations yields a single possible solution, including the rotation of the wrist, which, however, cannot be performed due to *boundary transgression*. The configuration of the opponent at this time is at the boundary of the configuration space manifold. Let us consider the $\mathcal{D}_{\mathcal{L}_k}$ which represents the manifold for the rotation angles of two joint axes of the wrist. The situation is depicted in Fig.10. The shape of $\mathcal{D}_{\mathcal{L}_k}$ was measured in the experiment. The black dot represents the projection of the configuration on $\mathcal{D}_{\mathcal{L}_k}$. The arrow originating from the dot represents the required joint angle velocities of the wrist. By calculation, it is $(-25.879189, -14.296033)$. The picture shows that the velocity is directed to the outside of $\mathcal{D}_{\mathcal{L}_k}$. Thus, the task is shown to be *infeasible* without the shoulder translation. It means that the opponent must be thrown down since the shoulder position must move downward in order to perform the task.

5. CONCLUSIONS

5.1. Summary

A model of human hands and arms which can decide whether the given task is feasible or not was presented. Hands and arms were modeled as an open-tree multibody system, which was a system of rigid bodies connected by the joints. The contact surface of a body with other bodies was approximated by a finite set of representative points of contact through which the representative forces were applied.

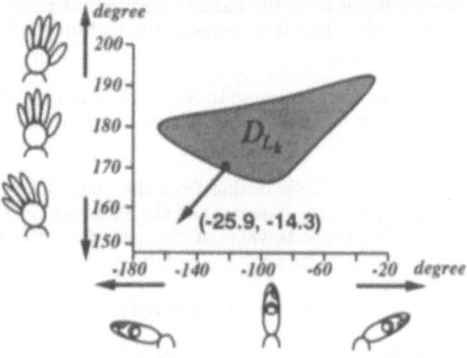

Figure 10: Boundary Transgression in *Kirigote*

The representative points of contact were viewed as the end-effectors, through which the hand or the arm can influence the other bodies.

Forward kinematic functions which map the configuration space manifold to the workspace manifold and their Jacobian matrices were formulated. The joint rotation limits and the dependencies between the joints were defined in the configuration space.

A task was considered as a set of the instantaneous motions of the end-effectors, and the task feasibility was defined using the concept of the movable space.

A procedure to check the task feasibility based on the model was presented. The causes which lead to the infeasible task were classified into three situations: singular configuration, boundary transgression, and disharmony.

Using the model of the hands and arms, one of the techniques of the *Shorinji Kempo*, *Kirigote*, was analyzed to demonstrate the usefulness of the model. The process of being thrown down was explained using the concept of task feasibility.

5.2. Future Work

One of the most challenging extensions of this research is to integrate the kinematic model studied in this paper with the dynamics. Inverse dynamics will be one of the tools when the dynamics is dealt with. Difficulty may arise when the system forms the kinematic loops. In general, when a loop is formed, the system of the dynamic equations cannot be solved unless any other constraints are imposed on the system.

The singular configurations of the system of the hand and arm when an end-effector is fixed can be enumerated. The problem, however, is not so simple if two or more end-effectors need to be considered simultaneously. Actually, there can be a situation where the approximation of the contact surface by the representative points of contact is not desirable. If more accuracy is needed, we should either increase the number of the end-effectors, or consider the infinite set of the end-effectors as a limit.

The techniques of the *Shorinji Kempo* may be classified according to the singular configurations. In fact, the classification of the techniques according to the form is known. The classification possibly has some relationship with the singular configurations.

The automation of the fitting process will be an important topic. Some hardware support will be necessary when a large number of degrees of freedom are dealt with. Using the colors and textures will be one way to accomplish the automation, although there may be some difficulty concerning the stability.

It will be interesting to consider the physiological features of the hand and the arm in relation with the degrees of freedom, the movable space, and the task feasibility. If, in the future, we use the robot arms instead of the real human hands in many areas, the understanding of the kinematic features of the human hands and arms will be considerably helpful.

The analysis of the kinematic features of the hands and arms in various fields of sports, arts, and performances will be of interest. The common characteristics may be extracted from a variety of the examples.

The results of this paper can be extended to the general systems other than the hand and the arm. In general, a system has the controllable parameters and the system states. When the singularity occurs, the system state cannot be completely controlled by the parameters. As a matter of fact, the singularity theory has been applied to many areas. The results of this paper are applicable to the systems whose parameters have their domains and depend on one another.

ACKNOWLEDGMENT

The authors are grateful to Dr. Yoshihisa Shinagawa and Dr. Jintae Lee of the Kunii Laboratory for their helpful comments. The authors also want to express appreciation for the cooperation of Mr. Kimishi Ishida of the Wacom Co., Ltd.

6. REFERENCES

Burdick JW IV (1988) Kinematic Analysis and Design of Redundant Robot Manipulators. PhD thesis, Stanford University.

Craig JJ (1986) Introduction to Robotics: Manipulation and Control. Addison-Wesley, Reading, Mass.

Gourret J, Magnenat-Thalmann N and Thalmann D (1989) Simulation of Object and Human Skin Deformations. Computer Graphics, Vol.23, No.3, pp.21-30.

Huston RL (1990) Multibody Dynamics. Butterworth-Heinemann.

Kane TR and Levinson DA (1983) The Use of Kane's Dynamical Equations in Robotics. The International Journal of Robotics Research, Vol.2, No.3, pp.3-20.

Kunii TL and Sun L (1990) Dynamic Analysis-Based Human Animation. CG International '90, Springer-Verlag, pp.3-15.

Landsmeer JMF (1963) The Coordination of Finger-Joint Motions. The Journal of Bone and Joint Surgery, Vol.45-A, No.8, pp.1654-1662.

Lee P, Wei S, Zhao J and Badler NI (1990) Strength Guided Motion. Computer Graphics, Vol.24, No.4, pp.253-262.

Monheit G and Badler NI (1991) A Kinematic Model of the Human Spine and Torso. IEEE Computer Graphics & Applications, Vol.11, No.2, pp.29-38.

Rijpkema H and Girard M (1991) Computer Animation of Knowledge-Based Human Grasping. Computer Graphics, Vol.25, No.4, pp.339-348.

Sun L (1989) Dynamics Model-based Human Motion Analysis and Animation. PhD thesis, the University of Tokyo.

Wang K (1992) Automated Input and Recognition of Human Body Motions Based on Image Segmentation. Master's thesis, the University of Tokyo.

398

BIOGRAPHICAL SKETCH

Tosiyasu L. Kunii is currently Professor of Information and Computer Science, the University of Tokyo.
He authored and edited more than 32 computer science books, and published more than 120 refereed academic/technical papers in computer science and applications areas.
Dr. Kunii is Honorary President of the Computer Graphics Society, Editor-in-Chief of *The Visual Computer: An International Journal of Computer Graphics* (Springer-Verlag), Associate Editor-in-Chief of *The Journal of Visualization and Computer Animation* (John Wiley & Sons) and on the Editorial Board of *IEEE Transactions on Knowledge and Data Engineering, VLDB Journal* and *IEEE Computer Graphics and Applications*. He is on the IFIP Modeling and Simulation Working Group, and the IFIP Computer Graphics Working Group. He is on the board of directors of Japan Society of Sports Industry and also of Japan Society of Simulation and Gaming.
He received the B.Sc., M.Sc., and D.Sc. degrees in chemistry all from the University of Tokyo in 1962, 1964, and 1967, respectively. He is a fellow of IEEE and a member of ACM, BCS, IPSJ and IEICE.
Address: Department of Information Science, Faculty of Science, the University of Tokyo, 7-3-1 Hongo, Bunkyo-ku, Tokyo 113 JAPAN.

Yukinobu Tsuchida received B.Sc. and M.Sc. degrees in information science from the University of Tokyo in 1991 and 1993, respectively. He is currently at Fanuc Ltd. This research was done while he was at the University of Tokyo. His research interests include computer graphics, computer vision, and robotics. He is a member of ACM and IPSJ.
Address: Department of Information Science, Faculty of Science, the University of Tokyo, 7-3-1 Hongo, Bunkyo-ku, Tokyo 113 JAPAN.

Tsunehiro Arai has been working at Headquarters of Shorinji Kempo Federation since 1968. He is currently a director of Educational and Technical Affairs Department. He has 28 years' experience of *Shorinji Kempo*.
Address: Shorinji Kempo Headquarters, 3-1-59, Hondori, Tadotsu-cho, Nakatado-gun, Kagawa 764 JAPAN.

Hiroshi Matsuda has been working at Headquarters of Shorinji Kempo Federation since 1982. He is currently an assistant director of Publishing Department and a chief editor of the monthly magazine *Shorinji Kempo*. He has 20 years' experience of *Shorinji Kempo*.
Address: Shorinji Kempo Tokyo Office, 1-3-5, Uehara, Shibuya-ku, Tokyo 151 JAPAN.

Masahiro Shirahama has been working at Headquarters of Shorinji Kempo Federation since 1984. He is currently an editor of the monthly magazine *Shorinji Kempo*. He has 18 years' experience of *Shorinji Kempo*.
Address: Shorinji Kempo Tokyo Office, 1-3-5, Uehara, Shibuya-ku, Tokyo 151 JAPAN.

Shinya Miura has been working at Headquarters of Shorinji Kempo Federation since 1986. He is currently at Publishing Department. He has 12 years' experience of *Shorinji Kempo*.
Address: Shorinji Kempo Tokyo Office, 1-3-5, Uehara, Shibuya-ku, Tokyo 151 JAPAN.

The Elastic Surface Layer Model for Animated Character Construction

Russell Turner and Daniel Thalmann

ABSTRACT

A model is described for creating three-dimensional animated characters. In this new type of layered construction technique, called the elastic surface layer model, a simulated elastically deformable skin surface is wrapped around a traditional kinematic articulated figure. Unlike previous layered models, the skin is free to slide along the underlying surface layers constrained by reaction forces which push the surface out and spring forces which pull the surface in to the underlying layers. By tuning the parameters of the physically-based model, a variety of surface shapes and behaviors can be obtained such as more realistic-looking skin deformation at the joints, skin sliding over muscles, and dynamic effects such as squash-and-stretch and follow-through. Since the elastic model derives all of its input forces from the underlying articulated figure, the animator may specify all of the physical properties of the character once, during the initial character design process, after which a complete animation sequence can be created using a traditional skeleton animation technique. A reasonably complex character at low surface resolution can be simulated at interactive speeds so than an animator can both design the character and animate it in a completely interactive, direct-manipulation environment. Once a motion sequence has been specified, the entire simulation can be recalculated at a higher surface resolution for better visual results. An implementation on a Silicon Graphics Iris workstation is described.

Keywords: Character Animation, Physically-Based Models, Deformation, Elasticity, Articulated Figures.

1. INTRODUCTION

Computer generated character animation remains an open research subject. While many other aspects of commercial animation have developed well-established computerized techniques, character animation is still, for the most part, the domain of the traditional animator drawing by hand. In the two-dimensional realm, computerized ink and paint, morphing and image processing have become standard tools. In the three-dimensional area, computer animation of backgrounds and rigid bodies are common techniques. Several commercial software systems now allow the creation and animation of articulated figures, however, at least two major problems still prevent 3D character animation from becoming versatile enough to be generally accepted by the commercial animation community.

The first problem is that of natural-looking motion of the articulated skeleton. This is without doubt a difficult problem because the skeletal motion of a real human or animal is a result of both its passive physical properties and its active nervous system activity. Much progress has been made in the development of kinematic techniques such as inverse kinematics and key-frame interpolation of joint angles [Girard 87], which provide good control at the expense of realistic-looking dynamics. Forward dynamic techniques [Armstrong 85], [Wilhelms 85], which can generate natural-looking motion, are nonetheless difficult to control. Spacetime constraint techniques [Witken 88], [Isaacs 87] hold much promise to provide both control and natural dynamics simultaneously, but they are currently limited to fairly simple articulated figures. For some time to come, practical articulated skeleton animation systems will probably rely on a hybrid combination of these techniques. We will not be addressing this problem in this paper.

The second problem is that of deformation of the skin surface shape. Many geometric deformation techniques from the area of solids modeling are available, such as global deformation [Barr 84] and free-form deformations [Sederberg 86]. A variety of surface modeling methods have been proposed for representing deformable animated characters from standard polygonal surface meshes to implicit surfaces such as soft objects [Bloomenthal 90] and parametric surfaces such as hierarchical B-splines [Forsey 88].These geometric techniques provide ease of control and rapid computation but they have little relation to the physical reality of a flesh and blood creature, and therefore tend to lack realism. In particular, they tend to represent characters either as geometric surfaces, or as uniform solids, both of which ignore the complex internal structure of human or animal anatomy. Physically-based deformable models [Terzopoulos 87], are based on the elastic and viscous properties of continuous media and therefore can produce very realistic looking simulations of deformable materials. Physically-based models, however, are usually difficult to control and therefore to be useful, elastic models must be constrained properly [Platt 88]. Because they represent continuous media as large numbers of discrete nodal elements, elastic models can also be very CPU-intensive, especially when simulating solids using three-dimensional lattices. However, elastic surfaces, simulated as two-dimensional lattices, require fewer numbers of discrete nodes to produce useful results and therefore are not as demanding of CPU time. It is now possible, using high-end workstations, to simulate a reasonably complex surface of a few hundred mass points in real-time.

The issue of speed is important because for 3D character animation to become practical, it must be possible to create and animate the characters interactively. However sophisticated the models become, whether animating simple animals or realistic-looking human characters, character animation will always be an essentially creative process and it is necessary that the software tools be accessible to non-technical, creative animators. For these reasons, we believe that a model for three-dimensional character animation must be developed that provides a compromise between interactive speed and realism, and between control and physically realistic behavior.

Fortunately, the two problems of skeleton animation and skin deformation can usually be separated, and for the remainder of this paper, we will present a new approach to the skin deformation problem for animated characters, relying on standard techniques for animating the articulated skeleton. This approach, called the elastic surface layer model, falls into a general class of what we call *elastic layered models* of animated character construction. In section 2 we review previous work in layered construction models and layered elastic models. In section 3 we describe the elastic surface layer model we have developed. Section 4 gives mathematical details of the physical simulation and force constraints. Section 5 discusses our implementation using the LEMAN system, and Section 5 presents our conclusions.

2. THE LAYERED APPROACH

For designing animated characters, a common approach taken by artists and traditional animators is to work in layers. First a stick figure is drawn, representing the skeleton, followed by rounded forms to represent the flesh, followed by the finished outline, representing the skin [Culhane 88]. This same sort of approach is taken in clay animation, where plasticene is wrapped around a metal armature.

2.1 Layered Models

It is therefore not surprising that the first computer animated characters should also be constructed in layers. Magnenat-Thalmann and Thalmann used a two-layered approach to construct human characters in the film "Rendez-vous à Montréal," [Magnenat-Thalmann 87], in which a digitized outer enveloped was deformed by an underlying skeleton using abstract muscle procedures. The film "Tony De Peltrie" used combinations of digitized facial expressions to deform a polygonal surface. Implicit surfaces, called soft objects or blobbies surrounding a stick figure skeleton have been used to create deformable characters [Bloomenthal 90]. Forsey used hierarchical B-splines with control points attached to a skeleton for modeling animals and human joints [Forsey 91]

One of the major advantages of layered computer models is that it allows the animation process to be divided into two stages: character construction, in which the behavior of the layers and attachment to the skeleton is defined, and character animation, in which only the skeleton motion is specified. The outer layers then derive all their input from the skeleton motion alone, greatly simplifying the animation process. One basic limitation with all of these character models is the absence of any physical basis for the model. Both the skeleton and the surface envelope are purely geometric models. Furthermore, outer layers are usually tightly bound to the underlying skeleton, preventing the skin from sliding along the underlying layers.

2.2   Layered Elastic Models

Layered elastic models add physically based elastic components to some or all of the layers to improve realism. A simple example of this type of approach is Pacific Data Images *Goop* system, in which a mass and spring with damping are attached to each vertex of a polygonal model [Walters 89]. Moving the model causes the vertex points to oscillate, causing a jello-like effect, however, the surface points are not attached to each other, so the skin has no surface-like physical behavior.

A more sophisticated examples of layered elastic construction for animated characters is found in the Critter system [Chadwick 89] in which a network of connected springs and masses is used to create a control point lattice for free-form deformations of the geometric surface. Some of the control points are bound to links of the underlying skeleton so that, when the skeleton is animated, the unattached mass points are influenced to move through the spring lattice. In this way, a physical simulation controls a solid deformation. Although the mass-spring lattice allows for shape control over the muscle deformation and a technique for bending at the joints, the skin is still fundamentally a geometric surface model, not a model of a physical skin.

A model for articulated figures is proposed by Gascuel et al [Gascuel 91] in which the control points for an interpolating spline surface are bound to a rigid bone layer by springs. The finite element method is used by Gourret et al [Gourret 89], who describe a human hand modeled as a volume element mesh surrounding bones, and Chen et al [Chen 92], who have developed a biomechanically-based model of muscles on bone.

A sophisticated example of a layered elastic model is used by Terzopoulos to implement facial animation [Terzopoulos 91]. In this model, an elastic solid simulation, consisting of a mass-spring lattice of depth three, is attached to a human skull model and deformed by muscles which take the form of force constraints between the skin surface and the underlying bone. The springs are biphasic to emulate the non-linear behavior of real skin, and volume preserving constraints simulate the effects of incompressible fatty tissue.

A limitation of most of these techniques is that they model the layers as components of a single deformable solid material. Although this material can vary its properties from point to point, his does not always capture the complexity of real anatomy in which the different layers can have very different mechanical properties and can be loosely bound to each other. It is therefore not easy to reproduce such effects as skin sliding over underlying muscle surfaces.

3.   THE ELASTIC SURFACE LAYER MODEL

We have developed the elastic surface layer model in an attempt to improve realism of the skin surface and to find a practical compromise between purely kinematic and purely dynamic layered modeling approaches. By modeling the skin as an independent elastic surface and using reaction constraints to push it outside the underlying layers, we can achieve more realistic skin behavior in a practical system for constructing and animating 3D characters. To explain how we do this, first let us step back and reexamine the fundamental layered character animation problem: modeling anatomy.

3.1   Modeling Anatomy

Human and animal character animation requires a careful study of anatomy and even the most stylized, animated characters still have an underlying structure which contributes to their outer shape and dynamics. How does one begin to try to construct a computer model of human or animal anatomy? Obviously, the anatomical figure is immensely complex, but it is possible to break its important components down into several well-defined layers that contribute to the overall visual appearance and behavior. Going from the inside out, these layers can be defined as: *skeleton, bone, muscle, fat, and skin*. On top of the skin layer can be added *hair* (or *fur*) and *clothing*, if desired, although this will not be addressed in this paper. From the point of view of creating a computer model, each of these layers has distinct geometrical and dynamic properties which make it suitable for particular modeling techniques.

Bones, for example, are for all practical purposes rigid bodies, and their arrangement in a skeleton can be modeled very well as an articulated hierarchy of rigid bodies. Muscles are highly deformable and furthermore the only structure under active control, so physically-based models of passive materials are probably not appropriate for modeling muscle shape. Geometrical models of deformable surfaces, with a few input parameters such as joint angle and tension, are probably the most useful in this case. The fat and skin layers, by contrast, are completely passive structures and therefore more amenable to physically-based simulation. The skin layer is characterized by being relatively thin and is therefore a good candidate for simulation using an elastic surface. The fat layer separates the muscle layer from the skin and can be defined by its thickness at each point on the skin.

3.2 The Character Animation Pipeline

An attractive aspect of this kind of layered breakdown is that, to a good approximation, each layer is dependent only on what is inside it, not the other way around. Therefore, it is possible to construct a character animation pipeline in which each stage of the pipeline adds another layer and can be modeled by a separate algorithm. For example, there exist a number of techniques for generating animated skeleton sequences. Output from an algorithm using any of these techniques can be used to derive the skeleton motion which can then drive the outer layers. This is not a perfect model, of course. In reality it is the muscles that drive the skeleton and not the other way around, skin and fat contribute mass which effects the dynamic motion of the joint, and collisions with other objects are transmitted back through the skin to the skeleton. Nonetheless, these situations can often be handled as special cases of feedback so that the pipeline model can make a good approximation under a variety of circumstances.

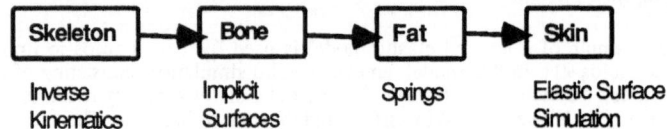

Figure 1: Example of a layered character animation pipeline

Another interesting aspect of the layered breakdown is that (with the possible exception of the skeleton motion) each successive layer is more and more visible and therefore requires more physical realism. Therefore it makes sense to build more sophisticated physically-based models for the outer layers while the inner layers can be simpler kinematic or geometric models. In fact, the only layer we can actually see is the skin layer, so it makes sense that this should be the starting point for a physically-based simulation.

3.3 A Hybrid Model

The different characteristics of the different anatomical layers suggest a hybrid model in which different modeling techniques are used at each stage of the pipeline to form the final layered model. Each layer uses the type of modeling technique most suited to its characteristics. Figure 2 shows a diagram of the different components of the elastic surface layer model. We start with the outer skin layer which we model as an physically-based simulation of an elastic surface. We then work inward, considering each successive layer as a constraint acting on the layer outside it.

3.4 Skin Layer

The skin layer is at the starting point for the elastic surface layer model and is the only layer that is purely physically based, using a simplified physical model of a continuous elastic surface. The surface is discretized using the finite difference technique and represented as a rectangular mesh of three-dimensional points, together with their physical characteristics (e.g. mass, elasticity) and their current state information (e.g. position, velocity). When the numerical solver is turned on, the state is evolved over time at a fixed simulation time step.[Terzopoulos 87].

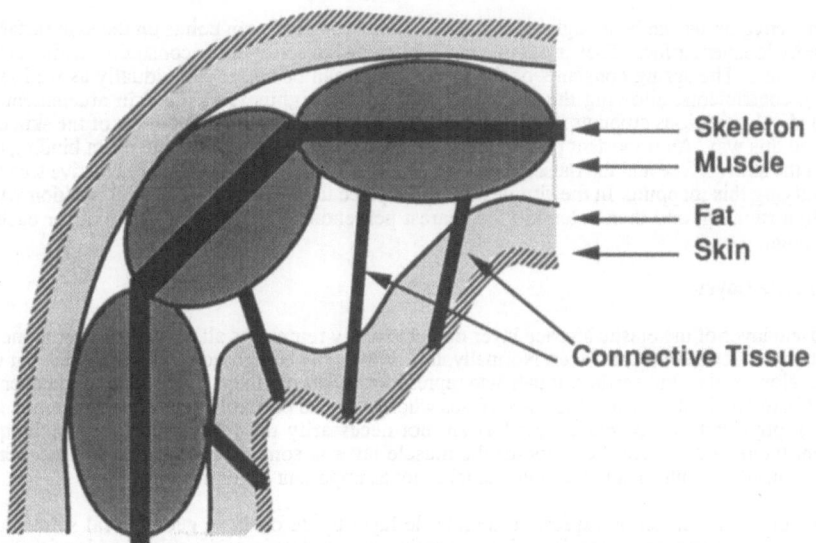

Figure 2: Components of the Elastic Surface Layer Model

The various physical parameters of the surface such as elasticity, rest metric, mass and damping, can all be specified at each point on the surface, allowing fine control of the intrinsic aspects of the surface behavior. Increasing the mass, for instance, increases the dynamic follow-through and squash-and-stretch effects of the skin, while increasing the damping density retards them. Globally adjusting the elasticity tensor affects the relative looseness or tightness of the skin, while selectively setting the elasticity tensor values at certain regions of the surface can simulate such effects such as wrinkles and tendons under the skin.

As the surface mesh evolves over time, external forces can be applied to each point. These forces constitute the constraints which bind it to the underlying surface layers. Two types of force constraints are used: reaction constraints, which force the surface to be on the outside of a given solid volume, and hookian spring constraints, which attract a given point on the surface to a particular point on the surface of the volume.

One of the advantages of using a rectangular mesh data structure to represent the skin is that it is fairly straightforward to increase or decrease the resolution of the mesh in response to the need for either fast interaction or high visual quality. All the current values of the mesh (e.g. position, velocity, elasticity, spring constants) are bilinearly interpolated to determine the values of the higher resolution points. In practice, we usually design our characters and animate them at a fairly low resolution (for interactive speed) and then increase the resolution to calculate a final sequence at simulation speed. The resulting sequence is stored as a large array of successive elastic surface meshes and can be played back at interactive rates and viewed from different angles to check the final animation. Then the entire sequence can be rendered off-line using a standard rendering package. As a final step, textures and colors can also be mapped onto the surface of the skin to simulate hair, fur, natural skin colors or clothing

3.5 Fat and Connective Tissue Layers

The fat and connective tissue layers both separate and attach the skin to the underlying muscle and bone layers. The repulsive component is the fat layer which is specified simply as a thickness between the skin and muscle layers and is implemented using reaction constraints to push the skin the required distance out from the underlying layers. This thickness can be specified at each point on the skin surface so that a considerable amount of sculpting of the final character's appearance can be performed simply by adjusting this parameter.

The connective tissue can be thought of as rubber bands strung between points on the skin surface and on the muscle layer surface. They are implemented as hookian spring force constraints acting between the two points. The spring constants of the rubber bands can be varied individually as well as their damping coefficients, allowing the degree of looseness or tightness of the skin attachment to be controlled. Also, various amounts of squash-and-stretch and follow-through effects of the skin can be controlled this way. An important parameter of the connective tissue layer is the exact binding points between the skin surface and the muscle layer surface. We have developed some interactive techniques for specifying this mapping. In the simplest case, we place the skeleton in a neutral position with the simulation running, and then calculate the nearest perpendicular muscle layer point for each skin surface point.

3.6 Muscle Layer

The muscle layer of the elastic surface layer model actually represents all of the solid components of the anatomy underneath the fat layer. Normally, this is primarily composed of muscle tissue, but where it comes close to the skin surface, it can also represent bone or cartilage. Since these components are either effectively rigid bodies (bone) or surfaces whose shape is primarily determined by active forces (muscle), physically-based elastic models are not necessarily the most appropriate technique to represent them. Also, since the shape of the muscle layer is somewhat obscured by the overlying layers, the need for a physically accurate model is not as important as for the skin.

We have therefore chosen to represent the muscle layer by deformable geometrical solid surfaces which the skin may not penetrate. Reaction constraints are used to force the skin outside of the muscle layer surface, but leave it free to slide along the surface until it finds an energy minimum. Since, in the worst case, every point on the surface must be tested for penetration, it is important that the muscle geometric models allow for quick inside/outside tests. For this we use spheres and implicit surfaces such as super quadrics which have a simple inside/outside function, together with global deformation functions [Barr 84]. The muscle shapes are attached as links to the skeleton joints so that they move as rigid components of an articulated figure. The flexing and bending of muscles is simulated by animating the parameters of the global deformations, either directly using key-frame interpolation, or by tying them to the joint angle values of the joints.

3.7 Skeleton Layer

We use the term skeleton in the computer animation sense of the word: a stick figure representing the positions and orientations of the joints which make up the articulated figure. The skeleton can be animated using a variety of techniques, as discussed in section 1. Fortunately, the problem of skeleton animation is largely orthogonal to the problem of deformation, given our pipeline model, and therefore we can treat the problems separately. For our purposes, we have chosen a simple key-frame interpolation method, together with an interactive inverse kinematic positioning technique [Girard 87]. This can easily be replaced with a more sophisticated method when desired.

To set the posture of the articulated figure, a portion of the skeleton forming a kinematic chain is selected by the user. Using interactive input devices, the end-effector of the chain is moved incrementally. This movement can be either a translation, a rotation or both. This differential vector is then multiplied by the inverse Jacobian of the kinematic chain to determine the corresponding differential joint angle values, which are added to the current joint angles [Klein 83]. This process is repeated for each event at interactive speeds so that the user has the impression of directly manipulating the skeleton by moving a particular joint.

Once a desired posture has been found, the user can store its joint angles as a key posture. A series of key postures can then be used to interpolate a smooth motion, using interpolating splines on the joint angles [Kochanek 84]. This motion sequence can be played back in real time, to check the animation, or in (usually non-real) simulated time to calculate an animation sequence at high surface resolution.

4. THE PHYSICAL SIMULATION

4.1 Deformable Surface

The deformable surface is modeled as a three-dimensional function of a two-dimensional material coordinate system, referred to as the u-coordinate system. Using the Lagrangian form, we can write the equation of motion for an elastically deformable surface as:

$$\mu\frac{\partial^2\bar{r}}{\partial t^2} + \gamma\frac{\partial\bar{r}}{\partial t} + \frac{\delta\mathcal{E}(\bar{r})}{\delta\bar{r}} = \bar{f} \tag{1}$$

where t is time, $\bar{r}(u_1,u_2,t)$ is the surface position, $\bar{f}(u_1,u_2,t)$ is the external applied force density, μ is the surface mass density, γ is the surface damping density, $\mathcal{E}(\bar{r})$ is the total elastic energy, and $\mathcal{E}(\bar{r})/\delta\bar{r}$ is the elastic force density. $\mathcal{E}(\bar{r})$, the total elastic energy of the surface, is a scalar-valued functional, that is, a single-valued function of the entire surface $\bar{r}(u_1,u_2,t)$. $\delta\mathcal{E}(\bar{r})/\delta\bar{r}$ is its variational derivative and represents the elastic force at each point on the surface [Gelfand 63]. The fact that this local quantity depends on a functional of the entire surface is the reason this kind of elastic model is non-linear. Note that this is an equation in force per u-coordinate area, or force density.

The choice of functional, $\mathcal{E}(\bar{r})$, is determined by the elastic properties of the surface and choosing a good model of these properties can help to make the solution of the equations easier. We use the elastic model proposed by [Terzopoulos 87] which defines the energy functional to be:

$$\mathcal{E}(\bar{r}) = \int_\Omega \sum_{i,j=1}^{2} \left(\eta_{ij}(G_{ij} - G_{ij}^0)^2 + \xi_{ij}(B_{ij} - B_{ij}^0)^2 \right) du_1 du_2 \tag{2}$$

where G_{ij} and G_{ij}^0 are the 2x2 symmetric current metric tensor and rest metric tensor, respectively, while B_{ij} and B_{ij}^0 are the current curvature and rest curvature tensors. The difference between the current and rest metric tensors is the metric strain tensor, which is the tensor analog of the displacement of a one-dimensional spring. The difference between the current and rest curvature tensors is the curvature strain. η_{ij} and ξ_{ij} are 2x2 symmetric "weighting functions", which determine the elasticity of the surface at each point, although they are not true elasticity tensors, which are rank four tensors. This places some limits on the range of elastic materials that can be represented. The variational derivative of this expression can then be approximated by the equation:

$$\frac{\mathcal{E}(\bar{r})}{\delta\bar{r}} = \sum_{i,j=1}^{2} -\frac{\partial}{\partial u_i}\left(\eta_{ij}(G_{ij} - G_{ij}^0)\frac{\partial\bar{r}}{\partial u_j}\right) + \frac{\partial^2}{\partial u_i \partial u_j}\left(\xi_{ij}(B_{ij} - B_{ij}^0)\frac{\partial^2\bar{r}}{\partial u_i \partial u_j}\right) \tag{3}$$

which is the elastic force in the force equation and is manageable enough to be solved numerically.

We now have a complete left-hand side of our force equation (1), which represents the behavior of an elastic surface over time. We can affect this behavior by adjusting various intrinsic properties associated with each point on the surface: the mass density, μ, which determines its inertia; the damping density, γ, which determines its viscous damping; the rest metric, G_{ij}^0 which determines its desired size; the stretching elasticity, η_{ij}, which determines its resistance to stretching; the rest curvature, B_{ij}^0, which determines its desired curvature; and the bending elasticity, ξ_{ij}, which determines its resistance to bending. Since skin does not have very much resistance to bending, and also to speed up the solution, we usually set ξ_{ij} to zero.

4.2 Environmental Forces

While the left-hand side of equation (1) represents the behavior of the passive skin layer of the elastic surface model, the right-hand side represents the active, driving input forces to the skin caused by the environment and the inner layers of the character model. The driving force term, $\vec{f}(u_1, u_2, t)$ is therefore composed of the sum of all the external and constraint forces acting on the surface:

$$\vec{f} = \vec{f}_G + \vec{f}_P + \vec{f}_S + \vec{f}_R \tag{4}$$

The first two of these, $\vec{f}_G$ = gravity and $\vec{f}_P$ = air pressure, are environmental forces which act on all surface points. The force of gravity is simply:

$$\vec{f}_G = \mu \vec{g} \tag{5}$$

where g is the acceleration of gravity (in the appropriate direction). The internal air-pressure force is:

$$\vec{f}_P = \frac{NRT}{V} a\hat{n} \tag{6}$$

where N is the amount of air in moles, R is the gas constant, V is the volume of the elastic surface, T is the temperature, and a is the ratio of surface area to coordinate area, and $\hat{n}$ is the unit vector pointing in the direction of the surface normal [Feynman 65].

4.3 Spring Constraint Forces

Each point on the elastic surface may be bound to a point on the underlying layers by a "rubber-band" constraint which exerts a spring force on the surface point. The rubber-band analogy is a good one because the force is attractive only and starts to act only beyond a given separation distance between the two points (the initial length of the rubber band). Beyond this separation distance, the force is hookian, i.e. proportional to the displacement. A spring damping term is also added to control oscillations caused by the spring forces. The force equation for the spring constraints can then be written as:

$$\vec{f}_S = -(k_S(\|\vec{x}\| - x_0) + k_D \vec{v}) \frac{\vec{x}}{\|\vec{x}\|} \tag{7}$$

where $\vec{x}$ is the difference vector from the fixed point to the surface point, x_0 is the initial length of the spring, k_S is the spring constant and k_D is the damping coefficient.

The spring constraints simulate the connective tissue which binds skin to muscle. By tuning the parameters of the springs (k_S, k_D and x_0), the animator can fine-tune the behavior of the skin. High values of k_S, for example, result in skin that clings tightly to the skeleton, while low values result in loose, floppy skin that hangs down below the skeleton under the influence of gravity. Adjusting the values of k_D controls how fast the skin follow-through dies down.

4.4 Reaction Constraint Forces

The reaction constraint forces act to force the skin surface outside the bone and muscle layers, preventing them from penetrating these surfaces. Unlike the environmental and spring constraints, which merely add forces to the system, reaction constraints remove "undesirable" forces (i.e. forces that cause penetration) and replacing them with forces that drive the elastic surface towards the constrain surface with critically damped motion [Platt 88]. "Desirable" forces (i.e. those that do not cause penetration) are retained. Figure 3a shows the important vector quantities of an element of the skin surface which is inside the constraint surface,

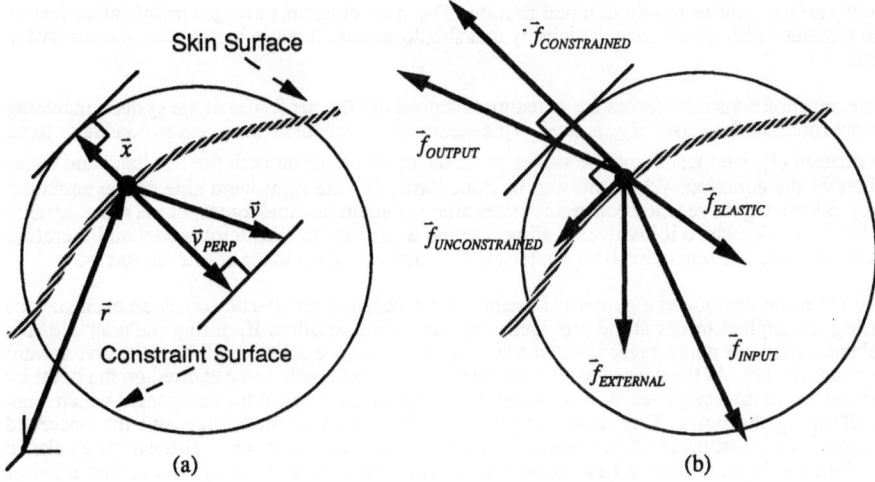

Figure 3: Reaction Constraint Force Components

where $\vec{r}$ is the position of the skin surface element, $\vec{v}$ is the velocity of the surface element, $\vec{v}_{PERP}$ is the component of the velocity perpendicular to the constraint surface, $\vec{x}$ is the perpendicular displacement vector to the constraint surface, $x = \|\vec{x}\|$ is the magnitude of $\vec{x}$, and $\hat{x} = \vec{x}/\|\vec{x}\|$ is the normal vector pointing in the direction of $\vec{x}$.

Figure 3b shows the vector forces acting on the surface element which are used to calculate the reaction constraint force, where $\vec{f}_{EXTERNAL} = \vec{f}_G + \vec{f}_P + \vec{f}_S$ is the sum of the external driving forces, $\vec{f}_{ELASTIC}$ is the sum of the internal elastic forces, $\vec{f}_{INPUT} = \vec{f}_{EXTERNAL} + \vec{f}_{ELASTIC}$ is the input force to the reaction constraint, $\vec{f}_{UNCONSTRAINED}$ is the unconstrained component of the input force, $\vec{f}_{CONSTRAINED}$ is the calculated constrained component, $\vec{f}_{OUTPUT} = \vec{f}_{CONSTRAINED} + \vec{f}_{UNCONSTRAINED}$ is the force output by the reaction constraint.

The reaction constraint calculation takes an input force, $\vec{f}_{INPUT}$ which consists of all of the forces acting on the surface element, both external forces (including forces from other constraints) and internal elastic forces. It then projects out from this vector the component perpendicular to the constraint surface to yield the unconstrained component, $\vec{f}_{UNCONSTRAINED}$.

$$\vec{f}_{UNCONSTRAINED} = \vec{f}_{INPUT} - (\vec{f}_{INPUT} \bullet \hat{x})\hat{x} \qquad (8)$$

The force necessary to drive the mass element toward the constraint surface with damped motion is then calculated. In the absense of any internal elastic forces, this force would be sufficient to make the mass element fit its constraint exactly. Since there are internal elastic forces on the left-hand side of the differential equation, however, we must counteract these on the right-hand side by subtracting out the component of the internal elastic force on the mass point, $\vec{f}_{ELASTIC}$, which is perpendicular to the constraint surface, yielding the final constraint force, $\vec{f}_{CONSTRAINED}$.

$$\vec{f}_{CONSTRAINED} = \mu(\omega_0^2 \vec{x} + \gamma_0 \vec{v}_{PROJ}) - (\vec{f}_{ELASTIC} \bullet \hat{x})\hat{x} \qquad (9)$$

where ω_0 and γ_0 are the spring and damping angular frequencies (inverses of the time constants), respectively, of the reaction constraint. When $\gamma_0 = 2\omega_0$ the surface element will move towards the constraint surface with critically damped motion. The time constants are generally set as fast as possible without causing numerical instability and should be significantly higher than the animation frame rate.

Therefore, reaction constraint forces are in reality functions of all other forces in the system, including the internal forces of the elastic model itself. This means that to calculate the reaction constraint term, $\vec{f}_R$, in equation (1), we must know the values of all the other forces on both the left-hand and right-hand sides of the equation. While this can be done easily for the right-hand side of the equation, simply by calculating the reaction constraint forces after the environmental forces, this is more difficult for the left-hand side since it involves getting into the details of the elasticity model and therefore decreases the functional separation between the elastic surface model and the constraint forces.

We have therefore developed a numerical method for estimating the elastic forces on each surface point using the applied forces at the previous time step in the solution. If, during the course of the physical simulation, we apply a reaction constraint force to a surface point, it will start to move toward the constraint surface. At the next time step, we can estimate the elastic force exerted on the point by taking the previous time step's reaction constraint force and subtracting out the component which went into accelerating the point. This difference between the actual applied force and the observed acceleration force is assumed to be the negative of the elastic force on the point. This estimated elastic force is then used to calculate a new value for the reaction constraint force. Using this form of feedback, the reaction constraint forces quickly grow until they become equal to the elastic forces, balancing them exactly when the mass point comes to rest at the constraint surface.

Since the reaction constraint forces only act perpendicularly to the bone and muscle layer surfaces, the skin surface is free to slide over these inner layers, eventually finding its own energy minimum within the constraints imposed on it. This results in a more realistic-looking effect because, like real skin, the skin surface is not tightly bound to a specific joint on the skeleton as in other elastic layered models.

4.5 Discretization And Solution

Although finite element methods are generally more powerful, finite difference methods require simpler data structures and numerical techniques, so following [Terzopoulos 87] we have chosen the finite difference technique. The surface is discretized as an MxN rectangular mesh of mass points at regular intervals in material coordinates. If we regard this entire mesh of points as a single MxNx3 dimensional vector, $\mathbf{r}$, we can write the canonical equation of motion for the surface as:

$$\mathbf{M}\frac{\partial^2 \mathbf{r}}{\partial t^2} + \mathbf{C}\frac{\partial \mathbf{r}}{\partial t} + \mathbf{K}(\mathbf{r}) = \mathbf{f} \tag{10}$$

Where $\mathbf{M}$ is the diagonal inertia matrix, $\mathbf{C}$ is the diagonal damping matrix, $\mathbf{K}$ is the diagonal banded stiffness matrix which results from discretizing the elastic force equation (3), and $\mathbf{f}$ is the vector of driving forces.

The positions of the mesh points can then be evolved through time from a given set of initial conditions using a semi-implicit integration procedure to solve a series of boundary value problems. See [Terzopoulos 87] for a more detailed description of the discretization process.

5. IMPLEMENTATION AND RESULTS

The elastic surface layer model for character animation has been implemented as part of the LEMAN (Layered Elastic Model ANimation) system, an animation system developed for studying layered elastic models at the Swiss Federal Institute of Technology. LEMAN is written in C using an object-oriented style and is built on top of the Fifth Dimension Toolkit [Turner 90] which runs on Silicon Graphics Iris workstations. The LEMAN system allows elastic surface layer model characters to be constructed and animated in a totally interactive, direct manipulation environment, using various multi-degree-of-freedom input devices such as the spaceball, dataglove and MIDI keyboard. Figure 4 shows several stages of a penguin character being constructed with the system.

Figure 4: Stages in the Construction of a Layered Elastic Character

Figure 5: Layered Elastic Character Deformation Under Various Skeleton Postures

To construct a character, a skeleton is first built interactively using the hierarchy-building tools. Muscle surfaces are then added to the skeleton joints. The skeleton kinematics may be tested at any point in the construction process using interactive inverse kinematics and key posture interpolation. When the muscle surfaces have been added, a rectangular surface mesh (initially in a spherical shape) is created and connected at both ends directly to the skeleton as fixed boundary conditions. At this point, the numerical solver can be started and, at periodic intervals, the surface is rendered on the screen, displaying a continuous simulation. Then the reaction constraints are turned on, pushing the skin surface outside the muscle layer. With the skeleton in a neutral position, individual surface points are then bound to the underlying bone and muscle layer, either automatically (by ray tracing a nearby surface point) or interactively using the mouse. The spring and damping constants are then adjusted to give the desired tightness or looseness of skin attachment. Finally, the thickness of the fat layer is adjusted, either as a global parameter or by sculpting individual points on the skin surface. The character construction process is entirely iterative, that is, the user may step back to any point in the process without losing work.

To animate a character, the user positions the skeleton into a sequence of key postures, either without the elastic surface, or with the simulation running at a low surface resolution for interactive speed. The resulting interpolated motion may then be played back at full speed to check the animation. Later, the resolution of the surface can be increased and the same motion played back in slow, simulation time to calculate a sequence for final rendering.

Using unoptimized code on an SGI Crimson with VGX graphics, we have been able to construct and animate full characters such as the penguin in Figure 5 at a surface resolution of 16 x 16 mass points in one tenth real-time. With a redraw rate set to five frames per second, which is just adequate for interactive work, about half the CPU time is spent redrawing the screen and half running the simulation. When scaled up to 32 x 32 mass points, the simulation slows down by a factor of eight to 1/80th real-time, which is still fast enough for calculating sequences for final rendering.

6. CONCLUSIONS AND FUTURE WORK

We believe that the elastic surface layer model is a promising approach to constructing animated three-dimensional characters. By modeling the skin as an separate elastic surface, which is free to slide along its underlying muscle layers while being held to it by attracting connective tissue, we have been able to simulate a rich variety of realistic-looking animation effects, with a conceptually simple model. Since the physical simulation is of an elastic surface only, while the underlying layers are geometrical models, we have been able to execute the model at interactive rates, allowing a three-dimensional, direct manipulation environment for layered character construction and animation.

One of the main limitations of the current implementation is the finite difference mesh, which has topological restrictions making it difficult to create surfaces with thin appendages (like arms and legs). We are planning to move to a finite element discretization, which should remove these restrictions. Addition of self-collision detection to the skin would allow greater deformations at the joints and more pronounced wrinkling. Adding dynamic properties to other layers such as the fat and muscle layers would also enhance realism

ACKNOWLEDGMENTS

The authors are deeply indebted to Enrico Gobbetti and Francis Balaguer for innumerable ideas, suggestions and 5D Toolkit software tools. We also wish to thank Prem Kalra, Ying Yang, Tsuneya Kurihara, Geoff Wyvill, and Tat-Seng Chua for valuable discussions. The penguin skin texture was created by Ling Wang using Wavefront software. This work was funded by the Swiss National Research Foundation.

REFERENCES

1. Armstrong WW, Green M (1985) The Dynamics of Articulated Rigid Bodies for Purposes of Animation, Proc. Graphics Interface '85, Montreal, pp.407-416
2. Barr AH (1981) Superquadrics and Angle Preserving Transformations, IEEE Computer Graphics and Applications, Vol. 1, No 1, pp.11-23

411

3. Barr AH (1984) Global and Local Deformations of Solid Primitives, Proc.SIGGRAPH '84, Computer Graphics, Vol. 18, No3, July 84
4. Bloomenthal J, Wyvill B. (1990) Interactive Techniques for Implicit Modeling, Proc. SIGGRAPH Symposium on Interactive 3D Graphics, Computer Graphics, Vol. 24, No2, pp.109-116
5. Chadwick J, Haumann DR, Parent RE (1989) Layered Construction for Deformable Animated Characters, Proc. SIGGRAPH '89, Computer Graphics, Vol. 23, No3, pp.234-243
6. Chen DT, Zeltzer D (1992) Pump It Up: Computer Animation of a Biomechanically Based Model of Muscle Using the Finite Element Method, Proc. SIGGRAPH'92, Computer Graphics, Vol. 26, No 2, pp.89-98
7. Culhane S (1988) Animation From Script To Screen, St. Martin's Press, New York 1988
8. Feynman RP, Leighton RB, Sands M (1965) The Feynman Lectures on Physics, Addison-Wesley, Reading Massachusetts 1965
9. Forsey DR (1991) A Surface Model for Skeleton-Based Character Animation, Proc. Second Eurographics Workshop on Animation and Simulation, INRIA/IRISA, Rennes, pp.55-74
10. Forsey DR. Bartels RH (1988) Hierarchical B-Spline Refinement, Proc. SIGGRAPH'88, Computer Graphics, Vol. 22, No4, pp.205-212
11. Gascuel MP, Verroust A, Puech C (1991) A Modelling System for Complex Deformable Bodies Suited to Animation and Collision Processing, The Journal of Visualization and Computer Animation, Vol. 2, No3, pp.82-91
12. Gelfand IM, Fomin SV, (1963) Calculus of Variations, Prentice-Hall, Englewood Cliffs, New Jersey 1963
13. Girard M (1987) Interactive Design of 3D Computer-Animated Legged Animal Motion, IEEE Computer Graphics and Applications, Vol. 7, No 6, pp.39-51
14. Gourret JP, Magnenat-Thalmann N, Thalmann D (1989) Simulation of Object and Human Skin Deformations in a Grasping Task, Proc. SIGGRAPH '89, Computer Graphics, Vol. 23, No 3, pp.21-30
15. Isaacs PM, Cohen MF (1987) Controlling Dynamic Simulation with Kinematic Constraints, Behavior Functions and Inverse Dynamics, Proc. SIGGRAPH'87, Computer Graphics, Vol. 21, No4, pp.215-224
16. Klein H, Review of Pseudoinverse Control for Use with Kinematically Redundant Manipulators, IEEE Transaction on Systems, Man and Cybernetics Vol SMC-132, No. 3, March/April '83
17. Kochanek DH, Bartels RH (1984) Interpolating Splines with Local Tension, Continuity, and Bias Control, Proc. SIGGRAPH '84, Computer Graphics, Vol. 18, pp.33-41
18. Lasseter J (1987) Principles of Traditional Animation Applied to 3D Computer Animation, Proc. SIGGRAPH '87, Computer Graphics, Vol. 21, No4, pp.35-44
19. Magnenat-Thalmann N, Thalmann D (1987) The Direction of Synthetic Actors in the Film Rendez-vous à Montréal, IEEE Computer Graphics and Applications, Vol. 7, No12, pp.9-19
20. Platt JC, Barr AH (1988) Constraint Method for Flexible Models, Proc.SIGGRAPH '88, Computer Graphics, Vol. 22, No4, pp.279-288
21. Sederberg TW, Parry SR (1986) Free-Form Deformations of Solid Geometric Models, Proc. SIGGRAPH'86 Computer Graphics, Vol. 20, No4, pp.151-160
22. Terzopoulos D, Platt JC, Barr AH, Fleischer K (1987) Elastically Deformable Models, Proc.SIGGRAPH'87, Computer Graphics, Vol. 21 No 4, pp.205-214
23. Terzopoulos D, Waters K (1991) Techniques for Realistic Facial Modeling and Animation, in: Magnenat Thalmann N, Thalmann D, Computer Animation '91, Springer-verlag, Tokyo, pp.59-74
24. Turner R, Gobbetti E, Balaguer F, Mangili A, Thalmann D, Magnenat-Thalmann N (1990) An Object-Oriented Methodology Using Dynamic Variables for Animation and Scientific Visualization, in: Chua TS, Kunii TL, CG International '90, Springer, Tokyo
25. Walters G. (1989) The Story of Waldo C. Graphic, 3D Character Animation By Computer, SIGGRAPH '89 Tutorial Notes.
26. Wilhelms J, Barsky BA (1985) Using Dynamics Analysis for the Animation of Articulated Bodies Such as Human and Robots, Proc. Graphics Interface '85, Montreal, pp.97-104
27. Witkin A, Fleischer K, Barr AH (1987) Energy Constraints on Parameterized Models, Proc. SIGGRAPH'87, Computer Graphics, Vol. 21, No4, pp.225-232
28. Witkin A, Kass M (1988) Spacetime Constraints, Proc. SIGGRAPH '88, Computer Graphics, Vol. 22, No4, pp.159-168

412

Russell Turner is a research assistant and doctoral candidate at the Computer Graphics Laboratory of the Swiss Federal Institute of Technology in Lausanne, Switzerland. He received his B.S. in Physics and his M.S. in Computer and Information Science from the University of Massachusetts at Amherst. He has also worked as a software engineer for V.I. Corporation of Amherst, Massachusetts. His research interests include animation, 3D interaction, physically-based modeling, and object-oriented graphics.

E-mail: russell.turner@di.epfl.ch

Daniel Thalmann is currently full Professor, Director of the Computer Graphics Laboratory and Head of the Computer Science Department at the Swiss Federal Institute of Technology in Lausanne, Switzerland. He is also adjunct Professor at the University of Montreal, Canada. He received his diploma in nuclear physics and Ph.D in Computer Science from the University of Geneva. He is coeditor-in-chief of the *Journal of Visualization and Computer Animation*, member of the editorial board of the *Visual Computer* and *the CADDM Journal* and cochairs the EUROGRAPHICS Working Group on Computer Simulation and Animation. Daniel Thalmann's research interests include 3D computer animation, image synthesis, virtual reality and scientific visualization. He has published more than 100 papers in these areas and is coauthor of several books including: *Computer Animation: Theory and Practice* and *Image Synthesis: Theory and Practice*. He is also codirector of several computer-generated films.

E-mail: daniel.thalmann@di.epfl.ch

The authors may be contacted at:

Computer Graphics Lab
Swiss Federal Institute of Technology
CH 1015 Lausanne, Switzerland
tel: ++41-21-693-5214   fax: ++ 41-21-693-5328

The GATI Client/Server Animation Toolkit

Chandrajit L. Bajaj and Steve Cutchin

ABSTRACT

This paper presents GATI, an animation server that provides for, distributed, potentially collaborative, soft real time interactive animation in two and three dimensions. The system supports a high level animation language based upon a commands/event paradigm. Examples are given of how the toolkit is being used in a distributed, collaborative geometrical modeling environment. GATI runs on unix platforms supporting the X-11 windowing environment and using the XS Graphics Libraries.

Keywords: algorithm animation, distributed animation, geometrical modeling, interactive animation

1 INTRODUCTION

Recently there has been great interest in algorithm animation, user interface animation and key-frame animation. Algorithm animation and user interface animation have concentrated almost exclusively on two-dimensional animation and key-frame animation systems have put great effort into generating photo-realistic three-dimensional animations that require hours per frame to generate. There exists in the area of computational geometry many problems that deal with a moderate number of graphical objects in three dimensions. With todays powerful graphics workstations it is longer necessary to limit animation to two-dimensions or to be satisfied with prolonged frame generation sequences for this particular class of problems.

We present in this paper GATI (GATI in sanskrit means speed), a system for general purpose two and three-dimensional interactive animation that runs on various hardware platforms and provides close to real time animation services. Close to real time in this context means that individual frames are rendered somewhere between 10 fps and 30 fps on average. However the real time constraint is not hard and prolonged frame generation rates are possible. GATI should be very useful in many areas of computational geometry and solid modeling. It could prove to be very useful as a visual debugger. GATI is a toolkit developed within the frame-work of a collaborative, distributed geometric software environment called SHASTRA[2]. The SHASTRA software environment provides a powerful substrate of tools for collaborative and distributed work, it also provides advanced networking facilities that ease the task of communicating between applications.

This paper presents an overview of the organization of the GATI animation system plus provides examples of how the system has been used to ease the creation of several geometric modeling and robotics applications and to provide animation services to other SHASTRA applications.

2 RELATED WORK

Much recent research has been done in the area of algorithm animation and animating user interfaces. Balsa[4] is a well known algorithm animation system. Tango[14] is another algorithm animation system based upon a path-transition paradigm. Both of these systems provide excellent facilities for generating two-dimensional animations of algorithms.

With respect to animated user interfaces Whizz[5] typifies a system for developing an animated interactive application. Whizz is based on a streams/event model and is limited to two-dimensional animation.

In the area of three dimensional animation systems a host of systems are available. Powerful keyframe animation systems are available from such companies as Wavefront Technologies Inc[10]. Alias Research Inc.[6] SOFTIMAGE Inc.[7], Vertigo Systems Inc.[9], Symbolics Inc.[8] and others. Also various kinds of animation systems have been developed at several universities as part of ongoing research projects into motion planning, dynamic simulation and animation scripting systems[13][12]. For instance DYNAMO[11] is a system for generating dynamic simulations via kinematic constraints, behavior functions, and inverse dynamics. A wide variety of animation packages are also available for the Macintosh and IBM compatibles. However most of the systems mentioned are single user, single workstation programs. In contrast GATI can simultaneously service multiple clients and allow multi-user interactions. Furthermore GATI can asynchronously support multiple views and can distribute its rendering over a network of workstations for distributed parallelism.

SHASTRA[2] is a highly extensible, distributed and collaborative geometric software environment consisting of a growing set of individually powerful and interoperable (client-server) toolkits which support collaborative design sessions. In the SHASTRA environment, the application toolkits listed below, run as independent processes on separate workstations having separate user interfaces (using X-11 and Motif). The application toolkits make use of a custom designed network library to communicate data structures conveniently between each other and manage multiple connections across a network.

1. The GANITH algebraic surface modeling toolkit provides symbolic and numeric computations on algebraic varieties.

2. The SHILP solid modeling and display toolkit manipulates curved solid objects with piecewise algebraic surfaces.

3. The VAIDAK medical imaging and model reconstruction toolkit manipulates medical image volume data.

4. The BHAUTIK physical analysis toolkit provides a graphical interface and functionality to set up and perform scientific and engineering simulations on geometric models.

GANITH provides the surface modeling infrastructure for SHILP and VAIDAK. Further, SHILP provides all the solid model manipulation and display functionality for skeletal structures reconstructed from CT/MRI image data in VAIDAK. GANITH, SHILP and VAIDAK provide BHAUTIK with a varied source of geometric domains. Collectively these toolkits provide a vast modeling infrastructure. GATI interoperates with GANITH, SHILP, VAIDAK and BHAUTIK toolkit processes and acts as their animation server.

3 SYSTEM MODEL - COMMANDS/EVENTS

The GATI animation paradigm is based on the basic client/server model. Animation applications are the clients of an animation server that accepts commands in a high-level animation language.

The animation server generates animation events that are sent to its clients. These events can be caused by mouse events (button press, motion) in animation windows or can be caused by the interaction of various animation objects within the animation environment. For example when an object has entered a certain region of a coordinate system or if an object has completed a specific animation command. This second set of events is useful in providing applications with the ability to interact asynchronously with the animations generated. A client can begin an animation and be signaled when the animation has completed.

The server can provide animation to multiple clients. The clients can each either generate separate animations or can collaborate on a single animation. This can be useful for a set of multiple processes working on a single task or possibly for a set of distributed interactive systems that each generate a portion of the animation.

This animation server to animation clients paradigm fits in nicely with the distributed and collaborative nature of the SHASTRA environment.

4 SYSTEM OVERVIEW

The GATI system consists of three primary components: An interactive animation server that is responsible for displaying the animations, A user library that is linked to animation clients to simplify communication between the server and the users client, and finally an interactive graphical editor that provides facilities for creating preset animations that can be used 'off-the-shelf' in user programs. These three components are described in detail in the following sections.

4.1 Animation Server

The GATI server provides interactive animation services to other SHASTRA applications, potentially even other GATI servers. The server accepts commands in a high level animation language and can generate animation events in response to user input and various graphical events. It supports multiple clients that can either share animations or have there own separate animations. It

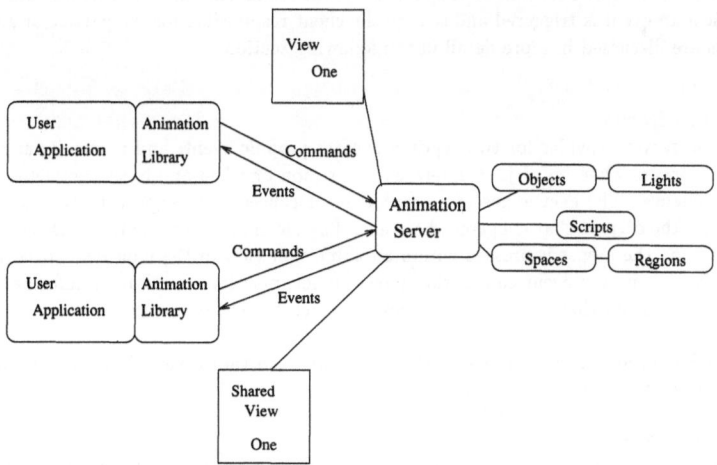

FIGURE 1: The Software Architecture of GATI

provides facilities for generating frame-by-frame movie files that can be used to play-back animations quickly or to use more powerful rendering programs to generate photo-realistic frames that can be saved on video-tape for high-quality animations.

4.1.1 Animation Language

The animator accepts commands from other SHASTRA applications in a high-level textual language that can be used to define complex animations. The language allows the definition of **movies** with a set of **objects, lights, spaces, scripts, views,** and **regions**. A host of operations can be performed on each of these items. The nature of these items are defined below.

object An object is a two or three dimensional graphical object represented internal as a set of polygons. Associated with every object is a collection of attributes that can alter the appearance of that object in an animation, for example color, material, orientation, etc.

lights The animator supports two kinds of light sources. Either local lights or infinite lights. Local lights exist within a coordinate system and can be seen in an animation. As such local lights can have polygonal representations associated with them. Infinite lights have no coordinate position and are represented primarily as a direction vector. Thus it is not possible to see an infinite light source. Only the effect that the light it generates is visible in a view.

spaces A space is an organizational device that allows for the creation of hierarchical models for animation. It also provides facilities for mixing two-dimensional animations and three-dimensional animations in a single animation. A space defines a local reference frame that can contain **objects, lights, regions** and other **spaces**. Spaces can contain both two-dimensional and three-dimensional **objects** and **spaces**. This ability to mix two and three dimensional animations can provide some powerful animation effects.

scripts scripts are nothing more than user-defined animations. A collection of animations can be collected together into a single script that can be later applied to multiple objects. This simplifies animation development, and provides simple mechanisms for having a collection of items undergo identical animations.

views views are actual on-screen windows and can be used to look at animations from different positions, angles and with different projections (orthographic versus perspective).

regions are used to mark subsections of spaces for event management. If an **object** enters or exits a **region** an event is triggered and sent to the client responsible for the particular animation. Events are discussed in more detail in the following section.

4.1.2 Animation Events

The animation server provides for two types of events: graphic events and mouse input events. A graphic event occurs when an **object** enters/exits a region or when an object completes a specific animation sequence. The occurrence of a graphic event causes a message to be sent to all clients that can access the **object** that triggered the event. The second class of events, mouse events, occur when a button on the mouse is pressed within an animation view or the mouse is moved within an animation view. A mouse event causes the space, object, position, and button information to be passed on to the clients that can access the view in which the event occurred.

Events must be turned on by sending explicit commands to the server. These animation events provide for interactive manipulation of animations.

4.1.3 Animation Commands

The animation language provides commands for creating all of the previously described objects as well as performing animations on them. It can perform rotations, translations, and scaling of objects , spaces, and lights. It supports changes in color and shade of objects and lights. Scripts can be defined and applied to objects, spaces, lights, and scripts. Events can be specified for objects, , lights, and regions. Recording can be turned on for any number of views so that an animation in a particular view can be saved and played back later.

4.2 User Library

The user library is a C library that must be linked to an application for it to take advantage of the Animation server. It provides utilities for sending animation commands to the server, specifying callback functions to handle animation events, loading saved objects, loading and saving animation scripts to files.

4.3 GATI Animation Editor

The GATI animation editor is an interactive graphical editor that allows animators to create and edit animation scripts that can be saved for later use.

4.4 Implementation Details

The GATI system has been implemented on a collection of unix workstations in a machine independent manner. It accomplishes this by using an extended version of the XS Graphics Libraries developed as a part of the SHASTRA project. The XS Graphics Libraries are a suite of 3D graphics libraries under X-11 that access system-dependent graphics facilities (and hardware) in a uniform, system-independent manner [1].

5 DISCUSSION OF PURPOSE

What are the benefits of GATI (Or why did we do it this way)? The design of the GATI system was motivated by the following four primary goals:

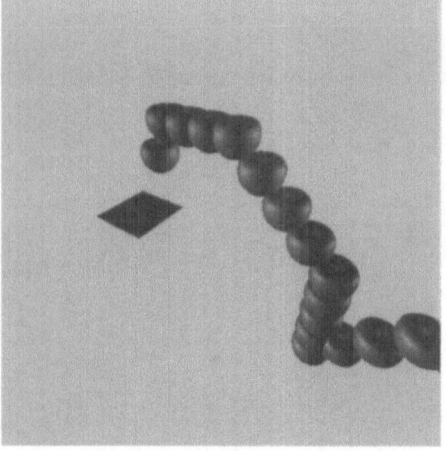

FIGURE 2: An apple moving along a simple path

```
# - a sample gati script for moving an apple

create gobject "apple" "apple.poly" ;
create gobject "square" "square.poly" ;
create view "bouncer" ;
create space "dancer" ;
create space "suber" ;
gobject set space "apple" "suber"  ;
gobject set space "square" "dancer" ;
space set space "suber" "dancer"  ;
view set space "bouncer" "dancer"  ;
translate space "dancer" ( -4.0 0.0 0.0 ) 1 ;
scale space "dancer" ( 0.5 0.5 0.5 )  1 ;
scale gobject "apple" ( 0.8 0.8 0.8 ) 2 ;
scale gobject "square" ( 2.5 2.5 2.5 ) 1 ;
translate gobject "apple" ( -1.0 1.0 0.0 ) 1 ;
define "curve" ( "obj1" )
    translate space "obj1" ( 1.6 1.6 0.0 ) 3;
    translate space "obj1" ( 1.6 0.0 0.0 ) 3;
    translate space "obj1" ( 1.6 -1.6 0.0 ) 4;
    translate space "obj1" ( 0.0 -1.6 0.0 ) 4;
 enddef

#now apply the curve to the object a few times

apply "curve" ( "suber" ) ;
apply "curve" ( "suber" ) ;
apply "curve" ( "suber" ) ;
```

FIGURE 3: A sample GATI script

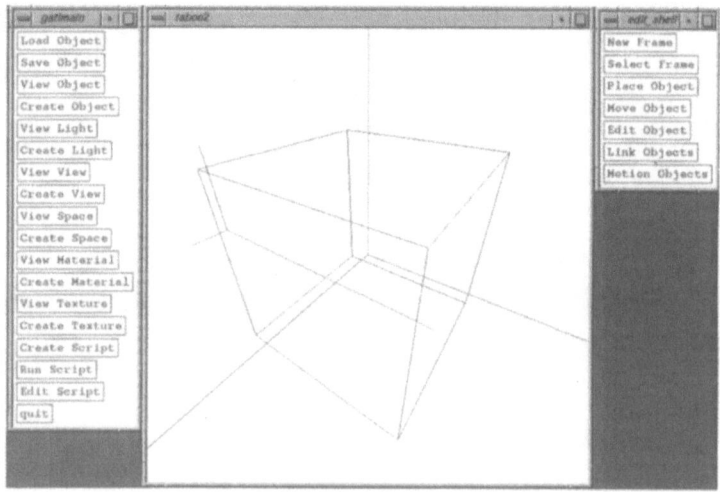

FIGURE 4: The GATI animation editor

- Provide a mechanism for experimenting with three dimensional algorithm animation.

- Provide mechanisms to ease the process of creating interactive animations for problems in computational geometry.

- Provide facilities for reasonable real-time performance as well as the capability of generating high quality animations if desired.

- Provide animation facilities to SHASTRA applications.

With these four goals as our driving influences we quickly discern that the system must be flexible, extensible, capable of collaboration, and distributed rendering to have any hope of fulfilling the goals. In the development of the system, programmer flexibility was almost always chosen over speed. Whenever possible two mechanisms are provided for output, one that is fast but yielding a lower resolution and another which is slow but capable of very high resolution. In attempting to fulfill these goals in the design we followed the principle of letting the programmer choose what mechanism he would like and providing him with many options.

This brings up the question of what do all of these features give us? In the following sections we will outline some examples of the versatility that these features provide to various SHASTRA applications. In the remainder of this section we will discuss some of the underlying reasons why we chose the goals that we did.

GATI is not an end system in and of itself. Hopefully it is a first step into several interesting and exciting areas in animation. By building GATI we have created a tool for investigating into the question of how can an algorithm be animated? Is it possible to animate an algorithm automatically? More fundamentally what is the relationship between the semantics of a complex algorithm and a particular visual representation of that program? Perhaps this question has no definitive answer but with GATI we can explore the possibilties and maybe find some 'good' answers.

GATI also provides us with a mechanism for testing the usefulness of animated debugging of programs. In the area of computational geometry this fits in very well With the inherent visualization associated with many problems.

Finally there is the interesting question of what about problems that we normally do not think of as having visual representations? Perhaps with GATI as tool into the investigation of these problems we can discover some new ways of looking at old problems that might lead to new results.

All of these questions and many more can be investigated with the functionality that GATI provides. GATI provides the mechanism for easily investigating the above questions and many more.

6 EXAMPLES

In this section we outline experiences with using GATI to implement some interactive animated applications within the area of geometric modeling and robotics.

GATI is being used in the development of an experimental algorithm for performing low cost obstacle avoidance, generating animations of families of implicit functions and an interactive application for manipulating the structure of molecules.

6.1 Motion Coordination

A recurring problem in robot motion planning is coordinating the motion of a collection of objects

420

while ensuring that none of the objects collide with each other. GATI provides many benefits when used for visualizing this particular problem. It provides immediate feedback to changes in the motion planning algorithm. It also removes from the application developer the burden of writing routines and functions for manipulating graphical objects. Thus allowing her to concentrate upon solving the motion planning problem and not delving into the details of how to draw and animate graphical objects on a workstation.

We have implemented an experimental motion planner that relies upon GATI for input and display. The motion planner is a prototyping application for experimenting with various heuristic and deterministic algorithms for motion planning. An initial problem that we are experimenting with is given n objects in three dimensional space, each with an initial position and final position, compute paths for the objects such that no two objects collide as they travel along these paths. We have developed a novel algorithm for this particular problem based on dynamic voronoi diagrams in two dimensions. The algorithm however is outside the scope of this document and is discussed in another paper.

The GATI animation system has provided a great deal of benefit in the development of this application. Particularly useful was the immediate feedback that was provided. This helped a great deal in the debugging process as it was visually obvious when the algorithm was performing incorrectly.

Figure 5 displays the paths of three moving objects from initial positions towards their goal positions moving in such a fashion as to ensure no collisions.

6.2 Mathematical Animations

GATI was used to enhance the capabilities of an existing SHASTRA application called GANITH[3]. GANITH provides tools for visualizing algebraic surfaces and performing complex manipulations of these surfaces. GATI provided GANITH with a mechanism for animating the presentation of a sequence of members of a family of implicit functions.

In figure 6 an overlay of a sequence of steps in an animation is shown. The picture is that of a

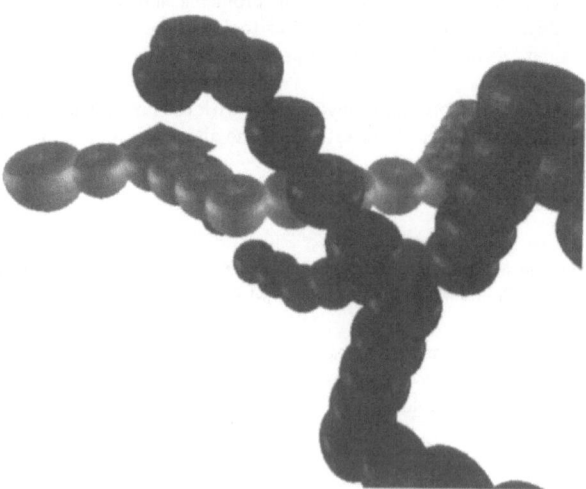

FIGURE 5: The paths of moving objects avoiding each other

421

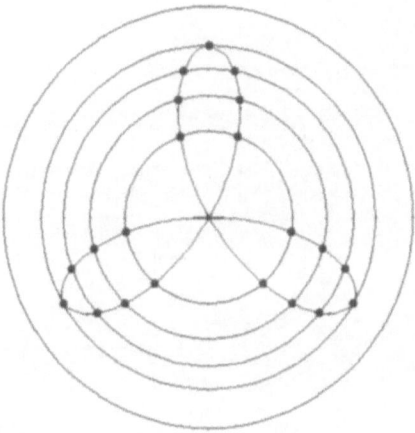

FIGURE 6: A family of algebraic curve intersections

family of concentric circles intersecting a quartic.

Figure 7 depicts a sequence of surfaces that smoothly join three pipes together. An animation of this type can be used to view and choose a surface that best joins three pipes and meets other visual criteria.

In figure 8 an overlay of snapshots of an animation depicting the intersection of families of surfaces is given.

6.3 Molecular Docking Animation

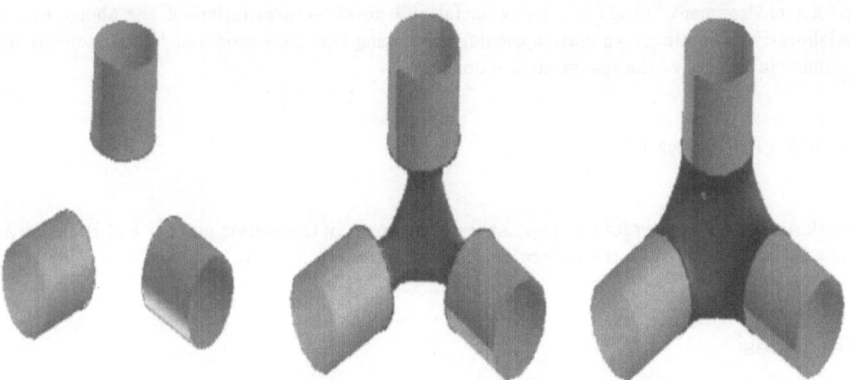

FIGURE 7: A family of smoothly joining surfaces

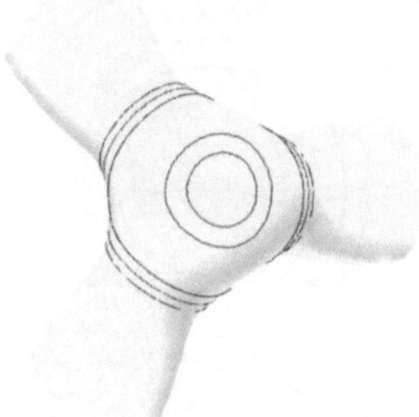

FIGURE 8: A family of intersecting surfaces with one surface shown

An interactive application was developed using GATI to visualize the 'docking' of drug and protein molecules under molecular Brownian motion.

The application reads in a description of the atom locations of a molecule from a file, computes the bonding information and then displays the molecule through GATI. Then either under program control (via the Gati Language) or a user can select two or more bonded atoms of the molecule. The angle between these bond atoms is varied with time and the structure of the molecule is updated and redisplayed. This provides for a animated view of how attractor drug molecules 'dock' with protein molecules under dynamic situations.

7 CONCLUSIONS

In this paper we have presented GATI an animation system for providing low cost real-time interactive three dimensional animation services to computational geometry applications within the SHASTRA environment. GATI has many useful and novel features including the ability to create collaborative animations, animation events, and mixing two-dimensional and three-dimensional animations via the use of the spaces abstraction.

8 ACKNOWLEDGEMENTS

We thank Assumpta Sabater for her help in the development of the motion planner and Dr. Andrew Royappa for his assistance in the molecular docking animation project.

References

[1] V. Anupam, C. Bajaj, A. Burnett, M. Fields, A. Royappa, and D. Schikore. *XS: A Hardware Independent Graphics and Windows Library.* Computer Science Technical Report, CAPO-91-

FIGURE 9: Two snapshots of an animated drug molecule

28, Purdue University, Department of Computer Sciences, 1991.

[2] V. Anupam, C. Bajaj, and A. Royappa. *The SHASTRA Distributed and Collaborative Geometric Design Environment*. Computer Science Technical Report, CAPO-91-38, Purdue University, Department of Computer Sciences, 1991.

[3] C. Bajaj and A. Royappa. *The GANITH Algebraic Geometry Toolkit*. *Proceedings of the First International Symposium on the Design and Implementation of Symbolic Computation Systems, Lecture Notes in Computer Science*, 1990.

[4] M. H. Brown. Algorithm Animation. PhD thesis, Brown University, 1987.

[5] Stéphane Chatty. *Defining the dynamic behavior of animated interfaces. In 5th IFIP Working Conference on Engineering for Human Computer Interaction*, 1992.

[6] Alias Research Inc. 110 richmond St. East, Suite 500, Toronto, Ontario, Canada m5c-1p1.

[7] SOFTIMAGE Inc. 3510, boul. St-Laurent, bureau 500, Montreal, Quebec, Canada, H2X 2V2.

[8] Symbolics Inc. 1401 Westwood Blvd, Los Angeles, CA 90024.

[9] Vertigo Systems International Inc. 119 W Pender St., Suite 221, Vancouver, BC, Canada v6b 1s5.

[10] Wavefront Technologies Inc. 530 East Montecito, Santa Barbara, CA 93101.

[11] Paul M. Isaacs and Michael F. Cohen. *Controlling Dynamic Simulation with Kinematic Constraints, Behavior Functions, and Inverse Dynamics. ACM COMPUTER GRAPHICS (Siggraph Proc. '87)*, 1987.

[12] N. Magnenat Thalmann and D. Thalmann. Computer Animation Theory and Practice. Springer Verlag, 1985.

[13] C. Reynolds. *Computer Animation with Scripts and Actors. Computer Graphics (Siggraph)*, 1982.

[14] John T. Stasko. *TANGO: A Framework and System for Algorithm Animation. Computer*, 1990.

Address: Department of Computer Science, Purdue University, West Lafayette, Indiana 47907, USA

Combined Visualization of Contour Levels and 3D Volumes in Molecular Graphics

André Deloff, Peter Fluekiger, and Jacques Weber

ABSTRACT

A new formalism has been developed to combine the representation of contour levels in arbitrary planes with the visualization of chemical properties as color-coded molecular envelopes or as isovalue rendered surfaces. This tool, which is characterized by a totally interactive and user-friendly input, has been integrated within our basic molecular graphics package MOLEKEL, which is used for molecular modeling applications on graphics workstations. After an overview of the design and practical implementation of this development, several applications are presented which underline its flexibility and utility in modeling the structure and reactivity of various chemical systems, ranging from pyrrole to $Cr(benzene)(CO)_3$ and C_{60} fullerene derivatives.

Keywords: scientific visualization, molecular modeling, chemical properties

INTRODUCTION

Scientific visualization has recently emerged as a critical component of computational science because of the high level of instantaneous perception of large data sets it offers (McCormick 1987; Mair 1992). Indeed, inasmuch as computerized modelization is nowadays an exploding topic in science and medicine, it is essential to visualize the results of such calculations and simulations to fully and rapidly comprehend their content, to provoke insights and to communicate them with others. These statements are of course totally applicable to molecular sciences since the possibility to generate realistic images of, e.g., DNA sequences, complex chemical systems and processes, etc., has undoubtedly paved the way to significant progresses in biotechnology and drug design (Ripka and Blaney 1991; Borman 1992).

In this context, molecular graphics (MG), which may be defined as the application of computer graphics to study molecular structure, function and interaction, has become an important tool in computer-assisted chemistry (Weber et al. 1991). It is indeed employed in conjunction with many modelizations performed on supercomputers or on workstations, where its role consists not only in visualizing molecular structures and properties, but also in interacting with simulations in real time, changing the building blocks of the investigated compounds, comparing geometries, displaying scenarios in which substrates dock and bind

424

to macromolecules, etc. Without exaggeration, it is possible to contend that the applications performed in this field have already led the chemists involved to change their way of thinking. For example, the developments recently achieved and allowing chemists to generate in real time the 3D molecular structures of unknown compounds and to search for specific 3D shape properties in large chemical databases are a key step towards the design of new biologically active species such as drugs, inhibitors, etc.

In addition to the tremendous progresses witnessed recently in the hardware and software of visualization tools, MG has also benefited from important methodological developments in computational chemistry (Ripka and Blaney 1991). To review just a few, fast and efficient 3D model builders are now available for both small systems and macromolecules (Rusinko et al. 1987); molecular dynamics methods allow the users to locate the global minimum on complex potential energy surfaces and simultaneously simulate the behavior of molecules in solution as a function of temperature (van Gunsteren and Berendsen 1990); powerful algorithms have been developed to generate realistic molecular surfaces as solvent accessible envelopes (Connolly 1983) and, last but not least, several approaches have been reported to rapidly evaluate some key local molecular properties such as hydrophobicity, electron densities, electrostatic potentials, reactivity indices, etc. (Ripka and Blaney 1991).

We have recently developed a quantum chemical method to rapidly evaluate the intermolecular interaction energy E_{int} between a substrate S and an incoming reactant R characterized by its electrophilic (i.e. electron acceptor) or nucleophilic (electron donor) behavior (Weber et al. 1991, 1992). The display of the E_{int} property is performed using two different techniques: (i) as a mapping of E_{int} values onto dot or solid models of the molecular surface of S by means of a standard color code; (ii) as isovalue surfaces of E_{int} with the usual rendering techniques leading to 3D perception. However, in several applications we have carried out recently and which were devoted to rather complex molecules with intricate shapes and several possible sites for favorable S-R interaction, both techniques of representation reveal their advantages and inconvenients but none of them is totally satisfactory. This explains why we have completed them with a simultaneous visualization of contour levels of E_{int} in arbitrary planes, chosen interactively, and this is the development we report in this paper.

In the first part, with a mostly technical content, the algorithms used and their implementation into our basic molecular graphics package MOLEKEL (Fluekiger 1992) will be described. Then, several applications of this very useful MG development to recent modelizations performed in our laboratory will be presented and discussed.

METHODS AND IMPLEMENTATION

Design of the Contouring Module

Two common approaches to visualize 3D volume data are: 1) extraction and visualization of two-dimensional slices through the volume; 2) imaging of selected data points forming two-dimensional isovalue surfaces within the volume (Wilhelms 1990; Watson 1992; Elvins 1992). This section deals with the first approach and its implementation in MOLEKEL (Fluekiger 1992). MOLEKEL is a versatile and powerful molecular graphics package allowing visualization of chemical systems and properties. The latter ones consist most often of three-dimensional datasets with one or several scalar values at each gridpoint of a lattice. Separate routines calculate these values on regular, Cartesian grids and supply them to modules creating images from volume data. MOLEKEL contains both the molecular (Connolly 1983) envelope and isovalue surface generating routines. The isovalue surfaces are composed of rendered triangles fitted to constant-value contour surfaces by the marching cubes procedure (Lorensen and Cline 1987). Even if the algorithm only traverses the volume once to extract the surface, this may become quite time consuming for large volumetric data sets and real-time threshold value adapting can usually not be performed. Another problem concerns the generation of the three-dimensional dataset itself which is equivalent to calculating some molecular property on a dense lattice. It is then obvious that the simpler, two-dimensional techniques used to visualize selected slices of data may still be very useful. Surface modeling is advantageous in many situations but a detailed view of two-dimensional slices of data containing a series of contour lines may provide a complementary image of selected data regions, especially if the contour planes may be combined with a solid, rendered model of isosurfaces.

Many general contouring programs, such as ContourXplore (Uniras Inc. 1992), are available but usually they offer very limited possibilities for representing molecules or for interfacing with specialized quantum chemistry packages. MOLEKEL was designed to meet the needs of data visualization in physical chemistry: the contouring option is a useful supplement and improves its functionality. On the other side, the possibility of simultaneous visualization of molecules, color-coded surfaces and contour planes surpasses the capabilities of most of the general contouring programs and gives the chemists an opportunity of creating both information-rich and suggestive images.

The basic strategy in developing the contouring package reflects the general principles of the design of MOLEKEL:

- A simple, user-friendly interface with buttons for basic operations like importing data, adding and deleting contours or contour planes and changing plane orientation in space. Both two and three-dimensional data arrays are accepted: two-dimensional arrays for fixed contour planes and three dimensional arrays for movable contour planes.

- Interactive, real-time contouring with sliders for changing the contour value and moving the contour plane. Only three principal plane orientations are possible (perpendicular to the X, Y, Z axes), no skewed planes are accepted.

These design rules are important for a fast, interactive scene building giving to the user the complete control of all contour planes in a friendly and extensive manner.

A typical scene to be represented using our system consists of a solid ball-and-stick model of a molecule with its imported scalar data field calculated on a regular 3D grid together with a

transparent or solid model of an isosurface and one or several
contour planes representing the main content of the data. The
complexity of the molecule and of its 3D data field often
requires many adjustments of plane positions, contour values,
viewing parameters and scaling factors before a satisfactory
visualization is obtained. To achieve a relatively fast scene
construction, the interactive, real-time contour and contour plane
redrawing are essential.

The choice of contour values is a very important task in data
visualization. The contouring routine redraws the selected contour
every time the threshold value is modified, which allows the user
to observe the changes of contour shape. New contours are added
after activating the "add contour" button and their values may be
adjusted with a slider. Once the desired values are selected, the
entire contour plane may be moved in real time along its normal
direction with the contour lines being instantaneously redrawn.
This sort of scanning the volume data has no advantage over
isosurface drawing for the simplest case of just one contour
value, however, moving the contour plane with two or more
different contour values may give us some more information about
the gradient behavior. Scanning data with contour planes in each
of the three main directions, i.e. along the axes X, Y, Z, is a
very useful way of visualizing global data properties.

Data Structure and Implementation

A contouring package based on the above concepts has been
implemented as a module inside MOLEKEL running on Silicon Graphics
workstations. The contouring routines are almost independent,
although they share the MOLEKEL user interface and some of its
internal data structures.

In addition, a procedure has been implemented to generate color-
filled contour maps, i.e the areas between successive contours can
be colored as a function of the property value. The use of rich
palette of colors allows an immediate perception of detailed
features of the property, such as the localization of extrema, the
changes of sign, etc.

All the graphics objects generated by the contouring module are
organized in a tree structured hierarchy which reflects the
natural order of image construction. Reusable linked list
structures are used throughout the code to manipulate all objects
(Sessions 1992) (Fig. 1). The plane object with its axes and 2D
data array is updated each time the user moves the plane position
slider or changes the plane orientation. The basic objects for
contour lines are lists of elements (straight line elements
scanned from a rectangular, regular data grid using a simplified,
two-dimensional version of marching cubes algorithm (Lorensen and
Cline 1987). These lists of elements displayed on the plane form
contour lines. Several contour lines together with a plane
definition form a contour plane object. The volume data set may
contain a list of contour plane objects .

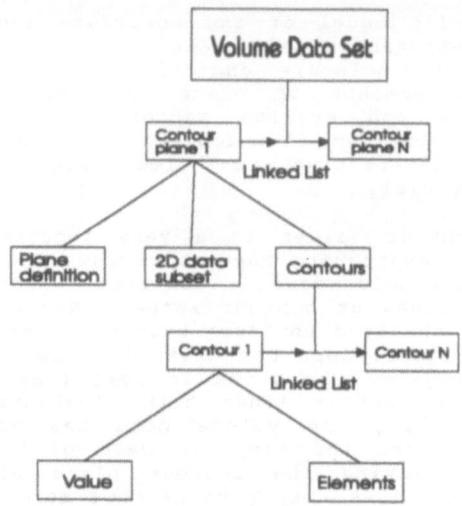

Fig.1. Tree structured hierarchy of the contour planes and levels generation.

Calculation of the Molecular Reactivity Index

As mentioned in the introduction, the molecular property we shall mainly use to illustrate our combined visualization technique is a local reactivity index made of the intermolecular interaction energy E_{int} between a substrate S and an incoming reactant R. Being a local property depending on the position r of the reactant R with respect to a fixed, rigid substrate S, E_{int} is calculated repeatedly at every point of a 3D lattice so as to lead to a dataset characterizing the most reactive regions within the molecular volume of S (Fig. 2).

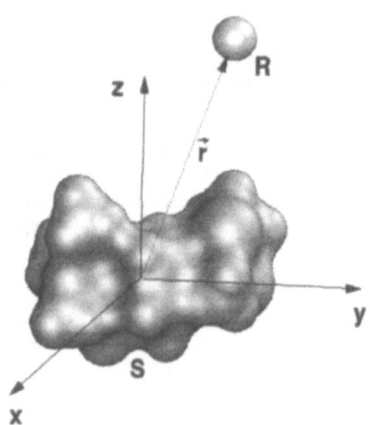

Fig. 2. Molecular substrate S and reactant R characterized by its position r. Moving R at every point on a 3D grid lattice generates the E_{int} dataset.

A convenient approximation is to partition E_{int} into several components:

$$E_{int}(\mathbf{r}) = E_{es}(\mathbf{r}) + E_{ct}(\mathbf{r}) + E_{ex}(\mathbf{r})$$

E_{es}, E_{ct} and E_{ex} being electrostatic, charge-transfer and exchange energy components, respectively. Both E_{es} and E_{ct} are evaluated in the framework of the extended Hückel (EH) quantum chemical method (Hoffmann 1963) using a reaction potential technique we have developed recently (Weber et al. 1992). The exchange term is calculated from a parametrized potential of Buckingham type (Weber et al 1992). The reactivity index is such that negative (or positive) values of E_{int} correspond to S-R attractive (repulsive) interactions. The regions where E_{int} is minimum are, therefore, the most reactive sites of S towards attack by R. To have E_{int} values that depend only on the position of R and not on its orientation, two spherically symmetric model reactants have been chosen: a naked proton for the electrophile (i.e. the electron acceptor) and an H^- anion for the nucleophile (electron donor).

Two different molecular graphics representations of E_{int} are commonly used: (i) in an initial stage, color-coded molecular surfaces of S by means of a mapping of E_{int} values, as they require to calculate this property at a considerably smaller number of points than the 3D lattice; (ii) in cases this mode of representation does not lead to a clear perception of the global minimum, isovalue surfaces of E_{int} represented as rendered models in 3D volume.

For both color-coded molecular surfaces and color-filled contour maps, the coding range from red to yellow to blue extends smoothly over the numerical range of the property represented from the most negative to the most positive values, the green color corresponding to a zero value. In the case of E_{int} this means that red zones correspond to preferred sites of attack.

RESULTS AND DISCUSSION

Our first application is devoted to the visualization of one-electron wave functions known in chemistry as molecular orbitals (MOs). It is indeed common in organic chemistry to describe the reactivity of chemical species using the characteristics of their frontier MOs, i.e. those corresponding to the highest occupied (HOMO) and lowest unoccupied (LUMO) electronic energy levels (Fleming 1976). For example, the characteristics of the HOMO of an organic substrate are predominant for describing the site and energy involved by an electrophilic attack such as a protonation reaction mechanism. According to these concepts, such an attack takes place preferentially on the atom or fragment which is the major contributor to the HOMO of the substrate.

Pyrrole (Fig. 3) is an interesting compound as it serves as a building block for several important biomolecules such as pigments. It is a planar molecule characterized by a rather low basicity. Examination of the HOMO of pyrrole (Fig. 4) shows that actually it has no contribution from the nitrogen atom, being mostly localized on the carbon centers of the penta-atomic cyclic system. On the opposite, the ante-HOMO, lying at lower (more

stable) energy than the HOMO (Fig. 5), displays a large
contribution from nitrogen arising mainly from the lone-pair
electrons of this atom.

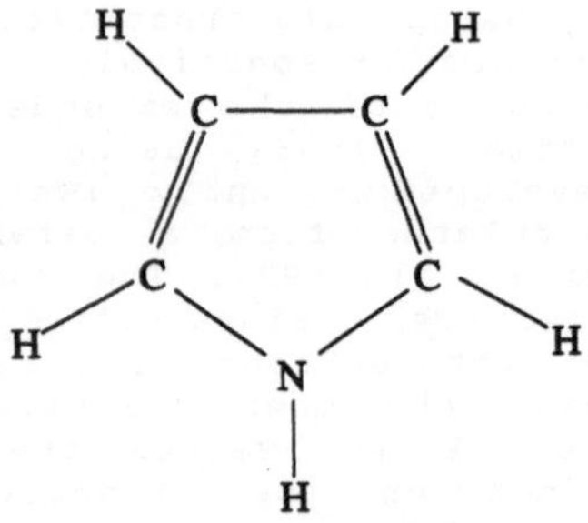

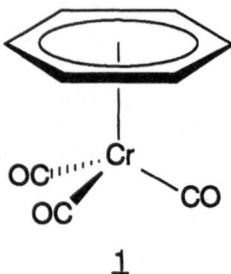

Fig. 3. Structure of the pyrrole molecule.

Being located at a more negative energy than the HOMO, the
electrons of the ante-HOMO wave function are therefore more stable
and less available for interaction with an incoming proton. This
simple reasoning explains easily the low basicity of this species.

Arguments based on frontier orbital theory are in general no
longer valid in organometallic chemistry, i.e. for compounds made
of organic ligands coordinated to metal center(s), since it is
here crucial to take into account all the MOs that could possibly
interact with the reactant, and not only the frontier ones. This
explains why it is then necessary to resort to more sophisticated
models such as the E_{int} reactivity index shortly described in
the previous section. Our next application will be concerned with
a textbook example of organometallic reactivity.

1

Fig. 6. Structure of the Cr(benzene)(CO)$_3$ complex **1**.

It has been shown that the electrophilic reactivity of a benzene
ring is remarkably increased by coordination to the Cr(CO)$_3$ moiety
(Kündig 1985). This allows us to understand why Cr(benzene)(CO)$_3$
(Fig. 6) and related species have important synthetic applications
in aromatic chemistry, particularly in view of the preparation of
regioselectively functionalized aromatics under mild conditions.

We would like now to use the E_{int} model to rationalize the basic mechanism of this enhanced electrophilic activity of benzene. Figures 7 and 8 present isoenergy surfaces of E_{int} calculated for both an isolated benzene ring and compound **1**, respectively, together with contour levels and color-filled contour maps in selected planes. It is immediately seen that, as expected, an important change in reactivity accompanies benzene complexation: whereas for an isolated benzene ring one observes a slightly negative (-1.2 kcal/mol) isoenergy envelope centered on the C_6 axis on both sides of the molecular plane and representative of a weak (van der Waals) interaction, the situation changes dramatically for the coordinated ring. In the latter case, a much more negative (-12.6 kcal/mol) isoenergy surface is found on the exo-face of benzene.

Let us turn now to a second reaction involving complex **1**. Indeed, Kündig et al. (1990) have recently shown that after the nucleophilic addition by, e.g., a reactive carbanion R^- has taken place on the exo-face of the ring, **1** may undergo in a subsequent step an electrophilic addition by a second reactant R'^+ directly to the metal atom.

However, whereas the experimental evidence clearly points out a direct attack of the chromium atom by R'^+, the detailed regioselectivity of this mechanism is unclear as conceivably the reactant R'^+ may approach the metal atom along several possible directions (Bernardinelli et al. 1992). We have therefore calculated the interaction energies between various substrates of general formula $[(C_6H_5R)Cr(Co)_2L]^-$ and an incoming electrophile so as to investigate the regioselectivity of this attack as a function of the type of ligand L substituting a CO group of the $Cr(CO)_3$ tripod.

The results show clearly that the direction of attack of R'^+ is dictated first by the size of ligand L (e.g., trans to L in the case of a bulky ligand L) and second by the position of substituent R on the benzene ring (e.g., trans to R in the case of a small ligand L) (Bernardinelli et al. 1992). This is perfectly illustrated by Fig. 9 which displays the color-coded molecular surface of $[(C_6H_5R)Cr(CO)_2L]$, with R=1,3-dithian and L=P(OCH_3)_3, together with selected contour levels of E_{int}. In this particular case, as the ligand L is rather bulky, the most reactive site is located trans to the phosphorus atom of L, i.e. close to the deep red zone of the molecular surface.

As a final example, we would like to turn to the modelization of the reactivity of the C_{60} molecule. The recent discovery of this fascinating compound (Kroto et al 1985), also known as "Buckminsterfullerene" or "footballene", has opened the way to important new applications: (i) in materials science, as alkali doped C_{60} crystals exhibit superconductivity with a T_c of 28 K for Rb_xC_{60}, (ii) in chemistry, as small molecules and ions can probably be trapped inside the cage and lead to inclusion compounds with unique properties. It was therefore interesting to apply our reactivity index to this system and to perform a theoretical investigation of the point (ii) mentioned above. In particular, we decided to study the behavior of the C_{60} cage in presence of a proton, as electrophilic additions to C_{60} have been shown recently to proceed readily in gas phase (McElvany and Callahan 1991). Our results show indeed that the C_{60} molecule is fairly reactive towards electrophiles: the calculated reactivity index (Figs. 10-12) exhibits negative values both inside and outside the cage, corresponding thus to attractive sites for an incoming (external) or trapped (internal) reactant. However, the global minimum of E_{int} lies outside the cage which suggests that, on purely electronic grounds, $C_{60}M$ is more stable when the electrophile M is bound externally to the cage. Clearly, molecular graphics developments such as that reported here may help the chemist identifying the most promising compounds to synthetize or designing the most suitable experiment to perform.

ACKNOWLEDGEMENTS

The authors are grateful to Professors C. Daul and E.P. Kündig for helpful discussions, and to Dr. P.Y. Morgantini, Mr. O. Schwalm and Mr. D. Stussi for assistance. This work is part of Project 20-29856.90 of the Swiss National Science Foundation.

REFERENCES

Bernardinelli G, Cunningham AF, Dupré C, Kündig EP, Stussi D, Weber J (1992) Experimental and theoretical investigation of asymmetric induction in the synthesis of disubstituted cyclohexadienes *via* chiral benzene chromium complexes. Chimia 46: 126-129

Borman S (1992) New 3-D search and *de novo* design techniques aid drug development. Chem. Eng. News 70 (32): 18-26

Connolly ML (1983) Solvent-accessible surfaces of proteins and nucleic acids. Science 221: 709-713

Elvins TT (1992) A survey of algorithms for volume visualization. Computer Graphics 26: 194-202

Fleming I (1976) Frontier Orbitals and Organic Chemical Reactions. Wiley, Chichester

Fluekiger P (1992) Development of the molecular graphics package Molekel and its application to selected problems in organic and organometallic chemistry. Ph.D. Thesis, University of Geneva

Hoffmann RJ (1963) An extended Hückel theory. I. Hydrocarbons. J.Chem Phys. 39: 1397-1412

Kroto HW, Heath JR, O'Brien SC, Curl RF, Smalley RE (1985) C_{60}: Buckminster-fullerene. Nature 318: 162-163

Kündig EP (1985) Recent advances in arene transformation reactions *via* chromium complexes. Pure and Appl. Chem. 57: 1855-1864

Kündig EP, Cunningham AF, Paglia P, Simmons DP, Bernardinelli G (1990) Trans-disubstituted cyclohexadienes *via* sequential addition of a carbon nucleophile and an electrophile to (η^6-benzene) tricarbonylchromium: scope of carbon electrophiles. Helv. Chim. Acta 73: 386-404

Lorensen WE and Cline HE (1987) Marching cubes: a high resolution 3D surface construction algorithm. Computer Graphics 21:163-170

Mair S (1992) Scientific Visualization: Snapshots from the Field. Computer Graphics 26: 178-190

McCormick BH, DeFanti TA, Brown MD (1987) Visualisation in Scientific Computing. Computer Graphics 21 (6)

McElvany SW, Callahan JH (1991) Chemical ionization of fullerenes. J. Phys. Chem. 95: 6186-6191

Ripka WC, Blaney JM (1991) Computer graphics and molecular modeling in the analysis of synthetic targets. Top. Stereochem. 20: 1-85

Rusinko A, Skell JM, Balducci R, Pearlman RS (1987) CONCORD, University of Texas at Austin, distributed by Tripos Associates, St. Louis, MO, USA

Sessions R (1992) Class Construction in C and C++. Prentice Hall, New York

Uniras Inc. (1992) ContourXplore. Uniras Inc. 376 Gladsaxevej, 2860 Soborg, Denmark

Van Gunsteren WF, Berendsen HJC (1990) Computer simulation of molecular dynamics: methodology, applications and perspectives in chemistry. Angew. Chem. Int. Ed. Engl. 29: 992-1023

Watson DF (1992) Contouring: a Guide to the Analysis and Display of Spatial Data. Pergamon, London

Weber J, Morgantini PY, Fluekiger P, Goursot A (1991) Recent developments in molecular graphics: visualisation of chemical structures and properties. Visual Computer 7: 158-169

Weber J, Stussi D, Fluekiger P, Morgantini PY, Kündig EP (1992) Development and applications of an extended-Hückel-based reactivity index for organometallic complexes. Comments Inorg. Chem. 14: 27-62

Wilhelms J (1990) In: Thalmann D, (ed) Scientific Visualization and Graphics Simulation. Wiley, Chichester, pp 77-93

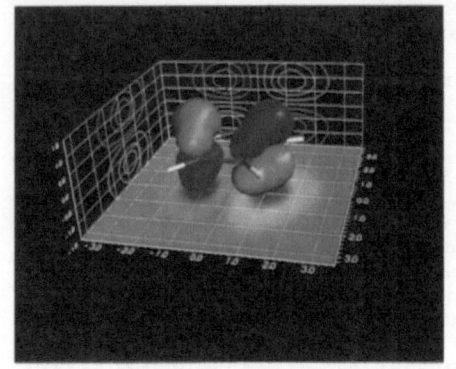

Fig. 4

Fig. 5

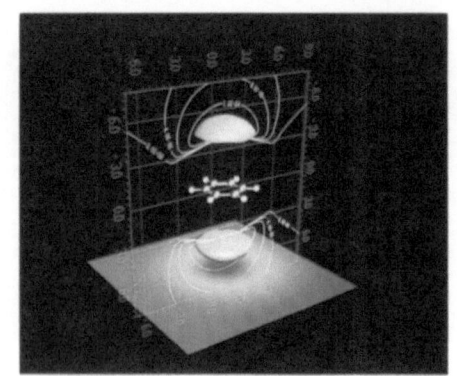

Fig. 7

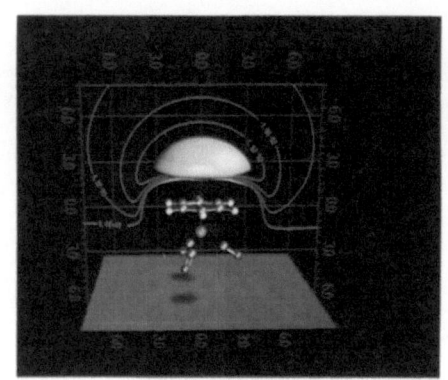

Fig. 8

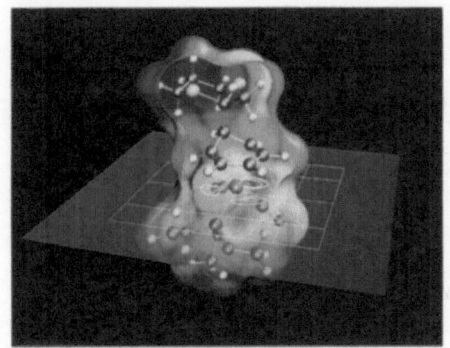

Fig. 9

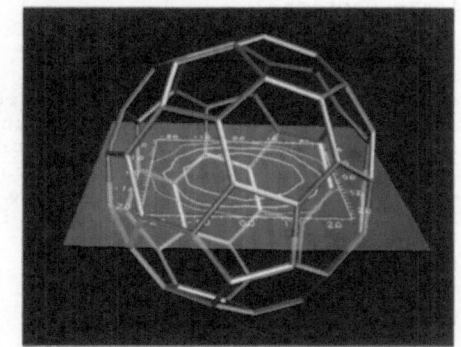

Fig. 10

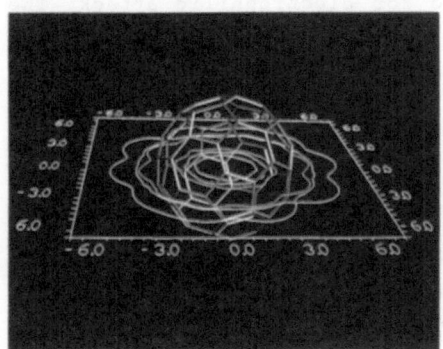

Fig. 11

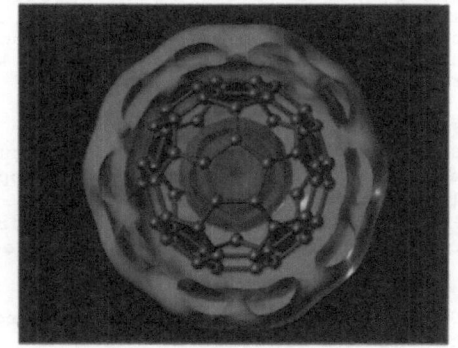

Fig. 12

Figure Captions

Fig. 4.
Solid model of the HOMO of pyrrole represented as red and blue
isosurfaces (at -0.06 atomic units) together with a stick model
of the structure of the compound. The horizontal and vertical
planes contain color-filled contour maps and contour levels,
respectively, generated from the MO values in the corresponding
planes. The scale of the axes is in Angstroems [A] (1A = 10^{-10} m).

Fig. 5.
Solid model of the ante-HOMO of pyrrole represented in the same
conditions as those of Fig. 4.

Fig. 7.
Structural model of benzene represented together wih solid models
(yellow lobes) of E_{int} isovalue surfaces at -1.2 kcal/mol
calculated for nucleophilic attack; the horizontal and vertical
planes contain color-filled contour maps and contour levels,
respectively, generated from E_{int} values.

Fig. 8.
Structural model of the $Cr(benzene)(CO)_3$ compound represented
together with a solid model (yellow lobe) of E_{int} isovalue surface
at -12.6 kcal/mol calculated for nucleophilic attack; the content
of the horizontal and vertical planes is the same as that
described in Fig. 7.

Fig. 9.
Solid model of the molecular surface of the ((1,3-dithian-2-
yl)cyclohexadienyl)$CrP(OCH_3)_3(CO)_2^-$ complex colored according to
the E_{int} reactivity index calculated for electrophilic attack. The
most reactive sites correspond to the red zones of the surface;
the horizontal plane contains some negative contour levels of E_{int}
at -220, -230, -250 and -260 kcal/mol from outside to inside,
respectively.

Fig. 10.
Stick model of the C_{60} molecule represented together with a
symmetry plane containing two opposite double bonds; the contour
levels drawn in this plane have been generated from a 3D grid of
E_{int} values calculated for electrophilic attack (color code of the
contours: pink: +15 kcal/mol , yellow: -15 kcal/mol).

Fig. 11.
Same as Fig. 11, but with a symmetry plane extending significantly
beyond the C_{60} cage.

Fig. 12.
Solid models of E_{int} isovalue surfaces at -21 kcal/mol (blue) and
-15 kcal/mol (red) calculated for electrophilic attack of C_{60}.

André Deloff works currently in the Computing Center of the University of Geneva (SEINF) and spends half of his time preparing his PhD thesis under the guidance of Professor Weber. Deloff received his MSc degree in physics from the University of Warsaw and his main research interests are interactive molecular graphics and parallel algorithms.
Address: Department of Physical Chemistry, University of Geneva, 30 Quai Ernest-Ansermet, 1211 Geneva 4, Switzerland

Peter F. Fluekiger obtained his Ph. D. in physical chemistry from the University of Geneva in 1992, where he developed the molecular graphics package MOLEKEL under the supervision of Prof. Jacques Weber. He is currently working at the Swiss Scientific Computing Center in Manno (Ticino) where he is developing software tools for interactive scientific visualization on high-performance graphics equipments.
Address: Centro Svizzero di Calcolo Scientifico, Via Cantonale, 6928 Manno, Switzerland

Jacques Weber is currently professor of computer-assisted chemistry at the University of Geneva. After completion of his PhD thesis in chemical physics in Geneva, he spent two years as a post-doc in the USA, working at the Quantum Theory Project of the University of Florida and at the IBM Research Laboratory of San Jose (California). His research interests include computational quantum chemistry, Monte Carlo and molecular dynamics simulations, and molecular graphics. In his recent research projects, supported by the Swiss National Science Foundation, Weber is combining different techniques deriving from these various fields so as to develop interactive molecular graphics tools for the prediction and interpretation of the structure and properties of chemical species. Weber was the organizer, or a member of the scientific committee, of several international congresses in computational chemistry and molecular graphics; in addition, he has authored and published over 160 refereed scientific papers in a broad range of chemistry and computer science journals.
Address: Department of Physical Chemistry, University of Geneva, 30 Quai Ernest-Ansermet, 1211 Geneva 4, Switzerland

Manufacturing Simulation for Turning Machine Centers

Abdelkader Belhi and Maurice Schneider

ABSTRACT

In order to control the machining process in turning machine centers, a software package was developed. This program has the advantage to be easily integrated in every CAD/CAM environment. It avoids machine breakdowns by checking interferences between moving objects in parallel with workpiece evolution. The operator is informed about the specific parameters of the machining process. These parameters are user modified to an appropriate application yielding a better result.

Keywords: CAD/CAM, collision, polyhedron, polygon, PHIGS, ARCHITECT, simulation, turning, clipping, intersection, boolean operations.

1. INTRODUCTION

Interferences between moving parts in a manufacturing machine can affect the production and cause serious damage that immobilizes the machine sometimes up to two weeks (a statistic made in 1982)[1]. Most of collisions are caused by human mistakes. In order to satisfy the efficiency requirements of turning centers with rotating tools, a software package for manufacturing simulation is developed. New concepts of computational geometry are introduced. A possibility of integration in CAD/CAM environment is offered.

The Aim of the manufacturing simulation is :

– to limit the preparation time in the workshop by the tool choice validation and by avoiding collision between moving parts. A simulation of a NC program gives more information about machining conditions (optional bloc level, feed potentiometer)

– to optimize the order of machining operations and reduce the lost time by a suitable parallel operation.

– to assist the operator in getting the right skills with low cost training. Testing a NC program on computer station without immobilizing the machine, offers the opportunity to detect all the written mistakes and to reduce the lost time.

This manuscript is organized as follows : a general presentation of the software package, structure of the data model, workpiece evolution and collision detection, and interactivity.

2. GENERAL PRESENTATION OF THE SOFTWARE PACKAGE

The main input of the simulation is based on the geometric machine model and the NC program of the machining part. All the data are translated in a neutral file easy to interpret. Then, a simulation

438

file is generated. In the process, 3D collision calculation is offered and workpiece evolution is visualized (in 2D and 3D). The order mode is simple, it was chosen similar to a tape recorder.

A tool catalog is added, the system has the possibility to be integrated in a CAD/CAM environment.

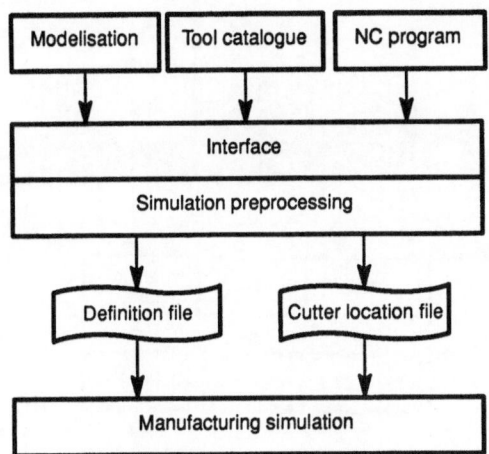

fig. 1. : CAD/CAM environment

Manufacturing simulation is laid as a complementary tool in CAD/CAM environment. The control of the process planning is assured, and the approach **down–top** was used (a geometric model of the workpiece is generated from the NC program).

3. MACHINE MODEL
3.1.MODELING THE ELEMENTS OF THE MACHINE

When simulating the motion of the machine, we should first choose a data model able to represent the machine geometry and the links among its various components.

3.1.1. LINKS BETWEEN VARIOUS ELEMENTS OF A MACHINE

The links among various elements of the machine are purely hierarchical. Indeed, it is possible to associate a tree to each machine. For more details, an example of assembly tree is presented :

- the slide parallel to the machine spindle is subordinated to the machine bed
- the cross slide is subordinated to the parallel slide
- the turret is subordinated to the cross slide.

This abstraction is very practical, because the motion of an element implies automatically an equivalent motion of its subordinates, which simplifies significantly the managements of moving elements.

According to the terminology defined for the simulation, an element of the hierarchic structure carries the name "object". Each link associates a parent object to one or more offspring objects. The intermediary objects are therefore both parents and offsprings.

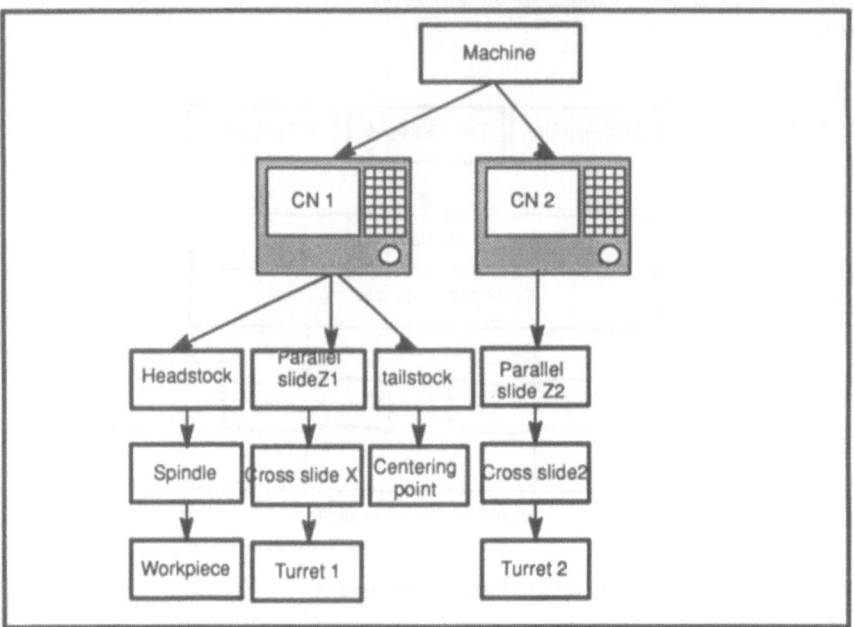

fig 2. : Gildemeister MD5–IT machine architecture

3.1.2. THE MACHINE GEOMETRY

The analysis tree yields the list of necessary objects to the modelling of the machine. The purpose of this section is to define its topology.

To speed up display procedures and improve the transportation of geometric data, a boundary representation approach was used. This approach is based on polyhedrons and polygons. Moreover it has the advantage to correspond to the data structure used by graphic libraries available on the market, in particular libraries based on the current standard (PHIGS[3]) and the ones based on the future standard (PEX).

In the simulation, an object may be a set of bodies, which have an hierarchic structure and represented by a set of polyhedrons.

Next, we give a summary of the used terminology:
– even body is named polyhedron
– a polyhedron is a set of polygons
– a polygon is a set of points.

3.2. MODELING THE MACHINE AXIS
3.2.1. LINKS BETWEEN THE CN AXIS AND THE MACHINE ELEMENTS

At this stage, the architecture and the geometry of the machine are known. However the correspondence between our objects and the axis generated by the CN has not been established yet; for example the parallel slider is associated to the Z CN axis.

3.2.2. KINEMATIC MODEL

The kinematic model of the turning center machine is extremely complex. Indeed the inertia of the various elements makes an exact computation of displacement times absolutely impossible.

Axis motion must be integrated in order to assure the simulation process. Every axis is defined by its kinematic attributes, the set of retained axis is:
– axis X, Y, Z, C
– tailstock (body and centering point)
– turret.
The main hypothesis of the kinematic model is defined as :
– acceleration and deceleration are considered as constant in rapid federate
– acceleration and deceleration are infinite with working federate.

3.3. MODELING TOOLS

Obviously, in order to be correctly represented, the tools should be modeled as other machine elements. Additional information will be supplied for each tool and for each one of its correctors:
–tool type,
–tool correction vector,
– all geometric machining parameters.

4. DATA MODEL

In this part, the data model is illustrated by examples of file:
–definition file:

fragment 1. : Partial File definition of Gildemeister MD5–IT turning center

```
// machine description

    OPEN_OBJECT "MACHINE"
        DEF_EDGE_COLOR LIGHTCYAN
        DEF_SOLID_COLOR LIGHTCYAN
        OPEN_POLYEDRE "CHARIOT_POUPEE"
            INS_LINEAR_REF -350.0 -170.0 0.0
            INS_BOX          700.0 -150.0 -500.0
        CLOSE_POLYEDRE
        OPEN_POLYEDRE "POUPEE"
            OPEN_POLYGONE "POUPEE"
                INS_POINT      -100.0 -170.0 0.0
                INS_POINT      -100.0   70.0 0.0
                INS_POINT       -50.0  120.0 0.0
                INS_POINT        50.0  120.0 0.0
                INS_POINT       100.0   70.0 0.0
                INS_POINT       100.0 -170.0 0.0
                INS_POINT      -100.0 -170.0 0.0
            CLOSE_POLYGONE
            EXTRUDE 0.0 0.0 -500.0
        CLOSE_POLYEDRE
    CLOSE_OBJECT
```

```
// Workpiece description
// La description du profil de la piece brute est variable et est donc importee
// depuis le fichier de description de la geometrie du brut

    OPEN_OBJECT "PIECE"
       DEF_EDGE_COLOR YELLOW
       DEF_SOLID_COLOR YELLOW
       INS_ROT_CENTER 0.0 0.0 0.0

#      include "$this.pdg"

    CLOSE_OBJECT

//Turret description

    OPEN_OBJECT "TOURELLE_1"
       DEF_EDGE_COLOR   LIGHTCYAN
       DEF_SOLID_COLOR LIGHTCYAN
       INS_ROT_CENTER 200.0 0.0 0.0
       OPEN_POLYEDRE "TOURELLE"
          INS_LINEAR_REF 200.0 0.0 0.0
          OPEN_POLYGONE "PROFIL_TOURELLE"
             INS_POINT 150.000 -160.000 0.000
             INS_POINT 170.000 -95.000 0.000
             INS_POINT 230.000 -30.000 0.000
             INS_POINT 230.000 30.000 0.000
             INS_POINT 213.564 49.904 0.000
             INS_POINT 167.272 99.724 0.000
             INS_POINT 140.981 184.186 0.000
             INS_POINT 89.019 214.186 0.000
             INS_POINT 63.564 209.904 0.000
             INS_POINT -2.728 194.724 0.000
             INS_POINT -89.019 214.186 0.000
             INS_POINT -140.981 184.186 0.000
             INS_POINT -150.000 160.000 0.000
             INS_POINT -170.000 95.000 0.000
             INS_POINT -230.000 30.000 0.000
             INS_POINT -230.000 -30.000 0.000
             INS_POINT -213.564 -49.904 0.000
            INS_POINT -167.272 -99.724 0.000
            INS_POINT -140.981 -184.186 0.000
            INS_POINT -89.019 -214.186 0.000
            INS_POINT -63.564 -209.904 0.000
            INS_POINT 2.728 -194.724 0.000
            INS_POINT 89.019 -214.186 0.000
            INS_POINT 140.981 -184.186 0.000
            INS_POINT 150.000 -160.000 0.000
          CLOSE_POLYGONE
          EXTRUDE 0.0 0.0 68.0
       CLOSE_POLYEDRE
    CLOSE_OBJECT

// Axis description

    OPEN_CN 1

#      ifdef $CONTREPOINTE
       OPEN_AXIS BCENTRE
          FROM $PARC_CONTREPOINTE
          ASS_OBJECT "CONTREPOINTE"
       CLOSE_AXIS
       OPEN_AXIS QUILL
          FROM $PARC_FOURREAU
          ASS_OBJECT "FOURREAU"
       CLOSE_AXIS
#      endif /* $CONTREPOINTE */

       OPEN_AXIS XAXIS
          FROM $X1_DEPART
```

```
        ASS_OBJECT "CHARIOTX_1"
    CLOSE_AXIS
    OPEN_AXIS ZAXIS
        FROM $Z1_DEPART
        ASS_OBJECT "CHARIOTZ_1"
    CLOSE_AXIS
    OPEN_AXIS CAXIS
        ASS_OBJECT "BROCHE"
    CLOSE_AXIS
    OPEN_AXIS PART
        ASS_OBJECT "PIECE"
    CLOSE_AXIS
    OPEN_AXIS TOOL
        ASS_OBJECT "TOURELLE_1" -1
    CLOSE_AXIS
CLOSE_CN
```

–cutter location file: This file is a translation of NC program related to an arbitrary mechanical part, written in CAM language, into natural language easy to interpret. An interface will be created between every CAM process and the simulation software.

5. WORKPIECE EVOLUTION

Calculation of the workpiece evolution in a simple turning mode is a 2D problem. All the machining operations are defined in the ZX plane. The mechanism of calculation is based on boolean operations of polygonal objects.

Geometric workpiece evolution is calculated basically on linear motion. The procedure of calculation is represented as:
– modeling the machining polygon
– determination of the intersection between the two polygons (workpiece polygon, machining polygon envelope). (see figure 3)

Generally, when two machining operations are executed simultaneously, calculation must be sequentially realized and the result is sent in the real time to the displayed workpiece.

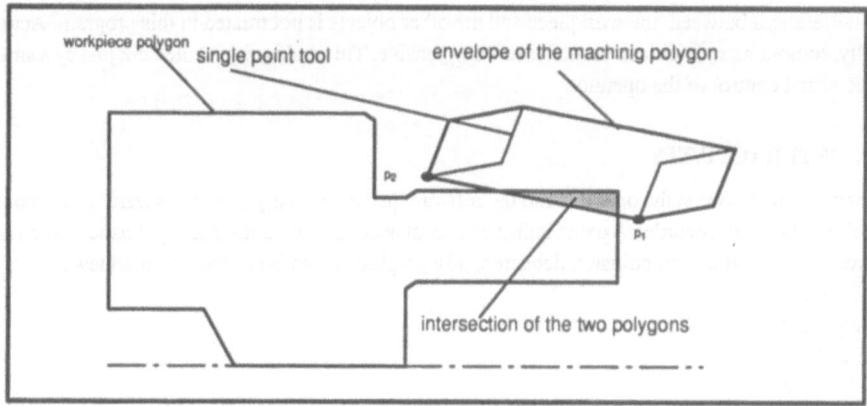

fig 3. : procedure of calculation

6. COLLISION DETECTION

Collision detection module is incorporated in the simulation process. Checking interference can be executed in parallel with workpiece evolution. In reality, calculation of collision between objects is static. Verification is realized only for displayed images.

–method: The program begins by clipping two objects (see fig.5) and comparing the two boxes. If there is an intersection, the treatment is continued by comparing every polyhedron to each other. The procedure can continue in different way polyhedron–polygon and edge–polygon.

The calculation of intersection in this case is limited to writing a routine of polygon–polygon intersection (convex or concave case).

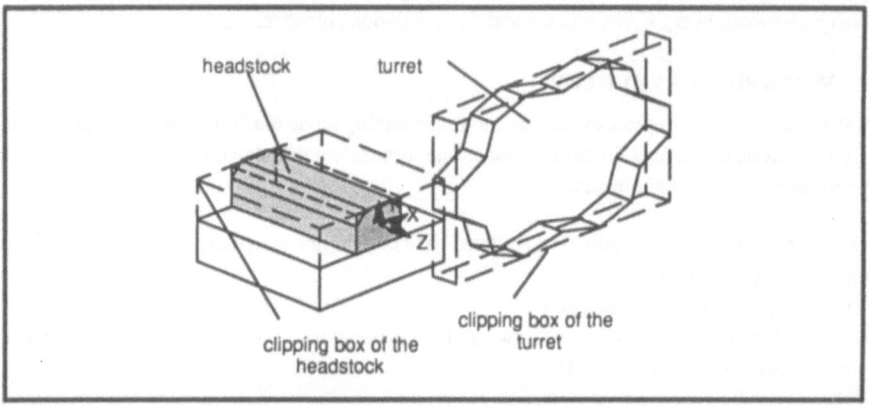

fig 4. : example of clipping objects.

Interferences between the workpiece and the other objects is not treated in this program. Actually, computing specific calculation is more expensive. This ambiguity is ruled out just by a simple visual control of the operator.

7. INTERACTIVITY

Interactivity between the operator and the software package is very straightforward. It was conceived like a type recorder. A menu indicates a set of needed commands (see fig 6) as activation of workpiece evolution or collision detection. The graphic screen is composed on 4 views:
–3D view,
–top view,
–inside view,
–right view.
A possibility of zooming a view is offered. Extending each view on graphic screen can be made with sectioning option.

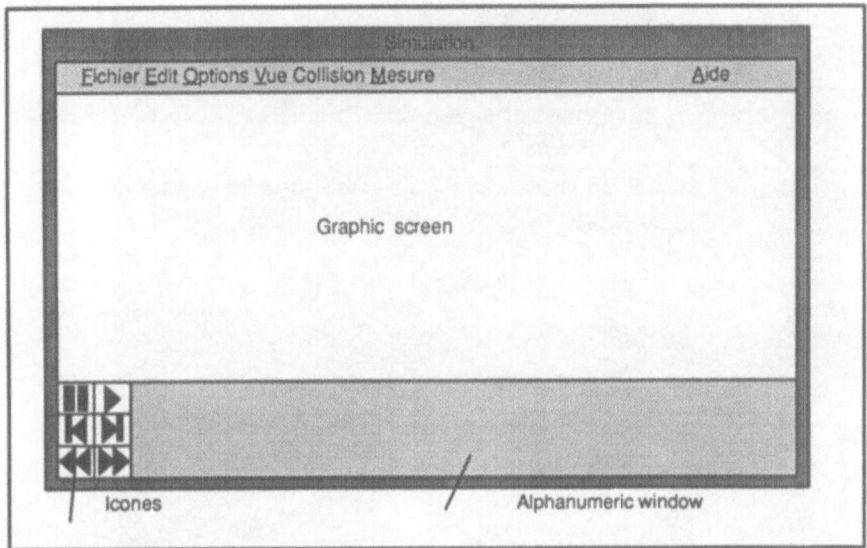

fig 5. : Illustration of the interactivity

Interactivity commands were designed by Architect tool [2].

8. CONCLUSION

In this software package, a down–top approach is used by for generating the workpiece geometric model based on NC program as input for the simulation process. An efficiency module of collision detection was integrated, which avoids the machine breakdowns.

The future work will involve the integration of milling operations for workpiece evolution in a 3D representation.

The simulation process can be useful for other machines like machine centers.

9. REFERENCES

–[1] Ulrich Pilland (1986), "Echtzeit–Kollisionschutz an NC–Drehmaschinen", Diss in Munchen Springer, Berlin

–[2] Hewlett Packard (1990), " HP interface Architect Developer's Guide "

–[3] Manuel, "FIGARO–PHIGS" (1991), Liant Software Corporation, U.S.A

446

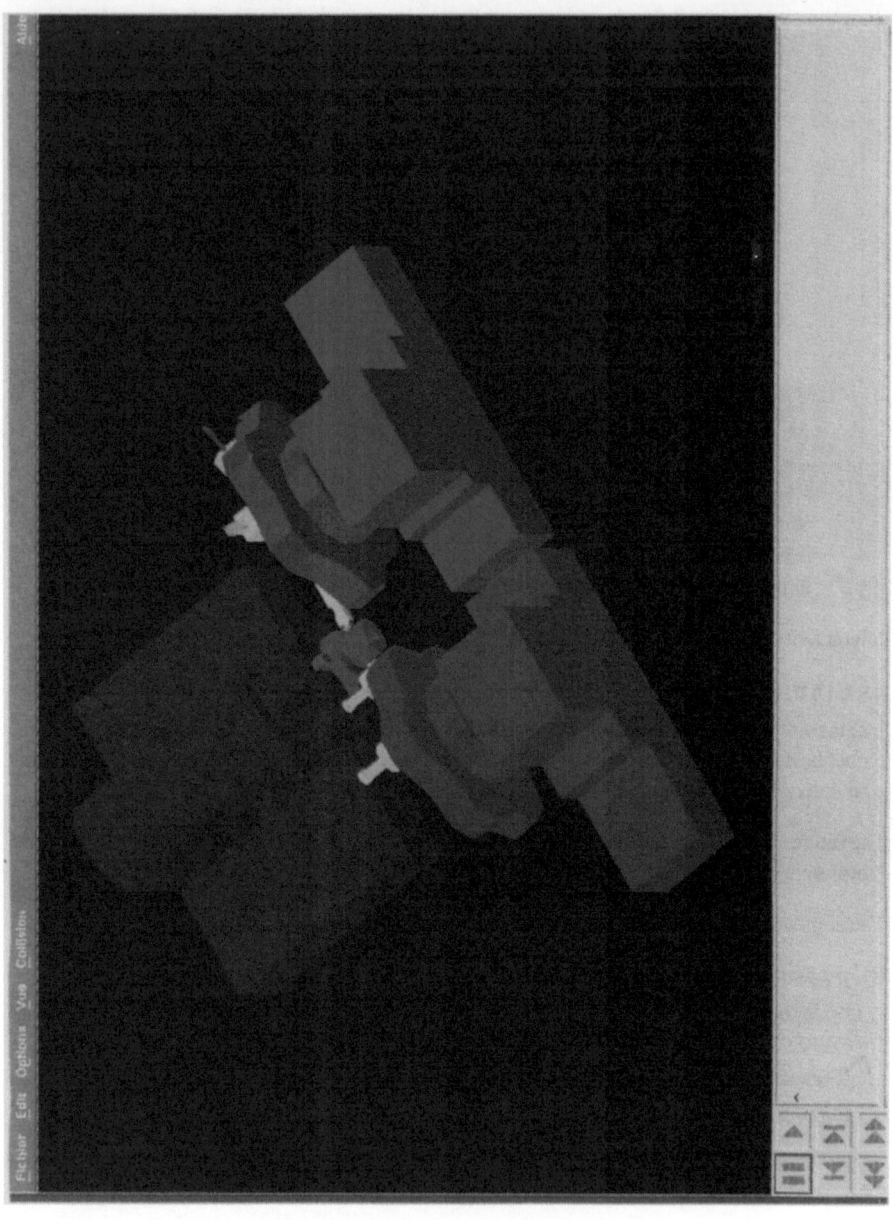

fig 6. : an Example of simulation for Gildemeister MD5–IT turning center

fig 7. : application for a machine center

Address: Computer Aided Design Laboratory, Mechanical Engineering Department,
          Swiss Federal Institute of Technology, CH 1015 Lausanne, Switzerland

Part V

Hardware and Parallel Processing

PROOF II: A Scalable Architecture for Future Highperformance Graphics Systems

Wolfgang Strasser and Andreas Schilling

ABSTRACT

PROOF II is an architecture for high-speed and high-quality raster image generation. The performance limitations of conventional architectures are overcome by distributing the rendering task to a pipeline of identical renderers with optimal cost/performance ratio. Each of the renderers generates a full-screen image of a fraction of the scene's primitives. The pixel data is transferred from one renderer to the next in the pipeline through special purpose list processors. They realize the EXACT A-buffer algorithm, which handles anti-aliasing and transparency correctly. Due to the pipeline structure the performance of PROOF II scales linearly with the number of renderers.

Keywords: scalable architecture, pipeline, EXACT A-buffer, anti-aliasing, transparency.

1   INTRODUCTION

Demanding applications such as scientific visualization, computer-aided design or virtual reality require graphics systems which are able to render complex scenes with high quality in real-time. Commercial systems have been successfully improved with respect to the number of polygons processable per second. For instance Hewlett Packard and Silicon Graphics claim for their high-end products 2 million polygons per second. Unfortunately the progress with respect to image quality is less impressive because of basic requirements like, correct anti-aliasing, true transparency and Phong-like shading are not supported by hardware.

The design of systems for much higher performance and improved image quality has to solve four major problems:

1) Improvement of floating-point performance for geometry processing

2) Elimination of the frame-buffer-access bottleneck

3) Acceleration of the rasterization

4) Correct hidden surface elimination on the pixel level including transparency handling

Another important design goal is the scalability of an architecture: it should be possible to achieve a constantly good cost/performance ratio from low to high performance machines (see Fig. 1).

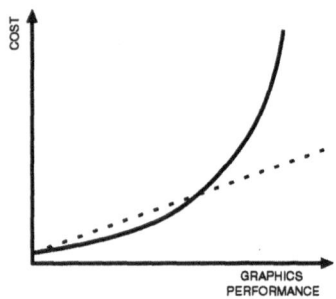

Figure 1: Price/Performance Ratio for Commercial Graphics Systems and Linearly Scalable Systems.

A detailed analysis of these problems for sample scenes can be found in [Foley et al. 1990] or [Jackèl 1992]. For example to render 100 000 Gouraud-shaded 50 pixel triangles for a 30 Hz refresh-rate requires roughly 1000

MFLOPS for geometry processing, 750 million integer operations for rasterization and about 200 – 300 million frame-buffer accesses, depending on the initially visible pixels. These specifications can be met only by parallel architectures.

The improvement of floating-point performance for geometry processing is achieved in available systems by distributing the primitives of a scene to a number of parallel floating-point processors (object-parallelism), which perform all geometry related operations like affine transformation, clipping, perspective transformation, back face culling, parameter calculation for illumination model etc. The SPIRIT Workstation [White et al. 1991] for instance uses up to twenty i860 processors offering more than 1 GFLOPS. The use of a general purpose offers extra flexibility for adding new features due to its programmability.

The elimination of the frame-buffer-access bottleneck is realized by building the frame buffer out of several interleaved banks, which multiples the effective access bandwidth by the number of banks. This scheme cannot be exploited too much, because of severe physical and economical constraints. E.g. the time for bankswitching cannot be shorter than, say 10ns etc. In other words this solution does not scale beyond available performance rates.

The acceleration of the rasterization beyond the performance of a single rasterizer can be achieved by applying object-parallelism again: if the load is too heavy for one rasterizer we must distribute it to many. Two options exist, namely dividing the screen into subscreens and object space or scene subdivision [Lindner 1979].

Screen subdivision works only, when the primitives of the scene are equally distributed over the whole screen, so that the rasterizer responsible for the subscreens have nearly equal shares of the load. Unfortunately many situations exist where alle the pictorial information is located in one or two subscreens. In this case the acceleration effect is rather bad compared to the number of installed processors. In addition screen-subdivision requires that each geometry processor has a high-speed link to all rasterizers.

Object-space subdivision distributes the primitives of the scene to the number of parallel rasterizers, each of which computes a full-screen image. This scheme fits perfectly to the parallel geometry processor concept. The combination of a geometry unit with a rasterizer can be considered as an elementary renderer unit (RU) which should offer an optimal cost/performance ratio and allow for scalability. In the compositing process to form the final image, visibility, anti-aliasing and transparency have to be calculated. Two options to realize a compositing network between the renderers exist: the binary comparator tree (Fig. 2) and the pipeline (Fig. 3). Molnar has described both versions and calls them image composition architectures [Molnar 1992]. In theory they are equivalent. Practical considerations led to the pipeline structure, which has been our choice for PROOF [Schneider 1988, Schneider 1990] already.

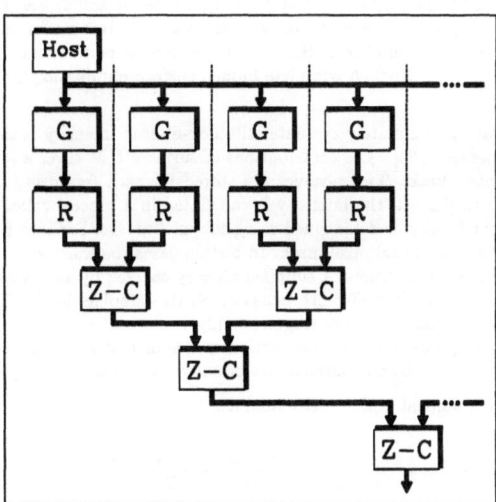

Figure 2: Binary comparator tree for image composition

Image composition architectures have the big advantage of linear scalability. The big disadvantage is the very high bandwidth needed for the communication between the renderers. Every pixel during every frame must pass through the pipeline. The data rate for a screensize of 1024 × 1024 pixels and a frame rate of 30 frames/sec.

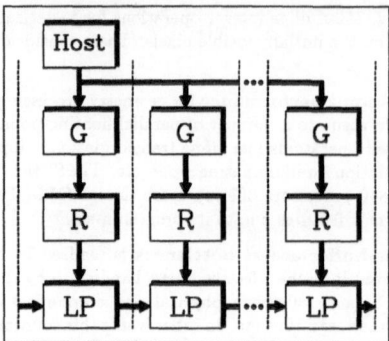

Figure 3: Pipeline with List Processors

is more than 1.8 GBytes/sec., if we assume that the information for one object consists of 32 Bytes and the average number of objects per pixel is 2.

This rate is the major technical problem of image composition architectures. It is independent of scene complexity but increases linearly with screen resolution.

The following sections concentrate on the issue of image quality and its solution by the EXACT A-buffer of PROOF II.

The rasterizer which relies on the performance of the IMAGE chip has been described in detail by [Dunnett et al. 1992].

2 THE ANTIALIASING PROBLEM

Rasterizing produces aliasing artifacts. If a box filter is used to perform anti-aliasing the brightness and color of edge pixels are functions of the pixel area covered by the objects as well as of the object colors. The ideal intensity would be described by the formula $I = \frac{1}{A} \sum_i I_i A_i$, where A_i and I_i are the areas and intensities of the visible surfaces within the pixel and A is the total pixel area. Subpixel masks can be used to calculate the fraction of the pixel area covered by an object. However, if the sample point is outside the polygon, its z-value is more or less useless for a correct HSE. A complete hidden surface elimination for the pixel area is required [Fiume et al. 1983].

A traditional algorithm that approximately evaluates the box-filtered intensity is the A-buffer Algorithm described by Carpenter [Carpenter 1984]. The contributions of surfaces that cover a pixel partially are arranged in a list that is sorted front-to-back. Two z-values are stored for each fragment, z_{min} and z_{max}. When all fragments have been added to the list, the intensity is calculated in a process called packing. Beginning with the frontmost object the contribution is determined using subpixel masks. For each fragment the exact covered pixel area is stored in addition to the subpixel mask. In certain cases the exact area can be used instead of the subpixel count to calculate the contribution. A subpixel already covered by an opaque object is excluded from further processing which results in a z-buffer-like behavior on the subpixel level. The difference to an actual z-buffer on the subpixel level is that for each fragment only two z values are stored per pixel. Intersecting surfaces are treated with an approximation. Intersection is assumed if the z ranges of two different objects overlap. It is further assumed that the two surfaces are oriented as indicated in Fig. 4.

The visible area of the front fragment is then calculated as:

$$Vis_{front} = \frac{Zmax_{next} - Zmin_{front}}{(Zmax - Zmin)_{front} + (Zmax - Zmin)_{next}}$$

The method will fail very often though, because it depends on assumptions that are hardly ever fulfilled. For example the surfaces in Fig. 5 are rendered exactly like the ones in Fig. 4 although one of the objects is not visible at all.

It should also be mentioned that other even more troublesome problem cases exist that are very difficult to handle. If only one z-value is available as in the z-buffer things become especially difficult. If the center of the

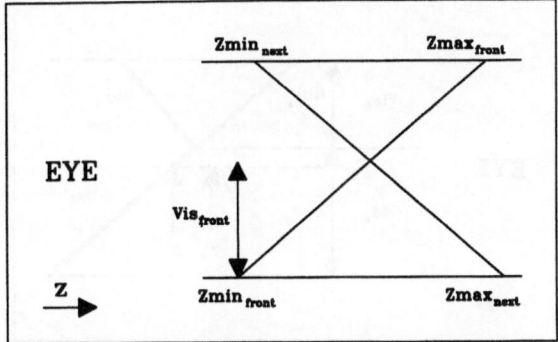

Figure 4: Visible fraction of front fragment ([Carpenter 1984]).

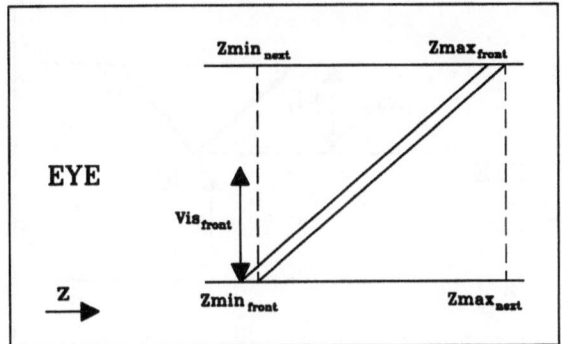

Figure 5: Front fragment should cover the whole pixel.

pixel where the z-values are sampled is outside of the object the z-values are nearly useless because they don't tell anything about the real location of the object if the slopes in z-direction are not known.

Some of the very common problem cases are shown in Fig. 6 - 8. The bold dashed objects are not drawn although they should be visible. These problems are not taken into account with most rendering algorithms.

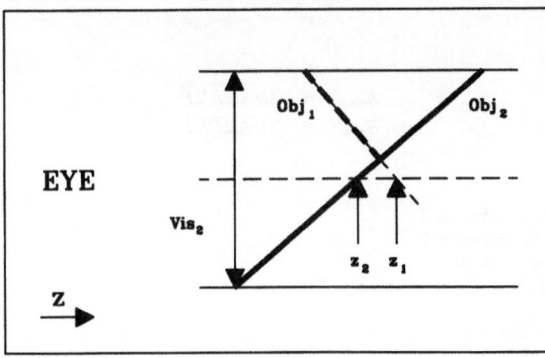

Figure 6: Object 1 disappears (z value sampled at pixel center seems further away).

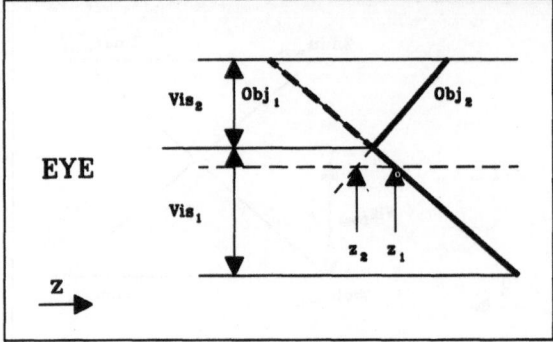

Figure 7: Object 2 shines through (z value sampled at pixel center seems closer).

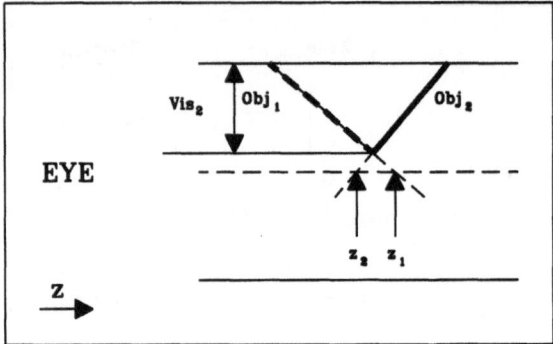

Figure 8: Object 1 disappears, but should be visible, object 2 is visible (situation similar to Fig. 6).

3 THE SOLUTION

If two objects (or the planes of the two objects resp.) intersect within a pixel a subpixel mask is generated which we call priority mask (P-mask). It indicates in which part of the pixel object #1 is in front of object #2. This subpixel mask is used to modify the edge subpixel masks of the two objects in the following way (see Fig. 9):

$$A_{new} = A\&\overline{A\&B\&\overline{P}} \tag{1}$$
$$B_{new} = B\&\overline{A\&B\&P} \tag{2}$$

where

A: edge subpixel mask for object # 1
B: edge subpixel mask for object # 2
P: P-mask for objects #1 and #2,
  plane #1 in front of plane #2 $\Rightarrow$ subpixel = 1

Two tasks remain to be solved:

1. The priority mask has to be calculated in an efficient way.

2. The decision has to be made, when two object planes intersect within a pixel's area.

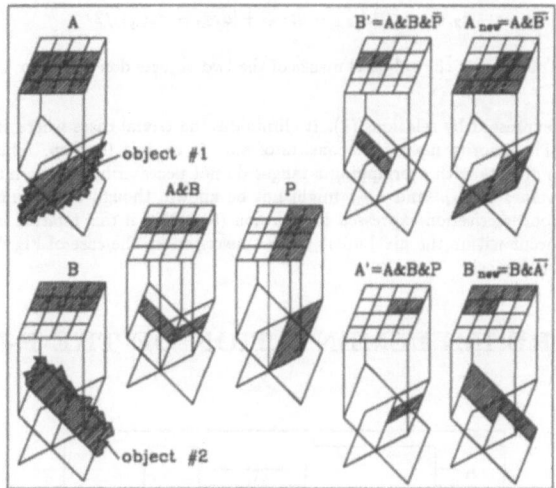

Figure 9: Generation of the modified edge subpixel masks A_{new} and B_{new} from the original edge subpixel masks A and B using the priority mask P. Shown is the subdivided pixel area, projected on the planes of two intersecting objects.

3.1 The Calculation of the Priority Mask

The priority mask generator uses the increments for the z value in the x and y directions dz_x and dz_y. (The values for the two objects are marked with indices, e.g. $dz_{1,x}$). The z-values at the pixel centers are known (z_1 and z_2). If we calculate the difference of the corresponding values for the two planes we get:

$$z = z_1 - z_2 \tag{3}$$
$$dz_x = dz_{1,x} - dz_{2,x} \tag{4}$$
$$dz_y = dz_{1,y} - dz_{2,y} \tag{5}$$

These parameters describe a plane that indicates, where plane #1 is in front of plane #2 by the sign of its z-value.

The representation of this plane with the above mentioned parameters resembles very much the representation of the polygon edges in some rendering systems, e.g. in the PIXEL PLANES system [Fuchs et al. 1989] or the IMAGE chip [Dunnett et al. 1992]. The mechanisms that exist to generate subpixel masks representing edges can therefore be used to generate the priority mask. A scheme producing subpixel masks that exactly represent the covered fraction of the pixel is described in [Schilling 1991].

3.2 Avoiding Priority Mask Generation

The generation of the priority mask is not very expensive. However, in a software implementation of the algorithm unnecessary calculations should be avoided where ever possible.

Several criteria can be used to reduce significantly the number of cases where the priority mask has to be calculated:

$$A\&B \neq 0 \tag{6}$$

$$z_{1min} < z_{2max} \quad \text{and} \quad z_{2min} < z_{1max} \tag{7}$$

or a much better criterion instead of (7):

$$z_2 - z_1 < (|dz_{2,x} - dz_{1,x}| + |dz_{2,y} - dz_{1,y}|)/2 \tag{8}$$

The first criterion (6) is obvious: if the subpixel masks of the two objects don't overlap, none of the objects can hide the other one.

The second criterion is expressed by relations (7). It eliminates the trivial cases where the z-ranges of the two objects don't overlap. The priority mask thus consists of only 1s or only 0s, resp. This criterion is not very strong however, because objects with overlapping z-ranges do not necessarily have to intersect each other (see e.g. Fig. 5). Also the values of z_{min} and z_{max} might not be known, though they could easily be calculated. This leads us to the stronger criterion expressed in equation (8). Only if this relation is true, an intersection of the two objects will occur within the pixel area. Using this criterion, the case of Fig. 5 is a trivial case with only 0s or 1s in the priority mask.

4   HARDWARE IMPLEMENTATION OF THE P-MASK GENERATION

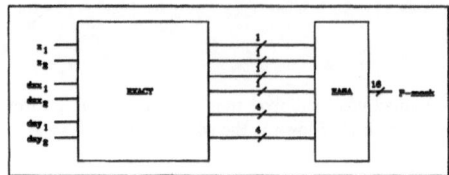

Figure 10: Block diagram of the P-mask generation on the EXACT-Chip

The block diagram of the P-mask generation is shown in Fig. 10. The block labelled EXACT takes two z-values and the corresponding increments as inputs and calculates from these values the parameters of the intersection line. These parameters are used to lookup the final P-mask. The contents of the corresponding lookup table can simply represent the order of the planes at the subpixel locations. It should however, be consistent with the method used for the generation of the coverage masks. The EXACT chip uses the EASA concept, described in detail in [Schilling 1991].

The design of the EXACT block (Fig.11) is intended to exploit parallelism as much as possible. Three parallel subtractors calculate the z-difference and the differences of the z-increments. The absolute values of the results are calculated in the next stage.

The resulting three values (z, dz_x and dz_y) are the parameters of the equation (9) for a straight line, the line of intersection between the two planes (origin of the coordinate system is the pixel center).

$$F(x,y) = z + x * dz_x + y * dz_y = 0 \tag{9}$$

This equation has to be normalized so that the parameters can be used to look up the resulting P-mask. The normalization could be performed by dividing the equation by $\sqrt{dz_x^2 + dz_y^2}$. However the square root can be avoided if we divide by the L_1-norm instead of the L_2-norm. This means that we divide by the sum of the absolute values of dz_x and dz_y.

The precision that is required so that the error introduced by the parameter calculation is smaller than one subpixel can be found if we apply the law of error propagation. For a 4×4 subpixel mask, only four bits are needed for each normalized parameter.

To keep the dividers simple (Fig. 12), barrel shifters are used to properly scale the input parameters.

5   SYSTEM ASPECTS

The EXACT-hardware is part of a new graphics system, PROOF II. The main concepts of its architecture are described in the following section.

457

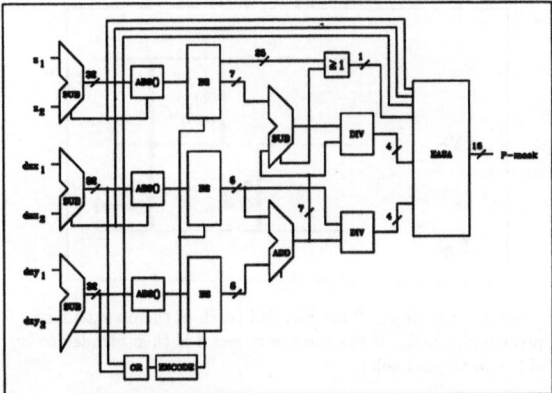

Figure 11: The P-mask generation on the EXACT-Chip ($\approx$ 12000 Gates)

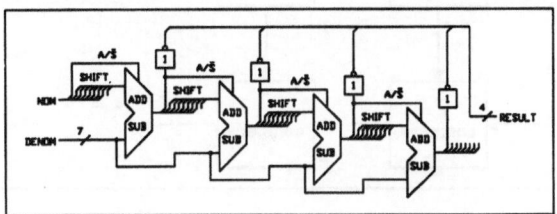

Figure 12: The Dividers on the EXACT-Chip

5.1 Processing of Lists — the Concept of the A-Buffer

A big difference between the A-buffer and a traditional z-buffer lies in the fact that in the A-buffer lists of contributions to each pixel are stored whereas in the z-buffer only one item per pixel has to be stored — the one currently closest to the viewer. Most rendering hardware today supports the z-buffer for obvious reasons: the list handling required by the A-buffer is much more difficult to implement in hardware. But there is no other solution to correct anti-aliasing and true transparency!

Anti-aliasing of edges implies the blending of the colors of different objects. There are cases in which the colors can be blended using a normal z-buffer. For example, if one object appears in front of another big object the colors can be blended with the weight factors A and $(1 - A)$, A being the pixel area covered by the second object. But what if three or more objects contribute to a pixel? A blending in the described way will lead to errors (see Fig. 13).

Transparency handling is the most obvious reason for the A-buffer. Assume several transparent objects covering a pixel. They have to be depth-sorted before their colors can be blended using the appropriate transparency factors and sorting requires that more than one object is stored.

5.2 The List Processing Pipeline

The pixel processing pipeline as a distributed z-buffer has been known quite a while. Cohen and Demetrescu presented such a processor pipeline already in 1980 Systems like the Triangle Processor and Normal Vector Shader System [Deering et al. 1988] or PixelFlow [Molnar 1992] use such a pipeline for image composition. As multiple z-buffer operations take place at the same time (see Fig. 14), the traditional frame buffer access bottleneck problem is solved in an elegant way. This might be a reason for this type of system to be more widely used in the future. Simply by adding more stages to the pipeline the rendering speed of the system can be increased indefinitely. The only penalty is a slightly increased latency time.

But now this pipeline architecture can not only be used as a z-buffer replacement; it is an outstanding architecture to perform the list processing required by the A-buffer algorithm. Schneider proposed in 1988 the PROOF

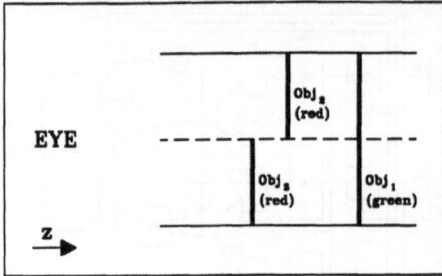

Figure 13: If the colors of object 1 and object 2 are blended (each of them contributing 50% to the final color), green will be part of the pixel color (25%). If the color of object 3 is then blended to the pixel color, green will erroneously still be part of the final pixel color.

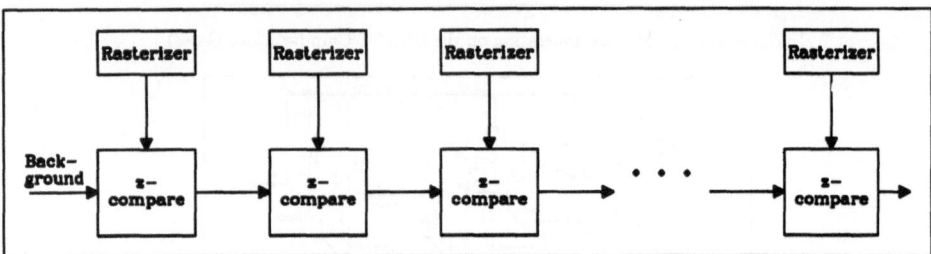

Figure 14: Pipeline of comparators performing n z-buffer operations simultaneously without problem of buffer access bottleneck. While e.g. the third comparator works on pixel #1, the second comparator works on pixel #2 and the first comparator is already working on Pixel #3.

system that uses a pipeline and transfers not only one object per pixel through the pipeline but a list of contributing objects for each pixel, similar to a proposal by [Weinberg 1981]. The hidden surface elimination was performed in a special post-processing stage. The architecture proposed here performs the whole list processing in list processors that contain the EXACT hardware for the hidden surface elimination on the subpixel level. Other features of the list processing pipeline, like image processing capabilities (filtering with arbitrary kernel) are not subject of this paper but also strong arguments for using such an architecture.

Figure 15 shows the block diagram of a list processor pipeline. The polygon descriptions are distributed in a round robin fashion among the RUs, which ensures a good load distribution with minimum effort. The RUs interpolate the z- and color-values (or resp. normals or texture coordinates) and send the sorted pixel contributions down to the list processors. Each RU is capable of rendering several thousand objects per second (about 20 MPixel/sec.).

The list processors, realized as ASICs, contain the described hardware for the EXACT algorithm and perform the modification of the subpixel masks coming from the RUs as well as the depth-sorting of the pixel contributions. Visible fragments are inserted into the lists at their appropriate positions which is important for transparent objects. Mutually intersecting transparent objects can be handled by splitting the subpixel mask of one of the objects in two parts: one in front of, the second behind the other object. The output of the pipeline consists of a depth sorted list of object contributions for each pixel, with nonoverlapping subpixel masks for opaque objects and transparent objects appearing in the correct sequence.

As each list processor can only handle one additional object per pixel, list processors that receive several objects for the same pixel flag all but the last of these objects as *not processed* and send them in front of the already processed list to the next stage. If this stage didn't receive an object from its RU for this pixel the last of the *not processed* objects is treated by this stage. If any objects remain unprocessed at the end of the pipeline the unprocessed pixels are cycled through the pipeline again to handle the unresolved objects. In order to keep the sequence of the pixels intact a FIFO is used to store the output of the pipeline during the recycling of the incompletely processed pixels. By adding several list processors without connected RUs to the end of the pipeline the probability for such cases can be significantly reduced.

The output of the pipeline can be directed to one of two RAM buffers (see Fig. 15). This allows the rendering

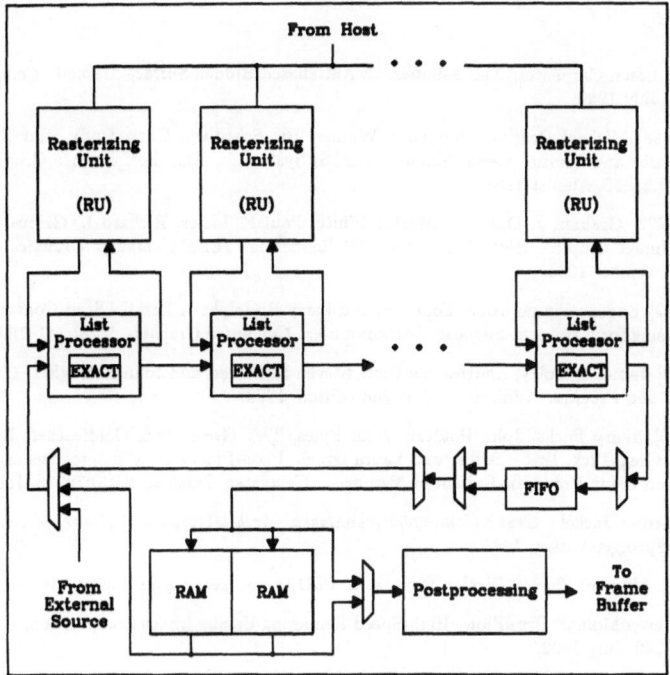

Figure 15: List Processor Pipeline Architecture

of scenes with changing parts. The static parts are rendered once into the RAM buffer. Then the RAM serves as input for the pipeline where only the changing parts have to be added for each frame. The RAM buffer is also used in other applications like image processing or form factor calculations for a radiosity algorithm. In the post-processing stage the transparency calculations are performed and the subpixel contributions are summed up.

6 CONCLUSION

PROOF II is an image composition architecture that scales linearly with the number of renderers and therefore has the potential of very high performance above todays commercial systems. In addition it supports unsurpassed image quality by implementing the EXACT A-buffer algorithm in hardware. All critical components, i.e. the geometry processor, the rasterizer with the IMAGE chip and the list processor with the EXACT chip, are programmable and therefore highly flexible for the implementation of new algorithms. PROOF II fulfills all demands on future high performance Graphics Systems including good cost/performance ratio.

Acknowledgements

We acknowledge Günther Knittel and Oliver Renz from our group and our partners from Sussex University for their suggestions and contributions.

This work is supported by the Commission of the European Communities through the SPIRIT Workstation project, ESPRIT Project No. 24 84.

References

[Carpenter 1984] Loren Carpenter. The A-buffer, an Antialiased Hidden Surface Method. *Computer Graphics*, 18(3):103–108, July 1984.

[Deering et al. 1988] Michael Deering, Stephanie Winner, Bic Schediwy, Chris Duffy, and Neil Hunt. The Triangle Processor and Normal Vector Shader: A VLSI System for High Performance Graphics. *Computer Graphics*, 22(4):21–30, August 1988.

[Dunnett et al. 1992] Graham J. Dunnett, Martin White, Paul F. Lister, Richard L. Grimsdale, and France Glemot. The Image Chip for High Performance 3D Rendering. *IEEE Computer Graphics & Applications*, 12(6):41–52, November 1992.

[Fiume et al. 1983] Eugene Fiume, Alain Fournier, and Larry Rudolph. A Parallel Scan Conversion Algorithm with Anti-Aliasing for a General-Purpose Ultracomputer. *Computer Graphics*, 17(3):141–150, July 1983.

[Foley et al. 1990] James D. Foley, Andries van Dam, Steven K. Feiner, and John F. Hughes. *Computer Graphics: Principles and Practice*. Addison-Wesley, 2nd edition, 1990.

[Fuchs et al. 1989] Henry Fuchs, John Poulton, John Eyles, Trey Greer, Jack Goldfeather, David Ellsworth, Steve Molnar, Greg Turk, Brice Tebbs, and Laura Israel. Pixel-Planes 5: A Heterogeneous Multiprocessor Graphics System Using Processor-Enhanced Memories. *Computer Graphics*, 23(3):79–88, July 1989.

[Jackèl 1992] Dietmar Jackèl. *Grafik-Computer:Grundlagen, Architekturen und Konzepte computergrafischer Sichtsysteme*. Springer-Verlag, 1992.

[Lindner 1979] R. Lindner. *Raster Display Processors*. PhD thesis, Technische Hochschule Darmstadt, 1979.

[Molnar 1992] Steven Molnar. PixelFlow: High-Speed Rendering Unsing Image Composition. *Computer Graphics*, 26(2):231–240, July 1992.

[Schilling 1991] Andreas G. Schilling. A New Simple and Efficient Antialiasing with Subpixel Masks. *Computer Graphics*, 25(4):133–141, July 1991.

[Schneider 1988] Bengt-Olaf Schneider. A Processor for an Object-Oriented Rendering System. *Computer Graphics Forum*, 7:301–310, 1988.

[Schneider 1990] Bengt-Olaf Schneider. *1An Object-Oriented System for High-Speed Image Generation*. PhD thesis, Eberhard-1Karls-Universität Tübingen, 1990.

[Weinberg 1981] Richard Weinberg. Parallel Processing Image Synthesis and Anti-Aliasing. *Computer Graphics*, 15(3):55–62, August 1981.

[White et al. 1991] Martin White, Graham J. Dunnett, Paul F. Lister, and Richard L. Grimsdale. The Spirit Workstation — Graphics Hardware. In José Encarnaçao, editor, *Eurographics 91: Graphics Research and Development in European Community Programmes*, pages 1–15. European Computer Graphics Association, Aire-la-Ville,Switzerland, 1991.

461

Wolfgang Straßer is full Professor of Computer Science, adjunct Professor of Mathematics and the founder and Director of the Computer Graphics Laboratory at Universität Tübingen, Germany, where research in Scientific Visualization, Geometric Modelling, Computer Vision and VLSI Design of high-performance graphics systems is done. From 1978 to 1986 he was Professor of Computer Science at Technical University Darmstadt, Germany. Before joining TU Darmstadt, he was head of the information processing department at Heinrich-Hertz-Institute in Berlin, where he developed communicating office workstations with Grundig and Nixdorf. He received his Ph.D. in Computer Science and his Dipl.-Ing. degree in Communications from Technical University in Berlin. Wolfgang Straßer has published more than 30 research papers and several books. He has given lectures and tutorials to the Eurographics Association, the German Computer Society and the British Computer Society. He is a consultant to government and industries.

Andreas Schilling is research and teaching assistant at the Computer Graphics Laboratory at Universität Tübingen, Germany since 1988. He had studied Physics at the same university and received his Dipl.-Phys. degree in 1987. He is involved in the development of graphics hardware in the context of the SPIRIT workstation project. His research interests include algorithms and hardware for realistic rendering.

The authors may be contacted at

Universität Tübingen
Wilhelm-Schickard-Institut für Informatik
Graphisch-Interaktive Systeme
Auf der Morgenstelle 10, C9
W - 7400 Tübingen
GERMANY
Tel.: ++49 7071 29 63 56
Fax.: ++49 7071 29 54 66
e-mail: strasser@gris.informatik.uni-tuebingen.de,
andreas@gris.informatik.uni-tuebingen.de

Realtime Synthesis of Super-Realistic Moving Goldfish Using Small-Scale Parallel Transputers

Hiroshi Dohi and Mitsuru Ishizuka

ABSTRACT

Parallel computer is one of important key technologies for achieving visual realism and natural behavior in realtime. This paper describes a transputer-based small-scale parallel computing system for synthesizing texture mapped *animated* goldfishes in realtime. It employs the techniques of a deformable three-dimensional wireframe model, texture mapping and linear movement compensation to generate realistic figure and natural motion. General purpose microprocessors are effectively used to realize a practical parallel computing system especially for visual data. Each transputer is controlled by small-sized packets, and responsible for generating own goldfish image. Network links connecting these transputers work in parallel to this purpose. This paper shows the result of the empirical trace of parallel computation on our prototype system. The total texture mapping performance for four goldfish synthesis is faster than 10 frames/sec on four transputers. This prototype system can also change the color of moving goldfishes with natural texture continuously by a luminance mapping technique.

Keywords: *Virtual environment, Texture mapping, Deformable objects, Parallel system, Transputer*

1 INTRODUCTION

The virtual environment has become one of the most important and most attractive research topics in computer graphics field (Bishop *et.al* 1992). Advances in computer and graphics will enable us to build a virtual world and a realtime interaction with it.

We have proposed a concept named visual software agent (VSA) as an interface surface between human and computer and have been working to realize it (Ishizuka 1991).

An important technical component of the VSA is realtime interactive graphics with three-dimensional deformable model. As an advanced human interface surface, the VSA is expected to eventually have the following features;

- reality,
- natural motion,
- wide communication spectrum, and
- intelligence.

To these ends, advanced graphics and computer technologies are to be integrated; for example, parallel computing for realtime image synthesis, texture mapping, knowledge-base etc.

462

 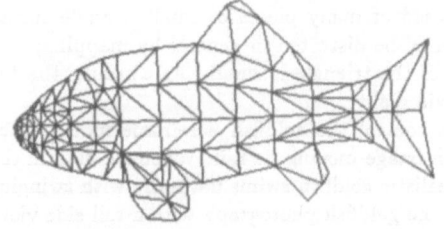

Fig. 1: 3-D goldfish wireframe model

We have so far built two prototypes of the VSA. One is an anthropomorphous VSA (Hasegawa 1992b) for advanced human interfaces, and another is a goldfish VSA for making naturalistic environment artificially (Lee 1991). These prototypes have been installed on SUN workstations and on our original parallel computing system.

A first important step for making a VSA system is to synthesize such realistic images that move in realtime on a display. To realize both reality and natural motion, the VSA adopts a texture mapping technique being applied to a three-dimensional deformable wireframe model. We don't necessarily need superfluous high-quality images for our application since the VSA is always moving. Rather, we need the realtime synthesis of moving images and quick response capability. Though texture mapping technique allows to generate realistic images, it requires high computational power compared with ordinary rendering techniques. This is a serious problem particularly for the synthesis of moving object.

There are many commercial graphic workstations/boards which can accelerate the rendering operation of image synthesis; however most of them have no support for texture mapping. Only a few high-end graphic workstations equip dedicated special hardware like a hardware texture mapper which enables realtime texture mapping; but they are very expensive. For example, IRIS VGX graphic subsystem executes graphic primitive operations on SIMD architecture, and the realtime texture mapping.

In this paper, we describes a new transputer-based small-scale parallel computing system and the goldfish VSA built on it. Each object (goldfish), instead of graphic primitive operation, is assigned to each processor element. Four realistic goldfishes swim (or fly) freely with swinging their tails in a virtual world. This prototype system can also change the color of moving gold-fishes with natural texture continuously by a luminance mapping technique. Four transputers provide necessary computational power particularly for visual data to realize this virtual world. The advantage of using general-purpose microprocessors instead of special-purpose processors is shown for this type of realtime synthesis of moving images.

2 METHOD AND ARCHITECTURE

2.1 Goldfish Visual Software Agent

Texture mapping (Heckbert 1986) is a technique which transcribes complex textures to any surface of objects. In the case of our goldfish VSA, for example, we decompose the photograph area of goldfish surface into many small triangles, then patch them to the surface of a three-dimensional goldfish model. Figure 1 shows our three-dimensional goldfish wireframe model, which is composed of many pieces of small triangle surface. The texture within the small triangle areas may be distorted in general by mapping; however, the texture can be restored when the area of the triangle is small. As a result, the texture mapping technique can give images with vivid reality.

Since we can control the goldfish wireframe model to bend its tail, it can be obtained a realistic goldfish image moving its tail. When we deform the wireframe model continuously in realtime, the realistic goldfish swims naturally with swinging its tail.

We use only one goldfish photograph with a full side view for the texture mapping. Since it must be able to generate the goldfish image from any view angles, we assume that the invisible side texture is identical to the visible side one. The wireframe model of goldfish is spindle-shaped; thus realistic images can be synthesized in spite of no image information from the views of a head and a tail. Therefore, the goldfish can conveniently texture-mapped with any viewing angle and then freely swim in a three-dimensional virtual world.

2.2 Hardware Configuration

We have already developed another visual computing system called TN–VIT (Transputer Network with VIT) suitable for realtime image synthesis by texture mapping (Hasegawa 1992a; 1992b). The VIT (Visual Interface to Transputers) is our original transputer board (Wongwarawipat 1991). It has a T800 transputer, 2MB local memory, 1MB frame buffer, and an access to/from a special image data bus. The special image data bus is 32-bits uni-directional synchronous links dedicated for image data transfer to an neighboring VIT. Image data written to each frame buffer is efficiently transferred via this image data bus without the commitment of CPU.

The TN–VIT system consists of 32 VITs and 16 TRAMs (standard transputer module) and is now under evaluation stage. In its current configuration, it mainly uses time-slice parallel processing with constant time interval; that is, assigns one frame image synthesis process to one VIT, and change output buffers in every certain period. It attains the synthesis of 25 frames/sec facial texture mapping with 32 VITs. However, it is hard to get quick response time because it takes more than one second for one transputer to complete one frame image.

We have designed and installed a new parallel transputer system for visual computing, which is also suitable to realize quick response after the issue of a drawing command as well as the realtime continuous movement of the object. The goal of this system is as follows;

- realtime texture mapping,

- quick response time (realtime interaction), and

- a compact-scale hardware (inexpensive for practical use)

We have emphasized the synthesis function of quick response and realtime movement rather than high-quality image production in our new hardware system design.

We have adopted the transputer T800 series (INMOS 1989) as our system's processor elements. The transputer T800 series is a 32-bits microprocessor and achieves the instruction throughput of 10 MIPS and 1.5 Mflops sustained by the processor speed of 20 MHz. Transputer architecture is designed for parallel processing; thus transputer is easily extensible as the building blocks of the transputer CPU. One transputer has four bi-directional serial links. These links which communication speed is 20Mbits/sec are used establish point-to-point connection.

Figure 2 shows hardware configuration of our system. The transputer network consists of three blocks; i.e. a root which communicates with a host workstation, a texture map engine, and a graphic board for video signal generation. The transputer for communicating with the workstation is called "root" transputer or *PE0* (Processor Element 0) in our system. The root

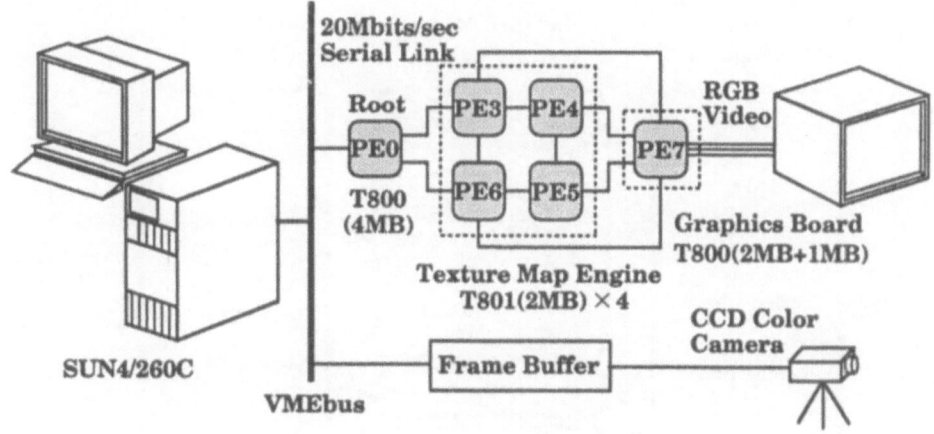

Fig. 2: Hardware configuration

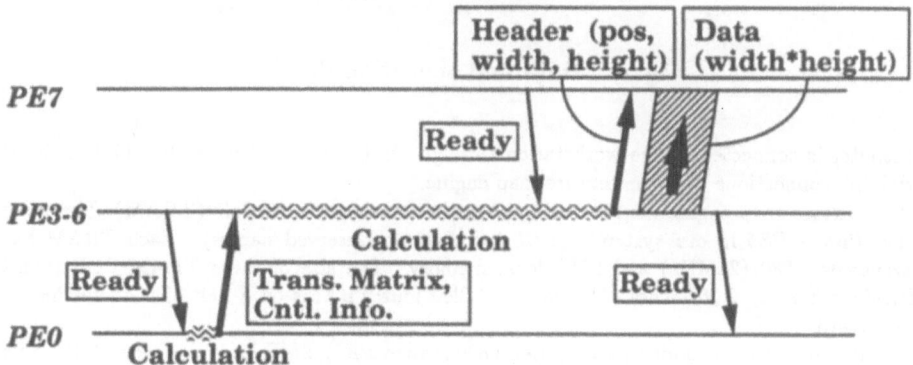

Fig. 5: System control protocol (1)

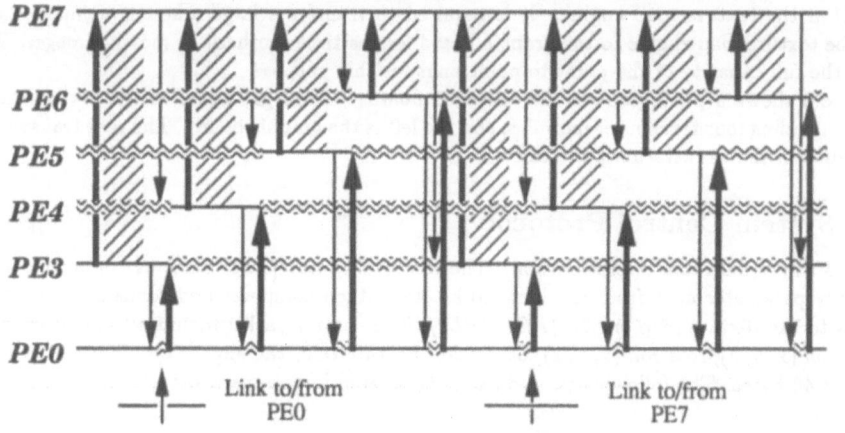

Fig. 6: System control protocol (2)

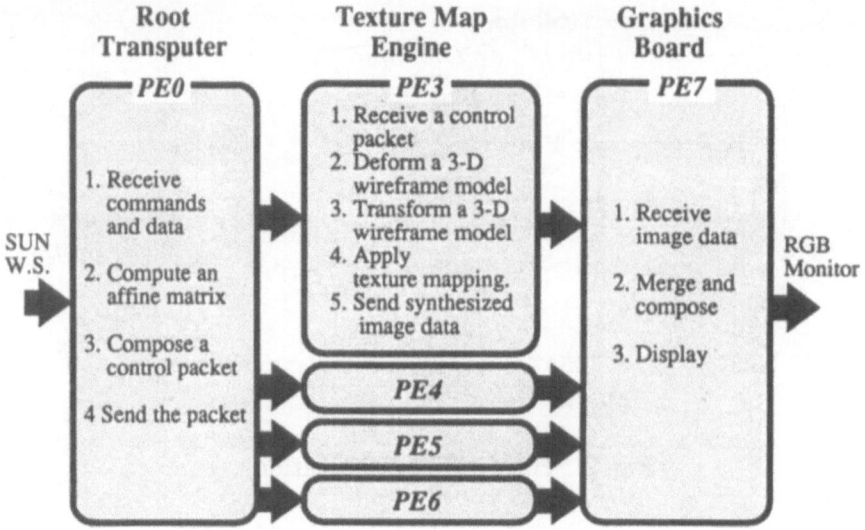

Fig. 4: Data and operation flow

transputer is connected to the workstation through VME bus. It also has two bi-directional serial-link connections with the texture map engine.

The texture map engine consists of four standard transputer modules(TRAM). These are called *PE3 – PE6* in our system. (*PE1* and *PE2* are reserved names). Each TRAM has a transputer T801(25MHz) and 2MB local memory. The size of these TRAM PCB (Size2 TRAM) is 3.66 by 2.15 inches. We have installed four TRAMs on a half of a double-height VME board.

The graphic board includes a transputer T800 (called *PE7*), 2MB local memory, 1MB frame buffer (dual port memory), and a D/A converter. It is installed on a double-height VME board. A graphic board receives image data synthesized by the texture map engine and then converts the data to RGB video signal. It has four serial link connections; that is, the graphic board has direct connections (a point-to-point bi-directional link) with each transputer module *(PE3 – PE6)* in the texture map engine. It is required to transfer a large amount of image data from the texture map engine to the graphic board for realtime synthesis of moving images. We utilize the full capacity of the point-to-point links for this purpose.

Figure 3 shows a photograph of the installed boards. The right board is the texture map engine including four transputer modules, and the left is the graphic board. The root transputer is installed in the workstation pedestal.

2.3 System Control Protocol

Figure 4 shows data and operation flow. The root transputer *(PE0)* receives commands and necessary parameter data from the host workstation, then composes and sends small control packets to the texture map engine *(PE3 – PE6)*. The control packet includes the information of position (x, y, z), rotation (x, y, z), base-color, posture (e.g. tail angle), etc. The size of this packet is 40 bytes. The following procedures are repeated in the operation;

Fig. 3: Texture map engine and graphic board

Fig. 7: Synthesized goldfishes image (normal)

Fig. 8: Synthesized goldfishes image (colored)

1. Wait a "Ready" packet from one of transputer modules *(PE3 – PE6)* in the texture map engine.

2. Receive commands and the data indicating a user input to which the goldfish responds from the host workstation. The data in the prototype implementation include the mouse position, the mouse button status etc. on X-window system in the host workstation.

3. Compute an affine matrix for the coordinates transformation of the goldfish from a wireframe model coordinates system to a virtual world coordinates system. Each goldfish has a different movement and position.

4. Compose a control packet by combining the affine matrix with other control parameters.

5. Send this packet to one of the transputer modules with idle state in the texture map engine.

At the starting time of operation, the texture map engine obtains information from the host workstation; i.e. the vertex positions of the three-dimensional wireframe model, sets of surface data, and texture image data. Each transputer module *(PE3 – PE6)* in the texture map engine repeats the following operations;

1. Send the "Ready" packet to the root transputer *(PE0)*.

2. Receive the control packet from the root transputer *(PE0)*.

3. Deform the wireframe model in the model coordinate system; e.g. bending backbone and swinging its tail.

4. Transform the model into the world coordinates system using the affine matrix received.

5. Apply texture mapping onto the transformed model.

6. Send this synthesized image data to the graphic board *(PE7)*.

Figure 5 and 6 depict the above communication protocol.

Four transputer modules *(PE3 – PE6)* work in parallel. They have equal priority and are identical. Suppose that four goldfishes are generated on four transputers; that is, one transputer is allocated for one goldfish. When two goldfish swim to disappear out of the screen, two transputers become to be allocated for one goldfish. The system can also assign one transputer to one goldfish and the rest three transputers to another goldfish if one is large or swims very fast. The system can change these types of processor allocation dynamically without changing the protocol.

For example, when the system controls four goldfishes, the root transputer sends four control packets to the texture map engine for generating one image. That is, four synthesized image data are merged and drawn onto a background image in the graphic board. Because the data transfer capacity of one standard serial link is insufficient for full-size image data, only modified parts from the previous frame are transferred. The image data header packet includes information of position, width and height of redrawing area. The image data (body) packet includes synthesized image data.

As a software development environment we have used EXPRESS ver. 3.2. (a product of PARALLELWARE Inc.) All software of our system is written in C language. The programs are cross-compiled on the host workstation, then downloaded to the transputers through a VME bus to be executed. The EXPRESS can record various types of events occurred during the operation period and the operation time. It contains several good tools for analyzing these profiled records. The results of the analysis can be graphically displayed. These are very useful for software optimization in a parallel system.

2.4 MOVING SUPER-REALISTIC GOLDFISH

It is well known that color is one of the significant factors for giving various impressions to human. However the aspects of color itself is not clear enough. Resembling colors tend to hide object contour and complementary colors increase the difference to some extent, whereas we can extract an object from even a monochrome image. Color may look differently depending on each person's subjective point of view. We have a general idea that the color of goldfish is red, red mingled with white and black, and black, etc. The word "red" has a certain range which is difficult for us to express by writing.

Our system can change the color of moving goldfish (deformable object) continuously for creative imagination according to two base-color parameters (Cr and Cb) in the control packet. The range of the parameters is 0 to 255. Each goldfish can change the color independently. In our prototype system, we use the position (X, Y) of the mouse on X-window system as an input to indicate the color. In this mode, the goldfishes are mapped by luminance (Y) value instead of RGB texture image value to keep their texture.

Twenty-four bits of RGB texture color information (8-bits each) are converted to a new color space YCrCb (8-bits each) in the texture map engine. The coefficient matrix of the conversion from RGB to YCrCb (CCIR601 1990) is as follows;

$$
\begin{aligned}
Y &= 0.299R + 0.587G + 0.114B \\
Cr &= 0.500R - 0.419G - 0.081B + 128 \\
Cb &= -0.169R - 0.331G + 0.500B + 128
\end{aligned}
$$

When the base-color parameter is changed, new RGB values of a color lookup table are assigned in the graphic board according to the parameter. Y value is an index of the color lookup table. It gives gray-scale color of the lookup table when other two parameters (Cr and Cb) are 128. The coefficient matrix of the conversion from YCrCb to RGB is as follows;

$$
\begin{aligned}
R &= Y + 1.402(Cr - 128) \\
G &= Y - 0.714(Cr - 128) - 0.344(Cb - 128) \\
B &= Y + 1.772(Cb - 128)
\end{aligned}
$$

Figure 7 and 8 show the example of "normal" goldfishes and "colored" goldfishes, respectively. The background is a real landscape.

In order to generate fascinating or appealing colors of the goldfish, we may be able to use the mutation of artificial genes as in the case of genetic algorithm. And this type of technology may become important to support or amplify human creativity by a computer.

3 EXPERIMENTAL RESULTS

Our goldfish wireframe model has about 400 vertices and about 400 surface patches. The system allocates four transputers for the synthesis of the moving goldfishes. Four synthesized goldfishes freely swim (or fly) with swinging their tails in a virtual world. The image of synthesized goldfishes has also perspective.

Figure 9 shows a part of execution profiling data, which is an output of the etool (execution profiler) on the EXPRESS. An elapse time is drawn along the x-axis and the y-axis is the processor number. A timer of each processor does not synchronize. The "exread" and the "exwrite" are synchronous communication functions supplied by the EXPRESS. The "exvread" and the "exvwrite" are also synchronous communication functions which are useful for two-dimensional block data transfer. "I/O" means communication functions from/to the host workstation; e.g. printf(), fread(), fwrite() etc. The "Ready" packet and the image data header are

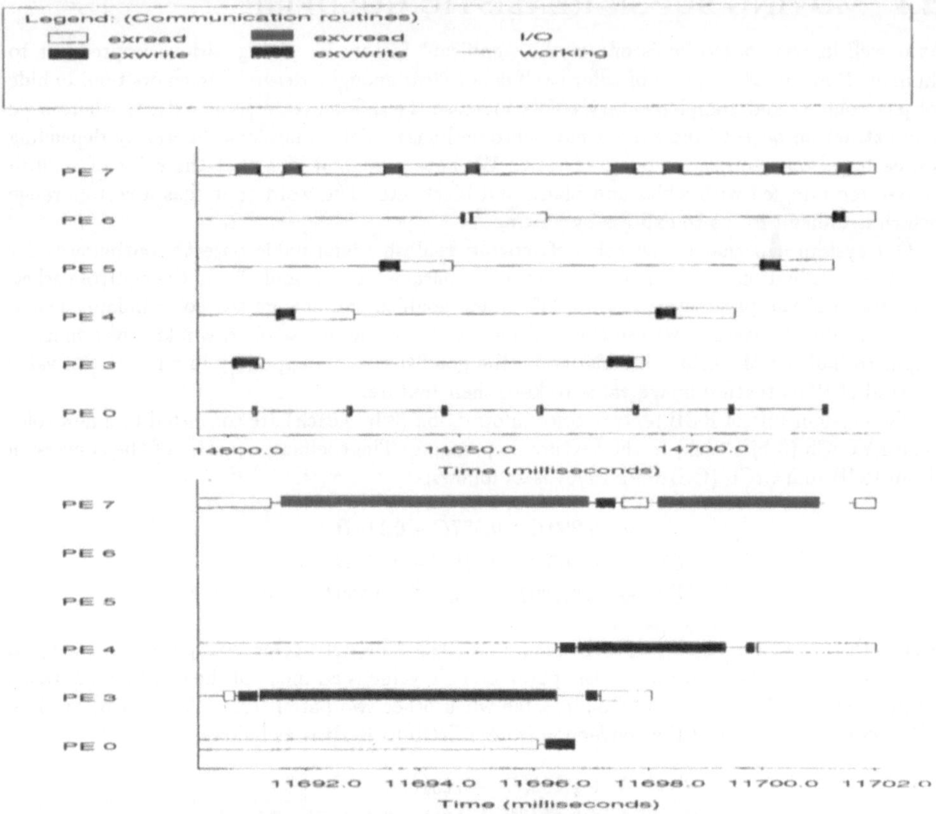

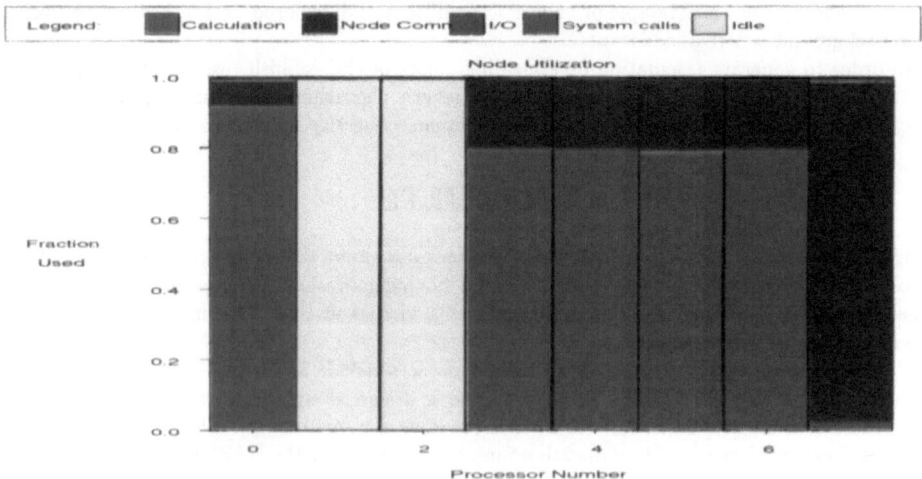

Fig. 9: Execution profile

Fig. 10: Communication profile

sent/received by using the exread/exwrite, and the body of the image data is sent/received by the exvread/exvwrite.

In this example, the root transputer *(PE0)* wakes up at intervals and sends the control packet to one of transputer modules with idle state in the texture map engine. If the root transputer wakes always up, it may be able to generate more image frames. However it increases the collision of operations, and causes the delay of input event handling.

Figure 10 depicts the analysis of a node utilization profile, which is an output of the ctool (communlcation profiler) on the EXPRESS. On the root transputer, a sleep function wastes the greater part of execution time. Four transputers *(PE3 - PE6)* in the texture map engine work almost equally in parallel, and spend about 75 - 80 % of the execution time for calculation. Total performance on four transputers is three times as fast as one transputer. In this profiler, waiting time for communication synchronization is accumulated in node communication time. execution time. On the graphic board, the communication with the texture map engine takes less than quarter of processing time and the rest is waiting time.

According to the measured profiling data, the total speed performance of the texture map engine containing four transputers is more than 10 frames/sec. The series of procedures (deformation of a three-dimensional wireframe model, transformation to the world coordinate system, and texture mapping) on each transputers takes less than 100 msec. Therefore the standard serial link speed (20Mbits/sec) of the transputer does not cause a performance bottle neck. Thus, if necessary, we can add more transputers easily to accelerate the processing speed.

4 CONCLUSION

This paper has described a transputer-based small-scale parallel computing system for synthesizing texture mapped *animated* goldfish in realtime. It employs the techniques of the deformable three-dimensional wireframe model and the texture mapping for generating reality and natural motion. Each object (goldfish), instead of graphic primitive operation, is assigned to each processor element. The result of the prototype implementation shows that the speed of the realistic image synthesis is fast enough for the real usage even if we use general purpose microprocessors. The prototype system of the goldfish VSA employs a new architecture of combining four transputers, and is easily extensible to accelerate the processing speed. The continuous color change of the moving deformable objects gives us an super-realistic and fantastic impression that can not obtained from static images.

References

[1] Bishop G, Fuchs H *et.al* (1992) Research directions in virtual environments. *Computer Graphics*, 26(3)

[2] CCIR Recommendation 601–2. (1990) *Encoding Parameters of Digital Television for Studios*

[3] Hasegawa O, Lee C-W, Wongwarawipat W, and Ishizuka M (1992a) A Real–time Visual Interactive System between Finger Signs and Synthesized Human Facial Images employing a transputer–based Parallel Computer. Visual Computing (Kunii T.L. ed.), 77–94. Springer-Verlag

[4] Hasegawa O, Lee C-W, Wongwarawipat W, and Ishizuka M (1992b) Realtime Synthesis of Human-like Agent in Response to User's Moving Image. *11th ICPR*, Hague

[5] Heckbert PS (1986) Survey of Texture Mapping. *IEEE CG&A*, 6(11), 56–67

472

[6] Ishizuka M, Hasegawa O, Wongwarawipat W, Lee C-W, and Dohi H (1991) Visual Software Agent (VSA) built on Transputer Network with Visual Interface (TN–VIT). *Proc. Computer World '91*, Osaka

[7] INMOS Limited. (1989) *The Transputer Databook*, second edition

[8] Lee C-W, Hasegawa O, Wongwarawipat W, Dohi H, and Ishizuka M (1991) Realistic Image Synthesis of a Deformable Living Thing based on Motion Understanding. *Journal of Visual Communication and Image Representation*, 2(4):345–354

[9] Wongwarawipat W, Lee C-W, Hasegawa O, Dohi H, and Ishizuka M (1991) Visual Software Agent built on Transputer Network with Visual Interface. *Transputing '91*, Sanyvale CA., IOS Press

Hiroshi DOHI received the B.S. and M.S. degrees in electrical engineering from Keio University in 1985 and 1987, respectively. He is a research staff member of the Institute of Industrial Science, University of Tokyo, Japan. He is a member of the ACM and the IPSJ. His research interests include human interface, computer architecture, and parallel computing.

Mitsuru ISHIZUKA received the B.S., M.S., and Ph.D. in electronic engineering from the University of Tokyo, and was visiting associate professor at Purdue University, Lafayette, Indiana, during 1980–1981. He has been a professor at the Faculty of Engineering, University of Tokyo, since 1992. He is now the chairman of the AI group at IPSJ (Information Processing Society of Japan). His research interests include artificial intelligence, computer vision and graphics, and parallel computing.

The authors may be contacted at:
Dept. of Information and Commun. Eng.,
Faculty of Eng., University of Tokyo
7–3–1, Hongo, Bunkyo–ku, Tokyo 113, JAPAN
E–mail: dohi@ee.t.u-tokyo.ac.jp

Parallel Volume Rendering Finite Element Data

Peter L. Williams

ABSTRACT

This paper describes a parallel system for interactive volume rendering large data sets from the finite element method or scattered data, as opposed to scanned or voxel data. The data is rendered using cell projection, without resampling it to a rectilinear mesh, and has been parallelized for a multiprocessor (MIMD) graphics workstation. The parallelization of the visibility ordering algorithms and the rendering process is described, and timings are presented. A method for coping with degeneracy found in irregular and curvilinear data sets is described. Using this system, data sets with over 1,000,000 cells have been rendered in 15-30 seconds, and with up to 100,000 cells in less than 2 seconds.

Key Words: volume rendering, finite element method, visibility ordering, parallelization, degeneracy.

1 INTRODUCTION

This paper describes a parallel system for interactive volume rendering large data sets from the finite element method or scattered data, as opposed to scanned or voxel data. The data is rendered without resampling it to a rectilinear mesh. Since irregular meshes can be highly refined in certain areas, resampling can result in an enormous increase in the size of the data set. Irregular meshes are often nonconvex; so it is essential that the volume renderer be capable of rendering nonconvex meshes. (If the boundary of a mesh S is also the boundary of the convex hull of S, then S is called a *convex* mesh; otherwise it is called a *nonconvex* mesh.)

Techniques for volume rendering irregular data have been reported, e.g. [Drebin et al 1988, Garrity 1990, Giertsen 1992a, Giertsen 1992b, Lucas 1992, Max et al 1990, Shirley and Tuchman 1990]. However, these methods have limitations such as: dealing only with convex meshes [Max et al 1990, Shirley and Tuchman 1990], not being interactive for large data sets [Garrity 1990, Giertsen 1992a, Giertsen 1992b, Lucas 1992], or resampling the data to a rectilinear mesh before rendering the data [Drebin et al 1988]. In addition, the method reported in [Lucas 1992] can result in artifacts in the image due to mis-sorting.

The system reported here uses cell projection, as opposed to ray tracing, for rendering the data. Each cell of the mesh is projected onto the screen in back-to-front order, thus requiring the cells to be visibility ordered. The cell's color and opacity contribution to each pixel is calculated and then composited with the pixel's existing color and opacity. A very accurate, but computationally intensive, cell projection algorithm is described by [Max et al 1990]. A fast approximation to this process, sometimes called a *splatting* algorithm, is given by [Shirley and Tuchman 1990]. Their algorithm is called the Projected Tetrahedra (PT) splatting algorithm. Two visibility ordering algorithms for the cells of irregular meshes, the Meshed Polyhedra Visibility Ordering (MPVO) algorithm and its adaptation for nonconvex meshes the MPVONC algorithm, are described by [Williams 1992a]. These visibility ordering algorithms in conjunction with the PT splatting algorithm form the basis of the system.

The basic system has been parallelized for a multiprocessor (MIMD) graphics workstation. The parallelization of the visibility ordering algorithms and the rendering process is described, and specific algorithms as well as timings are presented. In addition, a very simple, yet powerful, method for coping with degeneracy commonly found in irregular and curvilinear data sets is described.

A data set defined on a mesh generated by a conformed Delaunay triangulation can be rendered either as a convex mesh, where the cells lying outside the nonconvex domain of interest are marked invisible [Williams 1992a], or as a nonconvex mesh. Using such a mesh, the timing of the parallel volume rendering system when the MPVONC algorithm is used is compared with the timing when the regular MPVO algorithm is used.

The system described in the paper has volumetrically rendered images with over 1,000,000 cells in 15-30 seconds. Data sets with up to 100,000 cells can be rendered in less than 2 seconds. Useful information about the fine structure of the scalar field can be gained by watching the image being rendered.

2   OVERVIEW OF THE BASIC ALGORITHMS

In this section we review the splatting and visibility ordering algorithms. In splatting, as in splatting a snowball against a wall [Westover 1989], each cell is projected onto the screen in visibility order from back to front to build up a semitransparent image. The contribution of each cell to the image is proportional to the thickness of the splat. The splat is rendered as a set of triangles which have a common vertex at the point of maximum thickness of the splat. At this common vertex, the opacity is nonzero; at all other vertices the opacity is zero. The opacity and color at the vertices of each triangle is scan converted over the interior of the triangle.

An algorithm for splatting, called the Projected Tetrahedra (PT) algorithm is described in detail in [Shirley and Tuchman 1990]. That algorithm was modified and optimized for a high performance graphics workstation, as described in [Williams 1992c, Williams and Max 1992, Williams 1992b], for the purpose of the experiments described herein.

The Meshed Polyhedra Visibility Ordering (MPVO) algorithm, which orders the cells of convex meshes, and its adaptation for nonconvex meshes, the MPVONC algorithm, are described in detail in [Williams 1992a]. These algorithms are the basis for the work described in this paper.

An overview of the MPVO algorithm is as follows. First, the adjacency graph for the cells of a given convex mesh is constructed. Then, for any specified viewpoint, a visibility ordering can be computed simply by assigning a direction to each edge in the adjacency graph and then performing a topological sort of the graph. The adjacency graph can be reused for each new viewpoint and for each new data set defined on the same static mesh.

The direction assigned to each edge is determined by calculating a behind relation for the two cells connected by the edge. Informally, the behind relation is calculated as follows. Each edge corresponds to a face shared by two cells. That face defines a plane which in turn defines two half-spaces, each containing one of the cells. If we represent the behind relation by an arrow through the shared face, then the direction of the arrow is towards the cell whose half-space contains the viewpoint. To implement this, the plane equation for the shared face can be evaluated at the viewpoint. The adjacency graph and the plane equation coefficients can be computed and stored in a preprocessing step.

The preprocessing step is referred to as phase I. The phase where the arrows are directed for each face is referred to as phase II. Phase III is the topological sort. Either a breadth-first sort (BFS) or a depth-first sort (DFS) can be used for phase III of the MPVO algorithm.

The MPVO algorithm can be adapted to visibility order many acyclic nonconvex meshes. This modified algorithm, called the MPVONC algorithm, is really a heuristic; its limitations are discussed in detail in [Williams 1992a]. For all the nonconvex irregular meshes that it has been used for to date, it has performed satisfactorily.

An overview of the MPVONC algorithm is as follows. Construct the adjacency graph for the cells of the mesh. Set the arrows for each face in the same way as described above for the MPVO algorithm. Place all exterior cells that have one or more exterior faces with the arrow pointing outwards from the cell on a list L. Sort the cells on L by decreasing distance from the viewpoint to the centroid of the cell. Perform a DFS from each cell on L that is not marked. As each cell is output, mark it. Initially all cells are unmarked.

3   VOLUME RENDERING PARALLELIZATION

Massively parallel SIMD machines, such as the Connection Machine, usually have a nearest neighbor topology, such as a north-south-east-west (NEWS) interconnection scheme. Interactive volume rendering has been done on SIMD architectures, but only for data defined on rectilinear meshes which can take advantage of the NEWS topology.

The graph algorithms for visibility ordering an irregular mesh, and the associated data structures, do not seem suited to this topology. Finding ways to effectively apply massively parallel architectures with a NEWS topology to problems involving an irregular mesh is still a open problem. Future generations of SIMD machines that promise constant time communication between any two processors may remedy this problem. Therefore, a multiprocessor (MIMD) workstation with high performance graphics hardware was chosen for the parallelized volume rendering system described here.

The particular machine selected was the Silicon Graphics 4D/360VGX graphics workstation. The specific model

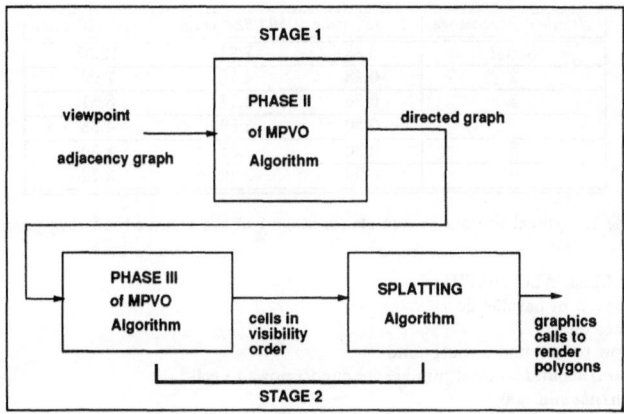

Figure 1: Overall runtime algorithm

used for the timings reported herein, both serial and parallel, had six 33MHz CPUs and 128 MB of physical memory. All algorithms were expressed using explicit parallelism. The timings reported are wall clock times. The hardware rendering engine is referred to herein as the *graphics pipe*.

When analyzing the algorithms, we use the notation $T_k(n)$ to mean the time complexity of the parallel algorithm when k processors are used. Phase II of the MPVO algorithm will now referred to as stage 1 of the volume rendering process. The combination of phase III of the MPVO algorithm and the splatting algorithm will be called stage 2. A diagram of the overall runtime algorithm is shown in Figure 1. For this paper, only tetrahedral cells are considered. If the cells are not tetrahedra, it is assumed the cells will be partitioned into tetrahedra in a preprocessing step.

Sections 3.1 and 3.2 describe the parallelization of the system when the MPVO algorithm is used. Section 3.3 describes the parallelization of the system using the MPVONC algorithm.

3.1 Parallelization of Stage 1 Using the MPVO Algorithm

In stage 1, the adjacency graph, which is created in a preprocessing step, is converted into a directed graph. This is done by evaluating the plane equation for each face in the mesh with the coordinates of the viewpoint and then setting the inbound/outbound arrow, as described in Section 2, for that face. In addition, all source cells, cells that have no arrows entering them, are located.

The parallel algorithm partitions the cells among all available processors. Each processor then sets the arrows for all faces of each cell for which it is responsible. Each processor maintains a shadow list to record the source cells it finds. After setting all arrows for a cell, the processor checks if that cell is a source cell. At the end of stage 1, the cells on all shadow lists are gathered into a single global Output List. Either one processor can do the gathering or it can be done in parallel.

The above procedure means the plane equation is evaluated twice for each shared face. Regardless, this method was faster than all alternative methods that were tested. For example, an alternative procedure is to evaluate all plane equations once by partitioning all faces among the available processors. Then an additional sweep of all cells is required to find the source cells. This alternative and a number of others are discussed [Williams 1992b].

Instead of shadow lists it is possible to use one global list for recording the source cells and require a lock to access it. Usually only a minority of the cells are source cells and so the list will not be accessed frequently. However, experiments showed that the use of one global list and a lock took 20% longer on average than the use of shadow lists.

The stage 1 algorithm is shown below. The complexity of the algorithm is $T_k(f) = O(f/k)$, where f is the number of faces in the mesh. Table 1 gives typical timings for 71,680, 593,920 and 1,003,520 tetrahedra for stage 1 of the volume rendering process. The serial times shown are for the most efficient serial algorithm, the algorithm described in [Williams 1992a]

Number Processors	71,680 cells	593,920 cells	1,003,520 cells
Serial	0.83	7.21	12.33
2	0.48	4.16	7.06
3	0.36	3.13	5.31
4	0.30	2.59	4.38
5	0.30	2.55	4.30
6	0.26	2.19	3.72

Table 1: Typical timings in seconds for stage 1 of the volume rendering process.

STAGE 1 PARALLEL ALGORITHM
    for all *cell ε Mesh* in parallel do
        for each face of *cell*
            set arrow to inbound or outbound
            set *cell.numInbound* to total number inbound arrows to cell
            if *cell.numInbound* = 0
                put *cell* on shadow list
    barrier
    move cells in shadow lists to Output List

3.2 Parallelization of Stage 2 Using the MPVO Algorithm

In stage 2, the directed graph created in stage 1 is enumerated in topological order. This results in a visibility ordering of the cells. Either a DFS or a BFS can be used for the topological sort. A BFS outputs sequences of cells, *layers*, that do not obstruct each other; therefore all cells in a layer can be rendered concurrently. Hence a BFS is preferable and is used here.

When stage 2 begins, the Output List contains the source cells gathered in stage 1. They constitute the first layer to be rendered. Their eligible successors constitute the next layer to be rendered, and so on. Since all cells on the Output List can be rendered concurrently, these cells can be partitioned among all available processors. A shadow list is maintained by each processor to store eligible successor cells it finds.

Each processor takes a cell from the Output List, splats it, waits on a spin lock to ensure mutually exclusive graphics calls, does the rendering, and then finds any eligible successors to that cell. When the Output List is empty, the layer is complete. The shadow lists are merged into the Output List and this procedure is repeated.

The eligible successors can be found quickly if each cell in the mesh keeps a count of the number of inbound arrow to it. Initially this number is set in stage 1. When a cell is output, all arrows from it to adjacent cells are removed and their counts updated. An adjacent cell can be rendered when its count is zero. A spin lock, as described below, is required when updating a cell's count.

STAGE 2 PARALLEL ALGORITHM
    while Output List not empty
        for all *cell ε* Output List in parallel do
            splat *cell*
            lock graphics pipe
                render *cell*
            unlock graphics pipe
            for each *face* of *cell*
                if *face* has outbound arrow to *adjCell*
                    lock *adjCell*
                        if *adjCell.numInbound* > 1
                            decrement *adjCell.numInbound*
                        else put *adjCell* on shadowList
                    unlock *adjCell*
        barrier
        move cells on shadowLists to Output List
        barrier
    end while

Number Processors	71,680 cells	593,920 cells	1,003,520 cells
Serial	0.45	4.34	7.61
2	0.61	5.81	10.45
3	0.45	4.28	7.69
4	0.38	3.52	6.31
5	0.34	3.13	5.57
6	0.33	2.97	5.22

Table 2: Typical timings in seconds for phase III of the MPVO algorithm.

Number Processors	71,680 cells	593,920 cells	1,003,520 cells
Serial	4.64	39.25	67.22
2	3.12	30.51	54.15
3	2.28	21.63	38.40
4	1.80	17.53	31.05
5	1.57	15.33	27.21
6	1.47	14.19	25.48

Table 3: Typical timings in seconds for stage 2 of the volume rendering process.

Hardware spin locks (hardlocks) are used to guarantee mutually exclusive access to (a) the shared variable in each cell containing the count of inbound arrows and (b) the graphics pipe. Only one lock is required for the graphics pipe. If there are enough hardlocks, one is assigned to each cell to protect the shared variable. If there are not enough hardlocks, there are two alternatives. Each hardlock can guard several cells, or multiplexed locks [Osterhaug 1987] can be used.

Multiplexed locks use a single hardlock to guard multiple softlocks. A softlock is a boolean software variable. Under multiplexed locks, each cell has its own softlock. In order to access a cell's shared variable, a process spins on that cell's softlock. Then it spins on the associated hardlock before locking the softlock. Once the softlock is locked, the hardlock is unlocked. This procedure maximizes simultaneous accesses.

The complexity of the stage 2 algorithm is $T_k(n+f) = O((n+f)/k)$, where f is the number of faces and n is the number of cells in the mesh. A processor may have to wait at a spin lock to access either a cell's shared variable or the graphics pipe. When 1,000 hardlocks were used to protect up to 1,000,000 cells, my experiments showed that an insignificant amount of time was spent waiting to access a cell's shared variable. On the other hand, considerable time was spent waiting for the graphics pipe spin lock. The rendering hardware was a bottleneck. This is the reason for the sublinear speedup shown in the tables of timings.

In graphics, surfaces are usually described as meshes of triangles. These meshes usually consist of several hundred or several thousand triangles. The SGI VGX graphics hardware is tuned to give maximum performance for such surface descriptions (tmeshes). In splatting, a tetrahedral cell is decomposed into from one to four triangles (3.5 on average for a typical irregular mesh), thus it is not possible to use the graphics hardware at its maximum efficiency. (Tmeshes were used whenever possible in this implementation. Their use resulted in a performance improvement of at least 35%. For example, for a tetrahedron which projects into a mesh of three triangles, if a tmesh is used, 12 graphics calls are needed instead of 24.) My experiments pinpointed the bottleneck to the Scan Conversion Subsystem of the SGI VGX graphics pipeline [Williams 1992b].

Timings for phase III of the MPVO algorithm (the BFS enumeration portion of stage 2) are given in Table 2. Timings for stage 2 of the volume rendering process are given in Table 3. Typical timings for the entire MPVO algorithm are given in Table 4. Table 5 shows typical timings for the entire volume rendering process (stages 1 and 2 combined) using the modified PT splatting method for 71,680, 593,920 and 1,003,520 cells. Several splatting approximation methods have been developed which are faster than the PT method [Williams 1992c]. They involve a trade-off of image accuracy/quality for faster generation time. Comparative timings for two of these methods, the Uniform Thickness Slab approximation (the fastest serial method) and the Voxel approximation (the fastest parallel method) are also shown in Table 5.

3.3 Parallelization Using the MPVONC Algorithm

Phase II of the basic MPVONC algorithm sets the arrows for every face in the mesh, finds all cells that have an exterior face with an outbound arrow and places them on a list L, sorts the cells on L as described in Section 2,

Number Processors	71,680 cells	593,920 cells	1,003,520 cells
Serial	1.28	11.55	19.94
2	1.09	9.91	29.05
3	0.81	7.61	13.00
4	0.68	6.11	10.69
5	0.64	5.68	9.87
6	0.59	5.16	8.94

Table 4: Typical timings in seconds for the entire MPVO algorithm.

	71,680 cells		593,920 cells		1,003,520 cells	
	PT	UTS/VOX	PT	UTS/VOX	PT	UTS/VOX
Serial	5.5	2.4	46.4	19.1	79.6	34.0
6 CPUs	1.8	1.1	16.5	10.1	30.2	16.3

Table 5: Typical timings in seconds for the entire volume rendering process using the modified PT splatting method compared with the use of the fastest serial and parallel splatting approximations to the PT method, the Uniform Thickness Slab (UTS) approximation and the Voxel (VOX) approximation, respectively. The MPVO algorithm was used in each case.

and locates all sink cells, cells which have no outbound arrows, placing them on the sink cell list. (The sink cell list is used as a basis for the DFS in phase III.) Since phase II of the algorithm accounts for a minority of the total volume rendering time and it involves a sort, it is not parallelized.

Phase III of MPVONC algorithm involves a DFS. It is known that a DFS is not significantly parallelizable; therefore, phase III is not significantly parallelizable. However, stage 2 as a whole (the combination of phase III and the splatting algorithm) can be parallelized to advantage. This parallel algorithm is now described.

Since a DFS does not output cells in layers that can be rendered concurrently, each cell must be rendered in the same order as it is output by the DFS. To deal with this, two queues are used, Q1 and Q2. One processor, call it proc0, is dedicated to performing the DFS; it places the cells output from the DFS in Q1. The remaining processors remove the cells from Q2 in order, splat them and then render them in the same order as they removed them from Q2. (This can be accomplished if the cells are removed from Q2 in order by processor number and the Lock Ordering algorithm given below is used when rendering.) After proc0 has enqueued a predetermined number STEPSIZE of cells on Q1, and the remaining processors have rendered the cells in Q2, the two queues are swapped. We refer to this as one cycle of the algorithm. Initially, Q2 is empty, so on the first cycle only proc0 is busy, the remaining processors are idle. On the last cycle, proc0 is idle while the remaining processors splat the cells in Q2.

A DFS algorithm is normally implemented as a recursive routine. However, to allow proc0 to synchronize with the remaining processors when it is time to swap the queues, the DFS algorithm is implemented without recursion using a stack. This algorithm is shown below for tetrahedra; however, it can be generalized to deal with any cells.

The following variables are initialized to false: *allDone, doneDFS, lastCycleSplatted*. The boolean variable *notVisited* is initially set to true for each cell. Since the value of the variable *allDone* is read by all processors, but is modified only by proc0, this must be announced to the compiler. Otherwise an optimizing compiler might remove apparently redundant references to *allDone* from the code of all processors other than proc0. It is common to announce this fact to the compiler by declaring such variables as *volatile*; we will follow that practice herein.

STAGE 2 PARALLEL ALGORITHM FOR NONCONVEX MESHES
```
if proc0
    for each cell on sink cell list
        if cell not visited
            mark cell visited
            face = 0
            push(cell); push(face)
            while not empty(stack)
                face = pop(stack); cell = top(stack)
                while face ≤ 3 /* for tetrahedra */
```

	13,499 cells	187,395 cells	287,962 cells	513,375 cells
Serial	1.15	14.37	24.74	38.44
6 CPUs	0.72	7.81	13.30	20.67

Table 6: Typical timings in seconds for volume rendering using the MPVONC algorithm with the PT Splatting algorithm. The number of exterior cells varied between 4% and 8% of the total number of cells. The STEPSIZE used in the parallel stage 2 algorithm for nonconvex meshes was 1000.

```
                if face has inbound arrow from adjCell
                    if adjCell not visited
                        mark adjCell visited
                        push(face + 1); push(adjCell)
                        cell = adjCell; face = 0
                    else
                        increment face
                    else increment face
                end while face ≤ 3
                cell = pop(stack)
                if Q1 has < STEPSIZE cells then enqueue cell on Q1
                else goto BAR
L1:             enqueue cell on Q1
            end while not empty(stack)
        end for each cell on sink cell list
        doneDFS = true
    else /* remaining CPUs */
L2:     while Q2 not empty
            remove cell from Q2 in order by processor number
            splat cell; render cell using Lock Ordering Algorithm.
    end else
BAR: barrier
    if proc0
        if lastCycleSplatted then allDone = true
        else swap Q1 and Q2
    barrier
    if not allDone
        if proc0
            if not doneDFS then goto L1
            else if not lastCycleSplatted
                lastCycleSplatted = true
                goto BAR /* to wait for last splatting cycle */
        else /* remaining processors */ goto L2
```

To ensure the cells are rendered in the same order as they are output by the DFS, an ordering algorithm is needed to control access to the graphics pipe. Such an algorithm is shown below; it assumes processors 1 to n will be rendering. The boolean array *waitLock* is initialized to true except for *waitLock[1]* which is set to false. This allows processor 1 to obtain a spin lock to access the graphics pipe. It is important that the array *waitLock* be declared to the compiler as volatile.

LOCK ORDERING ALGORITHM:
```
    while (waitLock[processor number]) busy-wait
    lock graphics pipe
        make graphics calls
        if processor number = n then waitLock[1] = false
        else waitLock[processor number + 1] = false
        waitLock[processor number] = true
    unlock graphics pipe
```

Typical timings for the above parallel algorithm for volume rendering data defined on meshes of several different sizes are shown in Table 6.

Number Processors	MPVO	MPVONC
Serial	32.66	36.01
6 CPUs	11.96	16.28

Table 7: Typical timings in seconds for volume rendering comparing the MPVO algorithm with the MPVONC algorithm for the same data set. The nonconvex data set has 362,712 tetrahedra; the convex version has 373,654 tetrahedra (including 10,942 imaginary cells). The PT splatting algorithm was used in both cases.

A large CFD data set defined on a mesh generated by a conformed Delaunay triangulation was produced by Tim Baker [Baker 1991]. He used a technique similar to that suggested in [Williams 1992a]. The mesh was generated over a convex domain even though the domain of interest was nonconvex. The vertices and cells lying outside the nonconvex region were retained for visualization and the remaining vertices and cells sent to the finite element solver.

This data set enabled the rendering of the data either as a convex mesh using the MPVO algorithm, where the cells lying outside the nonconvex domain of interest were marked imaginary, or as a nonconvex mesh using the MPVONC algorithm. Thus the volume rendering times for each of these two methods could be compared. The nonconvex mesh had 362,712 cells. The convex mesh had an additional 10,942 cells, the imaginary cells located inside the wing. Comparative timings for this experiment, both serial and parallel, are given in Table 7.

4 DEALING WITH DEGENERACY

Sophisticated techniques for dealing with degeneracy and numerical error in the MPVO visibility ordering algorithm are discussed in [Williams 1992a].

However, there is a very simple, yet powerful method for coping with degenerate cells which occur quite commonly in irregular and curvilinear data. Sometimes these degenerate cells will be created when the mesh coordinates are converted from double precision to single precision representation, especially in areas of the mesh which are highly refined.

If the vertices of the faces in a mesh are not enumerated in a consistent way, then the 'polarity' of the plane equations may not be consistent over the mesh. For tetrahedra, the signs of the plane equation coefficients, which determine the 'polarity' of the plane equation, can be set by evaluating the plane equation for a face of a cell with the coordinates of the cell vertex not used to define the face. If a cell is degenerate, the sign of the plane equation may be inconsistent. This can cause a cycle in the visibility ordering thus causing the visibility ordering algorithm to fail. Therefore it is essential that degenerate cells be properly dealt with. A useful method for doing this is now described. A beneficial side-effect of this method is that it results in the vertices of each face being recorded so they can be enumerated in counterclockwise order when viewed from outside. This can be useful for back face removal.

For tetrahedral meshes the following technique can be used so the sign of the plane equation, $pe(x, y, z) = Ax + By + Cz + D$, is consistent for each face for all cells. For each cell, index each face f by the local vertex number (0 .. 3) of the vertex v_f not used to define f. So, for example, face 1 has vertices $\{0,2,3\}$; face 3 has vertices $\{0,1,2\}$; etc. Using the convention that for the face whose vertex ordering is (i, j, k), the plane equation coefficients are:

$$A = y_i(z_j - z_k) + y_j(z_k - z_i) + y_k(z_i - z_j)$$
$$B = z_i(x_j - x_k) + z_j(x_k - x_i) + z_k(x_i - x_j)$$
$$C = x_i(y_j - y_k) + x_j(y_k - y_i) + x_k(y_i - y_j)$$
$$D = -x_i(y_j z_k - y_k z_j) - x_j(y_k z_i - y_i z_k) - x_k(y_i z_j - y_j z_i)$$

calculate these plane equation coefficients for face 3 of any nondegenerate cell, using the vertex ordering (0,1,2). If $pe(v_3) > 0$, swap the first two vertices of face 3. Propagate this ordering of the vertices to all the other cells in the mesh. For a right-handed coordinate system, the vertices are now recorded so they can be enumerated in counterclockwise order when viewed from outside the cell provided the following ordering is used: face 0: (3,2,1); face 1: (0,2,3); face 2: (3,1,0); face 3: (0,1,2). Now calculate the plane equation coefficients for each face of each cell using this vertex ordering. Mark all degenerate cells 'imaginary'. Imaginary cells are used in the visibility ordering process but are not output.

5 IMAGES OF NONCONVEX IRREGULAR DATA SETS

All volumetrically rendered images shown were generated using the parallel MPVONC algorithm and the modified PT splatting algorithm on a Silicon Graphics 4D/360VGX workstation. The times to generate these images are given in Table 6.

Figure 2 shows a volumetrically rendered image of the energy field from an airfoil flowfield generated by a CFD finite element simulation defined on a mesh of 287,962 tetrahedra. The data was generated at ICASE, NASA Langley.

Figure 3 shows a volumetrically rendered image of hot-spots in a simulated temperature field defined on an nonconvex irregular mesh of 13,499 tetrahedra whose boundary is a MBB-Gehäuse solid modeling benchmark. The mesh was generated using Sia Meshkat's CDSmesh [Meshkat 1991] which creates a conformed Delaunay triangulation.

The volume renderings shown in Figure 4 are of the velocity magnitude of coolant flow in a component of Electricité de France's Super Phoenix nuclear reactor. This N3S finite element method simulation is defined on a mesh of 12,936 tetrahedra.

ACKNOWLEDGEMENT

A helpful conversation was had with L. V. Kale regarding parallelization and with Herbert Edelsbrunner regarding degeneracy. I am grateful to Silicon Graphics Inc. for an equipment loan, and to Tim Baker at Princeton University, Sia Meshkat at IBM Almaden Research Lab, Dimitri Mavriplis at ICASE, NASA Langley and Germain Pot and Bruno Nitrosso at Electricite de France for generously providing data sets. I am also grateful to Sia Meshkat and IBM for the use of CDSmesh, an automatic mesh generator based on a conformed Delaunay triangulation. Peter Shirley and Allan Tuchman very generously supplied their implementation of the PT algorithm which I modified and optimized for the SGI VGX. The research described herein was performed at the Center for Supercomputing Research and Development and the National Center for Supercomputing Applications. This work was partially supported by the U. S. Department of Energy under Grant DE-FG02-85-ER25001, the Air Force Office of Scientific Research Grants AFOSR-90-0044, and Sun Microsystems Inc.

References

[Baker 1991] BAKER, T.J. Shape Reconstruction and Volume Meshing for Complex Solids. *Intl. J. Numerical Methods in Engin. 32 4* (1991), 665–675.

[Drebin et al 1988] DREBIN, R. A., CARPENTER, L., and HANRAHAN, P. Volume Rendering. *ACM SIGGRAPH Comput. Gr. 22 4* (Aug. 1988), 65–74.

[Garrity 1990] GARRITY, M. P. Raytracing Irregular Volume Data. *San Diego Workshop on Volume Visualization, Comput. Gr. 24 5* (Dec. 1990), 35–40.

[Giertsen 1992a] GIERTSEN, C. Volume Visualization of Sparse Irregular Meshes. *IEEE Comp. Gr. 12 2* (March 1992), 40–48.

[Giertsen 1992b] GIERTSEN, C. and TUCHMAN, A. Fast Volume Rendering with Embedded Geometric Primitives. *Visual Computing - Integrating Computer Graphics with Computer Vision*, T.L.Kunii (ed), Springer Verlag, 1992, pp. 253–271.

[Lucas 1992] LUCAS, B. A Scientific Visualization Renderer. *Proceedings Visualization '92*, Boston (Oct. 1992), 227–234.

[Max et al 1990] MAX, N., HANRAHAN, P., and CRAWFIS, R. Area and Volume Coherence for Efficient Visualization of 3D Scalar Functions. *San Diego Workshop on Volume Visualization, Comput. Gr. 24 5* (Dec 1990), 27–33.

[Meshkat 1991] MESHKAT, S. CDSmesh 3D Automatic Mesh Generator User's Guide and Reference. IBM Almaden Research Center, Oct. 1991.

[Osterhaug 1987] OSTERHAUG, A. *Guide to Parallel Programming*. Sequent Computer Systems, Beaverton, OR, 1987.

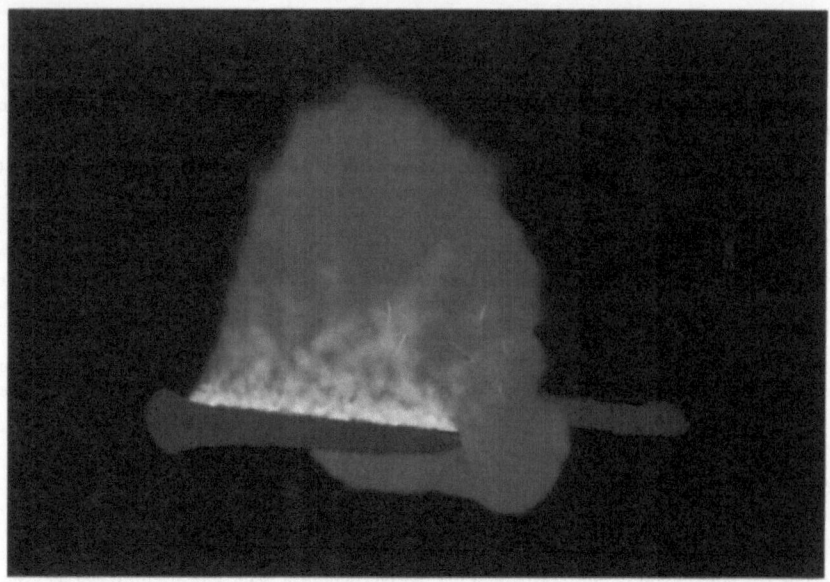

Figure 2: Volume rendered image of energy field around airfoil from CFD finite element simulation on mesh of 287,962 tetrahedra.

Figure 3: Volume rendered image of hot-spots in simulated temperature field over nonconvex unstructured mesh of 13,499 tetrahedra whose boundary is MBB-Gehäuse solid modeling benchmark.

483

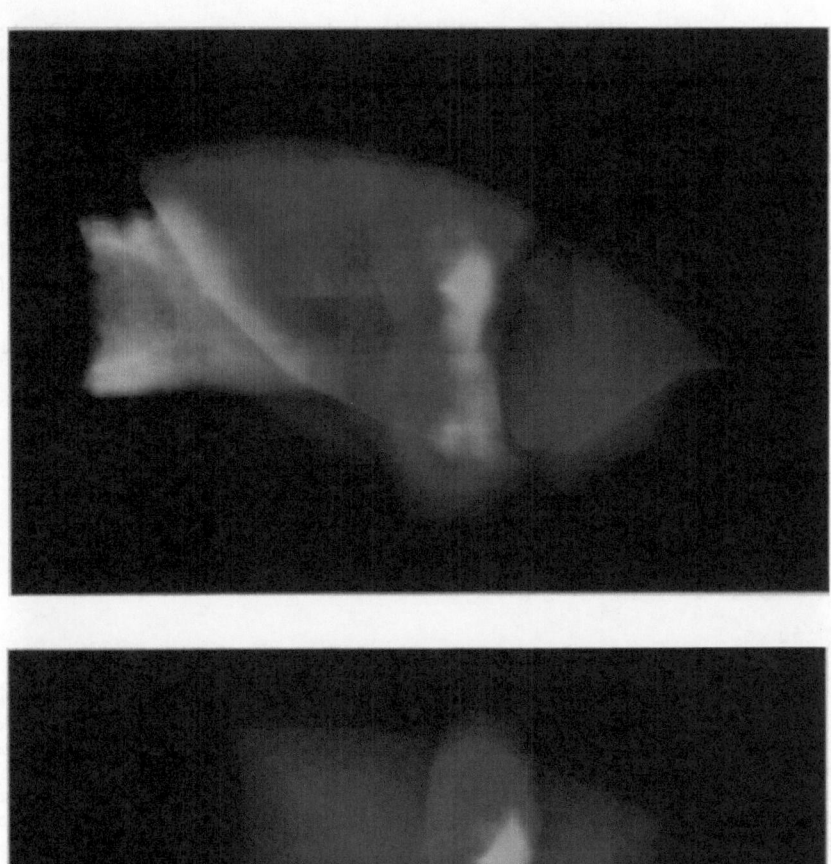

Figure 4: Volume rendered images of velocity magnitude of coolant flow in component of Electricité de France's Super Phoenix nuclear reactor. This N3S finite element simulation is defined on mesh of 12,936 tetrahedra.

484

[Shirley and Tuchman 1990] SHIRLEY, P. and TUCHMAN, A. A Polygonal Approximation to Direct Scalar Volume Rendering. *San Diego Workshop on Volume Visualization, Comput. Gr. 24 5* (Dec 1990), 63-70.

[Westover 1989] WESTOVER, L. Interactive Volume Rendering. *Proceedings Chapel Hill Workshop of Volume Visualization* (May 1989), 9-16.

[Williams 1992c] WILLIAMS, P. L. Interactive Splatting of Nonrectilinear Volumes. *Proceedings Visualization '92*, Boston (Oct. 1992), 37-44.

[Williams and Max 1992] WILLIAMS, P. L. and MAX, N. A Volume Density Optical Model. *Proceedings ACM SIGGRAPH 1992 Workshop on Volume Visualization*, Boston (Oct. 1992), 61-68.

[Williams 1992a] WILLIAMS, P. L. Visibility Ordering Meshed Polyhedra. *ACM Trans. on Graphics 11 2* (April 1992), 103-126.

[Williams 1992b] WILLIAMS, P. L. Interactive Direct Volume Rendering of Data Defined on Nonrectilinear Meshes. PhD thesis, Dept. of Computer Science, University of Illinois at Urbana-Champaign, 1992.

Peter L. Williams is an Assistant Professor of Computer Science at Harvey Mudd College. He received a BS in Engineering-Physics from the University of California at Berkeley and a PhD in Computer Science from the University of Illinois at Urbana. At the University of Illinois, he was a member of the Center for Supercomputing Research and Development and the National Center for Supercomputing Applications. His research interests are: scientific visualization (particularly volume rendering finite element and scattered data), parallel and distributed processing, real-time systems, and the use of computers to create innovative tools for science and engineering.

Address: Department of Computer Science, Harvey Mudd College, Claremont, CA 91711, USA. e-mail: williams@jarthur.claremont.edu Telephone: 909-621-8000 X3882. FAX: 909-621-8465.

Parallel Processing in Radiosity Calculations

Wim Lamotte, Frank Van Reeth, Luc Vandeurzen, and Eddy Flerackers

ABSTRACT

Global illumination models have recently received a considerable amount of attention in realistic image synthesis research. Especially radiosity methods for realizing the illumination in scenes exhibiting global Lambertian diffuse reflection have been reported upon. Since the introduction of the progressive refinement methodology, the performance of the early pioneering algorithms has been improved drastically. In this paper, we go a step further in improving the performance by utilizing parallel processing techniques. Concretely, we elucidate a transputer based approach for realizing a parallel ray tracing based progressive radiosity method.

Keywords : illumination, radiosity, parallel processing, transputer

1. INTRODUCTION

During the last years, a substantial amount of research regarding realistic image synthesis has been focused on the realisation of global illumination models. Especially models realizing solutions for global Lambertian diffuse reflections have received considerable attention. Two broad categories of approaches for solving the illumination problem in diffusely reflecting environments can be recognized. The first one is based on extensions to the traditional ray tracing algorithms (Cook 1986; Kajiya 1986). The second category incorporates radiosity algorithms (Cohen 1986; Cohen 1991; Goral 1984). One of the major advantages of the radiosity approach is that it results in a solution independent from the position of the viewer.

Although the early radiosity methods gave rise to the most realistically rendered images of that period, they suffered from a storage and time cost that were $O(n^2)$ - with n the number of elementary surface patches -, so they were not practical to be used for high complexity scenes. With the introduction of progressive radiosity algorithms, however, the performance has drastically improved (Cohen 1988; Wallace 1989). Moreover, additional features have been introduced around the radiosity theme that even futher enhance the image quality through the introduction of specular reflection (Chattopadhyay 1987; Sillion 1989) and mapping effects (Chen 1990), or even more improve performance via hierarchical representations and multigridding (Hanrahan 1991).

A next step upwards with respect to improving performance is to incorporate parallel computations to solve the radiosities. As the computations of the form factors take up most of the time, it could be worthwhile to parallelize them. Several approaches involving coarse-grained parallelism can be found in the literature (Baum 1990; Puech 1990; Recker 1990). They are based on parallel computation of the form factors with a hemi-cube alike technique to determine illumination.

In this paper, we describe parallelisation of the form factor computations based on ray tracing methods. The main arguments we can give for choosing this approach are the following : aliasing and undersampling problems are reduced; traditional advantages (non-physical light sources, shadow testing against exact geometries, ability to turn shadows on and off on a surface by surface basis, utilization of exact surface normals, shadows of semi-transparent surfaces) as mentioned in (Wallace 1989) remain; our transputer based graphics systems (Van Reeth 1991) doesn't include hidden surface removal hardware to heavily accelerate the hemi-cube method; transition towards inclusion of specular reflections (Chattopadhyay 1987; Sillion 1989) will be easier.

The succeeding overview section elucidates the various elements of the radiosity pipeline and highlights the formula's ultimately to be computed in parallel. The third section describes the hardware platform and gives a description of the way in which we implemented the parallelism. In section four results are presented, while conclusions are given in the last section.

2. THE RADIOSITY PIPELINE

2.1 Outline and Radiosity Equation

Radiosity algorithms generally follow a sequence of steps (hence the term pipeline) in order to come to a solution : (i) the scene is processed into a mesh of elements; (ii) the radiosities are calculated; and (iii) the result is interactively displayed. In this paper, we use the term element to indicate the small subdivided surfaces, while the term patch (or surface patch) is used to indicate the larger surfaces - including the original "input" polygons - themselves. The calculation of the radiosities ultimately produces the radiosity at the element vertices. The radiosity at the vertices of the elements is then used to calculate the colors at the vertices. Once this is done, the scene can be rendered from any view point at interactive rates using a Gouraud alike interpolation technique.

The calculation of the radiosities (given the assumption of global Lambertian diffuse illumination) narrows down to solving a set of equations in which the relation of energy leaving each surface element and arriving on each surface element is expressed :

$$B_{dAi} \; dAi = E_{dAi} \; dAi + \rho_{dAi} \int_j B_{dAj} \; F_{dAj\text{-}dAi} \; dAj \qquad [1]$$

where dAi is a differential surface area; B_{dAi} is the radiosity (energy per unit area) of differential area dAi; E_{dAi} is the energy emission of differential area dAi (i.e. a light source); ρ_{dAi} is the reflectivity of differential area dAi (a value between 0 and 1 indicating which fraction of the arriving light is reflected); and $F_{dAj\text{-}dAi}$ is the form factor from dAj to dAi (a value between 0 and 1 indicating which fraction of light leaving dAj arrives at dAi). As the number of differential areas is infinite, the number of radiosities to be calculated is also infinite. Hence, a discretized version of the above integral equation is used. In this approach the scene is discretized into finite areas rather than differential ones, resulting in the following equation:

$$B_{Ai} \; Ai = E_{Ai} \; Ai + \rho_{Ai} \sum_j B_{Aj} \; F_{Aj\text{-}Ai} \; Aj \qquad [2]$$

Using the reprocity relationship $F_{Ai\text{-}Aj} \; Ai = F_{Aj\text{-}Ai} \; Aj$ this becomes :

$$B_{Ai} = E_{Ai} + \rho_{Ai} \sum_j B_{Aj} \; F_{Ai\text{-}Aj} \qquad [3]$$

Hence we obtain a matrix of form factors that have to be calculated. The major advantage of the progressive refinement radiosity algorithms over the early brute force methods lies now in the fact that the matrix is solved incrementally, on a row by row basis, rather than as a whole. Each step in the progressive refinement (i) searches for the patch with the most energy left to be shot into the environment and (ii) calculates its influence on the other patches.

2.2 Form Factors in the Ray Tracing Approach

The form factor between differential areas depends on the distance r between the areas, as well as on their mutual orientation θi and θj (Fig. 1). In the initial radiosity reports, a hemicube algorithm is used to determine the form factors. An interesting alternative in computing the form factors is to use

487

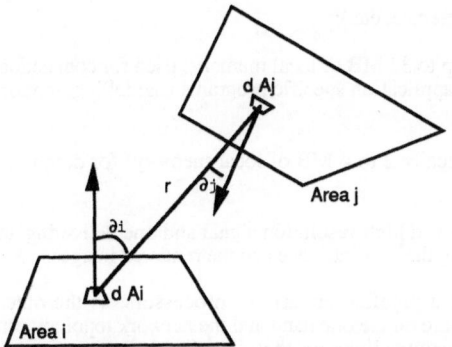

Fig. 1 Geometrical aspects regarding the form factors.

ray tracing (Wallace 1989). Instead of utilizing a hemi-cube to determine visibility on a discrete regularly spaced grid of space, now ray tracing is used to determine visibility between patches. As it is the goal to ultimately obtain radiosity values at the vertices of the elements in the scene, the ray tracing approach can provide a more convient solution. Indeed, by shooting rays from vertices to patches, the visibility and form factor values necessary for determining the radiosity can be computed directly at the positions on which they are needed without introducing a sampling problem. In this ray tracing methodology, a somewhat different form factor is utilized (Wallace 1989), as one now has to compute the form factor from an area A2 to a differential area dA1 at each vertex. For the case in which one subdivides the area A2 uniformly in n parts, the following form factor (including a visibility term δ_i) is to be computed :

$$dF_{A2\text{-}dA1} \quad = \quad dA1 \; \frac{1}{n} \sum_i \; \delta_i \; \frac{\cos \theta 1i \; \cos \theta 2i}{\pi \; r_i^2 + A2/n} \qquad [4]$$

The radiosity B1 at a vertex 1 received from an area A2 is consequently given by (Wallace 1989):

$$B1 \quad = \quad \rho 1 \; B2 \; A2 \; \frac{1}{n} \sum_i \; \delta_i \; \frac{\cos \theta 1i \; \cos \theta 2i}{\pi \; r_i^2 + A2/n} \qquad [5]$$

It is the parallel computation of a large set of these equations, in which the tracing of rays from the element vertices to sample points on the successive source patches (for determining δ_i) takes up the bulk of the computation, that will be the theme in the next section.

3. PARALLELIZING THE COMPUTATION OF THE FORM FACTORS

3.1 The Hardware Platform

During the definition of the radiosity project within the laboratory, an important condition was the fact that the implementation should be integrated into the existing image synthesis architecture, consisting of a parallel network of transputers (Van Reeth 1991). The transputer of the current generation is a 32-bit parallel processor sustaining 20 MIPS / 1.5 MFlops at 25 MHz. Each of its four serial links allow bidirectional synchronized communication with other members of the transputer family at 20 Mbit / sec.

The entire hardware platform of a graphics system in the lab consists of the following components:

• a PC, utilized as a host for booting the network and for housing the I/O equipment (mouse, graphical tablet & stylus, scanner, video recorder interface, etc.);

• host transputer boards (with transputers having up to 32 MB of local memory) used for connection with the PC and for storing the database as well as application specific programs (modelling, motion specification, programming environment, etc.);

• a farm of workers (with transputers having typically 2 to 4 MB of local memory) for doing the calculation intensive rendering computations.

• two graphics boards (one delivering a non-interlaced high-resolution signal and one delivering an interlaced true color PAL video signal) for displaying the user interface and the rendered images.

Our current system is topologically organized as a pipeline or farm of processors, as the other graphics algorithms in our system require this structure on the one hand and the network topology can only be configured by physically wiring the transputer links on the other hand. Other network topologies have been reported upon elsewhere (Chalmers 1991). Although we have been utilizing OCCAM (INMOS 1988) for implementing the system in the past, we are currently implementing more and more in a parallel version of the C programming language.

3.2 Distributing the Work

Given the available hardware facilities, several interrelated issues have to be tackled and kept in mind during the realization of a parallel algorithm: (i) which part of the overall algorithm is to be parallelized; (ii) how is the database to be distributed; and (iii) can the communication overhead stay low in comparison with the amount of work to be done. Regarding the former issue, there seems to be a general agreement on the fact that the computation of the form factors is the part to be parallelized, as it takes up the bulk of the computational resources. The latter two issues are closely related to *how* the parallelism is realized on a given platform, and will be elucidated in this section.

Several references can be found in the literature regarding parallelizing the radiosity algorithm. (Prior 1989) describes a solution in which the computational power of a transputer network is used for solving directly the form factor matrix in a distributed fashion. Although in some cases even superlineair expandability (based on the fact that the $O(n^2)$ data could be kept entirely in the distributed main memory, rather than on a virtual memory disk) is reported, we didn't want to follow this approach as it doesn't offer the advantages of progressive refinement methods. References to parallelizing the progressive radiosity method can be found in (Baum 1990; Puech 1990; Recker 1990). Moreover, we recently received reference to (but didn't as yet manage to get access to) additional work around parallel radiosity in (Chalmers 1989) and in Workshop reports (Purgathofer 1990; Chalmers 1991; Feda 1991; Guitton 1991; Jessel 1991). (Puech 1990) and (Recker 1990) introduce parallelism by distributing the progressive radiosity computations among a number of loosely coupled workstations, whereas (Baum 1990) utilizes the hardware accelerators and the (fixed set of) multiple processors within a single graphics workstation.

The latter three approaches are based upon a hemi-cube alike methodology for computing the form factors. The general topology of the distributed processes resemble the one given in Fig. 2. A master process (processor) selects the patch with the highest energy during the progressive refinement and

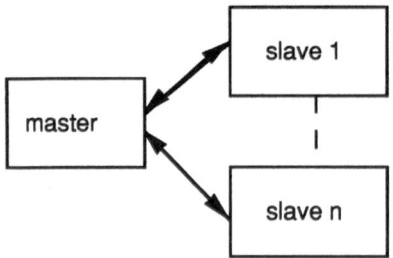

Fig. 2 Process topology in distributed form factor computation.

distributes the work, while the other slave processes (processors) have to compute the form factors of the selected patch in relation with the other patches in the scene. Because the entire scene is available to each of the slaves, a reasonable efficiency can be maintained. In the loosely coupled workstation approach, however, the network communication (with a reported bandwidth < 150K / sec) might become a bottleneck, especially when the number of stations increases (Recker 1990).

In our ray tracing based progressive radiosity implementation, we also utilize the master-slave approach: a transputer on the host boards (with up to 32 MB) acts as the master, whereas the transputers in the farm act as slaves; the master holds the element database and distributes the work, while a copy of the much coarser surface patch database is kept on each slave. Since each of the four bi-directional links in each of the transputers peak at 20 Mbit / sec, communication isn't forming a bottleneck (because the aggregate bandwith increases linearly with the number of processors in the system).

As inter-transputer communication takes place on a point-to-point relation, the functional topology (cfr. Fig. 2) is converted into the physical topology of Fig. 3.

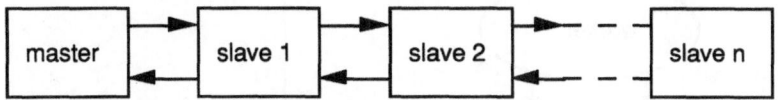

Fig. 3 Physical transputer topology.

In order to keep the slave processors usefully busy - in tracing rays from the vertices to different points on the source patches and in computing equation [5] - four important issues have to be borne in mind : granularity of the blocks sent to the slaves, buffering methodologies, process priorities and acceleration techniques.

Granularity
In the master-slaves methodology we utilize, it is the master who decides how much work is done by each of the slaves. For a given step in the iteration, (1) the surface with the largest amount of energy left to be radiated is selected by the master to be forwarded to each slave, after which (2) the radiosities can be calculated for each of the vertices in the element database (note : vertices shared by more than one element are processed only once). It is the work in step (2) that is performed in parallel. Rather than sending large chunks of work to a slave, as could be beneficial in a loosely coupled workstation approach, the size of the data packets carrying the element vertices to be processed by the slaves is kept much smaller in our closely coupled transputer network. Indeed, the more element vertices to be processed in a burst, the more rays that processor will have to fire and the longer it will take to finish its burst. Hence, a fine granularity is beneficial as it will ensure a low elapsed time of waiting processors at the end of a progressive iteration. On the other hand is it not beneficial to have too many timeconsuming synchronisations (i.e. bursts) in an iteration. These are conflicting requirements, so determining a good number of vertices to be processed in one burst is a far from trivial task: it depends on the average time it takes to trace a certain amount of rays through a scene, the complexity of the scene as well as on the number of processors in the system.

For each progressive iteration, we currently have the rule of thumb of synchronising between 50 and 100 times (this number goes up if the number of processors in the system gets larger). For scenes of a complexity alike the testing scene in Section 4, this means we send over between 2 to 8 vertices in a synchronisation: if V equals the number of vertices sent over in a synchronisation and S equals the number of sample points on the source patch, the number of rays to be traced in the entire iteration divided by V x S has to lie between 50 and 100, according to our rule of tumb.

Buffering and Priorities
In order to prevent a processor from going idle (regarding the tracing of rays and the evaluation of equation [5]) between the moment of having calculated the radiosities of the vertices sent over and the moment of receiving the next package to be calculated, it is necessary to buffer data (this might not be necessary in an approach where the work distribution is fixed beforehand, but we follow a dynamic work load in which the slaves ask for more work if they are finished). Given the fact that we were obliged to use physically a farm topology (Fig. 3) it moreover is important to see that the data

packages are send foreward and backward across the network as quickly as possible. Hence we utilize on each slave processor the (in transputer applications not uncommon) process structure of Fig. 4. The forward process receives data from a previous processor and checks if the data is sent over for the processor on which it resides. If this is the case, it will buffer the data packet; otherwise it will simply forward the packet to the next processor. The worker process does the actual computational job while the backward process simply ships data packets back down the farm. Hardware logic for context switching on the transputers ensures that scheduling and descheduling of processes on the processor is handled properly with minimal time penalties.

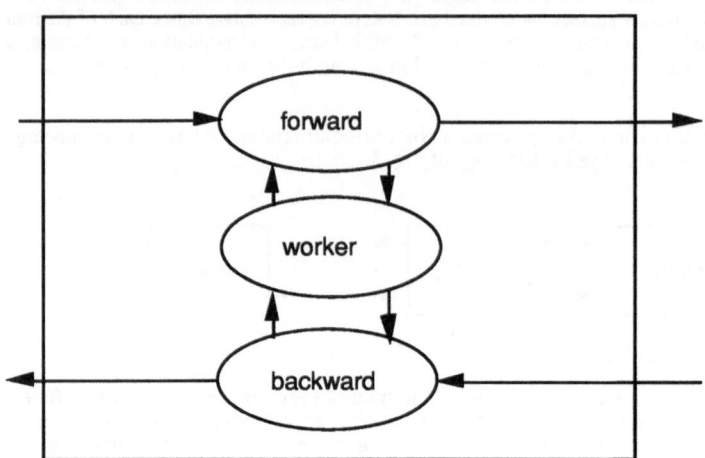

Fig. 4 Process structure on the slave processors.

It is important to notice that the forward and the backward process have to be given a higher priority than the work process, in order to prevent a considerable loss in performance. The main motivation for this is that a backlocking communication tends to hold up the other processors from doing their work properly. The philosophy behind this is that no matter what, the data always has to be transferred anyway, so one can better do it right away.

In alternative approaches, e.g., in which the vertex list is simply distributed equally among all the processors, the problem of finding a good granularity and the difficulty of finding a suitable fine grained communication methodology with appropriate priorities might not be present. However, these approaches would heavily suffer in keeping an optimal load balance, as some processors can coincidentally have been given a set of vertices which need a lot of work in comparison to other processors, introducing possibly much elapsed idle waiting time at the end of each iteration.

Additional Speed-up Techniques
It should be realized that conventional ray tracing (non- screen space based) speed-up techniques (Kaplan 1987) can still be applied in order to substantially improve performance even further. We implemented the voxel based algorithm of (Amanatides 1987) and found it to be particularly well suited. The fact that "typical" radiosity scenes - often building indoors consisting of coherently grouped surfaces - fit the voxel structure well, can account for this. The voxel structure we utilize has a size of 20 X 20 X 20. Currently, each worker has its copy of this structure, implying on average only a few thousand surface patches can be handled (note that the original input surfaces are stored in the voxel structure, and not the surface elements, as the ray tracing naturally is done on the non-subdivided input-surfaces). Our progress in the parallel ray tracing of large databases (Van Reeth 1993) will enable us to solve this duplication problem.

4. RESULTS

For a given scene, the timing results regarding the radiosity calculations heavily depend upon the following factors : (i) the number of original surface patches; (ii) the level of subdivision into surface elements; (iii) the maximum number of samples on the sources; (iv) the number of rays to be shot per vertex; and (v) the number of iterations in the solution.

Hence, it is difficult to find a "general" example for evaluating the solution. We try to overcome this problem by giving some basic timings on the basis of the testing scene of Fig. 5 on a network of 13 processors. This scene contains 238 original input surface patches, which are subdivided into 2029 surface elements. The number of points on which the radiosities have to be calculated is 3351.

Figure 6 shows 4 different steps in the progressive solution: from the 1st iteration (numbered 0), in steps of five, up to the 15th iteration. Depending on the energy source in a given iteration and the number of samples on a source, the number of rays to be traced varies from 4628 to 29575 (as the element vertices of surface patches behind the energy source don't have to be processed), giving respective calculation timings of 0.7 seconds to 4.1 seconds per iteration.

When we force the number of samples on a source to 16, we get the following timings (per iteration, in seconds) given the number of processors and the number of vertices in the iteration:

# processors :	4	7	10	13
# vertices				
1982	15.22	8.59	6.08	4.60
2743	24.04	13.49	9.52	7.25
3182	22.11	12.50	8.86	6.51
3251	25.75	14.54	10.23	7.80

As yet, we haven't had access to a system with more slaves than 13 slaves for testing the radiosity code, but our load balance of ray tracing large data bases on a large number of workers (Van Reeth 1993) indicates we can expect a further linear expandability (tested with up to 50 slaves).

(in between note: As the ray tracing is an important time consumer, it might be interesting if we give an impression of the traditional ray tracing speed: A 13 processor system generates a 768 X 576 resolution ray traced image (tree depth = 1) of the scene in Fig. 6 (with 4 point light sources) in 38 seconds if no shadowing nor anti-aliasing is used.)

5. CONCLUSION

In this paper, we presented a novel approach for parallelizing the calculation intensive parts of the ray tracing based progressive refinement radiosity method. It has been shown how a network of closely coupled parallel processors, in casu transputers, can be utilized for speeding up the performance linearly.

Future research is necessary to reveal what happens to the load balance in case of utilizing much more processors. Our own work will also involve a study around incorporation of parallel ray tracing software for large data bases. Moreover, it will be interesting to find out what happens to the expandability of the system if the visibility calculations can be done more quickly; e.g., by incorporating novel "less accurate" ray tracing approaches (cfr. conclusion in (Hanrahan 1991)) or by accompanying the transputers with state of the art RISC- or DSP-chips, sustaining a performance more than an order of magnitude larger than that of transputers.

ACKNOWLEDGEMENTS

We would like to thank all the colleagues in the lab for supporting the realization of this work. In particular, we would like to mention our feelings of appreciation to the people in the Graphics Group, for their direct contribution to the project. This work is partly funded by a grant from the Belgian National Fund for Scientific Research (NFWO).

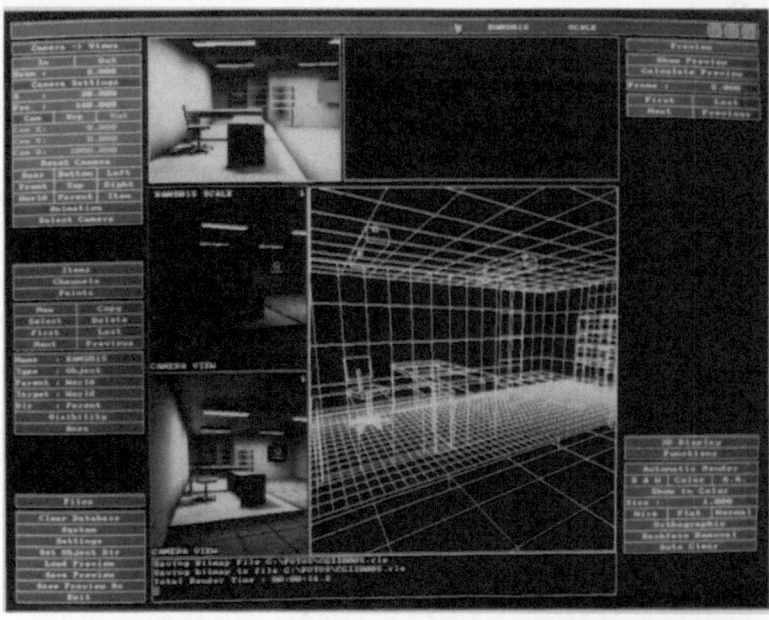

Fig. 5 Testing scene in our motion specification subsystem.

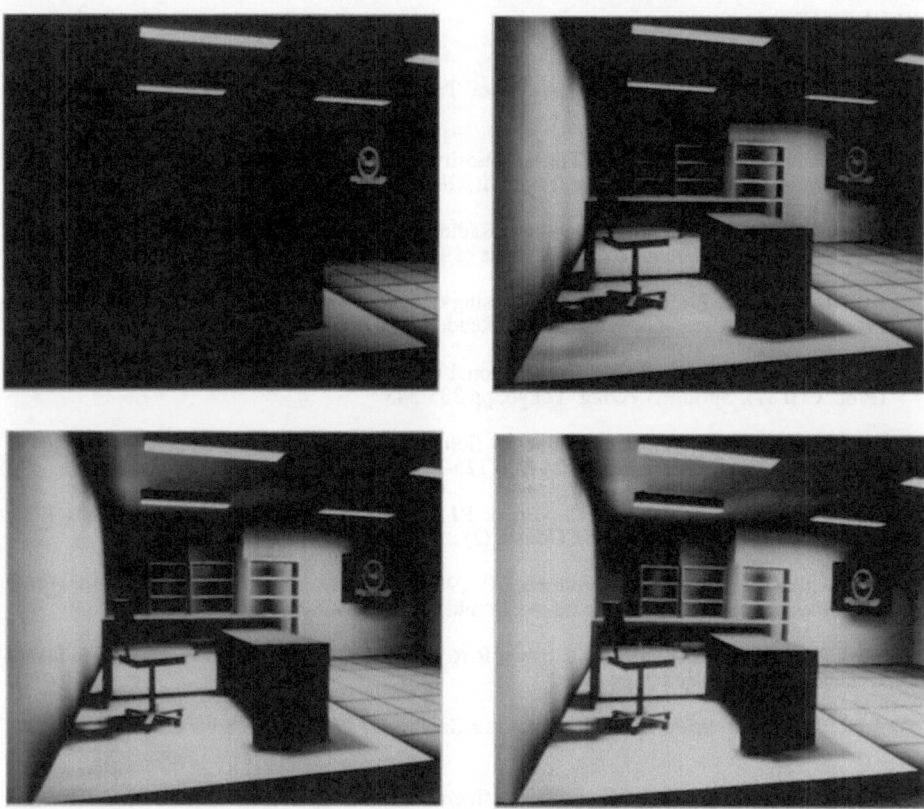

Fig. 6 Iterations 0, 5, 10 and 15 in the solution of the testing scene.
(The fine coloring effects are more apparent on the monitor screen.)

REFERENCES

Amanatides J, Woo A (1987) A Fast Voxel Traversal Algorithm for Ray Tracing. Proc. Eurographics'87 : 3-10

Baum DR, Winget JM (1990) Real Time Radiosity Through Parallel Processing and Hardware Acceleration. Computer Graphics (Proc. SIGGRAPH'90) 24 (2) : 67-75

Chalmers A, Paddon D (1989) Implementing a Radiosity Method Using a Parallel Adaptive System. Proc. First Int'l Conference on Applications of Transputers

Chalmers A, Paddon D (1991) Parallel Proccesing of Progressive Refinement Radiosity Methods Proc. Second Eurographics Workshop on Rendering, Barcelona

Chattopadhyay s, Fujimoto A (1987) Bi-directional Ray Tracing. Computer Graphics International (Proc. CGI'87), Springer-Verlag, Tokyo, pp 335-343

Chen H, Wu eH (1990) An Efficient Radiosity Solution for Bump Texture Generation. Computer Graphics (Proc. SIGGRAPH'90) 24 (2) : 125-134

Cohen MF, Greenberg DP, Immel DS, Brock PJ (1986) An Efficient Radiosity Approach for Realistic Image Synthesis. IEEE CG&A 6 (2) : 26-35

Cohen MF, Chen SE, Wallace JR, Greenberg DP (1988) A Progressive Refinement Approach to Fast Radiosity Image Generation. Computer Graphics (Proc. SIGGRAPH'88) 22 (3) : 75-84

Cohen MF (1991) Radiosity. In: D.F. Rogers, R.A. Earnshaw (eds.) State of the Art in Computer Graphics. Springer-Verlag pp 59-90

Cook RL (1986) Stocastic Sampling in Computer Graphics. ACM Transactions On Graphics 5 (3) : 51-72

Feda M, Purgathofer W (1991) Progressive Refinement Radiosity on a Transputer Network, Proc. Second Eurographics Workshop on Rendering, Barcelona

Goral CM, Torrance KE, Greenberg DP, Bataille B (1984) Modeling the Interaction of Light Between Diffuse Surfaces. Computer Graphics (Proc. SIGGRAPH'84) 18 (3) : 213-222

Guitton P, Roman J, Schick C (1991) Two Parallel Approaches for a Progressive Radiosity, Proc. Second Eurographics Workshop on Rendering, Barcelona

Hanrahan P, Salzman D, Aupperle L (1991) A Rapid Hierarchical Radiosity Algorithm. Computer Graphics (Proc. SIGGRAPH'91) 25 (4) : 197-206

INMOS Ltd. (1988) OCCAM2 Reference Manual. Prentice-Hall, New York London Toronto Sydney Tokyo

Jessel JP, Paulin M, Caubert R (1991) An Extended Radiosity using Parallel Ray-Traced Specular Transfers, Proc. Second Eurographics Workshop on Rendering, Barcelona

Kajiya JT (1986) The Rendering Equation. Computer Graphics (Proc. SIGGRAPH'86) 20 (4) : 143-150

Kaplan MR (1987) The Use of Spatial Coherence in Ray Tracing. In : Rogers DF, Earnshaw RA (eds.) Techniques for Computer Graphics. Springer-Verlag, pp 173-193

Prior D (1989) An Architecture That Exploits Parallelism In Radiosity Calculations. Proc. BCS Computer Graphics and Displays Group Seminar "Parallel Processing for Display", 7th April, London

Puech C, Sillion F, Vedel C (1990) Improving Interaction with Radiosity-Based Lighting Simulation

Programs. Computer Graphics (Proc. SIGGRAPH'90) 24 (2) : 51-57

Purgathofer W, Zeiller M (1990) Fast Radiosity by Parallelization. Proc. Eurographics Workshop on Photosimulation, Realism and Physics in Computer Graphics

Recker RJ, George DW Greenberg DP (1990) Acceleration Techniques for Progressive Refinement Radiosity. Computer Graphics (Proc. SIGGRAPH'90) 24 (2) : 59-66

Sillion F, Puech C (1989) A General Two-Pass Method Integrating Specular and Diffuse Reflection. Computer Graphics (Proc. SIGGRAPH'89) 23 (3) : 335-344

Van Reeth F, Flerackers E (1991) Utilizing Parallel Processing in Computer Animation. Proc. Computer Animation '91, Springer-Verlag Tokyo, pp 227-240

Van Reeth F, Lamotte W, Flerackers E (1993) Ray Tracing Large Scenes on a Parallel Architecture. paper submitted for the Eurographics'93 conference.

Wallace JR, Elmquist KA Haines EA (1989) A Ray Tracing Algorithm for Progressive Radiosity. Computer Graphics (Proc. SIGGRAPH'89) 23 (3) : 315-324

Frank Van Reeth is a research assistant at the Limburg University Center and a member of the research staff at the Applied Computer Science Laboratory in the same university. He obtained his Master's Degree in Computer Science in 1987 at the Free University of Brussels, Belgium. His current research interests include 3D rendering, animation, parallel processing and visual programming environments. He is a member of CGS.
Address: Applied Computer Science Laboratory, Limburg University Center, Universitaire Campus, B3590 Diepenbeek, Belgium

Eddy Flerackers is currently full Professor of Computer Science at the Limburg University Center, Belgium. He studied Physics at the University of Louvain, Belgium. He received his PhD in Physics in 1980 at the Free University of Brussels with a thesis on nuclear structure calculations. Since 1987 he is Director of the Applied Computer Science Laboratory at the Limburg University Center. His research interests include computer graphics, 3D computer animation, scientific visualization, simulation and programming environments.
Address: Applied Computer Science Laboratory, Limburg University Center, Universitaire Campus, B3590 Diepenbeek, Belgium

Wim Lamotte is a research assistant at the Limburg University Center and a member of the research staff at the Applied Computer Science Laboratory in the same university. He obtained his Master's Degree in Computer Science in 1988 at the Free University of Brussels, Belgium. His current research interests include ray tracing, computer animation and parallel processing.
Address: Applied Computer Science Laboratory, Limburg University Center, Universitaire Campus, B3590 Diepenbeek, Belgium

Luc Vandeurzen is currently an undergraduate student, finishing his Master's thesis on radiosity as a research assistant at the Applied Computer Science Laboratory in the Limburg University Center. His current research interests include realistic image synthesis in general and radiosity in particular.
Address: Applied Computer Science Laboratory, Limburg University Center, Universitaire Campus, B3590 Diepenbeek, Belgium

A Massively Parallel Processing Approach to Fast Photo-Realistic Image Synthesis

Hiroaki Kobayashi and Tadao Nakamura

ABSTRACT

Photo-realistic image synthesis based on the global illumination models is very time consuming and is not practical in the industrial world. This paper presents a new parallel processing scheme to accelerate photo-realistic image synthesis. A massively parallel processing system and its control scheme for this purpose are discussed. System behavior is also examined by using the queueing network model.

Keywords: massively parallel processing, photo-realistic image synthesis, radiosity, ray tracing

1. INTRODUCTION

Recently, photo-realistic image synthesis attracts much attention in many application areas such as visual simulation for landscape design and virtual reality. Photo-realistic image synthesis requires to calculate the pixel intensity of a screen by using the global illumination models, which consider the effect of inter-reflection between objects.

Global illumination models can be classified into two categories, *view-dependent global illumination models and view-independent global illumination models*. For view-dependent global illumination models, the sample points within the environment and their directions are determined both by the view position and by the discretization of the image plane. On the other hand, view-independent global illumination models treat view-independent illumination, which is inter-reflection between diffuse surfaces, and calculate surface intensity by sampling the environment with certain resolution that is independent of pixel resolution of an image plane.

As the most popular view-dependent global illumination model, ray-tracing is an elegant solution to photo-realistic image synthesis and can treat the effect of inter-reflection among specular surfaces and refractive surfaces (Whitted 1989). However, ray tracing cannot calculate the global illumination of the inter-reflection between diffuse surfaces because ray tracing ignores diffuse surfaces as second light sources and uses the local illumination model to calculate the intensity for diffusely reflected-light contribution. Besides, ray tracing is computationally expensive because of the enormous number of ray-object intersection calculations.

Approaches based on thermal-engineering models for the emission and reflection of radiation eliminate the need for the ambient-lighting term by providing a more accurate treatment of inter-object reflections. Radiosity algorithms assume the conservation of light energy in a closed environment (Cohen and Greenberg 1985). All energy emitted or reflected by every surface is accounted for by its reflection from or absorption by other surfaces. *Radiosity,* the rate at which energy leaves a surface, is the sum of the rates at which the surface emits energy and reflects or transmits it from that surface or other surfaces. Although radiosity algorithms do an excellent job of modeling inter-reflection between diffuse surfaces, it has some problems concerning the global lighting contributions caused by specular reflection and transmission. Besides, radiosity algorithms are also computationally expensive for calculating form-factors among surfaces and require large memory for storing them.

To overcome the disadvantages of each global illumination model and synthesize high quality images, two-path solutions that integrate both view-dependent and view-independent models have been proposed (Wallace et al. 1987; Sillion and Puech 1989). Although these approaches can synthesize very photo-realistic mages, they are very time-consuming and are not practical in the industrial world.

This paper proposes a new approach to the global illumination model for photo-realistic image synthesis and an acceleration scheme for the image synthesis by using massively parallel processing. This paper is organized as follows. In Section 2, we present a new global illumination model for massively parallel processing. Section 3 shows a concrete system architecture based on our parallel processing model and its control scheme. In Section 4, we discuss the system behavior by using the queueing network model. The paper concludes with Section 5.

2. A NEW GLOBAL ILLUMINATION MODEL FOR MASSIVELY PARALLEL PROCESSING

In image synthesis using the global illumination model, intensity calculation and reflection/refraction calculation for inter-reflection between objects are carried out on each object in an object space. Thus, computational efforts for image synthesis occur on each object, and can be localized. Therefore, it is natural to define objects as parallel tasks for image synthesis, and we propose an object-space parallel processing model for massively parallel processing of the global illumination. In the object-space parallel processing model, object information is distributed among local memories of processing elements (PEs) to realize an object space on the distributed memory system. Therefore, PEs do not need to have the shared memory for accessing object information as the common database. Rays that may cause inter-reflections travel within the parallel system by inter-PE communications. Each PE calculates the global illumination of objects within a local memory and transfers rays to appropriate PEs. Here, ray is modeled by a set of discretized rays with certain resolution, and each of discretized rays is independently traced in the parallel processing systems. Propagation of rays may cause many inter-PE communications. However, this does not lead the system to the non-linearity of the performance, because these communications can be solved locally between neighboring PEs that have the neighboring object information. Therefore, even though the parallel processing system has the large number of PEs, linear speed-up can be expected.

Our massively parallel processing for the global illumination has two phases: *a view-independent phase* based on the radiosity model and *a view-dependent phase* based on the ray tracing model. In the view-independent phase, the complete global propagation of light is approximated in order to determine the diffuse component of intensity for all surfaces. The view-dependent phase then uses the results of the view-independent phase as the basis for calculating specular component to the accuracy required by the view. For each pixel in the final image, the resulting specular component is added to the diffuse component, interpolated from the sample points in the view-independent phase. In the following, we present our parallel processing method based on the object-space parallel processing model for view-independent and view-dependent phases.

A) View-independent phase: In the view-independent phase, interrefrection among diffuse surfaces is calculated by using the radiosity model. The radiosity model describes an equilibrium energy balance within an enclosure. It is assumed that all emission and reflection processes are ideal diffuse. Thus, after reflection from a surface, the history of direction of a ray is lost. First, we briefly summarize the essential features of the radiosity model (Siegel and Howell 1972), and then present a parallel computation scheme in the view-independent phase.

The light leaving a surface (its radiosity) consists of self-emitted light and reflected or transmitted incident light. The amount of light arriving at a surface requires a complete specification of the geometric relationships among all reflecting and transmitting surfaces, as well as the light leaving every surface. This relationship is given by:

$$\text{Radiosity}_i = \text{Emission}_i + \text{Reflectivity}_i \int_{env} \text{Radiosity}_j \text{Form-factor}_{ij} \qquad (1)$$

Radiosity (B):   *The total rate of energy leaving a surface. Sum of emitted and reflected energy. (energy/unit time/unit area)*

Emission (E):   *The rate of energy (light) emitted from a surface. (energy/unit time/unit area)*

Reflectivity (ρ):   *The fraction of incident light that is reflected back into the environment. (unitless)*

Form-factor (F_{ij}):   *The fraction of the energy leaving surface i that lands on surface j. (unitless)*

If the environment is subdivided into discrete surface elements or "patches," for which a constant radiosity is assumed, a set of simultaneous equations can be generated to describe the interaction of light energy within the environment as follows:

$$B_i = E_i + \rho_i \, \Sigma \, B_j \, F_{ij} \qquad (2)$$

Now, we present a parallelization scheme of the radiosity model. Equation (2) describes the estimate of patch i's radiosity B_i based on the estimates of the other patch radiosities. In the object-space parallel processing model, radiosity transmission from patches in an object space is simulated. Therefore, a patch radiosity is further discretized with certain resolution, and these discretized radiosities are shot from a patch into the environment via inter-PE communications. To this end, we introduce the progressive refinement approach (Cohen et al. 1988) to our parallel computation model.

As presented in (Cohen et al. 1988), the radiosity shot from a patch into the environment is obtained as follows:

$$B_j \text{ due to } B_i = \rho_j \, B_i \, F_{ij} \, A_i \, / \, A_j \qquad \text{for all } j \qquad (3)$$

Given an estimate of $Bi,$ the contribution of patch i to the rest of the environment can be determined by evaluation Equation (3) for each patch j. To calculate form-factor Fij, we use the hemi-cube method (Cohen and Greenberg 1985). Therefore, a patch radiosity is discretized at the pixel level on the hemi-cube. We call each discretized radiosity a *delta-radiosity*. Delta-radiosities are shot from surfaces, and contributions of delta-radiosities to the environment are calculated in parallel.

In the system based on the object-space parallel processing model, each processing element calculates form-factors of each pixel on hemi-cube's surfaces to obtain each radiosity of pixels by evaluating Equation (3), and then issue these radiosities to the rest of environment through pixels. Radiosity propagation in an object space is achieved by inter-PE communications. In practice, the information needed for radiosity propagation is transferred between PEs as a *radiosity packet*. The PE, receiving a radiosity packet, performs radiosity-surface intersection calculations for objects within the local memory. If an intersecting object is detected, the radiosity of the packet is added to the surface radiosity of the object. If there is no intersecting object or an intersecting object causes reflection/refraction, the radiosity packet is transferred to the appropriate PE according to the direction of the radiosity propagation.

The radiosity after reflection/refraction must be attenuated according to the specular reflection/transmission coefficients of the intersecting object. Moreover, it should be stressed here that the discretization of the objects into patches is necessary only for the diffuse to diffuse inter-reflection calculation, and is harmful for the calculation of reflection and refraction. Therefore, surfaces of specular or transparent objects are not approximated by patches, and patch approximation is only required for diffuse reflective objects. This is controlled by each PE Figure 1 depicts the parallel radiosity propagation in the view-independent phase when an object space is subdivided into regular subspaces and these subspaces are allocated to different processing elements. For simplicity, Figure 1 shows parallel processing for delta-radiosities from only one surface. In practice, delta-radiosities from multiple surfaces can be processed in parallel.

500

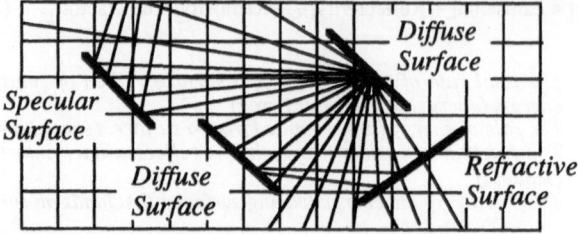

Figure 1. Object space parallel processing in the view-independent phase.

B) View-dependent phase: In this phase, for a given view, intensities for surface visible at each pixel on a screen are calculated. This calculation is based on the ray tracing model. Intensities of pixels are calculated by evaluating the following equation:

$$I = G + k_s S + k_t T \qquad (4)$$

where

G: *The intensity of diffuse reflection calculated in the view-independent phase.*

k_s: *The specular reflection coefficient.*

S: *The intensity of light incident from the direction of the specular reflection.*

k_t: *The transmission coefficient.*

T: *The intensity of light from the direction of transmission.*

For given view point and screen, rays through pixels on a

screen are issued to an object space, as *ray packets*, to find visible surfaces. Thus, ray packets are transferred to appropriate PEs according to the directions of rays. Each PE performs ray-object intersection calculations. When there is no intersecting object within the local memory, a ray packet is transferred to the next PE. On the other hand, if intersecting objects are detected, the intensity on the object derived from the patch radiosity in the view-independent phase are accumulated in the frame buffer. Moreover, if an intersecting object causes reflective/refractive rays, ray packets, involving the attenuation coefficient considering the whole reflection/refraction coefficients of past visited objects, are transferred to PEs according to the directions of reflection/refraction. When these secondary rays intersect with some objects, the intensity on the intersection is calculated by multiplying the attenuation coefficient by the radiosity of the intersecting object, and then is accumulated in the frame buffer. Notice that it is not necessary to check shadowing on the intersecting point because shadowing is already solved in view-independent phase. Figure 2 shows the object-space parallel processing in the view-dependent phase.

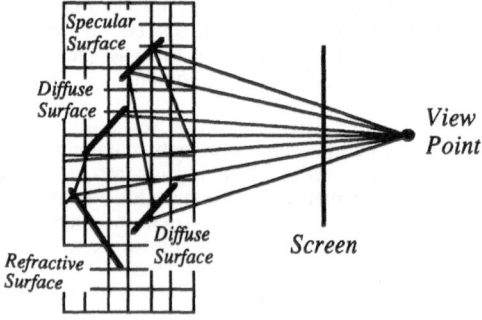

Figure 2. Object space parallel processing in the view-dependent phase.

4. A MASSIVELY PARALLEL PROCESSING SYSTEM FOR PHOTO-REALISTIC IMAGE SYNTHESIS

In this section, we will present a concrete system architecture based on the object-space parallel processing for the global illumination model as discussed in the previous section. Figure 3 depicts the system organization for two-dimensional parallel processing in which PEs are interconnected in the torus fashion. Of course, we can construct one-dimensional or three-dimensional parallel processing models in which PEs have two or six links along coordinate axes. The system consists of a *host computer*, *PEs*, a *frame buffer*, a *frame buffer controller* and a *display*. The host computer allocates object description to PEs via the system bus and controls the executions in the view-independent and view-dependent phases. The PE consists of a *Ray-Object Intersection Calculation Unit (ROIC unit)*, a *Radiosity/Intensity Calculation Unit (RIC unit)*, a *Secondary Ray Generation Unit (SRG unit)*, a *Direction Decision Unit (DD unit)*, a *Local Memory* and a *Network Interface Unit (NI unit)* as shown in Figure 4.

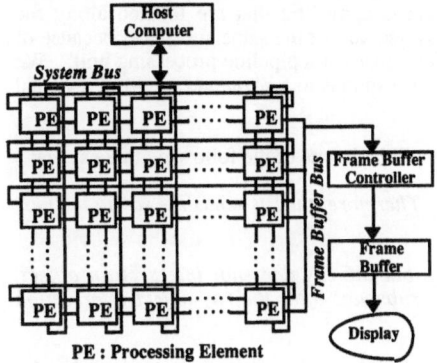

Figure 3 System architecture.

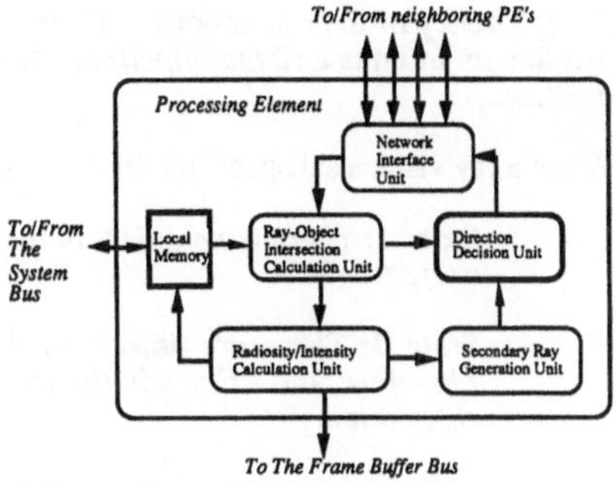

Figure 4. Structure of the processing elemets

Object description is stored in the local memory that has multiports for reads and writes. The ROIC unit receives ray/radiosity packets from the NI unit, and performs intersection calculations between rays and objects. If an intersecting surface is detected in the view-independent phase, the radiosity in the packet is added to the radiosity of the surface by the RIC unit. On the other hand, in the view-dependent phase, the RIC unit transfers the radiosity of the intersecting surface of the object, attenuated by the reflectivity in the packet, to the frame buffer controller via the frame buffer bus Then, the frame buffer controller accumulates the radiosity in the appropriate pixel value of the frame buffer. If there is no intersecting object with a radiosity/ray packet, or an intersecting object causes the secondary rays owing to reflection/refraction, the DD unit decides the next PEs, which have subspaces to be visited by the radiosities/rays, and sends these packets to the NI unit to realize ray/radiosity propagation. The units in the PE operate asynchronously and simultaneously, and realize circular pipeline processing.

As for an allocation scheme of object description on PEs, we equally divide an object space into subspaces and allocate subspaces at certain interval apart to one PE so that neighboring subspaces can be allocated to the different PEs. Since each object occupies several neighboring subspaces due to spatial coherence and computational loads related with the subspaces tend to concentrate in local space, this allocation scheme is able to distribute much heavier loads existing in local space to PEs approximately uniformly. Moreover, by dividing object space equally, we can effectively specify the subspaces pierced by rays by using the three-dimensional digital differential analyzer

(3DDDA) (Fujimoto et al. 1987). Since the 3DDDA is the high speed line generator based on incremental calculations, we introduce the 3DDDA to each PE to propagate radiosities and rays in a regularly subdivided object space.

5. DISCUSSIONS ABOUT THE SYSTEM BEHAVIOR

5.1 An Analytical Model

We are constructing a software simulator to evaluate the performance of our parallel processing system in detail. In this section, for preliminary evaluation, we make quantitative analysis of the system behavior by using the queueing network model (Kleinrock 1975). In particular, we discuss *virtual pipelines* constructed along the directions of rays.

In the object-space parallel processing, rays are processed by PEs that are located along the directions of the rays. Moreover, neighboring rays traverse almost the same subspaces because of the coherency of their directions. Therefore, these PEs construct a pipeline processing unit. We call this set of units a *virtual pipeline*, where each PE corresponds to a *segment* (*stage*) of a virtual pipeline.

When a ray visits a subspace, the PE with the subspace will be in one of the following three states:

>   *State A: There is no object in the subspace. Therefore, the PE sends the ray to the next subspace (PE).*

>   *State B: There are objects in the subspace, but the ray does not intersect an object. Therefore, the PE sends the ray to the next subspace after the ray-object intersection calculation.*

>   *State C: A ray intersects an object within the subspace, and tracing the ray is completed.*

Therefore, a ray is processed in a virtual pipeline as shown in Figure 5 until the ray intersects an object or the ray reaches out of an object space.

We define a simple analytical model for the object-space parallel processing by the queueing network model as shown in Figure 6. Here, we assume that the units in one PE operate sequentially, and model them as a single processing unit. The communication unit transfers rays to the next processing unit. Since the output of the communication unit becomes the input of the next processing unit, all rays enter the processing unit after leaving the communication unit. On the other hand, a part of rays leaving the processing unit may not enter the communication unit, since an intersecting object was detected. In Figure 6, P_0 generates a ray at the certain interval T_g. Here, let transition probabilities to the states A, B and C in each processing unit be P_A, P_B, and P_C, and processing times in the states A, B, and C be T_A, T_B, and T_C, respectively. Therefore, T_g is given as follows:

$$T_g = P_A T_A + P_B T_B + P_C T_C \qquad (5)$$

Since the probability of transferring a ray from the one processing unit to the next processing unit is $(1 - P_C)$, the mean arrival rate λ_i of rays at the *i-th* processing unit is obtained by

$$\lambda_i = (1 - P_C)^i / T_g \qquad (6)$$

Generally, the interarrival-time probability density function for rays and the service-time probability density function for each unit have the arbitrary probability densities However, for such a model, no exact analytic solution is yet known (Kleinrock 1975). Therefore, since each unit operates asynchronously, we assume the arrival of rays at each unit is the Poisson arrival and the

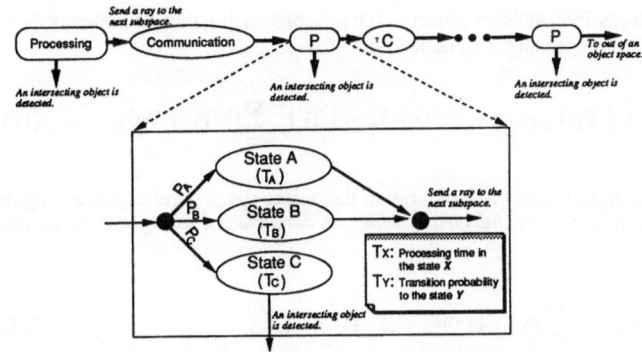

Figure 5. A state diagram of the object-space parallel processing.

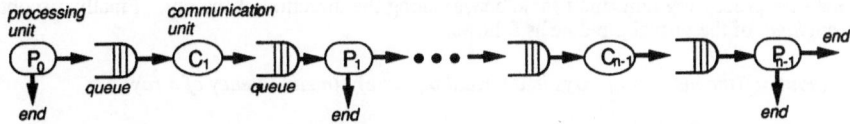

Figure 6. An analytical modelof the object-space parallel processing.

service-time probability density in the processing unit is the exponential probability density. As for the communication unit, the service-time is always constant because of the fixed length of ray/radiosity packets. Under these assumptions, we approximately model the processing unit and the communication unit as $M/M/1$ and $M/D/1$ queueing models, respectively. Here, in the notation $A/B/m$, A is the interarrival-time probability density, B the service-time probability density and m the number of servers. Moreover, M and D mean the exponential probability density (M stands for Markov) and the deterministic time, respectively. The assumption of an exponential interarrival probability is completely reasonable for any system that has a large number of independent customers that are rays in our model (Kleinrock 1975). Thus, we think that our queueing network model shows the mean system behavior in the steady state.

By using the Pollaczek-Khinchin equation (Kleinrock 1975) for $M/M/1$ and $M/D/1$ models, the mean waiting times WP_i and WC_i for each ray in the queues for the i-th processing unit and the i-th communication unit are given by:

-for the i-th processing unit

$$WP_i = (1 - P_C)^i T_g / (1 - (1 - P_C)^i)$$ (7)

-for the i-th communication unit

$$WC_i = (1 - P_C)^i T_t^2 / (2 (T_g - T_t (1 - P_C)^i))$$ (8)

Here, T_t is the processing time in the communication unit. Similarly, the mean numbers QP_i and QC_i of rays in the i-th units including rays in queues are:

-for the i-th processing unit,
$$QP_i = (1 - P_C)^i + (1 - P_C)^{2i} / (1 - (1 - P_C)^i)$$ (9)

-for the i-th communication unit.
$$QC_i = (1 - P_C)^i T_t / T_g + (1 - P_C)^{2i} T_t^2 / (2 (T_g^2 - (1 - P_C)^i T_t T_g))$$ (10)

Therefore, when a ray intersects an object in the *i-th* processing unit, the latency L_i of the ray in the object-space parallel processing is obtained by

$$L_i = i \, (P_A T_A + P_B T_B) / (P_A + P_B) + T_C + i \, T_t + \sum_{k=1}^{i} (WP_k + WC_k) \qquad (11)$$

Consequently, the mean latency *ML* of a ray in the object-space parallel processing (in other words, *the mean latency of a ray in the virtual pipeline constructed along the direction of the ray*) is obtained by

$$ML = \sum_{i=0}^{n-1} P_i L_i = \sum_{i=0}^{n-2} P_C (1-P_C)^i L_i + (1 - P_C)^{n-1} L_{n-1} \qquad (12)$$

Here, n is the number of processing units in the virtual pipeline, and P_i is the probability that a ray visits the *i-th* processing unit (the *i-th* subspace) along the direction of the ray. Finally, we obtain the *throughput* of the virtual pipeline as follows:

Throughput = (the number of rays in a virtual pipeline) / (mean latency of a ray)

$$= (1+ \sum_{i=1}^{n-1} (QP_i + QC_i)) / ML \qquad (13)$$

5.2 Experimental Results and Discussions

We assume that an object space is regularly subdivided into subspaces. In this case, we can approximately define P_A, P_B, and P_C as follows:

$$P_A = 1 - \alpha$$
$$P_B = \alpha(1 - \beta)$$
$$P_C = \alpha\beta$$

where,

   α: *The ratio of the number of the subspaces having objects to the number of subspaces in an object space.*
   β: *The mean occupation ratio of objects in a subspace.*

Moreover, we define the basic processing times as follows:

Intersection calculation time:	*4 (unit times)*
Next subspace calculation time:	*1*
Communication time:	*1*
Intensity calculation time:	*14*

These processing times were derived from actual program steps of each processing. We also assume that the mean number of spaces visited by a ray is *16*, which is based on the case that an object space is subdivided into 16^3 subspaces and each subspace is allocated to one processing unit.

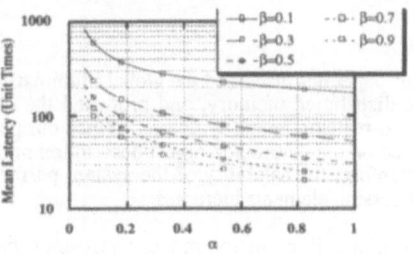

Figure 7 shows the mean latency of a ray in a virtual pipeline as a function of α for given β. The mean latency is very long when α and β is relatively small. As α and β approach 1.0, the mean latency is reduced. This is because a ray travels many subspaces until an intersecting object is detected, when objects are sparsely distributed in an object space. On the other hand, in the complicated environment ($\alpha \to 1.0$ and/or $\beta \to 1.0$), the probability of finding an intersecting object in the first few subspaces is very high. Thus, the mean latency is reduced.

Figure 7. Mean latency of a ray.

Figures 8-(a) and 8-(b) show the throughput of the virtual pipeline and the processing time for a ray as a function of α for given β, respectively. As Figure 8-(a) shows, the throughput of the virtual pipeline is very high, even though the mean latency is relatively long. This is because many processing units are activated by rays, and each processing unit performs the light processing, which is the next subspace determination by using the 3DDDA, when α and β are small. On the other hand, as α and β increase toward 1.0, the processing changes from the light processing to the relatively complicated processing, which includes intersection calculations and intensity calculations as well as next subspace calculations. This is clarified by Figure 8-(b), which is the processing time a ray. Figure 8-(b) shows that the processing time for a ray increases as α and β increase. Here, we point out that the processing time for a ray corresponds to the mean processing time of one processing unit, i.e., *mean segment (stage) time*, of a virtual pipeline, and its upper limit is determined by the processing within a subspace. Consequently, we conclude that the throughput of a virtual pipeline in the object-space parallel processing is always expected to be:

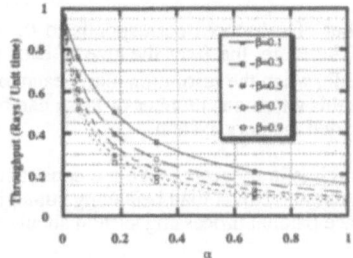

Figure 8-(a) Throughput of a virtual pipeline.

(Processing time within a subspace)$^{-1}$

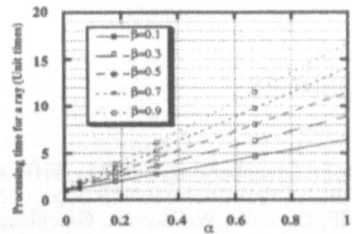

Figure 8-(b) Processing time for a ray.

Moreover, since many virtual pipelines will be constructed in an object space in practice, we will obtain the further accelerated performance of the object-space parallel processing. Pipeline processing within one PE as described in Section 3 also improves the throughput of a virtual pipeline, which reduce the processing time within a subspace. Of course, we must clarify these advantages of the object-space parallel processing by using the simulator we are constructing now.

6. CONCLUSIONS

This paper has discussed the global illumination model suited for massively parallel processing with the distributed memory, and proposed the object-space parallel processing approach to fast for photo-realistic image synthesis. Since our parallel processing model for the global illumination is based on the distributed object description in the parallel system, there is no global communication. Therefore, the salability of the system performance will be expected even though the number of processing elements increases.

Our global illumination model consists of the view-independent phase for inter-reflection among diffuse reflective surfaces and the view-dependent phase for intensity calculation for the object visible at each pixel on a screen. Since these two phases can be performed in parallel in the system, the system can render intermediate images at the early stage of image generation. The intermediate images are very useful. For example, by using them, we can finely re-subdivide surfaces of objects to render more accurate images. Combining this feature with massively parallel processing can realize the interactive environment in photo-realistic image synthesis.

The number of subspaces corresponds to the number of parallel tasks in our parallel processing model. Therefore, the finer the size of each subspace is, the larger the degree of parallelism is. For example, when the resolution along each axis is 1000, 10^6 parallel tasks are generated, and we think that this enormous number of tasks can be only solved by massively parallel processing with the distributed memory system.

This research is in progress. We are constructing a simulator to evaluating the parallel processing system in detail. Novel load balancing strategies to fully bring out the potential performance of the object-space parallel processing system should be also discussed and addressed as future work.

Acknowledgements

This work has been partially supported by the Tateisi Science and Technology Foundation.

REFERENCES

Cohen MF, Greenberg DP (1985) THE HEMI-CUBE: A RADIOSITY SOLUTION FOR COMPLEX ENVIRONMENTS. Proc. of SIGGRAPH'85:31-40.

Cohen MF, Chen SE, Wallace JR, Greenberg DP (1988) A Progressive Refinement Approach to Fast Radiosity Image Generation. Computer Graphics 22(4):75-84.

Fujimoto A, Tanaka T, Iwata K (1987) ARTS: Accelerated Ray-Tracing System. IEEE Computer Graphics and Applications:16-26.

Kleinrock L (1975) QUEUEING SYSTEM, VOLUME I: THEORY. John Wiley & Sons, Inc.

Siegel J, Howell JR (1972) THERMAL RADIATION HEAT TRANSFER. McGraw-Hill.

Sillion F, Puech C (1989) A General Two-Pass Method Integrating Specular and Diffuse Reflection. Proc. SIGGRAPH'89:335-344.

Wallace JR, Cohen MF, Greenberg DP (1987) A TWO-PASS SOLUTION TO THE RENDERING EQUATION: A SYNTHESIS OF RAY TRACING AND RADIOSITY METHODS. Proc. of SIGGRAPH'87: 311-320.

Whitted T (1980) An Improved Illumination Model for Shaded Display. CACM 23(6):343-349

Hiroaki Kobayashi is currently an assistant professor of Department of Machine Intelligence and Systems Engineering at Tohoku University, Sendai, Japan. His research interests include computer architecture, parallel processing systems and applications, and computer graphics. He received the B.E. degree in Communication Engineering, and the M.E. and D.E. degrees in Information Engineering from Tohoku University in 1983, 1985, and 1988, respectively. He is a member of the IEEE Computer Society, the ACM, the IEICE of Japan and the IPS of Japan.

Tadao Nakamura was born in Ube, Japan, on January 25, 1944. He received the Dr. of Eng. degree from Tohoku University. Since 1972 he has been a faculty member of the Faculty of Engineering of Tohoku University. He is currently a Professor of Computer Science in the Department of Machine Intelligence and Systems Engineering, Tohoku University. He has been studying computer architecture frequently at the Computer System Laboratory, Stanford University since 1983. His present research interests include computer architecture, supercomputer architecture, computer graphics, and distributed processing systems. He is an Editorial Board Member of The Visual Computer. He is also a Senior Member of the IEEE and a member of the IEICE of Japan, the IEEE COMSOC Communications Software Committee and the IEEE COMSOC Computer Communications Committee.

Address: Department of Machine Intelligence and Systems Engineering, Faculty of Engineering, Tohoku University, Sendai 980, JAPAN.

Real-Time Hardware for Image Edge-Thinning Using a New 11-Pixel Window

P.K. Sinha and F-Y Chen

ABSTRACT

A fast edge-thinning algorithm is developed with particular reference to real-time applications in computer vision and pattern analysis. This algorithm is based on a small set of erosion templates generated by a novel 11-pixel window. A hardware architecture containing ROM-based look-up tables is described for implementing the algorithm at video frame rate. A number of thinning algorithms are experimentally compared with the proposed algorithm. Experiments with real-world images are included.

Keywords: skeleton, thinning, erosion, real-time thinning, parallel thinning

1. INTRODUCTION

In digital image processing thinning is a procedure which transforms a given pattern into a 'line-like' representation. Such thin-line patterns have unit width and are often called skeletons in the literature. Use of skeletons in pattern recognition reduces the amount of data to be processed in the analysis. Therefore many thinning techniques have been developed and applied to various fields (Lam et al. 1992).

An ideal thinning algorithm should reduce the quantity of data, retain significant features of the patterns, and avoid noise. It has been commonly accepted that a good thinning algorithm should produce skeletons having the following properties:-

Connectivity: the thinning process should not alter the connectivity of the original patterns.

Thinness: the skeleton should converge to unit width even when the thinning process carries on.

Position: the resulting skeleton should lie closely to the medial axis of the pattern.

Immunity to noise: the algorithm should be insensitive to contour noise of the pattern.

Thinning algorithms are classified by Lam et al. (1992) into three groups: sequential, parallel, and non-iterative. In this paper we present a parallel one-pass thinning algorithm for binary images. Patterns are matched to a set of 11-pixel templates for decision of

508

deletion. Implementing this rule by table look-up, thinning can be performed at video frame rate.

This paper is organized as follows. Section 2 describes the background algorithm proposed by Stefanelli and Rosenfeld (1971), which is a modification of the fundamental algorithm (Rutovitz 1966) of parallel thinning. Our algorithm is presented in section 3. The experimental comparisons of our algorithm to others are given in section 4. In section 5, issues of the hardware implementation are addressed. Discussions and conclusions are in section 6.

2. BACKGROUND

In parallel thinning, skeletonization is performed iteratively. Pixels are examined for removal according to the result of the previous iteration. Once the conditions of removal are met, the corresponding pixels are marked. Marked pixels are then deleted at the end of each iteration simultaneously. Patterns are 'peeled' layer by layer in each iteration until one-pixel-wide skeletons are obtained. Since the decision of removal is made independently on each pixel, these algorithms are suitable for implementation on parallel processors.

This strategy is generally employed in various parallel algorithms. The difference is just the conditions of deletion. The conditions of Stefanelli and Rosenfeld (1971) may be re-written as below according to a nine-pixel neighbourhood shown in Fig. 1.

(a). $2 \leq B(p_1) \leq 6$
(b). $A(p_1) = 1$
(c). c1: $p_2 \, p_4 \, p_8 = 0$ or c2: $A(p_2) \neq 1$
(d). d1: $p_2 \, p_4 \, p_6 = 0$ or d2: $A(p_4) \neq 1$

Where the function of A(.) and B(.) are defined as:-
$A(p_1)$ is the number of white-to-black (0 to 1) transitions along the clockwise walk around the central pixel p_1.
$B(p_1)$ is the number of non-zero neighbours of p_1.

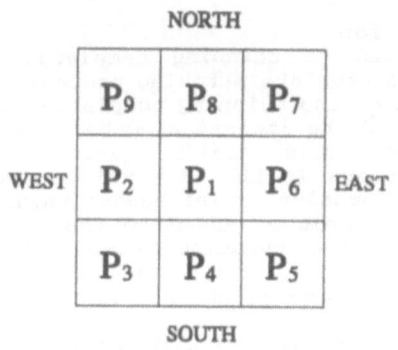

Fig. 1 Nine-pixel window

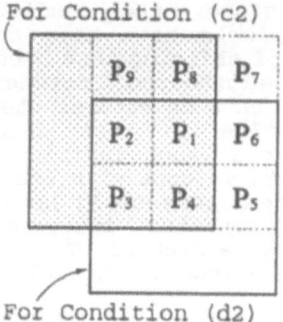

Fig. 2 Fifteen-pixel window

The idea of conditions (a) and (b) is to delete boundary pixels without creating holes or breaking patterns. Conditions (c) and (d) are used to preserve two-unit-wide lines from simultaneous erosion on both sides. This algorithm has the necessary properties discussed in section 1 and has been widely adopted. However, this algorithm may lead to excessive erosion in some patterns. Accordingly, various minor modifications have been made to yield better performance (e.g. Lu and Wang 1986).

In the algorithm proposed in this paper, the decision of deletion is made according to the pixel's 15-neighbourhood shown in Fig. 2. Compared with normal 3x3 windows, there are 3 'extra' pixels taken into account for each of the second halves of conditions (c) and (d), i.e., (c2) and (d2). These two sub-conditions are designed to indicate whether p_1 is on the east side (c2) or on the north side (d2) of a two-pixel-wide segment or not. If yes, p_1 should not be removed. These two sub-conditions may be simplified for the examinations of p_{10} and p_{11} respectively. A black pixel at p_{10} ($p_{10}=1$) implies that p_1 is NOT on the east side of a vertical two-pixel-wide segment and may be removed if other conditions (a, b, and d) are all met. Similarly, appearance of a black pixel at p_{11} in addition to satisfying conditions (a), (b) and (c) may lead to the removal of the corresponding central pixel. In this way, east and north sides of two-unit-wide lines are preserved. The local neighbourhood concerned, therefore, turns to an 11-pixel window shown in Fig. 3. The four conditions for removal are then changed to :-

(a). $2 \leq B(p_1) \leq 6$
(b). $A(p_1) = 1$
(c). c1) $p_2 p_4 p_8 = 0$ or c2) $p_{10} = 1$
(d). d1) $p_2 p_4 p_6 = 0$ or d2) $p_{11} = 1$

The number of all possible patterns which may appear in the 11-pixel window is 2^{11}. Amongst them, those which meet the modified four conditions are worked out and list in Fig. 4(a).

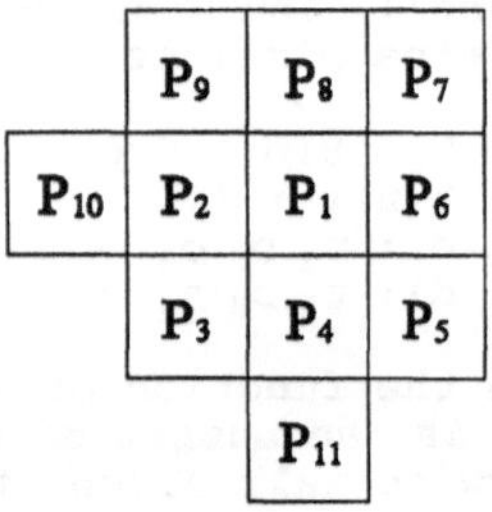

	P_9	P_8	P_7
P_{10}	P_2	P_1	P_6
	P_3	P_4	P_5
		P_{11}	

Fig. 3 11-pixel window used in our algorithm

3. PROPOSED NEW ALGORITHM

At this stage, the conditions for removing pixels have been converted to thinning templates. The procedure of thinning then becomes a template-matching process. Once a pixel's neighbourhood matches one of the thinning templates, it is marked and then deleted at the end of the iteration. Otherwise, the pixel's value is kept unchanged. This modification has two advantages: a) each individual pattern in the 11-pixel window is independent. To cope with excessive erosion or inadequate thinning, relevant templates could be removed from or added to the list of thinning templates independently; b) thinning templates are determinate beforehand. The procedure of thinning could be carried out as table look-up. A real-time implementation is thus possible.

We define a decimal equivalent number k for each individual pattern as

$$k = \sum_{n=1}^{11} P_n \cdot 2^{n-1}$$

511

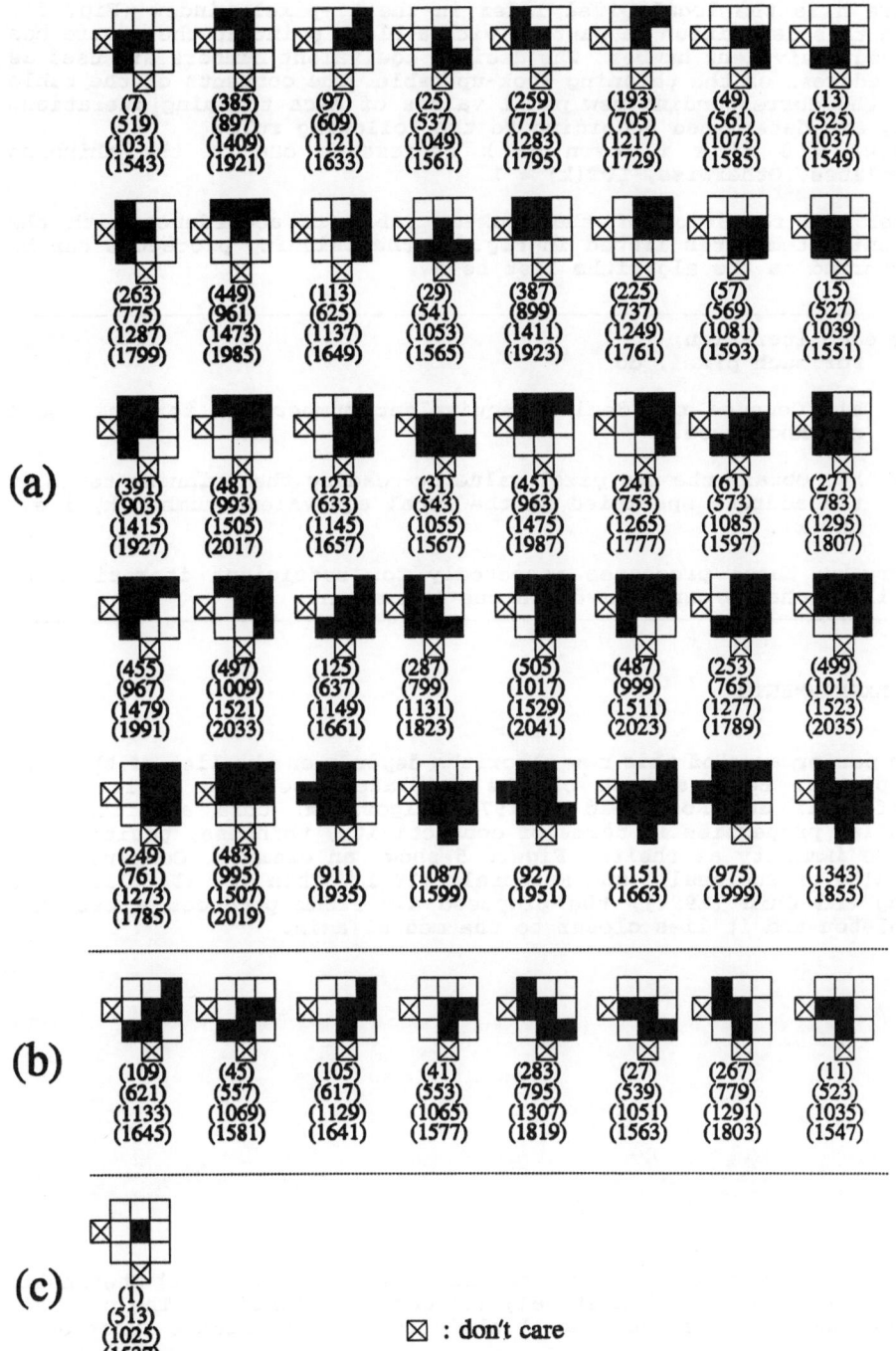

Fig. 4 Thinning templates with decimal equivalent numbers; (a) templates derived from Stefanelli and Rosenfeld (1971); (b) templates for two-unit-wide diagonal segments; (c) isolated pixel.

where n is the local pixel index in the 11-pixel window (Fig. 3). With this definition, a pattern with a black point at the centre has an odd equivalent number. The decimal equivalent numbers are used as the address of the thinning look-up table. The contents of the table are the corresponding new pixel values of each thinning iteration. They are determined according to the following rule:
LUT(k) = 0 if k is even or k represents one of the thinning templates. Otherwise, LUT(k) = 1.

After the formation of the look-up table in accordance with the thinning templates listed in Fig. 4, the thinning procedure can be performed as the algorithm list below.

For each iteration,
    For each pixel, do

    a). Compute the decimal equivalent number (k) for the local neighbourhood.

    b). Obtain the new pixel value by reading the thinning table at the address specified by the local equivalent number k, i.e., LUT(k).

Carry on these processes repeatedly for sufficient iterations or until no change can be made in one iteration.

---

4. EXPERIMENTS

The performance of this new algorithm depends on the list of thinning templates. Because most of the templates used are derived from Stefanelli and Rosenfeld's (1971) algorithm, this algorithm has similar properties in terms of connectivity, thinness, position and noise immunity as theirs. Figure 5 shows an example. Compared with results of Stefanelli and Rosenfeld (1971), Chin et. al. (1987) and Jang and Chin (1992), the proposed algorithm produces a smoother skeleton and it lies closer to the medial axis.

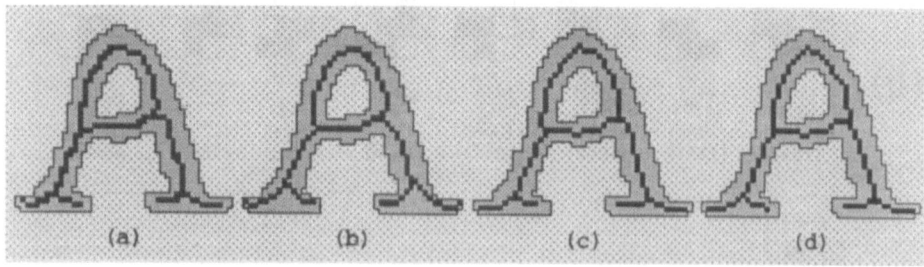

Fig. 5 A binary test pattern on different algorithms; (a) Stefanelli and Rosenfeld; (b) Chin et. al; (c) Jang and Chin; (d) The proposed algorithm. Only (d) has smooth skeleton near the middle junctions.

The templates in Fig. 4(b) and 4(c) are added for the reasons stated as follows. Templates in Fig. 4(b) are designed to remove the

northeast or northwest pixels on two-pixel-wide diagonal lines. With
them, two-pixel-wide diagonal segments will not vanish. Instead,
these segments are thinned down to one-pixel-wide. Some patterns
introduced by Lu and Wang (1986) are used for experiments. The new
algorithm is compared with various algorithms including Zhang and
Suen (1984), Lu and Wang (1986), Chin et. al. (1987), and Jang and
Chin (1992). It can be seen in Fig. 6 that the new algorithm is
superior to those of Zhang and Suen, Lu and Wang, and Chin et. al.
Results here are similar to Jang and Chin's but more symmetric.
Figure 4(c) shows an isolated pixel. Wether an isolated pixel should
be deleted or not is application-dependent. In applications like
blood cell counting, the user may wish to retain each individual
entry; those from object recognition area may wish to remove small
groups to yield 'clean' images, on the other hand. Figure 4(c) is
included because we are more interested in the latter. However,
templates may be easily excluded when necessary.

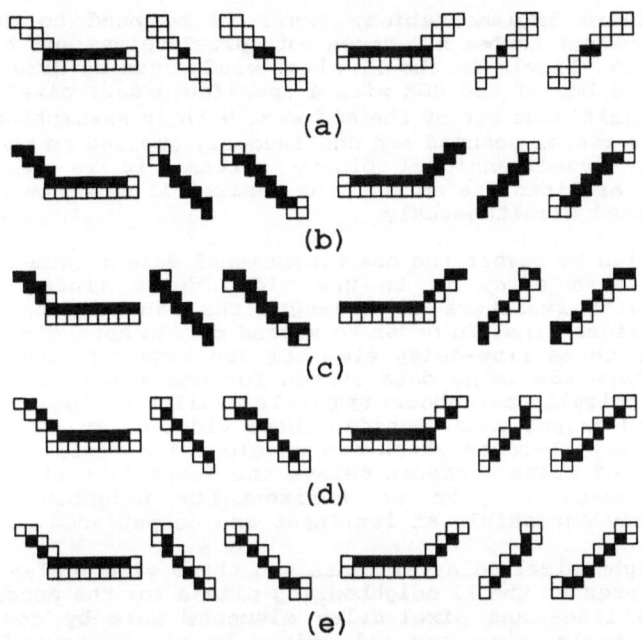

(a)

(b)

(c)

(d)

(e)

Fig. 6 Diagonal line segments tested by different algorithms; (a)
Zhang and Suen; (b) Lu and Wand; (c) Chin et. al.; (d) Jang and Chin;
(e) Our algorithm.

5. HARDWARE IMPLEMENTATION

Because the proposed thinning algorithm needs to compute the decimal
equivalent number for each pixel in every iteration when implemented
on a general purpose microprocessor, the processing speed is not fast
enough for real-time applications. An architecture is presented below
to realize the algorithm for binary images.

Thinning here is a sequence of table look-up tasks: the decimal equivalent number is derived from the local neighbourhood and applied as the address; the thinned image is then obtained by reading the contents of the table. To physically realize the thinning table, Read-Only Memory (ROM) is used to store the LUT table since its contents are pre-determined. Thinned new pixel values are saved at the corresponding locations specified by the equivalent numbers. In each iteration of thinning, image data flows into the address bus of the ROM and the thinned image data comes out from the data bus. Therefore, the thinned image data does not mix up with the input image data as it is required that image is refreshed at the end of each iteration. Several stages of these ROM blocks, each for one iteration, can be pipelined together for the necessary number of thinning iterations.

5.1 Architecture for one iteration

In the hardware implementation, there is no need to derive the decimal equivalent number k because both pixel values and ROM address bus are binary. Pixels in the 11-pixel window can be directly input to the address bus of the ROM with a specific order: pixel P_n to the nth least significant bit of the address. With an assumption that the image data is raster scanned and continuously applied to the thinning device as a one-dimensional binary stream, it is necessary to organize the architecture so that the desired 11 neighbouring pixels can be accessed simultaneously.

A common design to covert the one dimensional data stream into a two-dimensional data array is to use video delay lines, which are pipelined shift registers of a length the same as the number of pixels in a video line. In order to access pixels spreading over four video lines, three line-delay elements are required. Each of these elements delays the image data stream for one video line and makes a pair of vertically neighbouring pixels available simultaneously at its input and output ends. Besides these video delay lines, a small number of delay elements which are single shift registers are also needed. Each of these elements delays the image data stream for one pixel and makes a pair of horizontally neighbouring pixels simultaneously accessible at its input and output ends.

In total, eight pixel delay elements and three video delay lines are required to present the 11 neighbouring pixels for the access of ROM. As both the line- and pixel-delay elements work by counting the numbers of pixels, they are all driven by the system pixel clock which controls the image acquisition/transfer rate. The block diagram in Fig. 7 shows the architecture for one-iteration of thinning. D-type flip-flops (D-FF) and first-in-first-outs (FIFO) are used for pixel- and line-delay elements respectively. Note that the length of the FIFOs is determined by the resolution of the video scan line. The processing speed of this architecture is limited only by the access time of the ROMs.

5.2 End of thinning

Most of the existing thinning algorithms are proposed to terminate while no further thinning can be done (i.e., no more pixel value can be changed). This termination operation is difficult to implement with the above architecture. Therefore, a thinning machine may be

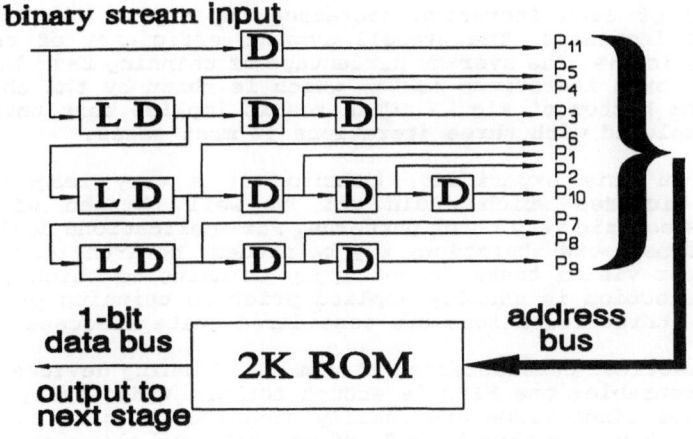

binary stream input

P₁₁
P₅
P₄
P₃
P₆
P₁
P₂
P₁₀
P₇
P₈
P₉

1-bit data bus

output to next stage

2K ROM

address bus

Fig. 7 Block diagram for one-stage thinning

built with the number of thinning devices determined by a) the resolution of the image systems (eg. 255 stages for 512x512 resolution), or b) the maximum width of possible patterns. The former method is impractical on the basis of implementation cost. With the second approach, the number of iterations needed is application-dependent. An incorrect estimation may result in incomplete thinning. However, full thinning is not necessary in most applications. A trade-off has then to be made between the "implementation cost" (in terms of processing time and price) and the "skeleton thinness" according to specific applications.

An estimation of the efficiency of each thinning iteration has been made as reference. The efficiency of any ith iteration may be defined as

$$\eta_i = \frac{N_i}{N_t}$$

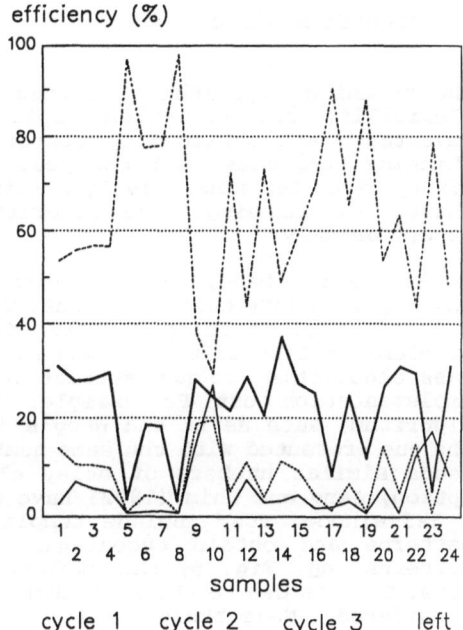

efficiency (%)

samples

cycle 1   cycle 2   cycle 3   left

Fig. 8 Efficiencies of individual iterations

where N_i is the number of points removed in the ith iteration, and N_t is the total number of points to be deleted during the complete thinning process. Figure 8 shows the efficiency of each of the first three iterations and percentage of the whole thinning task left after the first three iteration of 24 experiments. It is shown that the efficiency of each iteration decreases rapidly as the number of iterations increases. The overall average efficiency of the first iterations is 63%. The average percentage of thinning task left after the first three iterations is 7%, which is shown by the thin solid line on the bottom of Fig. 8. This result implies that thinning is almost completed with three iterations in most cases.

As shown in this experiment, thinning is a very image specific process. Pictures which could not be well thinned with three iterations contain very thick patterns. For applications dealing with such patterns, more iterations may be needed. Nevertheless, most of the computer vision tasks do not apply thinning to thick patterns. An edge detection is usually applied prior to thinning process. In this case, three iterations are considered quite adequate.

Another practical consideration also makes thinning devices of three stages favourable: one FIFO is enough for the video delay lines of three stages since FIFOs are usually organised as nine-bit wide. A thinning machine can thus be made of one FIFO and three octal D-FFs, each contains eight pixel-delay elements for one stage, together with three 2K ROMs.

6. DISCUSSION AND CONCLUSION

The thinning algorithm presented here has two advantages: design flexibility and real-time implementation capability. These two advantages are obtained by converting logical decision rules into thinning templates. All the possible patterns within the 11-pixel window have been exhaustively examined. Forty-nine templates are then chosen for thinning. This algorithm has been compared with others experimentally.

On the other hand, the algorithm presented has shortcomings in dealing with very thick patterns. The resulting skeletons tend to the concave sides of sharp corners. There are two ways to tackle this problem: utilize multiple passes or consider a larger window. Multi-pass algorithms are not attractive due to their comparatively high implementation cost. For example, the cost of implementing a two-pass algorithm, such as Lu and Wang's (1986), is about twice as that of the one presented with the same number of iterations, since each pass needs similar numbers of delay elements and ROMs. For the latter option, Jang and Chin (1992) have presented an algorithm which uses a 5x5 window. They include templates specially designed for thick patterns and obtain encouraging results. However, for ordinary patterns (eg. Fig. 5) the skeletons obtained are not as smooth as ours. This is due to the fact that local situations are not carefully considered. Nevertheless, it is difficult to examine all the possibilities (2^{25}) within the large window and the overall operational cost will increase if more templates are used. This problem has been left out since sharp and thick patterns do not exist so commonly in real world applications. Apart from this extreme condition, the new algorithm works well. Two sets of real world images processed by a software implementation are shown in Fig. 9 to illustrate its effectiveness.

An architecture for realization of the proposed thinning algorithm has also been described in this paper. The critical limit of the speed of this design is the access time of the ROMs. With fast bipolar ROMs, the thinning device is able to provide a capability of running at 33 MHz. A three-stage thinning machine has been built in the laboratory and is now fully operational, offering the features indicated above while working with a real-time edge detector. This machine has a cost estimated less than one ninth of that which uses IMS A110 (Inmos 1990) and is more compact physically.

ORIGINAL PICTURE   AFTER 3 ITERATIONS   THINNED PICTURE

(a)

ORIGINAL PICTURE   AFTER 3 ITERATIONS   THINNED PICTURE

(b)

Fig. 9   Thinning of a text image with the presented algorithm

REFERENCES

Chin RT, Wan HK, Stover DL, Iverson RD (1987), A one-pass thinning algorithm and its parallel implementation. Comput. Vision Graph. Image Process. 40: 30-40

Inmos (1990), Thinning digital patterns using the IMS A110. In: Image processing databook, 1st edn, Inmos, UK, pp 395-402

Jam L, Lee SW, Suen CY (1992), Thinning methodologies - a comprehensive survey. IEEE Trans. Pattern Anal. Mach. Intell. 14(9): 869-885

Jang BK, Chin RT (1992), One-pass parallel thinning: analysis, properties, and quantitative evaluation. IEEE Trans. Pattern Anal. Mach. Intell. 14(11): 1129-1140

Lu HE, Wang PSP (1986), A comment on "A fast parallel algorithm for thinning digital patterns". Commun. ACM 29(3): 239-242

Rutovitz D (1966), Pattern recognition. J. Roy. Stat. Soc. (A) 129: 504-530

Stefanelli R, Rosenfeld A (1971), Some parallel thinning algorithms for digital pictures. J. ACM 18(2): 255-264

Zhang TY, Suen CY (1984), A fast parallel algorithm for thinning digital patterns. Commun. ACM 27(3): 236-239

518

Pradip K. Sinha received the D.Phil degree in Control Engineering from the University of Sussex, England, in 1974, and was subsequently appointed a Post-Doctoral Research Fellow in Electronic and Control Engineering in the School of Engineering. He then joined the University of Warwick in 1977 as a lecturer in Engineering. Since 1988 he has been the Professor of Electronic Engineering at the Department of Engineering, University of Reading, England.

He has held several industrial consultancy posts in the UK, Europe, Japan and Taiwan. His current interests are in real-time control using parallel and adaptive techniques with particular reference to applications in vision-guided robots. He is the author of three books Multivariable control, Marcel Dekker, 1984; Microprocessors for Engineers, Ellis Horwood/Prentice-Hall, 1987; and Electromagnetic Suspension, IEE, London, 1987, and numerous journal and international conference papers in control, robotics and image processing.

Professor Sinha is a chartered Engineer, a member of the Institution of Electrical Engineers, London, and a member of the Institute of Measurement and Control, London.

Fa-Yu Chen received the B.S. degree in Electrophysic from the National Chiao-Tung University, Taiwan, in 1987. He was a teaching assistant in the NCTU in 1989. He is currently a Ph.D. student in the Department of Engineering, University of Reading, England. His research interests include computer vision, pattern recognition, and design of vision systems.

Address of both authors: Department of Engineering, University of Reading, P.O. Box-225, Reading RG6 2AY, England.

Parallel Creation of Linear Octrees from Quadtree Slices

Larry K. Swift, Theodore Johnson, and Panos E. Livadas

Abstract

Quadtrees and octrees are hierarchical data structures for efficiently storing image data. Quadtrees represent two dimensional images, while octrees are a generalization to three dimensions. The linear form of each is an abstraction of the tree structure to reduce storage requirements. We have developed a parallel algorithm to efficiently create a linear octree from quadtree *slices* of an object without the use of an intermediate data structure. We also propose the d-slice, which is a generalization of a quadtree and, octree which efficiently represents non-cubic volumes.

1 Introduction:

Modeling of three-dimensional objects applies to many areas of Computer Science, such as Computer Aided Design, Image Analysis, Virtual Reality. In each there is a need to model, represent and store 3d image data. Octrees are a data structure that meets these needs. Hunter proposes octrees in [2] and they are developed in [3], [4], [5] and [6]. Their creation is discussed in [8] using cross-sectional images, and in [7] using a boundary representation of a solid.

2 Octree Creation:

Our algorithm is based on the algorithm in [8] and [1] to the extent that octrees are created from quadtrees of serial slices. It has been altered to use linear quadtrees to create linear octrees, to remove the need for intermediate data structures, and to allow for parallelism.

2.1 Data at Intermediate Levels The input to the algorithm is an ordered series of linear quadtree slices, and the output is a linear octree. At intermediate stages in the processing, it is less clear what the data represents. This section will introduce some simple formulae to help clarify what the data represents at these stages.

A linear quadtree is comprised of simple codes, each representing a leaf node in the quadtree. The *linear codes* define the path from the root of the tree to the leaf node. Formally, a linear quadtree slice is a sequence of lexically (ie. depth-first-search) ordered codes: **slice** $= (c_1, c_2, \ldots, c_n)$ where each c_i is the linear code of a leaf. The code for a leaf is: $c_i = (q_1 q_2 \ldots q_j)$, where each q_s is the number of a child node and represents one step of the traversal from the root to the leaf. Finally, the *length* of a linear code c_i is the number of elements in the code (eg. the $length((q_1 \ldots q_j)) = j$).

Figure 1 shows a visual representation of our algorithm. linear quadtree slices of an image are repeatedly combined until a linear octree is produced. The numbers below each cube shows the linear code prior to processing, the numbers above show the converted code. The *combined* caption denotes where 2 lists are combined to create the input for the next level. The dashed lines denote where the division of work is for each level in the *processing tree*.

A linear quadtree that represents an area with dimensions $2^n \times 2^n$ can have codes with length at most n. Each of the original quadtree slices represents a volume 2^n units high, 2^n units wide, and 1 unit deep. As Figure 1 shows, when two slices are combined the result is a new *deeper slice* (abbreviated d-slice). Thus a quadtree is a 0-slice (with one unit of depth). Two 0-slices are combined to create a 1-slice (with two units of depth), two 1-slices are combined to create a 2-slice, and so on. In general, a d-slice at level d in the processing tree is 2^d units deep (assuming levels $0 \leq d \leq n$).

An element in a $2^n \times 2^n$ 0-slice that has n elements in its path is one unit high, one unit wide, and one unit deep. In general, any linear code observed at level d in the processing tree with length $\geq n - d$ must represent a volume of equal dimensions that cannot be subdivided or combined.

For example, look at the 1-slices in Figure 1. These are $2^2 \times 2^2 \times 2^1$ slices of a $2^2 \times 2^2 \times 2^2$ volume. Using these as a reference, we can introduce some generalizations about d-slices:

- A d-slice inside a $2^n \times 2^n \times 2^n$ volume is composed of $2^{n-d} \times 2^{n-d}$ cubes of dimension $2^d \times 2^d \times 2^d$.

519

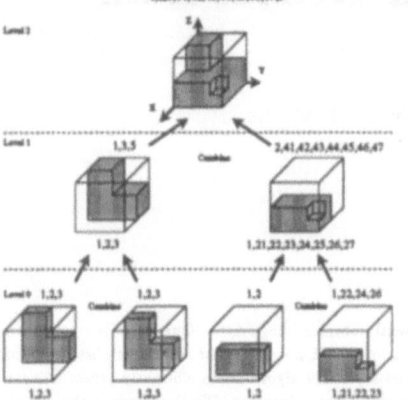

Figure 1: A visual representation of our algorithm.

Figure 2: The three cases.

- To index a particular voxel, first index to the cubic volume the voxel is in, then index within the cubic element.
- Indexing to the cubic volume is done using quadtree subdivision of the d-slice. Indexing within the cubic volume is performed using octree subdivision.
- A group of neighboring voxels that are the same color are combined using the rules of octree creation, a group of cubic volumes that are the same color are combined using the rules of quadtree creation.

The formal definition of a d-slice follows:

d-slice $= (c_1, c_2, \ldots, c_n)$ - lexically sorted.

$c_i = (q_1 \ q_2 \ldots q_j), \ j \leq d$ or

$c_i = (q_1 \ q_2 \ldots q_d \ o_1 \ o_2 \ldots o_n)$

q_i = a code element in quadtree notation (volume is subdivided into quadrants).

o_i = a code element in octree notation (volume is subdivided into octants).

A brief summary of the salient points:

1. a d-slice observed at level d $(1 \leq d \leq n)$ in the processing tree represents a $2^n \times 2^n \times 2^d$ volume.
2. a linear code with length s $(s < n - d)$ does not represent a cubic volume, and therefore is, a candidate for splitting or combining.
3. a linear code with length t $(t \geq n - d)$ represents a cubic volume that may not be split or combined.

Converting linear codes The interpretation of a d-slice code depends on d. Before two d-slices are combined into $d + 1$-slice, every d-slice code c_i must be converted into a $d + 1$-slice code:

- if length$(c_i) < n - d$ then $c_i = (q_1 \ldots q_j)$ and $(q_1 \ldots q_j) \to (q_1 \ldots q_j)$.
- if length$(c_i) \geq n - d$, then $c_i = (q_1 \ldots q_d o_{d+1} \ldots o_n)$, and $(q_1 \ldots q_d o_{d+1} \ldots o_n) \to (q_1 \ldots q_{d-1} o_d o_{d+1} \ldots o_n)$

The conversion of the d-th element from a quadtree child into an octtree child depends on whether the d-slice is on the top or the bottom:

1. If the d-slice is containing the code is closer to the Y-Z plane then it will use the following conversion formula: $o_{n-d} = 2q_{n-d} - 1$.
2. Otherwise, convert using the formula: $o_{n-d} = 2q_{n-d}$.

Since we know that slices are to be read in increasing X order, it is trivial to determine which of a pair of slices that are to be combined is closer to the Y-Z plane.

2.3 Combining Slices Once both slices in a pair are converted to $d+1$-slice representation, they are ready to be *combined*. During combination, we need to compare matching areas of the two d-slices to see if they are similarly colored. If such areas exist, they may represented by a single node of the $d+1$-slice. Since the list of codes for each d-slice is lexically ordered, finding matching areas is a simple matter of comparing the head of each list to that of its neighbor. Identical numbering of the elements indicates a matching area.

There are three possible cases that may occur when two codes are compared (illustrated in Figure 2):

1. The linear codes may be exactly equal.

2. The linear codes may be equal for the length of the of the shortest.

3. The linear codes are dissimilar.

The first case is illustrated several times in Figure 1. For example, when the two left-most 0-slices are combined the head of each list is 1. Since they are exactly equal, this element is removed from each list and a single 1 appears as input to the next level. This is repeated when 2 and 3 appear at the head of each list.

In the second case, as illustrated by Figure 2 one code represents an area that is a subarea of the other. When this is the case, one code (representing the larger area) is always shorter than the other. This code must be *split* (described below) so that its subareas may be compared with the shorter code, in the hope that one of these comparisons will fall into case 1. This case is shown in Figure 1 at the far right of level 0. After the 1 at the head of each list is removed (by case 1) the code 2 from the left 0-slice is compared to the code 22 from its neighbor. Since they are equal for the length of the shorter, the shortest code (2) is split to obtain 21,23,25, and 27.

In the final case, since the linear codes differ, this indicates that the two are not in the same area of the d-slice. Clearly, these are not candidates for combining. However, since the codes are lexically sorted, the code with the higher lexical value may match a code further down in the list of the lower valued code. Because of this, only the code with the lower lexical value will be removed. If the length of this linear code is less than $n-d$ it must be split until the resultant codes represent a cubic volume. The resulting code(s) should be sent as input to the next level. This case is represented at level 1 in Figure 1 where the head of the two lists are 1 and 2. These codes are dissimilar, so the one with the lower lexical value (1) is sent as input to the next level.

Splitting a code is similar to subdividing a quadrant when creating a quadtree. When we are sure that a linear code cannot be combined with a similar code from its neighbor, and its length $< n-d$ it must be split. The formal definition of splitting a code follows:

- $(q_1 \, q_2 \ldots q_j) \rightarrow (q_1 \, q_2 \ldots q_j \, 1) , (q_1 \, q_2 \ldots q_j \, 2) , (q_1 \, q_2 \ldots q_j \, 3) , (q_1 \, q_2 \ldots q_j \, 4)$

The only exception to this rule is when $j+1 = n-d$. Since we established in Section 2.1 that the $(n-d)^{th}$ element represents a volume, the new element in each of the resulting codes must be converted. The rules from Section 2.2 are used to convert the new elements (therefore, it is important to remember which d-slice the code came from).

2.4 The Algorithm We have already described the salient points of the algorithm. Each pair of d-slices requires a task. Assuming we start with 2^n quadtree slices, they will require 2^{n-1} tasks. These will create 2^{n-1} d-slices which will require 2^{n-2} tasks (and so on). It should be clear that the total number of tasks will be $\Sigma_{i=1}^{n} 2^{n-1} = 2^n - 1$. Each task consists of conversion of the pair of lists (representing the d-slices) and combining them to create a $d+1$-slice that will be used at the next level as input. The task at the next level that receives this data is referred to as the *parent task*. Some important points of the algorithm are given below:

- Conversion of the $(n-d)^{th}$ element in each linear code must be completed before attempting to combine. Remember that a code with $n-d$ elements represents a cubic volume at level d. If they are not converted first, two identical codes of length $n-d$ could mistakenly be considered for merging.

- When splitting a code, if the length of the resultant codes is $n-d$, then the last digit must also be converted to octree notation. The formula to be used depends on which d-slice the original code came from.

- Splitting ends when the resultant codes length is $n-d$. As explained in 2.1 this indicates that the volume represented by the code is now cubic, and cannot be further divided.

- If tasks are numbered sequentially starting with 1 as the root (the final two d-slices) to $2^n - 1$ (the initial 0-slices), then the parent's task number is as easy as integer division of the current task number by 2. Data received from an even-numbered task is from the right-child, data received from an odd-numbered task is from the left-child.

Initially, the quadtrees are placed in the input lists at the bottom of the processing tree. Each level is successively completed, and the output from a task is sent to the input list of its parent. The output of the task at level 1 will be the completed octree.

2.5 Parallel Approaches Since there is no dependency between neighboring tasks, the algorithm lends itself nicely to a parallel approach. Each level of the processing tree may be performed in parallel. However, a task on a new level may not start before its children on the previous one are finished, since the two for loops at the beginning of the algorithm in Code 1 cannot begin until all input to the task is available (this restriction will be removed in section 2.5).

Task Allocation We have laid out the basic issues in task allocation above, but not the specifics. The tasks cannot be performed in an arbitrary order, as this could lead to starvation, or deadlock. A simple but effective task allocation scheme is to number the tasks from top to bottom. Each processor selects a new task by decrementing a global task counter. More sophisticated allocation schemes can be devised to increase I/O parallelism and to decrease network traffic.

Pipelining It is possible to pipeline our algorithm. Rather than receiving all data from the queues onto lists, simply place all the codes from a single child onto a list until a code comes in from its sibling. At this time the codes at the head of each list can be converted, the appropriate action can be taken (Splitting, combining, whatever is required) and data sent up the processing tree to a parent task. Processing should continue until one of the two children has no data in its list. Then go back and receive more data from the children until there is again data in each list.

Since the entire input list from both children is not available, the conversion step cannot be considered to be complete before the combination step. This requires only that the data from each child be kept separate. As indicated in section 2.2 knowledge of whether a linear code came from a left, or right child is enough to know how to convert it. Therefore, we can assume that when two codes (one from the head of each list) are being considered for combination, that the tail of each code is converted, and we can use the knowledge of which child each code came from to convert the $(n - d)^{th}$ element of the path (assuming d is the current level). In this manner, it is possible to get many levels of the processing tree operating simultaneously on the data.

2.6 Analysis We note that the time to execute one d-slice combination step is linear in the size of the input and output. If sufficient processors are available, the time to compute the octree is the time to compute the critical path, or the path from the root to a leaf that processes the most data. If nodes on the critical path process c times as much data than average, the speedup of the algorithm is bounded by $2^n/cn$. By using the pipelining technique, the algorithm can support a parallelism of P as long as P tasks remain in the processing tree.

A precise estimate of the possible speedup that our algorithm supports depends on an estimate of c. Unfortunately, c is highly dependent on the input data, and is difficult to characterize. In our future research, we will implement and experimentally characterize the performance of our algorithm.

References

[1] H. H. Chen and T. S. Huang. A survey of construction and manipulation of octrees. *Computer Vision, Graphics and Image Processing*, 43(3):409–431, 1988.

[2] G. M. Hunter. *Efficient Computation and Data Structures for Graphics*. PhD thesis, Department of Electrical and Computer Science, Princeton University, Princeton, NJ, 1978.

[3] C. Jackins and S.L. Tanimoto. Oct-trees and their use in presenting three-dimensional objects. *Computer Graphics and Image Processing*, 14(3):249–270, 1980.

[4] D. Meagher. Octree encoding: A new technique for the representation, manipulation and display of arbitrary 3-d objects. Technical Report IPL-TR-80-111, Rensselaer Polytechnic Institute, Troy, NY, October 1980.

[5] D. R. Reddy and S. Rubin. Representation of three-dimensional objects. Technical Report CMU-CS-78-113, Carnegie-Mellon University, Pittsburgh, Penn, April 1978.

[6] S. N. Srihari. Hierarchical representation for serial section images. In *Proceedings, 5th International Conference on Pattern Recognition*, pages 1075–1080, December 1980.

[7] M. Tamminen and H. Samet. Efficient octree conversion by connectivity labeling. *Computer Graphics*, 18(3):43–51, July 1984.

[8] M. M. Yau and S. N. Srihari. A hierarchical data structure for multidimensional digital images. *Comm. ACM*, 26(7):504–515, July 1983.

Address: Department of Computer and Information Sciences, University of Florida, Gainesville, FL 32611, USA

A Graphical Hierarchical Flowchart Generator for Parallel Fortran Programs

Rajeev R. Raje, Daniel J. Pease, Sanjay D. Jejurikar, and Neng T. Lin

It is a well-known fact that the humans can process a large quantity of image
information in parallel, detecting and tracking complex visual patterns with an
incredible speed. In today's hi--tech world, the need for visualization is very
obvious. This need for visualization in the scientific domains is reflected as
graphical simulations and animations. The field of parallel processing is one
such excellent example where the graphical simulations can be of great assistance.

Parallel processing has become a necessary choice to meet the challenges and
demands posed by the various scientific and engineering applications. Programming
these parallel machines is hardly a trivial task. A great deal of visualization
is required to write correct and efficient parallel programs. A graphical tool
helping the user in this parallel programming development can be considered a
boon from the perspective of the user.

The parallel programming languages proposed have been mostly the **extensions** of
the popular sequential languages like Fortan or C. FORTAN is one such language
offered by IBM for the 3090 multi-processor. It has special constructs incorporated like **parallel case, parallel do**, etc.

This paper presents a hierarchical flowchart generator, which displays the flowchart of the user program written in Parallel FORTRAN for IBM 3090 multi-processor.
The flowchart generator has two components - **static** and **dynamic**. The static component is responsible for the graphical representation of the program in the form
of a flowchart. This allows the user to get a clear picture of the control flow.
The dynamic component indicates the information about the frequency of the execution of various constructs in the user program along with run--time simulation.
The combination of the two components helps the user to improve the readability
of the programs and assist in writing better and more efficient parallel programs,
thereby, aiding to exploit the parallelism to the maximum extent offered by the
IBM 3090 hardware.

The **statement-grouping algorithms** developed in this research are based on the
fan-ins and **fan-outs** of each statement in the program. Based on these algorithms,
statements which form a logical unit are grouped together and displayed as a single
block (at the higher level of abstraction) in the flowchart. Every further level
of abstraction decreases this grouping and at the lowest level the source code is
displayed. The flowchart thus created, is superimposed by the run--time frequency
data for each statement.

The hierarchical flowchart generator constitutes a part of an environment called
PFDE (Parallel Fortran Development Environment)[1] developed at Syracuse University.

Address: Dept. Electrical & Computer Engineering, Room 2-185, Center for Science and Technology
Syracuse University, Syracuse, New York 13244, USA

---

[1] This project was supported by IBM Corporation under contract OSP 353--9226.

A Graphical Hierarchical Flowchart Generator for Parallel Fortran Programs

Hans-Jörg Rein, Christoph Peter Gänger, C. Jeyukhar and Head T. Lan

Part VI

Image Processing

A Fast Algorithm for Digital Image Scaling

George Wolberg and Henry Massalin

ABSTRACT

This paper describes a fast algorithm for scaling digital images. Large performance gains are realized by reducing the number of convolution operations, and optimizing the evaluation of those that remain. We achieve this by decomposing the overall scale transformation into a cascade of smaller scale operations. As an image is progressively scaled towards the desired resolution, a multi-stage filter with kernels of varying size is applied. We show that this results in a significant reduction in the number of convolution operations. Furthermore, by constraining the manner in which the transformation is decomposed, we are able to derive optimal kernels and implement efficient convolvers. The convolvers are optimized in the sense that they require no multiplication; only lookup table and addition operations are necessary. This accelerates convolution and greatly extends the range of filters that may be feasibly applied for image scaling. The algorithm readily lends itself to efficient software and hardware implementation.

Keywords: Image scaling, fast convolution, multiresolution

1. INTRODUCTION

Image scaling is a geometric transformation that is used to resize digital images. This is a classic uniform resampling problem with widespread use in computer graphics and image processing. It plays a key role in many applications including pyramid construction (Chin 92; Meer 87), supersampling, multi-grid solutions (Vaidyanathan 93), and geometric normalization (Wolberg 90).

Despite a flurry of activity in this area, image scaling remains a computationally expensive operation. Its cost is dominated by convolution, which is necessary to bandlimit the discrete input and thereby mitigate undesirable reconstruction and aliasing artifacts. Convolution may prove to be prohibitively expensive, especially when large (high-quality) filter kernels or large scale factors are applied. This poses a quality-time tradeoff in which high-quality output must often be compromised in the interest of time. Not surprisingly, commonly used resampling filters utilize small kernels to achieve satisfactory processing rates.

This paper addresses the computational bottleneck imposed by convolution. The goal of this work is two-fold: to reduce the number of convolution operations, and to optimize the evaluation of those that remain. Although the quality-time tradeoff will always exist, accelerated image scaling promises to extend the range of high-quality resampling filters that may be feasibly applied. This stands to benefit many applications in such fields as computer graphics, computer vision, remote sensing, and medical imaging.

We present a fast algorithm for image scaling that progressively scales the image towards the desired resolution. Since each stage in the progression imposes different constraints on the resampling filter, we make use of a multi-stage filter with suitably tailored kernels that are each applied to its respective intermediate image. We demonstrate that by decomposing the overall scale transformation into a series of smaller scale operations, a significant reduction in the number of convolution operations is possible. Furthermore, by constraining the manner in which we decompose the transformation, we are able to derive optimal kernels and implement efficient convolvers. The convolvers are optimized in the sense that they require no multiplication; only lookup table accesses and addition operations are necessary. This makes the algorithm particularly attractive for both software and hardware implementation.

2. MAGNIFICATION

Image magnification is achieved by upsampling the discrete input image. The central component to this process is image reconstruction, an interpolation stage that fits a continuous function through the data samples. This serves to recover the continuous input image from its discrete representation so that it may be subjected to a higher sampling rate. In practice, magnification is usually implemented by interpolating only those points which are needed to produce the output image. For equally spaced data, interpolation can be expressed as

$$g(x) = \sum_{k=0}^{K-1} g_s(x_k) \dot{h}(x - x_k)$$

where g_s is the discrete input signal defined over integer values of x_k, g is the output signal defined over real values of x, and h is the interpolation kernel weighted by K data samples. The equation given above formulates interpolation as a convolution operation. Nearly always, h is a symmetric kernel, i.e., $h(-x) = h(x)$. In addition, h must satisfy the following two conditions in order to interpolate the data: $h(0) = 1$, and $h(k) = 0$ for all integer values of $k \neq 0$. This lets $g(x_k) = g_s(x_k)$, thereby allowing $g(x)$ to pass through the data.

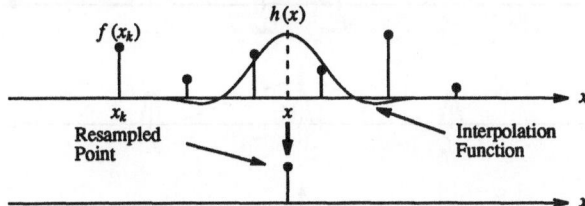

Figure 1: Interpolation of a single point.

The computation of one interpolated point is illustrated in Fig. 1. The interpolation kernel is centered at x, the location of the point to be interpolated. We refer to the kernel as a 4-point kernel because it extends over four points. In general, any kernel which extends over N data samples will be referred to as an N-point kernel in this paper. Note that this applies when the kernel is *not* centered at a data sample. Otherwise, the kernel will actually extend over $N+1$ samples but this case is not of interest to us since $g(x)$ is known to pass through the data.

The value of the point at x is equal to the sum of the values of the discrete input scaled by the corresponding values of the interpolation kernel. This follows directly from the definition of convolution. Unfortunately, this is computationally expensive for the wide kernels that are necessary to perform accurate interpolation.

A wide range of filters are now in common use. The shortest ones include the 1-point box and 2-point triangle filters used for nearest neighbor and linear interpolation, respectively. Superior results are possible with cubic convolution (Keys 81; Park 83). More recently, a two-parameter family of cubic filters was introduced to offer a broader range of behaviors (Mitchell 88). Applications requiring wider kernels typically use windowed sinc functions. Popular windows include the Hann, Hamming, Blackman, Kaiser, Gaussian, and Lanczos windows (Wolberg 90).

2.1. A Strategy For Reducing the Cost of Magnification

Consider the problem of magnifying a 1-D signal $g_s(x)$ by a factor of a, where $a \geq 1$. Let $g_s(x)$ consist of M samples, and let $h(x)$ be an N-point interpolation kernel. In the general case, the interpolation cost is $O(aMN)$ because $h(x)$ must be centered at aM equispaced positions in the input. For integer values of a, M of these positions is guaranteed to lie on the data samples themselves. Since the output at those positions is known, the cost of interpolation for integer values of a is $O((a-1)MN)$.

One apparent way of reducing this cost is to select a narrower kernel and compromise on reconstruction quality. This may be warranted if the spectrum $G(f)$ has a narrow bandwidth, with no high frequency components that can contribute significantly to postaliasing. Although we cannot predict the frequency content of $G(f)$, we can be sure that magnification will reduce its bandwidth relative to the new sampling rate. This suggests that a series of filters, with increasingly relaxed constraints, can be applied to a set of progressively magnified signals for reconstruction.

Figure 2 demonstates this reconstruction. It shows three stages in the magnification of a sampled signal with spectrum $G_s(f)$. The first stage applies a high-quality reconstruction filter to effectively bandlimit the signal to f_{max}. Notice that the reconstruction filter, drawn with dashed lines, must have a sharp cutoff to retain the baseband spectrum and discard the broadband replicas. That reconstructed signal is then enlarged and sampled to produce a signal with a narrower baseband bandwidth. Since there is now more space between replicas, the next reconstruction filter applied need not have a sharp cutoff. This is depicted in the second row of Fig. 2 by a filter with a wider transition band that slowly tapers off. The third row repeats this process, making use of an even poorer filter to bandlimit the magnified signal. In the spatial domain, these results imply that ever-smaller kernels can be applied in each stage for

528

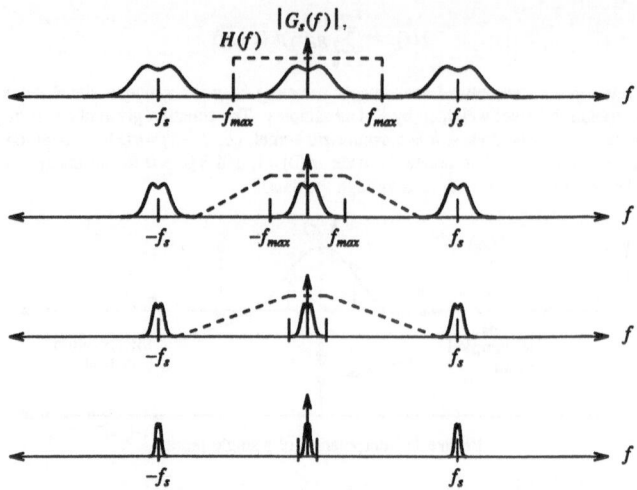

Figure 2: Spectra of a progressively magnified signal.

adequate interpolation. This cycle of reconstruction, enlargement, and sampling ends once the desired signal resolution is reached.

Let's assume for now that $a=2$ for each stage in the progression. In the example given above, three stages were necessary to achieve an overall eight-fold magnification. The total cost of interpolation is $O(MN_0+2MN_1+4MN_2)$, where N_i refers to the N_i-point kernel used in stage i. Collectively, these kernels comprise the *multi-stage filter* used to bandlimit the input and intermediate signals. The computational savings of using a multi-stage filter in this progressive approach is due to the fact that $N_2 < N_1 < N_0$, i.e., ever-smaller kernels are applied in successive stages. This proves to be cheaper than direct convolution with a single wide kernel ($N_0=N_1=N_2$) which was predicted earlier to have a cost of $O(7MN)$.

For K magnification stages, the cost of using a multi-stage filter is $O(\sum_{i=0}^{K-1} 2^i MN_i)$. This fares better than direct convolution, with a cost of $O((2^K-1)MN_0)$. Multi-stage filters are particularly attractive for large magnification factors, where more stages induce more savings. In addition, their low cost bears significant consequences on image quality. We are not deterred, for instance, from using superior reconstruction filters with wide kernels since they are applied early in the process when the signal has the fewest samples. As the size of the signal grows, we avoid prohibitively expensive convolution by turning to smaller kernels. This balance makes it feasible to apply higher quality filters than would otherwise be possible with direct convolution.

Multi-stage filters exploit the frequency characteristics of increasingly magnified signals to perform adequate nonideal reconstruction. Although the enlargement at each stage can be arbitrary, we choose to limit it to two-fold magnification. As we have seen earlier, it is computationally cheaper to deal with integer magnification factors, with two being the smallest. In addition, a two-fold magnifier readily lends itself to efficient software and hardware implementation. The next section discusses how to derive N-point kernels for several values of N.

2.2. Deriving Optimal Kernels

Interpolation kernels are generally continuous functions that may be centered anywhere in the input. The weights applied to the neighbors must be evaluated by sampling the centered kernel at positions coinciding with the input samples. In the case of two-fold magnification, the allowable set of positions at which we must sample the interpolation kernel is greatly reduced. Since the kernel can either be centered directly on the data samples or halfway between them, the kernel must be evaluated at half-unit intervals. An example of a 6-point kernel sampled for use in two-fold magnification is shown in Fig. 3.

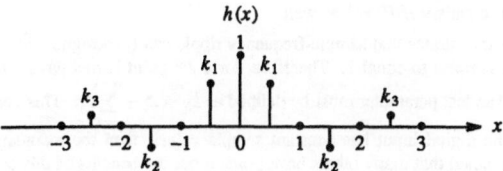

Figure 3: Kernel samples needed for two-fold magnification.

We note that those weights defined at integer values of x are applied when the kernel is centered on a data sample. In order to conform with the standard requirement of interpolation kernels, $h(0) = 1$ and $h(x) = 0$ for all nonzero integer values of x. This is necessary to guarantee that the output passes through the input. In practice, we avoid this computation at integer input coordinates by directly copying the input value to the output.

remainder of the weights are applied when the kernel is centered halfway between input samples. This results in ietric set of weights that offers several important benefits. First, the weights never have to be re-evaluated during-time because the kernel always maintains the same alignment with the data samples. Second, the number of iplications necessary to compute one output value is cut in half to reflect the number of distinct weights. Third, ι most importantly, symmetric weights allow us to express the frequency response of the kernel as a particularly mple closed-form expression. That expression shall be used to derive optimal kernel values.

We begin by noting that the kernel samples in Fig. 3 constitute a summation of symmetric impulse pairs:

$$h(x) = \delta(0) + \sum_{i=1}^{3} k_i \delta(x+i-.5) + k_i \delta(x-i+.5)$$

In order to compute $H(f)$, we make use of the well-known Fourier transform pair that relates symmetric impulse pairs in one domain to cosines in the other to give us:

$$H(f) = 1 + 2k_1 \cos(\pi f) + 2k_2 \cos(3\pi f) + 2k_3 \cos(5\pi f)$$

This result can be generalized to $2N$-point filters as follows:

$$H(f) = 1 + 2\sum_{i=1}^{N} k_i \cos((2i-1)\pi f)$$

Since our kernel samples are known to be symmetric, we now use N to refer to the number of distinct weights and $2N$ to refer to the filter support.

The above equation is a simple closed-form expression for $H(f)$ in terms of k_i. This result is significant because it now becomes possible to derive optimal kernel values by selecting those k_i's that minimize the difference between $H(f)$ and the ideal filter response. Due to point symmetry about $f=.5$, it is sufficient to directly minimize $H^2(f)$ over the stopband, i.e., $.5 \leq f \leq 1$. The square term ensures that the integrand $H(f)$ is always positive. We now use this least-squared error constraint to derive optimal kernels for several $2N$-point filters.

2.2.1. 2-Point Filters

The expression for $H(f)$ for a 2-point filter is $H(f) = 1 + 2k_1 \cos(\pi f)$. Minimizing $H^2(f)$ over the interval $.5 \leq f \leq 1$ gives us $k_1 = .63662$. Note that although we only minimized $H^2(f)$ over the stopband, the passband shares its same characteristics due to point symmetry about $f=.5$. This guarantees that any improvements made in the stopband will also reflect back into the passband.

Close inspection of this result reveals a problem: $H(1) \neq 0$, or equivalently $H(0) \neq 1$. This leads to an artifact known as *sample-frequency ripple* which produces a noticeable grid pattern on the image. Although the ideal filter (dashed) requires $H(f) = 0$ for $f > .5$, the failure to satisfy this condition at the sampling frequency $f=1$ is most disturbing because the strongest component of the signal (at $f=0$) is now aliasing as a high frequency (at $f=f_s=1$). This problem is remedied by constraining $H(1) = 0$. That gives us $0 = 1 + 2\sum_{i=1}^{N} k_i \cos((2i-1)\pi)$ which simply reduces to $1 = 2\sum_{i=1}^{N} k_i$. The 2-point filter is now fully constrained, forcing $k_1 = .5$ i.e., the usual triangle filter. Due to the point symmetry about $f = .5$, we also satisfy $H(0) = 1$ as well.

The equation given above demonstrates that sample-frequency ripple can be designed out of the filter by requiring the sum of all of the $2N$ kernel samples to equal 1. Therefore, for a $2N$-point kernel having N points on each side, there are $N-1$ free parameters. The last parameter must be defined as $k_N = .5 - \sum_{i=1}^{N-1} k_i$. This constraint enforces a *flat-field response*, meaning that if the digital input has constant sample values, then the reconstructed signal will also have constant value. It should be noted that many others have pointed out the benefits of this constraint (Mitchell 88).

2.2.2. 4-Point Filters

The expression for $H(f)$ for a 4-point filter is $H(f) = 1 + 2k_1\cos(\pi f) + (1-2k_1)\cos(3\pi f)$. Minimizing $H^2(f)$ over the interval $.5 \le f \le 1$ now yields $k_1 = .674413$. Plugging k_1 back into the above expression for k_N gives us the remaining kernel sample: $k_2 = -.174413$. The frequency response of this filter is labeled $H_{1/2}$ in Fig. 4a. Its stopband response is depicted more prominently in Fig. 4b. Although $H_{1/2}(1) = 0$ ensures that there is no sample-frequency ripple, its stopband response illustrates that there still remains plenty of frequency leakage, particularly near $f = 1$.

We are better served by introducing a transition region in which the frequency response $H(f)$ may smoothly drop from the passband to the stopband. This significantly reduces ringing because $H(f)$ can now be more closely approximated by the summation of cosines. Filter $H_{1/4}$ in Fig. 4 demonstrates the superior response gained by selecting kernel values that minimize $H^2(f)$ over the interval $.75 \le f \le 1$. The kernel values are now $k_1 = .587051$ and $k_2 = -.087051$. Although $H_{1/4}$ does not drop to 0 in the stopband as sharply as $H_{1/2}$, it does remain there more closely when it reaches $f = .75$. This proves to be a very important property for reconstruction filters used in magnification. As already demonstrated in Fig. 2, a flat passband/stopband response is more essential than a sharp cutoff, especially for increasingly enlarged images that can tolerate wide transition bands anyway.

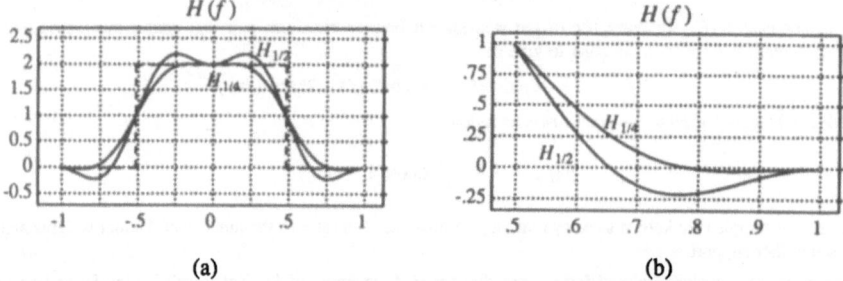

Figure 4: 4-point filters. (a) Spectrum; (b) Stopband response.

2.2.3. 6-Point Filters

The expression for $H(f)$ for a 6-point filter is

$$H(f) = 1 + 2k_1\cos(\pi f) + 2k_2\cos(3\pi f) + (1-2k_1-2k_2)\cos(5\pi f)$$

The kernel values for $H_{1/2}$, and $H_{1/4}$ are given below.

	k_1	k_2	k_3
$H_{1/2}$	.619374	-.229452	.110078
$H_{1/4}$	.600816	-.123529	.022713

Their frequency responses are shown in Fig. 5.

2.2.4. 8-Point Filters

The expression for $H(f)$ for an 8-point filter is

$$H(f) = 1 + 2k_1\cos(\pi f) + 2k_2\cos(3\pi f) + 2k_3\cos(5\pi f) + (1-2k_1-2k_2-2k_3)\cos(7\pi f)$$

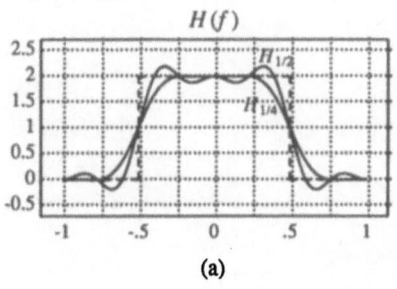
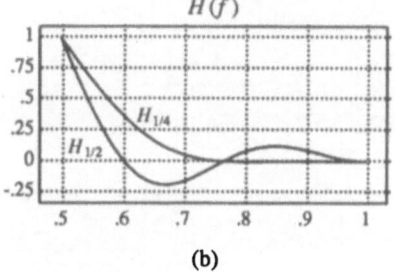

(a)   (b)

Figure 5: 6-point filters. (a) Spectrum; (b) Stopband response.
The kernel values for $H_{1/2}$ and $H_{1/4}$ are given below.

	k_1	k_2	k_3	k_4
$H_{1/2}$	.646422	-.202404	.137126	-.081144
$H_{1/4}$	.60964	-.142133	.0390404	-.0065474

Their frequency responses are shown in Fig. 6.

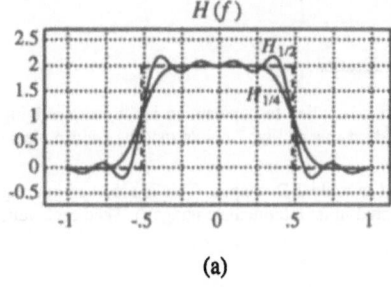
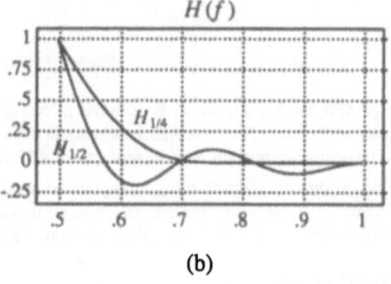

(a)   (b)

Figure 6: 8-point filters. (a) Spectrum; (b) Stopband response.

2.3. Magnification Algorithm

Multi-stage filters accelerate magnification by significantly reducing the number of convolution operations with each successive stage. Further savings are possible when each stage is limited to two-fold magnification. In this section, we examine several means for accelerating an individual stage, and propose a novel method for optimizing convolution. 1-D scanlines are considered here for simplicity. This will later be extended to 2-D using a separable implementation.

Two-fold magnification is essentially a cycle of fetch-convolve operations. Figure 7 illustrates this process on an input scanline consisting of five samples. Those samples are directly applied to even-addressed positions in a working buffer, trivially generating half of the magnified signal. The odd-addressed positions are reserved for the remaining output values that must be derived by interpolation. Since a 4-point kernel will be used in this example, padding is added to each end of the buffer so that the kernel has enough data to compute the interpolated results near the borders. The padding shown in the shaded areas of Fig. 7 is generated by reflecting the input values about the borders. Due to the nature of the interpolation, the right side needs one additional padding element more than the left side.

Convolution is applied directly on the input elements stored in the buffer, with the output interleaved among them. There is therefore a distance of two between successive input samples and successive interpolated output samples in the buffer. The two-fold magnification is implicit in this layout of the data. Since the kernel must now be applied to input data that has twice the inter-sample spacing, it too must be scaled to coincide with the samples. Therefore, the kernel samples must now lie at $x=0, \pm1, \pm3, \pm5, ...$ as opposed to $x=0, \pm.5, \pm1.5, \pm2.5, ...$ as in Fig. 3. This

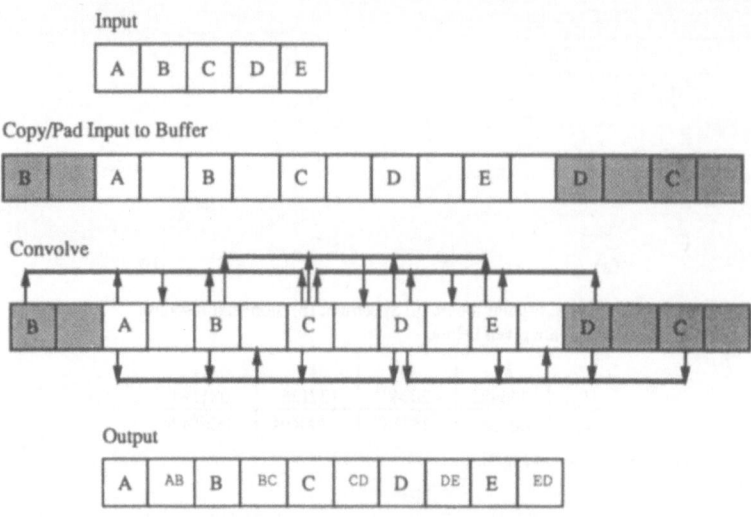

Figure 7: Two-fold magnification.

spacing permits the kernel, which is centered at odd addresses, to be applied to consecutive input samples lying at even buffer addresses. The convolution process is depicted in the third row of Fig. 7. Note that the padded elements prove to be necessary in computing output values *AB*, *DE*, and *ED*.

The 1-D algorithm magnification algorithm can be readily extended to scale 2-D images. This is achieved in a separable manner. First, each horizontal scanline (row) is scaled and stored in an intermediate image *I*. Then each vertical scanline (column) of *I* is scaled to produce the final output image.

3. MINIFICATION

Image minification is achieved by downsampling the discrete input image, in a manner akin to magnification. We have already established that magnification narrows each baseband replica in the spectrum, as demonstrated in Fig. 2. Due to the reciprocal relationship between the spatial and frequency domains, minification serves to broaden each replica. This introduces complications because there now exists the possibility that the replicas in the spectrum of the minified signal may overlap. This is a symptom of undersampling, and contributes to aliasing. Unlike the spurious high frequencies retained by nonideal reconstruction filters, the spectral components passed due to undersampling are more serious since they actually corrupt the components in the original signal.

The filtering necessary to combat aliasing is known as *antialiasing*. This is most typically done by low-pass filtering the input *before* sampling at the lower rate. This method, known as *prefiltering*, bandlimits (truncates) the signal spectrum to eliminate the offending high frequencies.

Minification is usually implemented by convolving the input with a low-pass filter centered at only those sparse positions which are needed to produce the output image. This procedure is identical to the interpolation performed for magnification. This should not be surprising since interpolation and prefiltering play similar roles: they convert the discrete input into a continuous signal that is suitable for resampling.

The only difference between prefiltering and interpolation is the shape of the filter kernel. Whereas the cutoff frequency f_c is held constant at .5 cycle/pixel for magnification, f_c must now vary with the scale factor: $f_c = .5a$ cycle/pixel for minification, where $0 < a < 1$ is the scale factor. This implies that minification requires a broader filter kernel whose width N is inversely proportional to the scale factor. As with magnification, we are faced with the same challenge to reduce the cost of high-quality low-pass filtering.

3.1. A Strategy For Reducing the Cost of Minification

Consider the problem of minifying a 1-D signal $g_s(x)$ by a factor of a, where $0 < a < 1$. Let $g_s(x)$ consist of M samples, and let filter $h(x)$ be an N-point kernel. The cost of prefiltering is $O(aMN)$ because $h(x)$ must be centered at aM equispaced positions in the input. For integer values of $1/a$, these positions coincide with the data samples themselves. In that case, N must be odd to accommodate symmetric kernels.

One apparent way of reducing this cost is to select a narrower kernel and accept more aliasing artifacts. This may be warranted if $G(f)$ has a narrow bandwidth, with no high frequency components that can contribute significantly to aliasing. As already noted, though, the value of N is inversely proportional to a, and so we must consider the scale factor as well. In general, the cost of prefiltering rises with decreasing a and higher bandwidth signals.

We can reduce this cost by minifying the signal in stages in a manner akin to magnification. This approach derives its benefit by exploiting relaxed filter constraints that can be applied to a set of progressively minified signals. A key observation to be made here is that the narrow slice of the spectrum that falls below $f_c = .5a$ will ultimately span the entire baseband bandwidth in the output. It is important that this frequency band remain uncorrupted as it grows in size with each successive stage. As we shall see, this may be achieved by applying a series of filters with increasingly tighter cutoff constraints in each stage of minification.

The progressive minification that we consider downsamples the input by a factor of two in each stage. For notational convenience, we refer to the frequency band between $-f_c$ and f_c as B_0. With each successive minification stage i, B_0 doubles in size to become B_i with a range of $0 \le |f| < 2^i f_c$. In order to prevent any degradation in B_i, ideal passband and stopband responses must be defined over $0 \le |f| < 2^i f_c$ and $.5 - 2^i f_c < |f| \le .5$, respectively. The ideal passband prevents the attenuation of B_i while the stopband guards against aliasing by preventing frequency foldover in B_{i+1} after the signal in stage i undergoes 2:1 minification.

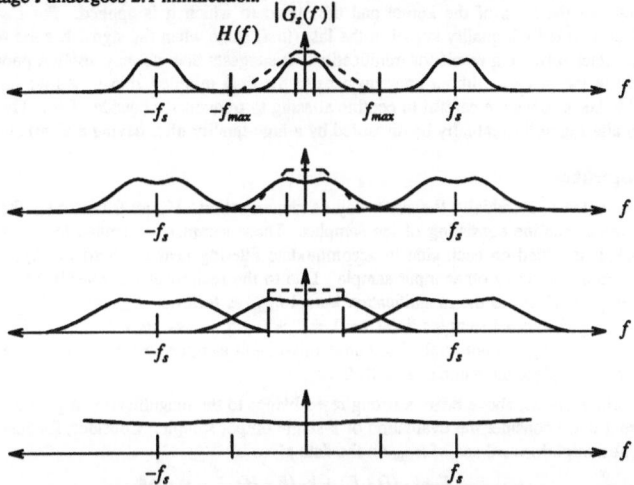

Figure 8: Spectra of a progressively minified signal.

Figure 8 demonstrates this process. It shows a sampled signal with spectrum $G_s(f)$ undergoing 8:1 minification as it passes through a succession of three 2:1 stages. The first stage applies a low-quality low-pass filter to the input. The filter, drawn with dashed lines, has a narrow passband that cuts off at $f_c = .0625$ cycles/pixel. This serves to retain B_0, the frequency band that will ultimately comprise the output spectrum. Unfortunately, the cutoff is not sharp, allowing some high frequencies to remain. That signal is then minified and resampled to produce the signal shown in the second row of Fig. 8. The high frequencies retained earlier now give rise to aliasing, as depicted by the overlapping spectral components.

Although the signal suffers from aliasing, B_1, which spans over $|f| < .125$, remains uncorrupted. This is due to our careful choice for the stopband range. By attenuating all frequency components in the range $.5 - .0625 < f \le .5$ in stage 0, the frequency components in the range $1-.125 < f \le 1$ are fully suppressed in stage 1. Therefore, frequency foldover onto the baseband from the adjacent replicas centered at $f = \pm 1$ have no effect on B_1. That signal is then prefiltered in stage 1 with a filter having ideal passband and stopband responses over $0 \le f < .125$ and $.5-.125 < f \le .5$, respectively. After scale reduction, aliasing is again present in the signal, as depicted in the third row of the figure. However, frequency foldover is now limited to the range $|f| > .25$, leaving B_2 untampered. Finally, a filter having a sharp cutoff at $f = .25$ is applied to retain B_2 before it doubles in size to become B_3, the final output spectrum.

In the example given above, three stages were necessary to achieve an overall eight-fold minification. The total cost of prefiltering is $O(MN_0 + .5MN_1 + .25MN_2)$, where N_i refers to the N_i-point kernel used in stage i. Collectively, these kernels comprise the multi-stage filter used to bandlimit the input and intermediate signals. The computational savings of using a multi-stage filter in this progressive approach is due to the fact that $N_0 < N_1 < N_2$, i.e., the smallest kernels are applied in the earliest stages. This proves to be cheaper than direct convolution with a single wide kernel having extent N_2/a (with $f_c = .5a$). For K minification stages, the cost of using a multi-stage filter is $O(\sum_{i=0}^{K-1} .5^i MN_i)$. This is particularly attractive for large-scale minification, where more stages induce more savings.

Several observations can be made about this process. First, the most relaxed constraints on the low-pass filter occur in the first stage of processing. Any low-quality filter may be applied as long as it has good response over the narrow passband and stopband ranges. Note that the filter is considered to be low-quality only in the sense that it has a wide transition band. As the passband and stopband regions become wider with each successive stage, the transition band becomes narrower until finally, the filter must have a sharp cutoff.

A second observation is that this process is the dual of that for magnification. Whereas the signal grows and the kernel size decreases with each successive stage of magnification, the opposite is true for minification. This maintains a desirable balance between the sizes of the kernel and the signal to which it is applied. For instance, minification (magnification) applies a wide high-quality kernel in the last (first) stage when the signal has the fewest samples. At first glance, this is a rather surprising result for minification. It suggests that we may apply a poor filter and thereby tolerate aliasing early in the process without consequences to the final minified signal. As we have already demonstrated, this is possible because we are careful to confine aliasing to frequencies outside of B_i. Those frequency components degraded by aliasing will eventually be discarded by a high-quality filter having a sharp cutoff.

3.2. Minification Algorithm

Minification is implemented in essentially the same way as magnification. Figure 9 illustrates the minification algorithm applied to an input scanline consisting of ten samples. Those samples are copied to a working buffer, where padding (shown shaded) is added on each side to accommodate filtering near the borders. The minification kernel $h_{min}(x)$ is centered directly on every other input sample. Due to the reciprocal relationship between the spatial and frequency domains, h_{min} is related to the magnification kernel h_{mag} as follows: $h_{min}(x) = .5h_{mag}(x/2)$. Since h_{min} is now twice as wide as h_{mag}, its kernel samples lie at $x = 0, \pm 1, \pm 3, \pm 5, \ldots$ as opposed to $x = 0, \pm .5, \pm 1.5, \pm 2.5, \ldots$ as in Fig. 3. This explains why h_{min} is not applied to consecutive input samples in Fig. 9. For instance, samples $B, D, E, F,$ and H, are filtered to replace the value of E with E'.

The minification algorithm shown above bears a strong resemblance to the magnification algorithm depicted in Fig. 7. This becomes apparent if we consider the evaluation of a single output sample. Consider, for instance, the computation of E' above. The straightforward use of h_{min} on the data gives us:

$$ E' = \frac{E + k_1(D+F) + k_2(B+H)}{2} = \frac{E + DF}{2} $$

where DF is the output of the magnification algorithm applied to samples $B, D, F,$ and H. This result shows that h_{min} differs only slightly from h_{mag}. Since h_{mag} is centered at odd addresses in between input samples, it does not apply $k_0 = 1$. The application of h_{mag} therefore only accounts for the weighting of samples $B, D, F,$ and H. The central data sample E must be added explicitly. That sum is divided by two because the weights applied by h_{mag} are not appropriate for minification, i.e., recall that $h_{min} = .5h_{mag}$.

These observations allow us to recast minification as a variation of the magnification algorithm. Since we simply want to average the even-addressed input elements with the interpolated results of the odd-addressed elements, only a slight modification to the algorithm shown in Fig. 7 need be done. This implies that minification can be implemented with the same software/hardware that is used to realize magnification. The resulting minification algorithm is illustrated in Fig. 10.

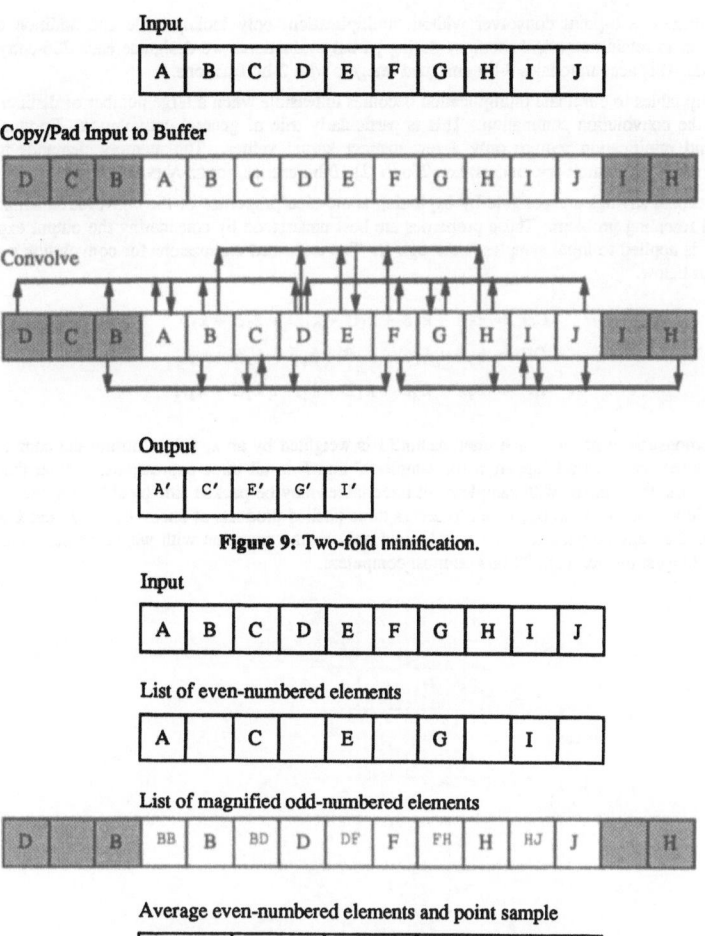

Input

A	B	C	D	E	F	G	H	I	J

Copy/Pad Input to Buffer

D	C	B	A	B	C	D	E	F	G	H	I	J	J	I	H

Convolve

D	C	B	A	B	C	D	E	F	G	H	I	J	J	I	H

Output

A′	C′	E′	G′	I′

Figure 9: Two-fold minification.

Input

A	B	C	D	E	F	G	H	I	J

List of even-numbered elements

A	C	E	G	I

List of magnified odd-numbered elements

D		B	BB	B	BD	D	DF	F	FH	H	HJ	J			H

Average even-numbered elements and point sample

(A+BB)/2	(C+BD)/2	(E+DF)/2	(G+FH)/2	(I+HJ)/2

Figure 10: Two-fold minification using magnification.

3.3. Fast Convolution

The most time-consuming operation in image scaling is convolution. Although the use of multi-stage filters helps reduce this cost, the core multiply-add operation remains costly. In this section, we describe an efficient means for implementing convolution using lookup table operations. For convenience, our discussion will assume that we are convolving 8-bit data with a 6-point kernel.

A 6-point kernel has only three kernel values: k_1, k_2, and k_3. Since each kernel value k_i can be applied to an integer in the range [0, 255], we may precompute their products and store them in three lookup tables tab_i, for $1 \leq i \leq 3$. The product of data sample s with weight k_i now reduces to a simple lookup table access, e.g., $tab_i[s]$. This makes it possible to implement a 6-point convolver without multiplication; only lookup table and addition operations are necessary. In order to retain numerical accuracy during partial evaluations, we designate each 256-entry lookup table to be 10-bits wide. This accommodates 8-bit unsigned integers with 2-bit fractions.

The use of lookup tables to eliminate multiplication becomes unfeasible when a large number of distinct kernel values are required in the convolution summation. This is particularly true of general convolution. Fortunately, two-fold magnification and minification require only a few distinct kernel values. The memory demands to support the corresponding lookup tables are very modest, i.e., $256(N/2)$ 10-bit entries, for an N-point kernel.

Further computational savings are possible by exploiting some nice properties of the convolution summation for our special two-fold rescaling problem. These properties are best understood by considering the output expressions after a 6-point kernel is applied to input samples A through H. The expanded expressions for convolution output CD, DE, and EF are given below.

$$CD = k_3A + k_2B + k_1C + k_1D + k_2E + k_3F$$

$$DE = k_3B + k_2C + k_1D + k_1E + k_2F + k_3G$$

$$EF = k_3C + k_2D + k_1E + k_1F + k_2G + k_3H$$

These results demonstrate a pattern: each input sample s is weighted by all k_i values during the course of advancing the kernel across the data. This is apparent for samples C and F in all three expressions. Rather than individually accessing each of the three tables with sample s, all three tables may be packed side-by-side into one wide table having 30 bits in width. This permits one index to access three packed products at once: k_3s, k_2s, and k_1s. The largest number of tables that may be packed together is limited only by the precision with which we store the products and the width of the longest integer, e.g., 32 bits on most computers.

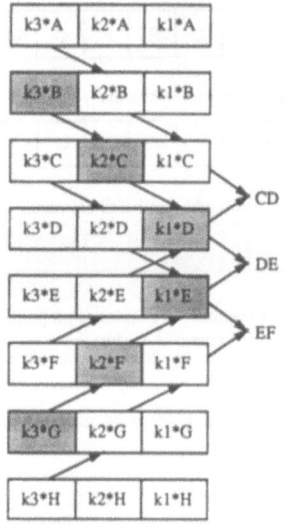

Figure 11: A fast convolver.

Figure 11 shows table entries for input samples A through H. Three 10-bit fields are used to pack three fixed point products. Each field is shown to be involved in some convolution summation, as denoted by the arrows, to compute output CD, DE (shown shaded), and EF. The organization of the data in this manner not only reduces the number of table accesses, but it also lends itself to a fast convolution algorithm requiring only shift and add operations. The downward (upward) arrows denote a sequence of right-shift (left-shift) and addition operations, beginning with the table entry for A (D). Let fwd and rev be two integers that store both sets of results. The first few shift-add operations produce fwd and rev with the following fields.

	fwd			rev	
k_3B	k_3A+k_2B	k_2A+k_1B	k_3E+k_2D	k_2E+k_1D	k_1E
k_3C	k_3B+k_2C	$k_3A+k_2B+k_1C$	$k_3F+k_2E+k_1D$	k_2F+k_1E	k_1F
k_3D	k_3C+k_2D	$k_3B+k_2C+k_1D$	$k_3G+k_2F+k_1E$	k_2G+k_1F	k_1G
k_3E	k_3D+k_2E	$k_3C+k_2D+k_1E$	$k_3H+k_2G+k_1F$	k_2H+k_1G	k_1H

Notice that the low-order 10-bit fields of fwd contain half of the convolution summation necessary to compute the output. The other half is contained in the high-order 10-bit fields of rev. By simply adding both fields together, the output values are generated.

This scheme is hampered by one complication: addition may cause one field to spill into the next, thereby corrupting its value. This will happen if a field value exceeds the range $[0, 2^8 - 1]$. We modify the fast convolver by adding a .25 bias to the k_2 field. The bias is removed from the computation when we add the low-order 10-bit field of fwd to the high-order 10-bit field of rev.

Operating with symmetric kernels has already been shown to reduce the number of arithmetic operations: $N/2$ multiplies and $N-1$ for an N-point kernel. This algorithm, however, does far better. It requires no multiplication (other than that needed to initialize lut), and a total of four adds per output sample, for a 6-point kernel. Furthermore, no distinction is made between 2-, 4-, and 6-point kernels because they are all packed into the same integer. That is, a 4-point kernel is actually implemented as a 6-point kernel with $k_3 = 0$. Since there is no additional penalty for using a 6-point kernel, we are induced to use a superior (6-point) filter at low cost. Larger kernels can be assembled by cascading integers together.

4. SUMMARY AND CONCLUSIONS

We have presented an algorithm to accelerate the scaling of digital images. Since scaling is an exercise in convolution, our goal has been to relieve the computational bottleneck by reducing the number of convolution operations and optimizing the evaluation of those that remain. In the process, we have also derived optimal kernels.

The algorithm is motivated by the observation that filtering constraints change as an image is progressively scaled towards the desired resolution. At each stage of processing, a different kernel is used to reflect these changing filtering requirements. The use of these multi-stage filter kernels is less costly than direct convolution. We have demonstrated that as the size of the input grows, we avoid prohibitively expensive convolution by turning to smaller kernels. The dual is true as well: as the input becomes increasingly decimated, the kernel size grows. This maintains a desirable balance between the kernel size and the signal size, i.e., large kernels are limited to small signals.

We have shown that the multi-stage filter has many desirable properties when the scale change across each stage is limited to a factor of two. Since each kernel is now guaranteed to be symmetric, its frequency response can be defined by a simple closed-form expression $H(f)$. This permits us to derive optimal kernels by solving for the unknown kernel samples that minimize the difference between $H(f)$ and the ideal filter. Optimal N-point kernels for even values of $N \le 8$ have been given.

A very interesting relationship is shown to exist between two-fold magnification and minification. We have shown that two-fold minification is achieved by averaging the even-addressed input elements with the interpolated results of the odd-addressed elements. This result implies that minification can be implemented with the same software/hardware used to realize magnification. Scale factors that are not powers of two are realized by scaling to the closest power of two and then applying direct convolution.

The final result of this paper has focused on optimizing the evaluation of the convolution summation. We achieve large performance gains by packing all weighted instances of an input sample into one 32-bit integer and then using these integers in a series of shift-add operations to compute the output. In this manner, we essentially mimic a pipelined vector processor on a general 32-bit computer. This approach will likely find increased use with the forthcoming generation of 64-bit computers. The additional bits will permit us to handle wider kernels at finer precision.

5. ACKNOWLEDGEMENTS

This work was supported in part by grants from the National Science Foundation (IRI-9157260) and The City University of New York PSC-CUNY Research Award Program (#663297).

6. REFERENCES

Chin F, Choi A, and Luo Y (1992) "Optimal Generating Kernels for Image Pyramids by Piecewise Fitting," *IEEE Trans. Pattern Analysis and Machine Intelligence*, vol. 14, no. 12, 1190-1198.

Keys RG (1981) "Cubic Convolution Interpolation for Digital Image Processing," *IEEE Trans. Acoust., Speech, Signal Process.*, vol. ASSP-29,pp. 1153-1160.

Meer P, Baugher ES, and Rosenfeld A (1987) "Frequency Domain Analysis and Synthesis of Image Pyramid Generating Kernels," *IEEE Trans. Pattern Analysis and Machine Intelligence*, vol. 9, no. 4, pp. 512-522.

Mitchell DP and Netravali AN (1988) "Reconstruction Filters in Computer Graphics," *Computer Graphics*, (SIGGRAPH '88 Proceedings), vol. 22, no. 4, pp. 221-228.

Park SK and Schowengerdt RA (1983) "Image Reconstruction by Parametric Cubic Convolution," *Computer Vision, Graphics, and Image Processing*, vol. 23, pp. 258-272.

Vaidyanathan PP (1993) *Multirate Systems and Filter Banks*, Prentice Hall, Englewood Cliffs, NJ.

Wolberg G (1990) *Digital Image Warping*, IEEE Computer Society Press, Los Alamitos, CA.

George Wolberg is currently an Assistant Professor in the Computer Science department at the City College of New York / CUNY, and an Adjunct Assistant Professor at Columbia University. He received the B.S. and M.S. degrees in Electrical Engineering from The Cooper Union, New York, NY, in 1985, and the Ph.D. degree in Computer Science from Columbia University, New York, NY, in 1990. During the summers between 1983 and 1989, he worked at AT&T Bell Laboratories, IBM Watson Research Center, and Fantastic Animation Machine. He spent the summer of 1990 at the Electrotechnical Laboratory in Tsukuba, Ibaraki, Japan, as a selected participant in the Summer Institute in Japan, a research program sponsored by the U.S. National Science Foundation and by the Science and Technology Agency of Japan.

Dr. Wolberg is the author of *Digital Image Warping* (IEEE Computer Society Press, 1990) and the recipient of a 1991 NSF Presidential Young Investigator Award. His research interests include image processing, computer graphics, and computer vision. He is a member of Tau Beta Pi, Eta Kappa Nu, and the IEEE Computer Society.

Address: Department of Computer Science
City College of New York
138th St. at Convent Ave., Rm. R8/206
New York, NY 10031
USA

email: wolberg@gemini.engr.ccny.cuny.edu
wolberg@cs.columbia.edu

Henry Massalin is currently a research scientist at Microunity Systems Engineering, Inc., in Sunnyvale, California. He received the B.S. and M.S. degrees in Electrical Engineering from The Cooper Union, New York, NY, in 1984, and the Ph.D. degree in Computer Science from Columbia University, New York, NY, in 1992. His dissertation concerns the structuring of an operating system kernel that creates executable machine code at runtime as a means of greatly improving its performance. His prototype operating system kernel - The Synthesis Kernel - runs on an experimental hardware platform that includes real-time audio and video input and output devices, and demonstates order- of-magnitue performance gains over comparable, traditionally-structured systems. He has taught Senior Projects Lab and Advanced Programming Methods at The Cooper Union during the semesters between 1986 and 1990.

Dr. Massalin is the recipient of the NCR Stakeholder Award for exellence in innovation, the IBM special Scholarship in I/O systems, and the USENIX scholarship. He is a member of Eta Kappa Nu. His other interests include computer music, radio-controlled cars, koalas, and giving people piggy-back rides.

Address: Microunity Systems Engineering
255 Caspian Dr
Sunnyvale, CA 94089
USA

email: qua@microunity.com
henry@cs.columbia.edu

A Method of Dynamic Image Montage and Simple Scene Model Construction for Landscape Simulation

Yutaka Soyama, Takami Yasuda, Shigeki Yokoi, and Jun-ichiro Toriwaki

Abstract

In this paper, first we present a method to generate dynamic images of a montage consisting of natural scene and images of newly planned constructions. Secondly, we propose a method to construct a simple scene model for landscape simulation basing upon video images of real scenes. The dynamic image montage system should include the dynamic image analysis such as extracting positions and directions of the video camera from sequential video images. It allows the dynamic image montage to be created efficiently. Furthermore, using the proposed simple scene model, we confirmed that this model could easily compute the positional relationship between each objects in the scene and synthesized montage images were realistic enough.

Key words : landscape simulation, dynamic image analysis, optical flow, montage, scene model construction

1. Introduction

Landscape simulation in its first stage was performed with users' satisfaction by line drawing objects alone, and compensation of its drawback primarily relies on users' imagination. Nowadays images for landscape simulation are required to be more real. Remarkable progress in computer graphics has made it possible to satisfy such requirement. In fact landscape simulation is expected to be applicable to present three dimensional (3D) pictures of newly planned constructions to users and to perform environmental assessments [Nakamae 1991]. We have developed a landscape simulation system for estimating effects of large-scale constructions such as an electric power line's tower in the electric power engineering.

In this paper, first we present a method to generate dynamic images of a montage consisting of natural scene and images of newly planned constructions. Secondly, we propose a method to construct a simple scene model for landscape simulation basing upon video images of real scenes.

The dynamic image montage can be synthesized with an object image to be planned generated by computer graphics and video images including natural scene. A conventional landscape simulation uses a still picture montage technique. This is a technique to synthesize an image of construction image and a still picture for the background, and can create realistic montage images [Nakamae 1986]. Our method is developed on the basis of the still montage technique. This technique needs to modify both the camera position where a background picture is taken and a view point of computer world when an image of planned objects is generated. Applying this technique to dynamic images, we must make this modification at every frame. This means a dynamic image montage is too time consuming and almost impossible. To overcome such difficulty we propose an automatic method to obtain the camera position at each video frame. It is possible that a dynamic image montage is created efficiently using our system. Additionally we apply this dynamic image montage to electric power line's towers, to make sure its usefulness. For example, we confirm that where the constructions are seen first, and how their forms change.

For landscape simulation with computer graphics, we need a scene model of terrain, trees and so on, in addition to models of newly planned constructions. One conventional method is that we make images of all objects by computer graphics. Another method uses a digital terrain model which is derived from aerial photographs and construction models in the computer world. In the former method, it is so difficult to create natural objects like trees as they are. In the latter method, several problems are mentioned including that unnatural images are generated when their view points are near the ground. A growth model of trees was reported as a natural objects modeling technique and may be applied to the former problem [Aono 1984]. For the latter one, some improvements were reported to get more natural images using high resolution aerial photographs when view points were near the ground [Kaneda 1990].

The objective of our study is to construct a simple scene model that may generate appropriate images when the view point is near the ground. In this paper, we propose a method to construct a 2.5-dimensional (2.5D) simple scene model using two pictures which are taken from different positions on the ground. The "2.5D" means that, although it does not have complete 3D information, we can obtain approximated positional relations among the objects in the scene by the model. This simple model has two advantage: One is that a scene model itself is created easily, and the other is that a rendering process using this model is remarkably simple. By applying the proposed method to a natural scene taken from a car, we confirmed that the 2.5D scene model could easily compute the positional relationship between each object in the scene and synthesized montage images were realistic enough. We also generated a stereo pair of images and animations by using this scene model in order to get more effective and impressive images for landscape simulation.

We describe the dynamic image montage and the construction of simple scene model in chapter 2 and 3, respectively.

2. Dynamic image montage

In our system, the procedure of making a montage video can be summarized as follows (Fig.1).

(Step 1) A video of actual landscape is prepared. We use in the experiment a video taken from a car running highland. Each frame of the video is digitized in order to store in computer memory.

(Step 2) 3D models of constructions are created in a computer using planned drawings of the constructions. <Construction modeling section>

(Step 3) The video image is analyzed in order to obtain the camera position and direction change from frame to frame. <Dynamic image analysis section>

(Step 4) Images of constructions are generated by computer graphics using camera information acquired in (Step 3). A montage video is created by synthesized by integrating their computer graphics images with actual video scenes. <Image montage section>

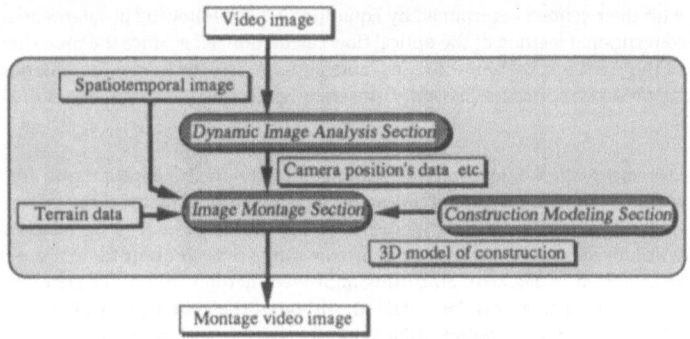

Fig.1   The overview of the dynamic image montage

Section 2.1 describes a procedure of dynamic image analysis. In sections 2.2 and 2.3, construction modeling and image montage are briefly explained, respectively. A resulting example of montage video using our method is provided in section 2.4.

2.1 Dynamic image analysis

In order to integrate an actual picture and a computer graphics image into a scene including images of constructions from a computer model, we have to know camera position and the direction of the actual pictures. Camera positions and directions usually change from frame to frame in a dynamic sequence of images, therefore we need to analyze them efficiently. Our system extracts camera positions and directions from video images which are used as the background. Video images used here are taken from a car running on a road without a special equipment such as a quakeproof stand. Therefore the video images include motion of the car, tremor due to rough road surface and shaking for car suspensions. Here we deal with video images which have no moving objects like a car running in the opposite lane.

Dynamic image analysis section consists of two parts: calculation of optical flows on the basis of the template matching, and calculation of camera movement using obtained optical flows.

2.1.1 Calculation of optical flows

In this section we describe first a conventional method of optical flow calculation, and then present an improved method to calculate more precise optical flows.

For an optical flow calculation we employ a template matching method. First of all, we cut out a rectangle region called the template from the n-th frame of the successive video images whose center point is $(c_x^{(n)}, c_y^{(n)})$. Template center points $(c_x^{(1)}, c_y^{(1)})$ in the first frame are chosen automatically by thresholding the outputs of edge detectors. For the (n+1)th frame, the most similar part to the template is found according to the following Equation (1). That is, we find the $(v_x^{(n)}, v_y^{(n)})$ which minimizes the following square error E_n,

$$E_n(v_x^{(n)}, v_y^{(n)}) = \sum_i \sum_j (L^{(n+1)}(i + v_x^{(n)}, j + v_y^{(n)}) - L^{(n)}(i, j))^2 \tag{1}$$

$$n=1,2,3,\ldots\ldots$$

where summation is performed for all i's and j's on the template, $(v_x^{(n)}, v_y^{(n)})$ is the difference of the template position between the n-th frame and the (n+1)th frame, and $L^{(n)}(x,y)$ is the intensity at the position (x,y) on the n-th frame.

Then, the center point of the template on the (n+1)th frame, $(c_x^{(n+1)}, c_y^{(n+1)})$, is given as follows:

$$c_x^{(n+1)} = c_x^{(n)} + v_x^{(n)} \tag{2}$$
$$c_y^{(n+1)} = c_y^{(n)} + v_y^{(n)}$$

Effects of the change of the shape of templates with the movement of a camera is reduced by updating the templates with their centers determined by Equation (2). The following problems arise when applying the above conventional method of the optical flow calculation. First, since the precision of $(v_x^{(n)}, v_y^{(n)})$ (a difference of the position between the n-th frame and the (n+1)th frame) in Equation (1) is of one pixel unit, quantization error occurs. Secondly, the error is accumulated gradually as the frame goes on in Equation (2).

Therefore, we developed a new improved method to get highly precise optical flows. For simplicity, let us consider the case of a one dimensional image. In the conventional method, the center point $c^{(n+1)}$ of the template on the (n+1)th frame is selected so that the square error $E^{(n+1)}$ becomes minimum as in Fig.2(a). In our improved method, we use an approximating curve in order to obtain a more accurate minimum error as shown in Fig.2(b). Since this improved method would not generate quantization error, more precise optical flows can be obtained. Although the center point of the template on the (n+1)th frame $c^{(n+1)}$ is found by Equation (3), it is hardly possible that $c^{(n+1)}$ exists on a pixel grid.

$$c^{(n+1)} = c^{(n)} + v^{(n)} \tag{3}$$

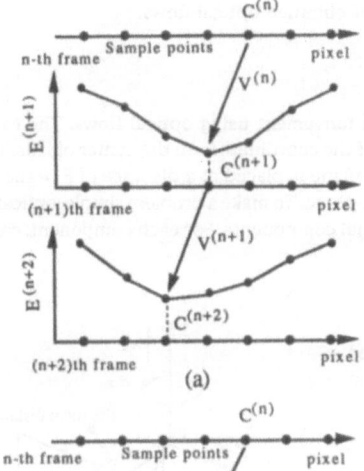

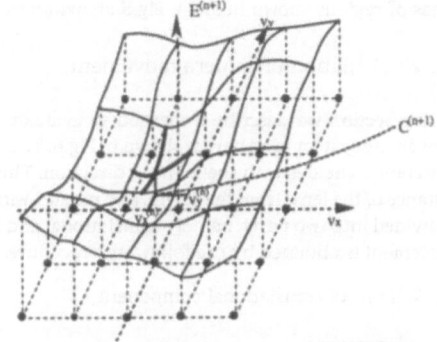

Fig.3 Approximating surface of the estimation error and its local minimum $(v_x^{(n)}, v_y^{(n)})$

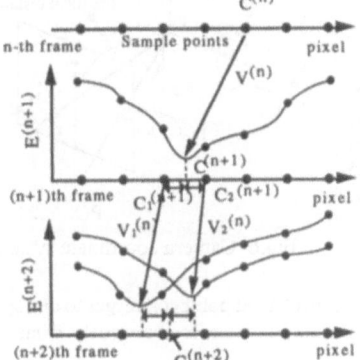

(b)

Fig.2 Optical flow calculation

(a)Conventional matching process

(b)Proposed highly precise matching process

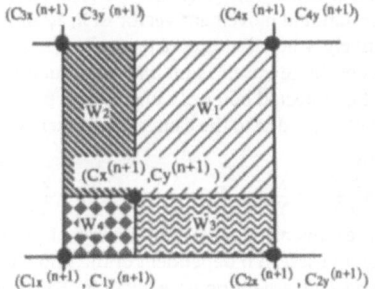

Fig.4 Nearest neighboring points and their weight values for 2D interpolation

However, a template must be on a pixel grid to execute a template matching calculation on the (n+1)th frame. To solve the problem, we adopt a linear interpolation method of obtaining the optical flows. The desired flow $v^{(n+1)}$ from (n+1)th frame to (n+2)th frame can be calculated by interpolating between $v_1^{(n+1)}$ and $v_2^{(n+1)}$, the optical flows of $c_1^{(n+1)}$ and $c_2^{(n+1)}$ which are the two nearest pixel grids from $c^{(n+1)}$.

We can easily extend this method to a two dimensional image. Fitting an approximating curved surface to the error values on the image as shown in Fig.3, the next center point $c^{(n+1)}$ and the optical flow $(v_x^{(n+1)}, v_y^{(n+1)})$ can be found which minimizes the error value in the way as in one dimensional case. The next optical flow $(v_x^{(n+1)}, v_y^{(n+1)})$ is derived by using a linear interpolation. This process is almost the same as in one dimensional case except that four nearest pixel grids from $c^{(n+1)}$ should be needed. We represent these four pixels as $(c_{1x}^{(n+1)}, c_{1y}^{(n+1)})$, $(c_{2x}^{(n+1)}, c_{2y}^{(n+1)})$, $(c_{3x}^{(n+1)}, c_{3y}^{(n+1)})$ and $(c_{4x}^{(n+1)}, c_{4y}^{(n+1)})$. After calculating the flows $(v_{1x}^{(n+1)}, v_{1y}^{(n+1)})$, $(v_{2x}^{(n+1)}, v_{2y}^{(n+1)})$, $(v_{3x}^{(n+1)}, v_{3y}^{(n+1)})$ and $(v_{4x}^{(n+1)}, v_{4y}^{(n+1)})$ for the four pixels, the desired flow $(v_x^{(n+1)}, v_y^{(n+1)})$ is obtained in Equation (4).

$$v_x^{(n+1)} = \frac{w_1 \cdot v_{1x}^{(n+1)} + w_2 \cdot v_{2x}^{(n+1)} + w_3 \cdot v_{3x}^{(n+1)} + w_4 \cdot v_{4x}^{(n+1)}}{w_1 + w_2 + w_3 + w_4} \qquad (4)$$

$$v_y^{(n+1)} = \frac{w_1 \cdot v_{1y}^{(n+1)} + w_2 \cdot v_{2y}^{(n+1)} + w_3 \cdot v_{3y}^{(n+1)} + w_4 \cdot v_{4y}^{(n+1)}}{w_1 + w_2 + w_3 + w_4}$$

where w_1, w_2, w_3, and w_4 are weight coefficients which are determined basing upon the corresponding areas of regions shown in Fig.4. Fig.5 shows an example of obtained optical flows.

2.1.2 Calculation of camera movement

In this section we describe a method to evaluate camera movement using optical flows. The camera coordinate system used here is shown in Fig.6. The origin of the coordinate is on the center of lens. Y-axis direction coincides with the viewing direction. The image plane is placed at a distance of F (= the focal distance of the lens) from the origin, and parallel with the XZ-plane. To make a problem simple, optical flow is divided into two parts, namely translational and rotational components. For each component, camera movement is obtained by the following procedure.

(1) Analysis of translational component

A point P(X,Y,Z) in the world coordinate system is projected onto the point p(x,y) in the screen coordinate system in Equation (5) (Fig.6),

$$x = \frac{X}{Y}F \quad , \quad y = \frac{Z}{Y}F \qquad (5)$$

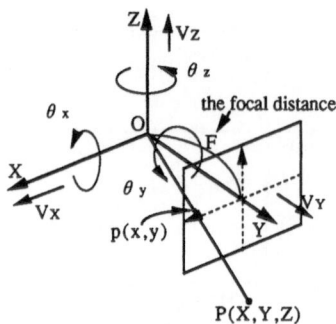

Fig.6 Camera coordinate system

Let us assume that V_x, V_y and V_z are X, Y, and Z components of the translational movement vector in X, Y, and Z directions, respectively, when the camera moves in translation with the world coordinate axis in a unit time (= a frame interval = 1/30 sec.). The projected point p(x,y) moves to p'(x',y') expressed by Equation (6) due to the camera movement with (V_x, V_y, V_z) in time t.

$$x' = \frac{X'}{Y'}F = \frac{X - V_x t}{Y - V_y t}F \quad , \quad y' = \frac{Z'}{Y'}F = \frac{Z - V_z t}{Y - V_y t}F \qquad (6)$$

When the movement of P(X,Y,Z) consists of translation only, its projected point converges to one specific point on the screen independent of the initial location of point P and determined uniquely from (V_x, V_y, V_z). This convergent point is given by Equation (7).

$$(x,y) = \left(\frac{V_x}{V_y}F, \frac{V_z}{V_y}F \right) \qquad (7)$$

This convergent point is called vanishing point [Nakatani 1980]. Equation (7) is derived from Equation (6) when t reaches infinity or minus infinity.

Therefore the velocity ratio of the camera is obtained from the vanishing point position in Equation (7). If there is more than one known point in the scene, all components of the translation vector can be derived by substituting Equation (7) into Equation (6).

(2) Analysis of rotational component

Let us assume that θ_x, θ_y and θ_z are clockwise rotation angles of the camera in a unit time with respect to X, Y, and Z axis, respectively. The following Equation (8) describes an approximate coordinate transformation corresponding to the camera rotation.

$$\begin{pmatrix} X' \\ Y' \\ Z' \end{pmatrix} = \begin{pmatrix} 1 & \theta_z & -\theta_y \\ -\theta_z & 1 & \theta_x \\ \theta_y & -\theta_x & 1 \end{pmatrix} \begin{pmatrix} X \\ Y \\ Z \end{pmatrix} \qquad (8)$$

where $(X,Y,Z)^T$ and $(X',Y',Z')^T$ are positions of point P before and after the rotation, respectively.

A projected point p'(x',y') after the rotation is given by following Equation (9) using both Equations (5) and (8):

$$x' = \frac{X'}{Y'}F = \frac{X + \theta_z \cdot Y - \theta_y \cdot Z}{-\theta_z \cdot X + Y + \theta_x \cdot Z}F = \frac{x + \theta_z \cdot F - \theta_y \cdot y}{-\theta_z \cdot x + F + \theta_x \cdot y}F \qquad (9)$$

$$y' = \frac{Z'}{Y'}F = \frac{\theta_y \cdot X - \theta_x \cdot Y + Z}{-\theta_z \cdot X + Y + \theta_x \cdot Z}F = \frac{\theta_y \cdot x - \theta_x \cdot F + y}{-\theta_z \cdot x + F + \theta_x \cdot y}F$$

Assuming that the camera movement includes only rotational component, a movement vector $(\delta x, \delta y)$ is related to the screen coordinates as follows [Kaneda 1990].

$$\delta x = x' - x = \theta_z \cdot F - \theta_y \cdot y - \frac{1}{F}(-\theta_z \cdot x + \theta_x \cdot y)x \quad (10)$$

$$\delta y = y' - y = -\theta_x \cdot F + \theta_y \cdot y - \frac{1}{F}(-\theta_z \cdot x + \theta_x \cdot y)y$$

where F is assumed to be large enough compared to $\theta_z x$ or $\theta_x y$.

(3) Analysis method when both components are included.

The optical flows usually consist of both translational and rotational components. Assuming that two rotational components θ_x and θ_z are to be zero, for the simplicity, the camera movement consists of translation components and rotational component θ_y. If we could rotate the optical flows $-\theta_y$ exactly in Equation (10), the resultant camera movement includes only translation and the optical flows converge to a vanishing point. Under this assumption, we can derive the convergent point in the following manner.

As shown in Fig.7 candidates for the convergent point or the vanishing point should be the intersections of the extracted optical flows. A candidate of the vanishing point (Pv_x, Pv_y) is derived by the following equation.

$$(Pv_x, Pv_y) = \frac{\sum_k (Px_k, Py_k) \times w_k}{\sum_k w_k} \quad (11)$$

where $w_k = |\delta x1_k \cdot \delta y2_k - \delta x2_k \cdot \delta y1_k|$ and (Px_k, Py_k) is the position of the k-th intersections of extended optical flows.

To specify the vanishing point, the following evaluating function is applied to all candidates (see Fig.8).

$$E_c = \frac{\sum_n (L_n |\delta x1_n \cdot \delta Pv_{yn} - \delta y1_n \cdot \delta Pv_{xn}|)}{\sum_n L_n} \quad (12)$$

where $L_n = \sqrt{\delta x1_n^2 + \delta y1_n^2}$ and n denotes the n-th optical flow.

The point minimizing E_c concerning θ_y is selected as the vanishing point. Actually, if we choose an optical flow of an object far from the camera position, translation components in the camera movement can be ignored since $X \gg V_x$, $Y \gg V_y$, and $Z \gg V_z$ in Equation (6). Therefore, using such optical flow we can obtain relatively accurate rotational components from Equation (10). The translation components are then derived by the optical flows of objects near the camera after suppressing the rotational movement obtained above.

The whole procedure to estimate the camera movement is summarized as Fig.9.

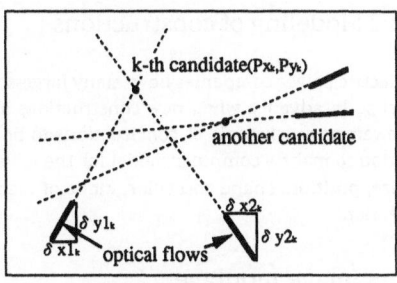

Fig.7   Candidates for the vanishing point

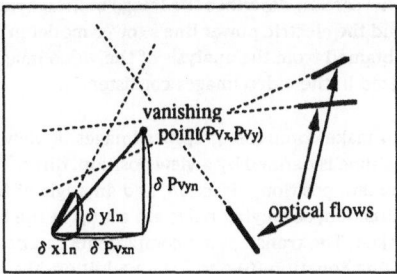

Fig.8   Estimation of the vanishing point

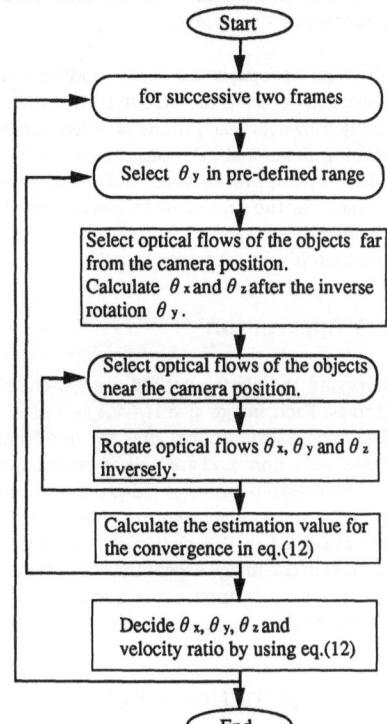

Fig.9   Flowchart of calculating camera
movement vectors

2.2 Modeling of constructions

Electric power companies have many large-scale constructions. It is usually important to evaluate landscape in advance when new constructions are planned. Here we use electric power transmission line towers as an example of constructions to be built. Several components should be taken into consideration to make a computer model for the tower, such as locations of planned towers, tower's component size, position, shape and color, kinds of insulators and their connection positions, and cable's weight, tension.

2.3 Image montage

This section describes the image montage method using results of video images' analysis in section 2.1 and the electric power line's tower model in section 2.2. The positions and directions of the camera are obtained from the analysis of the video images. Computer graphics images of towers should be synthesized in the video images consistently.

To make computer graphics images, a view volume is supposed in the tower model world. The view volume is defined by a view position, direction, and an angle of field. These parameters correspond to a camera position, direction, and an angle of field in the real world. To determine a camera position and direction, surveying poles are set up at the known positions in the real 3D world and video images are taken. The translational components can be obtained from V_x/V_y , V_z/V_y and the known pole positions using Equation (6) and (7). In addition, the camera position is found successively from frame to frame after the initial position of the camera is given. The direction of the view volume is also decided for every pair of successive frames after rotational components (θ_x, θ_y, θ_z) are calculated and the initial camera direction is given.

The next process is the depth modification. For example, this modification is needed in such case as towers' lower parts are hidden by front hills. The depth of towers from the camera position is calculated easily. However, each frame of video images does not have depth information so that information concerning positional relationship should be added for synthesizing the images. Then, pseudo depth is added to the first of video images in order to decide the rough positional relationship on the video images. For the successive frames, pseudo depths are applied semiautomatically. Pseudo depths are not necessarily too strict, if they are enough to decide the rough positional relationship between the divided subregions and the tower models.

2.4 Application

Applying the above method, we generate about 24 seconds montage video images which have 711 frames. Each image size is 640x480 pixels with 8 bits for each of red, green and blue components. Required computational time for one frame is 62.8 seconds and 47.4 seconds (CPU time) for optical flows' detections and analysis of camera movement on SGI IRIS 4D 320 VGX, respectively. An example of the synthesized montage video is shown in Fig.10. If the calculation of camera positions and directions fails, fluctuation between the video image and CG image appear. However, such marked fluctuation is not observed in this example. This example is the simplest one because the pseudo depths are the nearest in the image except the sky and none of segments newly appear with the movement of a camera. If new segments appear in a frame and the rough positional relationship changes, we must restart the depth modification process from that frame.

3. Construction of simple scene model

For landscape simulation with computer graphics, we need a scene model of terrain, trees and so on, in addition to models of newly planned constructions. We developed a method to construct a 2.5D simple scene model using two pictures. The strategy here is that objects in the scene are approximated by planes. Section 3.1 describes a construction of simple scene model. Section 3.2 provides examples of drawing.

3.1 2.5D scene model

An overview of a 2.5D simple scene model construction is described in this section. The 2.5D simple scene model is generated from only two pictures which are taken at different positions on the ground and camera parameters (the camera position (x,y,z) and the direction (θ_x, θ_y, θ_z)). We use a plane called "panel" for modeling objects in the scene such as hills and roads. "Panel" is an approximating plane of object in the scene shown in Fig.11.

\<Overview of a 2.5D simple scene model construction\>

(Step 1) Region division: One of the two input images is selected for the "basic image". We divide it into subregions which correspond to each object in the scene. Let us call this divided image "region label image". Each divided region of the "basic image" is used to determine the texture of each "panel".

(Step 2) Definition of panel planes: In order to obtain a panel plane for each subregion, three pairs of corresponding points are specified on the basic image and the other one taken by a camera as shown in Fig.12.

(Step 3) Texture mapping: Finally, we obtain the 2.5D scene model by mapping each texture on the subregions of the "basic image" to the correspondence "panel plane".

Original images used here are two frames selected from successive video images which are taken from a car running on a road. One of them is called "basic image" and the other is "image for measurements". The image size of one frame is 640x480 pixels with 8 bits for each color component; red, green and blue. The camera parameters of each frame are found by the method described in section 2.3.

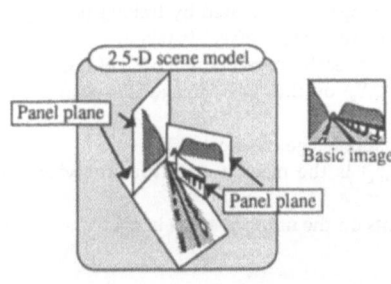

Fig.11 Conceptual illustration of 2.5 dimensional scene model

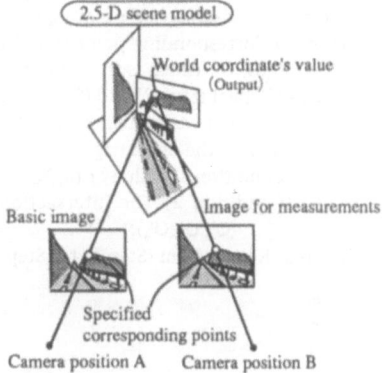

Fig.12 Definition of panel planes

(1) Region division

We apply the following region division processes to the "basic image". First, each pixel color value of the "basic image" is converted to a gray value using Equation (13).

$$y_{ij}=0.30R_{ij}+0.59G_{ij}+0.11B_{ij} \qquad (13)$$

where y_{ij}, R_{ij}, G_{ij} and B_{ij} are gray, red, green and blue intensity of a pixel (i,j), respectively.

Second, the median filter is applied to the gray image for noise reduction. Thirdly, the gray image is divided into regions by iterating region merging operation. The algorithm of iterative region merging is as follows: in the first stage, every pixel is regarded as different region. If a difference between the mean intensity in a region and the intensity of a neighboring pixel is less than a threshold, the pixel is merged to the region, otherwise not [Tomita 1979]. After this processing, a labeled image and an averaged gray value image are obtained. Here, the labeled image is the one in which each pixel has an integer representing the label of the subregion including that pixel, and the averaged gray value image is the one such that the intensity of all pixels in the same subregion is the mean intensity value of the subregion. This process is iterated until no pixel to be merged exists. Results are corrected manually if necessary. Fig.13 shows examples of "basic image" and "region label image". As the number of region increases, the approximation of an object in the scene becomes more exact but the calculation cost of the rendering increases. In this paper, we deal with a fairly rough approximate "panel".

(2) Definition of panel planes
Each panel plane equation is calculated for an approximating plane corresponding to each region in 3D space (Fig.12). In this process, points of the "basic image" and counterparts in the "image for measurements" are input manually. Three counterpart points are obtained for each panel. Next, positions those three points in the world coordinate system are calculated for each panel using known camera parameters. After then, a panel equation is determined using them.

(3) Generation of a new picture from an arbitrary view point
The following values in the 2.5D scene model are utilized to generate a picture observed from an arbitrary view point:
* texture of the "basic image" and its camera parameters,
* "region label image" corresponding to each "panel", and
* plane equation of each "panel".

Picture generation procedure is described as follows (see Fig.14).
Here, the panel plane k corresponds to the region with the label k.
 (Step 1) An equation of a straight line l is obtained by linking a point (X,Y) on a new drawing image and the view point (O'_x, O'_y, O'_z).
 (Step 2) An intersection point (x_k, y_k, z_k) where the line l meets the panel plane k is calculated.
 (Step 3) Corresponding point (X_k, Y_k) on the "basic image" is calculated by linking (x_k, y_k, z_k) and (O_x, O_y, O_z) which is the camera position at which the "basic image" is taken.
 (Step 4) Repeat (Step 2) and (Step 3) for all panels to get each intersection. If both of the following conditions are satisfied, the color value of (X_k, Y_k) on the "basic image" is substituted for (X,Y) on the new image.
 (Condition 1) Value of (X_k, Y_k) on the "region label image" is equal to k.
 (Condition 2) The intersection point (x_k, y_k, z_k) is the nearest one from the view point (O'_x, O'_y, O'_z).
 (Step 5) Repeat from (Step 1) to (Step 4) for all points on the new projected image.

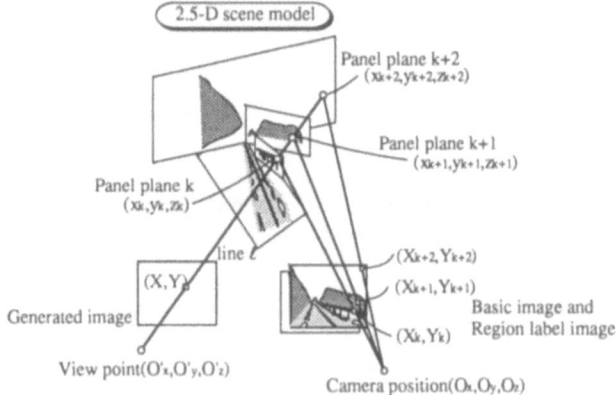

Fig.14 Illustration of new image generation algorithm

3.2 Applications

We use our 2.5D simple scene model in practical applications in order to confirm its efficacy.

(1) Montage image : Fig.15 shows an example of virtually generated montage image which would be seen at 5 meters ahead of the actual camera position for the "basic image". Since our 2.5D scene model has depth information between the planned constructions and the objects existing in the scene, a consistent montage image can be easily synthesized. In the conventional montage method, a background image does not have depth information so that information concerning positional relationship should be added for synthesizing the images. This work is so hard and time consuming when many images should be processed such as a dynamic image. In addition, the conventional montage image method can not generate an appropriate image viewed from an arbitrary position which is different from the position where the actual video is taken. By the proposed method we can obtain any montage image from an arbitrary viewing direction using the 2.5D scene model.

(2) Stereo pair of images : Fig.16 shows an example of stereo images with parallax. A stereo pair of images is sometimes effective for an observer to understand the positional relationships between the constructions and the scene. The depth of a road and a guardrail can be perceived with these stereo images.

(3) Dynamic landscape estimation : For a dynamic landscape estimation, we made a CG animation assuming that a viewing point is on a car running along a meandering driveway in highland. A few frames of the animation are shown in Fig.17. During this experiment, we understood that this model-based image generation dose not work well when the moving view point is too far from where the "basic image" is taken. It is necessary that our model should be updated by using another "basic image" when the view point moves too far from the camera position of the "basic image".

4. Conclusion

In this paper, we presented a method to synthesize dynamic image montage consisting of a video image of natural scene and a computer generated image of newly planned constructions. Additionally we proposed a method to construct a simple scene model using two pictures.

First, we considered dynamic image montage. Our system obtains the camera position from the video images by a simple method automatically, and synthesizes video images and construction images which are generated by computer consistently. We applied this dynamic image montage to constructions of electric power line's towers, and confirmed that montage video created by our system provides useful information for assessments of landscape. For example, we can confirm where the constructions are seen first, and how their forms change according to the movement of the view point.

Secondly, we proposed a method to construct a 2.5D simple scene model using two pictures which are taken from different positions on the ground. Using this scene model, we can generate images from arbitrary view points. We applied this method to generation of stereo images and the animation. Additionally in the example of montage image, we showed that it is easy to calculate depth relationship of the objects in the scene and construction models, and montage image is created so easily.

In an image made by 2.5D simple scene model gaps may be observed among "panels" as a view position moves because of the lack of texture. In this paper, we cope with this problem by a simple interpolation method. The generated image is coarse when a view point is near a "panel". More efficient and robust construction of the 2.5D scene model on the basis of more than two original pictures to overcome such gaps and to make the method applicable to synthesize a long animation remains to be studied in the future. We should also investigate the possibility of automatizing interactive works in our model construction.

Acknowledgments

We wish to thank Mr. Okamoto, Mr. Ishibuchi, Mr. Takashima and Mr. Hirano, Daikin Industries, Ltd. Our special thanks are due to the staffs and colleagues in our laboratory in Nagoya University and Electric Power R & D center, Chubu Electric Power Co., Inc. for valuable advice.

References

[Aono 1984] Aono M. and Kunii T. L. :"Botanical tree image generation", IEEE CG&A,Vol.4, No.5, pp.10-34 (May 1984)

[Kanatani 1988] Kanatani K. :"Transformation of Optical Flow by Camera Rotation", IEEE Trans.Patt.Anal.Mach.Intell.,PAMI-10,3, pp.131-143 (March 1988)

Fig.5 Optical flows

Fig.10   Examples of montage video images

Fig.13 An example of "basic image" and "region label image"

551

Fig.15   An example of displayed montage image

Fig.16   An example of the stereo pair of images

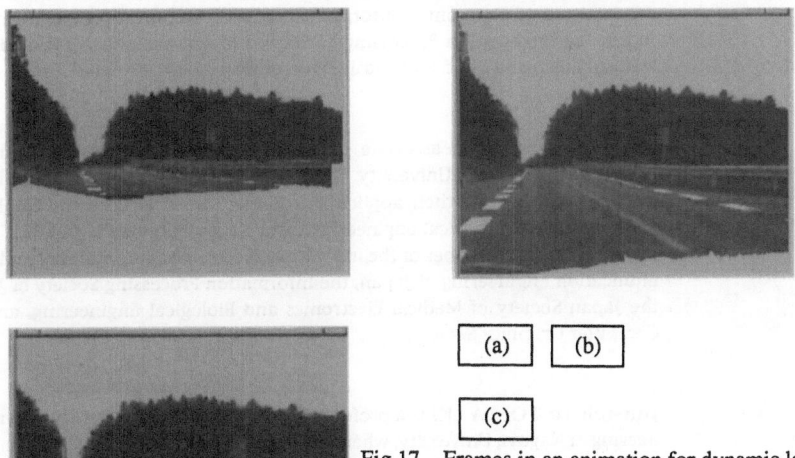

(a)   (b)

(c)

Fig.17   Frames in an animation for dynamic landscape estimation with our model.
Viewing points of these images are (a)5 meters
behind, (b)just the same as and (c)10 meters ahead
of, the camera position for the "basic image".

[Kaneda 1990] Kaneda K., Kato F., Nakamae E. and Nishita T. :"Three dimensional terrain modeling and display for environmental assessment", Compute Graphics, 23, 3, pp.207-214(1990)

[Nakamae 1986] Nakamae E., Harada K., Ishizaki T. and Nishita T. :"A montage method: The overlaying of the computer generated images onto a background photograph", Computer Graphics, 20, 4, pp.207-214 (1986)

[Nakamae 1991] Nakamae E., Kaneda K., Harada K., Miwa T., Nishita T. and Saiki R. :"Reliability of computer graphic image for visual assessment", The Visual Computer, 7, pp.138-148 (1991)

[Nakatani 1980] Nakatani H., Kimura S., Saito O. and Kitahasi T. :"Extraction of vanishing point and its application to scene analysis based on image sequence", Proc. 5th ICPR ,pp.370-372, (1980)

[Tomita 1979] Tomita F., Shirai Y. and Tsuji S. :"Description of textures by a structural analysis", Proc. 6th IJCAI, pp.884-889(1979)

Yutaka SOYAMA is a research engineer in Chubu Electric Power Co., Inc.. His research interests are computer graphics and its applications. He received BE in electronic engineering and ME in information engineering from Nagoya University in 1987 and 1989, respectively. He is a member of the Institute of Electronics, Information, and Communication Engineering of Japan and the Information Processing Society of Japan.

Address: Electric Power R & D Center, Chubu Electric Power Co., Inc., 20-1 Kitayama, Odaka-cho, Midori-ku, Nagoya-shi 459 Japan

Takami YASUDA is a research associate in the Department of Information Engineering at Nagoya University. His research interests are computer graphics and its applications to medicine. He received BE and ME in electronic engineering from Mie University in 1982 and 1984, respectively. He received a Ph.D. in information engineering from Nagoya University in 1989. He is a member of the Institute of Electronics, Information, and Communication Engineering of Japan, the Information Processing Society of Japan, and the Japan Society of Medical Electronics and Biological Engineering.

Shigeki YOKOI is an associate professor in the Department of Information Engineering at Nagoya University. His research involves computer graphics and image processing and their applications to medicine. He received BE, ME, and Ph.D. degrees in electrical engineering from Nagoya University in 1971, 1974, and 1977. He is a member of the Institute of Electronics, Information, and Communication Engineering of Japan, the Information Processing Society of Japan, the Japan Society of Medical Electronics and Biological Engineering, and the Computer Graphics Society.

Jun-ichiro TORIWAKI is a professor in the Department of Information Engineering at Nagoya University, where he teaches and performs research in pictorial patter recognition, biomedical image processing, and computer graphics and applications. He received his Ph.D. from Nagoya University in 1969. He is a member of IEEE, the Institute of Electronics, Information, and Communication Engineering of Japan, the Information Processing Society of Japan, and the Japan Society of Medical Electronics and Biological Engineering.

Address: Department of Information Engineering, Faculty of Engineering, Nagoya University, Furo-cho, Chikusa-ku, Nagoya-shi 464-01 Japan

A Necessary Condition of Block Edge Detection and Hierarchical Representations of the Kernel Form of the Hexagonal Grid

Z. J. Zheng

ABSTRACT

A necessary condition for block edge detection based on a hierarchical representation of the conjugate classification for the hexagonal grid is investigated in this paper. Constructing the operations of block edge detection, it is necessary to collect a set of 48 states as the structuring elements. To represent the selected state set, five hierarchical representations of the kernel form of the hexagonal grid and their inner classes, are illustrated and compared. Because the conjugate classification is an accurate class representation of structuring elements, its real implementation is very efficient. For the operation of 0 or 1 block edge detection, a speed-up ratio of more than 6-11 compared with the same activity performed by a standard implementation of mathematical morphology, can be observed. Sample processed pictures and their timing measurements are also illustrated.

Keywords: *edge detection, cellular automata, mathematical morphology, structuring element, hierarchical representation*

1   INTRODUCTION

For any binary image, block components should be the most impressive parts of the image composed of block edge points and block inner points respectively. How to separate block components from other parts is a difficult and practical problem in many image analysis and visual computing applications. Since a block component of a 2D binary image is a specific shape on a given grid, the possible number of structuring elements for block edges is much larger than the possible number of structuring elements for block inner points. Consequently, operations of block component detection are greatly dominanted by operations of block edge detection. Huge practical applications of computer vision and pattern recognition related to block edge detection make the block edge detection one of the most important operations of image analysis and processing. It is always possible to decompose a shape using a set of structuring elements (shape decomposition: Song 1990, Pitas 1989, Shapiro 1987), and then to extract the specific shape using elementary operations of mathematical morphology (τ-Openings: Dougherty 1992, Wilson 1992, Zhuang 1986). In order to reduce the computational complexity of operations, it is common to select a minimal number of structuring elements in order to establish a necessary condition for different applications. Because a specific shape should be decomposed into a large number of structuring elements (such as n structuring elements) and each structuring element requires at least one elementary operation (t units) to a relevant image, it is essential for mathematical morphology to spend a total of $n \times t$ processing units extracting the shape from the original image.

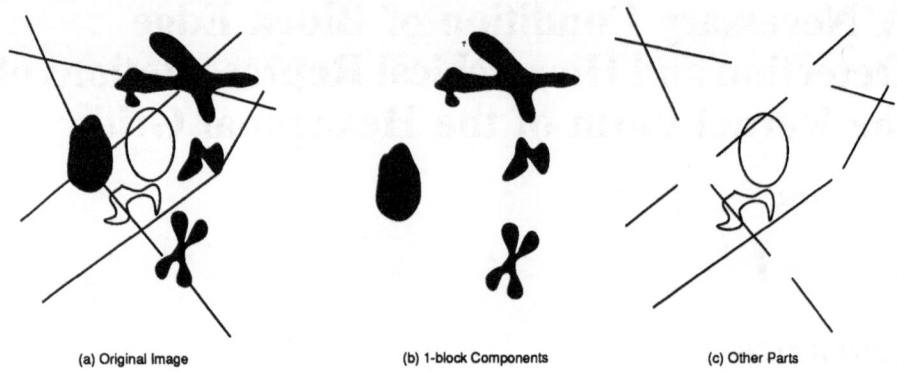

Figure 1: Identifying 1-Block Components from a Binary Image (a)-(c).

A necessary condition for efficient block edge detection on the hexagonal grid is investigated in this paper which is divided into seven sections. In section 2, the number of states needed to be selected for the problem of block component detection of the hexagonal grid is investigated. The relationships and connections between block component and block edge detection are explored and the symmetric operations to manage the relevant state set are investigated. In section 3, five classifications of the hexagonal grid (Boolean logic, symmetry function, crossing number, Golay transformation and conjugate transformation) are presented using a hierarchical approach. To distinguish each inner class from a specific classification, the state number of the class is evaluated and five relevant tree structures are illustrated. In section 4, a given state class with rotational invariance is selected to examine in what conditions a classification of the five schemes can represent the class precisely, in order to provide an exact solution for the operations of block edge detection. Except for the Boolean logic scheme, only the conjugate classification can use one inner class to represent block edge detection exactly. The relevant class of the other three schemes (symmetry function, crossing number and Golay transformation) contain the number of states double or multiple more than the requirements. Further refinement of the classes is required to split each class into an irreducible class set. In section 5, a necessary condition of the block edge detection of the hexagonal grid for the conjugate classification can be established. For convenient representation of the selected state set for block edge detection, the restricted conditions under logic plus arithmetic operations are examined, and the minimal number of the operations for block edge detection can be determined. In section 6, two sample picture sets of block edge detection, their timing measurements and speed-up ratios (0 or 1 block edge detection generated by an implemented prototype of the conjugate transformation), are illustrated; and finally in section 7 the main contributions of the paper are summarised.

2 A NECESSARY CONDITION OF STRUCTURING ELEMENTS FOR BLOCK COMPONENTS

For a clear explanation of block edge detection, it is convenient to start from a relevant example. First, the problem of block component detection is examined then to reveal the relationship between block component and edge detection. Figure 1(a) is a sample image composed of 1-block components and other structures (lines and junctions). It has been separated to 1-block components in Figure 1(b) and other structures in Figure 1(c). If we restrict the image to the

$$x_0 \qquad x_1$$

$$x_5 \qquad x \qquad x_2 \ , \qquad x_i \in \{0,1\}, X = (x, \cdots, x_i, \cdots, x_1, x_0), 0 \le i \le 5.$$

$$x_4 \qquad x_3$$

Figure 2: The Kernel Form of the Hexagonal Grid

hexagonal grid, is it feasible to perform similar operations mechanically?

To answer this question, it is necessary to analyze how many structuring elements are minimally required for block component detection. The simplest scheme for block component detection uses seven adjacent grid points (the kernel form of the hexagonal grid) as the structuring form. The kernel form is a regular form composed of 7 grid points for which one point x is at the centre and another 6 neighbouring points $x_0 - x_5$ are around it (shown in Figure 2). Each point is allowed to assume values of only 1 or 0; 7 points have fixed values as a state (structuring element), and there is a total of 128 states in the kernel form.

For any point x of an image, it is a *simple* block point if it has 2-6 neighbouring points which have the same value as x and which are one by one connected into a run cyclically. For any *component* of the image, if its all points are simple block points then it is a *simple block component*. In order to describe simple 1-block components, the following state set has to be selected as the structuring elements. There are 5 rotational invariant classes with a total of 25 states (24 states for 1-block edge points and 1 state for simple 1-block inner points shown in Figure 3). Conversely, for describing simple 0-block components, another conjugate state set has to be selected as the structuring elements. There are 5 rotational invariant classes with a total of 25 states too (24 states for 0-block edge points and 1 state for 0-block inner points shown in Figure 4).

Because any block component is composed of block edge plus inner points and only two structuring elements for inner points are used, the most complicated operations of block component detection obviously come from the operations of block edge detection. For representations of both 0 and 1 block edge points, a total of 48 states in 8 rotational invariant classes has to be selected as structuring elements. If we could get a simpler condition to identify these edge states, then it is helpful for simple block edge detection to get an efficient algorithm. Therefore, the requirements of looking for the efficient operations of block edge detection force us to investigate different representations of the state set of the kernel form of the hexagonal grid. From above discussion, we can establish the following lemma.

Lemma 2.0.1 *For any binary image of the hexagonal grid, if the kernel form of the grid is selected as the structuring form and only simple block edge points need to be identified, then it is necessary to select 48 structuring elements from its 128 state set. The selected structuring elements belong to 8 rotational invariant classes and each class contains exactly 6 states.*

Proof: For any simple edge point x, there must be 2-5 neighbouring points which have the same value as x and are $x_0 - x_5$ are arranged as two 0-1 runs cyclically. For any given state of a simple edge point, six rotational directions correspond to one rotational invariant class of six states. □

Morphological Patterns of Simple 1-Block Edges: 24 Patterns

```
{ 1  1     0  1            1  0    }
{ 0  1 , 0  1      1 ,···, 1   1  0 } ;
{ 0  0     0  0            0  0    }

{ 1  1     0  1            1  1    }
{ 0  1 , 0  1      1 ,···, 1   1  0 } ;
{ 0  0     0  1            0  0    }

{ 1  1     0  1            1  1    }
{ 0  1 , 0  1      1 ,···, 1   1  1 } ;
{ 0  1     1  1            0  0    }

{ 1  1     0  1            1  1    }
{ 0  1 , 1  1      1 ,···, 1   1  1 } .
{ 1  1     1  1            0  1    }
```

Morphological Patterns of 1-Inner elements: One Pattern, X = (1111111).

```
{    1  1    }
{  1   1   1 }
{    1  1    }
```

Figure 3: Structuring Elements of Simple 1-Block Components

Morphological Patterns of Simple 0-Block Edges: 24 Patterns

```
{ 0  0     1  0            0  1    }
{ 1  0 , 1  0      0 ,···, 0   0  1 } ,
{ 1  1     1  1            1  1    }

{ 0  0     1  0            0  0    }
{ 1  0 , 1  0      0 ,···, 0   0  1 } ;
{ 1  1     1  0            1  1    }

{ 0  0     1  0            0  0    }
{ 1  0 , 1  0      0 ,···, 0   0  0 } ;
{ 1  0     0  0            1  1    }

{ 0  0     1  0            0  0    }
{ 1  0 , 0  0      0 ,···, 0   0  0 } .
{ 0  0     0  0            1  0    }
```

Morphological Patterns of 0-Inner elements: One Pattern, X = (0000000).

```
{    0  0    }
{  0   0   0 }
{    0  0    }
```

Figure 4: Structuring Elements of Simple 0-Block Components

From an algebraic viewpoint, two types of symmetric operations can be identified to transform the structuring elements of block edge detection. The first one is the conjugation which establishes 0 to 1 and 1 to 0 symmetry. The second one is the rotation which manages six states into one rotationally invariant class. Another two conditions are simple connection and the number of the neighbouring points. Four conditions play the key role for the problem of simple block edge detection.

3 HIERARCHICAL REPRESENTATIONS OF THE KERNEL FORM OF THE HEXAGONAL GRID

The hexagonal grid plays a significant role in two dimensional image domains. How to represent the fundamental grouping of seven adjacent grid points (the kernel form) for the hexagonal grid is a key issue for any descriptive and analytic task on such images. In order to satisfy different circumstances (such as cellular automata, mathematical morphology and parallel Boolean logic computation), several representations of the kernel form of the hexagonal grid applicable to the binary images, have been developed. The comparable representations for other regular plane lattices also exist (Zheng 1993). For investigating block edge detection, five representation schemes using a hierarchical approach were selected for analysis and comparison. They are Boolean logic (lookup table), symmetric function (Gardner 1971), crossing number (Preston and Duff 1984, pp43-44), Golay transformation (Golay 1969) and conjugate classification (Zheng and Maeder 1992). Through hierarchical analysis, it is possible to abstract more information at intermediate levels then to give block edge detection an efficient representation.

The kernel form of the hexagonal grid is one point with six neighbouring points around it. When each point is allowed to assume values of only 0 or 1, there are in total 128 states corresponding to unique instances of the kernel form. From the mathematical point of view, a hierarchical classification of the kernel form is a specific procedure for decomposing the set of 128 states via several intermediate stages, into 128 individual sets in which each set contains one state. If we let the 128 state set be a root node and define an inclusion relation among sets, we can then establish a graphical description for a specific representation scheme using a tree in which each intermediate stage set is a node. The number of states in the set is recorded at the node and sets with an inclusion relation have a branch or a unidirectional path between them. From this description, two tree structures are *structurally-equivalent*, if it is possible to define a 1-1 mapping from one structure to another. However, two substructures of two trees are *equivalent*, if one state set of whole relevant classes of a substructure is equal to the state set of whole relevant classes of another substructure.

In order to provide a comparison, only the number of individual levels in the structure and the number of states in the level are considered. Let w_i^j be the i-th level and j-th node, then the five representations can be shown in Figure 5.

3.1 Boolean Logic Scheme (Look-up Table)

The state set is directly decomposed into 128 individual sets without intermediate nodes shown in Figure 5(a). Two Levels: one root and 128 leaves. $w_0^0 = 128; \{w_1^j\} = \{1\}, 0 \leq j \leq 127$.

3.2 Symmetry Function Scheme (Conway: Game of life)

Each state in a node has a fixed number of 1-elements. A total of 8 nodes can be distinguished. Three Levels: one root, 8 nodes and 128 leaves shown in Figure 5(b). $w_0^0 = 128; w_1^j = \binom{7}{j}, 0 \leq$

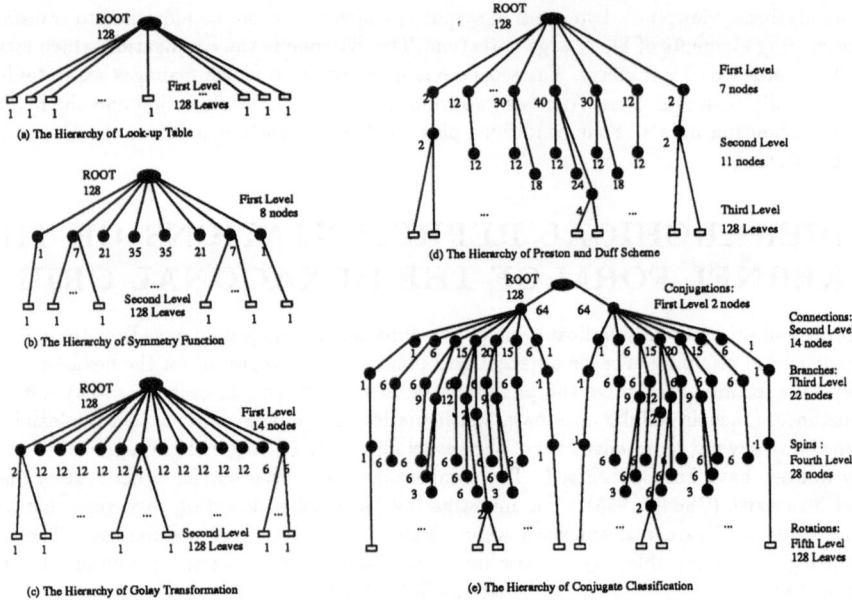

Figure 5: Five Hierarchical Trees of the Kernel Form of the Hexagonal Grid (a)-(e)

$j \leq 7, \{w_1^j\} = \{1, 7, 21, 35\}; \{w_2^j\} = \{1\}, 0 \leq j \leq 127.$

3.3 Golay Transformation Scheme (Golay)

Six neighbour points of two states in a node can be congruent by rotation. A total of 14 sets with rotational symmetry are distinguished. Three Levels: one root, 14 nodes and 128 leaves are shown in Figure 5(c). $w_0^0 = 128; \{w_1^j\} = \{2, 4, 6, 12\}, 0 \leq j \leq 13; \{w_2^j\} = \{1\}, 0 \leq j \leq 127.$

3.4 Crossing Number Scheme (Preston and Duff)

The first level of 7 nodes is related to states with the same number of 1-elements in six neighbour points; the second level of 11 nodes can be distinguished by the number of crossings in a state. Four Levels: one root, 7 nodes, 11 nodes and 128 leaves are shown in Figure 5(d). $w_0^0 = 128; w_1^j = 2 * \binom{6}{j}, 0 \leq j \leq 6, \{w_1^j\} = \{2, 12, 30, 40\}; \{w_2^j\} = \{2, 4, 12, 18\}, 0 \leq j \leq 10; \{w_3^j\} = \{1\}, 0 \leq j \leq 127.$

3.5 Conjugate Classification (Zheng and Maeder)

The first level is divided into 2 sets by the value of the centre point (0 or 1); the second level of 14 nodes is distinguished by the number of six neighbouring points with the same value of the centre point; the third level of 22 nodes is dependent on the number of branches in each state and the fourth level of 28 nodes has the property of rotational invariant in which any two states in a node can be congruent by rotation. Six Levels: one root, 2 nodes, 14 nodes, 22 nodes, 28 nodes and 128 leaves are shown in Figure 5(e). $w_0^0 = 128; \{w_1^j\} = \{64\}, 0 \leq j \leq$

$1; \{w_2^j\} = \{1, 6, 15, 20\}, 0 \leq j \leq 13; \{w_3^j\} = \{1, 2, 6, 9\}, 0 \leq j \leq 21; \{w_4^j\} = \{1, 2, 3, 6\}, 0 \leq j \leq 27; \{w_5^j\} = \{1\}, 0 \leq j \leq 127.$

Comparing the five classifications, they all have a root containing 128 states and 128 leaves. For a given tree, the nodes in different levels would have inclusion relations. However, nodes in the same level are a partition of the 128 states. Any two nodes of a given level do not have a common state. Because of the partition property, the number of states in a node at a lower level usually contain a smaller number of states than the number of a relevant node at a higher level. In order to establish an efficient representation, it is necessary for the comparison of any two substructures in five classifications to choose their corresponding levels as high as possible and then to establish an equivalent relationship between selected two substructures.

4 NODES IN HIERARCHICAL REPRESENTATIONS

The five hierarchical representations are composed of a different number of levels and their inner classes contain a different number of states. From the structural viewpoint, the simplest tree is the look-up table without any intermediate node. However, the most complex tree is the conjugate classification composed of two balanced subtrees which are split from the root. In order to determine what specific scheme can be directly applied to block edge detection, it is helpful to analyze relevant intermediate nodes. For a convenient comparison, only one class of rotationally invariant states of two 1-neighbouring points is selected and relevant classes of five representations are illustrated in Figure 6. Other classes of rotationally invariant states have similar properties.

It is interesting that both the look-up table and a certain level of the conjugate classification can provide the equivalent state set for the selected class. But the three other schemes contain at least a double number of states which is more than the real requirement. However, it is necessary to do further operations in order to distinguish relevant states from irrelevant ones. Because only the conjugate transformation can support the precise description for the selected classes of block edge detection, it is necessary to investigate the best level of the conjugate classification in detail for more efficient representations of block edge detection.

5 A Necessary Condition of the Conjugate Classification for Simple Block Edge Detection

The conjugate classification of the kernel form of the hexagonal grid are established by Zheng and Maeder (1992). For convenient description, the classification can be briefly described as following.

5.1 The Conjugate Classification of The Kernel Form

The *kernel form* of the hexagonal grid is a point with six neighbouring points around it. When each point is allowed to assume values of only 0 or 1, there is a total of 128 states corresponding to unique instances of the kernel form. From the state set of 128 states and the inclusion relation of set theory, we can use a tree of six levels to represent the conjugate classification. Each level contains 128 states and each node is a subset of states. Any two nodes in the same level do not contain the same state. If we let the 128 state set be the root, then the first level can be divided into one state set G and one conjugate state set $\tilde{G}$ dependent on the value of the centre point x, $x \in \{0, 1\}$. The second level of 14 nodes $\{_pG, _p\tilde{G}\}$ can be distinguished by p, the number of connections, $0 \leq p \leq 6$, that is, the number of six neighbouring points with the same value of

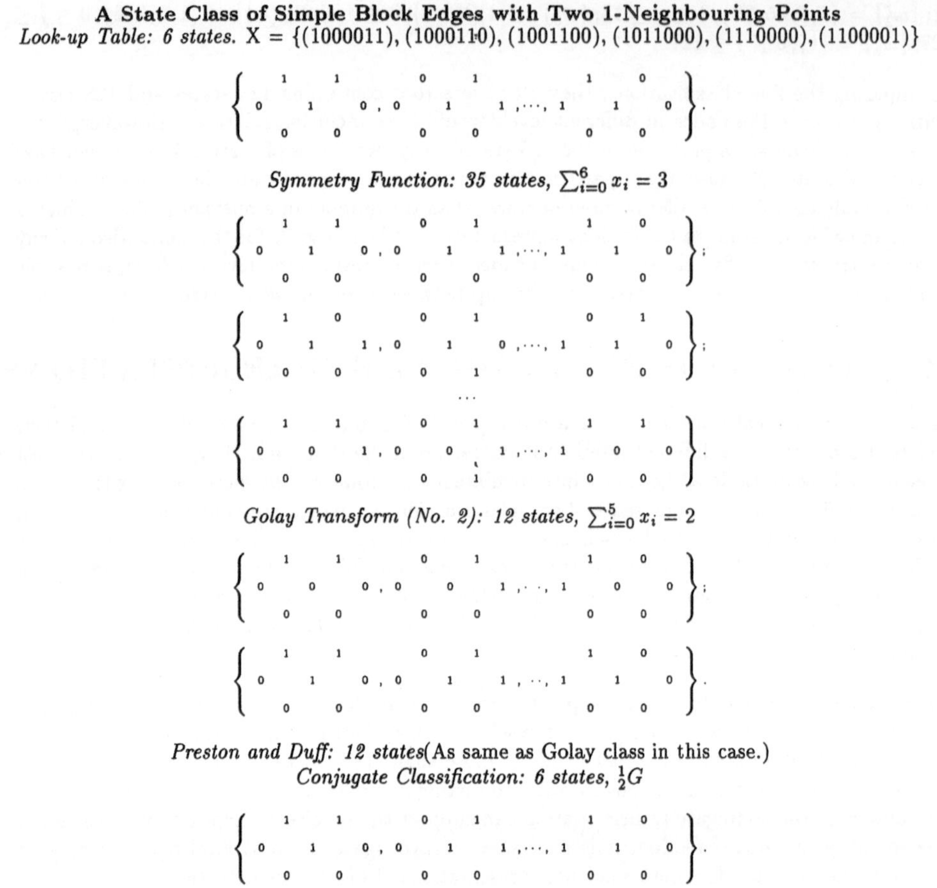

A State Class of Simple Block Edges with Two 1-Neighbouring Points

Look-up Table: 6 states. $X = \{(1000011), (1000110), (1001100), (1011000), (1110000), (1100001)\}$

$$\left\{ \begin{array}{ccc} 1 & 1 & 0 \\ 0 & 1 & 0 \\ 0 & 0 & 0 \end{array} , \begin{array}{ccc} 1 & & 1 \\ 0 & 1 & 1 \\ 0 & 0 & \end{array} , \cdots , \begin{array}{ccc} 1 & 0 \\ 1 & 1 & 0 \\ 0 & 0 \end{array} \right\} .$$

Symmetry Function: 35 states, $\sum_{i=0}^{6} x_i = 3$

$$\left\{ \begin{array}{ccc} 1 & 1 & 0 \\ 0 & 1 & 0 \\ 0 & 0 & 0 \end{array} , \begin{array}{ccc} 1 & & 1 \\ 0 & 1 & 1 \\ 0 & 0 & \end{array} , \cdots , \begin{array}{ccc} 1 & 0 \\ 1 & 1 & 0 \\ 0 & 0 \end{array} \right\} ;$$

$$\left\{ \begin{array}{ccc} 1 & 0 & 0 \\ 0 & 1 & 1 \\ 0 & 0 & 0 \end{array} , \begin{array}{ccc} 1 & & 0 \\ 0 & 1 & 1 \\ 0 & 0 & \end{array} , \cdots , \begin{array}{ccc} 0 & 1 \\ 1 & 1 & 0 \\ 0 & 0 \end{array} \right\} ;$$

$$\cdots$$

$$\left\{ \begin{array}{ccc} 1 & 1 & 0 \\ 0 & 0 & 1 \\ 0 & 0 & 0 \end{array} , \begin{array}{ccc} 1 & & 0 \\ 0 & 1 & 1 \\ 0 & 0 & \end{array} , \cdots , \begin{array}{ccc} 1 & 1 \\ 0 & 0 & 0 \\ 0 & 0 \end{array} \right\} .$$

Golay Transform (No. 2): 12 states, $\sum_{i=0}^{5} x_i = 2$

$$\left\{ \begin{array}{ccc} 1 & 1 & 0 \\ 0 & 0 & 0 \\ 0 & 0 & 0 \end{array} , \begin{array}{ccc} 1 & & 0 \\ 0 & 1 & 1 \\ 0 & 0 & \end{array} , \cdots , \begin{array}{ccc} 1 & 0 \\ 0 & 0 & 0 \\ 0 & 0 \end{array} \right\} ;$$

$$\left\{ \begin{array}{ccc} 1 & 1 & 0 \\ 0 & 1 & 0 \\ 0 & 0 & 0 \end{array} , \begin{array}{ccc} 1 & & 1 \\ 0 & 1 & 1 \\ 0 & 0 & \end{array} , \cdots , \begin{array}{ccc} 1 & 0 \\ 1 & 1 & 0 \\ 0 & 0 \end{array} \right\} .$$

Preston and Duff: 12 states(As same as Golay class in this case.)

Conjugate Classification: 6 states, $\frac{1}{2}G$

$$\left\{ \begin{array}{ccc} 1 & 1 & 0 \\ 0 & 1 & 0 \\ 0 & 0 & 0 \end{array} , \begin{array}{ccc} 1 & & 1 \\ 0 & 1 & 1 \\ 0 & 0 & \end{array} , \cdots , \begin{array}{ccc} 1 & 0 \\ 1 & 1 & 0 \\ 0 & 0 \end{array} \right\} .$$

Figure 6: A Class of Rotational Invariant in Five Representations

the centre point. The third level of 22 nodes $\{^q_p G\}$ and $\{^q_p \widetilde{G}\}$ is related to q which corresponds to the number of branches, $0 \le q \le 3$ (the number of runs of the six neighbouring points with the same value of the centre point in each state). The fourth level of 28 nodes $\{^q_p G^s\}$ and $\{^q_p \widetilde{G}^s\}$ has the property of rotational invariant in which any two states in a node can be congruent by rotation, and s denotes the number of spins, $s \in \{0, 1\}$. The fifth level of 128 leaves $\{^q_p G^s_r\}$ and $\{^q_p \widetilde{G}^s_r\}$ has the simple relation to the respected state, and r denotes the number of rotations $0 \le r \le 6$. In short, the conjugate classification is a tree of six levels: one root, 2 nodes, 14 nodes, 22 nodes, 28 nodes and 128 leaves. Each node of the tree is a class of states with 1-5 calculable parameters. The whole structure of the classification has been shown in Figure 5(b). We use (x, p, q, s, r) to denote five calculable parameters of this classification.

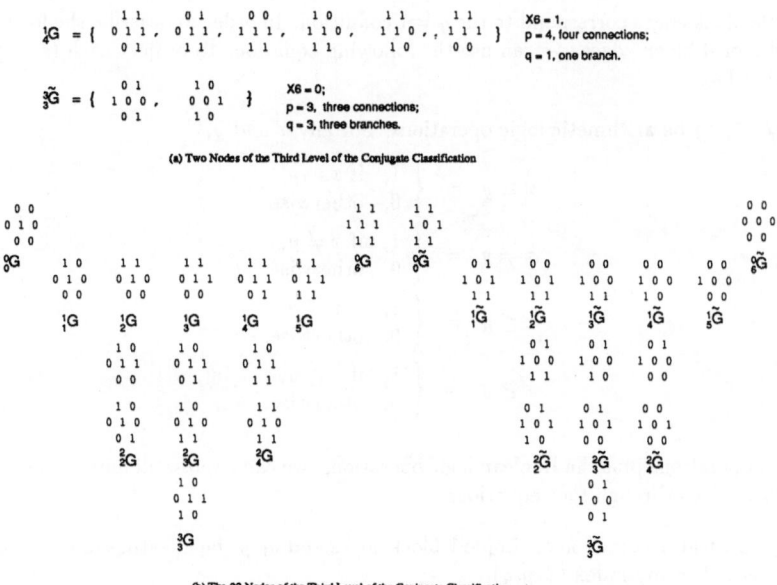

(a) Two Nodes of the Third Level of the Conjugate Classification

(b) The 22 Nodes of the Third Level of the Conjugate Classification

Figure 7: The Third Level of the Conjugate Classification

5.2 The Relevant Level for Block Edge Detection

The hierarchical structure of the conjugate classification provides a flexible framework for supporting different applications. It is obvious that x or (x,p) is not enough to describe the selected classes. However, it is sufficient to use three parameters (x,p,q) for the description. For current application, we only need to restrict our investigation to the third level of the conjugate classification: that is, the substructure of the tree in the third level of 22 nodes $\{^q_p G\}$ and $\{^q_p \widetilde{G}\}$.

The third level of the conjugate classification is illustrated in Figure 7. Some details of two nodes are explained in Figure 7(a), and their 22 nodes are shown in Figure 7(b).

In order to describe the selected structuring elements, only $\{^1_2 G, ^1_3 G, ^1_4 G, ^1_5 G, ^1_2 \widetilde{G}, ^1_3 \widetilde{G}, ^1_4 \widetilde{G}, ^1_5 \widetilde{G}\}$ nodes of the third level of the conjugate classification, are relevant. Their combinations can satisfy most applications of block edge detection and exactly satisfy the applications of simple block edge detection.

Proposition 5.2.1 *The third level of the conjugate classification can provide a necessary and sufficient representation for the eight classes of simple block edge points of the hexagonal grid.*

Proof: The structure itself contains all selected classes that can be distinguished each other, it is sufficient to support any combination of the classes. Neither $(x,p), (x,q), (p,q)$ nor $(x), (p), (q)$ can represent the required classes. So it is necessary for block edge detection to use the third level. □

5.3 The Calculable Condition of Block Edge Detection

For any class of the third level of the conjugate classification, there are three parameters (x,p,q): conjugation, connection and branch, $x \in \{0,1\}, p \in \{0,1,\cdots,6\}$ and $q \in \{0,1,2,3\}$.

The simple block edges correspond to the $q = 1$ condition. In order to describe the four selected classes of 1 or 0 block edges, we can use the following equations to project each (x, p, q) index into a 0-1 value.

Let $\{\equiv, \neq, \leq, \geq\}$ be arithmetic logic operations. For any x and y,

$$x \equiv y = \begin{cases} 1, & \text{if } x = y; \\ 0, & \text{otherwise.} \end{cases}$$

$$x \neq y = \begin{cases} 1, & \text{if } x \neq y; \\ 0, & \text{otherwise.} \end{cases}$$

$$x \leq y = \begin{cases} 1, & \text{if } x \leq y; \\ 0, & \text{otherwise.} \end{cases}$$

$$x \geq y = \begin{cases} 1, & \text{if } ^{,} \geq y; \\ 0, & \text{otherwise.} \end{cases}$$

Using four operations plus the Boolean logic operations, we can express all four classes of simple 0 or 1 block edges through four equations.

Let y_1, y_2 be a feature function of simple 1-block edges and $\tilde{y}_1, \tilde{y}_2$ be a feature function of simple 0-block edges. For any index (x, p, q),

$$
\begin{aligned}
y_1(x, p, q) &= (x \equiv 1) \cap (q \equiv 1) \cap ((p \equiv 2) \cup (p \equiv 3) \cup (p \equiv 4) \cup (p \equiv 5)); \textbf{Type A} \\
y_2(x, p, q) &= (x \equiv 1) \cap (q \equiv 1) \cap (p \geq 2); \textbf{Type B} \\
\tilde{y}_1(x, p, q) &= (x \neq 1) \cup (q \neq 1) \cup ((p \neq 2) \cap (p \neq 3) \cap (p \neq 4) \cap (p \neq 5)); \textbf{Type A} \\
\tilde{y}_2(x, p, q) &= (x \neq 1) \cup (q \neq 1) \cup (p \leq 1); \textbf{Type B}
\end{aligned}
$$

Proposition 5.3.1 *For any* (x, p, q), $y_1 = y_2$ *and* $\tilde{y}_1 = \tilde{y}_2$.

Proof: Each index (x, p, q) has certain values, two equations of Type A and B describe the same condition, one equation collects all relevant classes and another equation uses the order property of p. □

Corollary 5.3.2 *For any* (x, p, q), *if* $y_1 = 1$ *then* x *is a simple 1-block edge point.*

Corollary 5.3.3 *For any* (x, p, q), *if* $\tilde{y}_1 = 0$ *then* x *is a simple 0-block edge point.*

Proposition 5.3.4 *For* $\{\equiv, \neq, \leq, \geq\}$ *operations, if each operation can be performed in one unit period, then to identify four classes of simple block edges we can say that they have the same computational complexity as to identify one class of the third level of the conjugate classification.*

Proof: It is necessary to identify a class using three parameters. The equation has to be a Type B form. □

Let t_A or t_B be the units to perform a Type A or Type B equation.

Corollary 5.3.5 *For any optimal operation of simple block edge detection, its performing time measurement t is between t_A and t_B. That is,*

$$t_B \leq t \leq t_A.$$

Using specific properties of the conjugate classification, we have arrived at our conclusion. From the above proposition 5.3.4 and corollary 5.3.5, the complexity of simple block edge detection can be reduced to one time period by identifying a single class and it cannot be reduced further. This necessary condition has significant potential applications in different edge detection.

Table 1: Time Measurements of Two Schemes

Function	Class	State	CT(unit)	Morph(unit)	Speed-up	Fig
Full Edges	1	1	86	38	0.44	Fig.8&9(g)
One Class	1	6	86	230	2.6	Fig.8&9(b,c,d,e)
Block Edges	4	24	142	968	6.8	Fig.8&9(f) Type A
Block Edges	4	24	88	968	11	Fig.8&9(f) Type B

Note: Where Class is the number of relevant classes for the function, State is the number of involved states, CT is the average number of time units taken by Conjugate Transformation, Morph is the average number of time units taken by Mathematical Morphology, Speed-up is equal to Morph/CT and Fig indicates relevant figures.

6   USING THE CONJUGATE CLASSIFICATION

In order to illustrate the advantage of the conjugate classification, two sets of sample pictures of binary images for block edge detection are shown in Figure 8 and Figure 9 for 1-block edges and 0-block edges respectively in Appendix A. The pictures are generated from an implemented prototype of the *conjugate transformation* of the hexagonal grid (Zheng and Maeder 1993). The conjugate transformation can support any combination of the selected classes from the 22 nodes of the third level of the conjugate classification. Because of the capability of the class representation to efficiently identify states, the implementation of the conjugate transformation on the hexagonal grid is very efficient. A speed-up ratio of more than 6-11, compared with the same activity (0 or 1 block edge detection) performed by a standard implementation of mathematical morphology, can be observed. The results shown in Table 1 provide numerical measurements of the speed-up ratio of running times of two compared programs on IRIX 4.0.5 System V, Silicon Graphics Iris 4D/25. The unit of the measurement time is 1/60 second.

Because each tree has one root and 128 leaves, the conjugate classification contains the largest number of nodes among them. A complex structure can usually be mapped into a simple one but it is not always possible to directly do the reverse mapping operation. As shown by Zheng and Maeder (1992), the other representations can be generated from the conjugate classification.

7   CONCLUSION

From both representation and implementation, the proposed solution of simple block edge detection based on the conjugate classification is superior to other schemes in the condition of representing combined classes of multiple structuring elements. Using the precise class information, the 48 states of the structuring elements for simple block edge detection can be drastically reduced to one simple equation. This classification, therefore, provides a general structural description of relationships between adjacent spatial data points as a fundamental paradigm for image analysis and processing operations of binary images on the hexagonal grid.

Acknowledgements: The author would like to express gratitude for the financial support of ADCSS Awards and Monash University's Department of Computer Science for granting a Scholarship for towards the undertaking of this work, Dr. Anthony Maeder for encouraging supervisions, and Mrs. Patrizia Rossi and Dr. Imants Svalbe for editing and proofreading this paper.

REFERENCES

E.R. Dougherty (1992) *An Introduction to Morphological Image Processing*, SPIE Optical Engineering Press.

M. Gardner (1971). "On Cellular Automata, Self-reproduction, the Garden of Eden and the Game 'life'," *Scientific American* 224(2), pp112-117.

M.J.E. Golay (1969). "Hexagonal Parallel Pattern Transformations" *IEEE Trans. Comput.* Vol.18, pp733-740.

K.S. Huang, B.K. Jenkins and A.A. Sawchuk (1989). "Binary Image Algebra and Optical Cellular Logic Processor Design", *CVGIP* Vol. 45, pp 295-345.

I. Pitas and A. Venetsanopoulos (1989) "Morphological Shape Decomposition," *IEEE Trans. Pattern Anal. Machine Intell.*, Vol. 11, No. 7, July, 1989.

K. Preston, Jr and M.J.B. Duff (1984). *Modern Cellular Automata: Theory and Application* Plenum Press, New York.

L. Shapiro, R. MacDonald and S. Sternberg (1987) "Ordered Structural Shape Matching with Primitive Extraction by Mathematical Morphology," *Pattern Recognition*, Vol. 20, No. 1, 1987.

J. Song and E.J. Delp (1990) "The Analysis of Morphological Filters with Multiple Structuring Elements," *CVGIP* Vol. 50, pp 308-328.

S.S. Wilson (1992) "Theory of Matrix Morphology," *IEEE Trans. Patt. Anal. Machine Intell.*, Vol.14 No. 6, pp 636-652.

Z.J. Zheng and A.J. Maeder (1992). "The Conjugate Classification of the Kernel Form of the Hexagonal Grid" *Modern Geometric Computing for Visualization*, T.L. Kunii and Y. Shinagawa (Eds), Springer-Verlag, Tokyo, pp73-89.

Z.J. Zheng and A.J. Maeder (1993). "The Elementary Equation of the Conjugate Transformation for the Hexagonal Grid" *Modeling in Computer Graphics - Methods and Application*, B. Falcidieno and T.L. Kunii (Eds), IFIP Series on Computer Graphics, Springer-Verlag, Berlin Heidelberg.

Z.J. Zheng (1993). "The Conjugate Transformation of the Regular Plane Lattices for Binary Images", Ph.D Thesis (not submitted), Department of Computer Science, Monash University.

X. Zhuang and R.M. Haralick (1986). "Morphological Structuring Element Decomposition," *CVGIP* Vol. 35, pp 370-382.

Author's Biography:

Zhijie Zheng is a PhD student in the Department of Computer Science, Monash University. He graduated with B.Sc (Physics) and M.Sc (Computer Science) from Yunnan University and Graduate School of Chinese Science and Technology University, P. R. China, in 1978 and 1981 respectively. He joined the Institute of Computing Technology(ICT), Academia Sinica as a researcher in 1981. From 1983, he was a lecturer of ICT. During the period of 1987-1990, he was a visiting scientist at the Institute of Systems Science(ISS), National University of Singapore. He worked in the fields of parallel algorithms, architecture, combinatorics, interconnection network topology, Chinese output processing, image processing, antialiasing, graphics, parallel and VLSI architecture, convexity, pattern recognition, visualization and computer vision. He is currently researching the conjugate transformation of digital images for his PhD.

Address: Department of Computer Science, Monash University, Clayton, Vic. 3168, Australia.
Email: zheng@bruce.cs.monash.edu.au

565

Appendix A.

(a) The Original Image

(b) $\frac{1}{2}G$ class of (a)

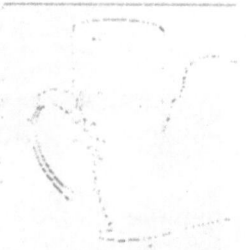

(d) $\frac{1}{4}G$ class of (a)

(e) $\frac{1}{5}G$ class of (a)

(f) 1-Block Edges of (a)

(c) $\frac{1}{3}G$ class of (a)

Figure 8: Sample Pictures of Black-ground (a)-(g). (a) original image (256 by 256), (b)-(e) sample images; (f) = (b) ∪ (c) ∪ (d) ∪ (e)) and (g) = (a) ∩ $\neg_6^0 G$.

(g) 1-Full Edges of (a)

(a) The Original Image

(b) $\frac{1}{2}\widetilde{G}$ class of (a)

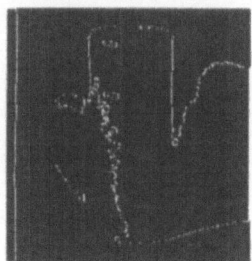

(c) $\frac{1}{3}\widetilde{G}$ class of (a)

Figure 9: Sample Pictures of White-ground (a)-(g). (a) original image (256 by 256), (b)-(e) sample images; (f) = (b) ∩ (c) ∩ (d) ∩ (e)) and (g) = (a) ∪ $\neg_8^0\widetilde{G}$.

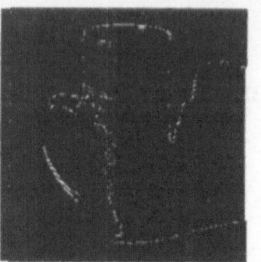

(d) $\frac{1}{4}\widetilde{G}$ class of (a)

(e) $\frac{1}{5}\widetilde{G}$ class of (a)

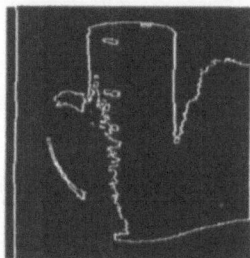

(f) 0-Block Edges of (a)

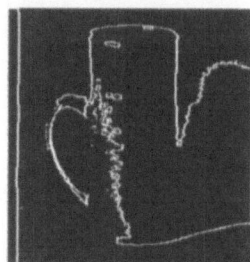

(g) 0-Full Edges of (a)

Partial Surface Identification Based on 3-D Multiple Spatial Filtering

Keisuke Iwasaki, Kenji Mochizuki, and Fumio Kishino

ABSTRACT
This paper proposes a new feature extraction technique for a 3-D surface, based on multiple spatial filtering, and also shows the usefulness of applying the feature to partial shape identification and pose estimation. This method incorporates the trajectory of a point on a surface caused by multiple filtering as characteristics of the point, and can be used robustly for searching feature points and estimating poses of even curved and complex shapes.

The basic concept, the extraction procedure for a shape taken by a range finder, the method for partial surface identification, and experimental results are presented.

KEYWORDS : 3-D Surface, Feature extraction, Multiple filtering, Pose estimation, Model-based vision.

1 INTRODUCTION

Matching a 3-D shape to a model in a database is one of the main issues in computer vision (low, 1/2 level) (Jain and Hoffman 1988; Fan et al. 1989; Brady et al. 1989), along with indexing 3-D objects for the teleconference with realistic sensations (Harashima and Kishino 1991). In this process, the feature extraction of the 3-D shape is one of the keys that reduce the error and computational cost in the matching step. In this field, differential geometric characteristics, e.g. surface curvature (Brady et al. 1985) or its sign map (Besl 1988), surface normal (Jain and Hoffman 1988) or the Gaussian image (Brou 1984), are well-known features on the 3-D surface, because of the following advantages: 1)View-point invariance and 2)Mathematical tractability. However, they also have the following drawbacks:

Sensitive to noise : For extraction, differential methods are used in the neighbor of a point on a surface, so a small error in the input may cause big errors in the extracted values. To avoid this, some works have employed refining methods by iteration (Sander and Zucker 1990; Besl 1988) or pre-processing filtering (Hoffman and Jain 1987; Besl and Jain 1988).
Coarse surface information is not included : Differential geometric features are fundamentally local characteristics, so upper level processes like segmentation (Besl 1988) are necessary to obtain the global characteristics of a surface.

These drawbacks complicate the upper level processes (segmentation, pose-estimation, recognition, etc.).

In this paper, we propose a new feature extraction technique for a 3-D surface, based on multiple spatial filtering of the surface, and also show the usefulness of applying the feature to partial shape identification and pose estimation.

This technique extends the scale-space filtering (Witkin 1983), applied to 2-D shape description and recognition (Asada and Brady 1986; Mokhtarian and Mackworth 1986), to 3-D surfaces. By utilizing the trajectory of a point on the surface caused by 3-D spatial multiple filtering, each point on a surface can have a robust value and direction; this facilitates feature point detection and pose estimation, of even curved and complex shapes like the face of a human head.

In the following sections, we report a method for partial shape identification. Section 2 describes the technique for feature extraction of a 3-D surface. Section 3 describes the method for pose estimation and partial shape identification. Section 4 describes some experimental results applied to facial-part identification, and Section 5 presents the discussion and conclusion.

2 FEATURE EXTRACTION

2.1 Basic Concept of Feature Extraction

A three-dimensional surface is described by two parameters(u, v) as

$$S(u, v) = (\ x(u, v)\quad y(u, v)\quad z(u, v)\ )^T \tag{1}$$

where T denotes the transposition. Let p_0 be a point $S(u_0, v_0)$. Then, as a result of convolutional filtering

$$p_1 = \begin{pmatrix} \iint x(k, l)h(u_0 - k, v_0 - l)dkdl \\ \iint y(k, l)h(u_0 - k, v_0 - l)dkdl \\ \iint z(k, l)h(u_0 - k, v_0 - l)dkdl \end{pmatrix}, \tag{2}$$

and the point p_0 moves to point p_1, where $h(u, v)$ is the filter impulse response. In this case, if we choose

1. The axes (u, v) are *perpendicularly crossing* each other at point p_0.
2. The coordinates of the axes are *distances from a point p_0 along the surface*.
3. The filter impulse response is *symmetrically circular with compact support* and $\iint h(k, l)dkdl = 1$.

then the trajectory of the point moving in 3-D space, $\overrightarrow{p_0 p_1}$, becomes congruent against the rotation and translation as

$$R(p_1 - p_0) + T = (Rp_1 + T) - (Rp_0 + T) \tag{3}$$

where R is a 3×3 rotation matrix and T is a 1×3 translation vector (See Appendix A).

Next, we explain multiple filtering. Let us assume a set of compact and circular symmetric low-pass filters whose radii are in the order of $r_0 < r_1 < \dots < r_{N-1}$, where r_i is the filter radius and N is the number of filters. When a surface is filtered by this set of filters, the point on the surface moves to certain locations according to the filter radii and makes a trajectory in 3-D space (Fig. 1(a)). This trajectory is independent of the rotation and translation of the surface.

In this case, the length of the trajectory registers the degree of convexity/concavity (like curvature) and its course registers the direction of the convexity/concavity (like surface normal) relative to the neighbor of the point. So, the length of the trajectory is considered a view-point invariant feature and its course is considered the attitude information of the surface around the point, which includes surface information from coarse to fine according to the radii of filters along the surface.

2.2 Description of the Trajectory

Figure 1(a) illustrates the trajectory of a point moved by filtering. We describe the trajectory like a space curve as follows so that it is described uniquely.

$$\text{Speed:}\quad \nu_l(i, j) = \|\ \overrightarrow{v}_l(i, j)\ \| \quad (0 \le i < M, 0 \le j < N, 0 \le l < L) \tag{4}$$

$$\text{Curvature:}\quad \kappa_l(i, j) = cos^{-1}(\overrightarrow{t}_l(i, j) \cdot \overrightarrow{t}_{l-1}(i, j)) \quad (0 \le i < M, 0 \le j < N, 1 \le l < L) \tag{5}$$

$$\text{Torsion:}\quad \eta(i, j) = cos^{-1}(\overrightarrow{b}_{l+1}(i, j) \cdot \overrightarrow{b}_l(i, j)) \quad (0 \le i < M, 0 \le j < N, 1 \le l < L - 1) \tag{6}$$

$$\text{where,}\quad \overrightarrow{v}_l(i, j) = \overrightarrow{p_l(i, j)p_{l+1}(i, j)}, \quad \overrightarrow{t}_l(i, j) = \frac{\overrightarrow{v}_l(i, j)}{\nu_l(i, j)}, \quad \overrightarrow{b}_l(i, j) = \frac{\overrightarrow{t}_l(i, j) \times \overrightarrow{t}_{l-1}(i, j)}{\|\ \overrightarrow{t}_l(i, j) \times \overrightarrow{t}_{l-1}(i, j)\ \|} \tag{7}$$

$\times$: outer product of vector,　　　: dot product of vector.

As shown in Fig. 1(c) and (d), *speed ν*, *curvature κ*, and *torsion τ* represent the distance between two points, change in trajectory direction, and torsion of the trajectory direction, respectively. When the number of filters is L, $3L - 6$ ($L \ge 3$) variations of feature values are registered for each point.

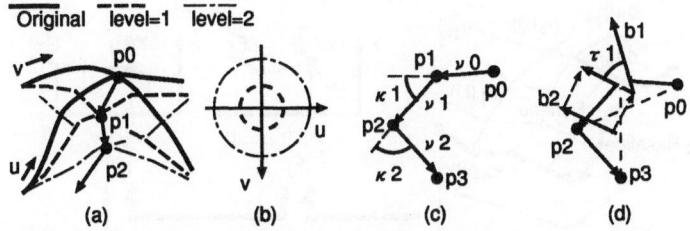

Fig. 1: Trajectory of a Point by Filtering

A point p_0 on the original surface is moved to p_1 and p_2 according to the filter radii. In this case, the radii are characterized as $r_1 < r_2$. p_1 and p_2 are moved by the filters with radii r_1 and r_2, respectively. The level denotes the index of filter.

2.3 Filtering Technique

To achieve the filtering expressed by Eq. 2 for each point on a surface taken by a range finder, two difficulties must be overcome regarding computational cost: 1) Calculating the distance between each pair of points and 2) Increasing the convolutional calculation that accompanies the radii of filters. In this section, we propose a low-cost method of approximating this filtering.

2.3.1 Coordinate System

A shape taken by a range finder is described by range image $f(i,j)$. This paper mainly deals with a cylindrical coordinated range image $r = f(\theta, z)$ (for example, taken by a Cyberware Digitizer), but an orthogonal coordinated range image $z = f(x,y)$ can be processed in a similar manner. In these cases, when we select the directions of the axes on a surface as a projection of the range image axes onto the surface, the axes on the surface cross approximately perpendicularly. So, when the impulse response of a filter is separable as $h(i,j) = h_1(i)h_2(j)$, one-dimensional convolution can be calculated alternatively as

$$h * f = \Sigma_j \Sigma_i h(i,j) f(u-i, v-j) = \Sigma_j h_2(j) \Sigma_i h_1(i) f(u-i, v-j) \tag{8}$$

2.3.2 Adoption of HDC

We also employ Hierarchical Discrete Correlation (HDC) (Burt 1981) to reduce computational cost. HDC is a low-cost technique for deriving convolutional integrals that achieve convolution of wide support by recursive weighted summation of a few points, that is

$$g_0(x) = f(x) , \quad g_l(x) = \sum_{i=-m}^{m} w(i) g_{l-1}(x - id^{l-1}) \quad (l > 1) \tag{9}$$

where, when $m = 2$, $d = 2$, $w(0) = 0.4$, $w(1) = w(-1) = 0.25$, and $w(2) = w(-2) = 0.05$, Gaussian low-pass filters ($\sigma = 0.56d^l$) are approximated by only five-point convolution at each level.

2.3.3 Filtering 3-D surface

Utilizing the above mentioned techniques, we extend filtering to the 3-D surface by alternative and recursive one-dimensional convolution as follows.

First, we define the terms used below (Fig. 2(a)).

Original surface: $\{ p_o(i,j) = (x(i,j), y(i,j), z(i,j))^T | 0 \le i < M, 0 \le j < N \}$ (10)

Surface at l-th level: $\{ p_l(i,j) = (x_l(i,j), y_l(i,j), z_l(i,j))^T | 0 \le i < M, 0 \le j < N \}$ (11)

i-Baseline, j-Baseline: $\{ p_o(i,0) | i = 0, 1, ..., M-1 \}, \quad \{ p_o(0,j) | j = 0, 1, ..., N-1 \}$ (12)

Distance from $p_o(i,j)$ to each baseline:

$$d_i(0,j) = 0, \quad d_i(i,j) = \Sigma_{k=1}^{i} \| p(k,j) - p(k-1,j) \| \tag{13}$$

$$d_j(i,0) = 0, \quad d_j(i,j) = \Sigma_{k=1}^{j} \| p(i,k) - p(i,k-1) \| \tag{14}$$

where (i,j) is a pixel index of a range image and l ($0 \le l < Lev$) is a level index.

The filtering procedure is described in Fig. 3 and examples of filtered shapes and trajectories are shown in Fig. 6.

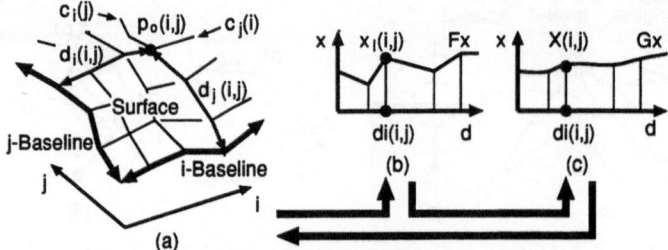

Fig. 2: Scenario of Filtering

(a) shows terms used in the text. (b) is an illustration of a function of distance along a surface (d) vs. coordinates (x, y, z). (c) is an illustration of the convoluted function of (b) by HDC. Only the x coordinate is shown in (b) and (c) but the y and z coordinates are processed similarly.

Step 0 :	Set original surface to the 0-th level's surface ($p_0 = p_o$). Set l to 1. Calculate the distance along the surface from each point to each baseline for all points.
Step 1 :	Make slices $c_j = (x(i,j), y(i,j), z(i,j))^T$ $(i = 0, 1, .., M - 1)$ along the i-direction for all j and do the next procedure for all c_j
Step 1.1 :	Make one-dimensional functions $x = F_x(d)$, $y = F_y(d)$, $z = F_z(d)$ where the coordinates of the functions are distance d_j vs. $x/y/z$ coordinate values for each point (Fig. 2(b)).
Step 1.2 :	Calculate HDC of the l-th level for F_x, F_y, F_z (Fig. 2(c)). Filtered signals are described as $X = G_x(d)$, $Y = G_y(d)$, $Z = G_z(d)$
Step 1.3 :	Results X, Y, Z in the i-direction and the l-th level are obtained by sampling the signals at the original absissa for each point (Fig. 2(c)). $X(i,j) = G_x(d_j(i,j))$, $Y(i,j) = G_y(d_j(i,j))$, $Z(i,j) = G_z(d_j(i,j))$ Intermediate surface is made by a set of (X, Y, Z)
Step 2 :	Make slices $c_i = (X(i,j), Y(i,j), Z(i,j))^T$ $(j = 0, 1, .., N - 1)$ along the j-direction for all i. Do the same procedure as in Step 1 for all c_i and set the result of this step to the l-th level surface.
Step 3 :	Set l to $l + 1$. Repeat Step 1 and Step 2 to the predetermined level.

Fig. 3: The Filtering Procedure

3 POSE ESTIMATION AND SHAPE IDENTIFICATION

In this section, we present a method for pose estimation and partial shape identification by using the trajectory mentioned above. This method is based on point-to-point correspondence of two shapes (a test shape and a model shape) e.g. like covering a test shape with the mask of a model shape. In this procedure, identification of a partial shape is done in the procedure for pose estimation, so we describe this while explaining the pose estimating steps.

3.1 Overview of Pose Estimation

Let us assume that two 3-D objects A (a model shape) and B (a test shape) are given. If these shapes have the same parts, by estimating six pose parameters of B relative to A, a part of B can be covered with a part of A correctly. If these two are totally different, however, A can not cover B by estimation of any pose parameters. So this method identifies a part of a test shape while estimating its pose relative to a model shape.

To estimate the pose parameters R, T, at least three correspondences between two objects are necessary in a general case. However, when the objects are complex like human heads, it is difficult to match three or more points. The proposed feature, however, makes it possible to estimate the pose by less than three correspondences because we can obtain a robust direction for the trajectories for each point on a surface.

The scenario of this method is very simple as shown in Fig. 4(a). Let Ta, Tb be the trajectory of a point Pa, Pb on shape A, B, respectively where point Pb corresponds to 'Pa. If it is possible to find the correspondence between Pa and Pb, the pose parameters are obtained by fitting Tb to Ta unless the trajectories are straight.

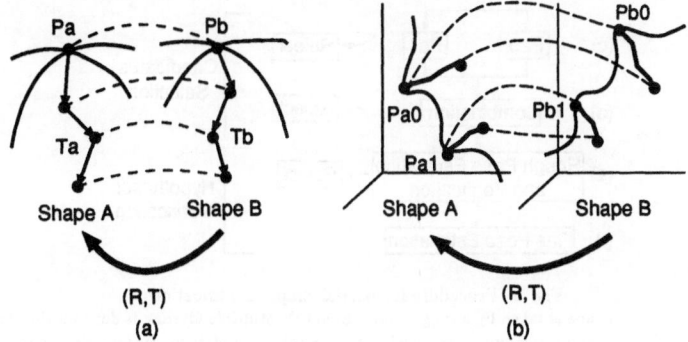

Fig. 4: Scenario of Pose Estimation

To perform this trajectory fitting, we have to search for the corresponding points on each shape. We should choose points with large *speed* values to make the matching easier. This is because a large *speed* is caused by a big convexity or concavity on the surface around a point; as a result, there are not many points on big 'bumps' in a shape. However, the *torsions* of the trajectory become critical when the *speeds* are large at every level, i.e., when the trajectory is almost straight. Therefore, we use two-point correspondences of long trajectories as shown in Fig. 4(b), and make them fit together. The merits of pose estimation by two-point correspondences are:

1. In addition to the values of *speed*, we can use the distance between two points (e.g. Pa_0 and Pa_1 in Fig. 4) to select candidates for these points consequently, we can have a smaller number of candidates.
2. Pose estimation becomes more stable because when two corresponding points are found, we have twice as much information as when there is one correspondence for fitting the trajectories.
3. It can save computational cost. If we have to find three corresponding points, we have to test three distances between three points besides the feature values of the three points in the selection of candidates.

This idea leads us to searching for candidate points for each model point. The candidates for the corresponding points are searched for on a test shape utilizing the *speed* values of the trajectories and the distance between the points. If no points are selected in this step, the model shape is rejected. If many points are selected, however, the poses made by these points are held for the next step as 'rough pose hypotheses'.

After estimating rough poses by selected candidates, we identify the surface utilizing additional points called 'verification points' to verify the pose hypotheses. These verification points are set on the part of a model we want to identify (See Fig. 7 for example). If a hypothesis is accurate, the correlation between the test shape and the verification points translated by the pose hypothesis is expected to be high, whereas if the test shape is different from the model shape, the correlation for all hypotheses are small. In this step, the test shape is rejected if the correlations are small. If there exist pose hypotheses that give high correlations, the best pose hypothesis giving the highest correlation is selected for finer pose estimation.

The finest pose is estimated by point to point correspondence of the verification points beginning with the best pose hypothesis as the initial pose, and as a result, the finest pose and corresponding verification points on the test shape are found. An overview of the procedure is shown in Fig. 5.

3.2 Procedure

3.2.1 Initial Condition
First, we have to know:

- Two trajectories of points P_{a0} and P_{a1} of model shape A for searching and fitting.

$$Ta_p^{(l)} = (x_{ap}^{(l)}, y_{ap}^{(l)}, z_{ap}^{(l)})^T \quad (l = 0, ..., Lev - 1, \quad p = 0, 1)$$

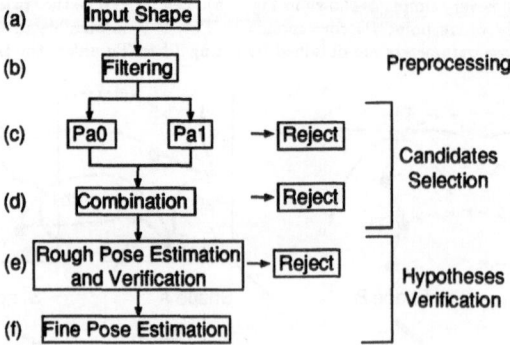

Fig. 5: Procedure for partial shape identification
Step (a): A test shape is taken by a range finder. Step (b): Multiple filtering is done on the shape, and the *speed* values for each point are calculated. Step (c): Candidate points for points Pa_0, Pa_1 are selected by thresholding the *speed* values of each point. Step (d): For every pair of candidate points for Pa_0 and Pa_1, the distance between them is tested. Step (e): The best pair is selected by rough pose estimation and verification of the pose. Step (f): The finest pose parameters are estimated by refining the rough pose.

where l is the level of filtering and p is an index of two points.
- Values of *speeds* of trajectories Ta_p.

$$Na_p^{(l)} = \| Ta_p^{(l+1)} - Ta_p^{(l)} \| /2^l \tag{15}$$

where 2^l normalizes the speed value for each level.
- Distance between points P_{a0} and P_{a1}.

$$D_a = \| Pa_0 - Pa_1 \| = \| Ta_0^{(0)} - Ta_1^{(0)} \|$$
$$= \sqrt{(x_{a0}^{(0)} - x_{a1}^{(0)})^2 + (y_{a0}^{(0)} - y_{a1}^{(0)})^2 + (z_{a0}^{(0)} - z_{a1}^{(0)})^2} \tag{16}$$

- Verification points and their trajectories.

$$\{Pa_p | p = 2, ..., N_v - 1\}, \quad \{Ta_p^{(l)} | p = 2, ..., N_v - 1\} \tag{17}$$

where N_v is the number of verification points.

3.2.2 Filtering
A test shape taken by the range finder is filtered as mentioned in Subsection 2.3 from level 0 to level $Lev - 1$. The *speed* values (Eq. 18) are calculated for all trajectories , $\{Tb^{(l)}(i,j) | l = 0, ..., Lev - 1\}$, of points $Pb(i,j)$ on the surface. Here, (i,j) are the coordinates of the range image.

$$Nb^{(l)}(i,j) = \| Tb^{(l+1)}(i,j) - Tb^{(l)}(i,j) \| /2^l \tag{18}$$

3.2.3 Candidate Selection
Candidates for two points are selected by thresholding $Nb^{(l)}$. A point is regarded as a candidate for point Pa_p when the *speed* values satisfy the following condition.

$$E_p(i,j) = \sum_{l=0}^{Lev-1} |Nb^{(l)}(i,j) - Na_p^{(l)}| < \theta_p \tag{19}$$

where θ_p is the predetermined threshold for Pa_p. If no candidates are selected, this test shape is rejected.

As a result, candidates for two points are selected. We term these candidate points and trajectories

$$\text{Candidates for point} Pa_0 : Pb(i_m, j_m), \quad Tb^{(l)}(i_m, j_m) \quad (m = 0, ..., M - 1) \tag{20}$$
$$\text{Candidates for point} Pa_1 : Pb(i_n, j_n), \quad Tb^{(l)}(i_n, j_n) \quad (n = 0, .., N - 1) \tag{21}$$

where m and n represent the candidate indexes and M and N represent the number of candidates.

3.2.4 Combination Selection

From among the candidates selected above, we further select candidate combinations. In the previous step, M and N points are selected and there are $M \times N$ candidate combinations. This step reduces the number of candidates that are selected unexpectedly so as to save computational cost for the following procedure.

We narrow down the number of combinations by thresholding the distances between all combinations of $Pb(i_m, j_m)$ and $Pb(i_n, j_n)$. If

$$abs(\| Pb(i_m, j_m) - Pb(i_n, j_n) \| - D_a) < \theta_d \qquad (22)$$

then the combination of m and n is selected as a candidate combination. Here, θ_d is the predetermined threshold for the distance. If no combination is selected, the test shape is rejected. As a result, we have the combination:

$$Cb(k) = \{Pb(i_{mk}, j_{mk}), Pb(i_{nk}, j_{nk})\} \quad (k = 0, ..., N_c - 1, \quad N_c \leq N \times M)$$

where k and N_c are an index and the number of selected combinations, respectively.

3.2.5 Rough Pose Estimation and Verification

In this step, we estimate rough poses by two-trajectories fitting and verify the pose hypotheses by correlating two shapes with the verification points. This step consists of the following procedures.

1 For all candidate combinations $C_b(k)$, do the next procedure.

    1.1 Estimate pose parameters by fitting two trajectories. The trajectories of elected pairs contain $Lev \times 2$ points for pose estimation. Let us term these trajectories:

$$Tb_0^{(l)} = (x_{mk0}^{(l)}, y_{mk0}^{(l)}, z_{mk0}^{(l)})^T, \quad Tb_1^{(l)} = (x_{nk1}^{(l)}, y_{nk1}^{(l)}, z_{nk1}^{(l)})^T \qquad (23)$$

These points and the trajectories of model $Ta_0^{(l)}, Ta_1^{(l)}$ are fitted by the least square method. Rotation matrix R and translation vector T are estimated so as to minimize error

$$E_i(k) = \sum_{l=0}^{Lev-1} \sum_{p=0}^{1} ((RTb_p^{(l)} + T) - Ta_p^{(l)})^2 \qquad (24)$$

We denote the pose parameters estimated here as $\{Ro(k), To(k) | k = 0, ... N_c - 1\}$ where k is an index of a candidate combination.

    1.2 By using estimated poses, the correlation of two shapes $corr(k)$ is calculated by

$$corr(k) = \frac{1}{N_v} \Sigma_{p=0}^{N_v-1} \|(Ro(k)Pa_p + To(k)) - Pb_p\| \qquad (25)$$

where Pa_p is a verification point on a model shape and Pb_p is a point on a test shape nearest from $Ro(k)Pa_p + To(k)$. In this expression, a high correlation gives a small value to $corr(k)$.

2 The combination ko that gives the smallest value of $corr(k)$ is selected.

3 If the value $corr(ko)$ does not satisfy the thresholding of Eq. 26, the test shape is rejected.

$$corr(ko) < \theta_c \qquad (26)$$

As a result of this step, the best combination $Cb(ko)$ that passed the thresholding (Eq. 26) is held, if it exists.

3.2.6 Fine Pose Estimation

In this step, finer pose parameters are estimated to identify the position of a model shape on a test shape. A finer pose is estimated by finding the pose parameters R, T that minimize the cost function

$$cost = \Sigma_{p=0}^{N_v-1} dis(R(k)Pa_p + T(k), Pb) \qquad (27)$$

$$dis(Pa_p, Pb) = \{\|Pa_p - Pb_p\| - \lambda\|Va_p - Vb_p\|\} \qquad (28)$$

where Va_p and Vb_q are the feature vector for points Pa_p and Pb_p, respectively. This expression means that the cost function is a weighted sum of 'distance on input space' and 'distance on feature space'. By minimizing this, the nearest points both in the input space and in the feature space are found for each verification point as well as R, T. We use the $Nb^{(l)}$ of a point as a feature vector so that the feature space is an $Lev - 1$ dimensional space. The procedure consists of the following steps:

1 Begin with the pose parameters $(Ro(ko), To(ko))$ for the initial pose.

2 Rotate and translate the verification points of the model shape.

3 For each verification point, search for the point on the test shape that gives the smallest value of $dis(Pa_p, Pb)$ as correspondent point Pb_q.

4 A new pose that minimizes $corr()$ value is estimated by the correspondence made in the previous step.

5 If the pose is not changed from the previous iteration, then the final pose is estimated;
    else repeat from the step 2

4 EXPERIMENTS

In this section, we report some experimental results of the method mentioned above. We selected the face part of a human head as an examples of a model shape (Fig. 7) because a human head is curved and complex. The verification points are selected manually as shown in Fig. 7; they consist of 15 points including the tip of the nose (Pa_0) and the center of the chin (Pa_1) for two-trajectory fitting.

4.1 Experimental Conditions

The shapes shown in Fig. 8(b)-(h) are test shapes for this experiment whereas (a) is the model shape. The range finder we used was a Cyberware model 4020/PS Digitizer. This range finder can obtain a shape as a cylindrical range image $r = f(\theta, z)$. In the range images shown in this paper, abscissas, ordinates, and brightness are denoted θ , z , and r, respectively. In the experiments, the resolution for range images was 128 × 128 pixel (16384 points). One pixel on the z axis was 3.2 mm, one level of 256 in brightness was 1 mm , and one pixel on the θ axis was about 2.8 degrees ($\simeq \frac{360}{128}$).

The filtering was done using the procedure proposed in Subsection 2.3. The HDC parameters were the same as those shown in Fig. 6. In this case, the filtering took about 1 $min.$ for each level with Sun $SS2$. Examples of filtered shapes and the trajectories are shown in Fig. 6. The number of levels was 5 so we had 6 points in a trajectory including the original point.

Candidates for the top of the nose and the chin were selected by the thresholding expressed in Eq. 19. θ_0, θ_1, the threshold for the nose and the chin, were both 0.3.

Combinations of candidates were tested and selected by Eq. 22. θ_d was set to $\sqrt{3}/2$, i.e. half the length of the diagonal direction of a unit cube.

With the selected combinations, the pose parameters were calculated by minimizing the error (Eq. 24). We estimated the parameters in these experiments as follows.

1. The center of rotation is fixed to the center of gravities of $Tb_p^{(l)}$ and $Ta_p^{(l)}$ ($l = 0, ..Lev - 1, p = 0, 1$) and the center of gravities of the trajectories are fitted.
2. Rotation matrix R is estimated by the non-iterating method described in (Kanatani 1990).
3. Translation vector T is calculated by the movement of the center and estimated matrix.

We determined the threshold θ_c to be $\sqrt{3}$. This means that for each verification point, there exists a point within approximately the length of the diagonal direction of a unit cube.

4.2 Results

Table 1 shows the identification capabilities. In the candidate selection, the numbers of candidates are narrowed down to very small values compared with the total number of points on a test shape (128 × 128 in those experiment). In particular, totally different shapes (g), (d) are rejected in the candidate selection, so no detailed verification and estimation are necessary.

Even if a different shape passed the candidate selection, the numbers of candidate combinations are small so computational cost can be saved in the verification step. And the $corr(ko)$ values in the verification step designate obvious differences between identical shapes and different shapes, so it is easy to reject different shapes in the verification step. The values of identical shapes (b), (c), and (d) also suggest that the rough poses are approximately correct. Shapes different from the model shape are all rejected.

Table 2 shows the error of the estimated pose parameters for each identified shape compared with the original poses. The estimated poses contain only small errors. The error for pose estimation can be reduced by increasing the number of verification points. However, increasing the number of verification points leads to an increase in computational cost in the verification step and for fine pose estimation, so the number of verification points should be selected according to the desirable accuracy for each application.

Figure 9 shows the estimated parts and corresponding points mapped onto range images. For each test shape, the facial part is estimated almost correctly as well as the corresponding points for each verification point.

Table 1: Results of Identification

Test shape	# of candidates			$corr$*1	Rejected step*2
	Nose	Chin	Combinations		
(b)	11	137	47	0.80	-
(c)	21	89	66	0.85	-
(d)	16	96	55	1.08	-
(e)	7	15	10	6.15	(e)
(f)	6	59	1	11.48	(e)
(g)	0	95	-	-	(c)
(h)	0	0	-	-	(c)

*1: The column of 'corr' shows the values of $corr(ko)$ (Eq. 25). *2: The column 'Rejected step' shows the step in Fig. 5 where a test shape is rejected.

Table 2: Error of estimated pose

Test shape	Error of Estimated Pose			Original Pose	
	Rotation (θ, ϕ, ψ)*degree	Translation (tx, ty, tz)*pixel	Itera-tions	Rotation (θ, ϕ, ψ)*degree	Translation (tx, ty, tz)*pixel
(b)	(-2.2, 1.1, 2.7)	(-1.4, -2.5, 1.0)	6	(20.0, 10.0, 25.0)	(11.1, 21.6, 68.8)
(c)	(-1.9, 1.7, 4.1)	(-1.8, -0.5, -1.1)	6	(45.0, 20.0, 0.0)	(21.8, 42.5, 85.5)
(d)	(2.4, 0.6, 1.9)	(0.5, 0.2, -2.7)	7	(70.0, -10.0, 0.0)	(-11.1, 59.2, 106)

* Parameters for rotation and translation are described as in Appendix B.

5 CONCLUSION

We have presented a new feature extraction technique and an identification method for a three-dimensional surface. This proposed technique can extract robust view-point invariant shape information coarse to fine around a point to make it easier to locate the point to be matched.

With the involved filtering, a point on the surface gets a trajectory with robust coarse-to-fine shape information, making it possible to estimate a pose with less than three points of correspondences. Furthermore, we applied this idea to identification of partial shapes and proved the effectiveness of this method. In this method, shapes totally different from a model shape are rejected early in the procedure by simply thresholding the values, so computational costs is reduced. And finally, this method performs excellent congruency matching.

In the step for pose estimation, points on a test shape corresponding to points on a model shape are obtained as byproducts. We are planning to extend this method to enable it to search for corresponding points between different shapes e.g. faces of different persons, for the description and recognition of a shape.

ACKNOWLEDGMENT
The authors would like to thank Prof. Narendra Ahuja of the University of Illinois, Dr. Kouhei Habara and Dr. Nobuyoshi Terashima of ATR Communication Systems Research Laboratories and the members of the Artificial Intelligence Department for their helpful discussions on this subject.

Appendix A
We want to find out why the length of the vector caused by filtering is independent of rotation.

We assume that the impulse response of the filter is symmetrically circular and the total impulse response is equal to 1 with compact support, that is,

$$h(u, v) = h(r) = h(\sqrt{u^2 + v^2}) , \qquad \iint h(u, v) du dv = 1 \qquad (29)$$

Let a surface S_o be: $S_o(u, v) = (x(u, v) \quad y(u, v) \quad z(u, v))^T$, where (u, v) are axes crossing perpendicularly at a point $p_o = So(u_o, v_o)$ on surface S_o and the coordinates of these axes are distances along the axes.

On surface S_o, vector V_o of point p_o moved to p_1 by filtering is:

$$V_o = p_1 - p_o = \begin{pmatrix} \iint x(k,l)h(u_o - k, v_o - l)dkdl - x(u_o, v_o) \\ \iint y(k,l)h(u_o - k, v_o - l)dkdl - y(u_o, v_o) \\ \iint z(k,l)h(u_o - k, v_o - l)dkdl - z(u_o, v_o) \end{pmatrix} = \begin{pmatrix} v_x & v_y & v_z \end{pmatrix}^T \qquad (30)$$

This vector V_o is independent of the selection of axes as long as it satisfies the condition mentioned above.

Next, let the surface S_r be a translated surface of S_o by R and T as

$$S_r(u,v) = R\begin{pmatrix} x(u,v) & y(u,v) & z(u,v) \end{pmatrix}^T + T \qquad (31)$$

where R and T are :

$$R = \begin{pmatrix} a_{00} & a_{01} & a_{02} \\ a_{10} & a_{11} & a_{12} \\ a_{20} & a_{21} & a_{22} \end{pmatrix} \quad , \quad T = \begin{pmatrix} t_x & t_y & t_z \end{pmatrix}^T \qquad (32)$$

On surface S_r, point p_o corresponds to

$$p_r = Rp_o + T = R(x(u_o, v_o), y(u_o, v_o), z(u_o, v_o))^T + T \qquad (33)$$

Then, vector V_r of point p_r moved to p_s by the same filtering as Eq. 30, is expressed and modified as

$$V_r = p_s - p_r \qquad (34)$$

$$= \begin{pmatrix} \iint\{a_{00}x(k,l) + a_{01}y(k,l) + a_{02}z(k,l) + t_x\}h(u_o - k, v_o - l)dkdl \\ \quad -\{a_{00}x(u_o, v_o) + a_{01}y(u_o, v_o) + a_{02}z(u_o, v_o) + t_x\} \\ \iint\{a_{10}x(k,l) + a_{11}y(k,l) + a_{12}z(k,l) + t_y\}h(u_o - k, v_o - l)dkdl \\ \quad -\{a_{10}x(u_o, v_o) + a_{11}y(u_o, v_o) + a_{12}z(u_o, v_o) + t_y\} \\ \iint\{a_{20}x(k,l) + a_{21}y(k,l) + a_{22}z(k,l) + t_z\}h(u_o - k, v_o - l)dkdl \\ \quad -\{a_{20}x(u_o, v_o) + a_{21}y(u_o, v_o) + a_{22}z(u_o, v_o) + t_z\} \end{pmatrix}$$

$$= \begin{pmatrix} a_{00}v_x + a_{01}v_y + a_{02}v_z + t_x\{\iint h(u_o - k, v_o - l)dkdl - 1\} \\ a_{10}v_x + a_{11}v_y + a_{12}v_z + t_y\{\iint h(u_o - k, v_o - l)dkdl - 1\} \\ a_{20}v_x + a_{21}v_y + a_{22}v_z + t_z\{\iint h(u_o - k, v_o - l)dkdl - 1\} \end{pmatrix} = \begin{pmatrix} a_{00} & a_{01} & a_{02} \\ a_{10} & a_{11} & a_{12} \\ a_{20} & a_{21} & a_{22} \end{pmatrix} \begin{pmatrix} v_x & v_y & v_z \end{pmatrix}^T$$

$$= Rv_o = R(p_1 - p_o) = (Rp_1 + T) - (Rp_o + T)$$

The selection of axes is independent as long as it satisfies the condition mentioned above and matrix R is a rotation matrix, the length of the vector is independent of rotation and translation.

Appendix B

We denote parameter R by θ, ϕ, ψ as Eq. 35 and T by t_x, t_y, t_z as similar to Eq. 32

$$R = \begin{pmatrix} \cos\phi\cos\psi & -\cos\phi\sin\psi & -\sin\phi \\ -\sin\theta\sin\phi\cos\psi + \cos\theta\sin\psi & \sin\theta\sin\phi\sin\psi + \cos\theta\cos\psi & -\sin\theta\cos\phi \\ \cos\theta\sin\phi\cos\psi + \sin\theta\sin\psi & -\cos\theta\sin\phi\sin\psi + \sin\theta\cos\psi & \cos\theta\cos\phi \end{pmatrix} \qquad (35)$$

References

Asada H, Brady M (1986) The Curvature Primal Sketch. *IEEE Trans.*, PAMI-8(1):2–14.

Besl PJ *Surfaces in Range Image Understanding* Springer-Verlag.

Besl PJ, Jain RC (1988) Segmentetion Through Variable-Order Surface Fitting. *IEEE Trans.*, PAMI-10(2):167–192.

Brady JP, Nandhakumar N, Aggarwal JK (1989) Recent Progress in the Recognition of Objects from Range Data. *IEEE Trans.*, PAMI-11(11):1140–1157.

Brady M, Ponce J, Yuille A, Asada H (1985) Describing Surfaces. *CVGIP*, 32(1):1–28.

Brou P Using the Gaussian Image to Find the Orientation of Objects. *The International Journal of Robotics Research*, 3(4):89–125.

Burt PJ Fast Filter Transform for Image Processing. *CGIP*, 16:20–51.

Fan T, Medioni G, Neavatia R (1989) Recognizing 3-D objects Using Surface descriptions. *IEEE Trans.*, PAMI-11(11):1140–1157.

Hoffman R, Jain AK (1987) Segmentation and Classification of Range Images. *IEEE Trans.*, PAMI-9(5):608–620.

Harashima H, Kishino F (1991) Intelligent Image Coding and Communications with Realistic Sensations - Recent Trends -. *The Transaction of the IEICE*, E-74(6):1582–1592.

Jain AK, Hoffman R (1988) Evidence-Based Recognition of 3-D Objects. *IEEE Trans.*, PAMI-10(6):783–802.

Kanatani K *Group-Theoretical Methods in Image Understanding* Springer.

Mokhtarian F, Mackworth A (1986) Scale-Based Description and Recognition of Planar Curves and Two-Dimensional Shapes. *IEEE Trans.*, PAMI-8(1):34–43.

Sander PT, Zucker SW (1990) Inferring Surface Trace and Differential Structure from 3-D Images. *IEEE Trans.*, PAMI-12(9):833–854.

Witkin A Scale Space Filtering. In *Proc. 8th Int. Joint Conf. on Artificial Intell.*, pages 1019–1022.

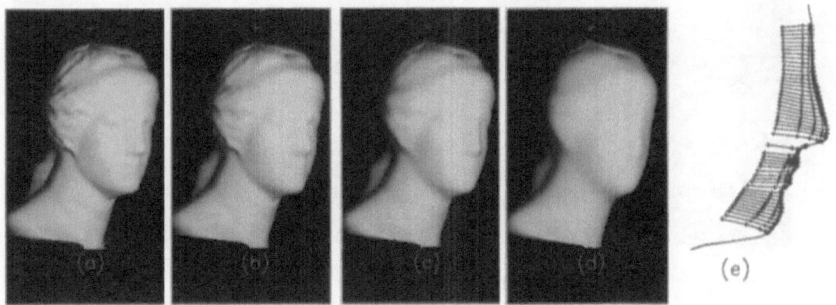

Fig. 6: Examples of Filtered Shapes and Trajectories

Original shape (a) is taken from a laser range finder whose output is a cylindrical coordinated range image. (b),(c) and (d) show filtered shapes at 1st to 3rd level, respectively. (e) shows the trajectories of the profile around the nose at 0 to 5th level. Parameters of HDC are $m = 2$, $d = 2$, $w(0) = 0.4$, $w(1) = w(-1) = 0.25$, $w(2) = w(-2) = 0.05$ to approximate gaussian low-pass filters.

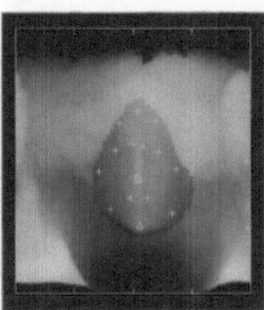

Fig. 7: A model shape and its verification points

The model shape (Fig. 8(a)) is displayed as a cylindrical range image. We are going to identify the facial part (bluish part). Verification points are marked on the facial part. The points for $Pa0$ and $Pa1$ are marked □ and △, respectively. The other verification points are marked +.

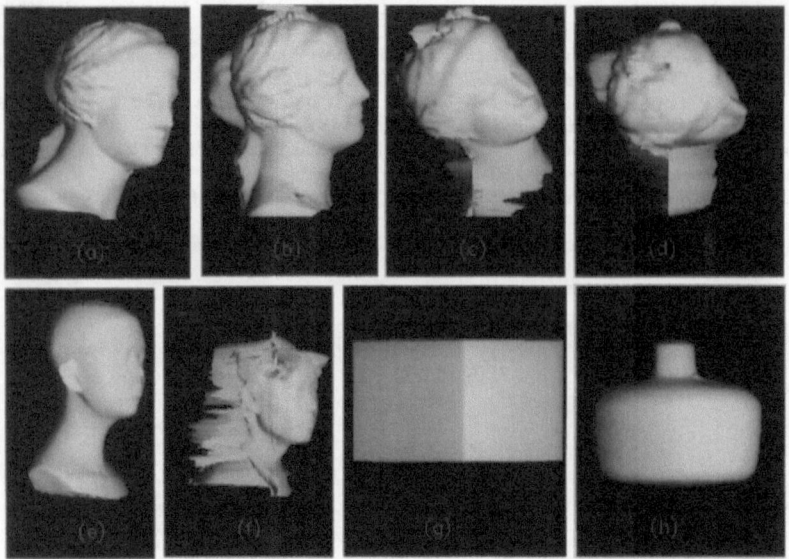

Fig. 8: Input shapes for the experiments

(a) is an original shape taken from a range finder.(b), (c), and (d) are generated by certain pose parameters from object (a). (e), (f), (g), and (h) are different shapes taken from a range finder.

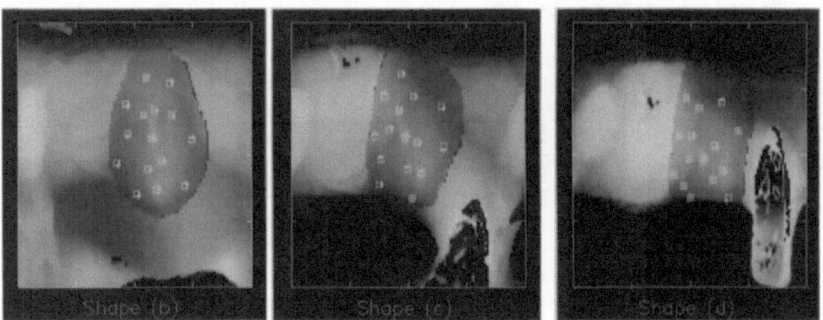

Fig. 9: Estimated parts on test shapes

A bluish part is estimated to be a facial part for each shape. A reddish parts along the edge of the bluish part indicate the error. □ indicates estimated corresponding point for each verification point whereas + indicates the correct corresponding point.

579

BIOGRAPHY

Keisuke Iwasaki received the B.E. degree from Osaka University, Osaka, Japan, in 1984. In 1984, he joined Sharp Corporation, where he has been involved in research and development of image processing and image database systems. He has been a researcher of the Artificial Intelligence Department, ATR Communication Systems Research Laboratories since mid-1991. His research interests include computer vision, image processing and computational geometry. He is a member of IEICE.

Kenji Mochizuki received the B.E. and M.E. degrees from Dosisya University, Kyoto, Japan, in 1976 and 1978, respectively. In 1978, he joined the Electrical Communication Laboratories, Nippon Telegraph and Telephone Corporation, where he has been involved in research and development of magnetic memories and autonomous robot systems. He has been a senior researcher of the Artificial Intelligence Department, ATR Communication Systems Research Laboratories since 1990. He is a member of the society of Instrument and Control Engineers, Japanese Society for Artificial Intelligence and IEICE.

Fumio Kishino received the B.E. and M.E. degrees from Nagoya Institute of Technology, in 1969 and 1971 respectively. In 1971, he joined the Electrical Communication Laboratories, Nippon Telegraph and Telephone Corporation, where he has been involved in research and development of image processing and visual communication systems. In mid-1989, he joined ATR Communication Systems Research Laboratories, becoming the head of the Artificial Intelligence Department. He is a member of IEEE, IEICE and ITEJ.

Address: ATR Communication Systems Research Laboratories, 2-2, Hikaridai, Seika-cho, Soraku-gun, Kyoto, 619-02 Japan.

Analysis and Recognition of Medical Images: 1. Elastic Deformation Transformation

Ronghua Yan and Naoyuki Tokuda

ABSTRACT

Due to considerably large morphometric variability in human organs such as brains, an accurate transformation of the pre-generated model to a patient's image space is a prerequisite to a successful implementation of a deformable model-based recognition method. We have found the two dimensional thin-plate spline transformation and particularly its three-dimensional version of Bookstein (1989,1991) is both efficient and accurate using only a small number of landmarks in the transformation. Surprisingly the accuracy of the three-dimentional thin-hyperplate spline transformation is as good as that of two-dimentions with the same number (26) of landmarks used. It is further demonstrated that the transformation can be improved interactively by successive applications of transformations, adding landmarks where differences are large.

Keywords: CT and MRI data, landmark, model-based recognition, thin-plate (thin-hyperplate) spline transformation

1. INTRODUCTION

Vision constitutes the richest and the most important of all the five sense modalities of human beings. This is evidenced by the proportion of the brain that is dedicated to vision; the occipital cortex where visual signals are processed, together with portions of the cerebral cortex that appear to be dedicated to vision, occupy approximately one fourth of the brain's volume. Of all human activities, in fact, perception and/or image recognition represents a highest level of human intelligence. Segmentation and feature extraction constitutes the core information processing required in image recognition. Much early work in image processing has been devoted to generating filters in detecting low level image features like edges with these filtered output being used for image recognition. When a simple general-purpose segmentation method is used at low level, however, we immediately encounter difficulties because there seems no easy way left for improving the often partial and unpredictable results of low level modules at the higher levels of the system. Once lost at low levels, amending or correcting errors or omissions by recovering the lost information at higher level segmentation of the system is next to impossible (Kapouleas 1990). One scheme suggested to overcome these difficulties is to make full use of a priori knowledge of the images in the form of a model in implementing segmentation and feature extraction. This so-called model-based recognition makes use of, firstly, structural information of a 'most typical model' of the images sought including their shapes and sizes and secondly, detailed statistical knowledge provided by the model involved (Bennett & Craw 1991). In medical applications, the model is represented often by an anatomical atlas of a region of interest

such as brain or abdomen depending on our interest. The present approach basically follows the model-based recognition as a first step to the task of automatic image recognition.

A problem still remains in medical applications of the model-based recognition, however, because we must deal with considerably large morphometric variability of individual organs largely due to individual anatomical differences (see the original images of figures 1 and 2 in § 4 for typical differences). In fact, no two organs or sections can be the same between any two individuals. Although a model can be built taking averages of a large amount of healthy organs, it can not be general enough to build a model capable of fitting and absorbing widely varying types of individual differences without applying some form of transformations. We see then a need for a transformation of mapping individual organs to a model organ. Several methods are suggested including the global affine transformation or local interactive adjustments (Bennett & Craw 1991; Bozma & Duncan 1991; Worrall et al. 1991). The affine transformation can only deal with uniform translation, magnification, rotation and/or shear deformation and so can not be effective in dealing with the present case of non-uniform complex deformation.

A most promising scheme has been developed by Bookstein (1989, 1991). Bookstein's method is a non-linear deformation transformation mapping the model organ to a target organ under the paradigm of a minimum bending energy when the given organ is subjected to specified displacements at various positions of the objects in proportion to variances from the model. Note that these points marked by displacements are called 'landmarks' of the transformation upon which the effectiveness of the transformation critically depends. By extensive experiments, we show that the present method of elastic deformation is not only very efficient in the complexity of computations but also in precision of the transformation. Because the spline interpolation of curves and surfaces is based on the same principle of a minimn bending moment (Bookstein 1989, 1991), these methods are called the TPS (Thin-Plate Spline) and the THS (Thin-Hyperplate Spline) method applicable to two- and three-dimensional cases respectively.

As a first step to automatizing image recognition, we will examine closely the effectiveness of the deformation transformation by mapping a model organ of an atlas to CT or MRI medical images. The data used for transformation are sets of MRI or CT brain volume image data. Without losing any generality, we may choose one set as the model organ while the other set as a target organ to which the model configuration is mapped. The precision of mapping critically depends on the number and locations of landmarks chosen along the external boundary region for two-dimensional case or over the boundary surface of the organs for three-dimensional cases. The selection of landmarks is quite flexible in our approach. In fact, depending on the outcome of the transformation, we can apply the transformation recursively adding landmarks at such points we want an improvement in transformation. This capability of successive refinement of the transformation is an additional advantageous feature of our approach. We will show how we can improve the accuracy of transformation successively by adding landmarks where differences are largest without affecting other parts of contours largely due to localized effects of landmrks (see comments in § 2.1 below).

Another advantage of the present method is an efficient implementation of surface rendering. Vertices of a model represented in geometrical data based on meshes, triangular patches, or polyhedrons can be mapped to an object space quite easily using a constrained number of landmarks. All we have to do in surface rendering of a mapped space is to recalculate the surface normals of each vertex. See fig. 12 and 13 for its demonstration where the effect of a bumped displacement is localized.

2. DEFORMABLE MODEL

The deformation model is based upon a space warp mapping function. The theory was first introduced in the 1970's as an interpolation theory of curved surfaces. The theory is now applied to the medical imaging field as a general-purpose warping utility. The landmarks of the objects of an image are mapped under the paradigm of a minimum bending energy onto a target plane, generating a mapping between different shape of the same object. The method can also be easily extended to 3D space.

2.1 Two-Dimensional TPS Model of Bookstein

Consider mapping a set of n points $\{p_i\}$ onto another set of n points $\{p_i'\}$ in two-dimentional space.

$$f(p_i) = p_i' \qquad i=1,2,...,n \qquad (1)$$

Here n is called the number of landmarks specified along the profile. f is a mapping function of (p_i) onto $\{p_i'\}$. There would be infinite solutions to that problem. Consider minimizing the following functional over a class of interpolation functions

$$I_f = \iint_{R^2} \left[\left(\frac{\partial^2 f}{\partial x^2}\right)^2 + 2\left(\frac{\partial^2 f}{\partial x \partial y}\right)^2 + \left(\frac{\partial^2 f}{\partial y^2}\right)^2 \right] dxdy \qquad (2)$$

Since the term within the bracket, $\left(\frac{\partial^2 f}{\partial x^2}\right)^2 + 2\left(\frac{\partial^2 f}{\partial x \partial y}\right)^2 + \left(\frac{\partial^2 f}{\partial y^2}\right)^2$,

is proportional to the bending energy at the point (x,y), equation (2) is equivalent to minimizing the bending energy all over the space. A class of minimizing function f can be constructed from a fundamental solution to a biharmonic equation:

$$\Delta^2 U = 0 \qquad U(r) = r^2 \log r^2 \qquad (r = \sqrt{x^2 + y^2}) \qquad (3)$$

Let $r_{ij} = |p_i - p_j|$ denote the distance between points i and j, and define K, P, L, Y as,

$$K = \begin{bmatrix} 0 & U(r_{12}) & ... & U(r_{1n}) \\ U(r_{21}) & 0 & ... & U(r_{2n}) \\ ... & ... & ... & ... \\ U(r_{n1}) & U(r_{n2}) & ... & 0 \end{bmatrix}_{n \times n} ,$$

$$P = \begin{bmatrix} 1 & x_1 & y_1 \\ 1 & x_2 & y_2 \\ ... & ... & ... \\ 1 & x_n & y_n \end{bmatrix}_{3 \times n} ,$$

$$L = \begin{bmatrix} K & P \\ P^T & 0 \end{bmatrix}_{(n+3) \times (n+3)} ,$$

$$Y = \begin{bmatrix} \dot{x}_1 & \dot{x}_2 & \cdots & \dot{x}_n & 0 & 0 & 0 \\ \dot{y}_1 & \dot{y}_2 & \cdots & \dot{y}_n & 0 & 0 & 0 \end{bmatrix}^T \quad ,$$

$$L^{-1}Y = \begin{bmatrix} w_{11} & w_{12} & \cdots & w_{1n} & a_1 & a_{1x} & a_{1y} \\ w_{21} & w_{22} & \cdots & w_{2n} & a_2 & a_{2x} & a_{2y} \end{bmatrix}^T \quad . \tag{4}$$

Here T denotes a matrix transpose operator.

Function f(x,y) can be represented everywhere in the plane as,

$$f_x(x,y) = a_1 + a_{1x} + a_{1y} + \sum_{i=1}^{n} w_{1i}U(|P_i - (x,y)|) \quad ,$$

$$f_y(x,y) = a_2 + a_{2x} + a_{2y} + \sum_{i=1}^{n} w_{2i}U(|P_i - (x,y)|) \quad . \tag{5}$$

We note that vector function $\{f_x, f_y\}$ is invariant under translation or rotation of either set of landmarks. That means the deformation transformation is not affected by the location or position of the object relative to the model space.

Bookstein (1989) shows that the specification of landmarks affect the transformation locally, their effect dying out like 1/r away from the regions. This means that if the result of transformation is unsatisfactory at some location, we may add one or more pairs of points as landmarks setting up transformation iteratively. The transformation thus improves interactively with successive transformation. See fig. 5 and 6 of §4 where marked improvement is observed in the contour of eyeballs of fig. 6 when landmarks are added along the eyeballs.

2.2 Three-Dimensional THS Model

An extension of two-dimensional TPS theory to three dimensions is straightforward. Noting that the fundamental solution of the biharmonic equation is now,

$$U(r) = |r| \quad . \tag{6}$$

the three-dimensional space mapping function f can be expressed as:

$$f_x(x,y,z) = a_1 + a_{1x} + a_{1y} + a_{1z} + \sum_{i=1}^{n} w_{1i}U(|P_i - (x,y,z)|) \quad ,$$

$$f_y(x,y,z) = a_2 + a_{2x} + a_{2y} + a_{2z} + \sum_{i=1}^{n} w_{2i}U(|P_i - (x,y,z)|) \quad ,$$

$$f_z(x,y,z) = a_3 + a_{3x} + a_{3y} + a_{3z} + \sum_{i=1}^{n} w_{3i}U(|P_i - (x,y,z)|) \quad . \tag{7}$$

Here the only difference from the two-dimension of §2.1 is the inversion of (n+4)×(n+4) matrix in stead of (n+3)×(n+3) matrix.

By mimicking TPS in two dimension, we may call this method as THS "Thin-Hyperplate spline" method.

3. DEFORMABLE MODEL-BASED RECOGNITION

3.1 Basic Consideration

We will explain below why the deformable transformation described above plays a significant role in the analysis and recognition of images.

a. A small number of landmarks are sufficient:
In spite of considerably large individual anatomical differences between organs such
as brain, we all know that the basic anatomical structure remains the same. So as
long as landmarks chosen characterize the key features of an organ, we are able to
build a well-fitted space mapping between the models and objects.

b. Pre-defined model:
Neither CT nor MRI images can be free from noise. This is more distinct for organs
of soft tissue in CT images and of bone in MRI images. In dealing with noise-affected
images, a most effective method is the model-based recognition scheme whereby some
pre-defined contour of specific objects is taken into account in extracting objects. We
see then that the present mapping is a necessity in building a bridge to image recognition.

As we have discussed above, image recognition depends critically on the selection and
recognition of landmarks we choose along objects image interactively. Image recognition rate is expected to rise with recognition rate of landmarks.

3.2 Procedure of Recognition

A typical step for image recognition process will be sketched below.

a. Using two-dimensional slices of CT or MRI brain image data, we manually extract
the contour of Regions Of Interest (ROI). This ROI can be alternatively extracted from
anatomical atlas of brain of course. Three-dimensional Volume Of Interest (VOI) can
easily be obtained by extending the cross-sectional slices to three dimensions. A set
of landmarks will be chosen by first taking into account the key featuring positions
which characterize the organs or tissues and then the key featuring positions of the
boundary contour or surfaces of an organs for correct space mapping. The selection
of landmarks affects the subsequent ease of image recognition.

b. Once a pair sets of landmarks are chosen on the object and model images, we apply
TPS or THS warp functions depending on two-dimensional or three-dimensional cases
respectively. The transformation is applied only on the vertices of the model. The
accuracy of the transformation can be evaluated by an evaluation functions such as
equation (8) below. If it does not satisfy the pre-set standard, we can add one or more
landmarks where errors are large and recalculate the deformation transformation iteratively until the goal is satisfied.

c. For more accurate recognition processing, the output of the transformation along with
the original object image data then can be fed in as an input for further processing.
We may use the contour or surface information to guide the search of recognition, like
contour tracking method (Bennett & Craw 1991 or Ueda et al. 1992).

4. EXPERIMENTS

The MRI and CT data used in our experiments are obtained through the courtesy of Toshiba Medical Engineering. The data are analyzed by an AVS software using Kubota Vistra/B Workstation.

4.1 Two-Dimensional Transformation

As we have mentioned in §1 already, we may use as a model one of the CT or MRI image data manually. Figure 1 shows the original image data we have used as a model while fig. 2 a target object to be recognized. Figures 3 and 4 show the manually extracted original contours of the model and of the object respectively with landmarks shown along the contours. The number of landmarks chosen vary from 0(namely original), 8, 12, 18 up to 26 points.

To assess the accuracy of the transformation we define the following evaluation function of the transformation;

$$V_{2d} = \frac{A_1 \cap A_2}{A_1 \cup A_2} \tag{8}$$

Here A_i represents the area of an i-th object (i=1,2), with $\cap$ and $\cup$ representing the logical 'AND' and 'OR'. The results of all tests are shown in Table 1. The area is computed directly by counting the numbers of pixels within the ROI.

The results of TPS transformation of the model to the object contour image are shown in fig. 5 and 6. Figure 5 has 18 landmarks with none specified along the pair of eyeballs while fig. 6 has 26 landmarks with 4 marks each specified now along eyeballs. We see that added landmarks along eyeballs improves the accuracy of eyeball transformation significantly without affecting the transformation of other portions. This is well documented in the numerical values of an evaluation function of Table 1. A grey scale image of the transformed object of fig. 1 is shown in fig. 7 for reference purpose where greyscale levels are interpolated by taking averages of nearby four points.

Table 1. The evaluation result of two-dimensional mapping

Number of LandMarks			Test 1	Test 2			Test 3		
Total	Contour	Eyeball	Contour	Contour	Right Eyeball	Left Eyeball	Contour	Right Eyeball	Left Eyeball
0	(Original Image)		73.75 %	80.87 %	69.40 %	31.96 %	80.51 %	17.85 %	18.36 %
8	8	0	93.24 %	94.55 %	60.02 %	50.46 %	96.88 %	60.53 %	60.35 %
12	12	0	95.30 %	95.37 %	76.80 %	65.56 %	95.01 %	69.09 %	82.66 %
18	18	0	96.74 %	97.55 %	67.74 %	64.29 %	97.78 %	55.85 %	71.97 %
26	18	8		97.69 %	94.22 %	90.08 %	97.84 %	91.89 %	93.62 %

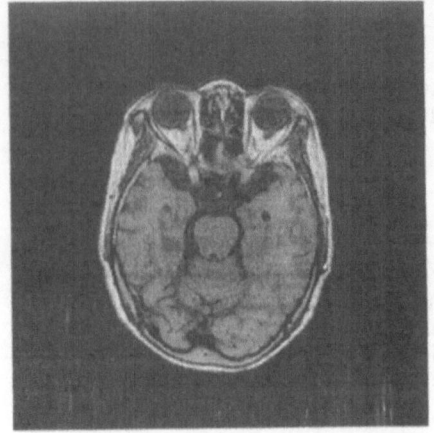

Fig. 1. Original MRI image 1

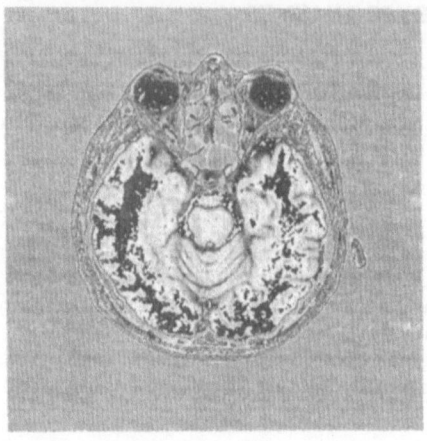

Fig. 2. Original MRI image 2

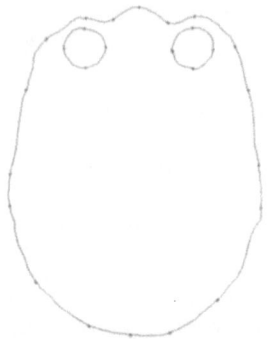

Fig. 3. Contour and landmarks of image 1

Fig. 4. Contour and landmarks of image 2

Fig. 5. Mapped result using 18 landmarks
with no landmarks along eyeballs

Fig. 6. Mapped result using 26 landmarks
with 8 landmarks along eyeballs

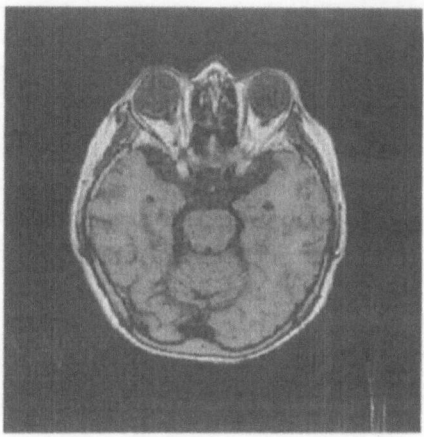

Fig. 7. Mapped result of image 1 in grey scale

4.2 Three Dimensional Transformation

We will now apply the transformation to the three-dimensional VOI regions directly. We have now used a CT data set as a model, since the surface of a model can more easily be extracted from CT images. In fact, the surface is now segmented automatically by a low level segmentation. To facilitate visual comparison, images of fig. 8 and 9 are shown as observed on horizontal slices about 10 mm apart. Figure 8 is the original image before we have applied the transformation while fig. 9 and 10 show images after we have applied Bookstein's THS transformation with 14 and 26 landmarks respectively. Figure 10 shows the surface rendering of the three-dimensional object into the transformed space where the transformation is applied on vertices only with surface normals being recomputed afterwards.

Figures 11 and 12 show the effect of sueface redering more clearly where the pot is subjected to a heavy bump. Since the bump inflicted is localized, the recalculation of the surface normals is extended only locally.

The evaluation function used in three dimension is similar to two dimension where an area is computed on slices and a volume is obtained by multiplying the distance between slices.

$$V_{3d} = \frac{V_1 \cap V_2}{V_1 \cup V_2} \qquad (9)$$

the V_i represente the volume of the objects and the result was shown in Table 2.

It is remarkable that as compared with the two-dimensional transformation, the accuracy of three dimensional transformation is almost equally accurate with the same number of 26 landmarks specified.

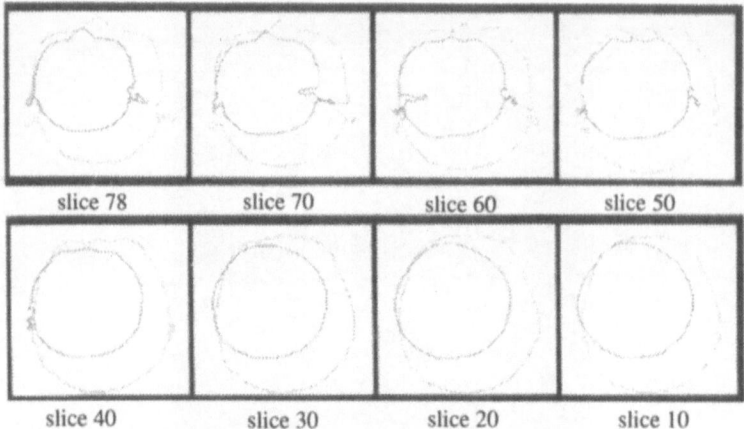

Fig. 8.   The original slices of the model and object

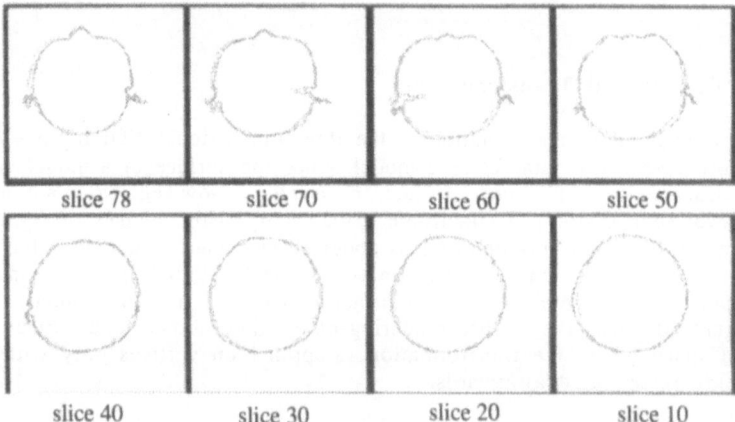

Fig. 9.   The map of 14 landmarks of the model and object

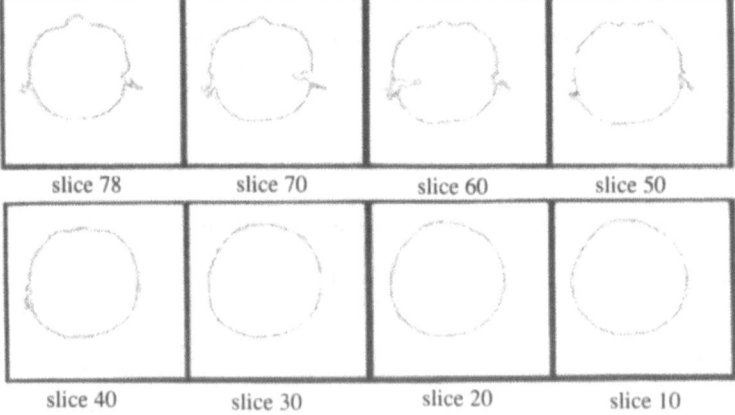

Fig. 10.   The map of 26 landmarks of the model and object

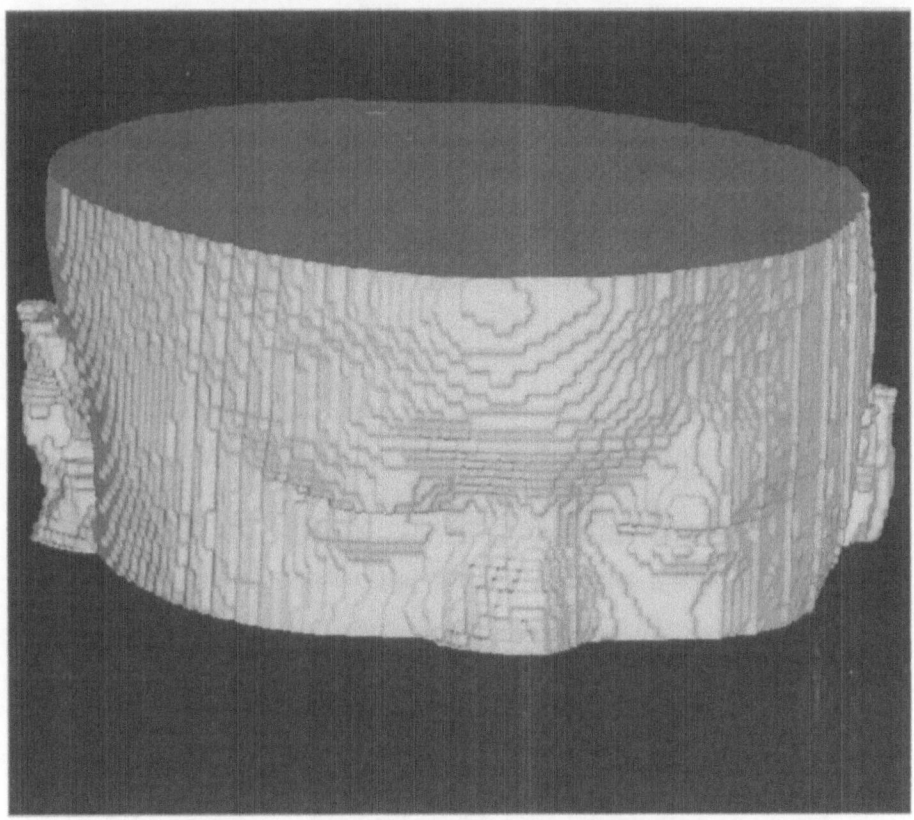

Fig. 11. The surface rendering of three-dimensional object

Table 2   The evaluation result of three-dimensional mapping

Number of LandMarks	Test 1
0 (Original Image)	55.94 %
8	88.72 %
14	90.91 %
18	92.49 %
26	93.36 %

Fig. 12. Surface redering of geometrical object

Fig. 13. Surface redering of the object with a bump after THS transformation

5. CONCLUSION

The main contribution of this paper is an introduction of the deformation transformation into the model-based recognition.

Our analysis shows that the thin-plate spline and thin-hyperplate spline methods applicable to two- and three-dimensions respectively are both efficient and accurate. Surprisingly this is more so in three-dimensional cases. 26 landmarks in three-dimensions seem adequate to ensure the accuracy of 94%! Since the complexity involved in the matrix inversion of $(n+4) \times (n+4)$ in 3D and $(n+3) \times (n+3)$ in 2D is marginal, the complexity of mapping depends largely on the number of geometric points to be mapped.

Using a simple space transformation, we are able to establish an equivalent relation prevailing between the pre-set experts knowledge and the image data we must analyze. The present approach should play an important role in searching and implementing an automatic image recognition process where experts knowledge may not be readily available.
A problem remains in selection of the landmarks in object space which are done interactively now. If ill-chosen, additional landmarks merely deteriorate the accuracy of transformation. Then we have to discard the landmarks and/or add additional landmarks for improvement.

Professor Kergosien suggested to one of the author (NT) that the homotopy theory (Kergosien 1991; Shinagawa & kunii 1991, Shinagawa et al. 1991) provides a more accurate means of surface reconstruction even where a singularity forms in some part of the surfaces under analysis. We are now examining such approach, because abnormal images with severely affected lesions may now be brought into our recognition process, undoubtedly adding the importance of the method in medical applications.

Note added in proof; Evans et al. (1991) which came to our attention after completing the paper applies also Bookstein's transformation to brain regions but discusses only the quantitative feature of the transformation. Our approach discusses the more fundamatal aspect of the transformation.

ACKNOWLEDGEMENTS

We extend our sincere appreciation to Mr. Saito and Iida of Toshiba Medical Engineering Co., Ltd. for providing valuable CT and MRI data. Without their help, this work would not even have started. Professor Y. Kergosien has encouraged the authors to undertake research in medical imaging field by showing radiological facilities of University of Paris-Sud. Professor Miyamichi of Utsunomiya University together with members of our Research Group have been helpful in encouraging our research efforts. And we also had a useful discussion with Mr. T. Miyazawa, M. Kimura of Tokyo Research Laboratory, IBM Japan Ltd. The first author have been supported by a research-in-aid grant from Ashigin International Foundation of Ashikaga Bank for years. We are grateful to all of them.

REFERENCES

Bennett A, Craw I (1991)   Finding Image Features Using Deformable Templates And Detailed Prior Statistical Knowledge. British Machine Vision Conference. 233-239.

Bookstein FL (1989) Principal Warps: Thin-Plate Splines and Decomposition of Deformation. IEEE Transactions on Pattern Analysis and Machine Intelligence: 11(6): 567-585.

Bookstein FL (1991) Thin-Plate Splines and the Atlas Problem for Biomedical Images. 12th Int. Conf. IPMI'91. 326-342.

Bozma HI, Duncan JS (1991) Model-based Recognition of Multiple Deformable Objects Using a Game-Theoretic Framework. 12th Int. Conf. IPMI'91. 358-372.

Evans AC, Dai W, Collins L, Neelin P, Marrett S (1991) Warping of a computerized 3-D atlas to match brain image volumes for quantitative neuroanatomical and functional analysis. SPIE Image Processing 1445. 236-246.

Kapouleas I (1990) Segmentation and Feature Extraction for Magnetic Resonance Brain Image Analysis. 10th Int. Conf. on Pattern Recognition. 583-590.

Kergosien YL (1991) Generic Sign Systems in Medical Imaging. IEEE Computer Graphics and Applications 11(5). 46-65.

Shinagawa Y, Kunii TL (1991) The homotopy model: a generalized model for smooth surface generation from cross sectional data. Visual Computer 7. 72-86.

Shinagawa Y, Kunii TL, Kergosien YL (1991) Surface Coding Based on Morse Theory. IEEE Computer Graphics and Applications 11(5). 66-78.

Ueda N, Mase K, Suenaga Y (1992) A Contour Tracking Method Using Elastic Contour Model and Energy Minimization Approach. Tran. Inst. Electron. Inf. Commun. Eng. D-II (Japan) J75-D-II(1). 111-120.

Worrall AD, Marslin RF, Sullivan GD, Baker KD (1991) Model-based Tracking. British Machine Vision Conference. 310-318.

Ronghua Yan is a second year master student at Utsunomiya University majoring in Computer Science. He has been engaged in research in image compression for Fax transmission and computer graphics.
Yan has obtained a BS in computer science from Fudan University in Shanghai, China in 1982. He had joined Shanghai Institute of Computer Technology as a researcher staff during 1982 to 1989 on computer network and expert system.

Naoyuki Tokuda is a Professor of Computer Science at Utsunomiya University. His present research interest includes computer graphics, probabilistic reasoning and intelligent tutoring system in artificial intelligence field, algorithmic analysis .of sorting methods and informatics education. He has previously published many papers in the field of applied mathematics including fluid mechanics and phase change analysis of Stefan problems involving heat and mass transfer.
Tokuda has received his BSc,MSc and Ph.d degrees from Yokohama National University in 1959, Stanford University in 1962 and University of Michigan in 1966 respectively, and D.Sc from University of Tokyo in 1975. He has been a research fellow at DAMTP, University of Cambridge during 1969-1971 and also at Mathematics Department at Southamptom University during 1971-1972.
Address: Faculty of General Education, Utsunomiya University, Utsunomiya, Japan 321
FAX: 286-35-3171   Tel: 286-36-1515 ext. 571
e-mail   tokuda@jsrv02.utsunomiya-u.ac.jp

Image Segmentation Using Color Information and Its Application in Colonscopy

Imdad Ali Ismaili and Duncan F. Gillies

ABSTRACT

An image segmentation algorithm, based on human colour perception, has been designed and implemented. An image in the RGB space is obtained through a conventional frame grabber. It is transformed into a perceptual colour space (HSI) and a histogram is constructed to estimate the size of any required feature. A regular decomposition of the image is then made, in which each node contains statistical information about the colour attributes of the pixels in the corresponding region. The best node is selected as a seed, and a merging process then obtains the boundary of the region. The algorithm has been tested on the identification of fluid in colon images observed through a conventional endoscope. In the intended application the segmentation will be part of a control system, and will enable the instrument to suck fluid out of the human colon automatically. Preliminary results suggest that a fast and accurate segmentation can be obtained using simple preceptual colour criteria. Real time performance could be achieved by implementing the algorithm on a small pyramid architecture.

1. INTRODUCTION

Image segmentation is the process of grouping the components of an image into meaningful units that are homogeneous with respect to one or more characteristic. Achieving an adequate image partition depends mainly on devising techniques to detect uniformity and then isolating the corresponding subsets of the picture. Many techniques have been suggested to accomplish image segmentation, such as edge detection, region growing, clustering and histogram thresholding. In colour image segmentation a variety of region based segmentation methods have been used some based on the perceptual attributes of colour (colour quality, purity, perceived brightness).

Colour image segmentation based on a multidimensional histogram thresholding scheme was suggested by Ohlander [1978]. He used threshold values obtained from three different colour coordinate systems (RGB, YIQ, and HSI). The technique takes a region of the image and uses the histograms of nine redundant attribute values to determine a threshold in one of the colour components. This threshold is used to split the region into smaller parts.

Ali [1977] has performed image segmentation by partitioning the picture into regions according to decision surfaces in a three dimensional normalized colour space. The space consisted of intensity and two normalized chromaticity coordinates. The system allows the user to specify, interactively, a decision surface on x-y, I-y, and I-x coordinates. This is then applied to the pixels of digitized scene so that the feature points falling within the volume, defined by the bounded surface are selected. The technique is similar to the clustering technique that Ohlander investigated using multiple histograms. An extension of this method for scene analysis based on an interactive system for second order decision surfaces was suggested by Sarabi [1981]. The system provides a means of solving the problem of extracting the regions which possess known colour characteristics. When there is no *a priori* knowledge about the scene, and we need to perform a general purpose colour segmentation, he proposed the use of a colour clustering method for image segmentation. The algorithm starts by creating a colour histogram of the colour coordinates (X, Y, I) of each image point. This colour histogram is based on the use of a three dimensional binary tree which is referred as the XYI-histogram. The purpose of using the binary tree was to reduce the XYI dimensionality. An image with NxN elements would be expected to have 1/5 N*N to 1/10 N*N histogram entries. A similar clustering image segmentation technique was used by Schacter [1976]. The major difference between

594

Schacter and Sarabi is that Schacter used a multidimensional histogram in the RGB image values (the method does not comply with the human perception system) while Sarabi used normalised colour coordinates, the intensity and two chromaticity coordinates. Otha [1980] has suggested three colour features for three orthogonal coordinates which he used in colour image segmentation, using a recursive thresholding scheme.

For colour edge detection Akira [1986] proposed an entropy operator which calculates the entropy of brightness, hue and saturation in a local region of the image. The entropy is large when the distribution of any selected feature is uniform and is small when the distribution of the selected feature is not uniform. The edges are marked at points where the entropy is very small. It is claimed that the method can work very well when images are noise free or colour balanced.

Image segmentation based on a recursive thresholding method for colour images was suggested by Shoji [1986]. He performed image segmentation in terms of three perceptual attributes. The input image was mapped pixel by pixel into the Munsell colour space and then the statistics of each image attribute was represented by three independent histograms. The most significant peak selection from the set of three histograms was based on the shape analysis of each peak of the histograms.

A colour clustering technique for image segmentation was proposed by Celenk [1990]. The method operates in a uniform colour coordinate system (L*,a*,b*) defined by the CIE, Wyszeck, et al. [1982]. The image cluster is detected in a set of circular-cylindrical decision elements of the colour space. The surfaces of the decision elements are formed with constant lightness and constant chromaticity loci. Each surface is obtained from the respective histograms of the Hue, Saturation and Lightness coordinates of the image data or the extracted feature vector.

Image segmentation based on a perceptual colour system was performed by Hiroshi [1991]. His work used an indoor controlled environment with a uniform white background. Scenes were segmented by using the threshold derived from the chroma histogram. For outdoor, or uncontrolled, environments he suggested an effective tone colour method. Effective tone of colour is a measure related to the psychological effect a colour has on a human. For example a blue colour arguably has a calming effect, and is represented on a negative axis, while a red colour, having the opposite effect is shown on a positive axis. The Munsell colour solid is based on this property and has got a very complex shape in that the distance between the value axis and colours with pronounced psychological effect (red, orange) is larger than the corresponding distance for passive colours (blue). Based on hue and brightness the image data was assigned the chroma value accordingly and then segmentation was performed.

2. COLOUR AND ITS PERCEPTION.

Colour is a subjective sensation, experienced through the light sensitive mechanism of the eye. The stimulus for vision is light energy, which is usually seen by reflection from or transmission through an object that modifies the quantity of light and produces the colour attributes of an object. The visible light spectrum is one portion out of the whole gamut of electromagnetic radiation. The limits of the visible spectrum are loosely regarded as terminating at the wavelength of 380 nm on the short wave side and at 700 nm on the long wavelength side.

We possess in the eye individual photoreceptors or light sensitive cells at the back of the retina which transduce the light energy into nerve energy. These photoreceptors contain a light-sensitive, or visual pigment. There are two kinds of photoreceptors, known as rods and cones because of their structural appearance under the light microscope. The rods are not used for colour vision, which is solely the domain of the cone receptors Travis [1991]. There is only one visual pigment common to all the rod receptors and a single visual pigment can only identify the number of quanta absorbed, and not the wavelength of those quanta Jollands [1984]. They are thus sensitive to movement, shape, and texture, and additionally are extremely sensitive to small amounts of light. At high levels of illumination they play little part in vision.

In the centre of the retina is a small pit called the fovea (about 1 mm in diameter), in which there are no rod receptors but only cones. Some seven million of these cones are tightly packed in it. These cones fall into three separate classes. The three classes have respective maximal sensitivity placed by Wald, Mark,and MacNichol at about 430, 450 and 570 nm, and by Chander and Das at 480, 540 and 570 nm Chamberlin [1980]. These wavelengths correspond to the Blue, Red and Green radiation. The CIE colour matching system, universally adopted, is based on this trichromatic model of colour, in which any colour can be matched with combination of red, green, and blue primary colours.

Determination of psychometric parameters of the colour is based on the opponent colour theory which is claimed to model human colour vision Joann [1989]. The theory behind opponancy of colours is based on the assumption that all colours are coded by the eye and brain into Bl-W (achromatic), Red-Green and Yellow-Blue (chromatic) signals MacDonald [1989]. In this system colours are mutually exclusive in that a colour cannot be red and green at the same time, or yellow and blue at the same time, but colour can be described as red *and* blue as in the case of purple.

Based on these assumptions a variety of colour models have been proposed, such as the Lab and Luv systems, defined by CIE (Wyszecki [1982], Bllimeyer [1981]), A C_1 C_2 colour model (Faugeras [1977]), I_1 I_2 I_3 (Otha [1980]), and HSV and HLS colour models (Burger [1989], Foley [1982], Travis [1991]). These colour models are all transformations of the RGB system and most of them are used in the computer vision domain.The psychometric parameters in these colour models have orthogonal coordinates. They are usually represented using a cylindrical coordinate system in which r and θ represent the chromatic information and z represents brightness or lightness of the colour under study.

Due to the low computational cost, we have selected the HSI colour model (Ballard [1982], Gonzales [1992]), for colour analysis. Hue, saturation, and intensity in this model are defined as follows:

$$H = \cos^{-1}\{\frac{1/2[(R-G)+(R-B)]}{[(R-G)^2+(R-B)(G-B)]^{1/2}}\}$$

Hue = H   if B ≤ G

Hue = 2 * π - H   if B > G.

$$S = 1 - \frac{3}{(R+G+B)}[\min(R,G,B)]$$

$$I = \frac{(R+G+B)}{3}$$

The hue is measured as an angle between 0 and 360 degrees (0, 120, 240 for red, green, and blue respectively). Saturation is a percentage between 0% and 100%, which measures the purity of the colour.

3. REGION ORIENTED SEGMENTATION

Region oriented segmentation techniques are based on dividing the image into sub-regions on the basis of a uniformity test, which may include intensity variation, colour variation, texture variation or other measures. These techniques are categorised as merging, splitting, and split and merge.

Region merging, sometimes called region growing, looks for groups of pixels around a seed with one or more similar properties (intensity, chroma, or hue). Connectedness is an important concept of region growing and frequently four connectedness or eight connectedness is used. In the simplest form, the method starts with one pixel and then examines its neighbours in order to decide whether they possess similar properties. If they do, then they are aggregated in a group. In some of the cases there is no prior knowledge about the initial seeds that properly represent the regions of interest. In this case the histogram of the image is constructed and the most dominant intensity points are used to determine the attributes of the initial seeds. The regions are then grown until some homogeneity criterion is broken.

Many different forms of this basic method have been suggested for image segmentation. For example, Levine and Shaheen [1981] have grown image regions by merging as many neighbouring pixels as possible on the colour features. A threshold was adopted according to the coherence of the regions for limiting the growth of less uniform regions. Pavlidis [1982] has suggested a uniformity approach which can be extended for regular texture segmentation. One can evaluate the co-occurrence matrices over small groups of regions and then compare the adjacent matrices, if they are similar then regions are of the same texture and may be merged. In the work of Barrow and Popplestone [1971] the criterion was the difference of the average levels of the adjacent regions. If the difference was less than a threshold, then the adjacent regions were merged. In the merging process a selected region is taken and tested against all adjacent regions. Those which may be merged with it are merged simultaneously and a new region is created. Muerle and Allen [1986] used a three stage approach for region merging. Firstly the entire image is segmented into square blocks of size 2×2, 4×4 etc.; secondly, a statistical measure is computed for each of these blocks and finally a regional neighbour search method is adopted to merge the regions of similar statistics. The statistical measure for a region is updated after every merge operation, which may provide a more accurate description of the regions formed by curved surfaces where there is a steady gradient in light intensity. Brice and Fennema [1970] applied a region merging method on the atomic regions of constant grey level. The atomic regions are merged on the basis of two heuristics which examine the boundary between adjacent regions. Adjacent regions are merged if the boundary between them is weak and the resulting region has a shorter boundary than the original ones.

Region splitting is the opposite approach to region merging. Splitting starts with the whole image which is considered as one region. It is then divided successively into smaller regions until the resulting region satisfies the uniformity criterion. Normally the histogram of a coherent or uniform region is unimodal. Therefore when a region has multimodal histogram, an attempt is made to partition the image in such manner that the histograms of resulting regions be unimodal. The successful use of this method was reported by Ohlander [1978] and Ohta [1980] individually, using a recursive region splitting technique. The method uses a histogram thresholding technique to segment the image. A set of histograms is constructed for a specific set of features, then each of these histograms is searched for distinct peaks. The best peak is selected and the image is split into regions based on this thresholding of the histogram.

The principle of split and merge is to partition the image into regions in a regular way, and then apply some statistical methods to determine a measure of similarity between each of the regions. This measure may be variation in texture, variation in colour attributes or only in intensity in the case of achromatic images. Once this measure is complete the image is taken for the next step of processing.

The next step is normally a homogeneity test for each of the regions. The regions that are homogeneous are tested for merging with their neighbours; the regions that do not satisfy the homogeneity criterion will be split further into more subregions. After a split is made, a merge is attempted. This merge procedure will attempt to merge every region with its neighbouring regions if the resulting region is acceptable to the homogeneity test. The procedure terminates when there is no region to be split or merged. An efficient quadtree algorithm based on these ideas was produced by Horowitz and Pavlidis [1974]. The nodes of the quadtree correspond to the square regions and the leaves represent the regions of single pixels. Each node has particular associated value, which is a function of particular attributes (brightness, hue, or saturation) of corresponding region. Efficient implementations of split and merge algorithms are usually based on pyramid structures [Khan 1989].

In a regular pyramidal decomposition using a quadtree data structure, the data at the nodes can be computed recursively, starting at the pixels and working up to the root. Typical transformations used compute properties such as mean, variance, standard deviation, and entropy. They offer currently the most computationally efficient way of segmenting images. To date however, little work has been done in applying colour criteria within pyramid architectures.

The methods for colour segmentation that have been adopted so far work on the whole image, or a large part of it, and therfore do not give satisfactory results when several different regions conform to one property. Although the histogram processing and thresholding may be done fast and efficiently, further, sequential processing is inevitably necessary to find the boundaries of regions. The methods also suffer an important drawback in cases where regions for segmentation contain an irregular texture. Thresholding or clustering within some colour space will result in a disconnected image in cases where the pixels of a coherent region are a mixture of two or more colours or intensities. Such textures do occur frequently in natural images, and our particular application is a good example. Most texture is loosely divided into three categories namely deterministic texture, structural texture, and stochastic texture. Deterministic texture can be described by mathematical formulas or a regular arrangement of well-defined primitives according to defined placement rules. A structural pattern is viewed as a layout of certain primitives according to some placement rules in which spatial variations on primitives and placement rules are permitted. Finally a stochastic texture can be viewed a texture which does not posses any globally perceivable regularities, periodicities or orientations (random dot pattern). This third category best describes the regions we wish to segment.

Statistical approaches describe texture by statistical rules which govern the distribution and the relation of the grey levels. Methods which have been tried include: *grey level dependence matrix* (GLDM) Julesz [1983], *generalized spatial dependence matrix* (GSDM) Davis [1978], *histogram and autocorrelation function analysis* (HAFA) Song [1983], *Fourier power spectrum analysis* (FPSA) Dastous [1984] , *grey level difference approach* (GLDA) Weszka [1976] and Conners [1980], *grey level edge element analysis* (GLEA) Marr [1982], *grey level run length* (GLRL) Galloway [1974], Haralic [1979], *grey level profile analysis* (GRPA), *and local linear convolution method* (LLCM) Laws [1980]. Other methods, based on breaking the texture down into its basic units and identifying repetition pattern have been used. These methods, although useful for deterministic or structural textures, are inappropriate for the types of image that we are dealing with.

To overcome these difficulties, we have developed a new method which uses a regular decomposition of the image and conventional split and merge techniques. In our case, the coherence of a region is established by comparing properties of its histogram either with an expected norm, or with those of its neighbours or children. In the most general case, a difference measure between two normalised histograms can be computed by summing the squared difference between corresponding points. Nodes may be merged if their histograms are sufficiently close, or split if the histogram of any child differs from the parent. If the histogram properties of the required region are known, then nodes can be tested as a quadtree is built, and marked if they conform to the criteria. The algorithm depends on the expectation that distribution of colour or intensity data within a coherent region remains roughly constant within a small window when it is moved accross the region. The size to which the window can be reduced is a property of the application. The accuracy of the method clearly depends on the number of histogram points that are processed. For example, where great accuracy is required, high resolution histograms of both hue and saturation could be used, and, where shading is not expected, the intensity histogram could also be incorporated in the measure. This would result in an expensive coherence test for each split or merge operation. However, for real time performance, the histograms could be reduced to a few bands.

4. APPLICATION IN ENDOSCOPY

The segmentation algorithm outlined above has been tested using endoscopic images of the human colon. The endoscope is a medical instrument for examining the inner surfaces of the human body. It is typically used for diagnosis and treatment of colon and upper gastrointestinal diseases including cancer. More modern systems use a CCD camera mounted in the tip, which transmits an image electrically for viewing on a TV monitor. The instrument has an operating channel allowing the passage of fine flexible therapeutic instruments (e.g. biopsy forceps) from a port in the endoscope head. They allow the removal of colonic polyps and direct attack on bleeding lesions. The operating channel is also used for aspiration of fluid by pressing the suction button.

The endoscope consultant controls the instrument by steering the tip with two mechanical wheels and simultaneously by pushing or pulling the shaft. The shaft is relatively torque stable so that he can also apply rotatory movements to the tip. In addition to these control actions he makes diagnostic decisions or therapeutic actions in each particular case.

The difficulties involved in using the endoscope are well known, and so our primary objective is to use machine vision to simplify endoscopic procedures and spare the endoscopist from some of the tasks he has to carry out concurrently, thus leaving him to concentrate on the diagnostic and therapeutic aspects of colonscopy. Earlier work Khan [1989], Sucar [1991] and Rashid [1991] has demonstrated that automatic navigation of the endoscope is possible. This project concerns the detection and removal of fluid present in the colon through inadequate bowel preparation which obstructs the view of the mucosal surface, on which evidence of cancer, or other diseases may be present.

4.1 Algorithm for fluid identification

An endoscopist uses two obvious visual clues to identify fluid for removal: *colour and relative motion.* Our present study considers only the colour information. The merging criterion was chosen after analysing the fluid attributes and the structure of the colon surface. Fluid in the colon gets its colour from small particles which are present due to inadequate bowel preparation. These move with the water producing a transparent yellowish green fluid through which the colon surface, with its irregular white and red texture, is sometimes seen. The simplest techniques, such as thresholding or clustering based on the some measure of similarity within a group, are not suitable for extracting the complete region of interest. Uniformity criteria based on mean, variance, and standard deviation are also unsuitable, as merging of the neighbouring areas may not be possible with these techniques. Thus an approach based on properties of the histogram, as described in section 3, was employed in our algorithm

A further constraint of the application is the need for real time time performance, and so we have selected a simple histogram property for our uniformity criterion. It is the proportion of the dominant feature in any area. The dominant feature being defined by one band of the normalised histogram. At any node the proportion of the dominant feature can be simply computed from the sum of the numbers of pixels in the desired histogram band of its children:

$$T = w_{k1} + w_{k2} + w_{k2} + w_{k3}$$

and the proportion is given by:

$$T_{PDF} = [w_{k1} + w_{k2} + w_{k2} + w_{k3}] / A_T$$

where A_T is the size of the image at level k+1 and is given by

$$A_T = 2^n \times 2^n$$

where $n = N - L$

This simple criterion ensures very fast computation, and has proved sufficiently accurate for this purpose. The algorithm is divided into the following distinct steps for extracting the region of interest.

Step 1: *Estimation of the approximate area of the fluid*

A hue histogram of the given image is constructed using HSI colour space. The approximate area covered by fluid is estimated from this histogram (see Figures 1 and 2).

Step 2: *Extraction of the seed region*

A regular quadtree decomposition of the image is made, going down to blocks of 2×2 pixels thus reducing the image resolution to half. The properties belonging to a node at level k+1, including the proportion of the dominant feature, are calculated recursively.

This process continues until a root is reached (L = 0). During this process each node is examined for coherence. The nodes which satisfy the uniformity criterion are marked.

Step 3: *Merging neighbouring regions*

After identifying the largest uniform seed region, adjacent areas of the extracted region are examined and merged if they do not violate the merging criterion. The merging of the neighbouring areas may be performed either at the same level of the pyramid or by using the lower nodes in the tree for making more accurate boundaries. This Merging process continues until the new region size approximates the size of required feature estimated in step 1, or until no merge is possible.

The formulation of colour criteria for merging based on the histogram of hue, is, as far as we know, employed for the first time in our algorithm.

5. Results

The algorithm has been implemented on PC 486/33MHZ hosting a Quintek Mosaiq, real time image capturing card, based on an Inmos T805 transputer. The system grabs the image from video recorder in full colour, with up to 4Mbytes of video buffer. The C language has been used to implement the algorithm with special functions which interact with the Mosiaq card using the transputer. The host processor is used as a server which only handles input/output transactions.

The technique has been tested for number of endoscopic images taken inside a human colon. The current implementation takes approximately 4 seconds to identify the feature of interest The result of applying this technique on two selected colon images along with their histograms is shown in Figure 1 and Figure 2.

Table 1 shows the results of the algorithm on a number of representative colon images, with and without fluid. The present approach of identifying fluid in the colon works well in most cases. However, it occasionally marks the wrong feature as a feature of interest. There are two reasons for this:

(i) The endoscope gets red, green, and blue frames in sequence. In the case of rapid movement of the endoscope in the human colon, the RGB planes are sometimes taken out of register and this gives the illusion of specularties of different colours. These colour specularties sometimes resemble the fluid and are marked as a true feature. The incorrect results shown in row2 of table 1 are due to these problems.

(ii) Other matter, sometimes present in the colon, has the same characteristics as the fluid does and is also marked as fluid. The errors due to these cases are shown in row3 of table 1.

Table 1:Segmentation Results

NO.	Number of images with fluid	Number of images without fluid	Identified correctly %	Identified incorrectly %
1	120		85.83	14.16
2		290	83.1	16.9
3		125	31.1	68.9

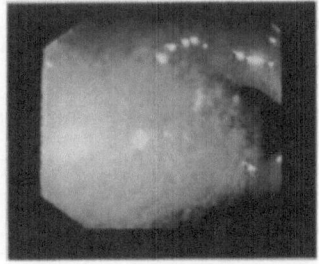

Original colon image.   Identification of fluid after segmentation

Figure 1. Histogram of the input image.

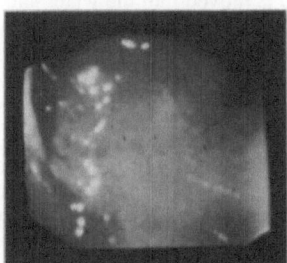
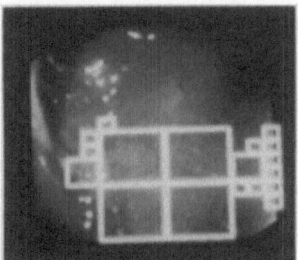

Original colon image.   Identification of fluid after segmentation

Figure 2. Histogram of the input image.

It is possible to avoid the first problem since artifacts produced by the rapid movement of the instrument, have characteristics that are are differènt statistically from the regions of fluid, in that variance in hue, saturation, and in intensity is comparatively lower than that of true features. This fact could be utilised to improve the algorithm in this application.

The second problem could be avoided using either by utilising more histogram properties, or by means of motion information. The latter is also one of the clues that expert endoscopist uses to identify the fluid when there is an ambiguity between fluid and other matter. The work is in progress and we hope that the combination of region based segmentation, including other histogram properties, and motion information will provide us with satisfactorily results.

6. CONCLUSION AND FUTURE WORK

Although only the simplest of histogram properties was used in this study, it never the less indicates that coherence criteria, based on properties of a region's hue histogram, can produce segmentations that are not possible using the established statistical measures, or by using the older thresholding or clustering techniques. Moreover, the method has proved to be sufficiently fast that real time performance can be achieved with a speed up of roughly twenty times. Since the proposed algorithm is based on a quadtree, it would be possible to achieve this speed up by mapping it onto a four branching pyramid structure with only three levels. Currently, we are engaged in further work to establish the more general properties of this type of algorithm, and to investigate the effect of other simple colour space histogram properties which can be employed in segmentation algorithms.

Regarding the application, our overall aim was to find simple and fast machine vision techniques to identify and remove fluid from the colon automatically during endoscopy. Tracing of the fluid in a sequence of images provides the most important part of the information required to enable the construction of a control system in which the instrument tip is moved into the water and fluid is sucked out without intervention by the doctor.

ACKNOWLEDGEMENTS

The authors would like to express their thanks to: The Ministry of Education, Government of Pakistan, Institute of Physics & Technology, for a grant enabling Mr Ismaili to conduct this research, The Olympus Optical Company, Tokyo, for providing equipment and Dr. Christopher Williams at St. Mark's Hospital London, for his enthusiasm, encouragement and video tapes of colonscopy.

REFERENCES

Akira Shiozaki, *Edge Extraction Using Entropy Operator,* Computer Vision, graphics, and Image Processing 36, 1.9.1986.

Ali M., W. N. Martin, and J. K. Aggarwal, *Color-based computer Analysis of Aerial Photographs,* Computer Graphics and image Processing 9, 1979.

Ballard, Dana H. and Christopher M. Brown, *Computer Vision*, Prentic-Hall, New Yark, 1981.

Billmeyer, F. W. and M. Saltzman, *Principles of Color Technology*, Wiley, New York, 1981.

Borrow, H.G., Popplestone, R.J., *Relational Description of picture Processing,* Machine Intelligence Vol. 6, 1971.

Brice, C.R., Fennema, C.L., *Scene Analysis Using Regions,* Artificial Intelligence, 1970.

Burger, P. and Gillies D., *Interactive Computer Graphics,* Addison Wesley,Workingham, 1989.

Celenk Mehemet, *A Color clustering Technique for Image Segmentation,* Computer Vision, Graphics, and Image Processing 52, 145-170 (1990).

Chamberlin, G. J. and Chamberlin D. G., *Colour its Measurement, Computation and Application,* Heyden, London, 1980.

Conners R. W., et al, *A Theoretical Comparison of Texture algorithms,* IEEE Trans. Pattern Anal. machine Intell., vol. PAMI-2 1980.

Dastous, F. et al., *Texture Discrimination based on detailed measure of the power spectrum,* Proc. of the 7th International Conference on Pattern recognition, Montreal, Canada, July 30 - Aug. 2, 83-86.

Davis L. et al., *Texture Analysis Using Generalized Co-occurrence Matrices,* in pattern Recognition and Image Processing conference, Chicogo, IL.

Faugeras, Olivier D., *Digital Colour Image Processing within the framwork of a Human Visual Model,* IEEE transactions on Acoustics, Speech, and Signal Processing Vol. ASSP-27, August 1977.

Galloway M, *Texture Analysis Using Grey Level Run Length,* Computer Graphics and Image Processing, vol.4, 1974.

Gonzalez Rafael C., and Richard C Woods, *Digital Image processing,* Addison-Wesley, 1992.

Haralic R. M, *Statistical and Structural Approaches to Texture,* proc. of IEEE, vol.67, 1979.

Hiroshi T, Shuichi Nishio, *A Study of Image Segmentation using a Perceptual Color System,* SPIE Vol. 1607 Intelligent Robots and Computer Vision, 1991.

Horowitz, S.L., Pavilids, *Picture Segmentation by Directed Split and Merge Procedure,* Proc. of the Second International Joint Conference on Pattern Recognition, Aug., 1974.

Joann M, Taylor, Gerald M. Murch, and Paul A. McManus, *A Uniform Perceptual Color System for Display Users,* Proceedings of the SID, Vol. 30/1, 1989.

Jollands, David Ed. by, *Sight, Light, and Colour,* Cambridge, London, 1984.

Julesz B., et al, *The Fundamental Elements in Preattentive Vision and Perception of Texture,* The Bell Syst Tech J, vol.62, 1983.

Khan, Gul Nawas, *Machine Vision for Endoscope control and Navigation, Ph.D Thesis,* Imperial College of Science, Technology and Medicine, London, 1989.

MacDonald, Lindsay W and Stephen A R Scrivener, *Colours in the Mind,* Presented at Computer Graphics, 1989.

Marr D., Vision, W.H.Freeman, 1982.

Muerle, J.L., Allen, D.C., *Experimental Evaluation of Techniques for Automatic Segmentation of objects in a Complex Scene,* Thompson Washington, 1968.

Ohlander R, Keith Price, and D. Raj Reddy, *Picture Segmentation Using a Recursive Region Splitting Method,* Computer Graphics and image processing 8, 1978.

Ohta Yu-ichi, Takeo Kanade, and Toshiyukai sakai, *Colour Information for Region Segmentation,* Computer graphics and Image Processing 13, 1980.

Pavlidis T., *Algorithms for Graphics and Image processing,* Spriger-Verlag, 1982.

Rashid, Haroon, *Shape from Shading and Motion Parameter Estimation Under Near Light Source Illumination,* Ph.D Thesis, Imperial College of Science, Technology and Medicine, London, 1991.

Sarabi Alireza and J. K. Aggarwal, *Segmentation of Chromatic Images,* Pattern recognition Vol. 13, No. 6, 1981.

Shacter B., L. S. Davis, and A. Rosenfeld, *Scene Segmentation by Detection in Color spaces,* SIGART Newsletter No. 58 June 1976.

Shoji Tominaga, *Colour Image Segmentation using Three Perceptual Attributes,* Proceedings IEEE, 1986.

Song De Ma and A. Gagalowicz, *Natural Texture Synthesis with the Control of the Autocorrelation and Histogram Parameters,* Proc. of 3rd Scandinavian Conf. on Image analysis, July 1983.

Sucar L E, *Probabilistic Reasoning in Knowledge-Based Vision Systems, Ph.D Thesis,* Imperial College of Science, Technology and Medicine, London, 1991.

Travis, David, *Effective Color Displays Theory and Practice,* Academic, London, 1991.

Weszka J. S., et al., *A Comparative Study of Texture Measure for Terrain Classification,* IEEE Trans. Syst., Man, Cybern., vol.SMC-6, Apr.1976.

Wyszecki, Gunter and W. S. Stiles, *Color Science: Concepts and Methods, Quantitation Data and Formulae,* Wiley, New York, 1982.

BIOGRAPHIES

Imdad Ali Ismaili received a BSc in 1984 and MSc in 1985 in Electronics from University of Sindh at Jamshoro. He was employed as a lecturer in the Institute of Physics & Technology in Jamshoro from 1986 to 1990 when he was awarded scholarship by the Government of Pakistan to undertake his present studies for a Ph.D degree in Computer Vision at Imperial College of Science, Technology & Medicine, London UK.
Address: Department of Computing, Imperial Collee of Science Technology and Medicine, 180, Queen's Gate, London SW7 2BZ, UK.

Duncan Gillies graduated from Cambridge University with a degree in Engineering Science in 1971. He subsequently obtained the MSc Degree in Computing and a PhD in the area of artificial intelligence from London University. After teaching for six years at the Polytechnic of the South Bank, he moved to the Department of Computing in Imperial College where he is now a Senior Lecturer. His research interests are in graphics and computer vision.
Address: Department of Computing, Imperial Collee of Science Technology and Medicine, 180, Queen's Gate, London SW7 2BZ, UK.

A Multi-Processor Vision System

Pradip K. Sinha and Fa-Yu Chen

This paper describes the architectural design of a fast and flexible multi-processor vision system with particular reference to on-line industrial applications. The vision has the following features:

Transputer-based: the Inmos transputer provides high processing speed and easy inter-connection between transputers. The system needs no hardware modification while being connected to other transputer-based systems (Inmos 1989a).
Self-contained: the system accepts and outputs CCIR video signals. It may work as a stand-alone system capable of carrying out various functions.
Fast: a number of low-level processing including 3x3 convolutions, table look-up, and edge thinning are carried out at video frame rate to yield high processing speed for on-line applications.
Non-destructive overlay: patterns in a separate memory can be superimposed onto the display image without damages to the original image data. This mechanism may be used for indication of object/pattern identification and location.
Flexible: the vision system is dynamically configurable by software.

The vision system consists of a real-time front-end and a transputer. The real-time front-end is designed to enhance the system performance on object/pattern recognition. An IMS A110 signal processor (Inmos 1989b) works in conjunction with an edge thinning machine (Sinha and Chen 1993) to produce thinned binary edge images at video frame rate. The images produced by this front-end are stored into a frame buffer which is memory mapped onto the transputer. Higher level processing is then carried out by the transputer. Using the memory mapping technique, the transputer can access the image data without transfer delay. As a combination of a fast pre-processor and a general main processor, the system yields very high speed in specific functions while maintaining the ability of implementing various complex algorithms. Besides these two processors, a 16-bit transputer is assigned to the system management: configuration of the IMS A110, the overlay memory and the system register. A working prototype of this vision system has been built and tested at the University of Reading. It has been used to guide a robot manipulator for picking up objects.

REFERENCES

Inmos (1989a) The transputer databook, 2nd ed., Inmos, UK
Inmos (1989b) The digital signal processing databook, Inmos, UK
Sinha PK, Chen FY (1993) Real-time hardware for image edge-thinning using a new 11-pixel window, accepted by CG International '93

Address: Dept. of Engineering, University of Reading, P.O. Box 225, Reading RG6 2AY, England

A Multi-Processor Vision System

Pradip K. Sinha and Le Yu Chen

Conference Organization

CONFERENCE CHAIR: Daniel Thalmann, EPFL, Switzerland

INTERNATIONAL COORDINATOR: Rae A. Earnshaw, University of Leeds, UK

PROGRAM CHAIR: Nadia Magnenat Thalmann, University of Geneva, Switzerland

PROGRAM COMMITTEE

H. Biéri	University of Bern, Switzerland
Tat-Seng Chua	National University of Singapore
Rae A. Earnshaw	University of Leeds, UK
Pierre-Jean Erard	University of Neuchâtel, Switzerland
Bianca. Falcidieno	University of Genova, Italy
G. E. Farin	Arizona State University, USA
André Gagalowicz	INRIA, France
Mike Gigante	Royal Melbourne Institute of Technology, Australia
Arie Kaufman	State University of New York at Stony Brook, USA
F. Kimura	University of Tokyo, Japan
Tosiyasu L. Kunii	University of Tokyo, Japan
H. Maurer	Technische Universität Graz, Austria
Toshi Minami	Kogakuin University, Japan
S.P. Mudur	National Centre for Software Technology, India
Eihachiro Nakamae	University of Hiroshima, Japan
Nicholas Patrikalakis	MIT, USA
Bernard Péroche	Ecole des Mines de Saint-Etienne, France
D. Roesner	FAW Ulm, Germany
David F. Rogers	US Naval Academy, USA
Larry Rosenblum	Office of Naval Research, USA
Hanan Samet	University of Maryland, USA
Harold Santo	Technical University of Lisbon, Portugal
Alfred Schmitt	University of Karlsruhe, Germany
Peter Stucki	University of Zürich, Switzerland
Yasuito Suenaga	NTT Human Interface Labs, Japan
Yuzuru Tanaka	Hokkaido University, Japan
Zesheng Tang	Tsinghua University, Beijing, China
Mario Tokoro	Sony Computer Science Laboratory, Japan
Godfried T. Toussaint	McGill University, Canada
Denis Vandorpe	Université Claude Bernard Lyon-1, France
Brian Wyvill	University of Calgary, Canada
Geoff Wyvill	University of Otago, New Zealand
David Zeltzer	MIT, USA

External Reviewers

Organized by: **Computer Graphics Society**
Swiss Federal Institute of Technology
University of Geneva

In Cooperation with: **IEEE Computer Society**
British Computer Society
Eurographics
IFIP WG 5.10

Author Index

Keyword Index